PRISON SCHOOL

Akira Hiramoto

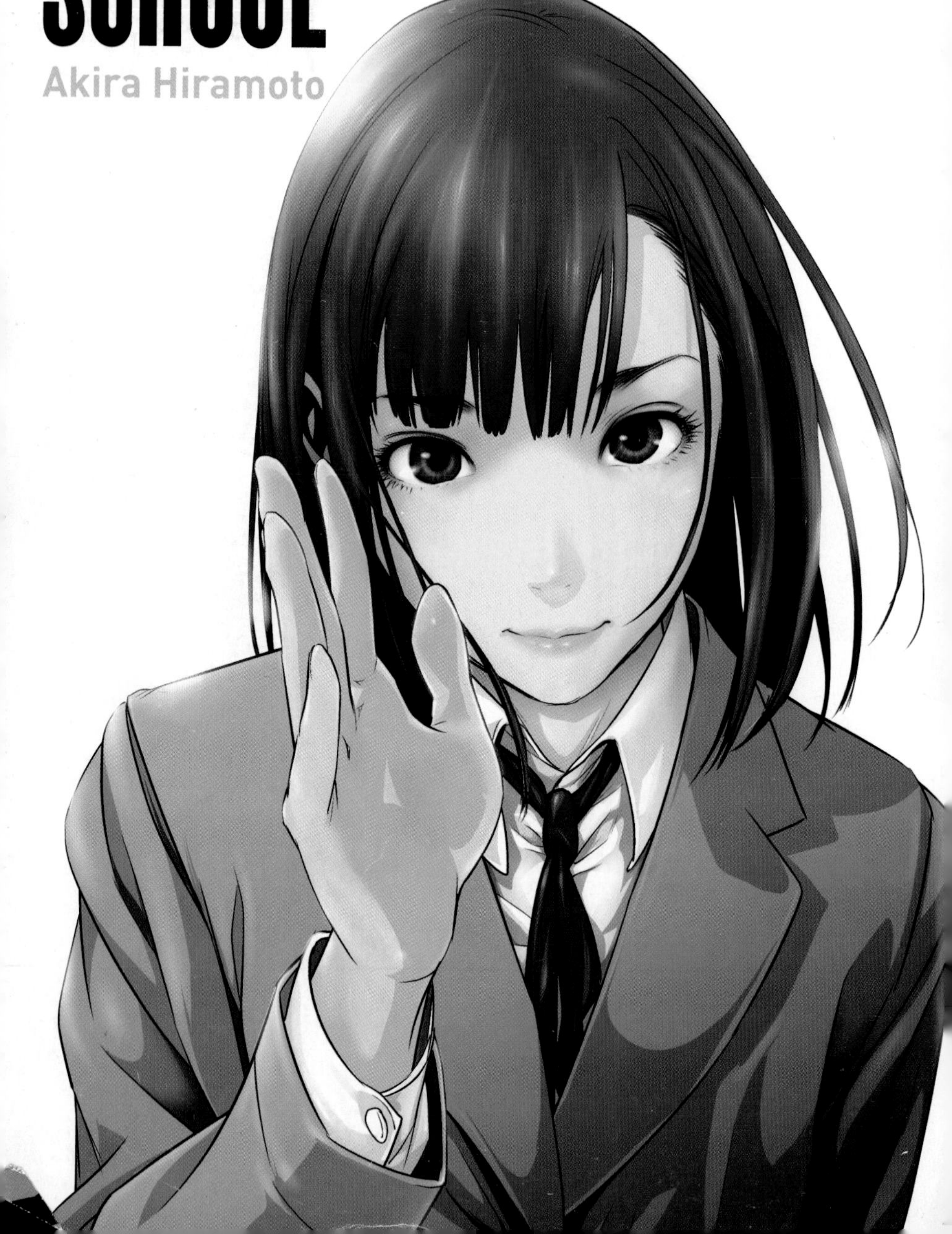

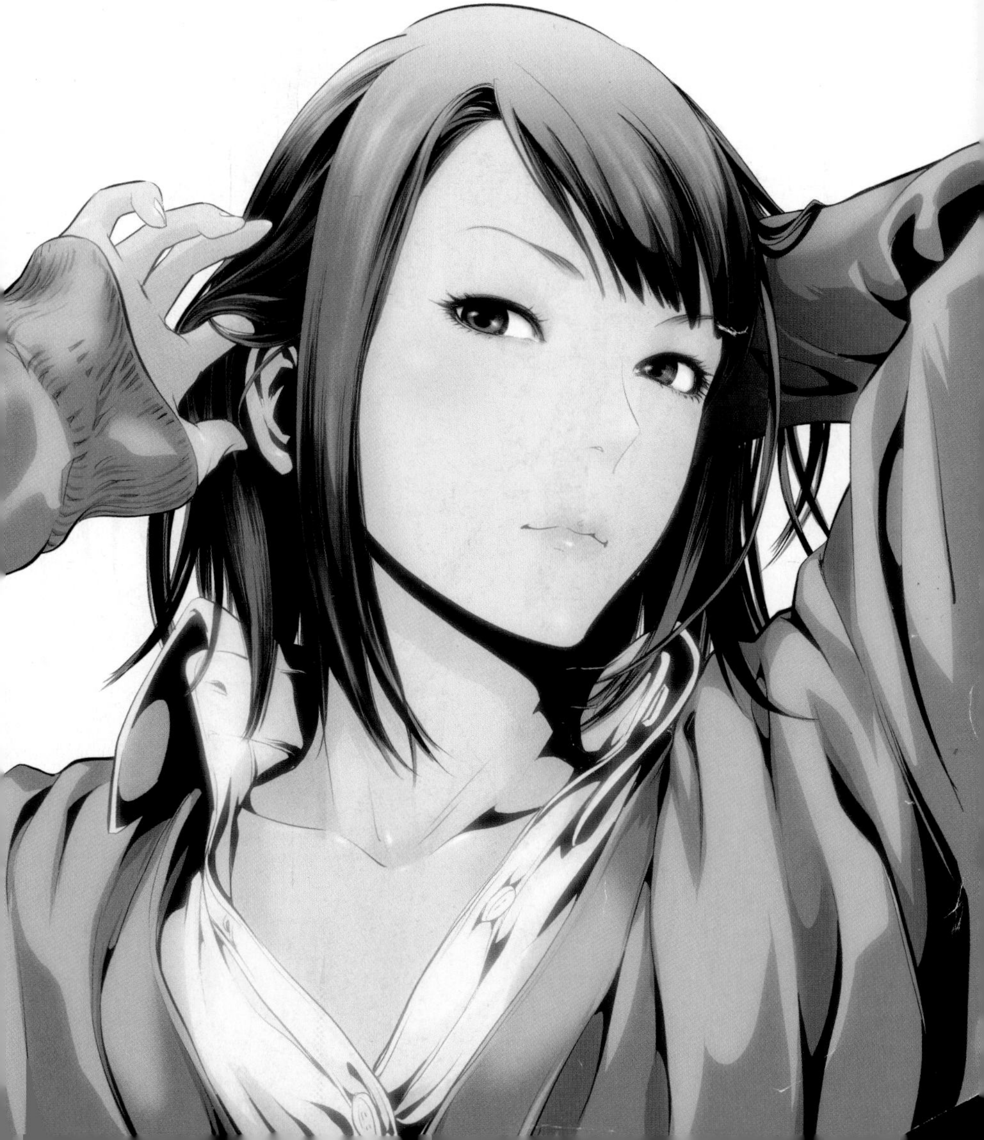

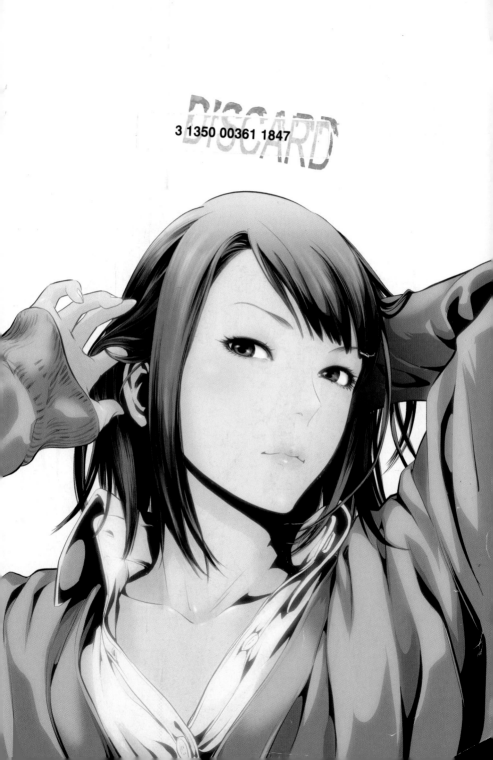

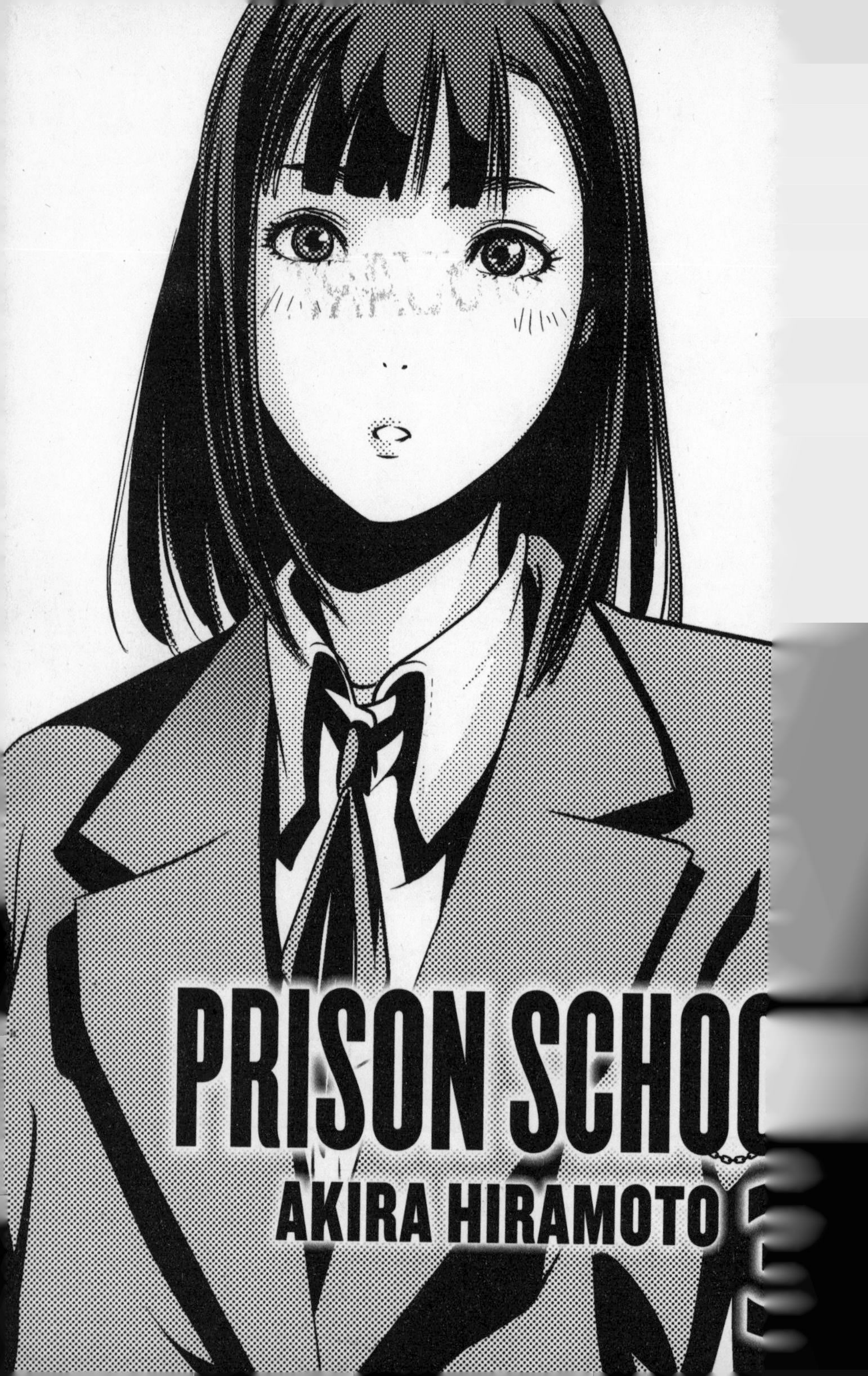
PRISON SCHOO
AKIRA HIRAMOTO

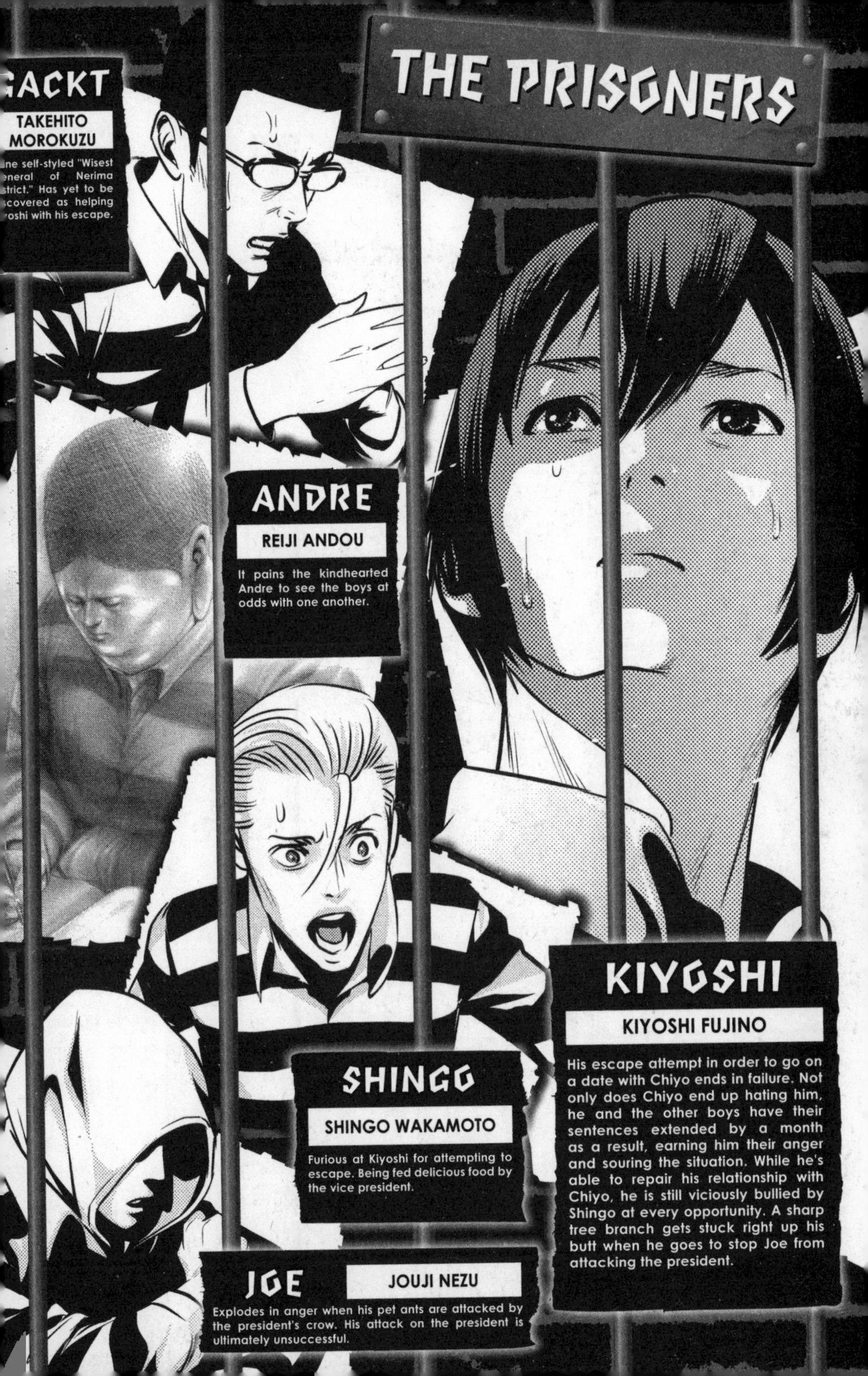
THE PRISONERS
ACKT
TAKEHITO MOROKUZU
ne self-styled "Wisest eneral of Nerima strict." Has yet to be scovered as helping oshi with his escape.
ANDRE
REIJI ANDOU
It pains the kindhearted Andre to see the boys at odds with one another.
KIYOSHI
KIYOSHI FUJINO
His escape attempt in order to go on a date with Chiyo ends in failure. Not only does Chiyo end up hating him, he and the other boys have their sentences extended by a month as a result, earning him their anger and souring the situation. While he's able to repair his relationship with Chiyo, he is still viciously bullied by Shingo at every opportunity. A sharp tree branch gets stuck right up his butt when he goes to stop Joe from attacking the president.
SHINGO
SHINGO WAKAMOTO
Furious at Kiyoshi for attempting to escape. Being fed delicious food by the vice president.
JOE
JOUJI NEZU
Explodes in anger when his pet ants are attacked by the president's crow. His attack on the president is ultimately unsuccessful.

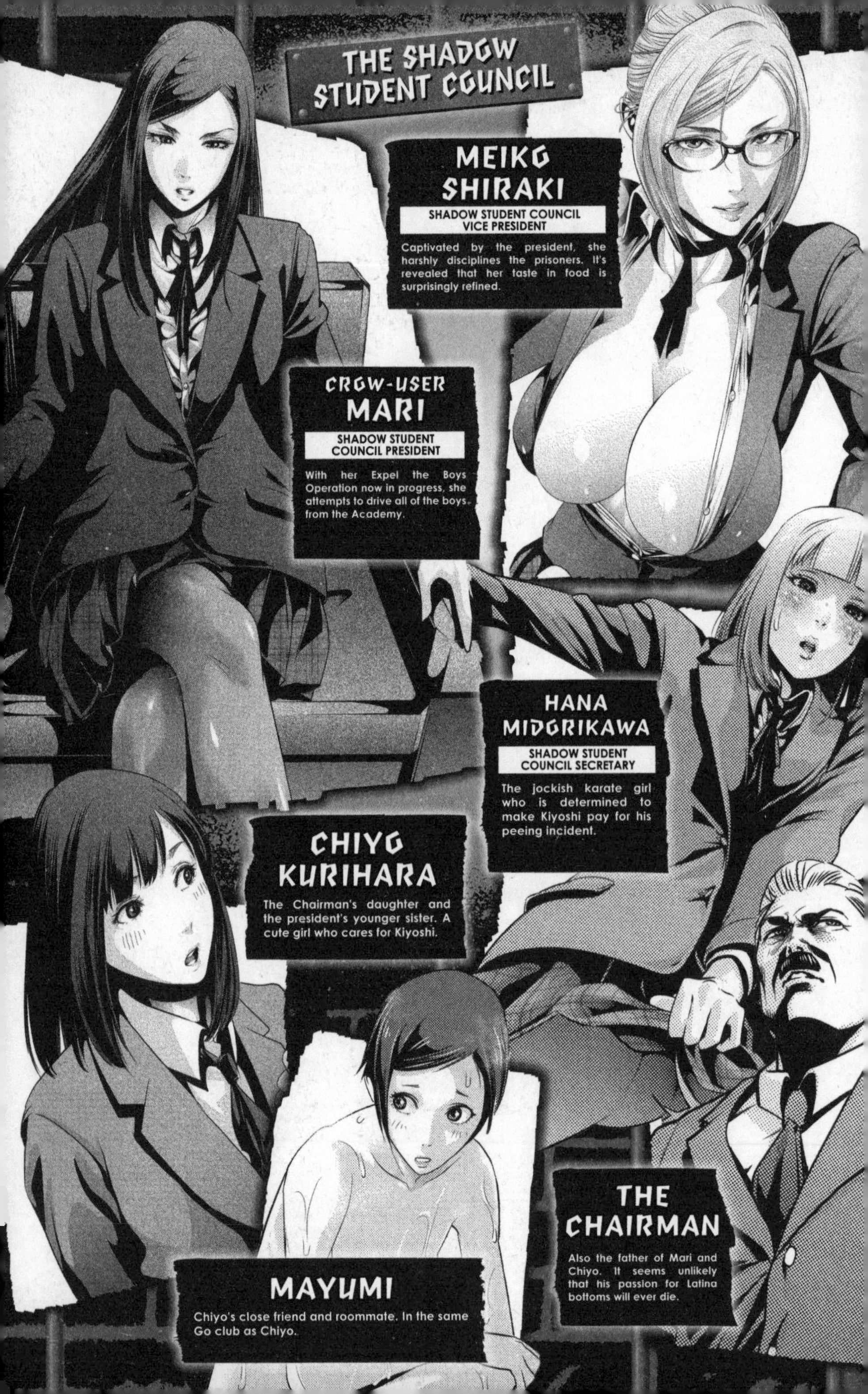
THE SHADOW STUDENT COUNCIL
MEIKO SHIRAKI
SHADOW STUDENT COUNCIL VICE PRESIDENT
Captivated by the president, she harshly disciplines the prisoners. It's revealed that her taste in food is surprisingly refined.
CROW-USER MARI
SHADOW STUDENT COUNCIL PRESIDENT
With her Expel the Boys Operation now in progress, she attempts to drive all of the boys from the Academy.
HANA MIDORIKAWA
SHADOW STUDENT COUNCIL SECRETARY
The jockish karate girl who is determined to make Kiyoshi pay for his peeing incident.
CHIYO KURIHARA
The Chairman's daughter and the president's younger sister. A cute girl who cares for Kiyoshi.
THE CHAIRMAN
Also the father of Mari and Chiyo. It seems unlikely that his passion for Latina bottoms will ever die.
MAYUMI
Chiyo's close friend and roommate. In the same Go club as Chiyo.

CONTENTS

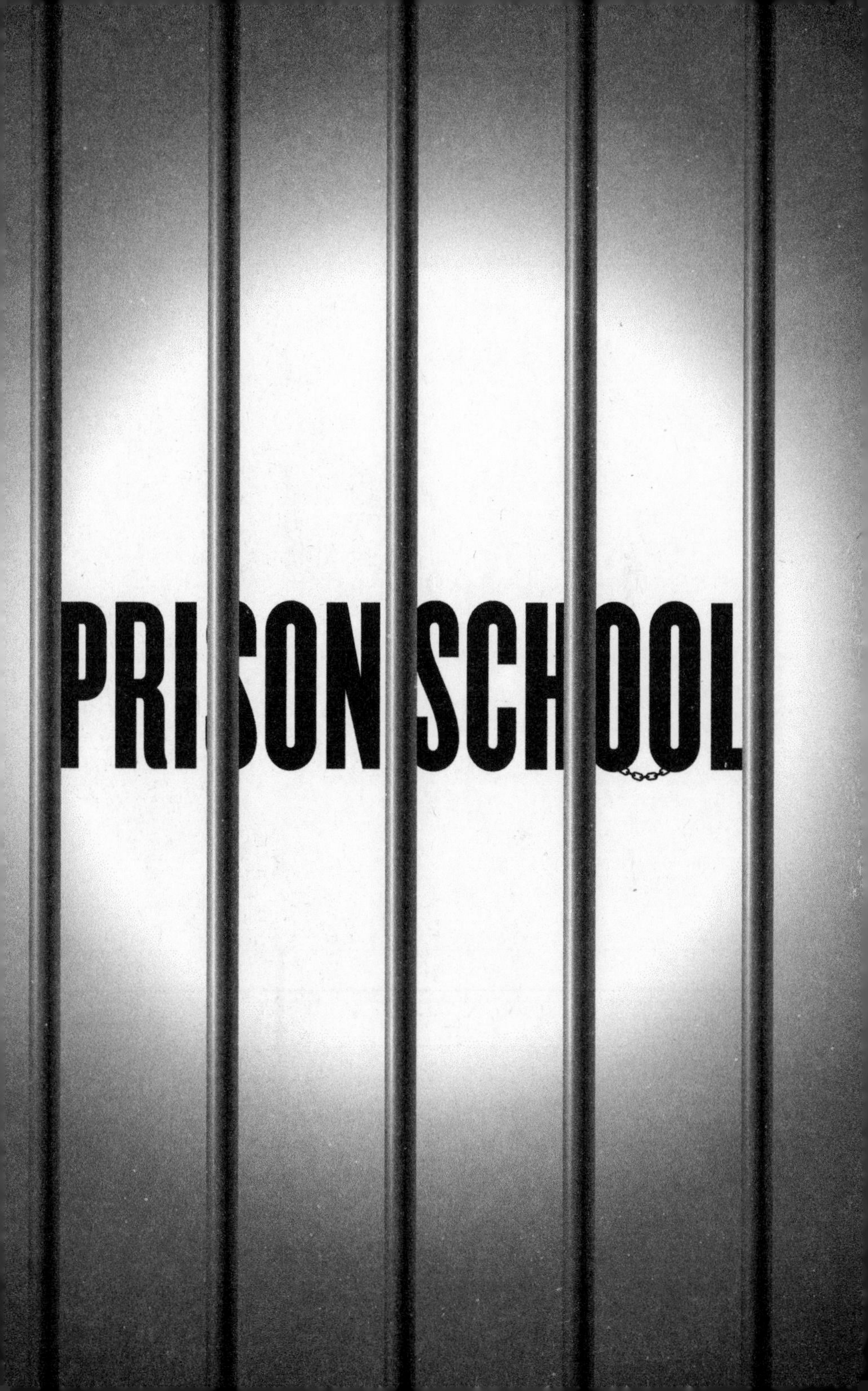
PRISON SCHOOL

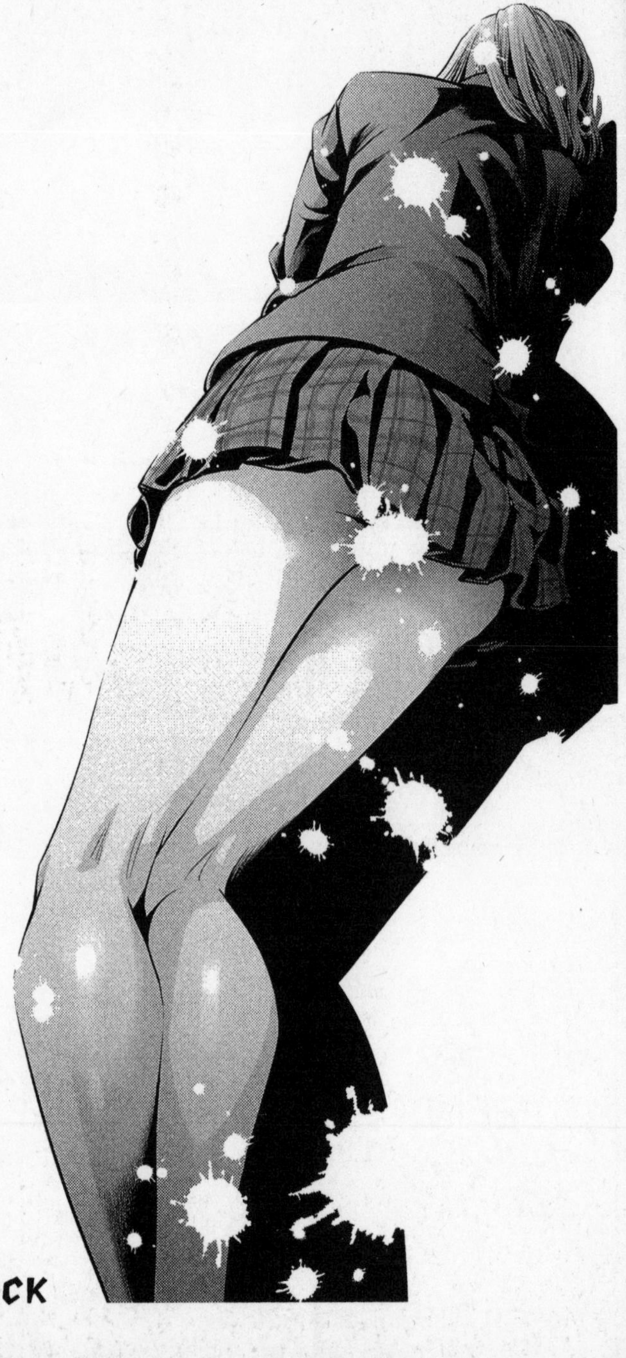

CHAPTER 39: HANA'S COUNTERATTACK

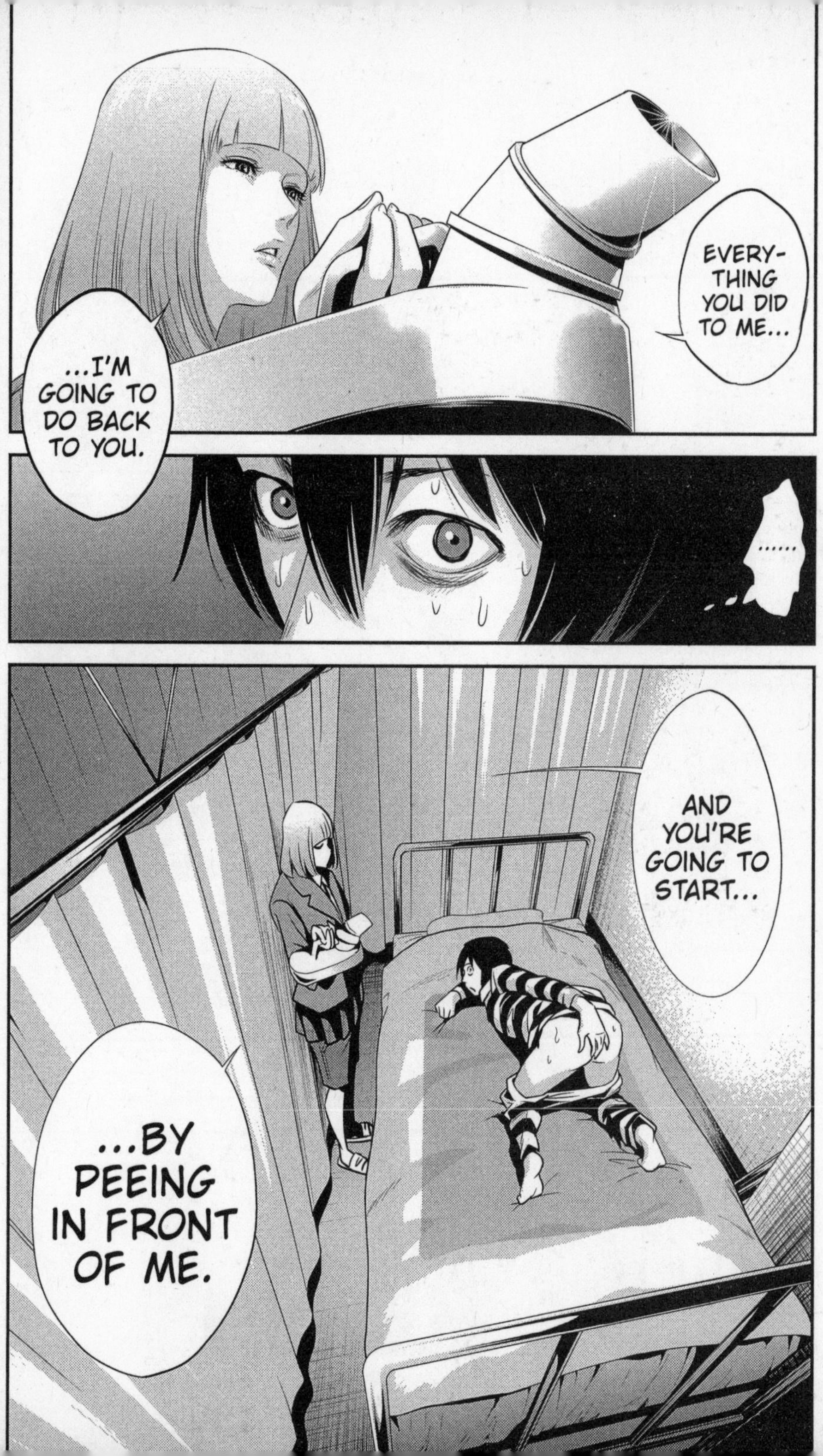
EVERY-THING YOU DID TO ME...
...I'M GOING TO DO BACK TO YOU.
......
AND YOU'RE GOING TO START...
...BY PEEING IN FRONT OF ME.

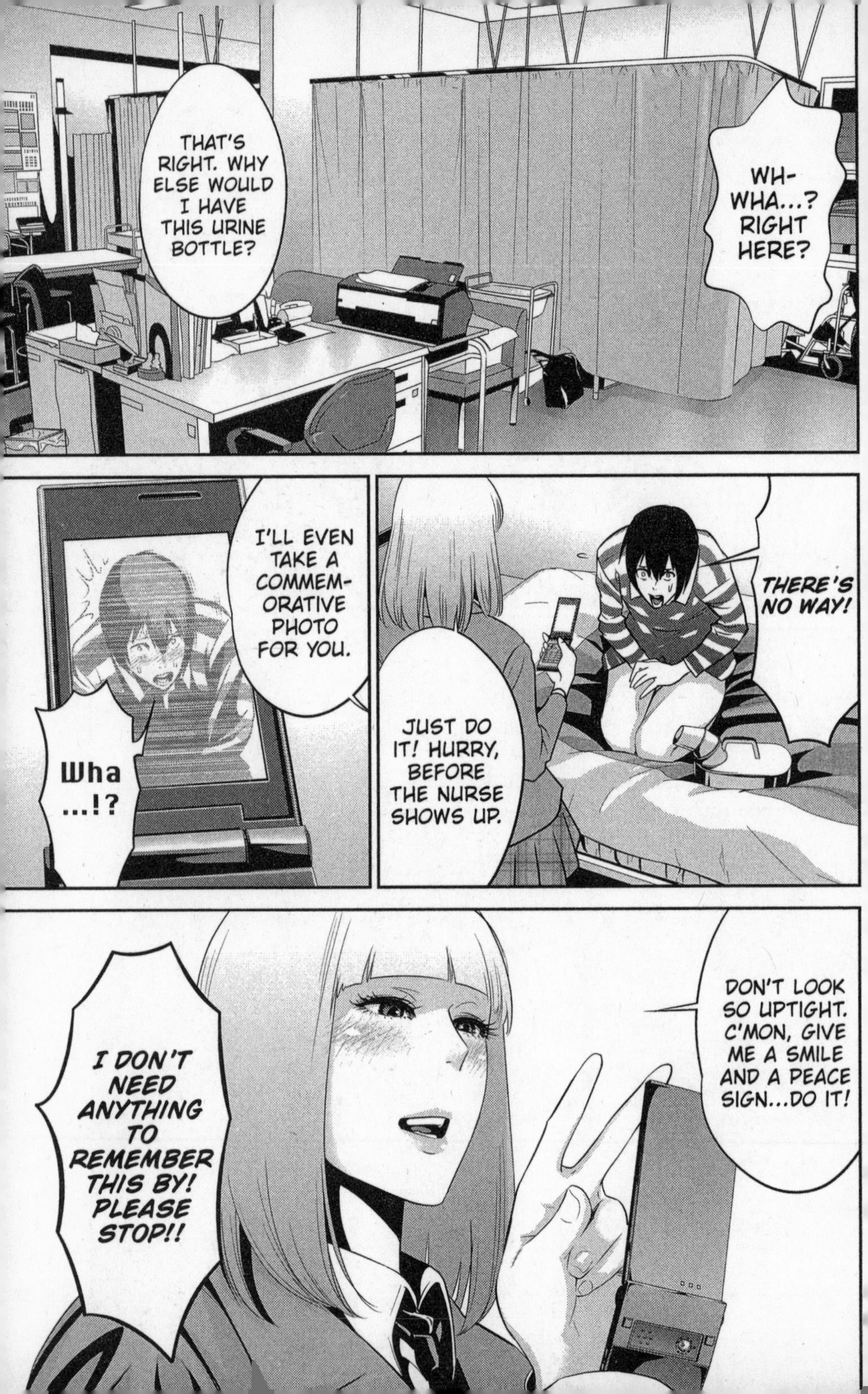
WH- WHA...? RIGHT HERE?
THAT'S RIGHT. WHY ELSE WOULD I HAVE THIS URINE BOTTLE?
THERE'S NO WAY!
JUST DO IT! HURRY, BEFORE THE NURSE SHOWS UP.
I'LL EVEN TAKE A COMMEMORATIVE PHOTO FOR YOU.
Wha ...!?
DON'T LOOK SO UPTIGHT. C'MON, GIVE ME A SMILE AND A PEACE SIGN...DO IT!
I DON'T NEED ANYTHING TO REMEMBER THIS BY! PLEASE STOP!!

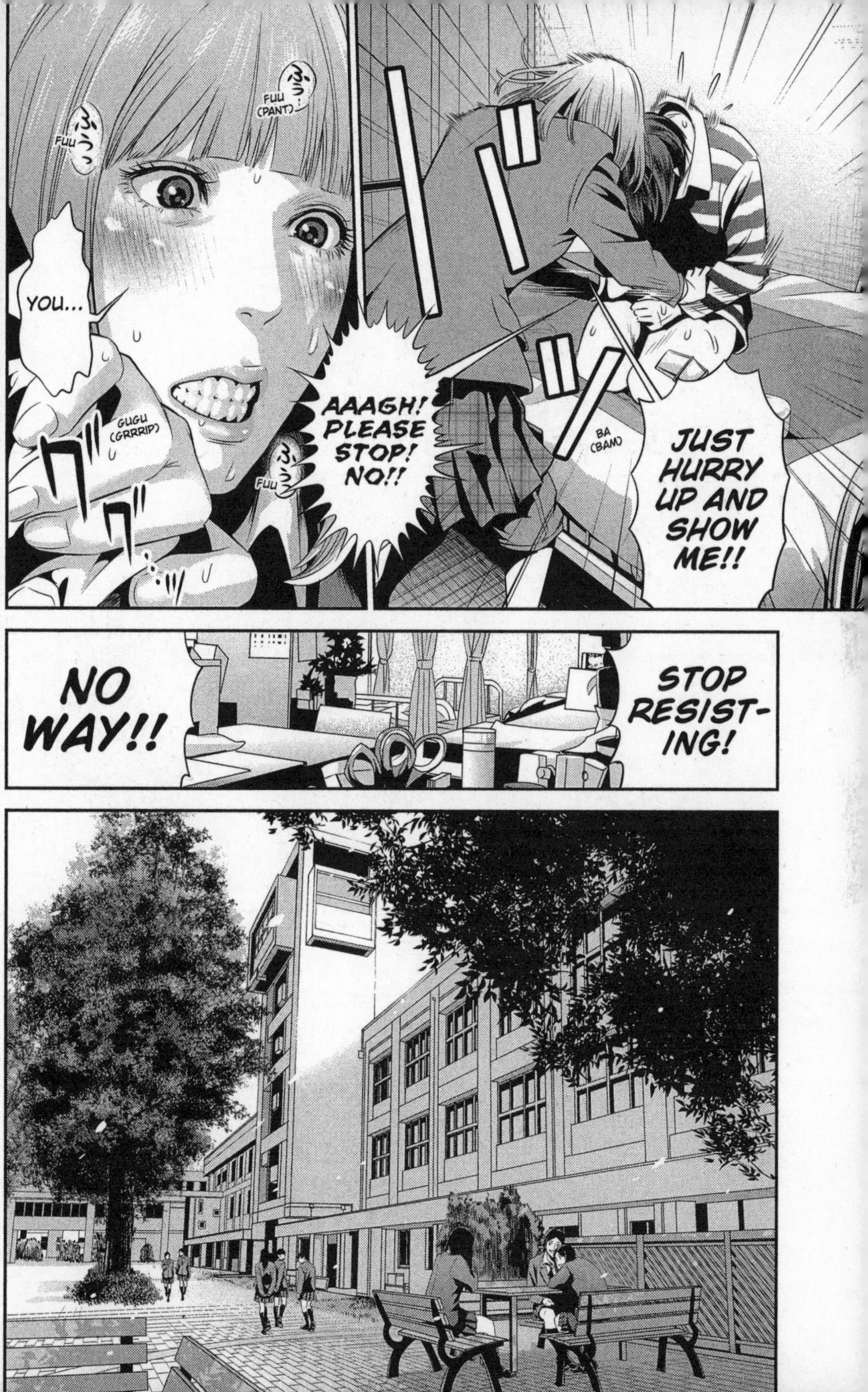
JUST HURRY UP AND SHOW ME!!
BA (BAM)
AAAGH! PLEASE STOP! NO!!
FUU (PANT)
FUU
YOU...
GUGU (GRRRIP)
FUU
STOP RESIST-ING!
NO WAY!!

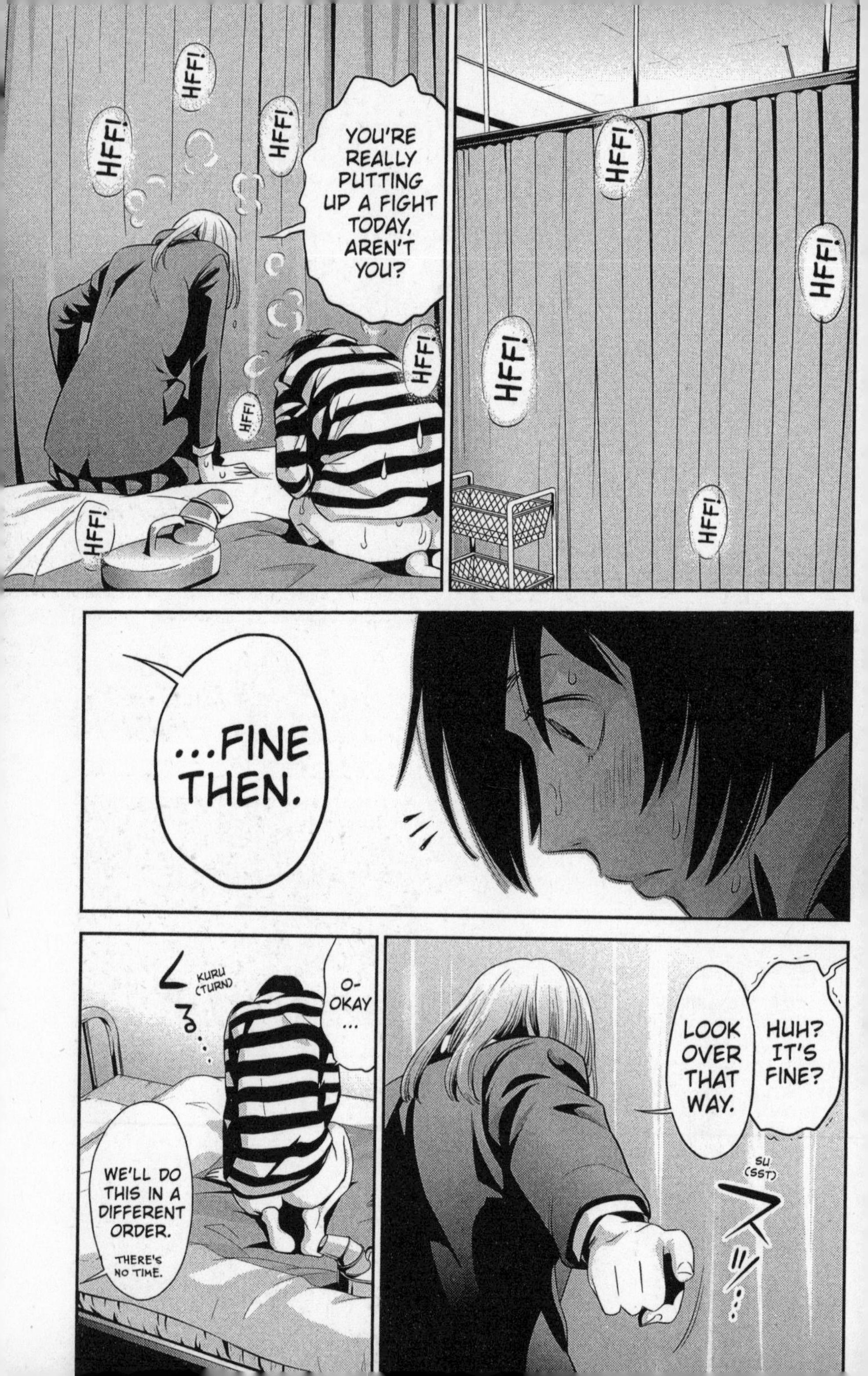
HFF!
HFF!
HFF!
HFF!
HFF!
YOU'RE REALLY PUTTING UP A FIGHT TODAY, AREN'T YOU?
HFF!
HFF!
HFF!
HFF!
HFF!
...FINE THEN.
HUH? IT'S FINE?
LOOK OVER THAT WAY.
SU (SST)
O-OKAY...
KURU (TURN)
WE'LL DO THIS IN A DIFFERENT ORDER.
THERE'S NO TIME.

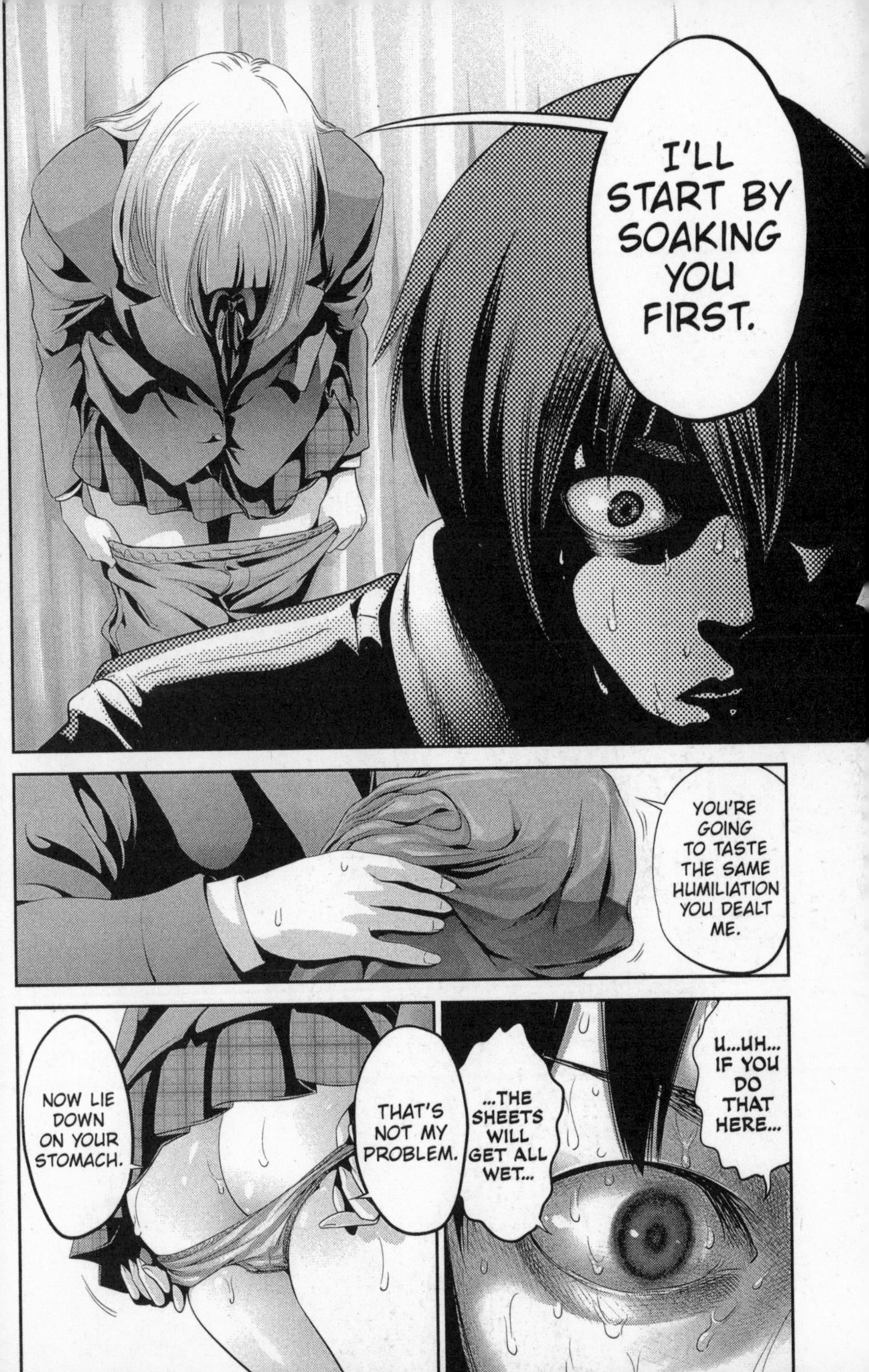
I'LL START BY SOAKING YOU FIRST.
YOU'RE GOING TO TASTE THE SAME HUMILIATION YOU DEALT ME.
U...UH... IF YOU DO THAT HERE...
...THE SHEETS WILL GET ALL WET...
THAT'S NOT MY PROBLEM.
NOW LIE DOWN ON YOUR STOMACH.

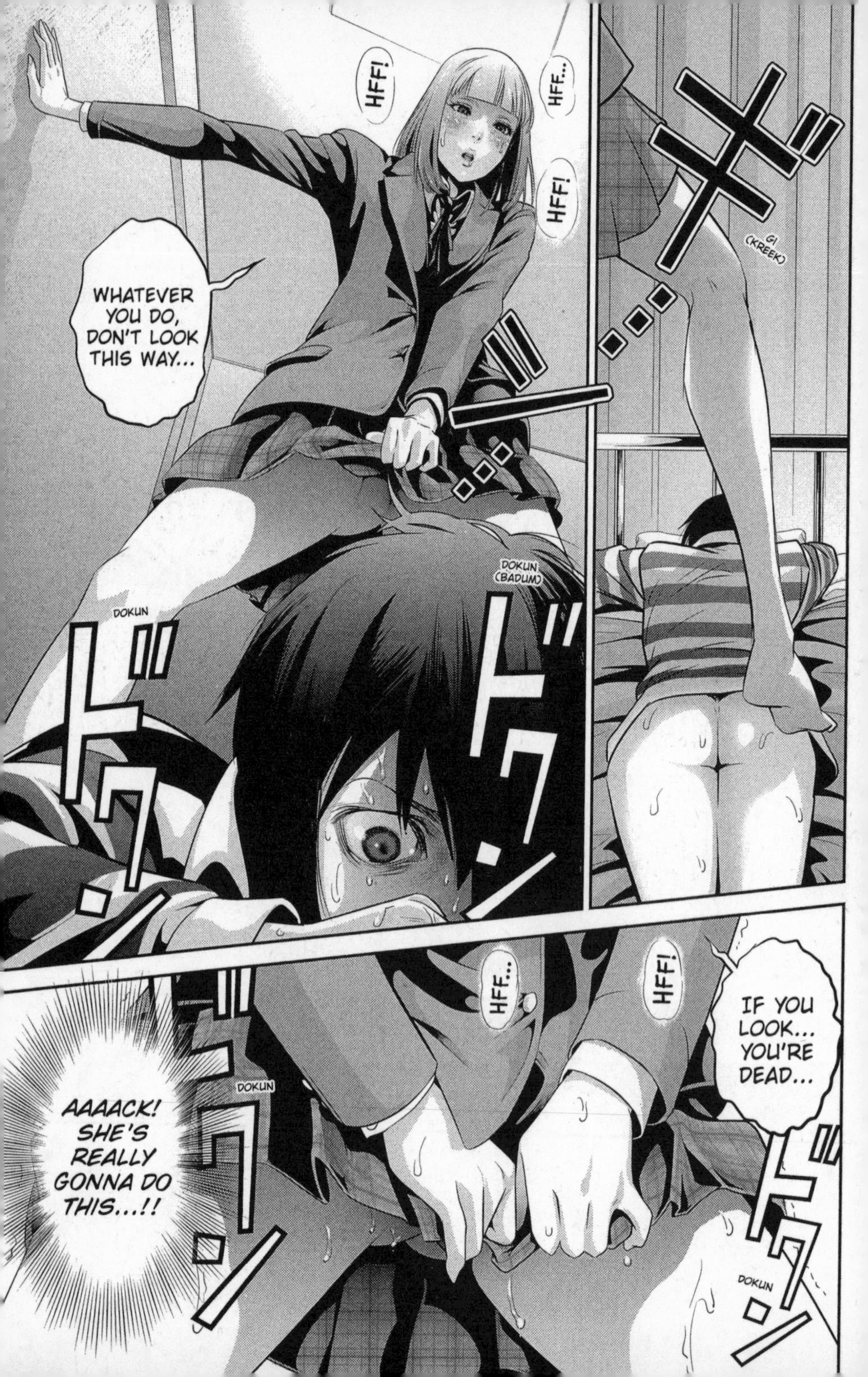
GI (KREEK)
HFF...
HFF!
HFF!
WHATEVER YOU DO, DON'T LOOK THIS WAY...
DOKUN (BADUM)
DOKUN
HFF!
IF YOU LOOK... YOU'RE DEAD...
HFF...
DOKUN
AAAACK! SHE'S REALLY GONNA DO THIS...!!
DOKUN

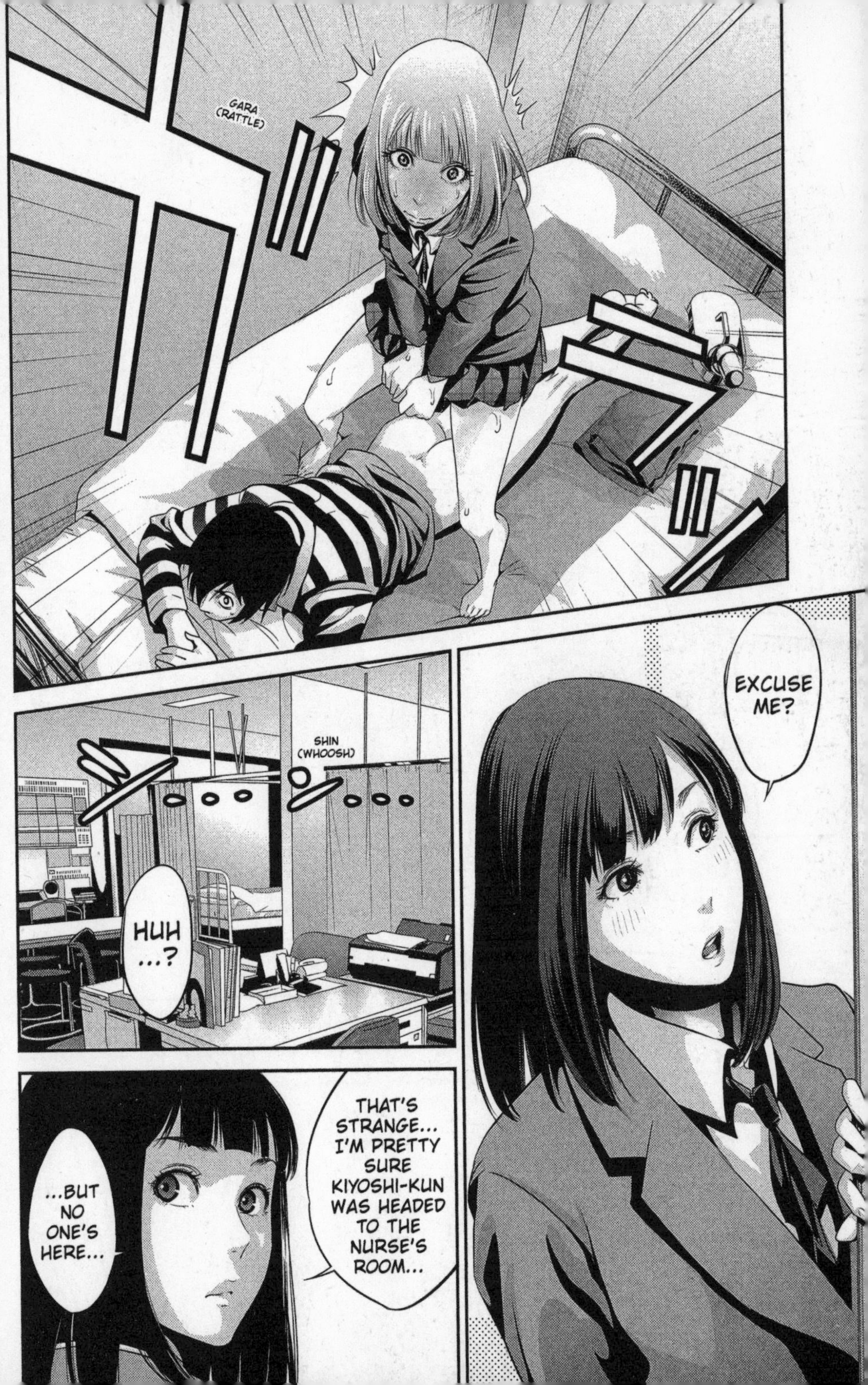
GARA (RATTLE)
EXCUSE ME?
SHIN (WHOOSH)
HUH ...?
THAT'S STRANGE... I'M PRETTY SURE KIYOSHI-KUN WAS HEADED TO THE NURSE'S ROOM...
...BUT NO ONE'S HERE...

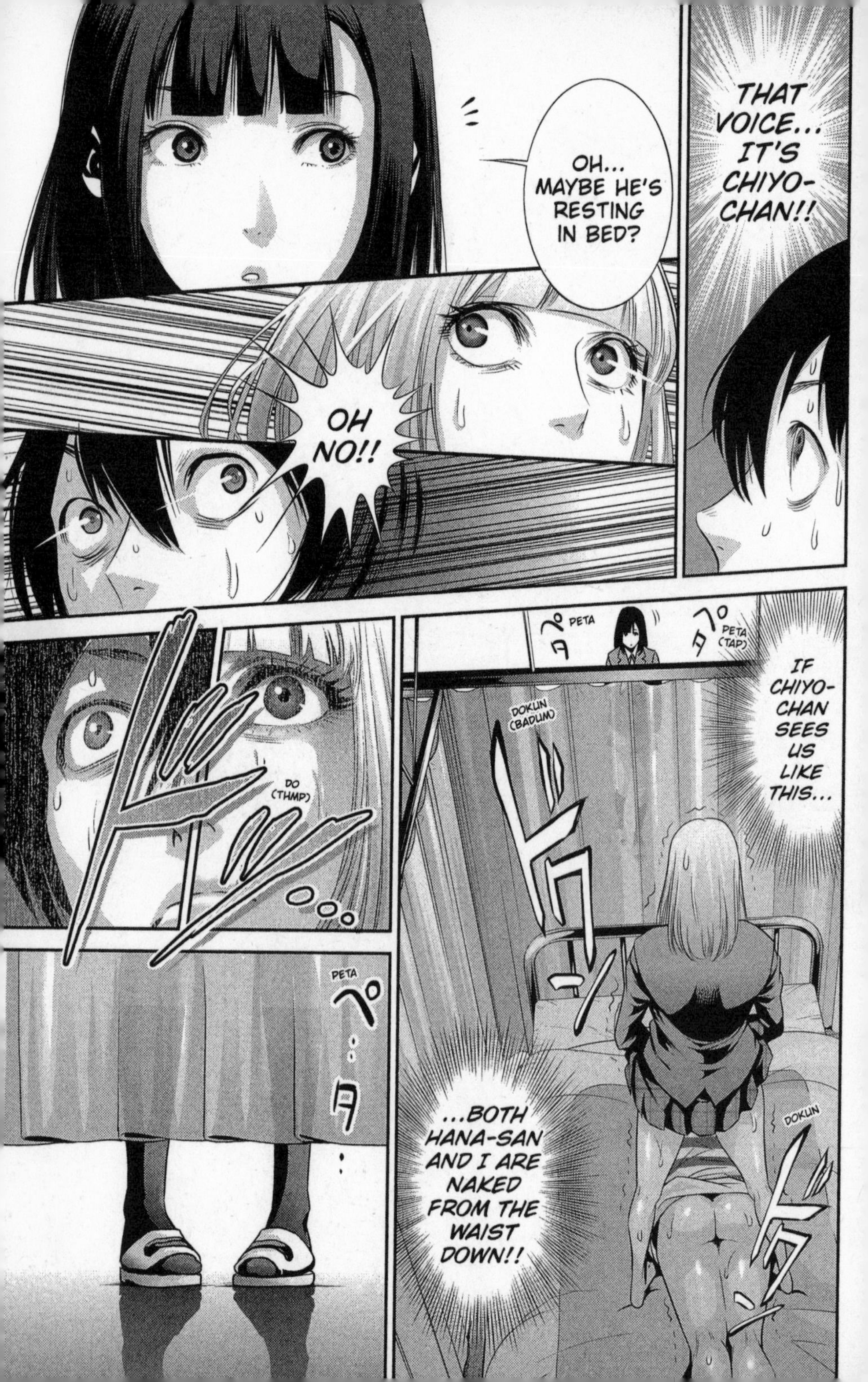
OH... MAYBE HE'S RESTING IN BED?
THAT VOICE... IT'S CHIYO-CHAN!!
OH NO!!
DO (THMP)
PETA
PETA (TAP)
IF CHIYO-CHAN SEES US LIKE THIS...
DOKUN (BADUM)
...BOTH HANA-SAN AND I ARE NAKED FROM THE WAIST DOWN!!
DOKUN
PETA

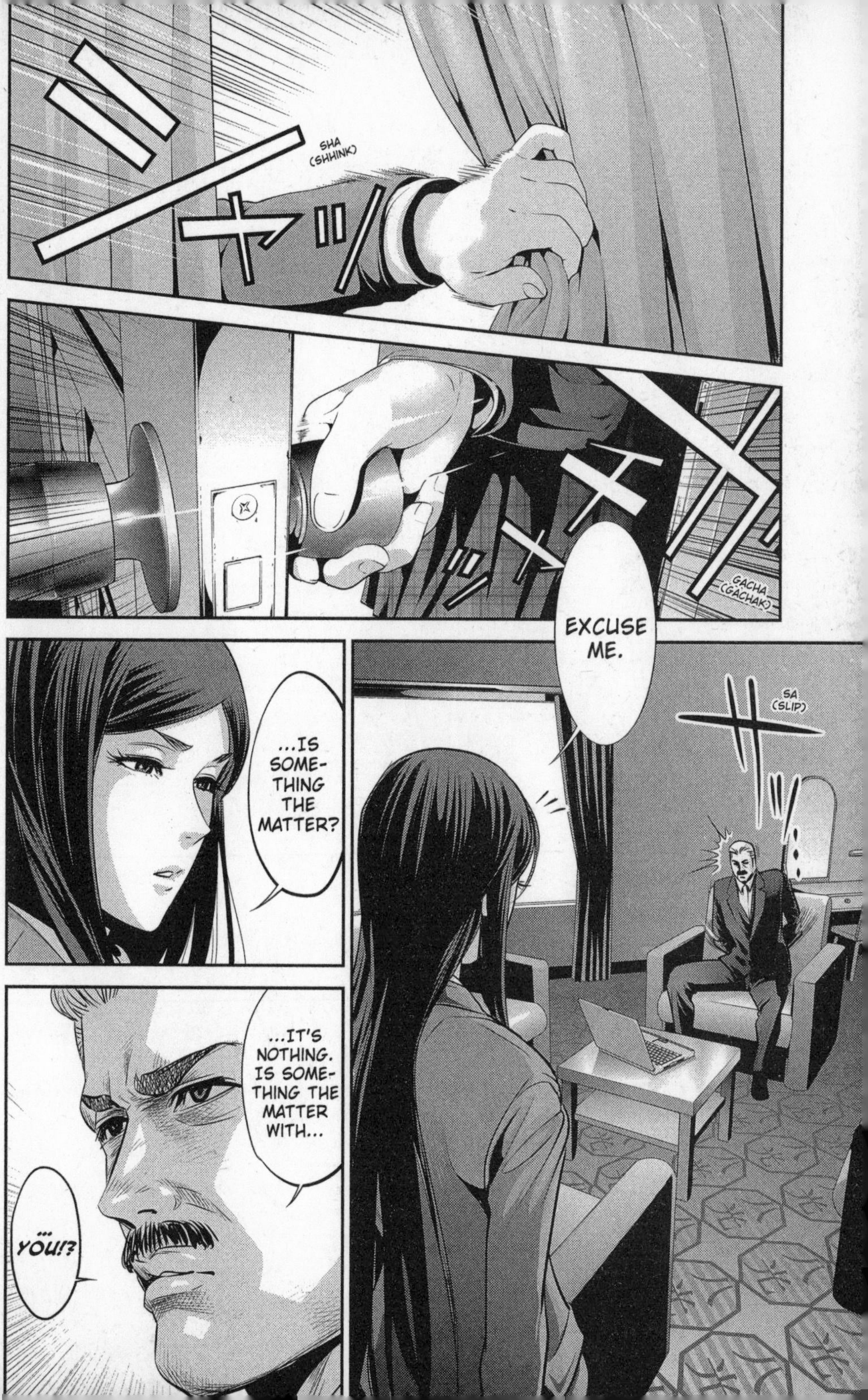
SHA
(SHHINK)
GACHA
(GACHAK)
EXCUSE ME.
SA
(SLIP)
...IS SOME-THING THE MATTER?
...IT'S NOTHING. IS SOME-THING THE MATTER WITH...
...YOU!?

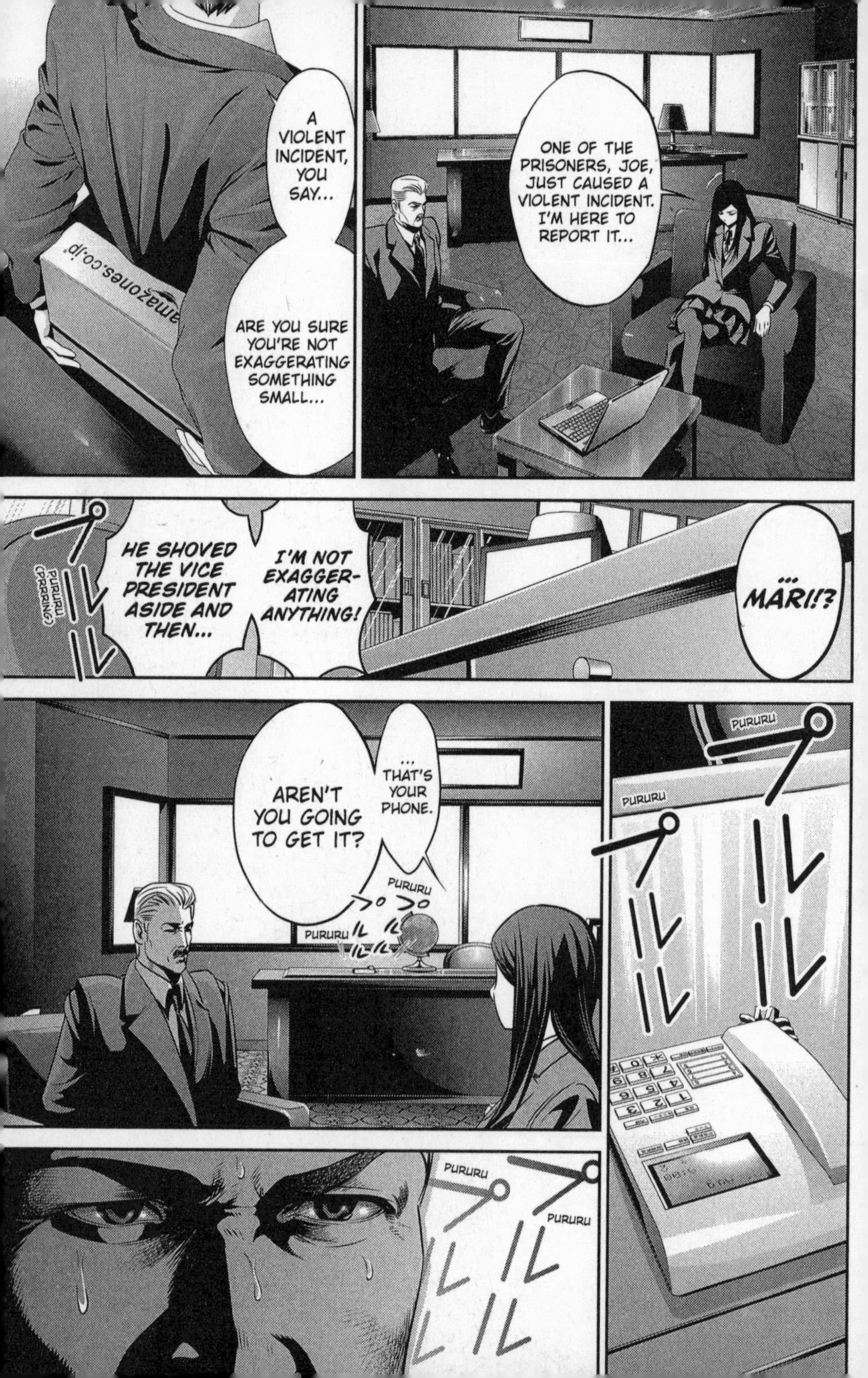
ONE OF THE PRISONERS, JOE, JUST CAUSED A VIOLENT INCIDENT. I'M HERE TO REPORT IT...
A VIOLENT INCIDENT, YOU SAY...
amazones.co.jp
ARE YOU SURE YOU'RE NOT EXAGGERATING SOMETHING SMALL...
...MÄRI!?
I'M NOT EXAGGER-ATING ANYTHING!
HE SHOVED THE VICE PRESIDENT ASIDE AND THEN...
PURURU (PRRRING)
PURURU
PURURU
...THAT'S YOUR PHONE.
AREN'T YOU GOING TO GET IT?
PURURU
PURURU
PURURU
PURURU

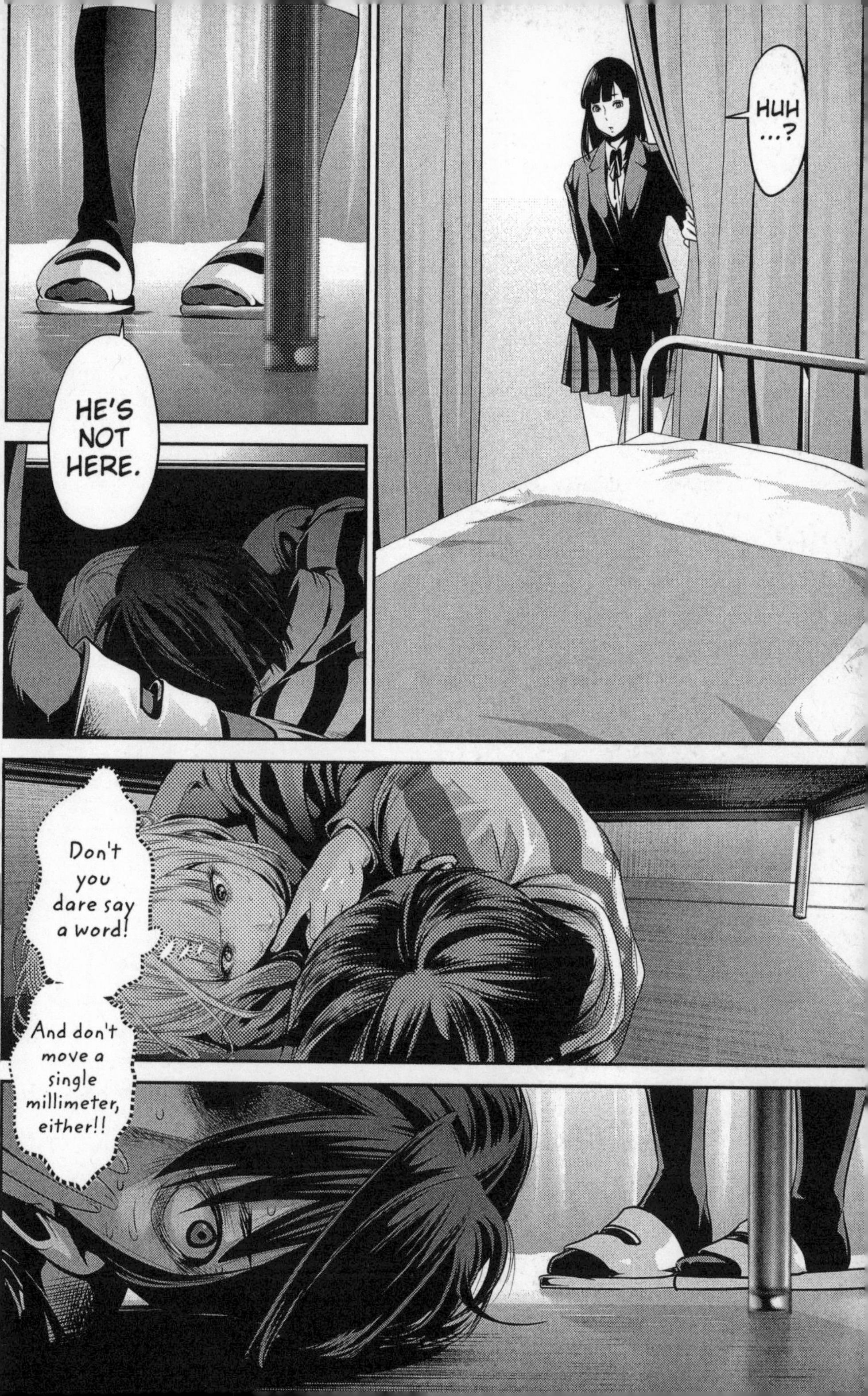
HUH ...?
HE'S NOT HERE.
Don't you dare say a word!
And don't move a single millimeter, either!!

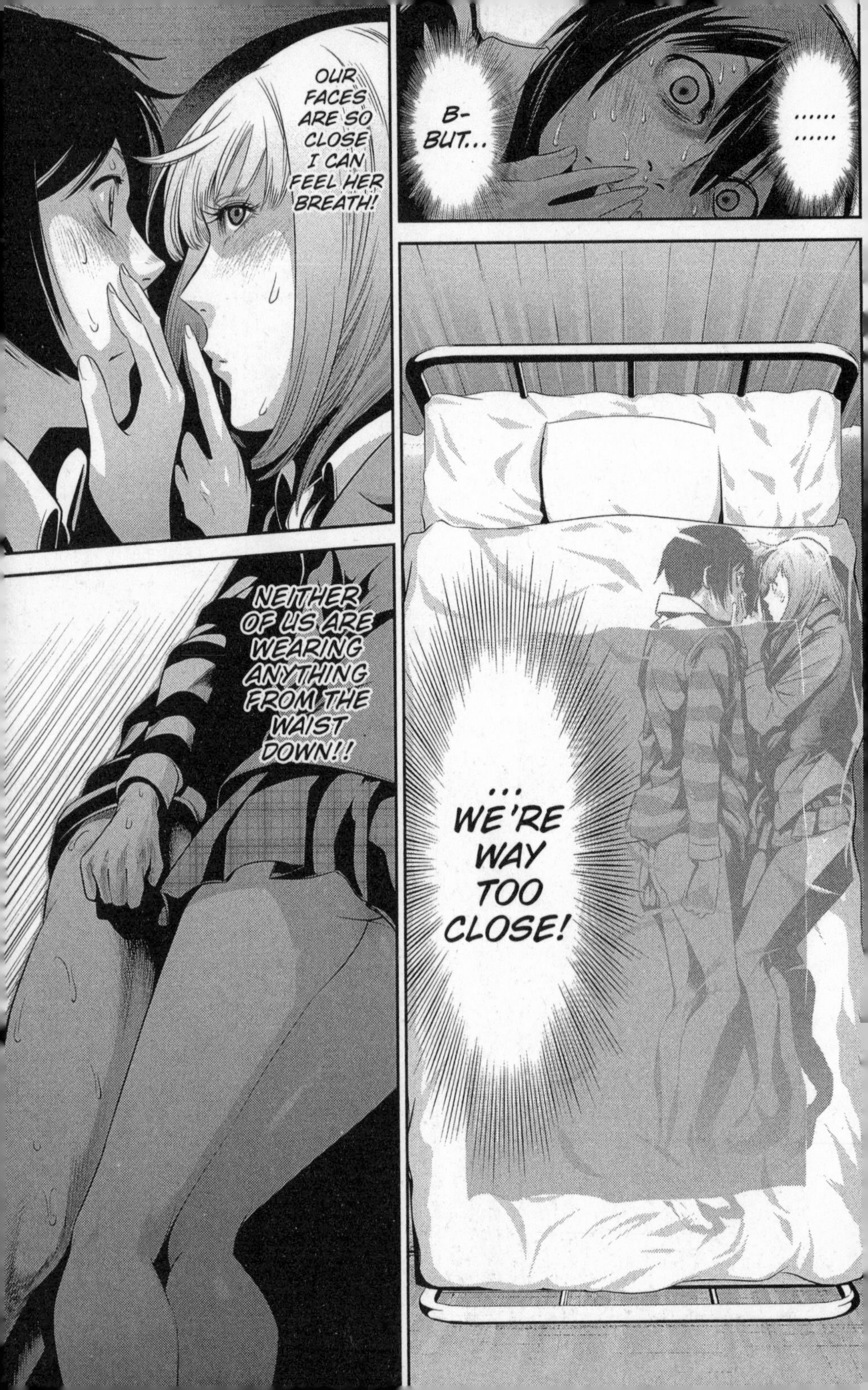

....
B- BUT...
OUR FACES ARE SO CLOSE I CAN FEEL HER BREATH!
NEITHER OF US ARE WEARING ANYTHING FROM THE WAIST DOWN!!
... WE'RE WAY TOO CLOSE!

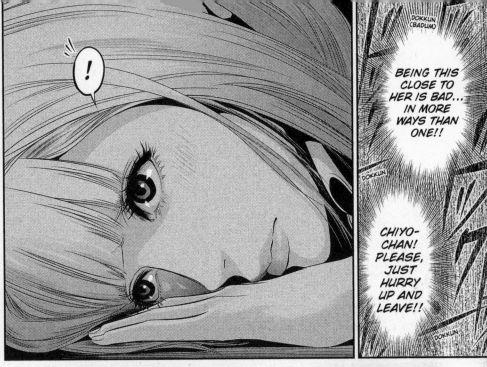

DOKKUN
(BADUM)

BEING THIS CLOSE TO HER IS BAD... IN MORE WAYS THAN ONE!!

DOKKUN

CHIYO-CHAN! PLEASE, JUST HURRY UP AND LEAVE!!

DOKKUN

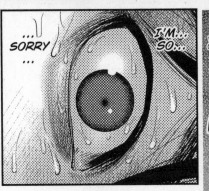

...SORRY...

I'M... SO...

HUKURI
(SPROING)

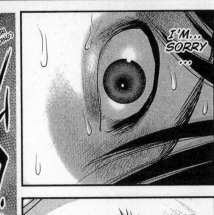

I'M... SORRY...

WHAT IS IT...?

THERE'S... SOMETHING PRESSING AGAINST MY THIGH...

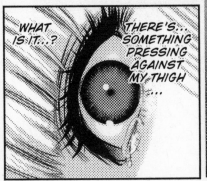

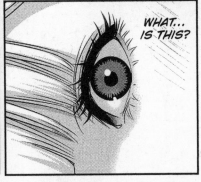

WHAT... IS THIS?

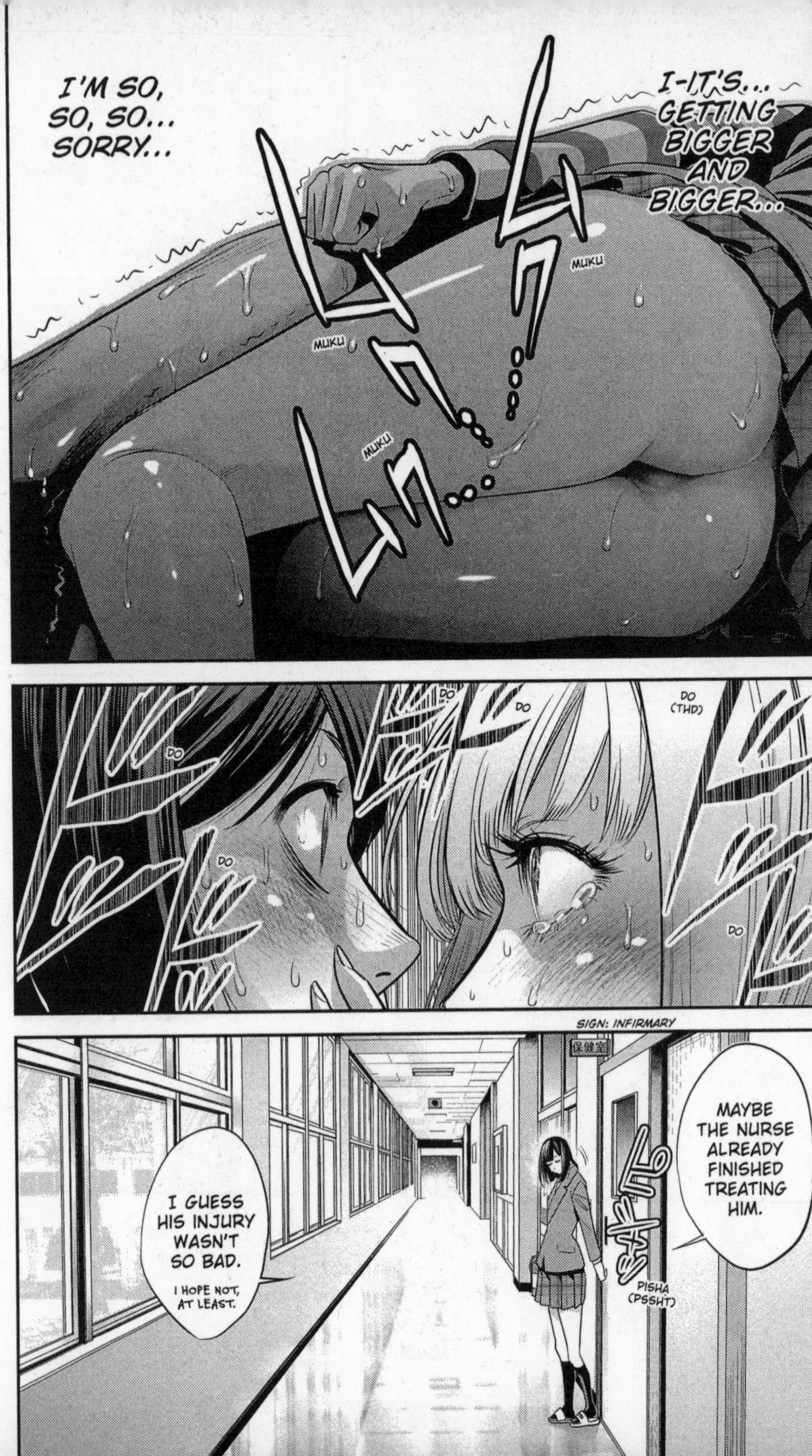
I-IT'S... GETTING BIGGER AND BIGGER...
I'M SO, SO, SO... SORRY...
MUKU
MUKU
MUKU
DO (THD)
DO
DO
DO
DO
DO
SIGN: INFIRMARY
保健室
MAYBE THE NURSE ALREADY FINISHED TREATING HIM.
PISHA (PSSHT)
I GUESS HIS INJURY WASN'T SO BAD.
I HOPE NOT, AT LEAST.

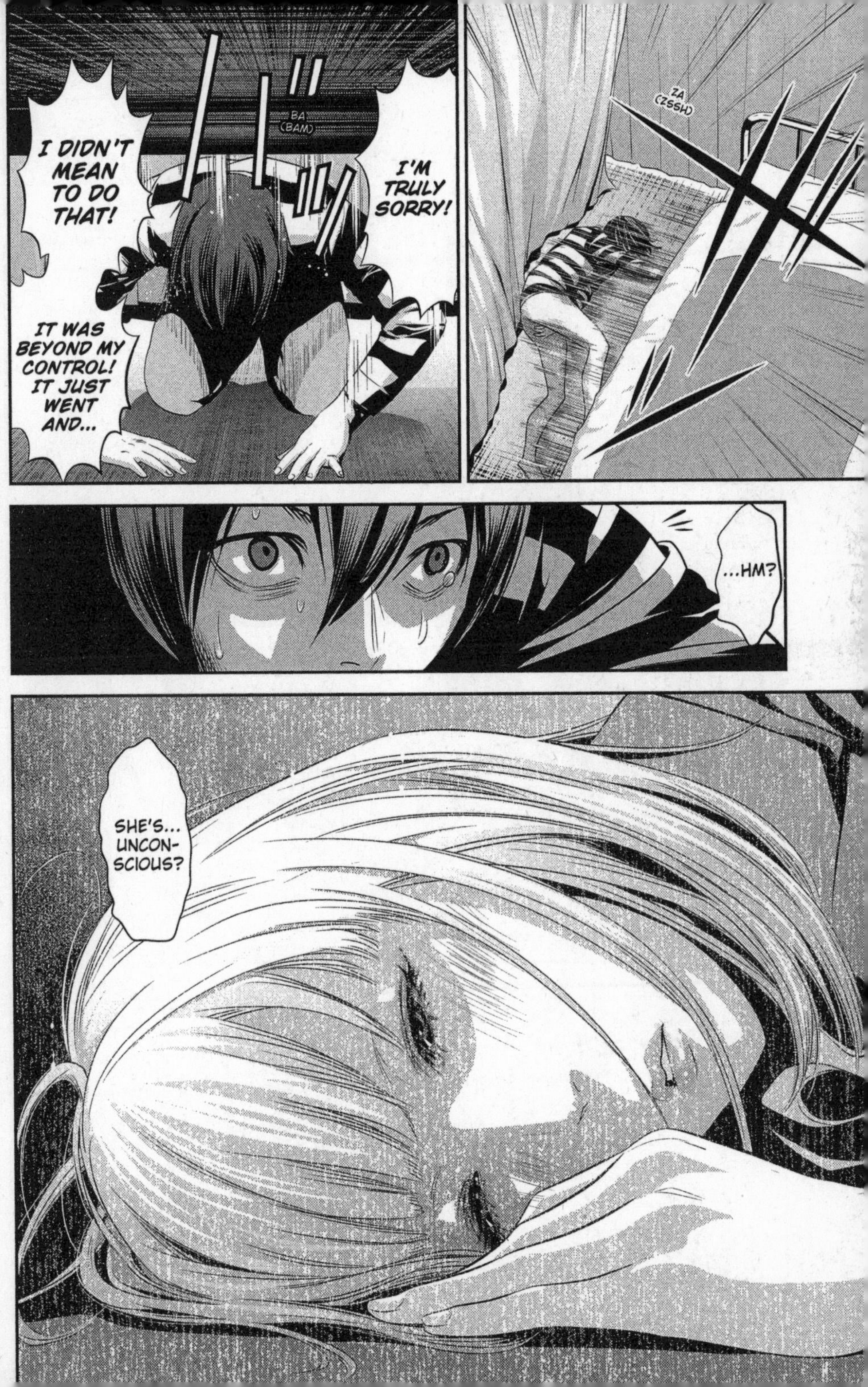
ZA (ZSSH)
BA (BAM)
I'M TRULY SORRY!
I DIDN'T MEAN TO DO THAT!
IT WAS BEYOND MY CONTROL! IT JUST WENT AND...
...HM?
SHE'S... UNCON-SCIOUS?

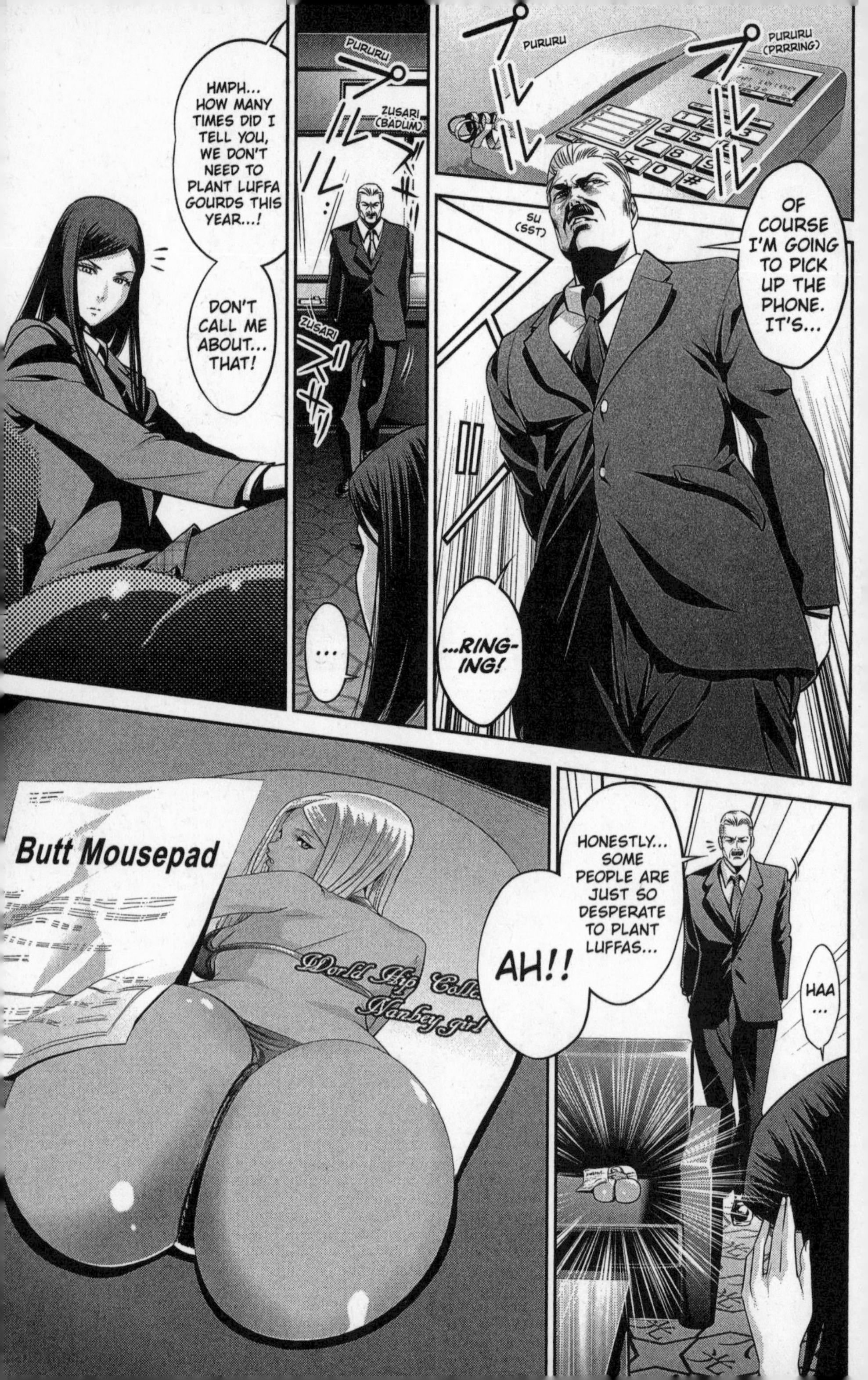
PURURU
PURURU (PRRRING)
SU (SST)
OF COURSE I'M GOING TO PICK UP THE PHONE. IT'S...
...RING-ING!
PURURU
ZUSARI (BADUM)
ZUSARI
...
HMPH... HOW MANY TIMES DID I TELL YOU, WE DON'T NEED TO PLANT LUFFA GOURDS THIS YEAR...!
DON'T CALL ME ABOUT... THAT!
HONESTLY... SOME PEOPLE ARE JUST SO DESPERATE TO PLANT LUFFAS...
HAA ...
AH!!
Butt Mousepad
World Hip Colle
Nanbey girl

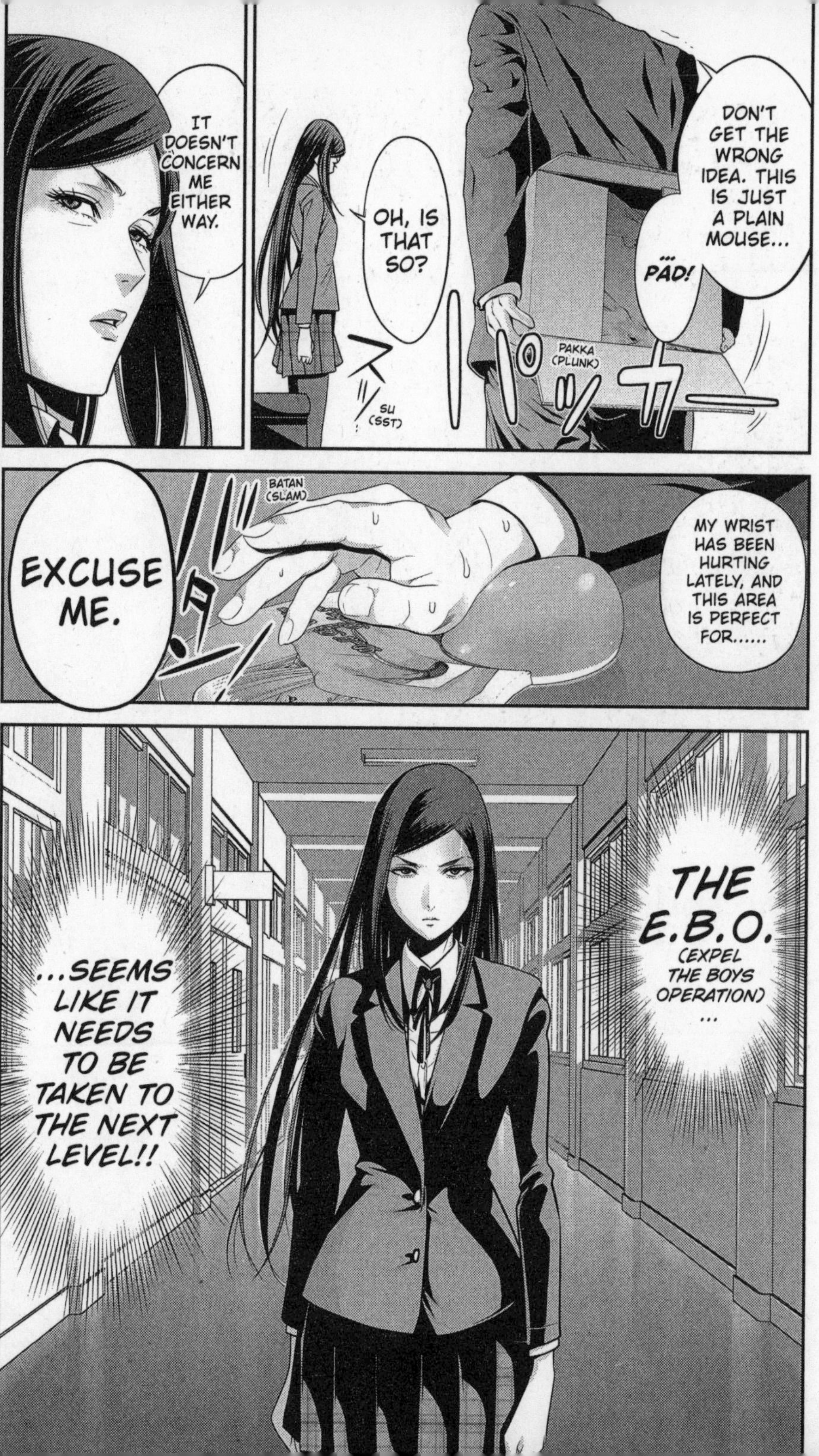
DON'T GET THE WRONG IDEA. THIS IS JUST A PLAIN MOUSE...
...PÄD!
PAKKA (PLUNK)
OH, IS THAT SO?
SU (SST)
IT DOESN'T CONCERN ME EITHER WAY.
MY WRIST HAS BEEN HURTING LATELY, AND THIS AREA IS PERFECT FOR......
BATAN (SLAM)
EXCUSE ME.
THE E.B.O. (EXPEL THE BOYS OPERATION) ...
...SEEMS LIKE IT NEEDS TO BE TAKEN TO THE NEXT LEVEL!!

CHAPTER 40: PATHS OF GLORY!

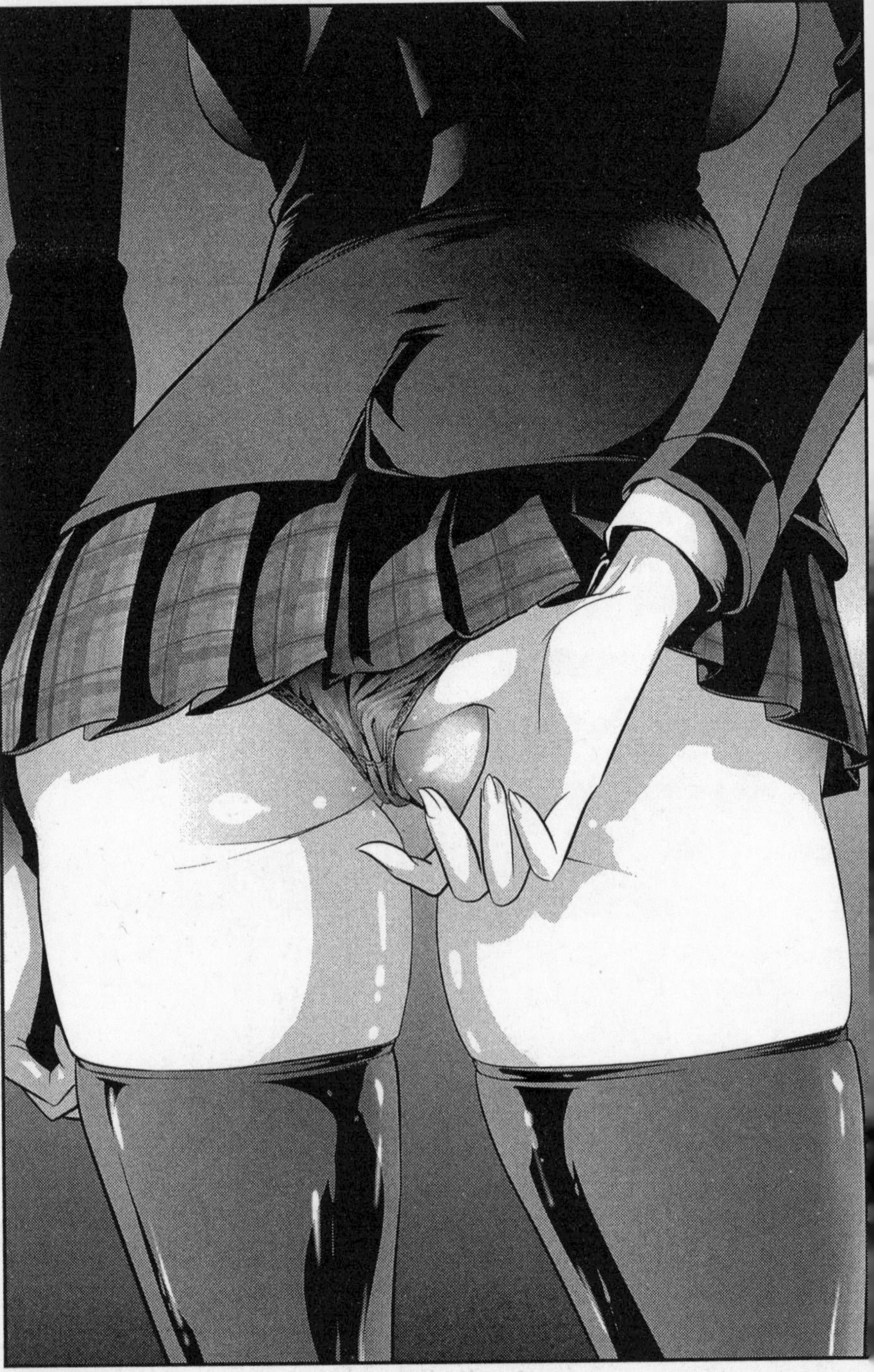

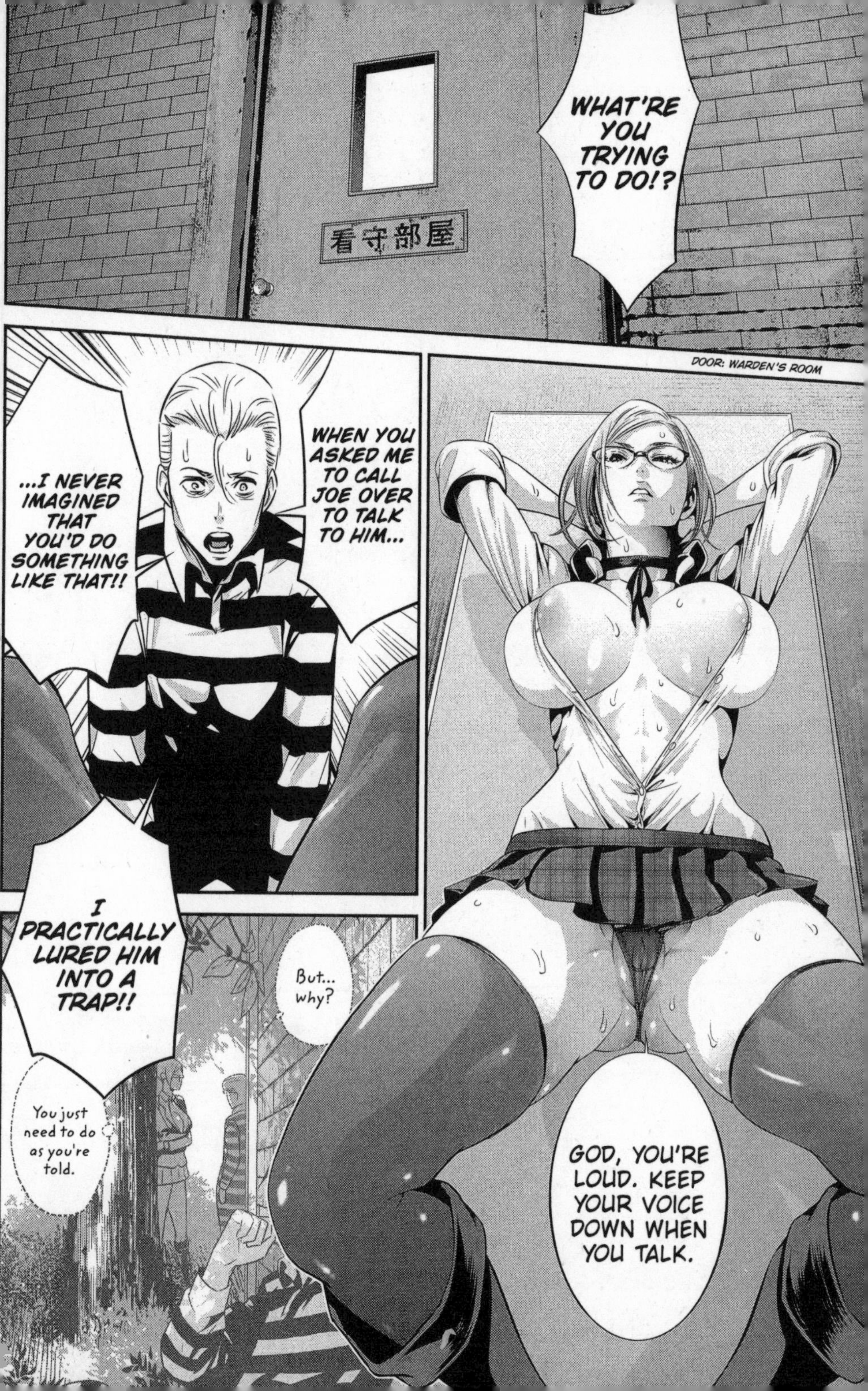
WHAT'RE YOU TRYING TO DO!?
看守部屋
DOOR: WARDEN'S ROOM
WHEN YOU ASKED ME TO CALL JOE OVER TO TALK TO HIM...
...I NEVER IMAGINED THAT YOU'D DO SOMETHING LIKE THAT!!
I PRACTICALLY LURED HIM INTO A TRAP!!
But... why?
You just need to do as you're told.
GOD, YOU'RE LOUD. KEEP YOUR VOICE DOWN WHEN YOU TALK.

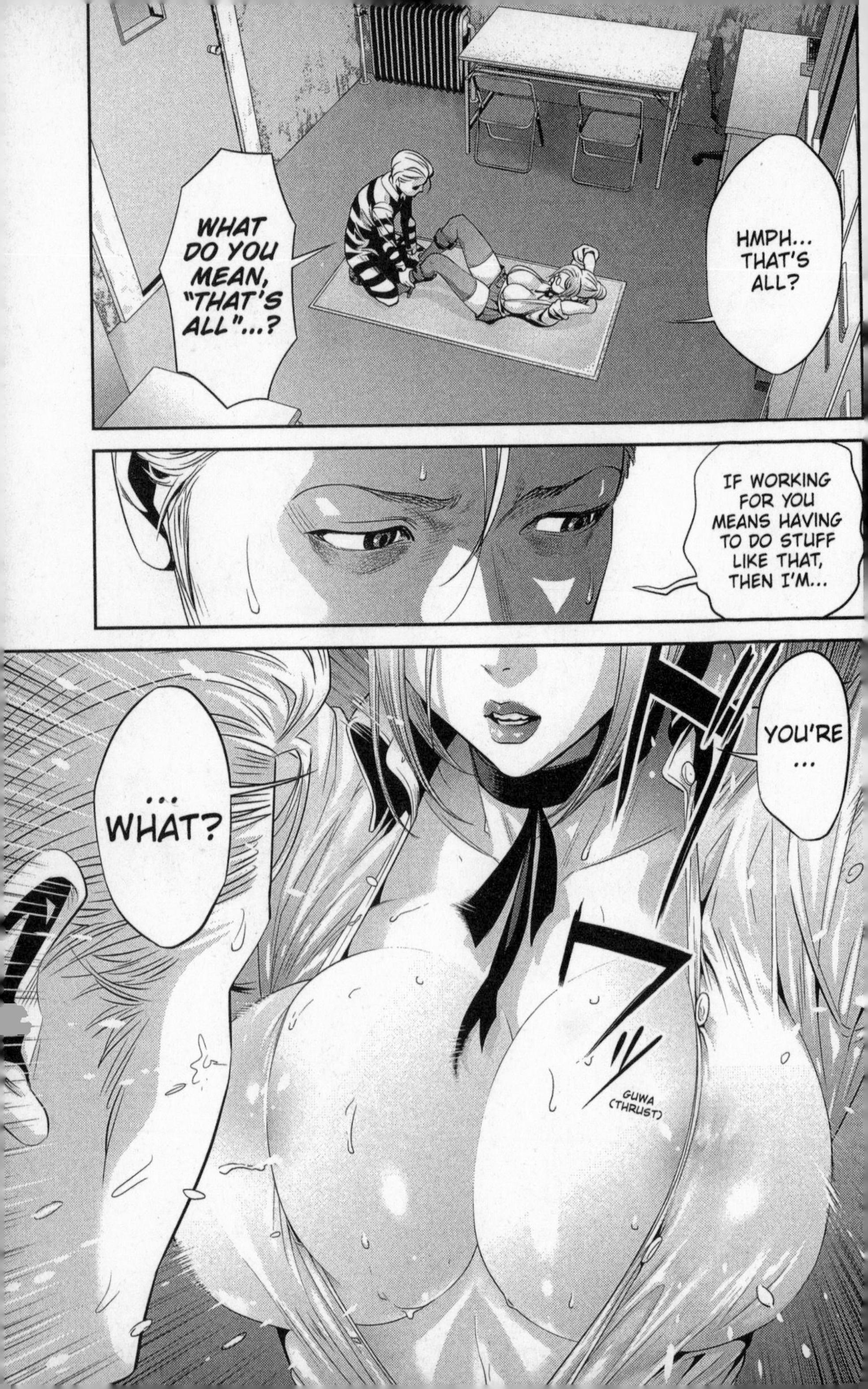
HMPH... THAT'S ALL?
WHAT DO YOU MEAN, "THAT'S ALL"...?
IF WORKING FOR YOU MEANS HAVING TO DO STUFF LIKE THAT, THEN I'M...
YOU'RE ...
... WHAT?
GUWA (THRUST)

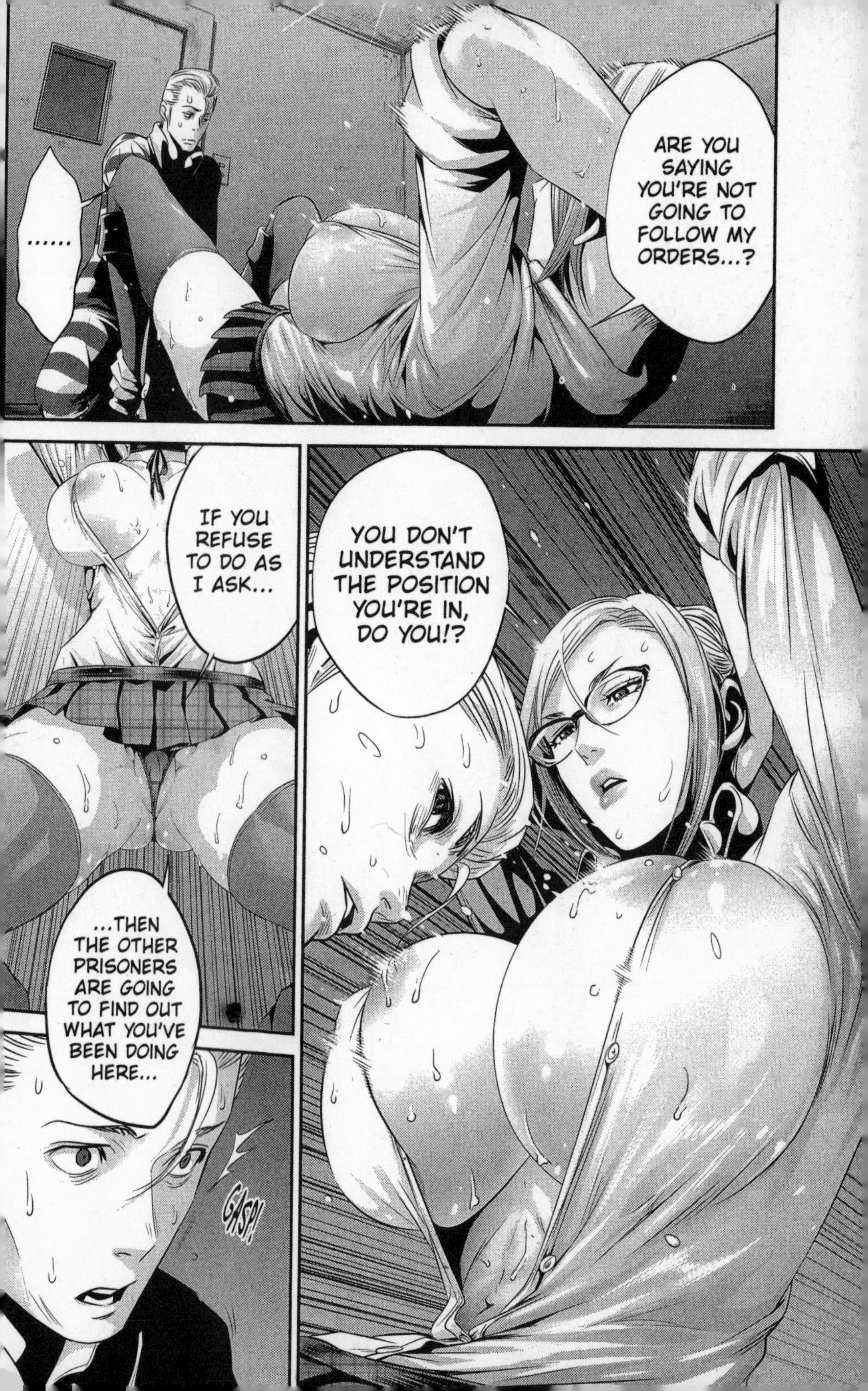
ARE YOU SAYING YOU'RE NOT GOING TO FOLLOW MY ORDERS...?
......
YOU DON'T UNDERSTAND THE POSITION YOU'RE IN, DO YOU!?
IF YOU REFUSE TO DO AS I ASK...
...THEN THE OTHER PRISONERS ARE GOING TO FIND OUT WHAT YOU'VE BEEN DOING HERE...
GASP!

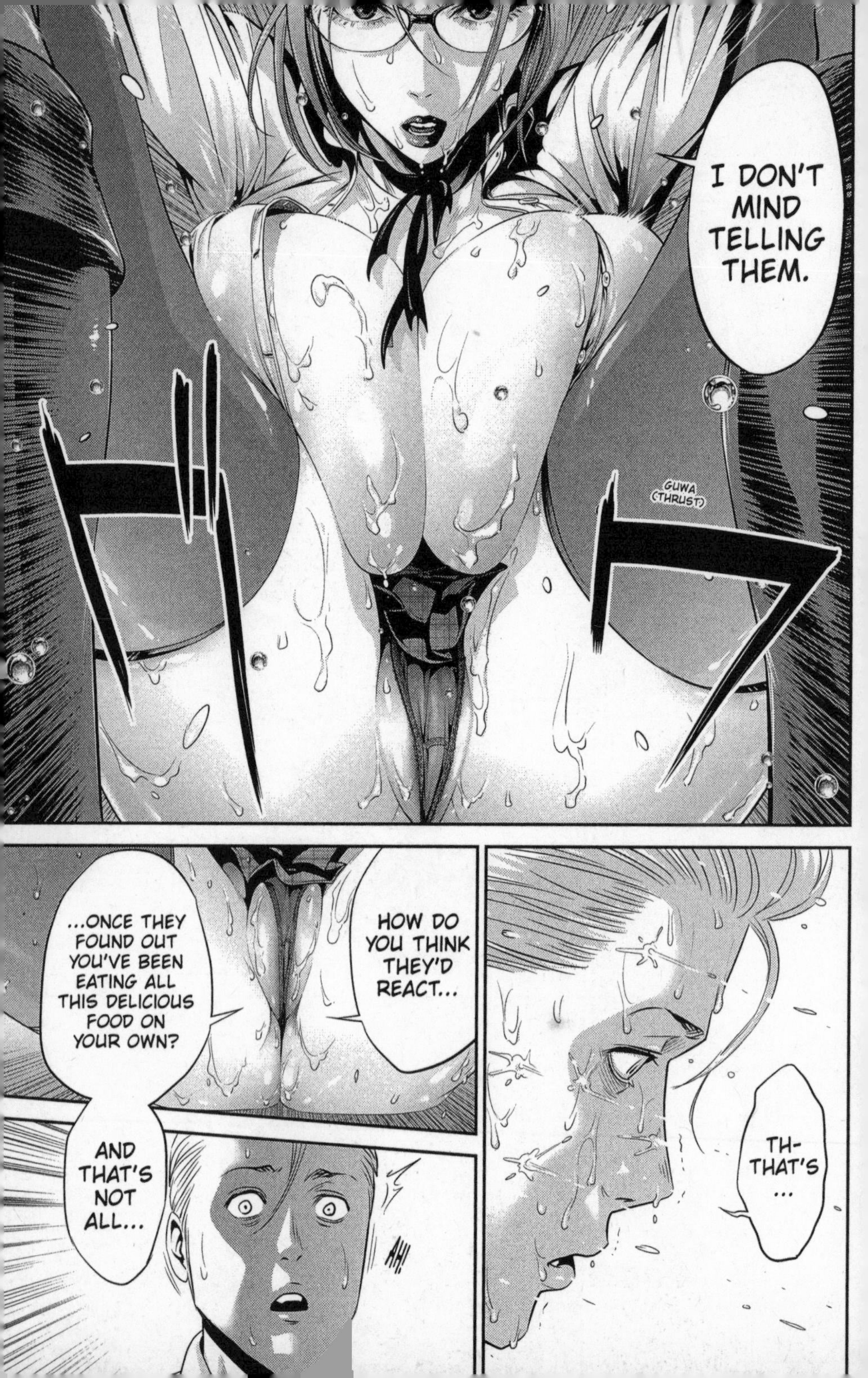
I DON'T MIND TELLING THEM.
GUWA (THRUST)
HOW DO YOU THINK THEY'D REACT...
...ONCE THEY FOUND OUT YOU'VE BEEN EATING ALL THIS DELICIOUS FOOD ON YOUR OWN?
TH-THAT'S...
AND THAT'S NOT ALL...
AH!

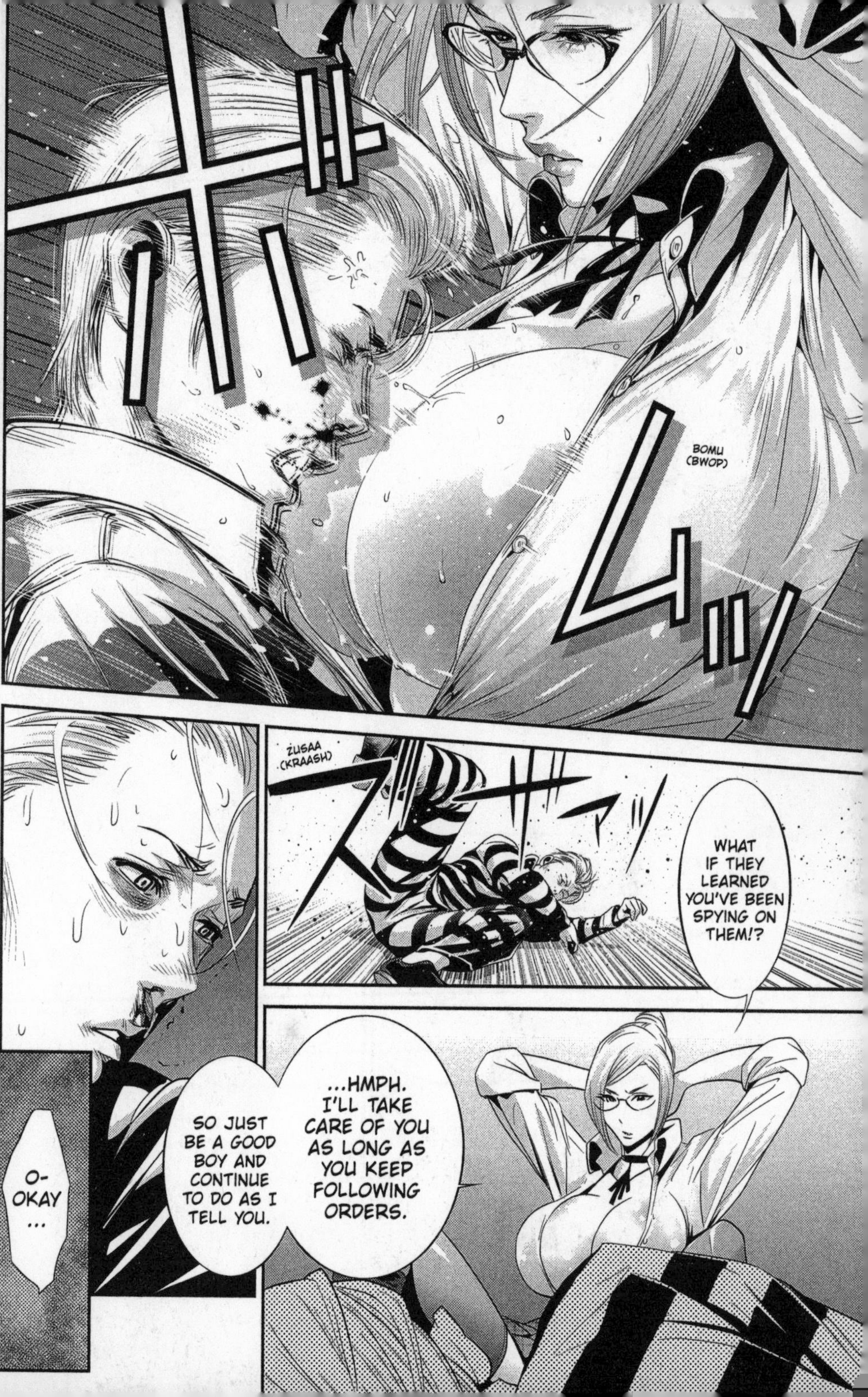
BOMU (BWOP)
ZUSAA (KRAASH)
WHAT IF THEY LEARNED YOU'VE BEEN SPYING ON THEM!?
...HMPH. I'LL TAKE CARE OF YOU AS LONG AS YOU KEEP FOLLOWING ORDERS.
SO JUST BE A GOOD BOY AND CONTINUE TO DO AS I TELL YOU.
O-OKAY ...

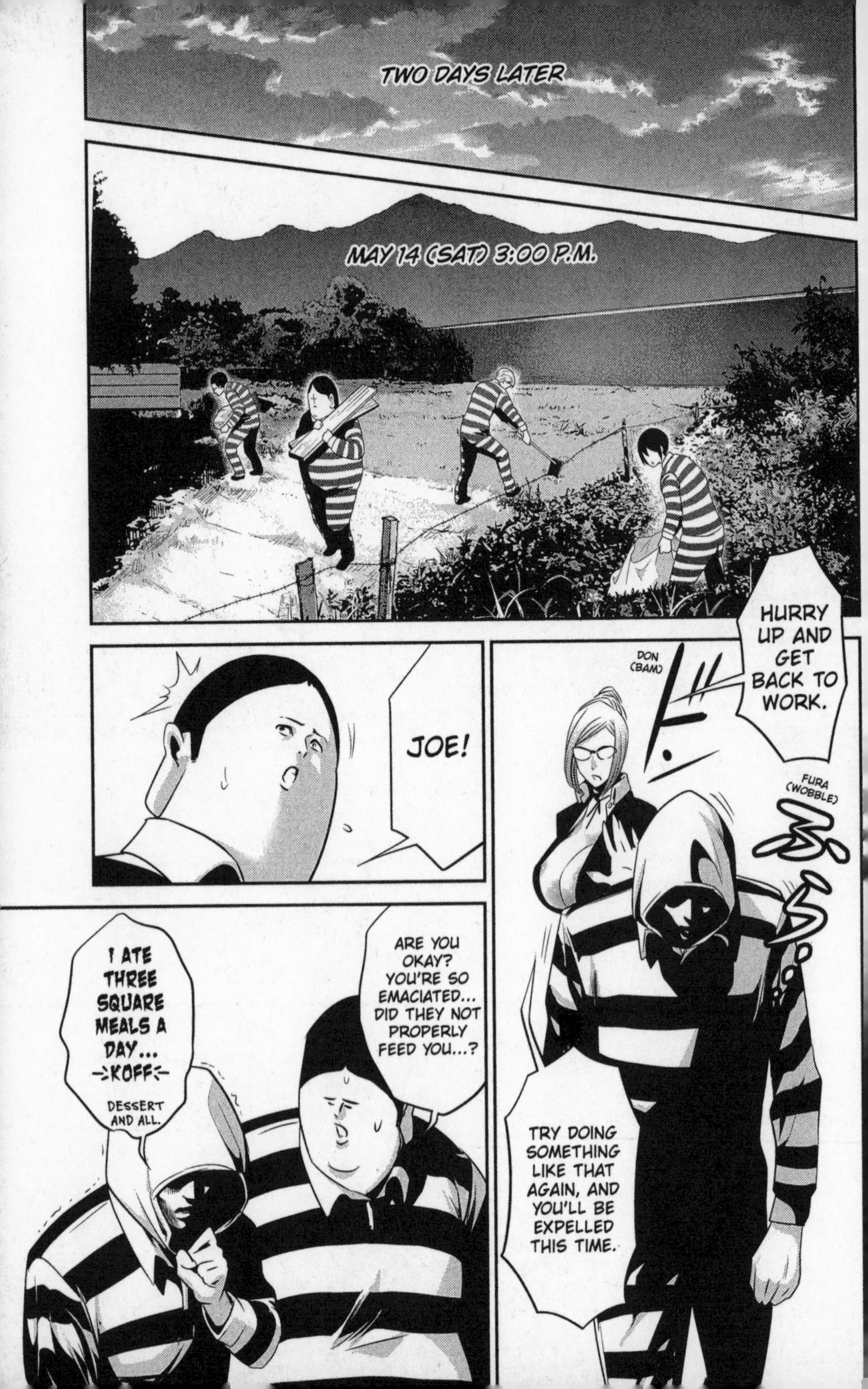
TWO DAYS LATER
MAY 14 (SAT) 3:00 P.M.
HURRY UP AND GET BACK TO WORK.
DON (BAM)
FURA (WOBBLE)
TRY DOING SOMETHING LIKE THAT AGAIN, AND YOU'LL BE EXPELLED THIS TIME.
JOE!
ARE YOU OKAY? YOU'RE SO EMACIATED... DID THEY NOT PROPERLY FEED YOU...?
I ATE THREE SQUARE MEALS A DAY... -KOFF-
DESSERT AND ALL.

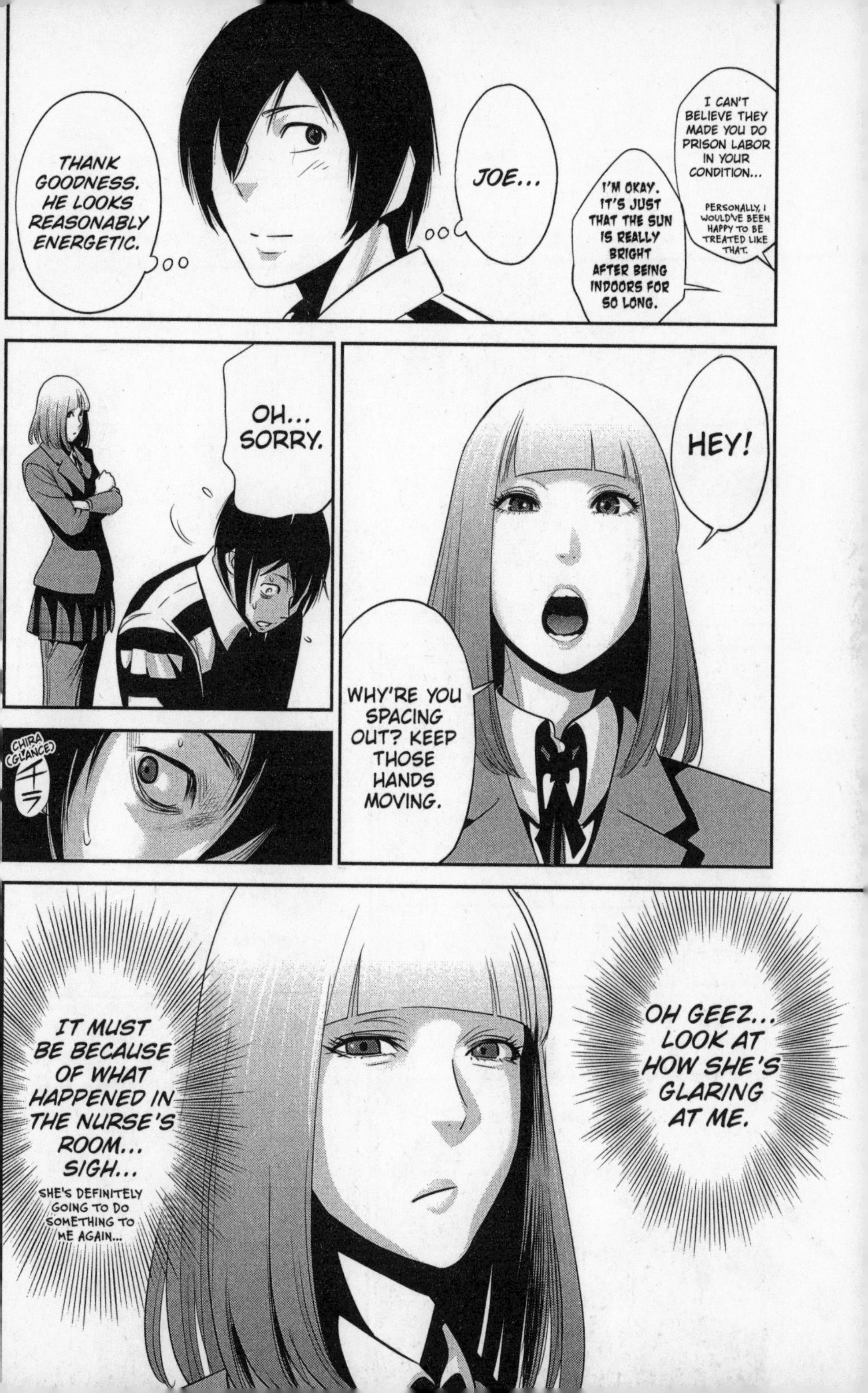
I CAN'T BELIEVE THEY MADE YOU DO PRISON LABOR IN YOUR CONDITION...
PERSONALLY, I WOULD'VE BEEN HAPPY TO BE TREATED LIKE THAT.
I'M OKAY. IT'S JUST THAT THE SUN IS REALLY BRIGHT AFTER BEING INDOORS FOR SO LONG.
JOE...
THANK GOODNESS. HE LOOKS REASONABLY ENERGETIC.
HEY!
WHY'RE YOU SPACING OUT? KEEP THOSE HANDS MOVING.
OH... SORRY.
CHIRA (GLANCE)
チラ
OH GEEZ... LOOK AT HOW SHE'S GLARING AT ME.
IT MUST BE BECAUSE OF WHAT HAPPENED IN THE NURSE'S ROOM... SIGH...
SHE'S DEFINITELY GOING TO DO SOMETHING TO ME AGAIN...

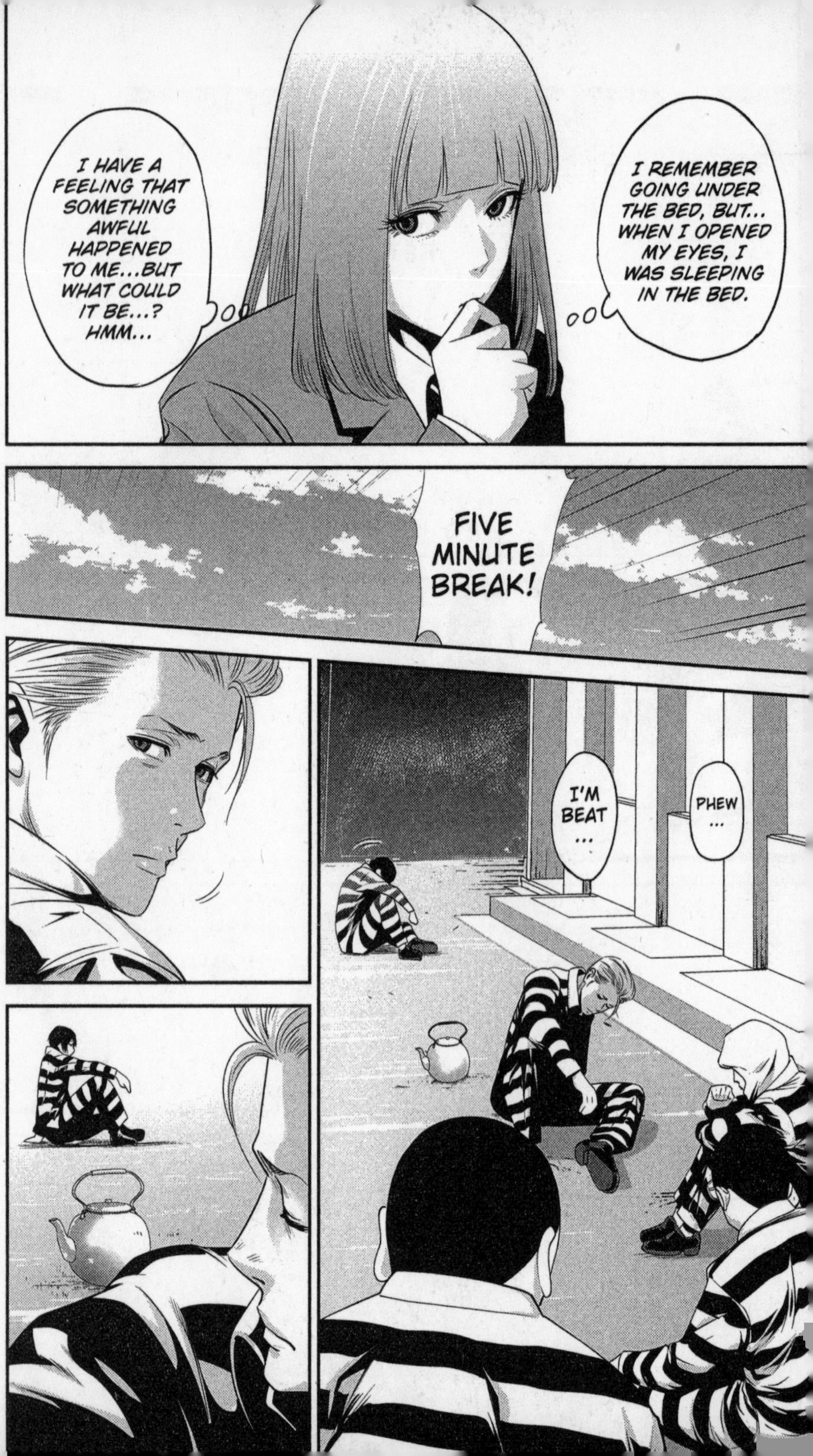
I REMEMBER GOING UNDER THE BED, BUT... WHEN I OPENED MY EYES, I WAS SLEEPING IN THE BED.
I HAVE A FEELING THAT SOMETHING AWFUL HAPPENED TO ME...BUT WHAT COULD IT BE...? HMM...
FIVE MINUTE BREAK!
PHEW ...
I'M BEAT ...

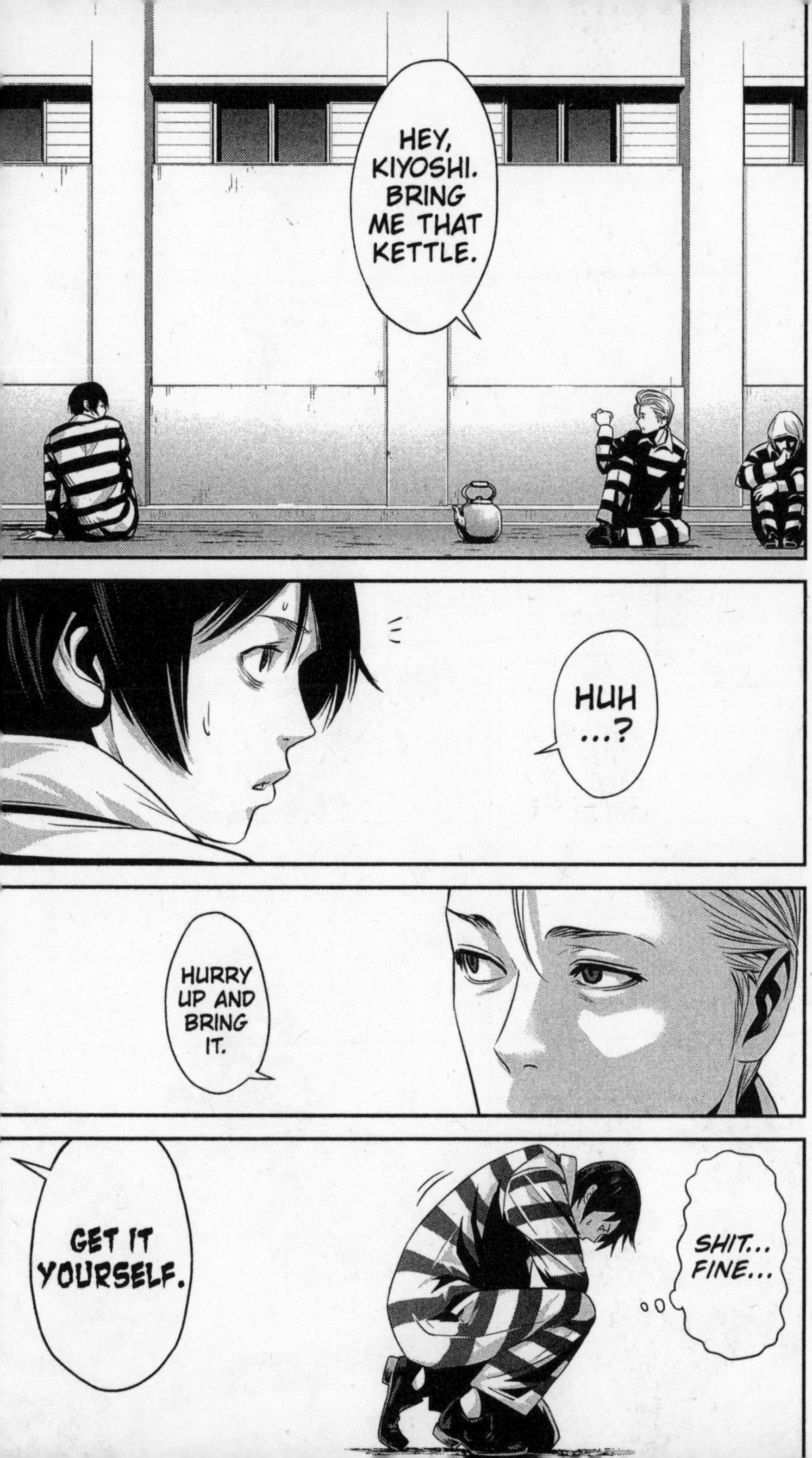
HEY, KIYOSHI. BRING ME THAT KETTLE.
HUH ...?
HURRY UP AND BRING IT.
SHIT... FINE...
GET IT YOURSELF.

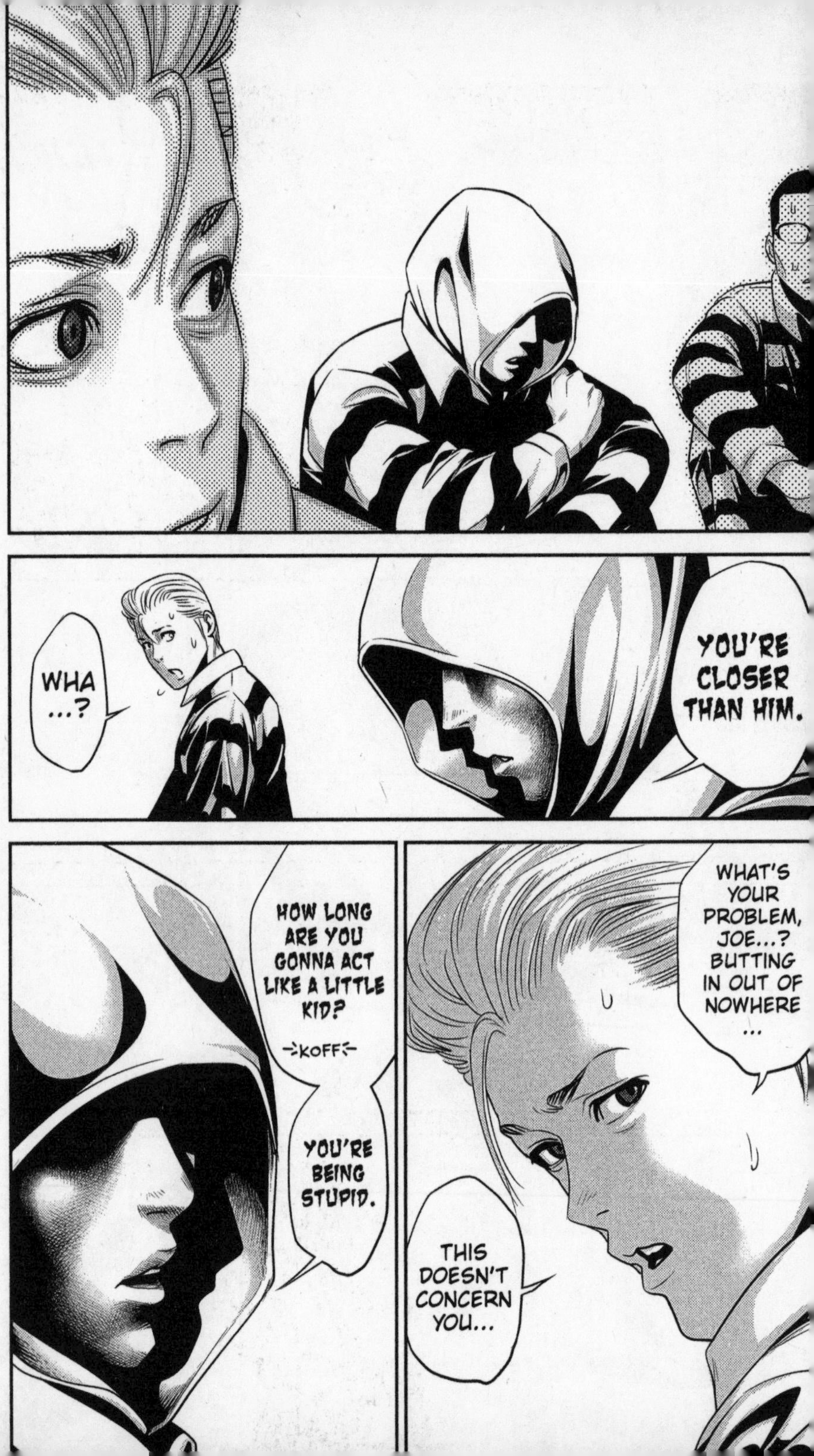
YOU'RE CLOSER THAN HIM.
WHA ...?
WHAT'S YOUR PROBLEM, JOE...? BUTTING IN OUT OF NOWHERE ...
THIS DOESN'T CONCERN YOU...
HOW LONG ARE YOU GONNA ACT LIKE A LITTLE KID?
KOFF
YOU'RE BEING STUPID.

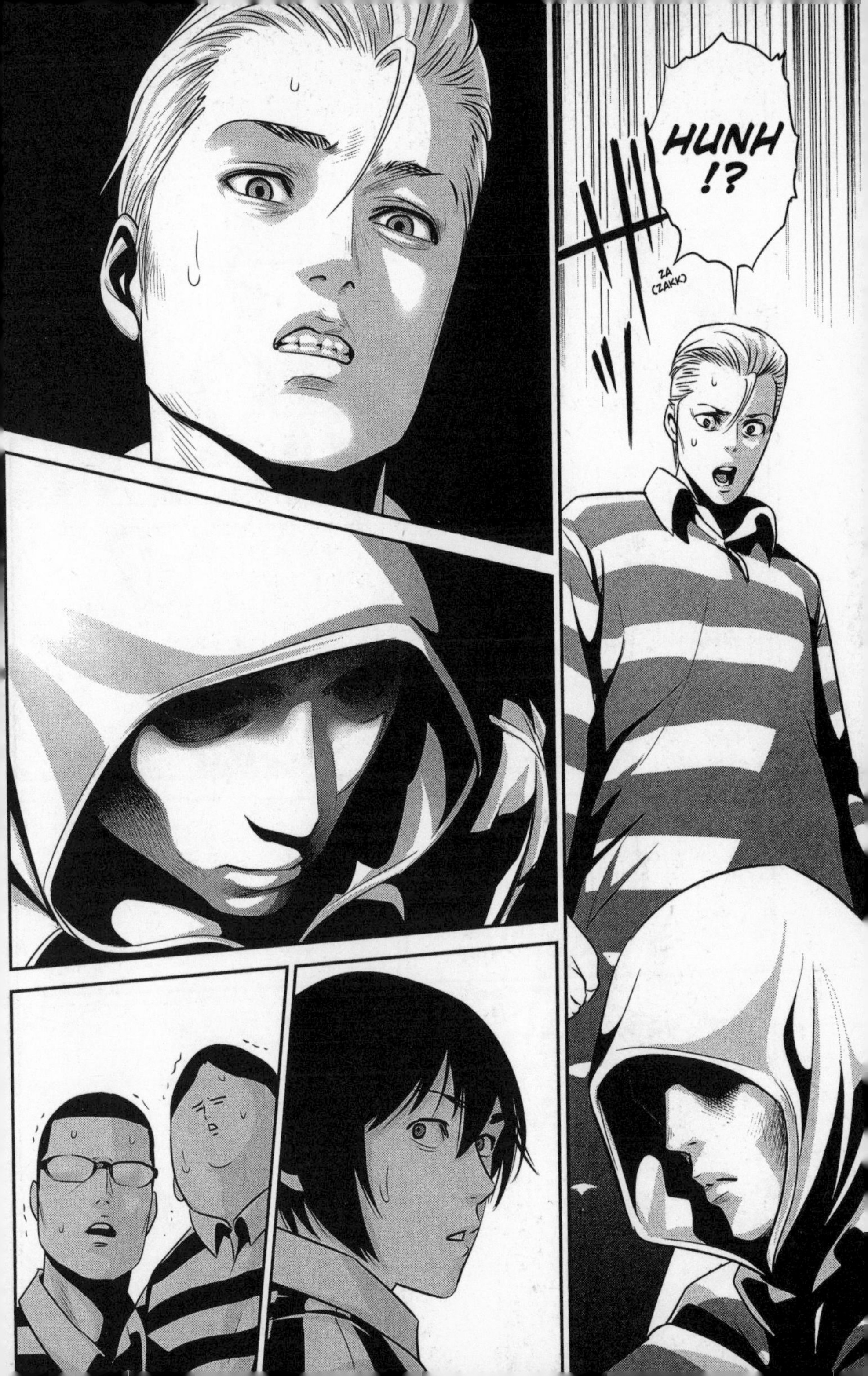
HUNH !?
ZA (ZAKK)

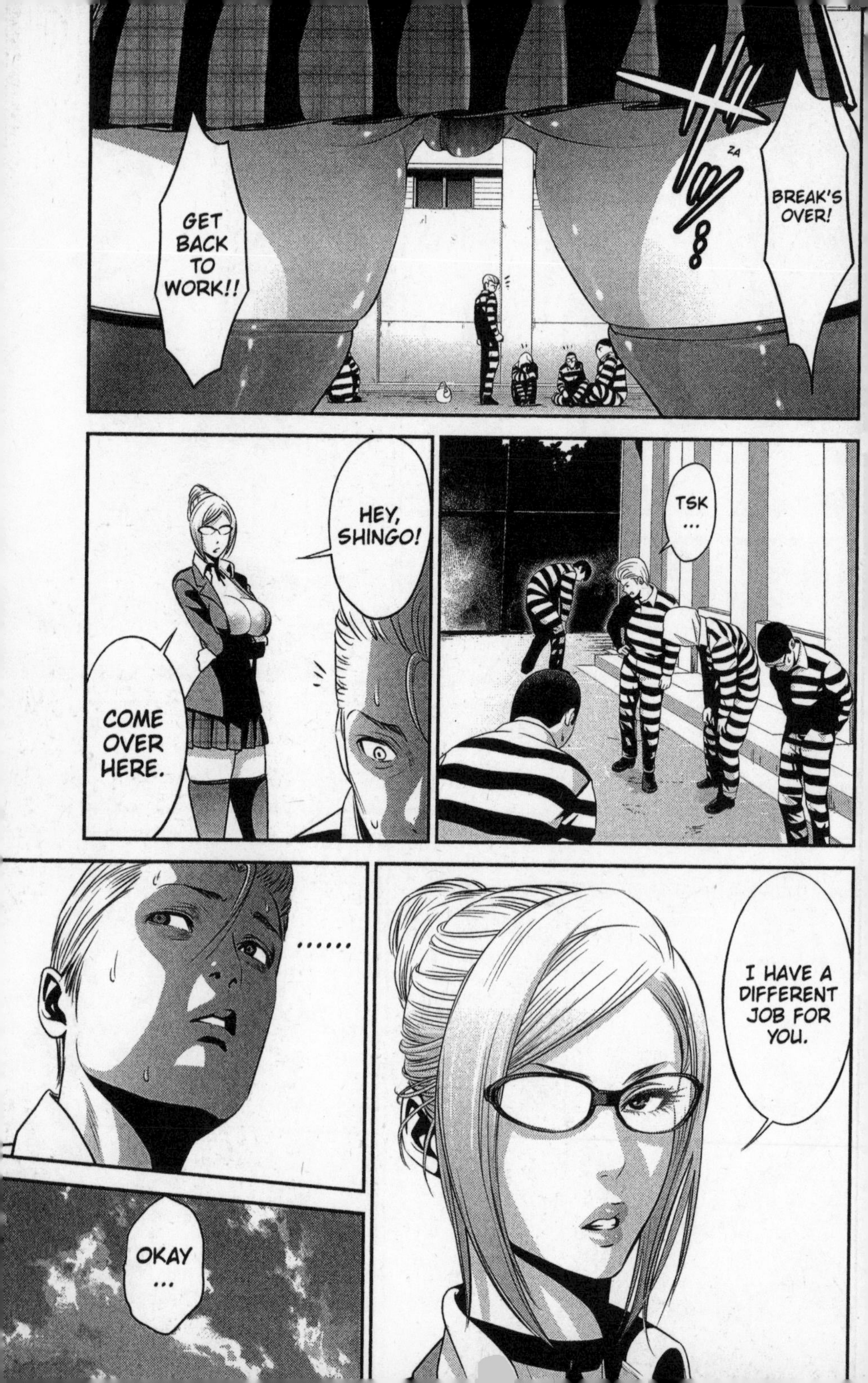
ZA
BREAK'S OVER!
GET BACK TO WORK!!
TSK ...
HEY, SHINGO!
COME OVER HERE.
I HAVE A DIFFERENT JOB FOR YOU.
......
OKAY ...

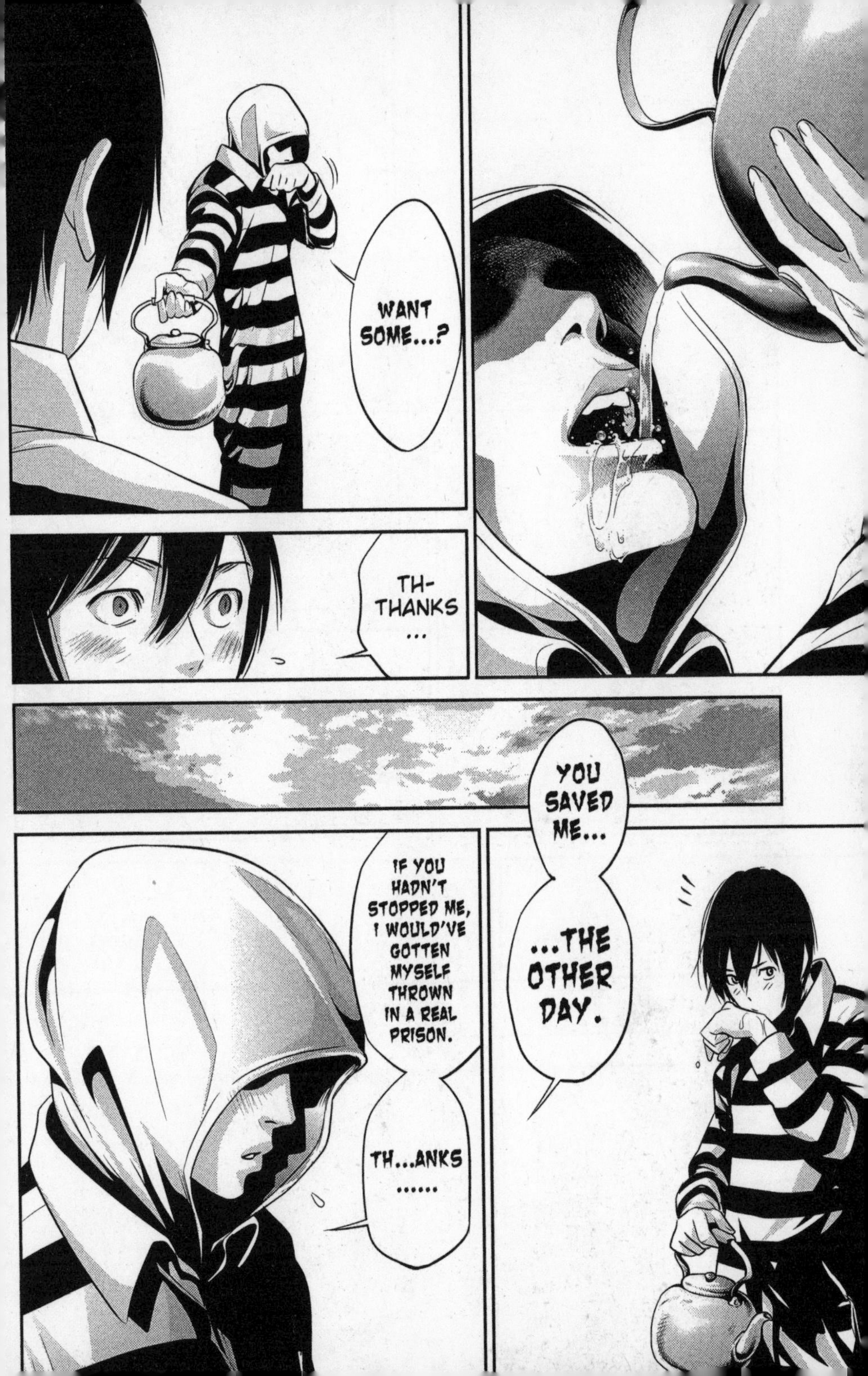
WANT SOME...?
TH-THANKS ...
YOU SAVED ME...
...THE OTHER DAY.
IF YOU HADN'T STOPPED ME, I WOULD'VE GOTTEN MYSELF THROWN IN A REAL PRISON.
TH...ANKS ......

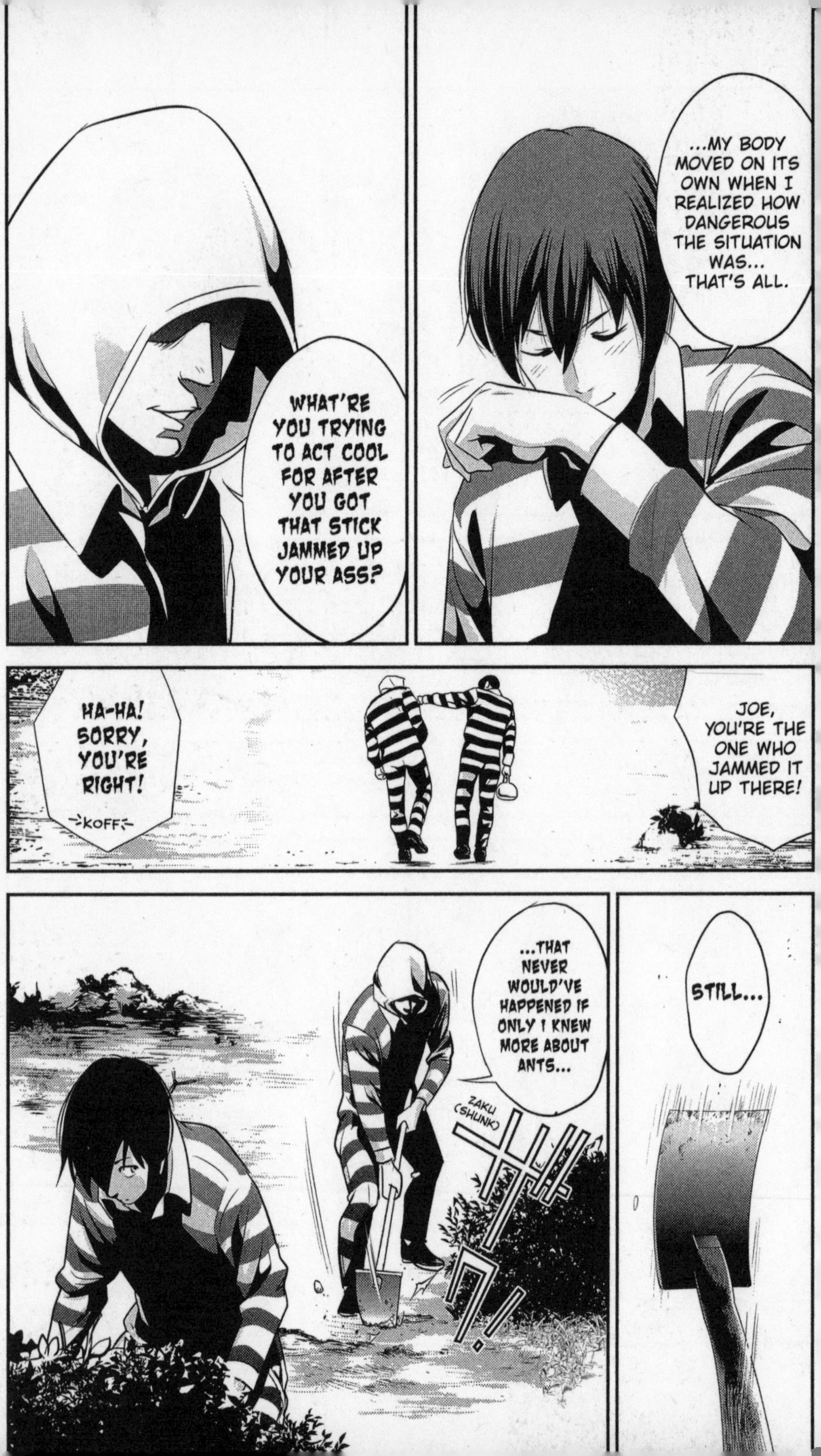
...MY BODY MOVED ON ITS OWN WHEN I REALIZED HOW DANGEROUS THE SITUATION WAS... THAT'S ALL.
WHAT'RE YOU TRYING TO ACT COOL FOR AFTER YOU GOT THAT STICK JAMMED UP YOUR ASS?
JOE, YOU'RE THE ONE WHO JAMMED IT UP THERE!
HA-HA! SORRY, YOU'RE RIGHT!
KOFF
STILL...
...THAT NEVER WOULD'VE HAPPENED IF ONLY I KNEW MORE ABOUT ANTS...
ZAKU (SHUNK)

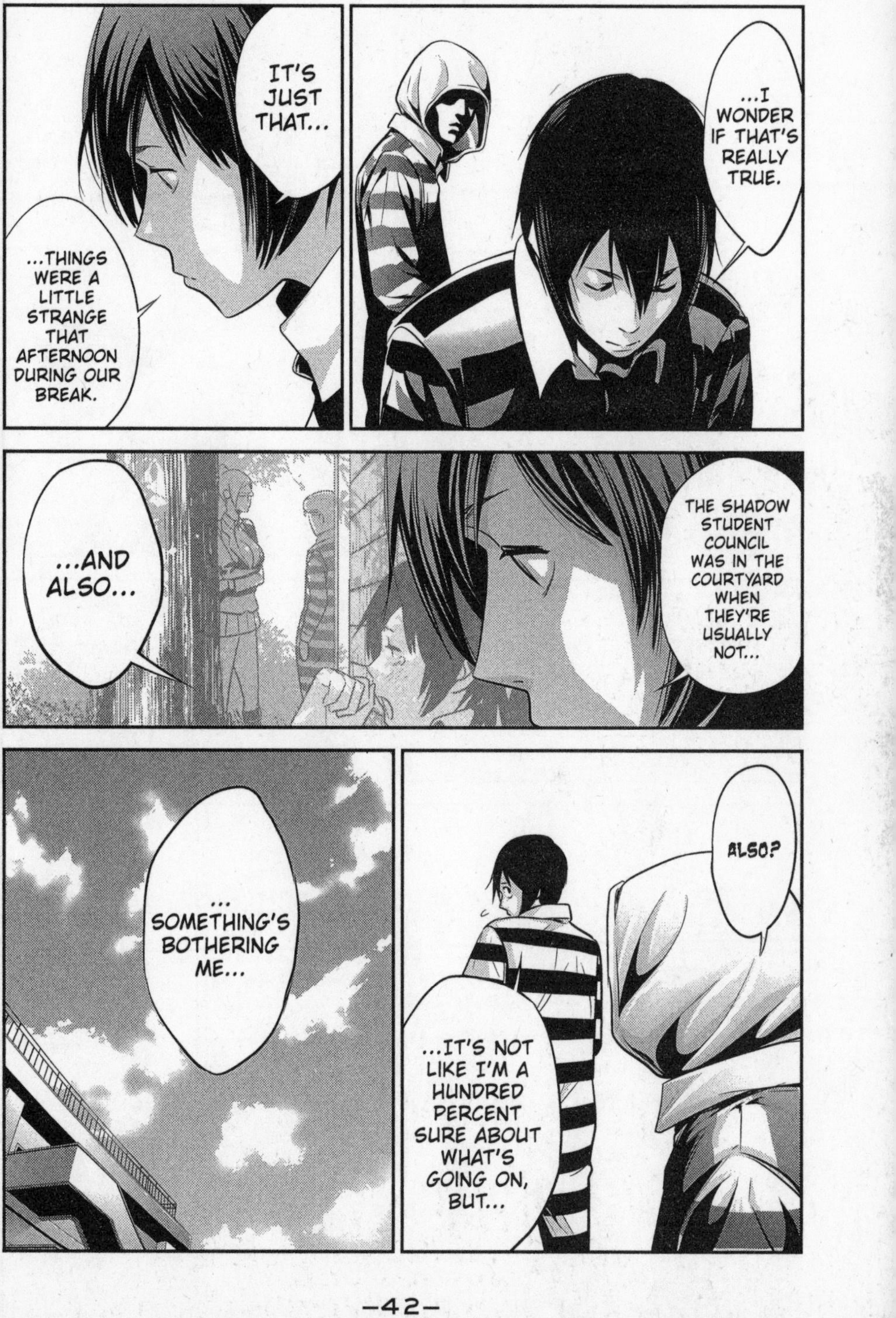
...I WONDER IF THAT'S REALLY TRUE.
IT'S JUST THAT...
...THINGS WERE A LITTLE STRANGE THAT AFTERNOON DURING OUR BREAK.
THE SHADOW STUDENT COUNCIL WAS IN THE COURTYARD WHEN THEY'RE USUALLY NOT...
...AND ALSO...
ALSO?
...IT'S NOT LIKE I'M A HUNDRED PERCENT SURE ABOUT WHAT'S GOING ON, BUT...
... SOMETHING'S BOTHERING ME...

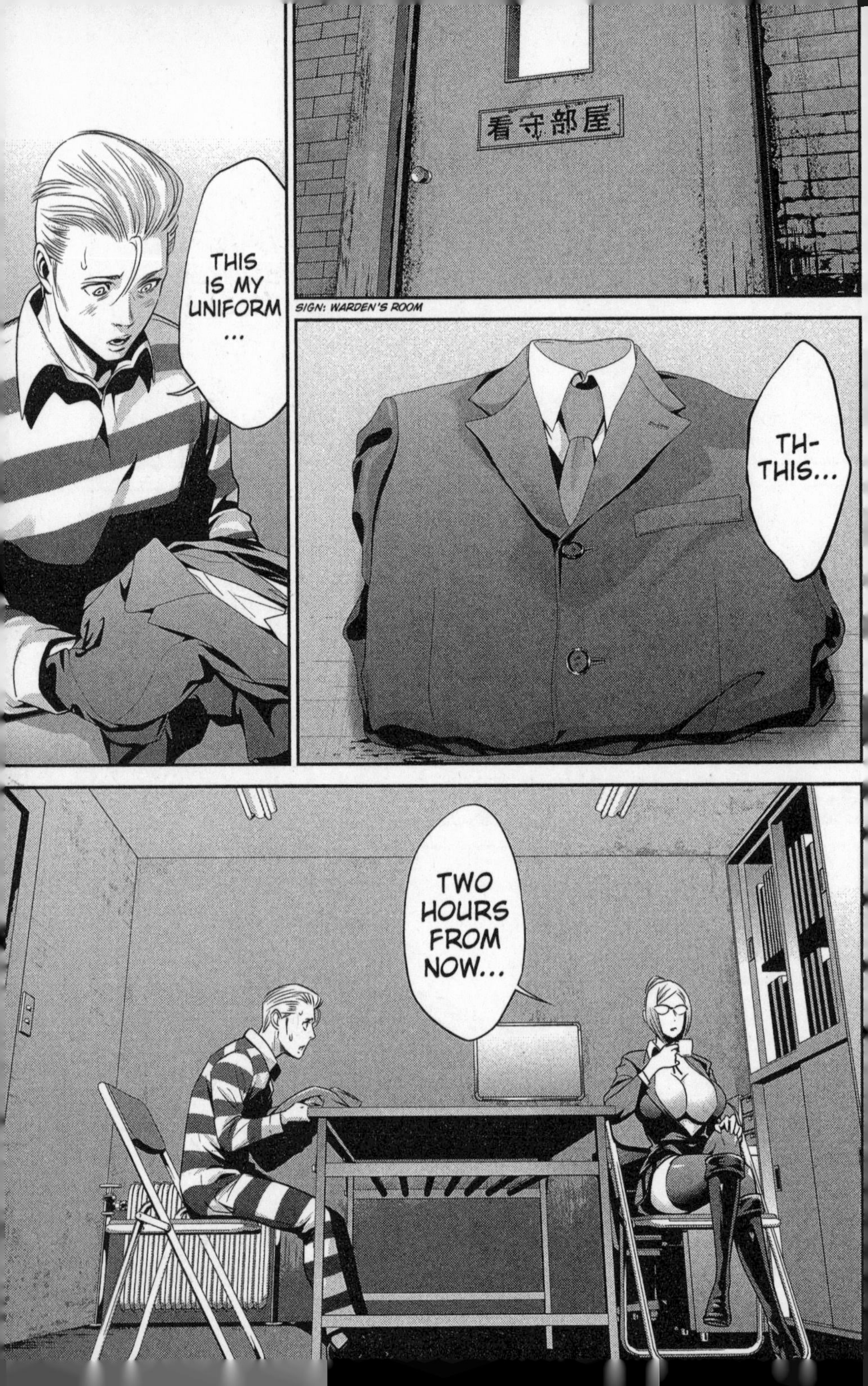
看守部屋
SIGN: WARDEN'S ROOM
TH-THIS...
THIS IS MY UNIFORM ...
TWO HOURS FROM NOW...

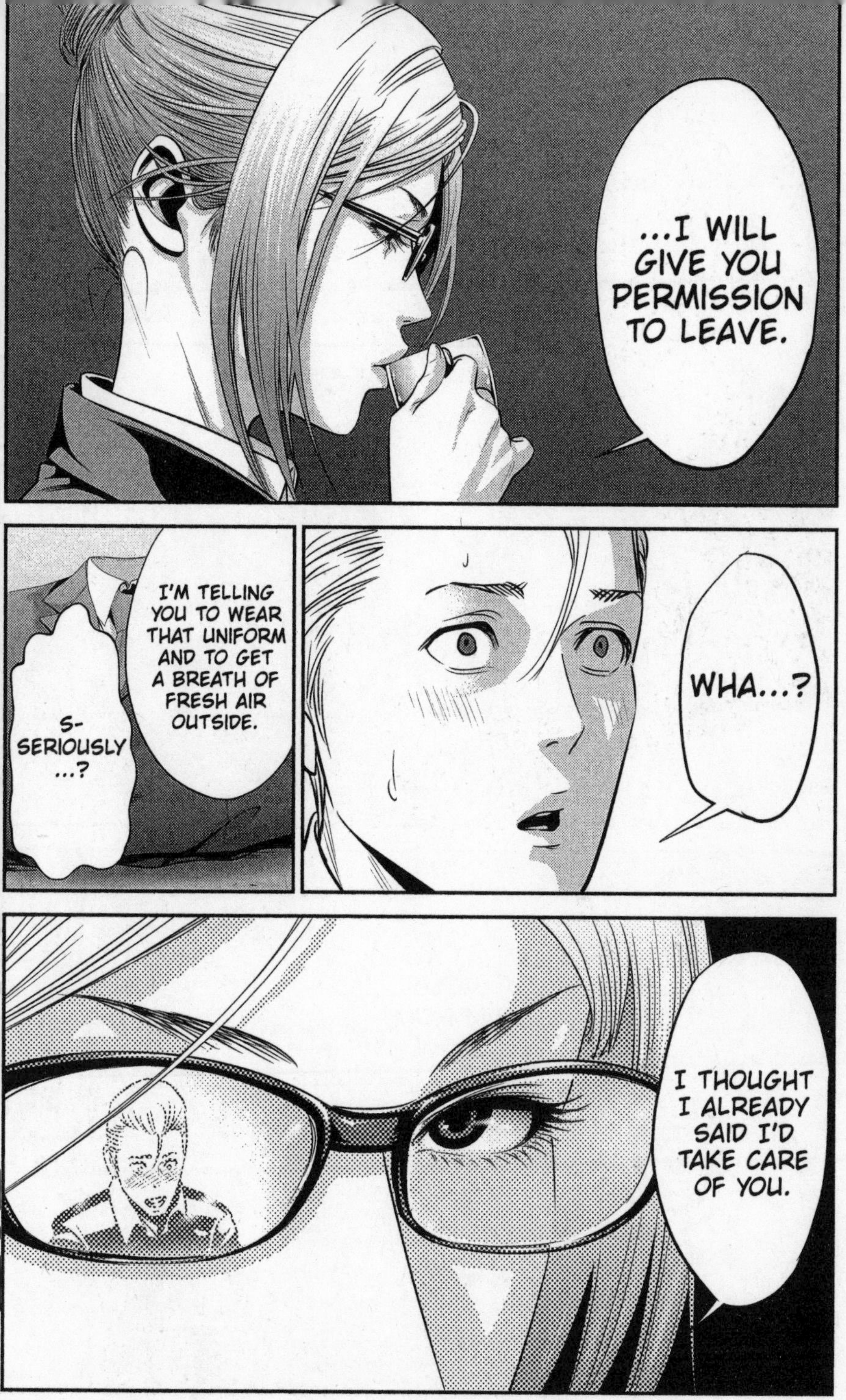
...I WILL GIVE YOU PERMISSION TO LEAVE.
WHA...?
I'M TELLING YOU TO WEAR THAT UNIFORM AND TO GET A BREATH OF FRESH AIR OUTSIDE.
S-SERIOUSLY...?
I THOUGHT I ALREADY SAID I'D TAKE CARE OF YOU.

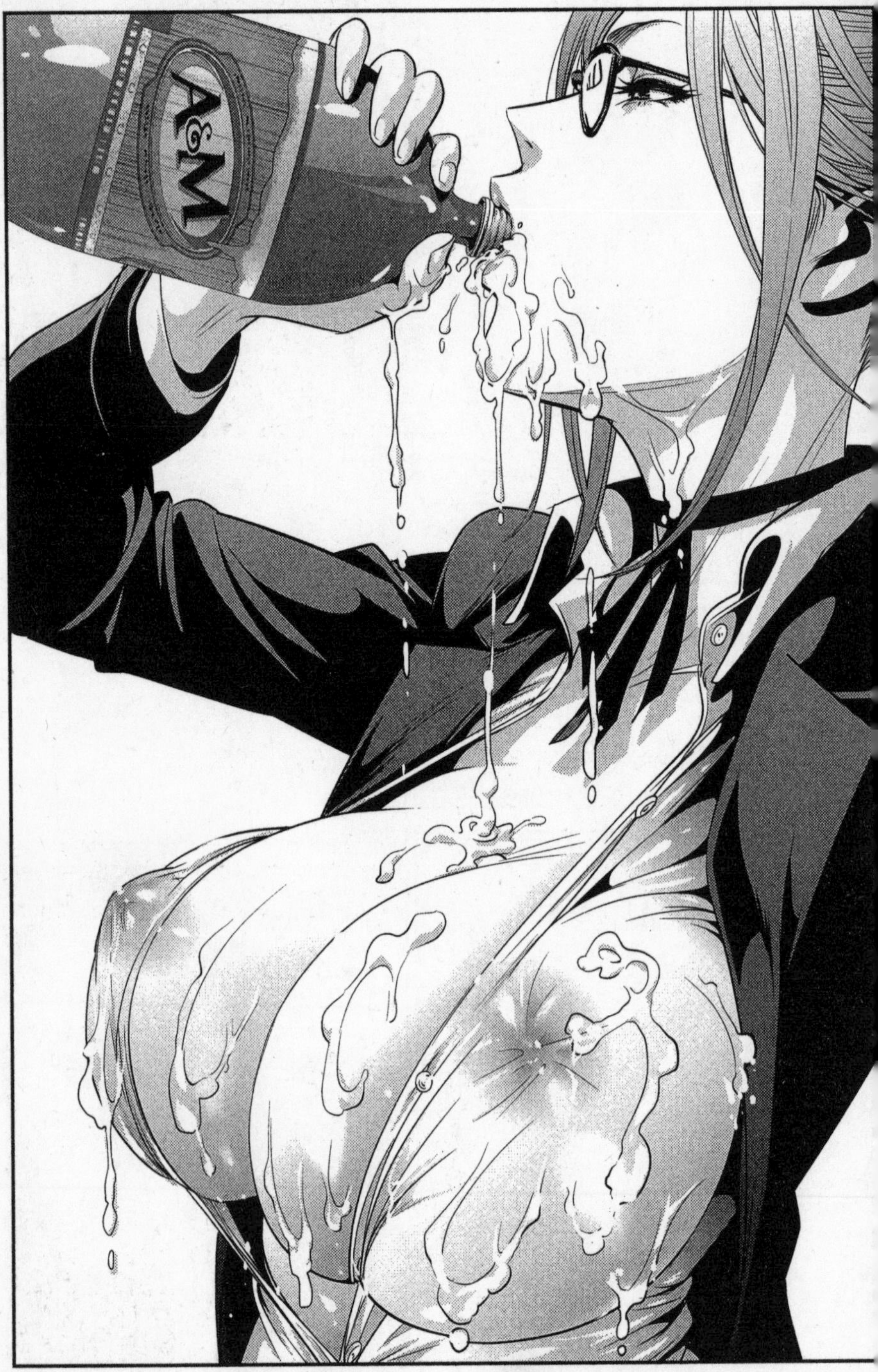
A&M

CHAPTER 41: SPLASH

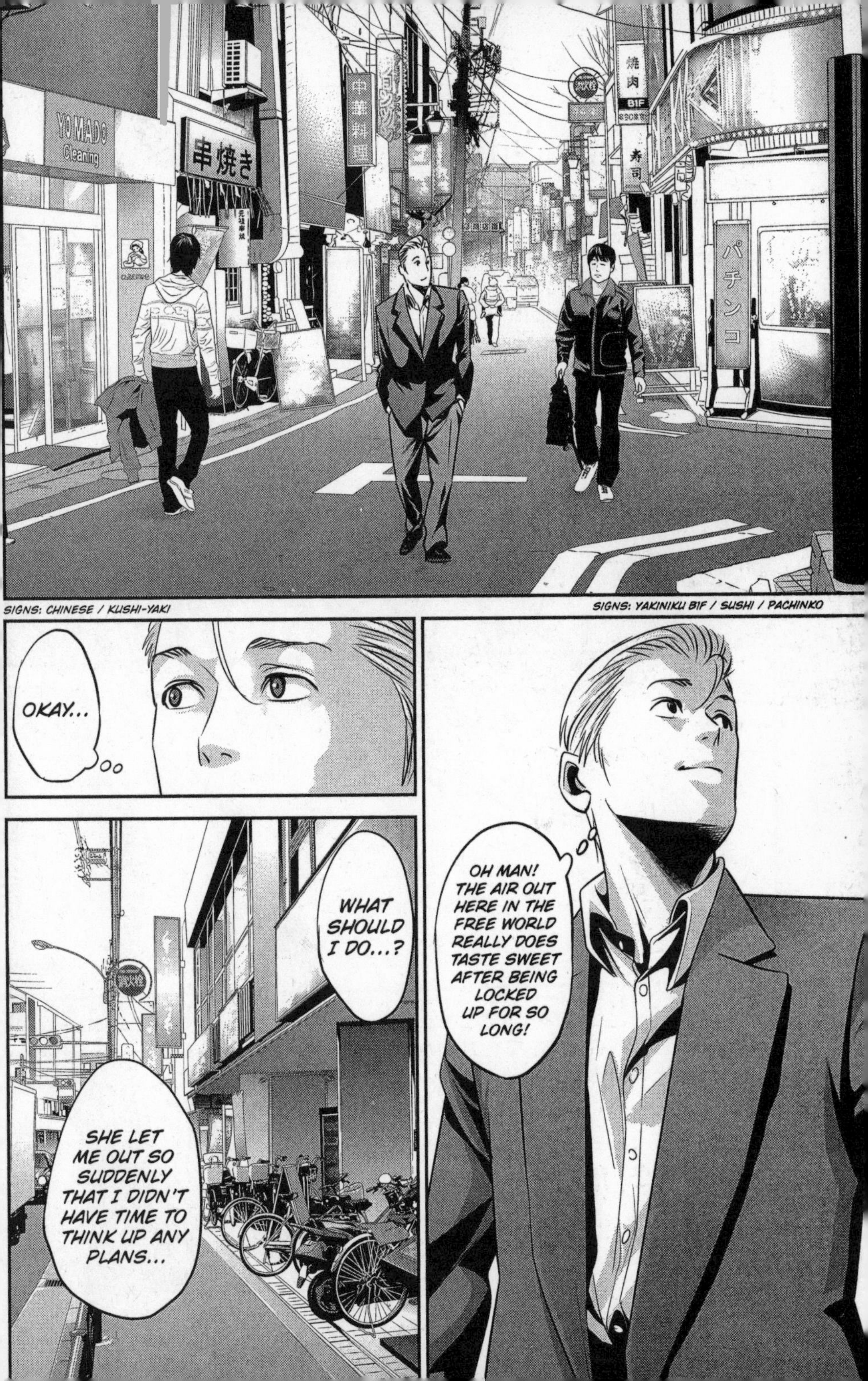
SIGNS: YAKINIKU B1F / SUSHI / PACHINKO
SIGNS: CHINESE / KUSHI-YAKI
OH MAN! THE AIR OUT HERE IN THE FREE WORLD REALLY DOES TASTE SWEET AFTER BEING LOCKED UP FOR SO LONG!
OKAY...
WHAT SHOULD I DO...?
SHE LET ME OUT SO SUDDENLY THAT I DIDN'T HAVE TIME TO THINK UP ANY PLANS...

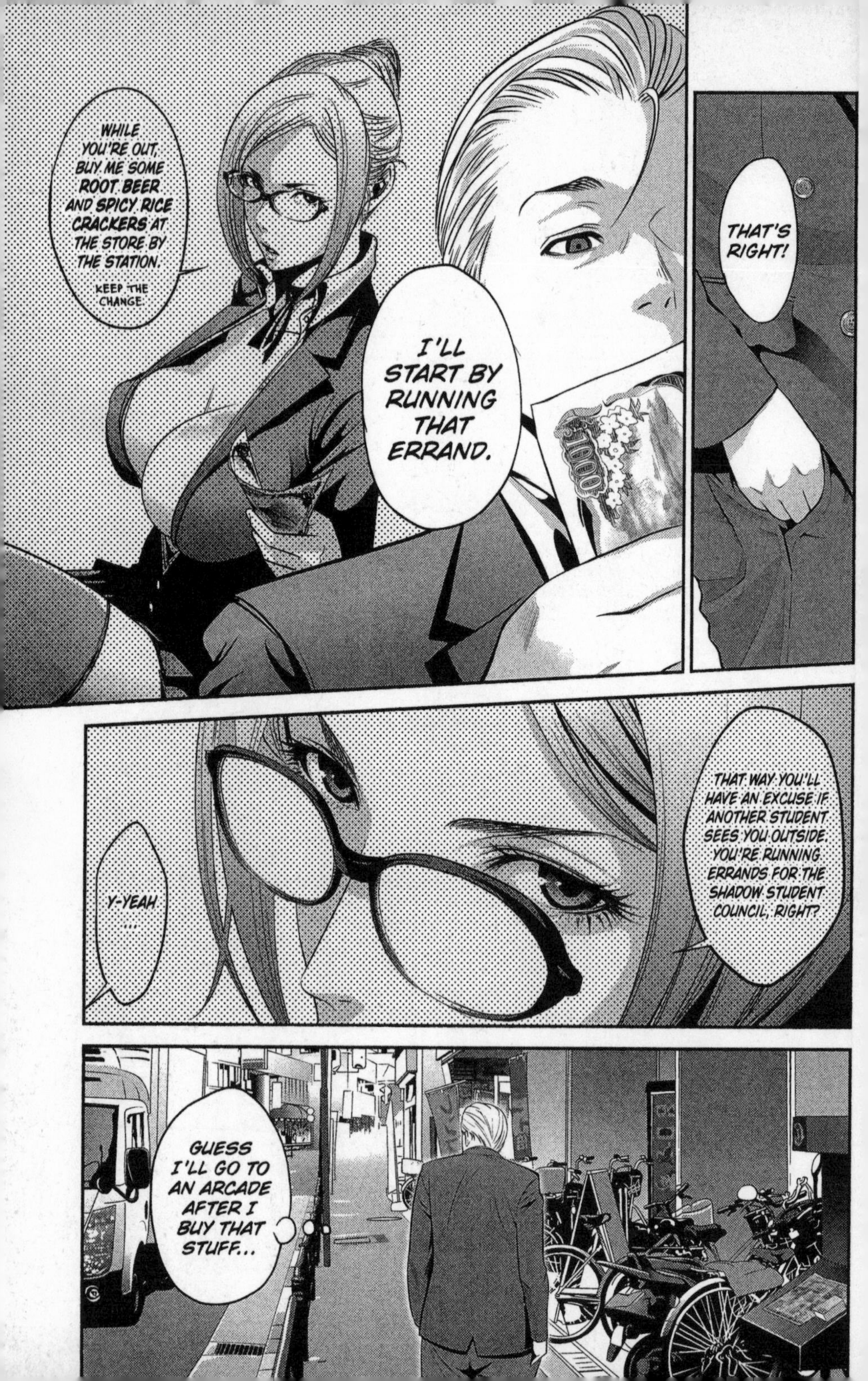
THAT'S RIGHT!
I'LL START BY RUNNING THAT ERRAND.
WHILE YOU'RE OUT, BUY ME SOME ROOT BEER AND SPICY RICE CRACKERS AT THE STORE BY THE STATION.
KEEP THE CHANGE.
THAT WAY YOU'LL HAVE AN EXCUSE IF ANOTHER STUDENT SEES YOU OUTSIDE. YOU'RE RUNNING ERRANDS FOR THE SHADOW STUDENT COUNCIL, RIGHT?
Y-YEAH ...
GUESS I'LL GO TO AN ARCADE AFTER I BUY THAT STUFF...

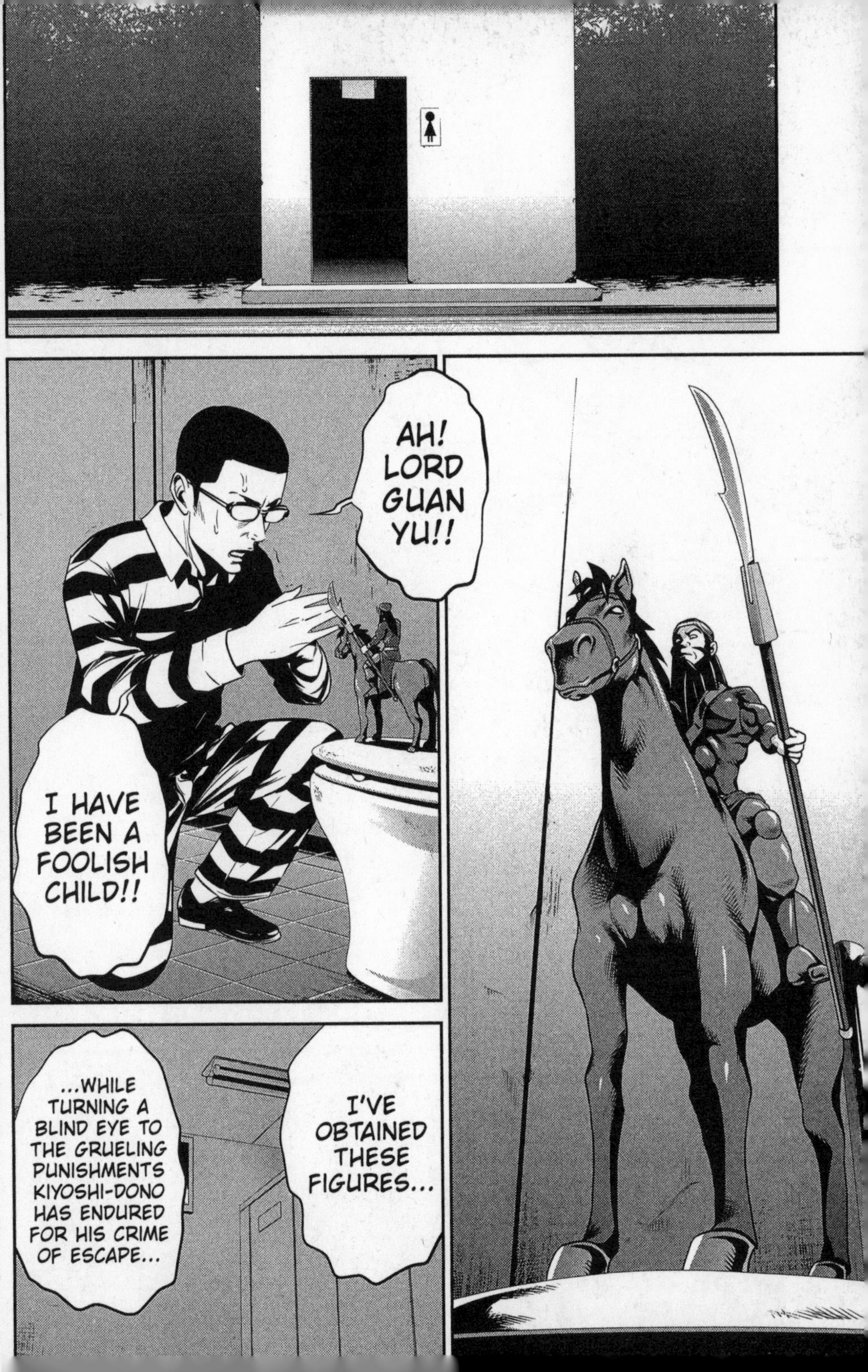
AH! LORD GUAN YU!!
I HAVE BEEN A FOOLISH CHILD!!
I'VE OBTAINED THESE FIGURES...
...WHILE TURNING A BLIND EYE TO THE GRUELING PUNISHMENTS KIYOSHI-DONO HAS ENDURED FOR HIS CRIME OF ESCAPE...

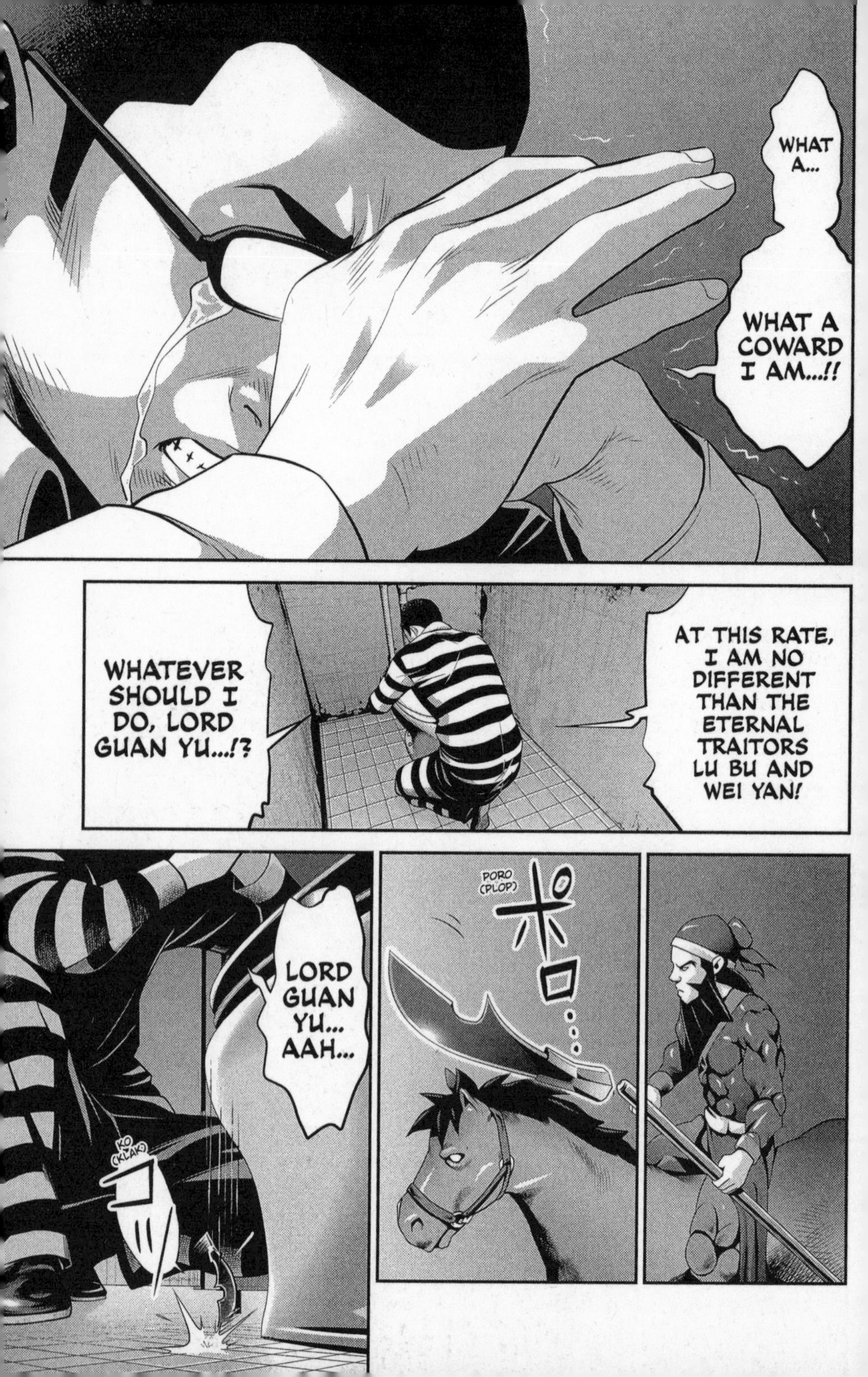
WHAT A...
WHAT A COWARD I AM...!!
AT THIS RATE, I AM NO DIFFERENT THAN THE ETERNAL TRAITORS LU BU AND WEI YAN!
WHATEVER SHOULD I DO, LORD GUAN YU...!?
PORO (PLOP)
LORD GUAN YU... AAH...
KO (KLAK)

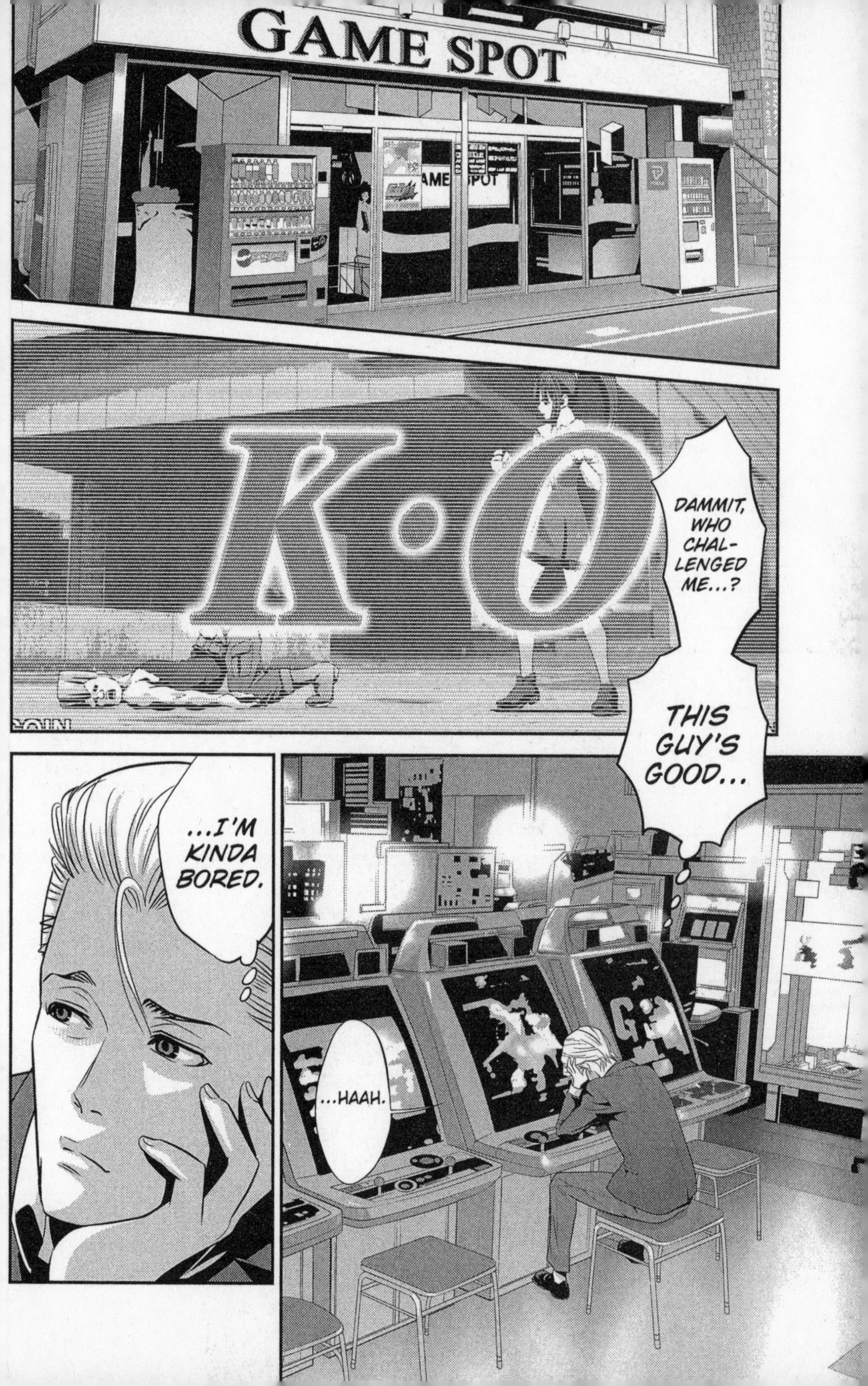
GAME SPOT
GAME SPOT
K.O
DAMMIT, WHO CHAL-LENGED ME...?
THIS GUY'S GOOD...
...HAAH.
...I'M KINDA BORED.

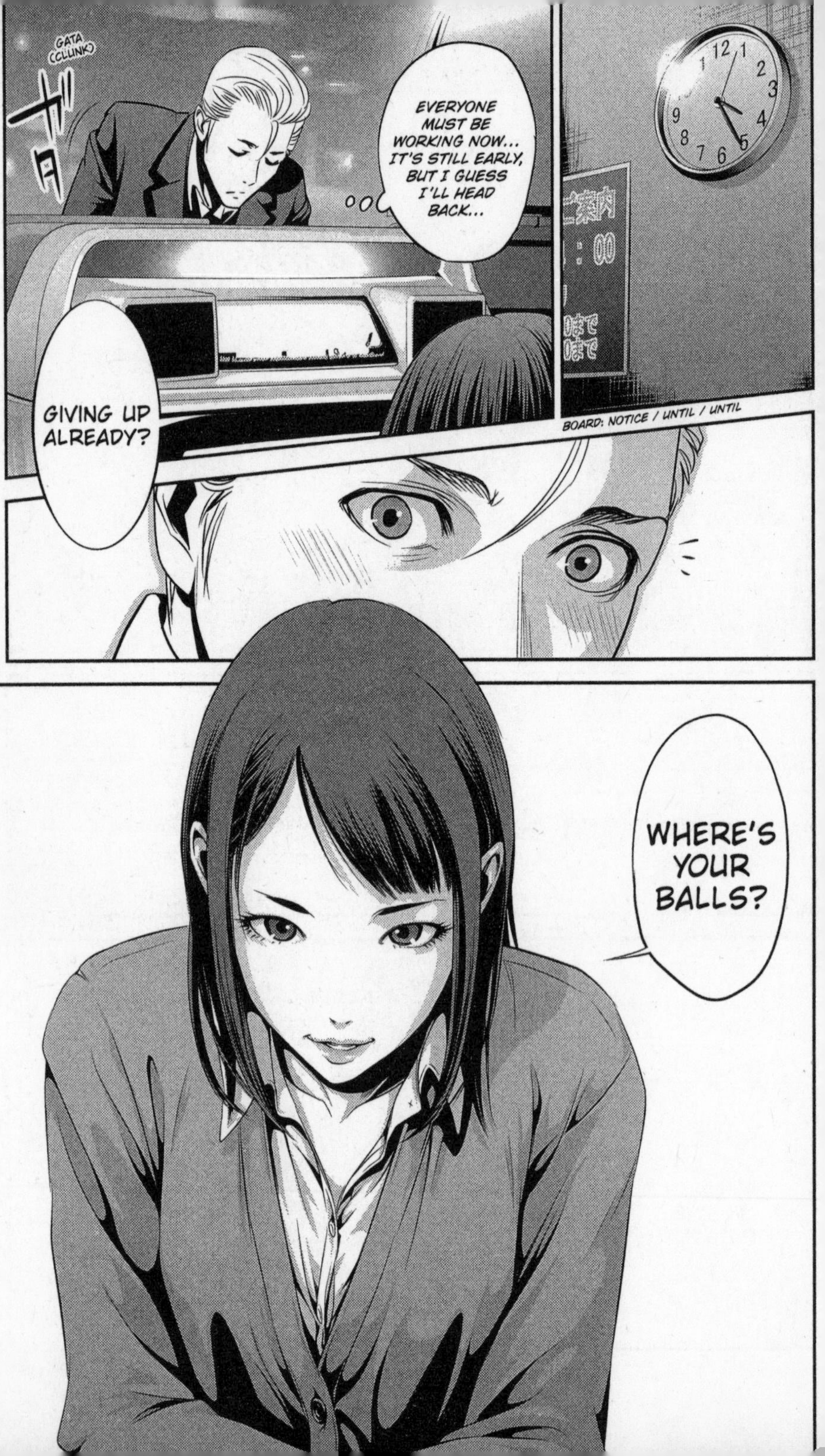
BOARD: NOTICE / UNTIL / UNTIL
GATA (CLLINK)
EVERYONE MUST BE WORKING NOW... IT'S STILL EARLY, BUT I GUESS I'LL HEAD BACK...
GIVING UP ALREADY?
WHERE'S YOUR BALLS?

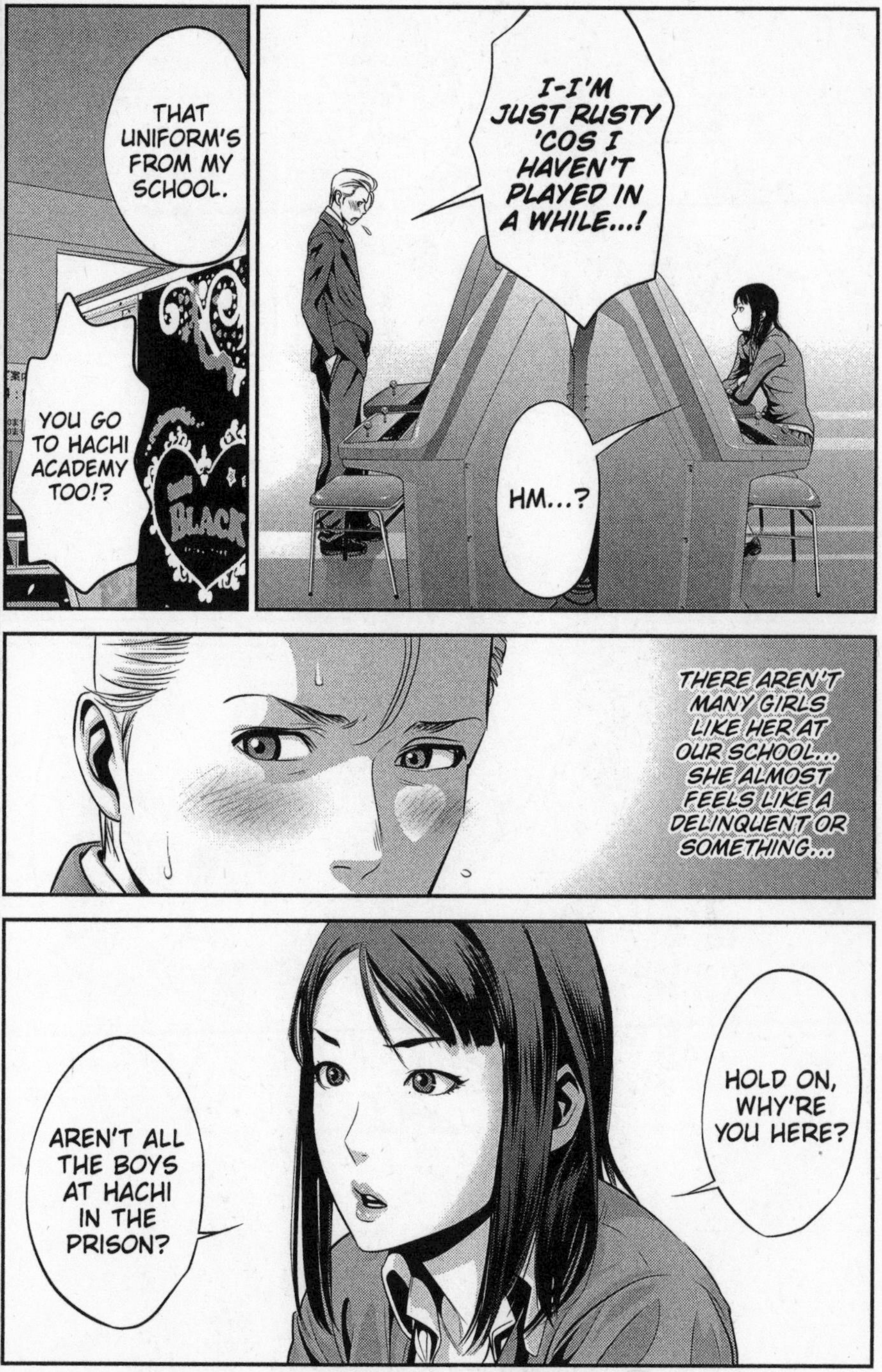
I-I'M JUST RUSTY 'COS I HAVEN'T PLAYED IN A WHILE...!
HM...?
THAT UNIFORM'S FROM MY SCHOOL.
YOU GO TO HACHI ACADEMY TOO!?
BLACK
THERE AREN'T MANY GIRLS LIKE HER AT OUR SCHOOL... SHE ALMOST FEELS LIKE A DELINQUENT OR SOMETHING...
HOLD ON, WHY'RE YOU HERE?
AREN'T ALL THE BOYS AT HACHI IN THE PRISON?

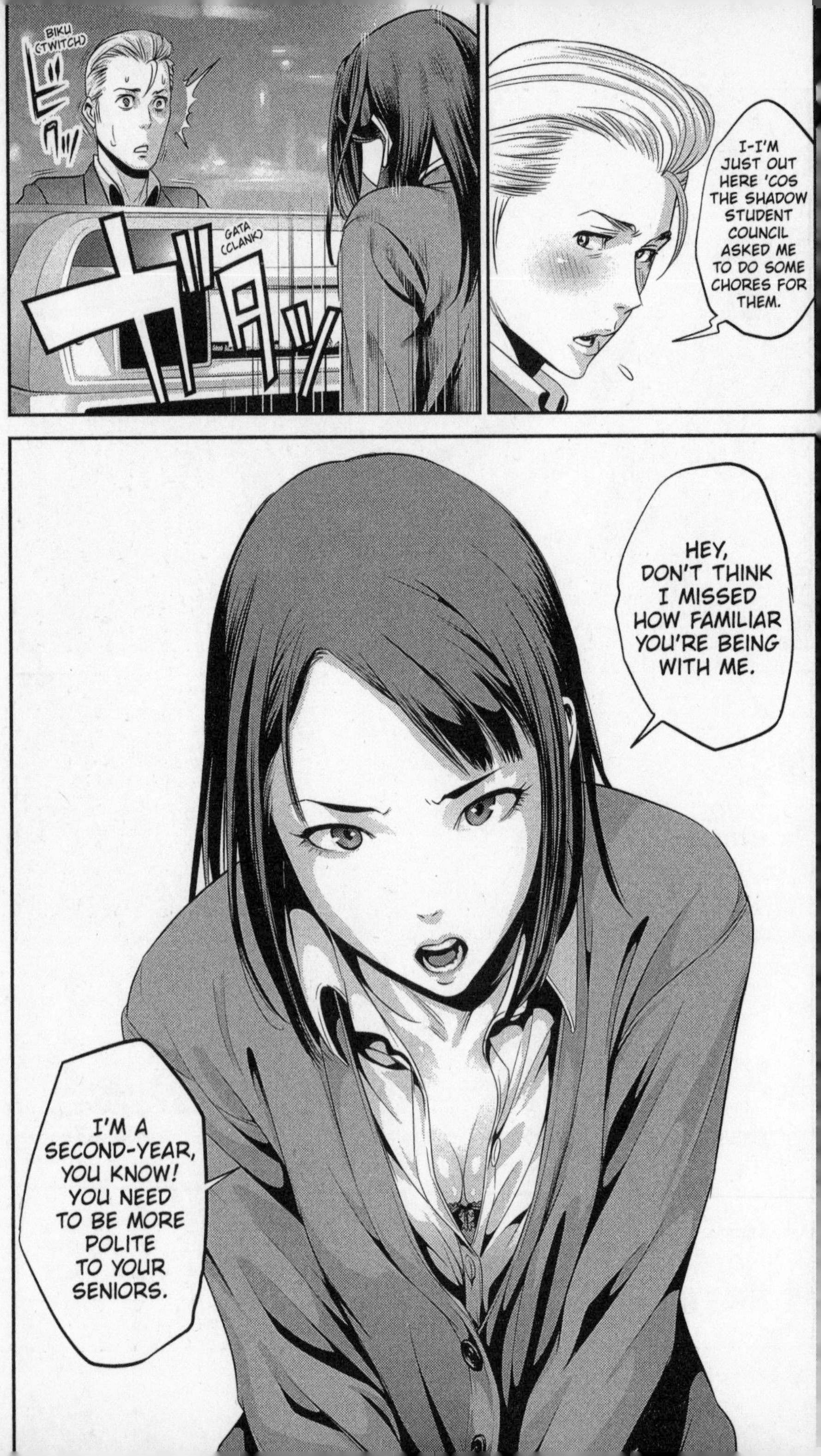
I-I'M JUST OUT HERE 'COS THE SHADOW STUDENT COUNCIL ASKED ME TO DO SOME CHORES FOR THEM.
GATA (CLANK)
BIKU (TWITCH)
HEY, DON'T THINK I MISSED HOW FAMILIAR YOU'RE BEING WITH ME.
I'M A SECOND-YEAR, YOU KNOW! YOU NEED TO BE MORE POLITE TO YOUR SENIORS.

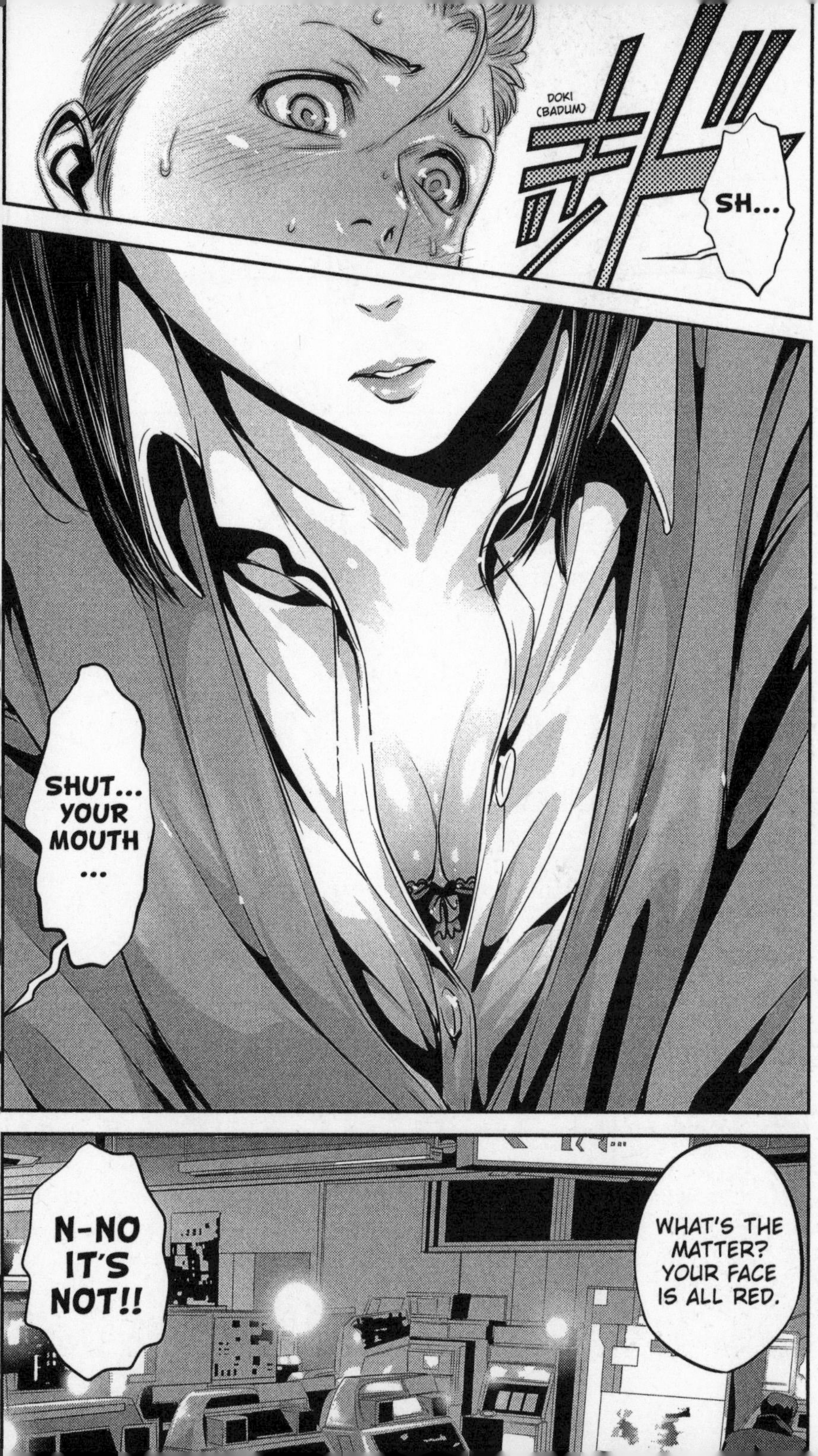

DOKI (BADUM)
SH...
SHUT... YOUR MOUTH ...
WHAT'S THE MATTER? YOUR FACE IS ALL RED.
N-NO IT'S NOT!!

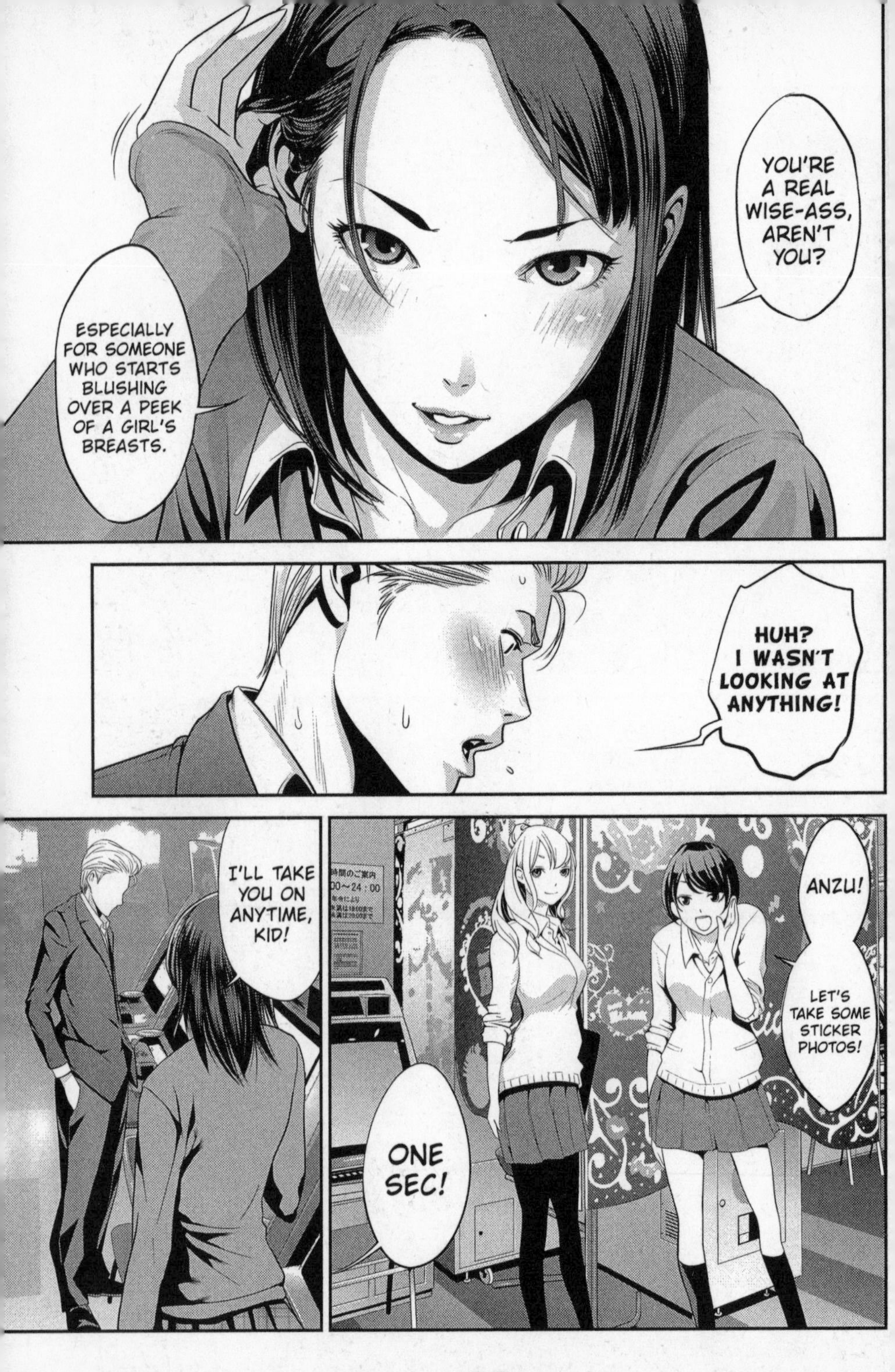
YOU'RE A REAL WISE-ASS, AREN'T YOU?
ESPECIALLY FOR SOMEONE WHO STARTS BLUSHING OVER A PEEK OF A GIRL'S BREASTS.
HUH? I WASN'T LOOKING AT ANYTHING!
ANZU!
LET'S TAKE SOME STICKER PHOTOS!
ONE SEC!
I'LL TAKE YOU ON ANYTIME, KID!

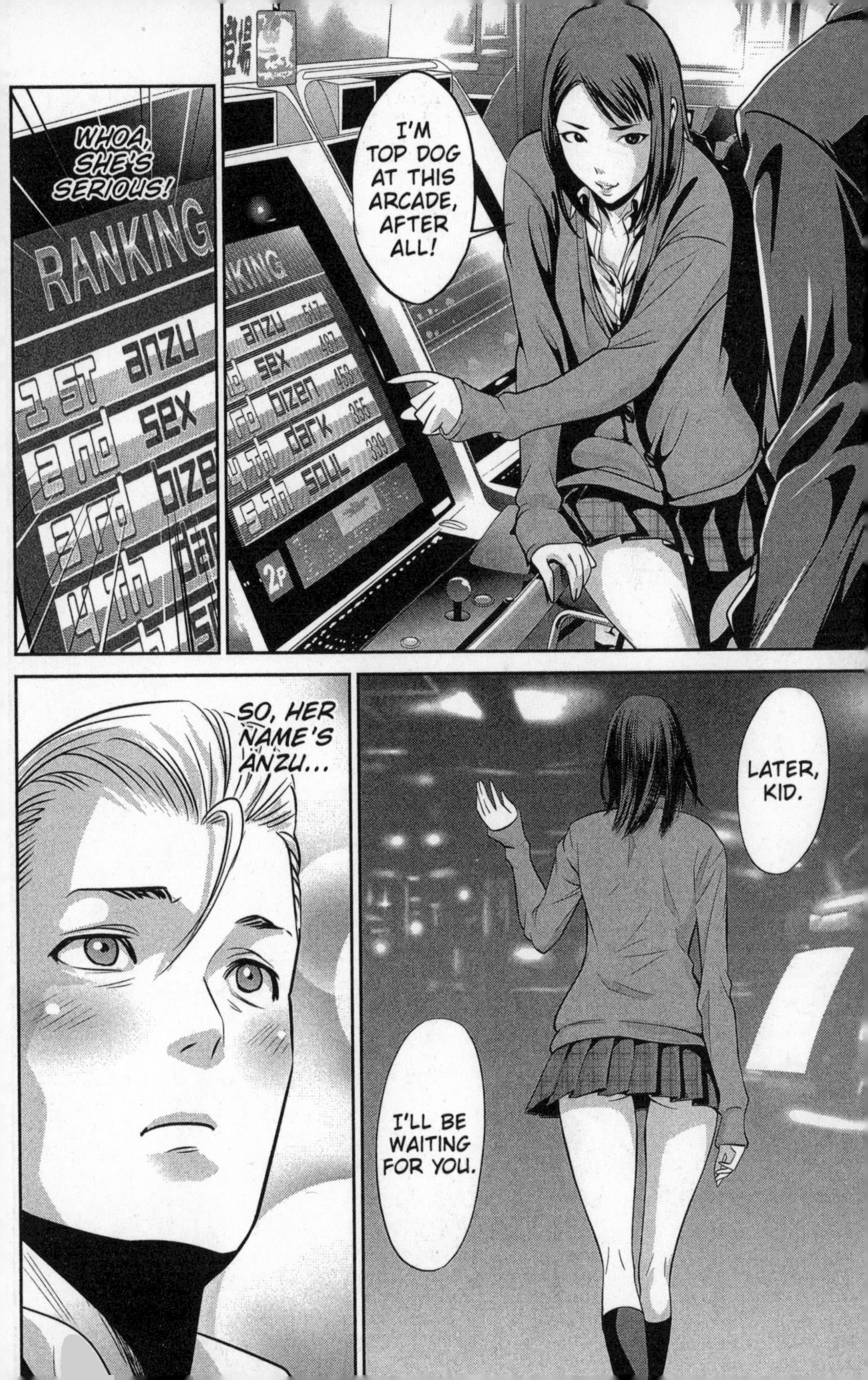
I'M TOP DOG AT THIS ARCADE, AFTER ALL!
RANKING
anzu
sex
bizen
dark
SOUL
2P
WHOA, SHE'S SERIOUS!
RANKING
1 ST anzu
2 nd sex
3 rd
LATER, KID.
I'LL BE WAITING FOR YOU.
SO, HER NAME'S ANZU...

SIGN: WARDEN'S ROOM

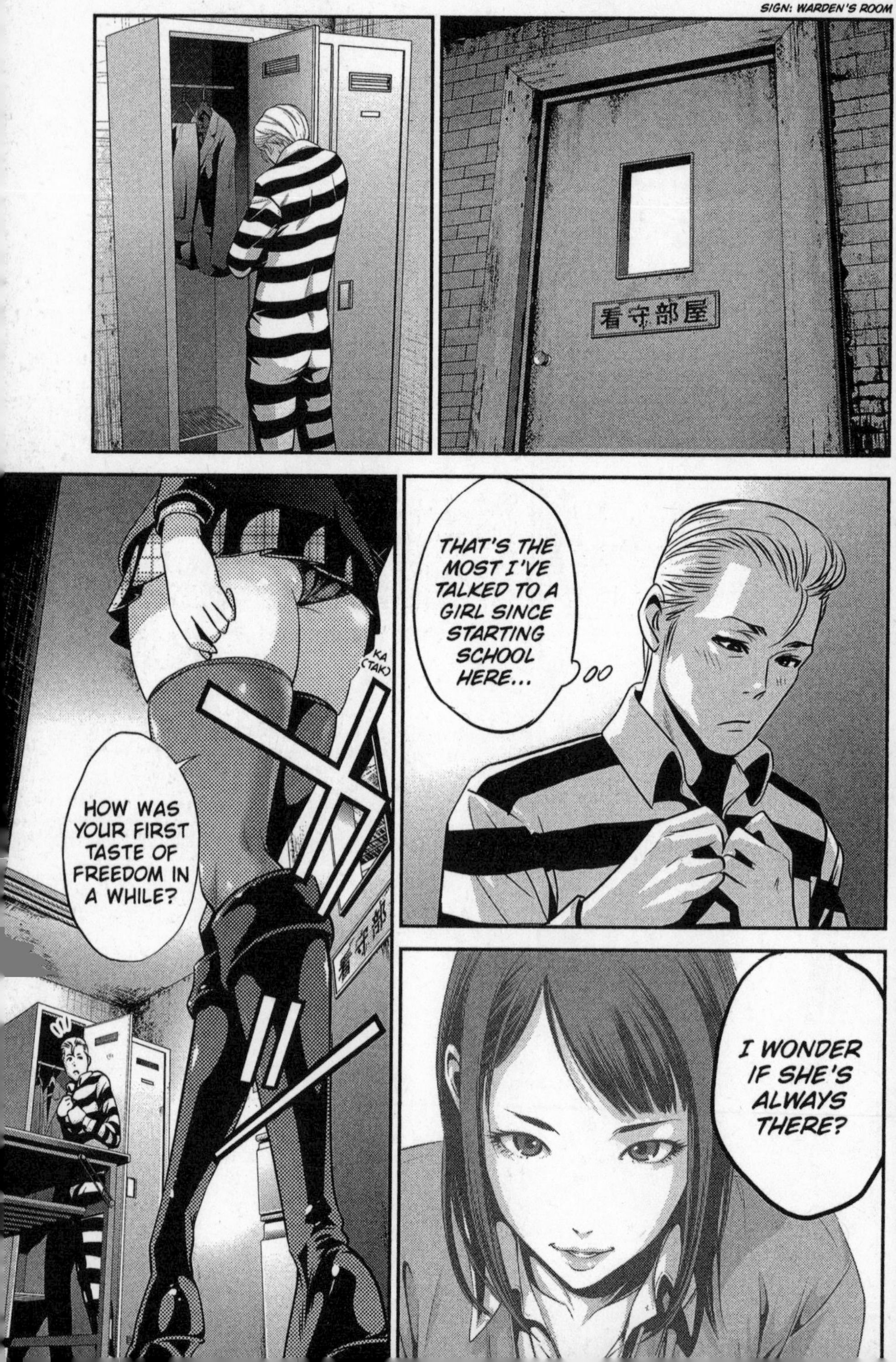
看守部屋
THAT'S THE MOST I'VE TALKED TO A GIRL SINCE STARTING SCHOOL HERE...
I WONDER IF SHE'S ALWAYS THERE?
KA (TAK)
HOW WAS YOUR FIRST TASTE OF FREEDOM IN A WHILE?
看守部

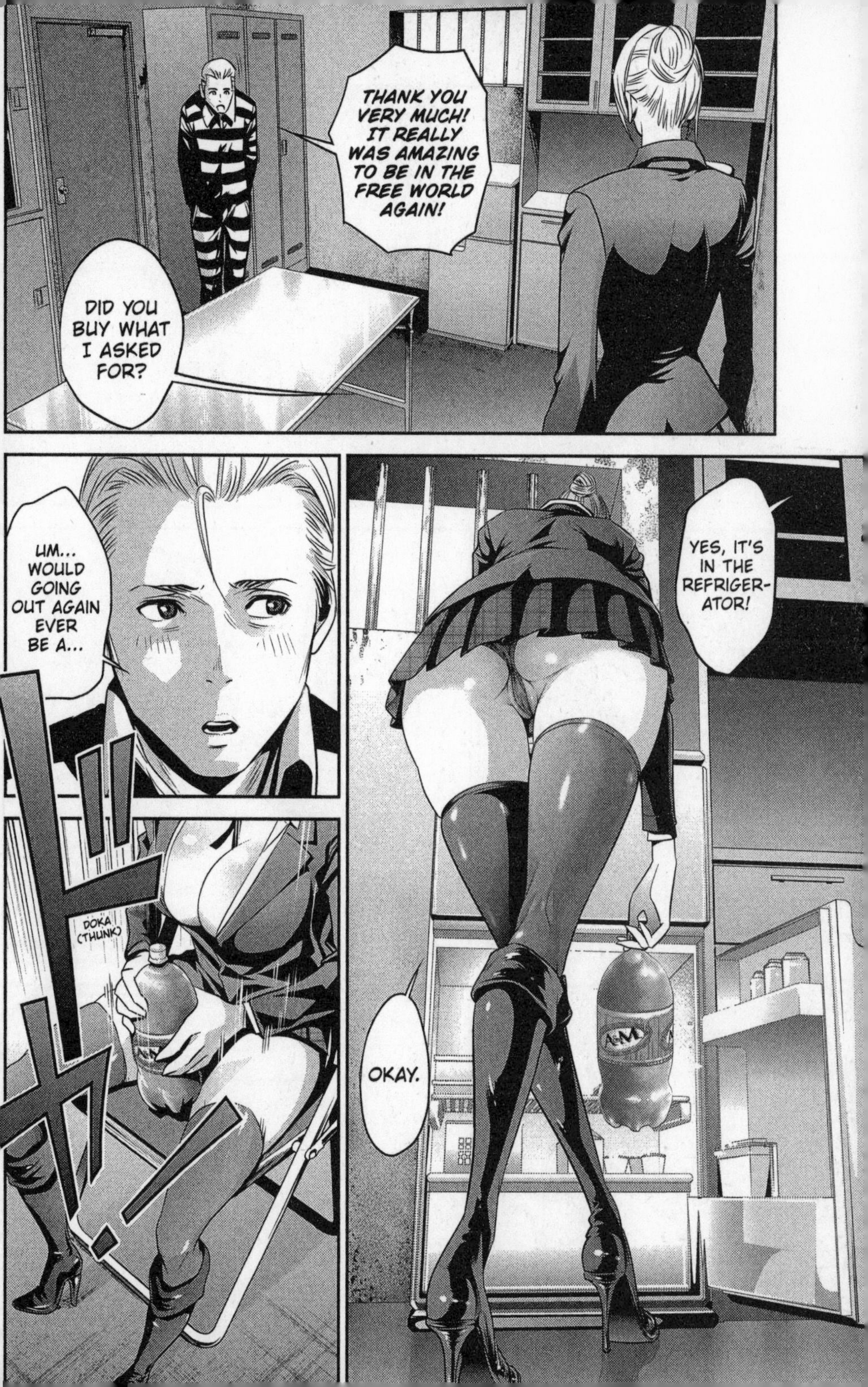
THANK YOU VERY MUCH! IT REALLY WAS AMAZING TO BE IN THE FREE WORLD AGAIN!
DID YOU BUY WHAT I ASKED FOR?
YES, IT'S IN THE REFRIGER-ATOR!
OKAY.
UM... WOULD GOING OUT AGAIN EVER BE A...
DOKA (THUNK)

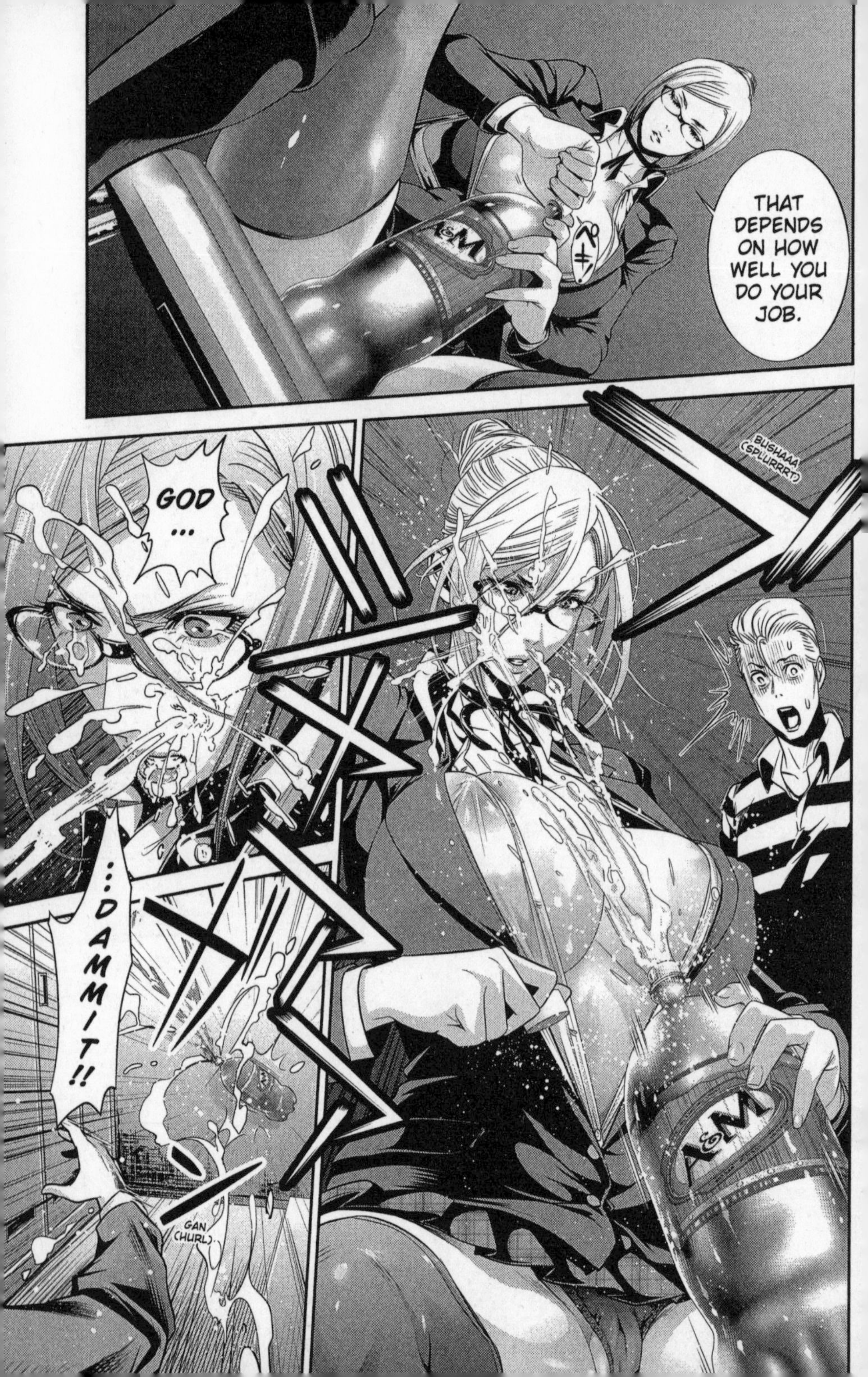
THAT DEPENDS ON HOW WELL YOU DO YOUR JOB.
BUSHAA (SPLURRRT)
GOD ...
...DAMMIT!!
GAN (HURL)

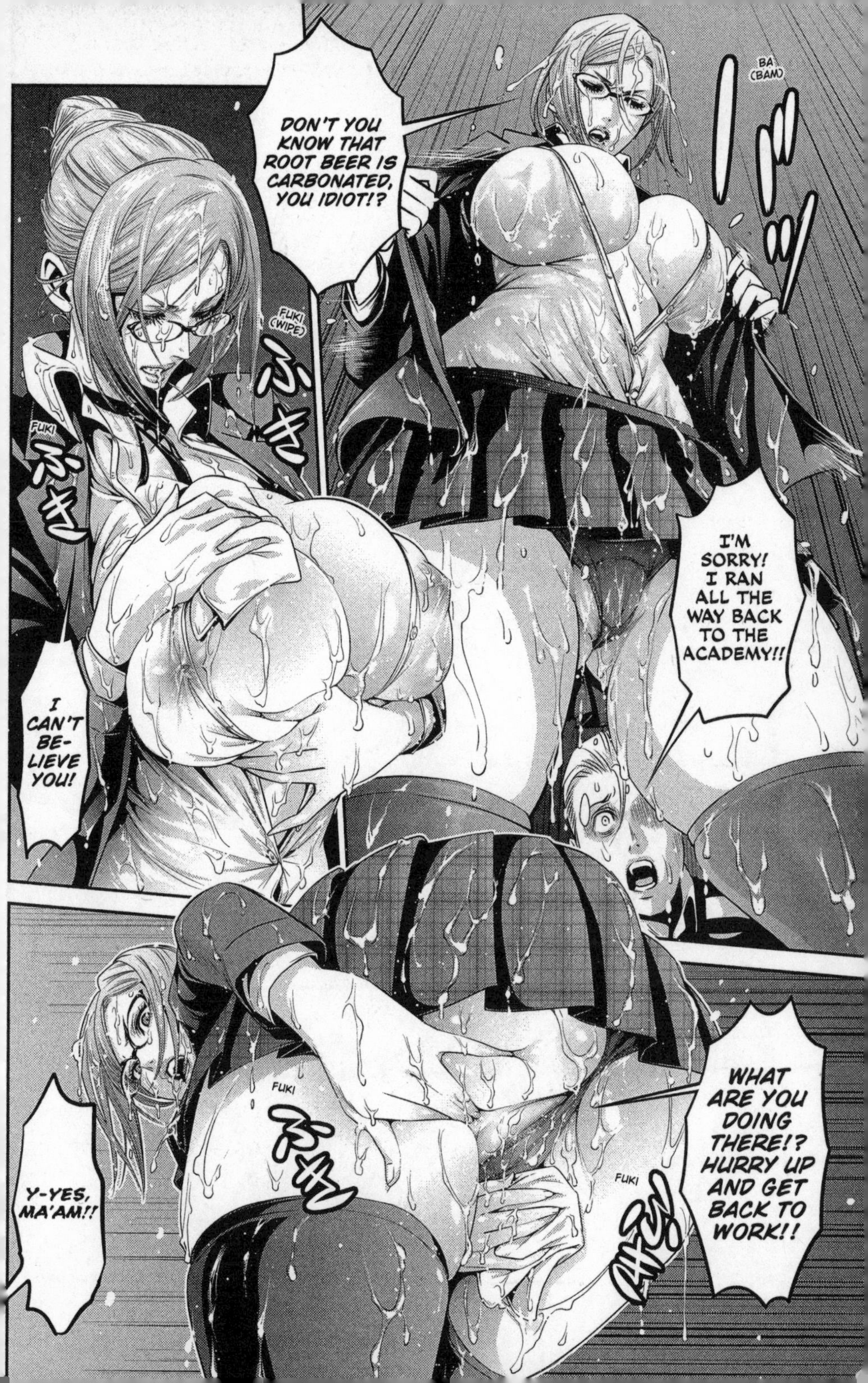
BA (BAM)
DON'T YOU KNOW THAT ROOT BEER IS CARBONATED, YOU IDIOT!?
I'M SORRY! I RAN ALL THE WAY BACK TO THE ACADEMY!!
FUKI (WIPE)
ふき
FUKI
ふき
I CAN'T BE-LIEVE YOU!
WHAT ARE YOU DOING THERE!? HURRY UP AND GET BACK TO WORK!!
FUKI
FUKI
Y-YES, MA'AM!!

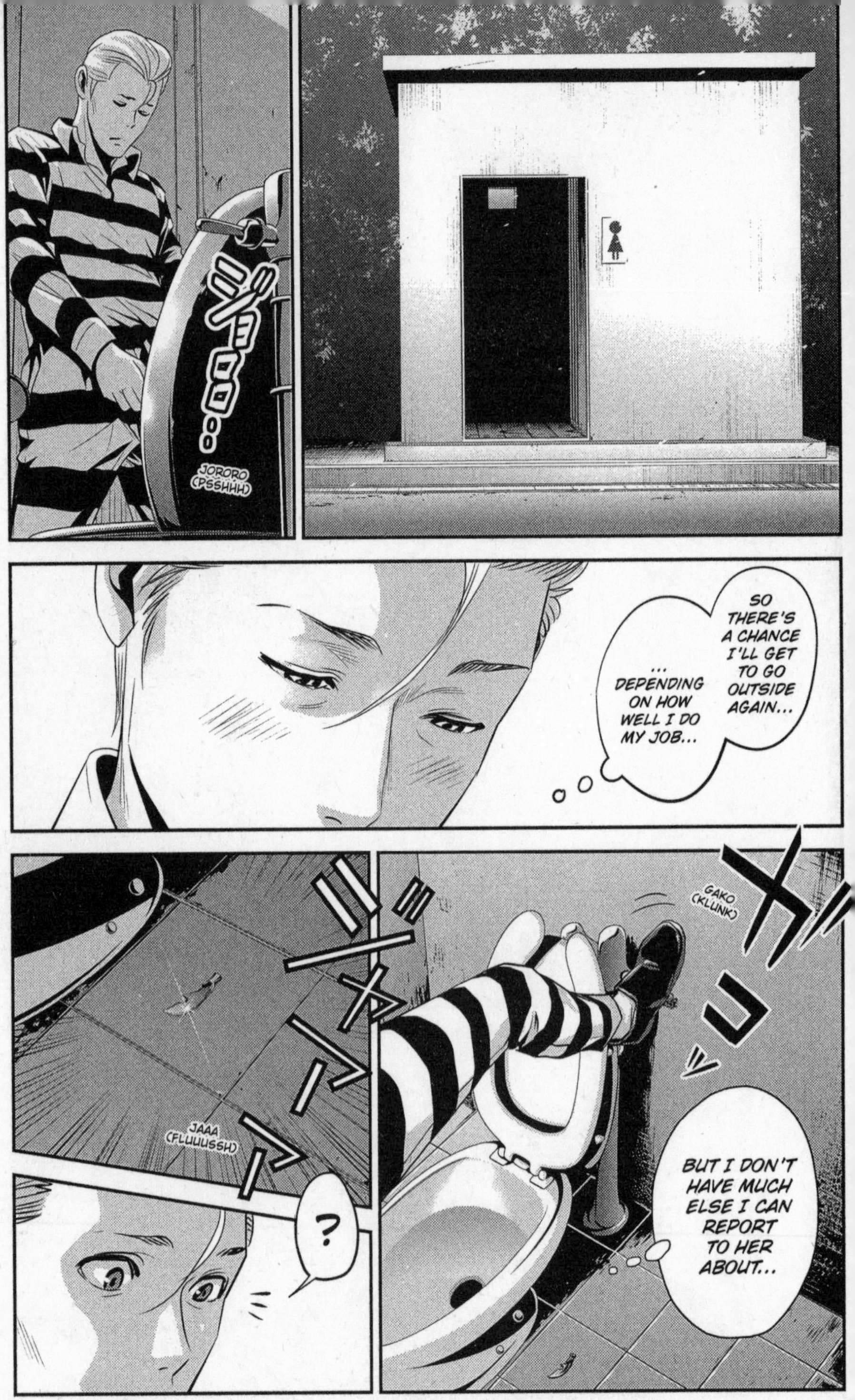
JORORO (PSSHHH)
SO THERE'S A CHANCE I'LL GET TO GO OUTSIDE AGAIN...
... DEPENDING ON HOW WELL I DO MY JOB...
GAKO (KLUNK)
BUT I DON'T HAVE MUCH ELSE I CAN REPORT TO HER ABOUT...
JAAA (FLUUUSSH)
?

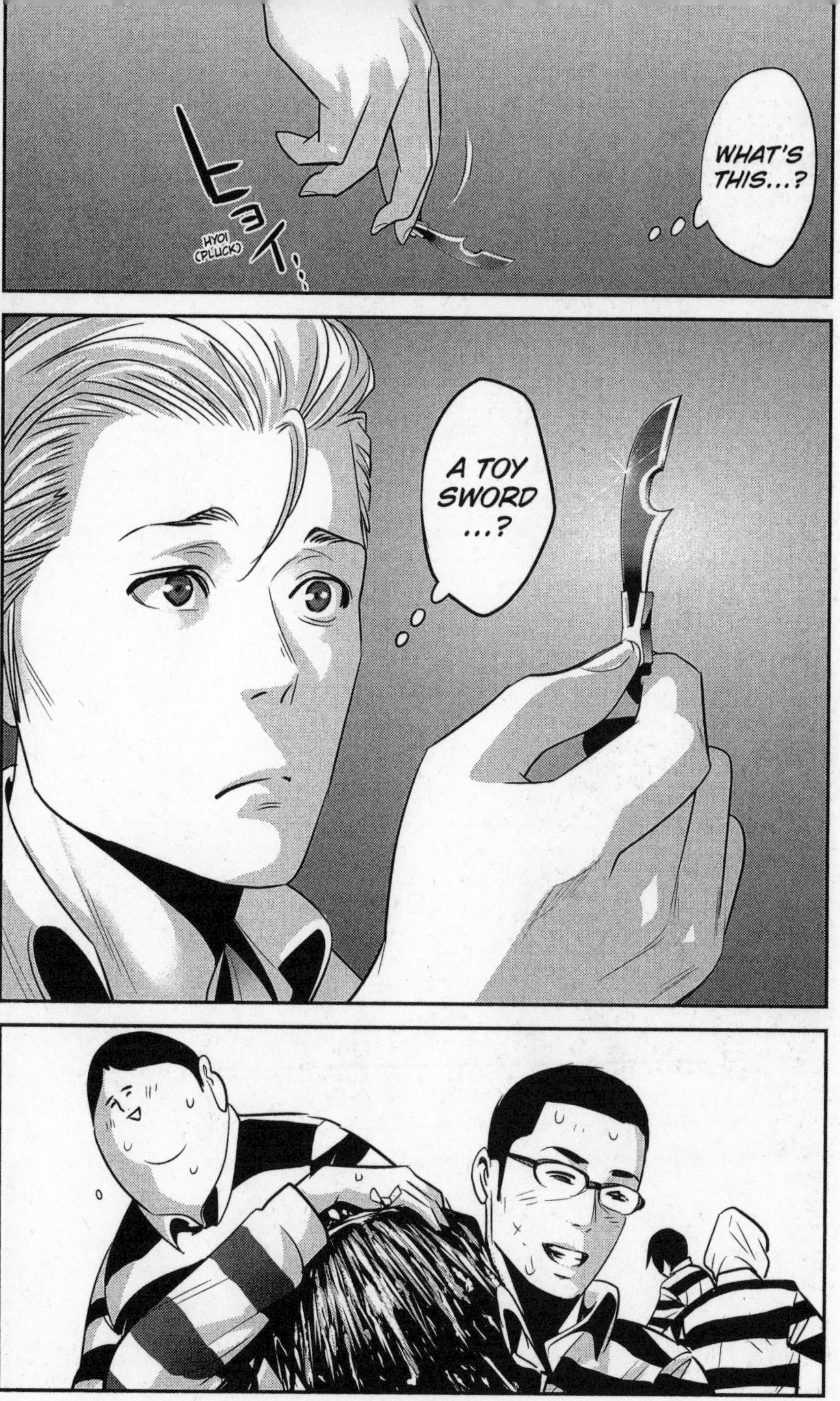
WHAT'S THIS...?
ヒョイ
HYOI (PLUCK)
A TOY SWORD ...?

CHAPTER 42: MEIKOTOUILLE

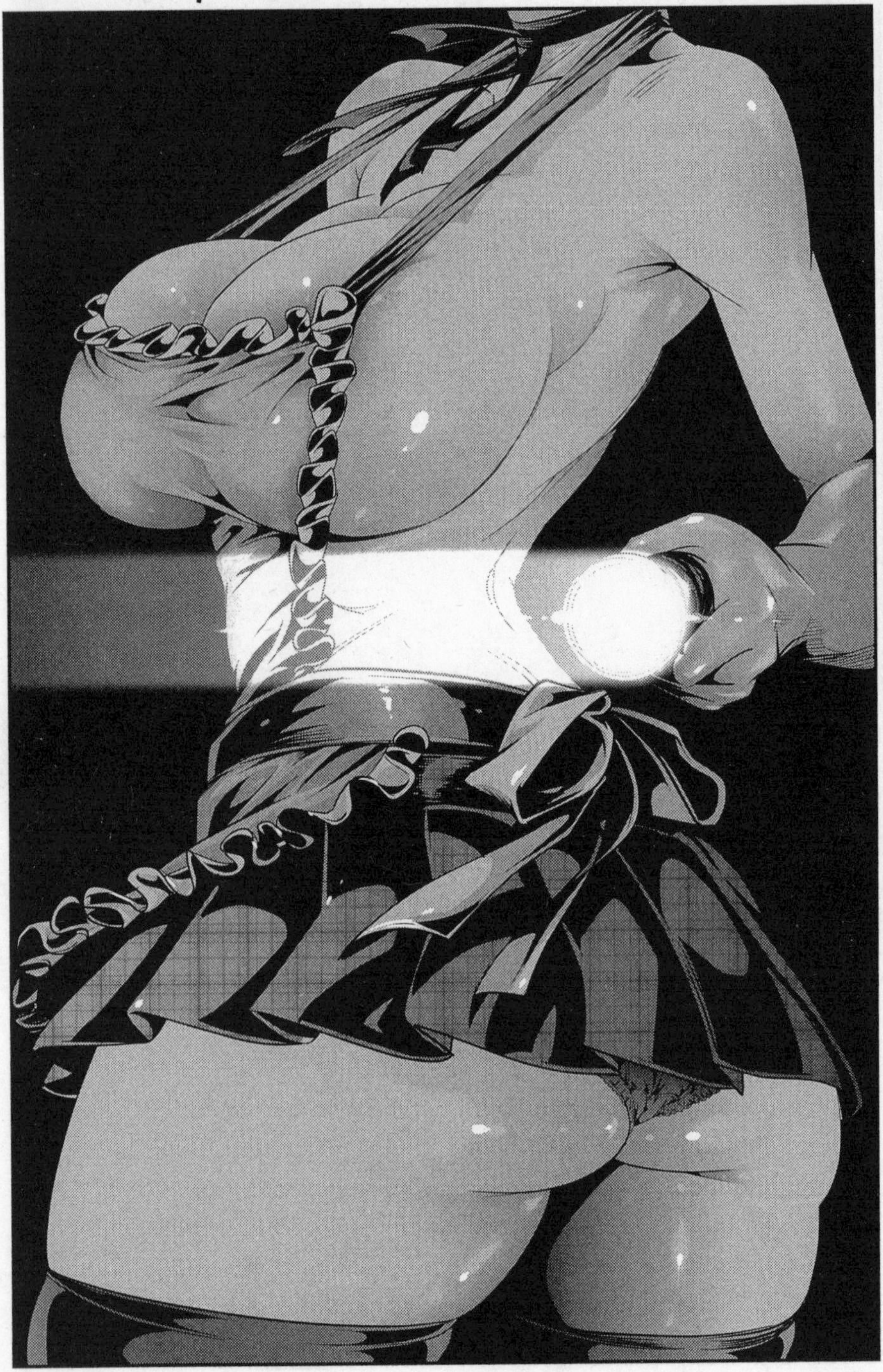

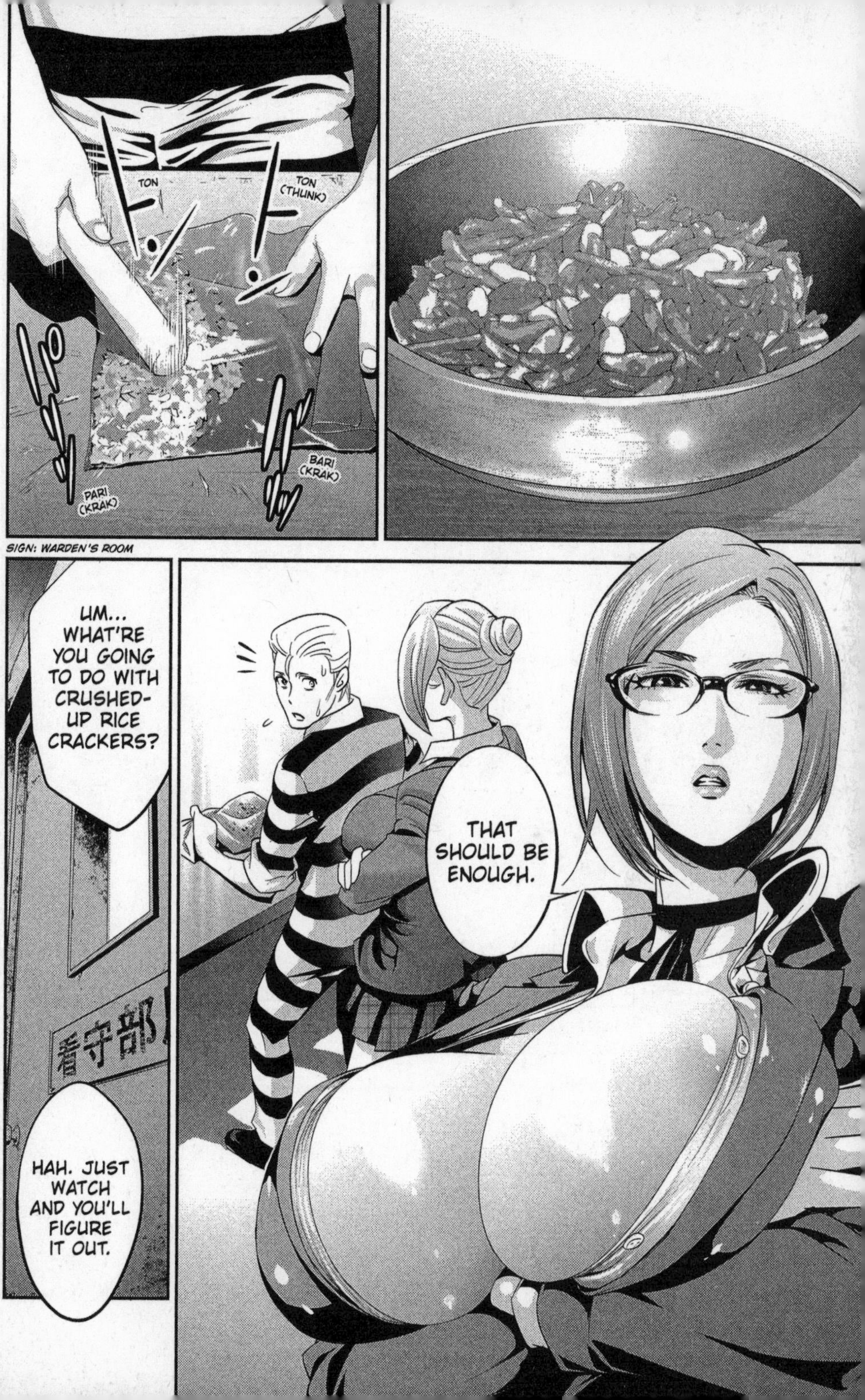
TON
TON (THUNK)
BARI (KRAK)
PARI (KRAK)
SIGN: WARDEN'S ROOM
THAT SHOULD BE ENOUGH.
UM... WHAT'RE YOU GOING TO DO WITH CRUSHED-UP RICE CRACKERS?
看守部
HAH. JUST WATCH AND YOU'LL FIGURE IT OUT.

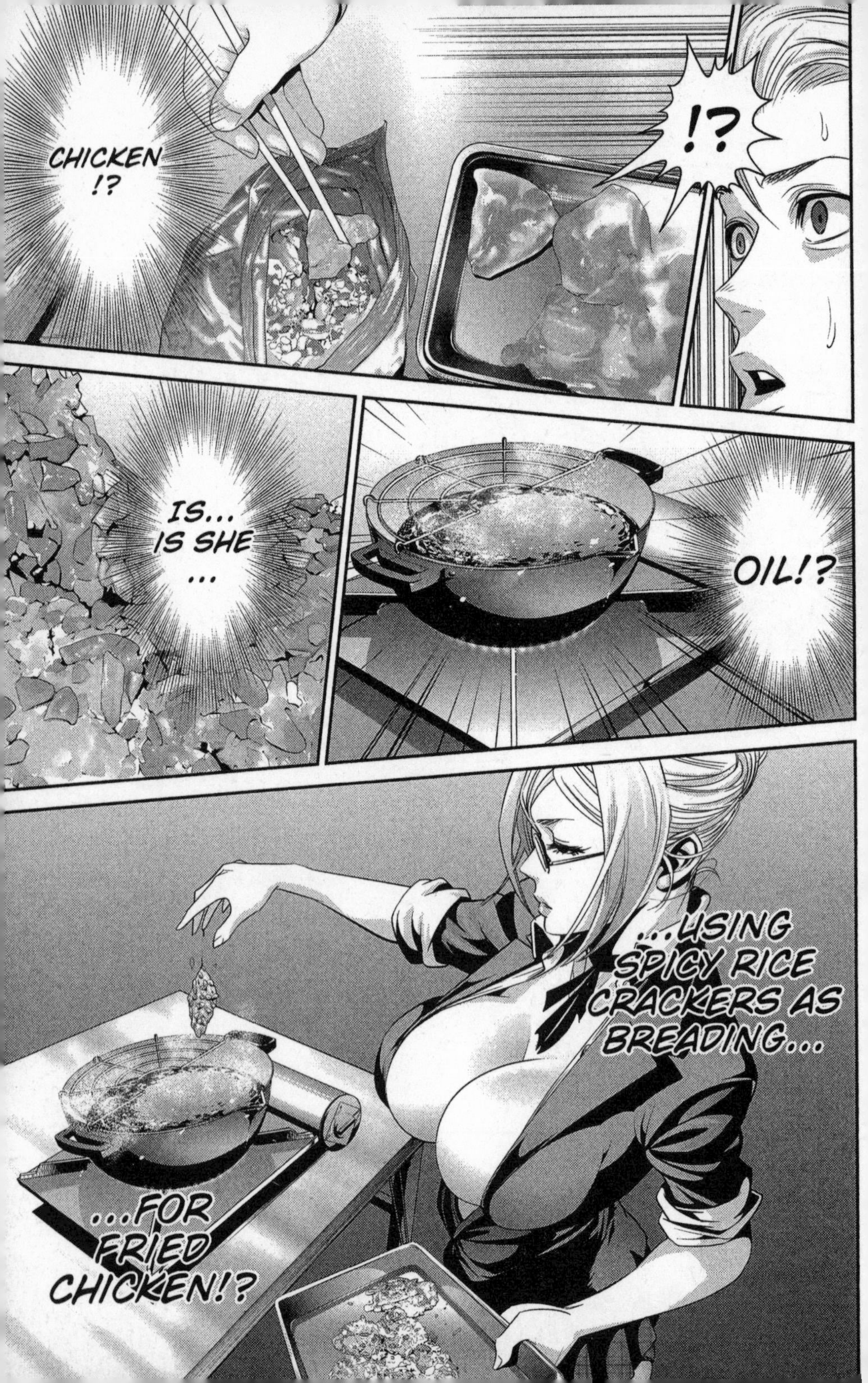
!?
CHICKEN !?
OIL!?
IS... IS SHE ...
...USING SPICY RICE CRACKERS AS BREADING...
...FOR FRIED CHICKEN!?

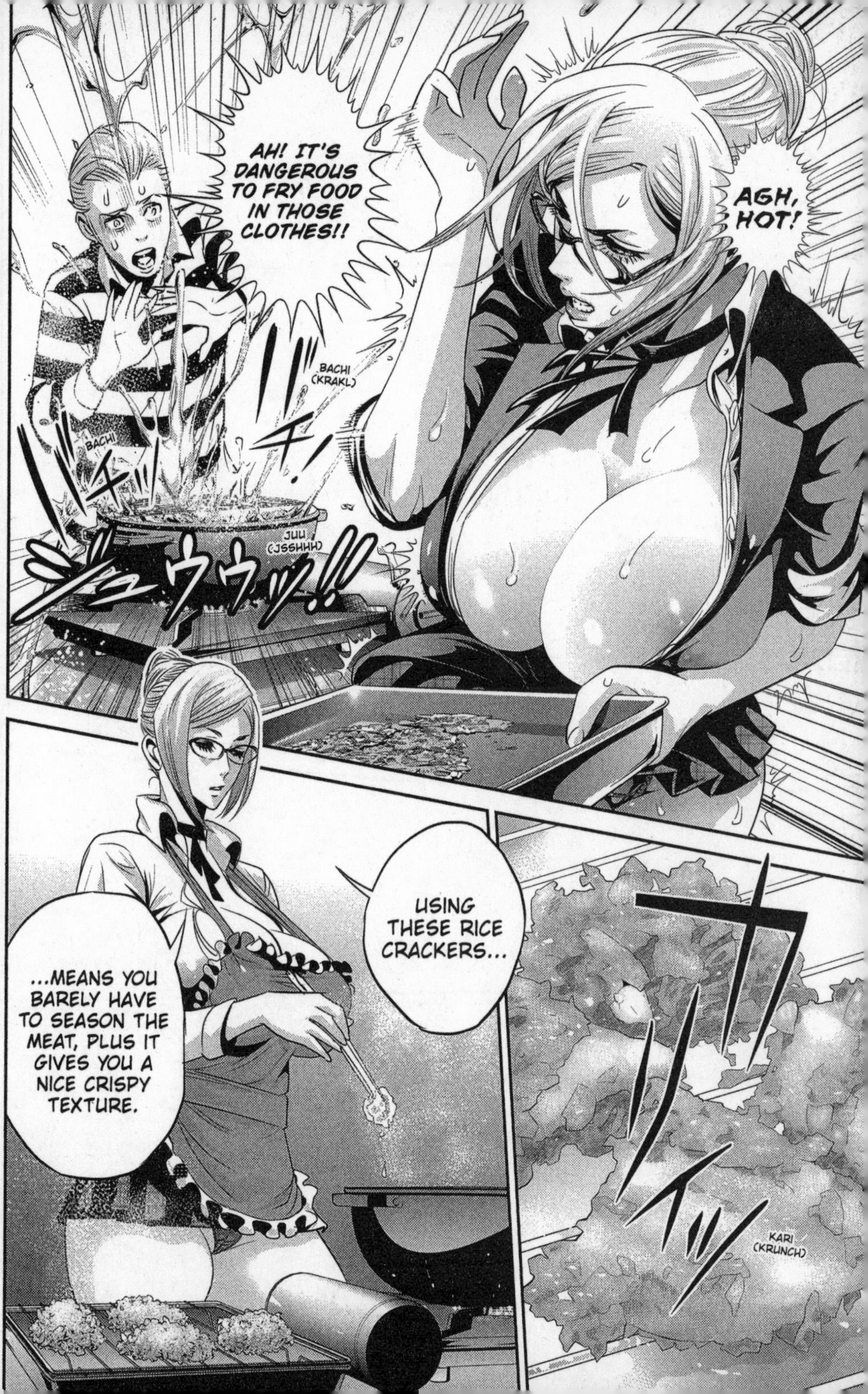
AGH, HOT!
AH! IT'S DANGEROUS TO FRY FOOD IN THOSE CLOTHES!!
BACHI (KRAKL)
BACHI
JUU (JSSHHH)
KARI (KRUNCH)
USING THESE RICE CRACKERS...
...MEANS YOU BARELY HAVE TO SEASON THE MEAT, PLUS IT GIVES YOU A NICE CRISPY TEXTURE.

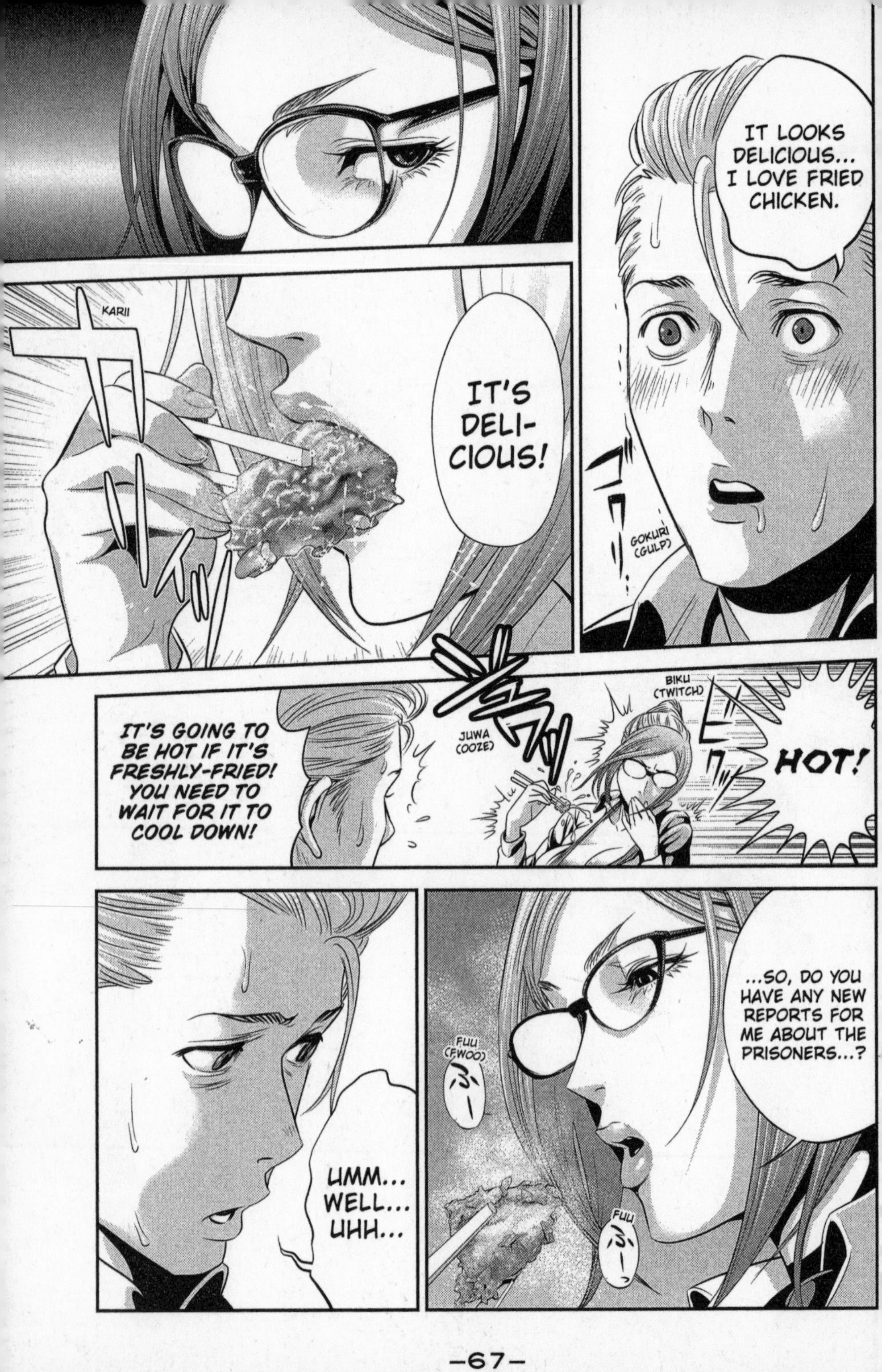
IT LOOKS DELICIOUS... I LOVE FRIED CHICKEN.
GOKURI (GULP)
IT'S DELI-CIOUS!
KARII
HOT!
BIKU (TWITCH)
JUWA (COOZE)
IT'S GOING TO BE HOT IF IT'S FRESHLY-FRIED! YOU NEED TO WAIT FOR IT TO COOL DOWN!
...SO, DO YOU HAVE ANY NEW REPORTS FOR ME ABOUT THE PRISONERS...?
FUU (FWOO)
ふー
FUU
ふー
UMM... WELL... UHH...

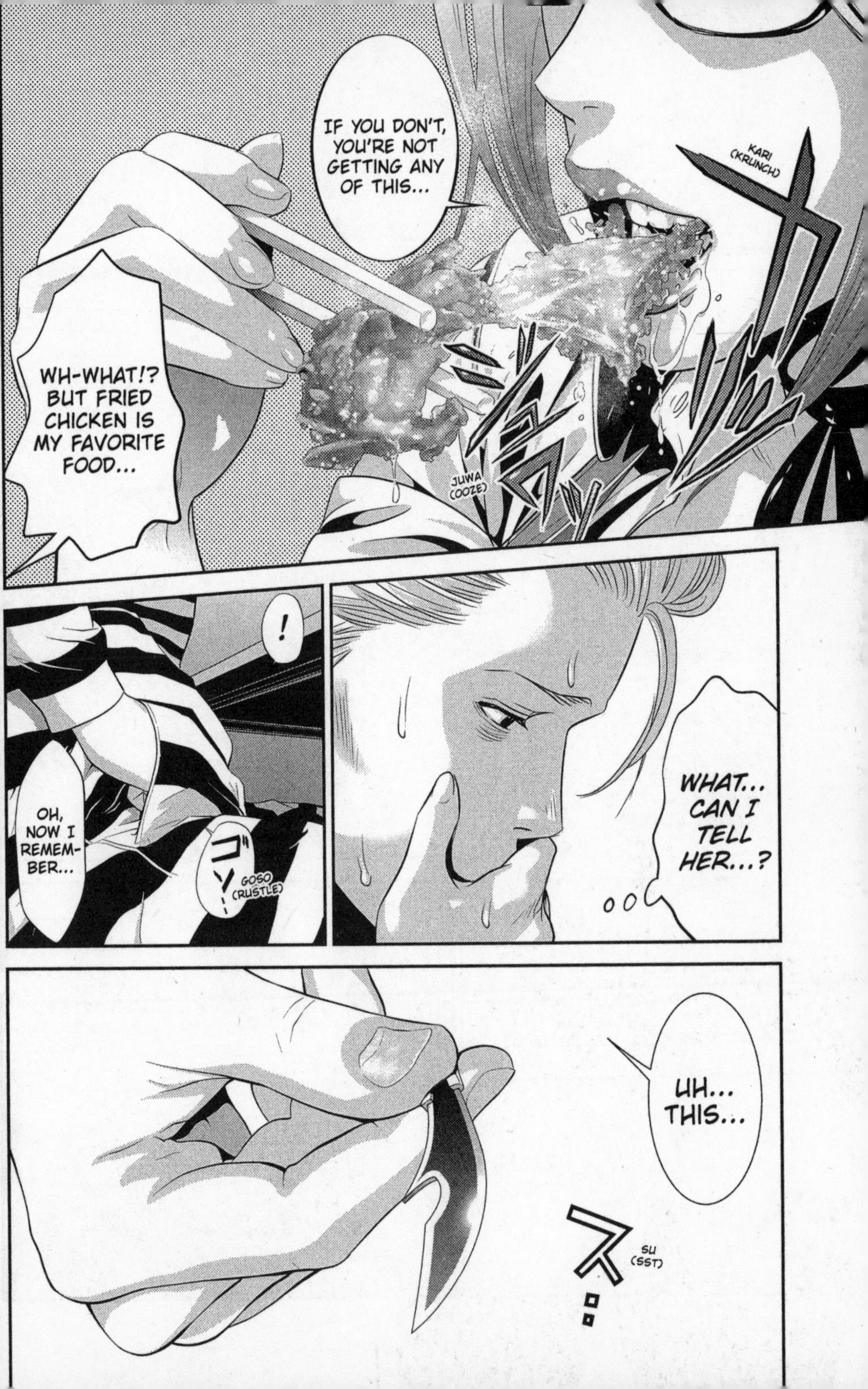
IF YOU DON'T, YOU'RE NOT GETTING ANY OF THIS...
KARI (KRUNCH)
JUWA (OOZE)
WH-WHAT!? BUT FRIED CHICKEN IS MY FAVORITE FOOD...
WHAT... CAN I TELL HER...?
!
OH, NOW I REMEMBER...
GOSO (RUSTLE)
UH... THIS...
SU (SST)

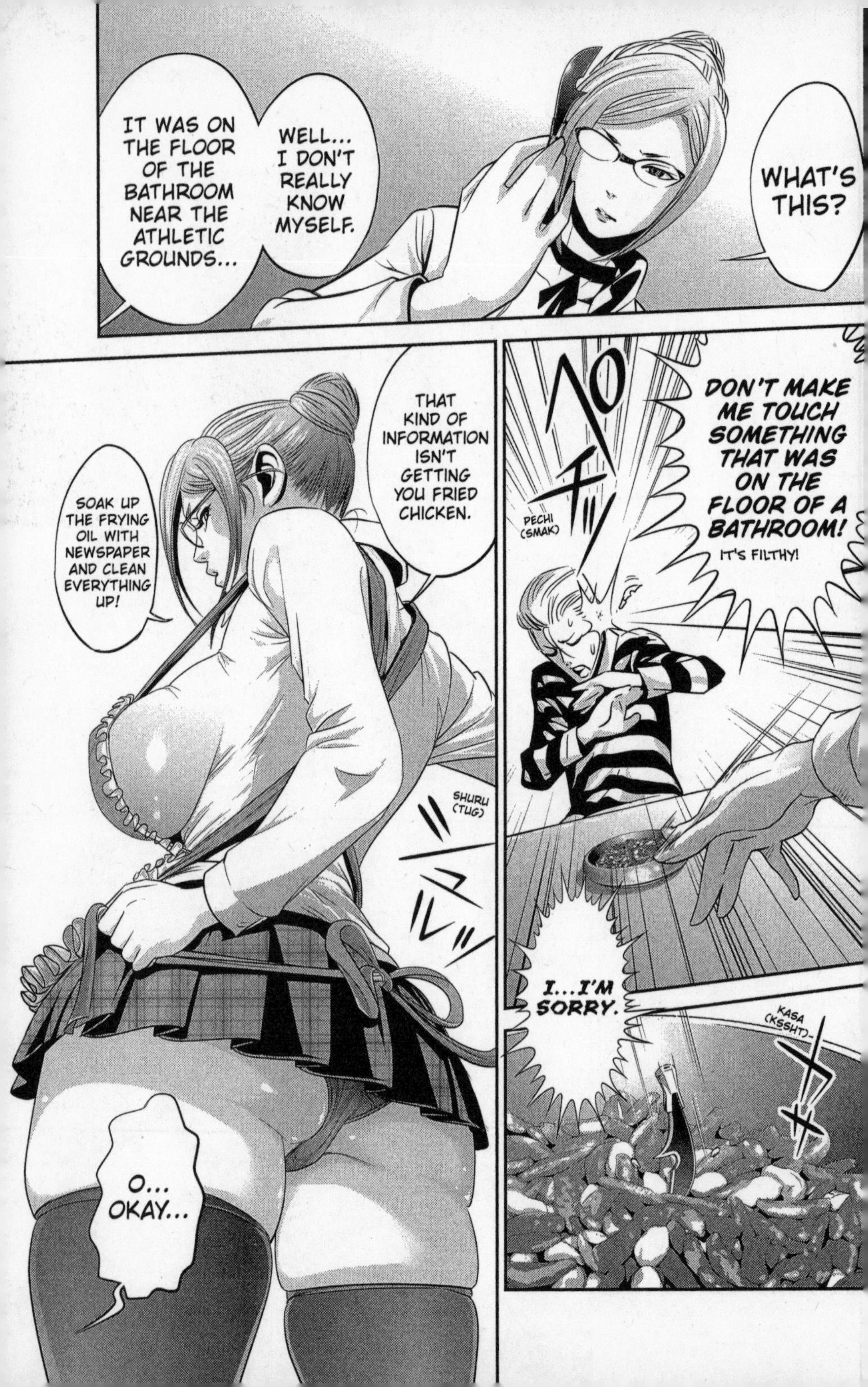
WHAT'S THIS?
WELL... I DON'T REALLY KNOW MYSELF.
IT WAS ON THE FLOOR OF THE BATHROOM NEAR THE ATHLETIC GROUNDS...
PECHI (SMAK)
DON'T MAKE ME TOUCH SOMETHING THAT WAS ON THE FLOOR OF A BATHROOM!
IT'S FILTHY!
I...I'M SORRY.
KASA (KSSHT)
THAT KIND OF INFORMATION ISN'T GETTING YOU FRIED CHICKEN.
SOAK UP THE FRYING OIL WITH NEWSPAPER AND CLEAN EVERYTHING UP!
SHURU (TUG)
O... OKAY...

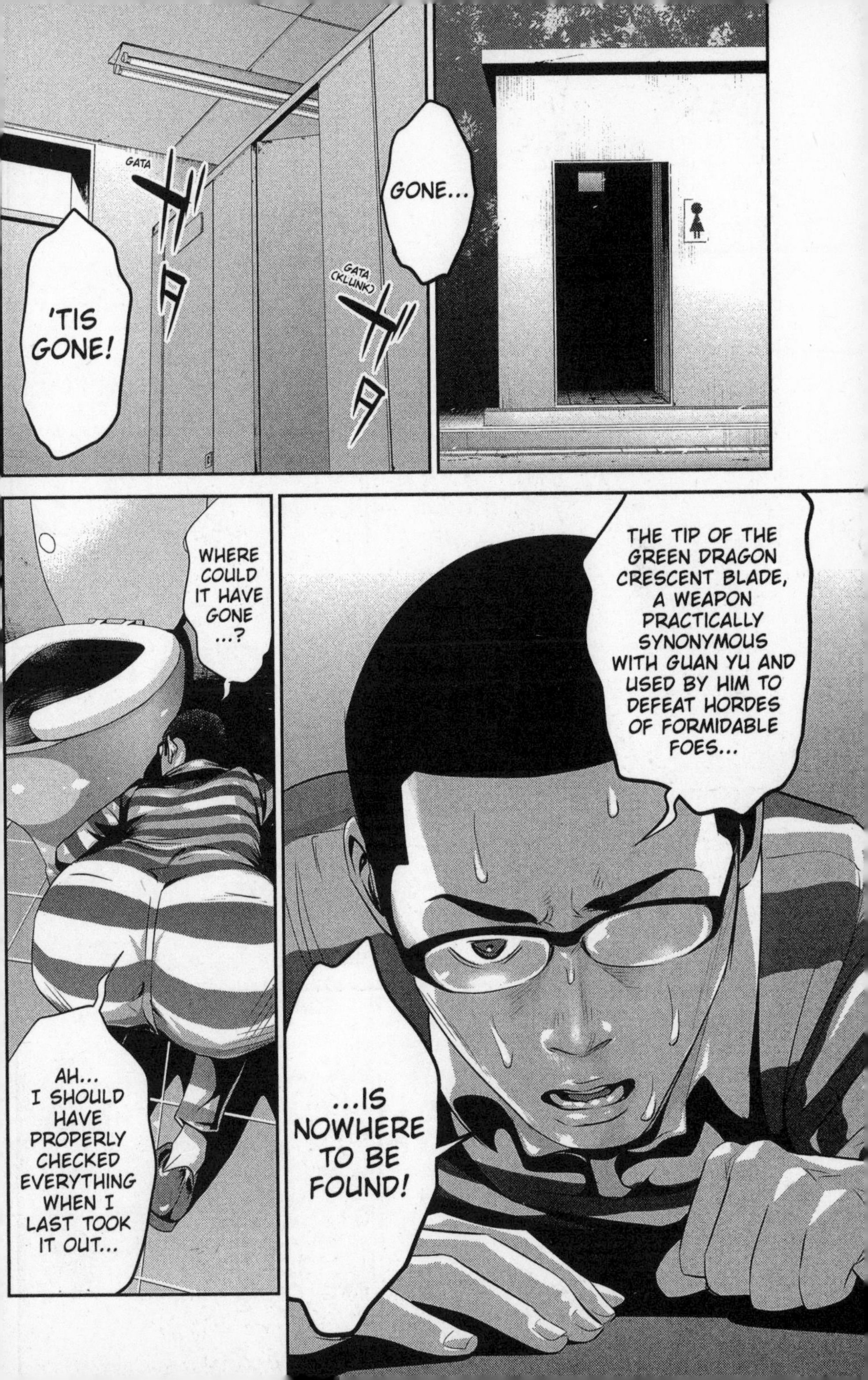
GONE...
GATA (KLUNK)
GATA
'TIS GONE!
THE TIP OF THE GREEN DRAGON CRESCENT BLADE, A WEAPON PRACTICALLY SYNONYMOUS WITH GUAN YU AND USED BY HIM TO DEFEAT HORDES OF FORMIDABLE FOES...
...IS NOWHERE TO BE FOUND!
WHERE COULD IT HAVE GONE ...?
AH... I SHOULD HAVE PROPERLY CHECKED EVERYTHING WHEN I LAST TOOK IT OUT...

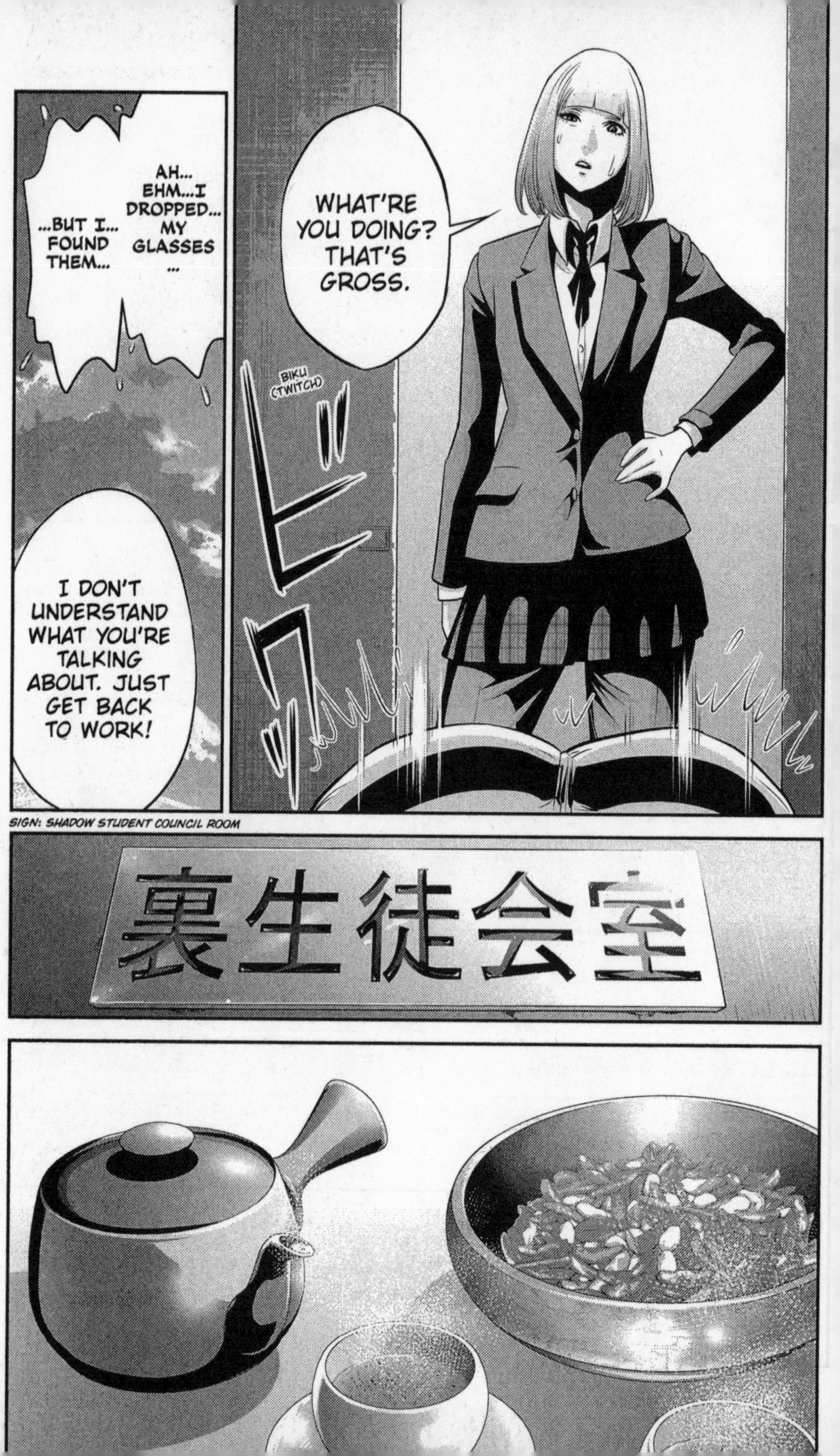
WHAT'RE YOU DOING? THAT'S GROSS.
BIKU (TWITCH)
ビクッ
AH... EHM...I DROPPED... MY GLASSES ...
...BUT I... FOUND THEM...
I DON'T UNDERSTAND WHAT YOU'RE TALKING ABOUT. JUST GET BACK TO WORK!
SIGN: SHADOW STUDENT COUNCIL ROOM
裏生徒会室

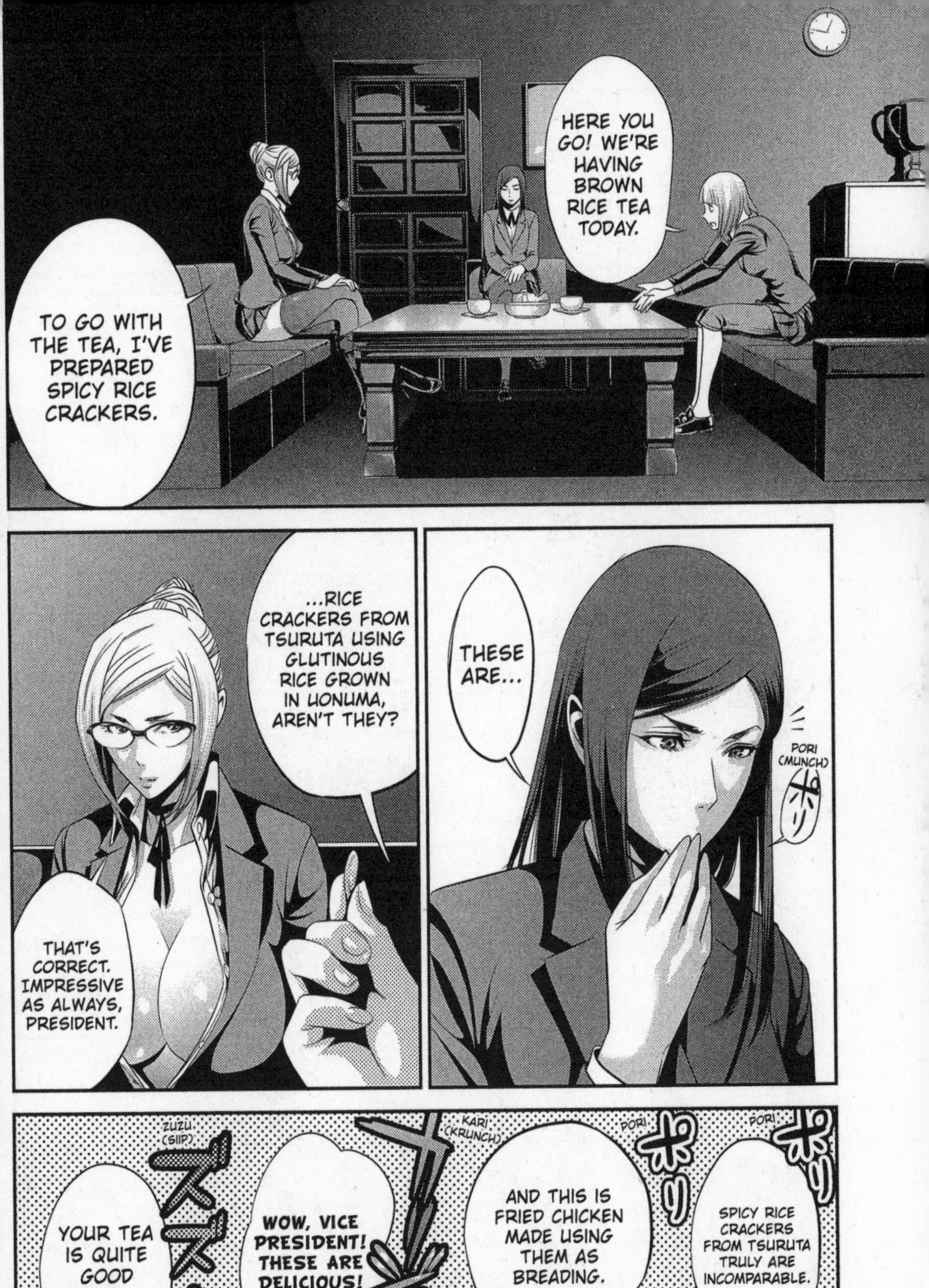
HERE YOU GO! WE'RE HAVING BROWN RICE TEA TODAY.
TO GO WITH THE TEA, I'VE PREPARED SPICY RICE CRACKERS.
THESE ARE...
PORI (MUNCH)
...RICE CRACKERS FROM TSURUTA USING GLUTINOUS RICE GROWN IN UONUMA, AREN'T THEY?
THAT'S CORRECT. IMPRESSIVE AS ALWAYS, PRESIDENT.
PORI
SPICY RICE CRACKERS FROM TSURUTA TRULY ARE INCOMPARABLE.
PORI
AND THIS IS FRIED CHICKEN MADE USING THEM AS BREADING.
KARI (KRUNCH)
JUWA (OOZE)
WOW, VICE PRESIDENT! THESE ARE DELICIOUS!
ZUZU (SIIP)
YOUR TEA IS QUITE GOOD TOO, HANA.

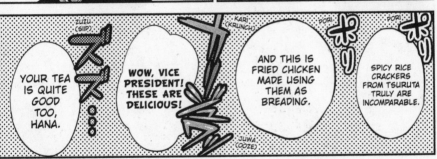

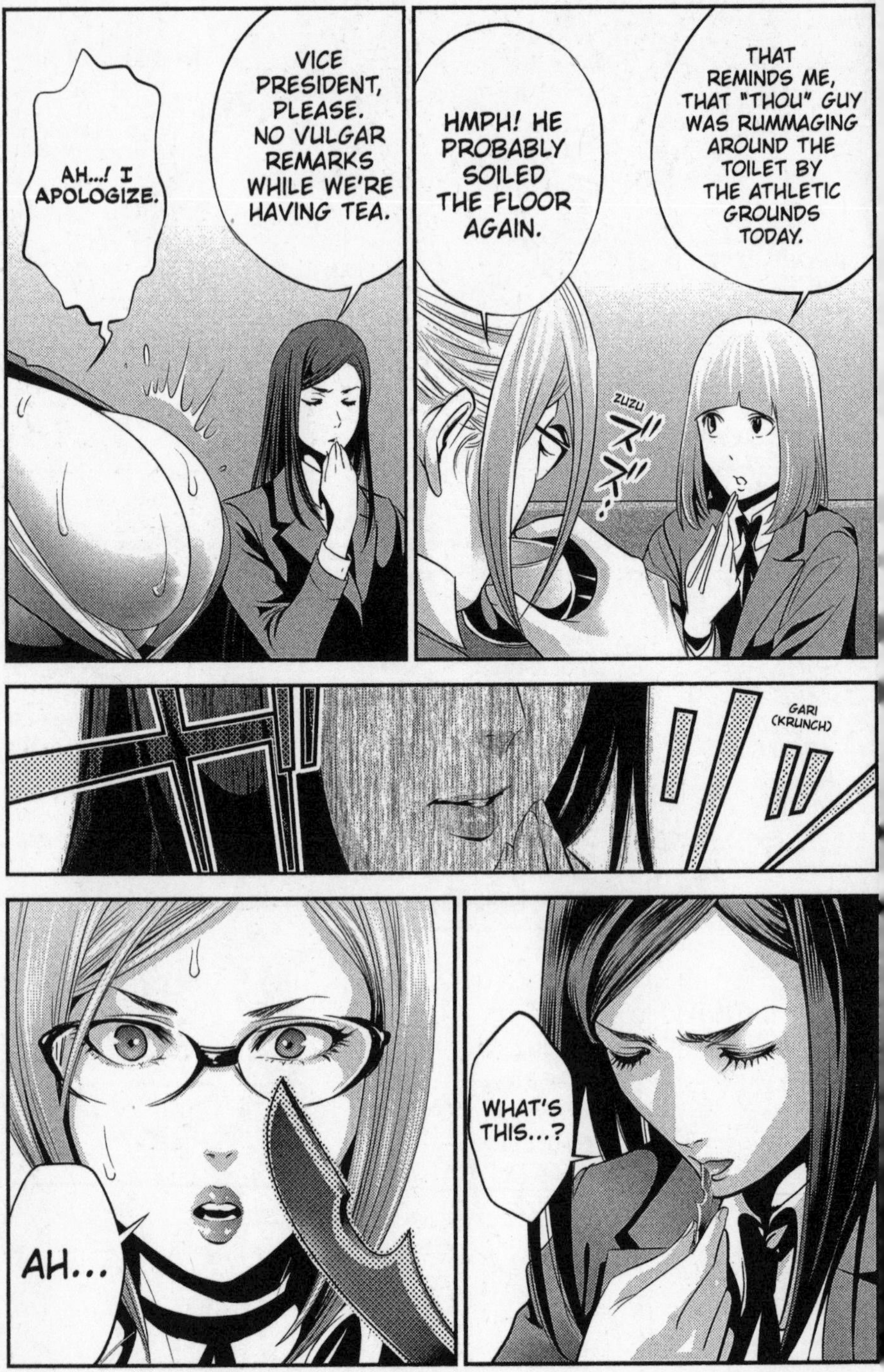
THAT REMINDS ME, THAT "THOU" GUY WAS RUMMAGING AROUND THE TOILET BY THE ATHLETIC GROUNDS TODAY.
HMPH! HE PROBABLY SOILED THE FLOOR AGAIN.
ZUZU
VICE PRESIDENT, PLEASE. NO VULGAR REMARKS WHILE WE'RE HAVING TEA.
AH...! I APOLOGIZE.
GARI (KRUNCH)
WHAT'S THIS...?
AH...

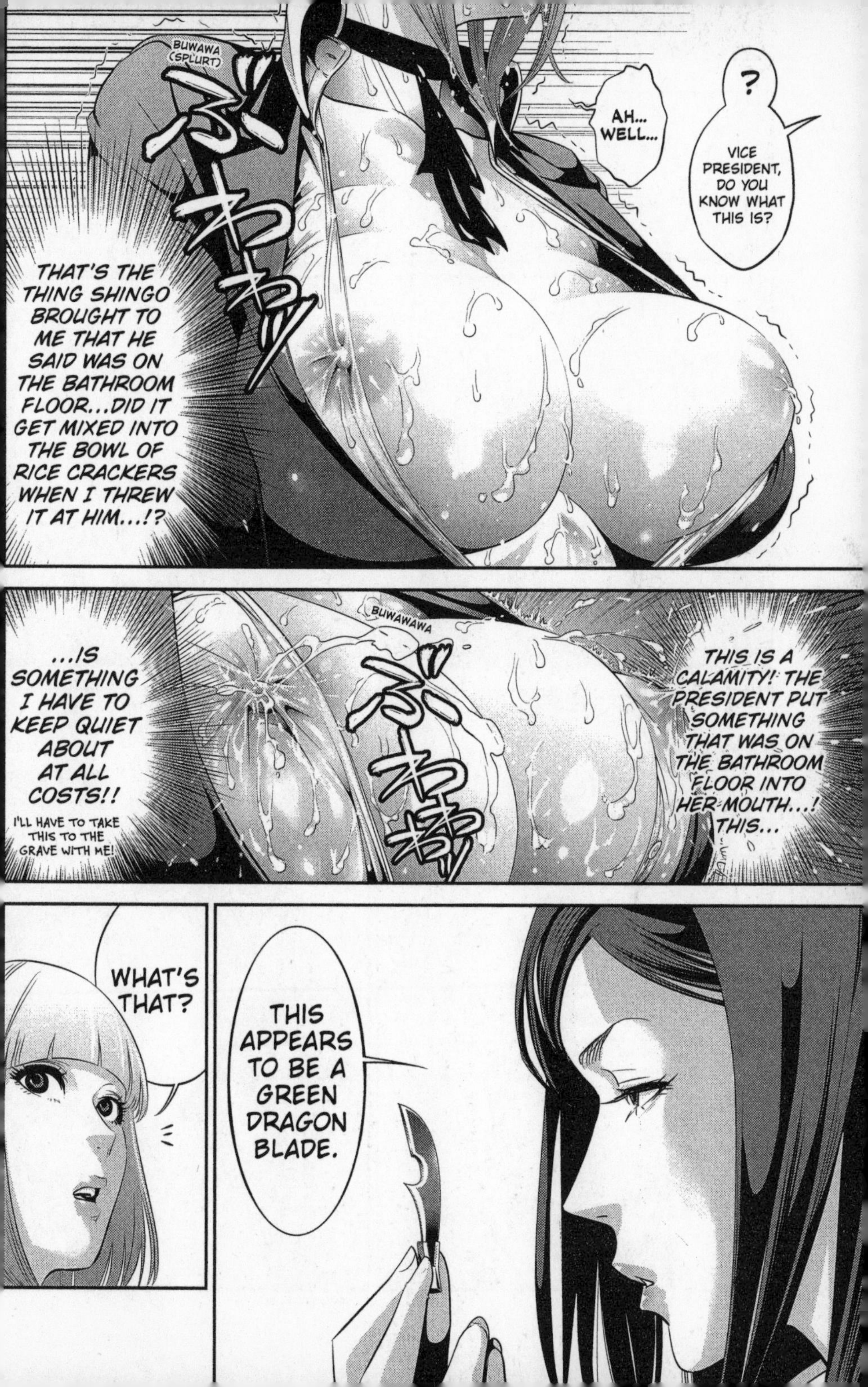
?
VICE PRESIDENT, DO YOU KNOW WHAT THIS IS?
AH... WELL...
BUWAWA (SPLURT)
THAT'S THE THING SHINGO BROUGHT TO ME THAT HE SAID WAS ON THE BATHROOM FLOOR...DID IT GET MIXED INTO THE BOWL OF RICE CRACKERS WHEN I THREW IT AT HIM...!?
THIS IS A CALAMITY! THE PRESIDENT PUT SOMETHING THAT WAS ON THE BATHROOM FLOOR INTO HER MOUTH...! THIS...
BUWAWAWA
...IS SOMETHING I HAVE TO KEEP QUIET ABOUT AT ALL COSTS!!
I'LL HAVE TO TAKE THIS TO THE GRAVE WITH ME!
THIS APPEARS TO BE A GREEN DRAGON BLADE.
WHAT'S THAT?

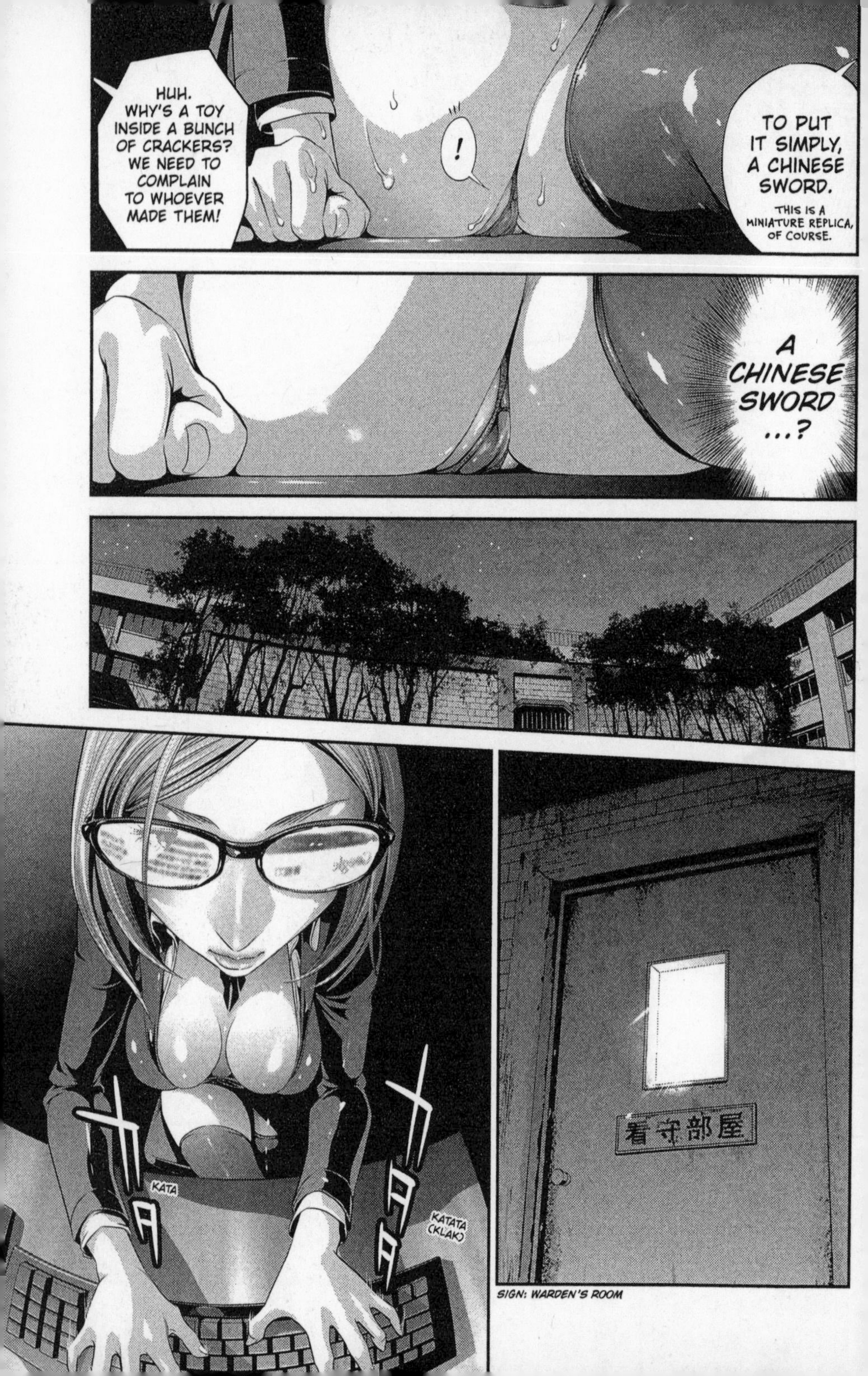
TO PUT IT SIMPLY, A CHINESE SWORD.
THIS IS A MINIATURE REPLICA, OF COURSE.
!
HUH. WHY'S A TOY INSIDE A BUNCH OF CRACKERS? WE NEED TO COMPLAIN TO WHOEVER MADE THEM!
A CHINESE SWORD ...?
看守部屋
SIGN: WARDEN'S ROOM
KATATA (KLAK)
KATA

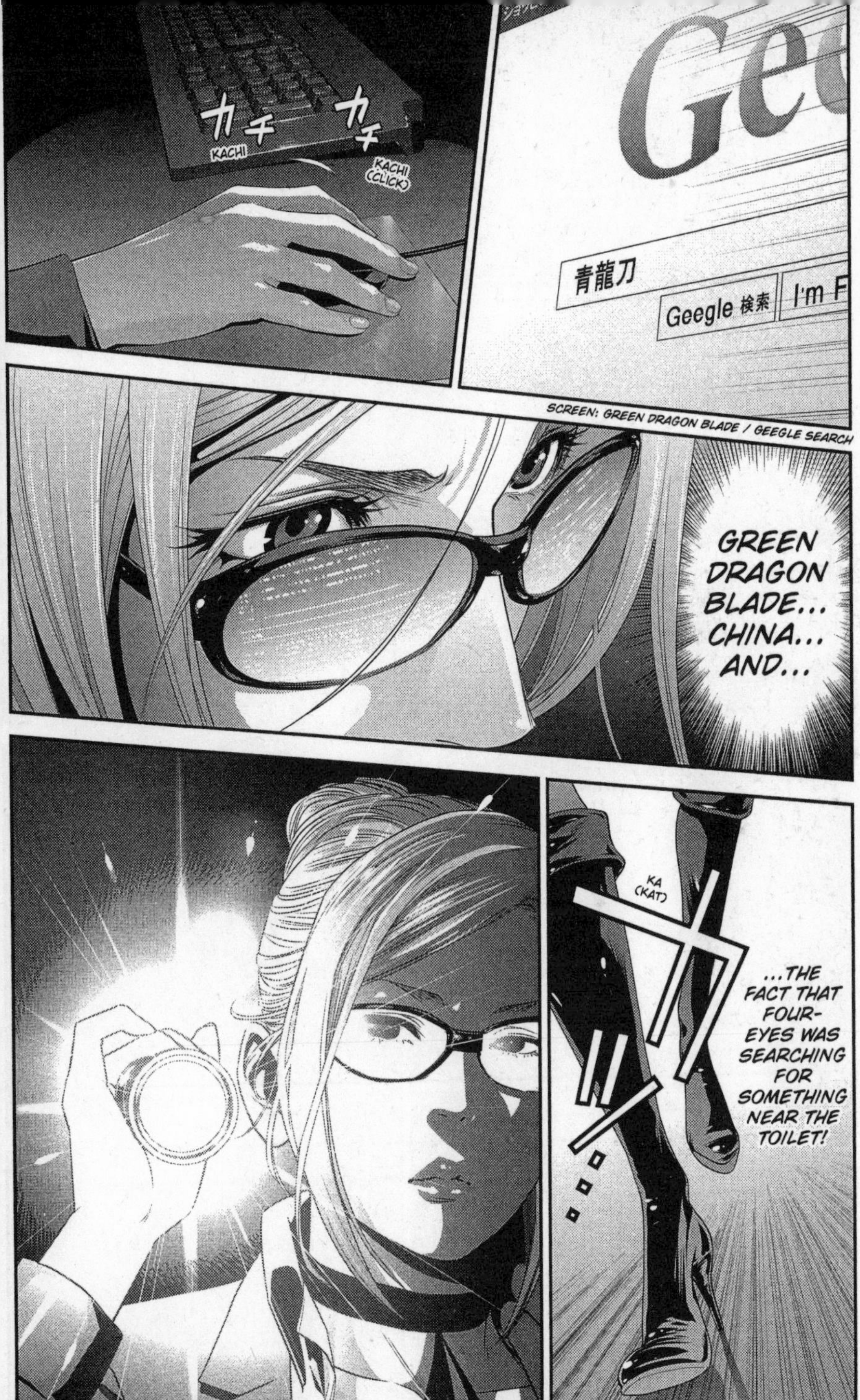
青龍刀
Geegle 検索
I'm F
カチ
KACHI
カチ
KACHI (CLICK)
SCREEN: GREEN DRAGON BLADE / GEEGLE SEARCH
GREEN DRAGON BLADE... CHINA... AND...
KA (KAT)
...THE FACT THAT FOUR-EYES WAS SEARCHING FOR SOMETHING NEAR THE TOILET!

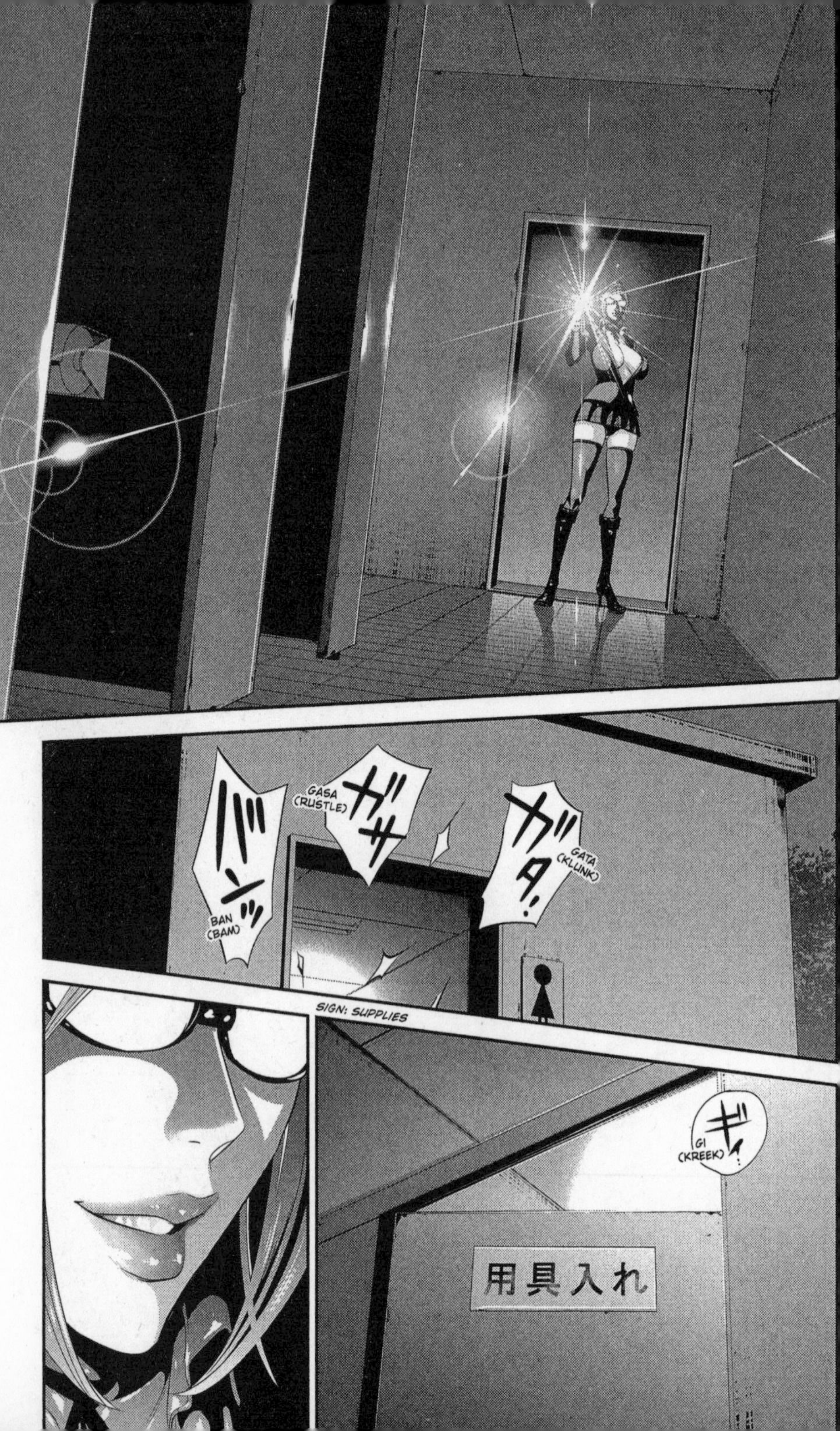
ガタッ!
GATA (KLUNK)
ガサ
GASA (RUSTLE)
バンッ
BAN (BAM)
SIGN: SUPPLIES
ギィ
GI (KREEK)
用具入れ

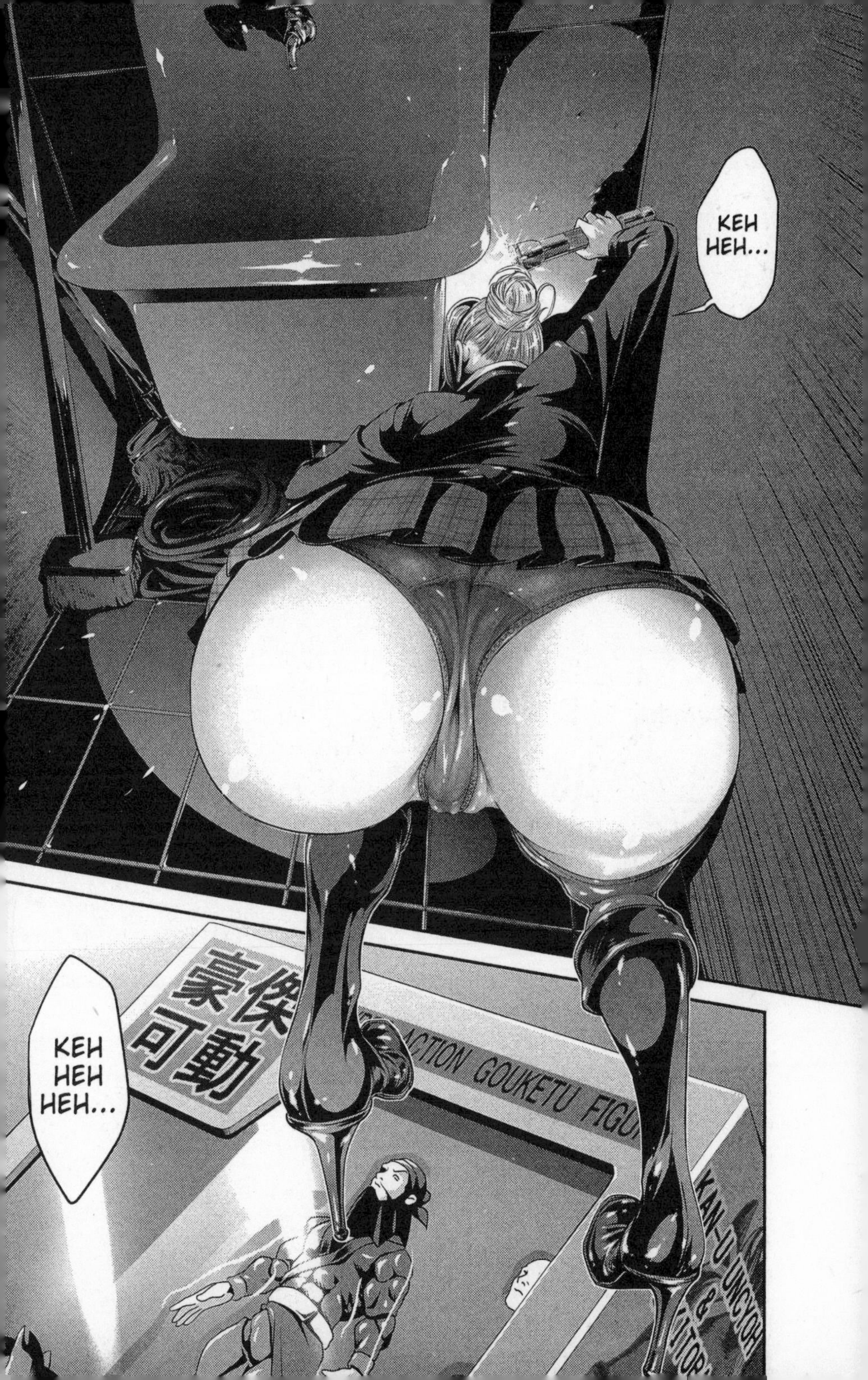
KEH HEH...
豪傑
可動
ACTION GOUKETU
KAN-U-UNCYOH &
KEH HEH HEH...

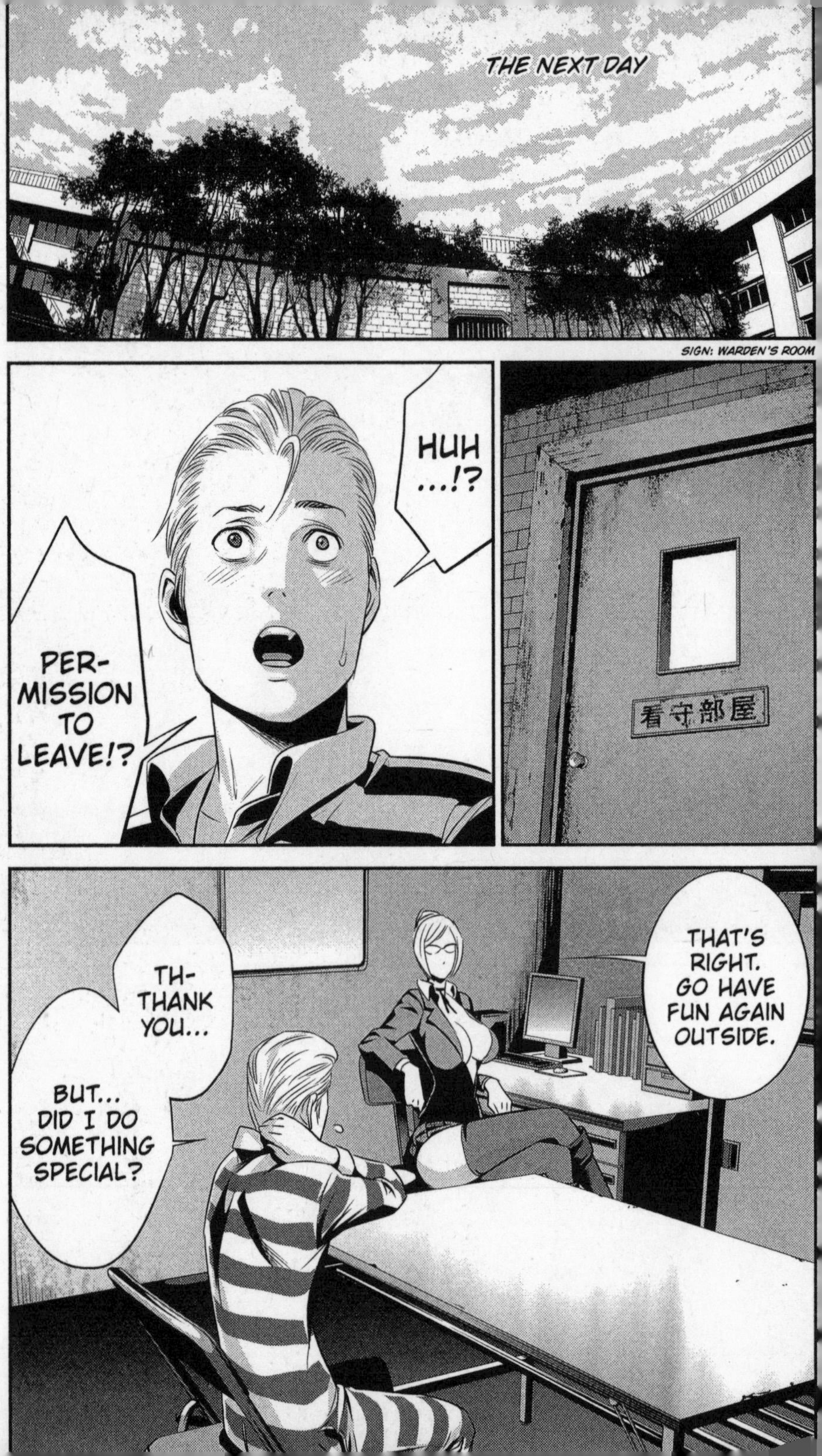
THE NEXT DAY
SIGN: WARDEN'S ROOM
看守部屋
HUH ...!?
PER-MISSION TO LEAVE!?
THAT'S RIGHT. GO HAVE FUN AGAIN OUTSIDE.
TH-THANK YOU...
BUT... DID I DO SOMETHING SPECIAL?

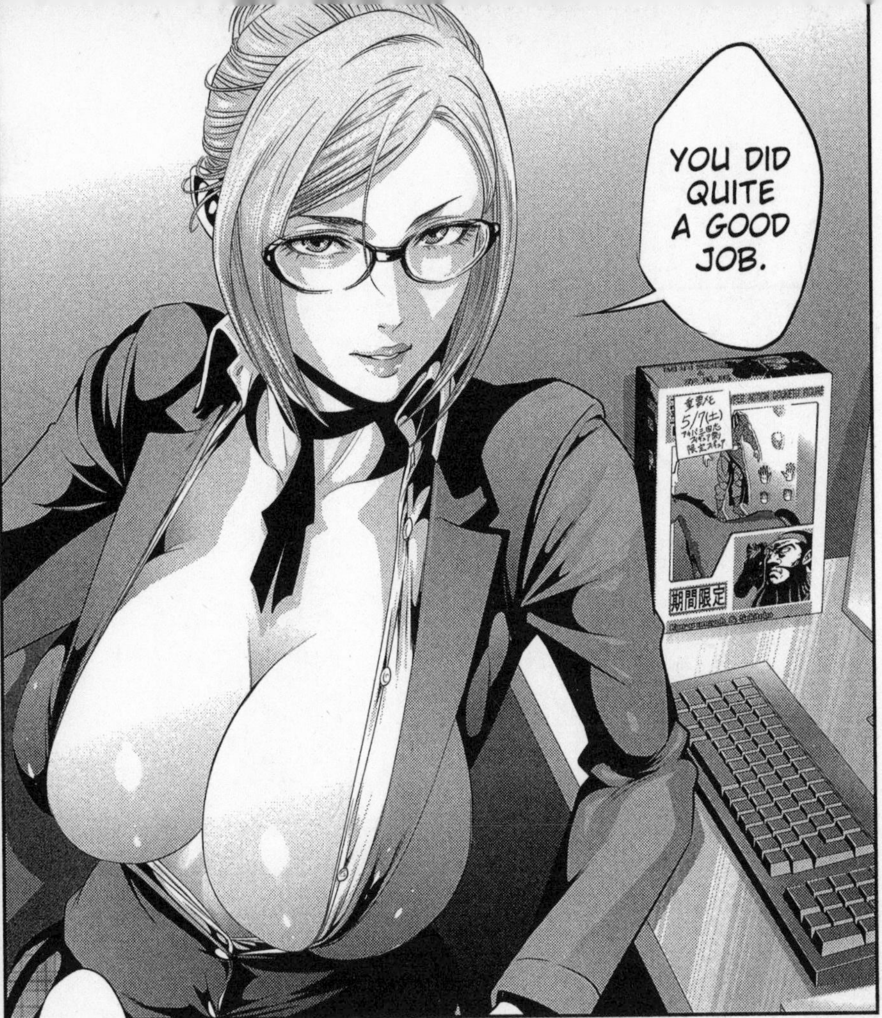
YOU DID QUITE A GOOD JOB.
HYPER ACTION GOUKETU FIGURE
期間限定

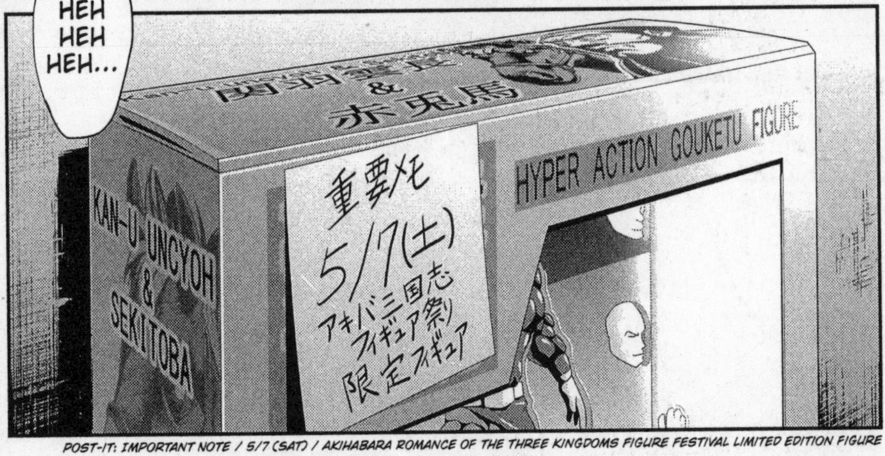
HEH HEH HEH...
赤兎馬
HYPER ACTION GOUKETU FIGURE
KAN-U UNCYOH & SEKITOBA
重要メモ
5/7(土)
アキバ三国志
フィギュア祭り
限定フィギュア

POST-IT: IMPORTANT NOTE / 5/7 (SAT) / AKIHABARA ROMANCE OF THE THREE KINGDOMS FIGURE FESTIVAL LIMITED EDITION FIGURE

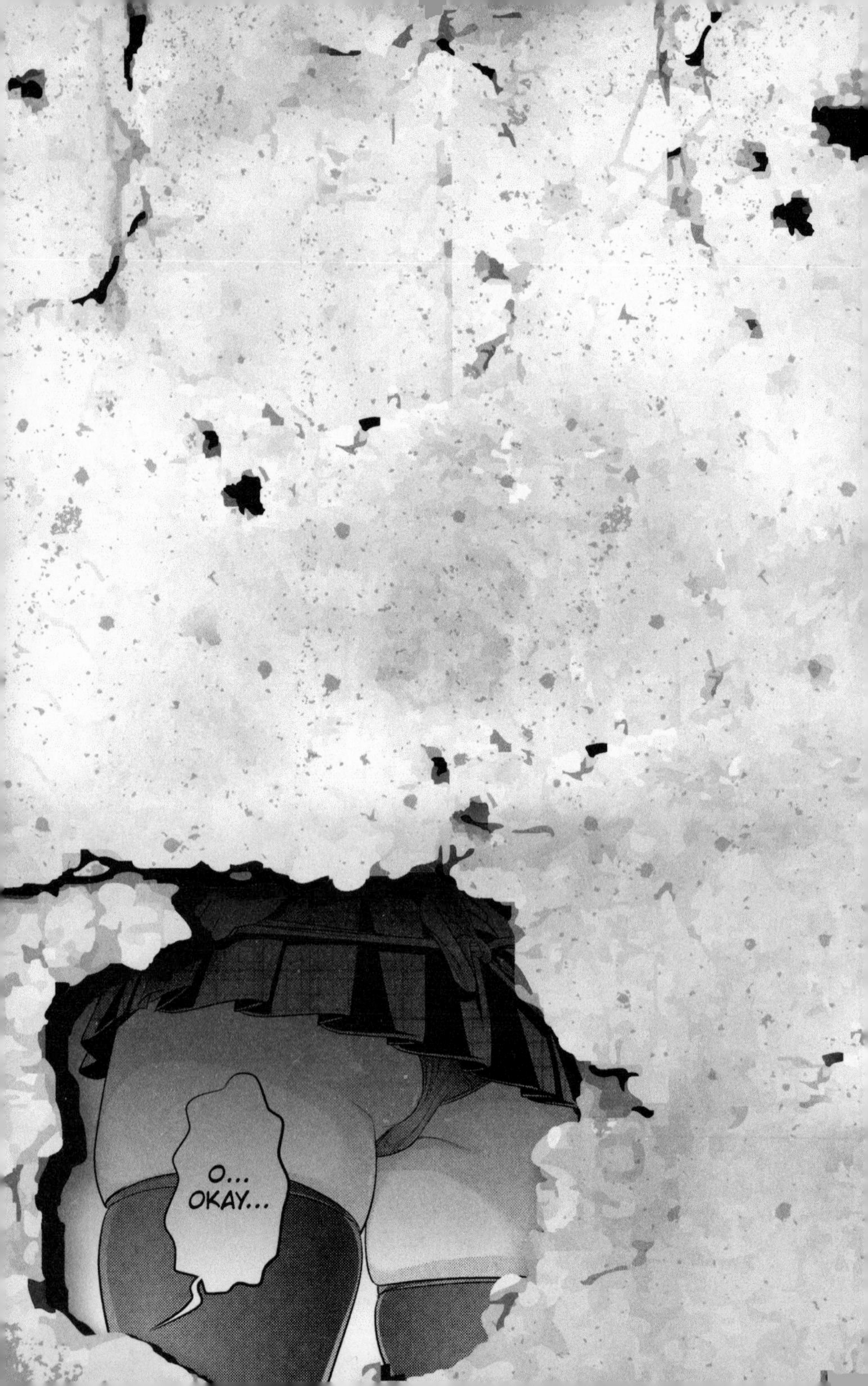
O... OKAY...

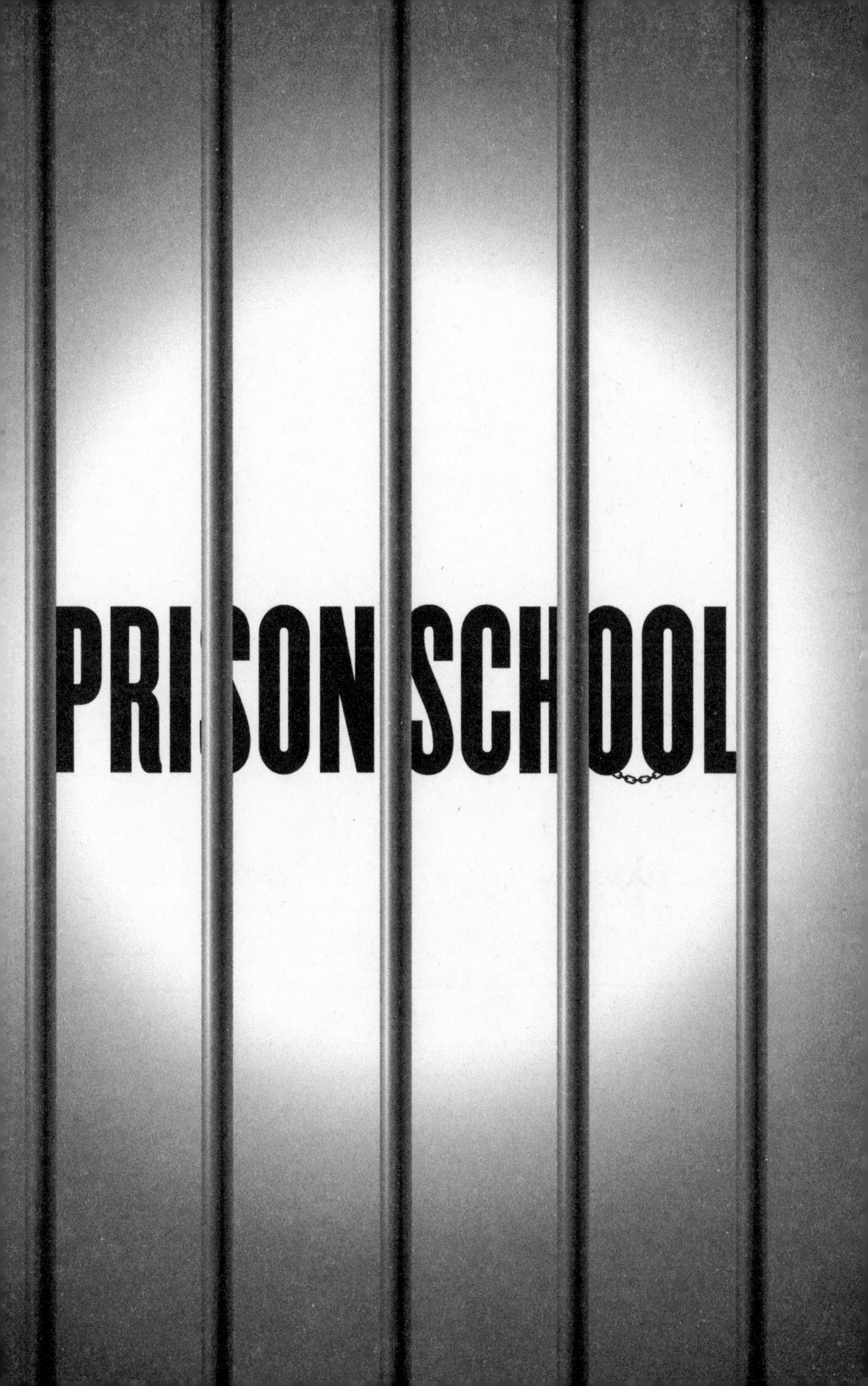
PRISON SCHOOL

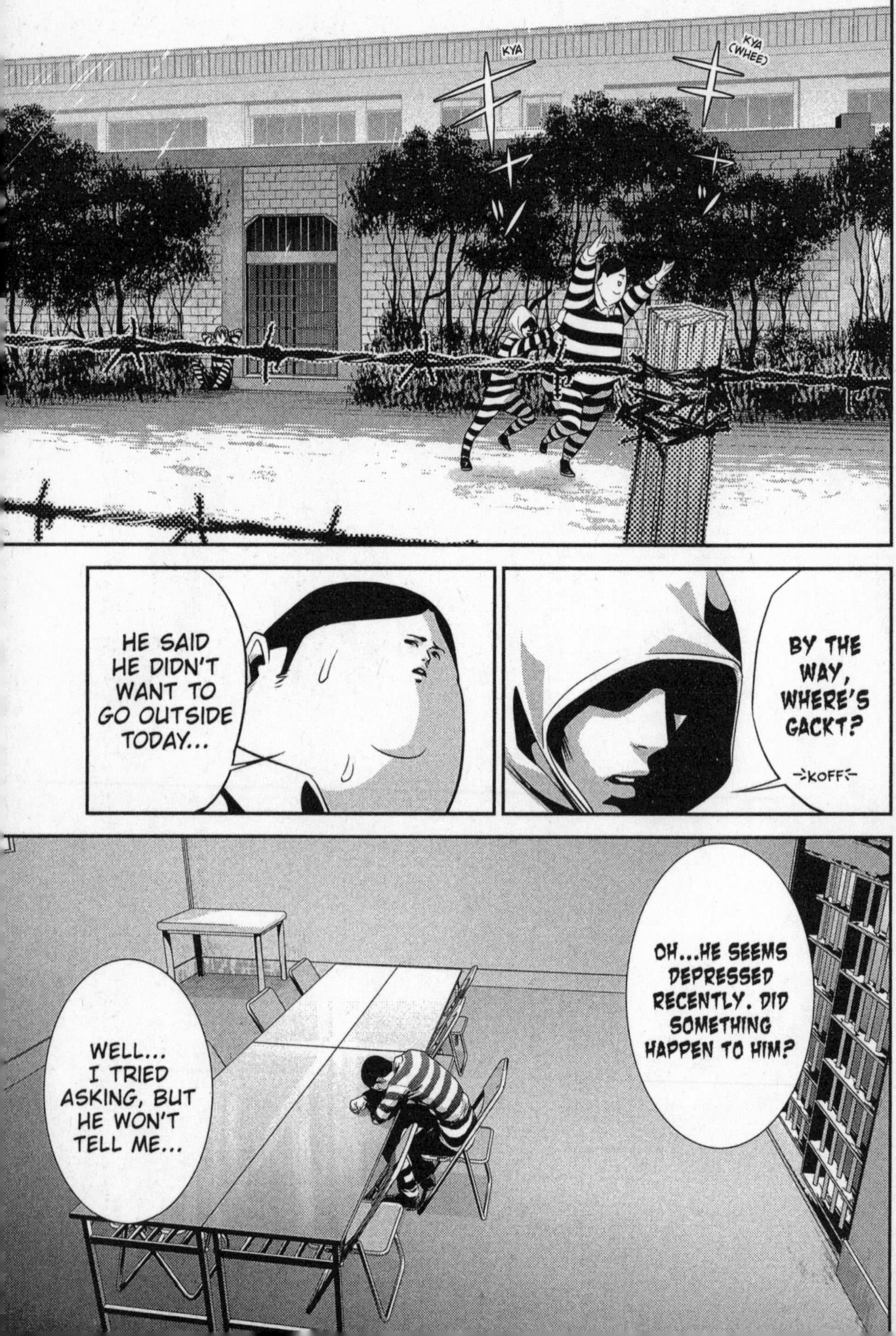
KYA (WHEE)
KYA
BY THE WAY, WHERE'S GACKT?
KOFF
HE SAID HE DIDN'T WANT TO GO OUTSIDE TODAY...
OH...HE SEEMS DEPRESSED RECENTLY. DID SOMETHING HAPPEN TO HIM?
WELL... I TRIED ASKING, BUT HE WON'T TELL ME...

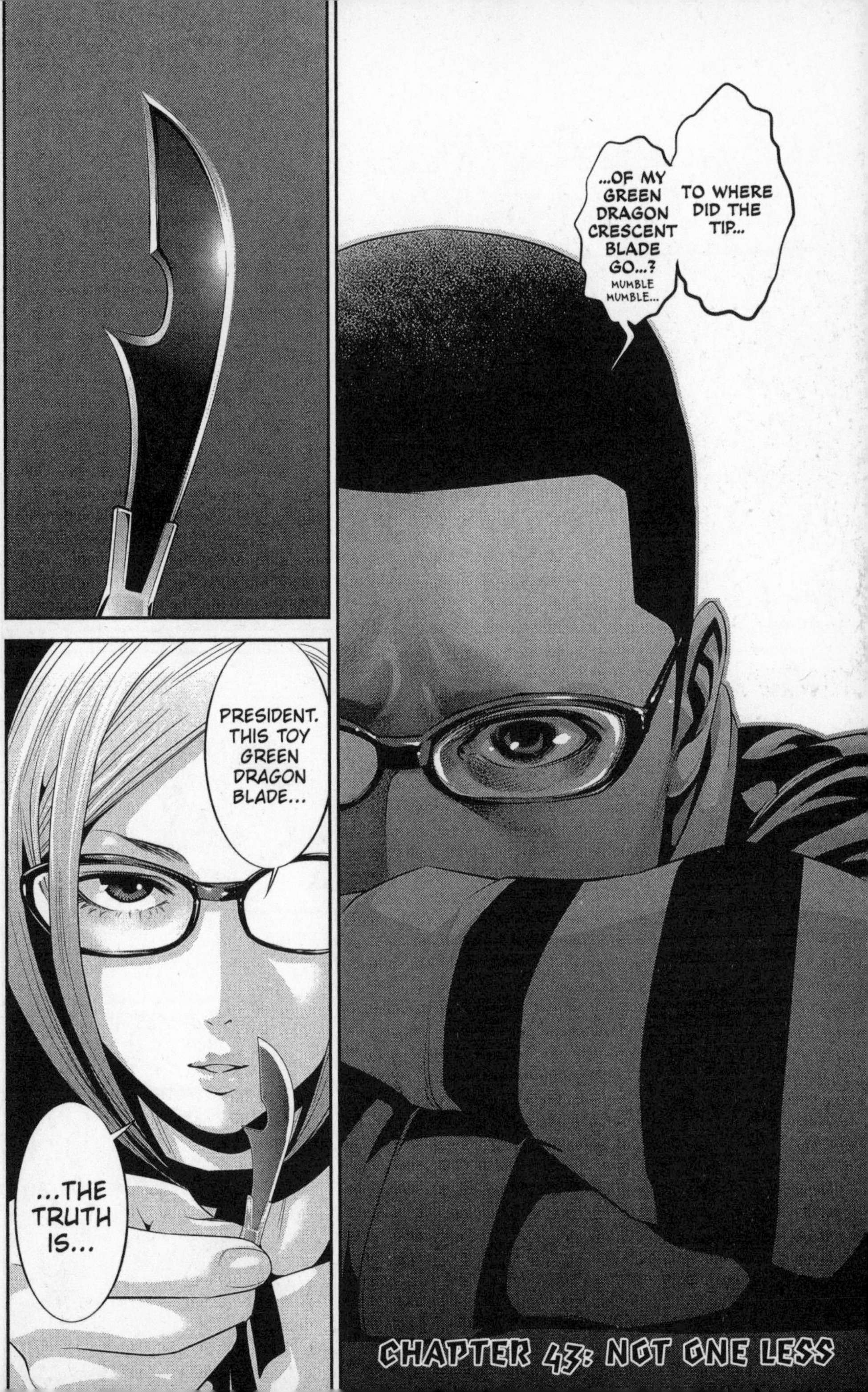
TO WHERE DID THE TIP...
...OF MY GREEN DRAGON CRESCENT BLADE GO...? MUMBLE MUMBLE...
CHAPTER 43: NOT ONE LESS
PRESIDENT. THIS TOY GREEN DRAGON BLADE...
...THE TRUTH IS...

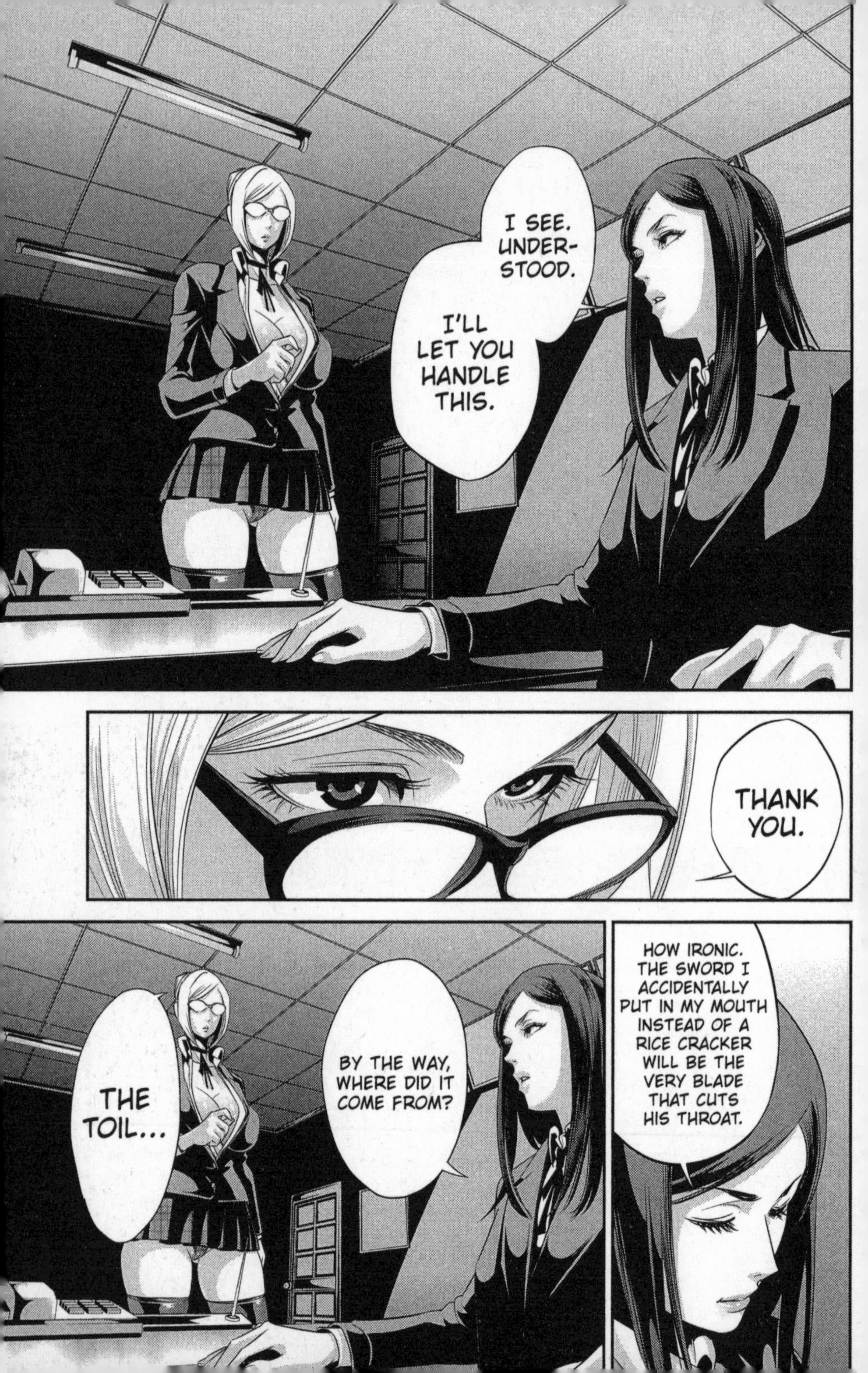
I SEE. UNDER-STOOD.
I'LL LET YOU HANDLE THIS.
THANK YOU.
HOW IRONIC. THE SWORD I ACCIDENTALLY PUT IN MY MOUTH INSTEAD OF A RICE CRACKER WILL BE THE VERY BLADE THAT CUTS HIS THROAT.
BY THE WAY, WHERE DID IT COME FROM?
THE TOIL...

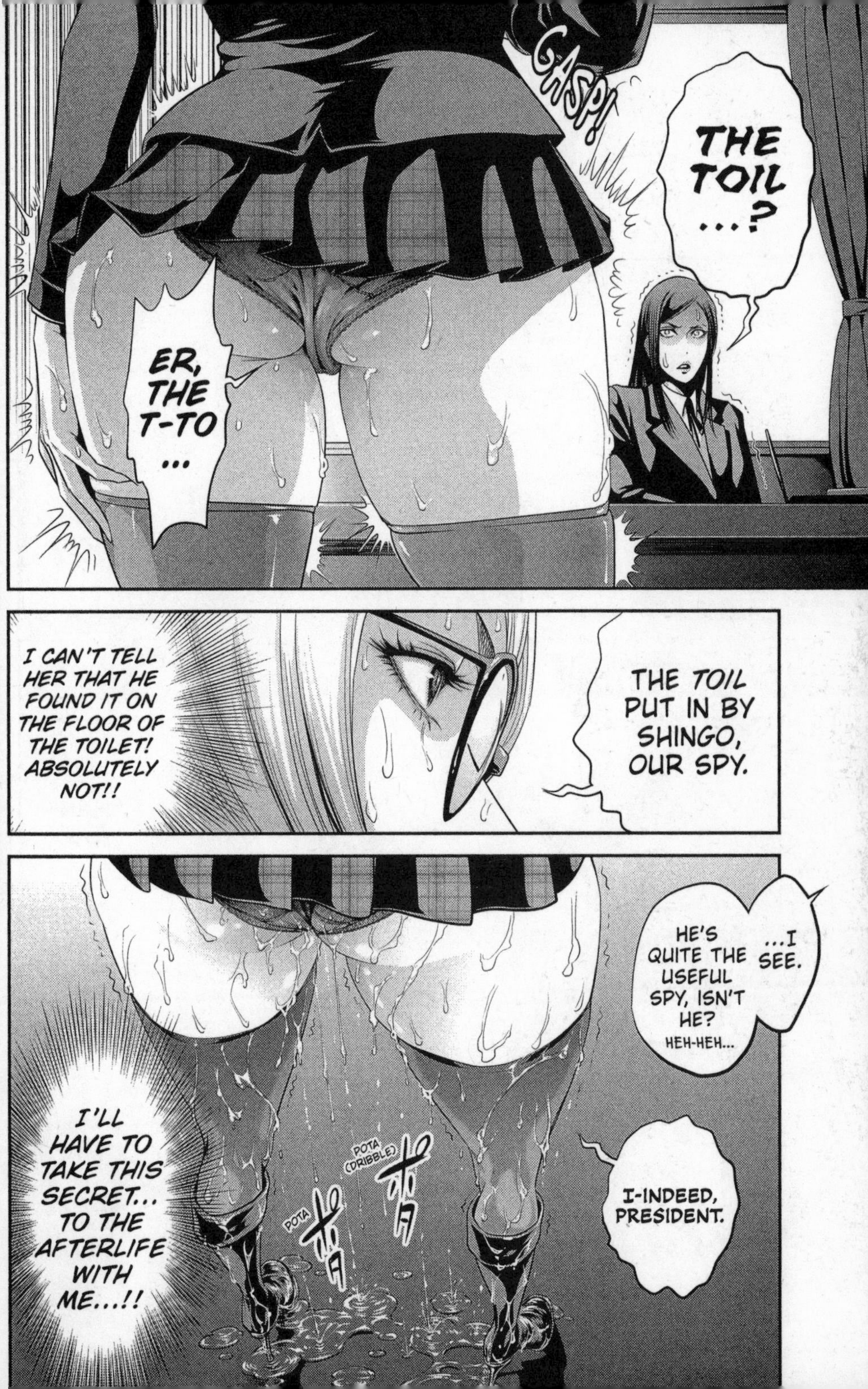
GASP!
ER, THE T-TO...
THE TOIL...?
THE TOIL PUT IN BY SHINGO, OUR SPY.
I CAN'T TELL HER THAT HE FOUND IT ON THE FLOOR OF THE TOILET! ABSOLUTELY NOT!!
...I SEE.
HE'S QUITE THE USEFUL SPY, ISN'T HE? HEH-HEH...
I-INDEED, PRESIDENT.
POTA (DRIBBLE)
POTA
I'LL HAVE TO TAKE THIS SECRET... TO THE AFTERLIFE WITH ME...!!

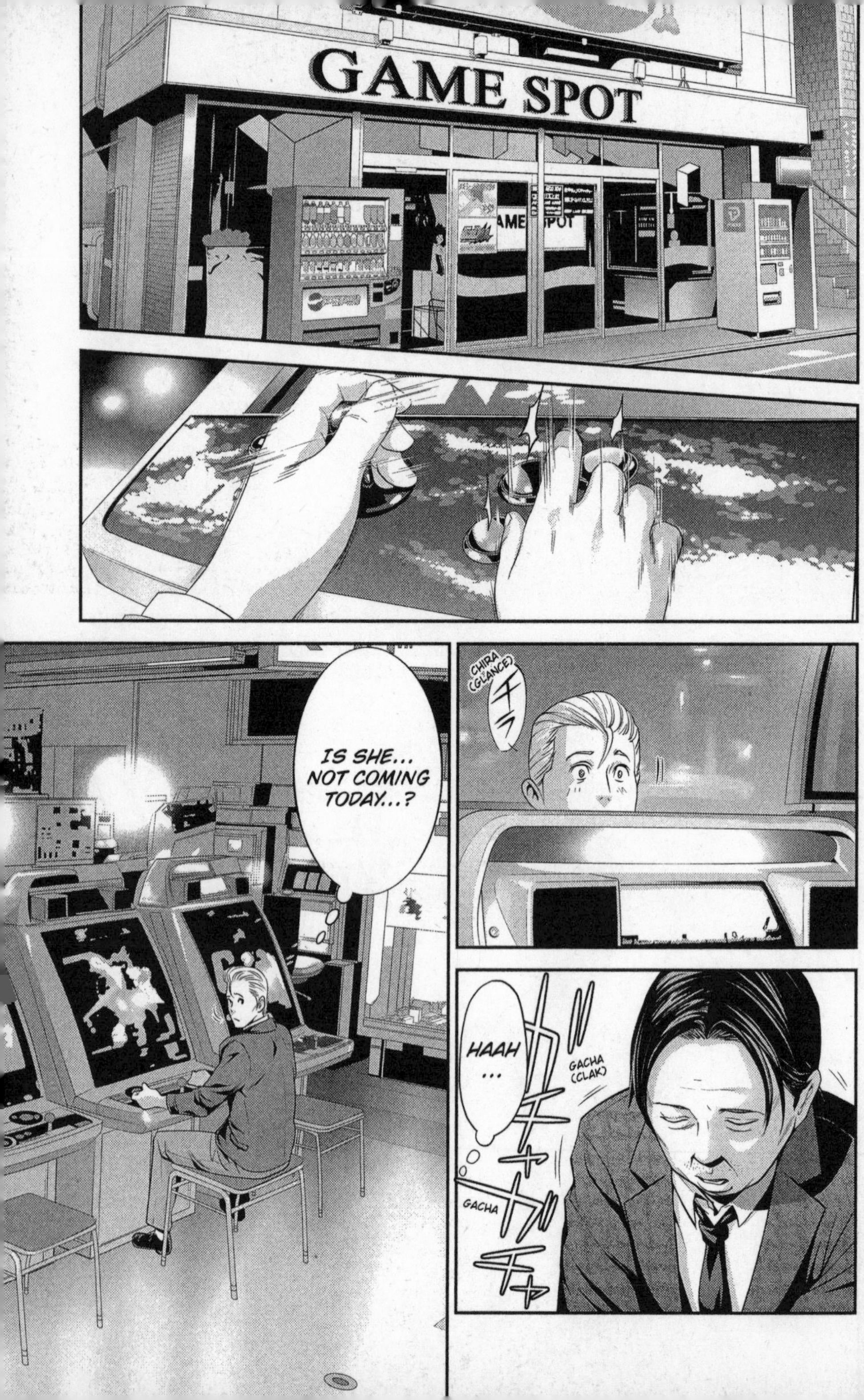
GAME SPOT
GAME SPOT
CHIRA (GLANCE)
HAAH...
GACHA (CLAK)
GACHA
IS SHE... NOT COMING TODAY...?

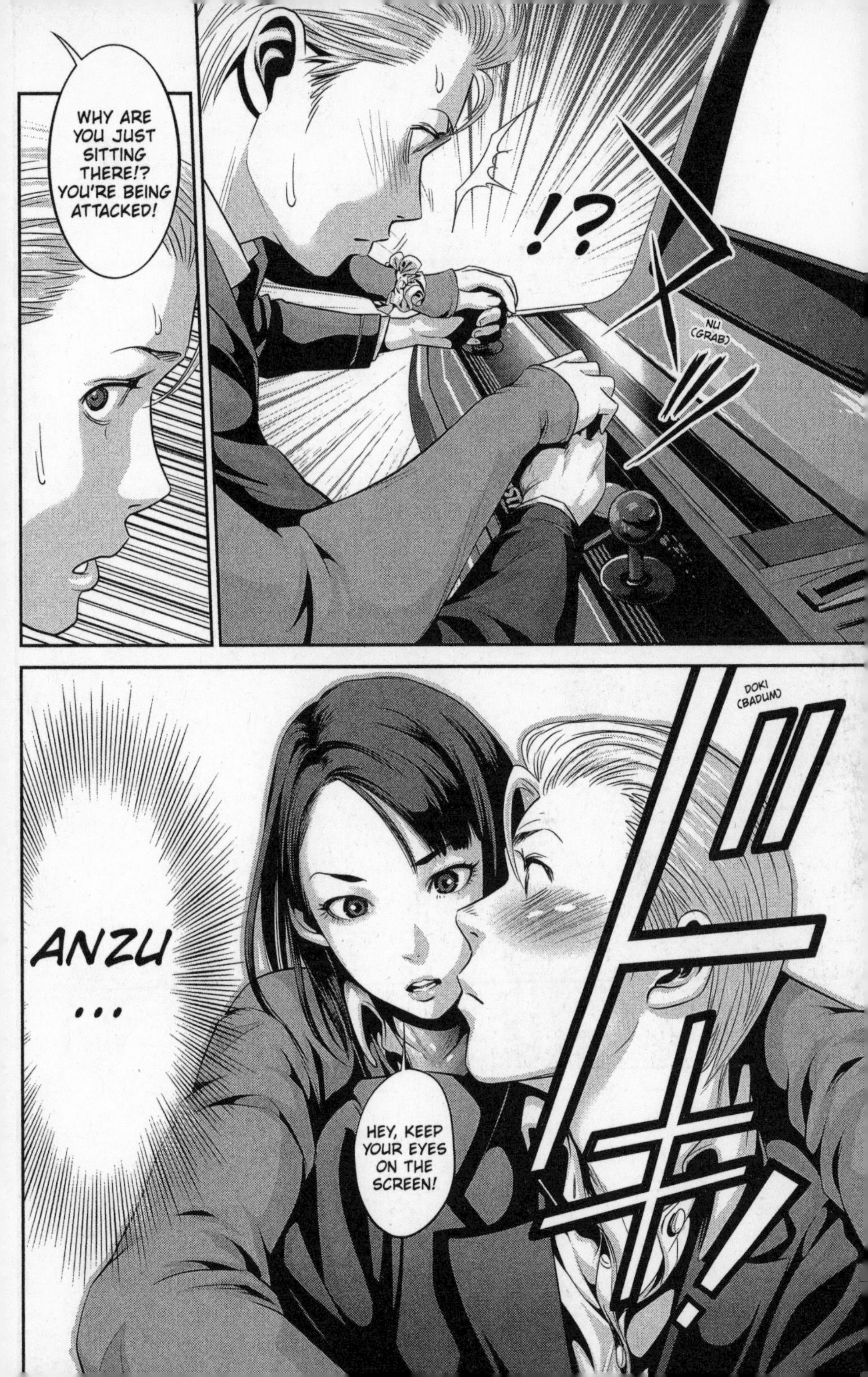
!?
NU (GRAB)
WHY ARE YOU JUST SITTING THERE!? YOU'RE BEING ATTACKED!
DOKI (BADUM)
ANZU ...
HEY, KEEP YOUR EYES ON THE SCREEN!

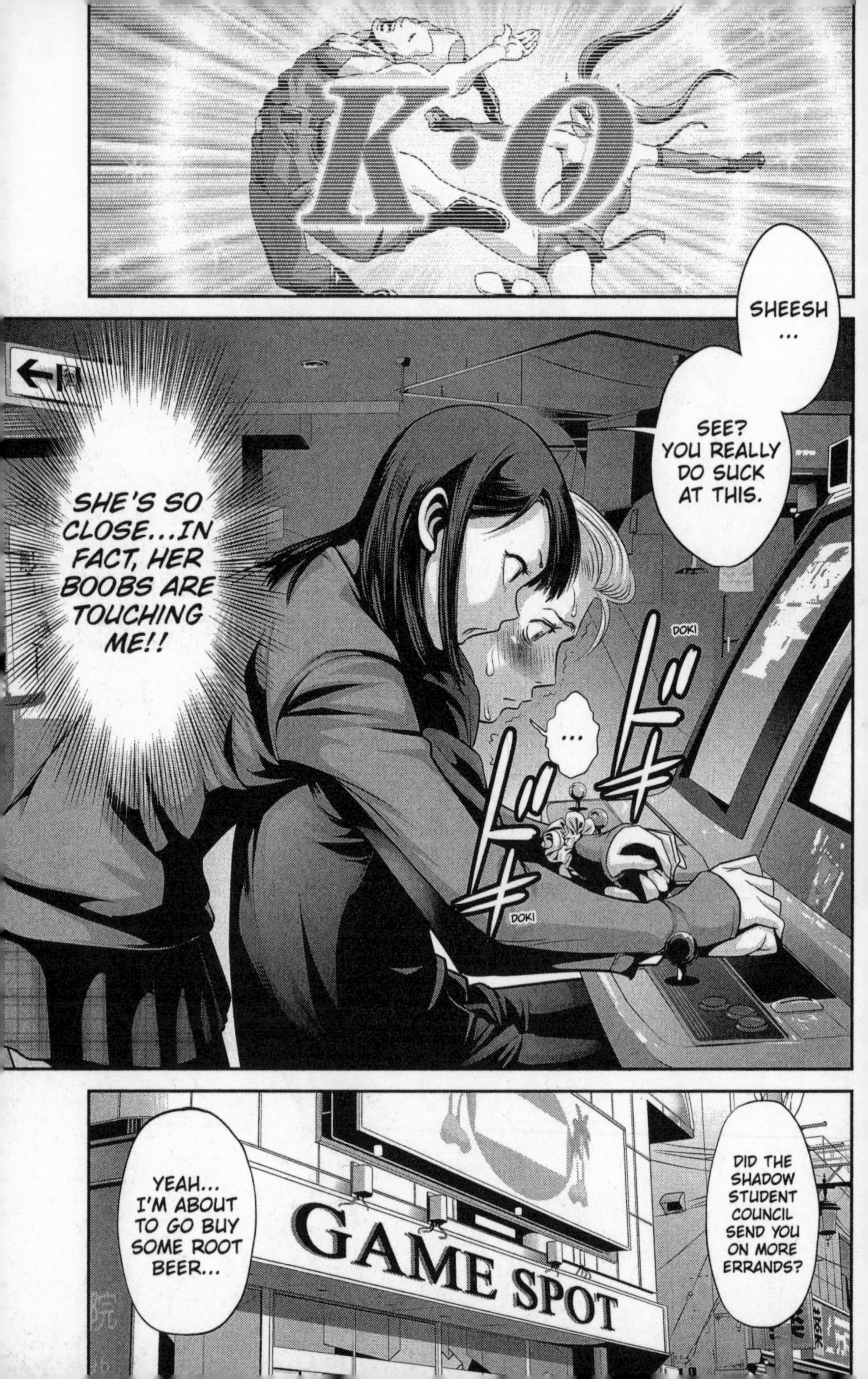
K.O
SHEESH...
SEE? YOU REALLY DO SUCK AT THIS.
DOKI
...
DOKI
SHE'S SO CLOSE...IN FACT, HER BOOBS ARE TOUCHING ME!!
DID THE SHADOW STUDENT COUNCIL SEND YOU ON MORE ERRANDS?
YEAH... I'M ABOUT TO GO BUY SOME ROOT BEER...
GAME SPOT

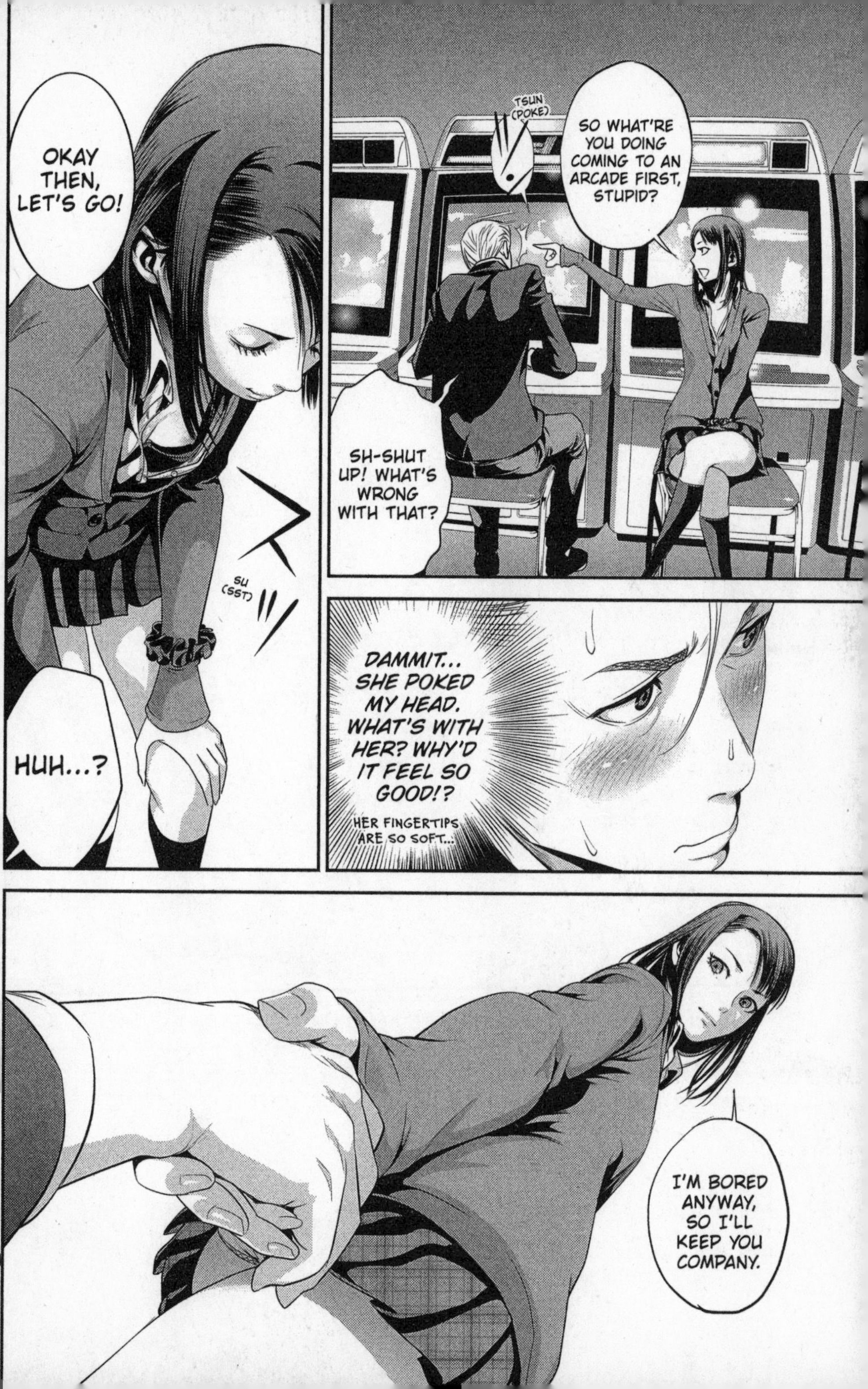
SO WHAT'RE YOU DOING COMING TO AN ARCADE FIRST, STUPID?
TSUN (POKE)
SH-SHUT UP! WHAT'S WRONG WITH THAT?
DAMMIT... SHE POKED MY HEAD. WHAT'S WITH HER? WHY'D IT FEEL SO GOOD!?
HER FINGERTIPS ARE SO SOFT...
OKAY THEN, LET'S GO!
SU (SST)
HUH...?
I'M BORED ANYWAY, SO I'LL KEEP YOU COMPANY.

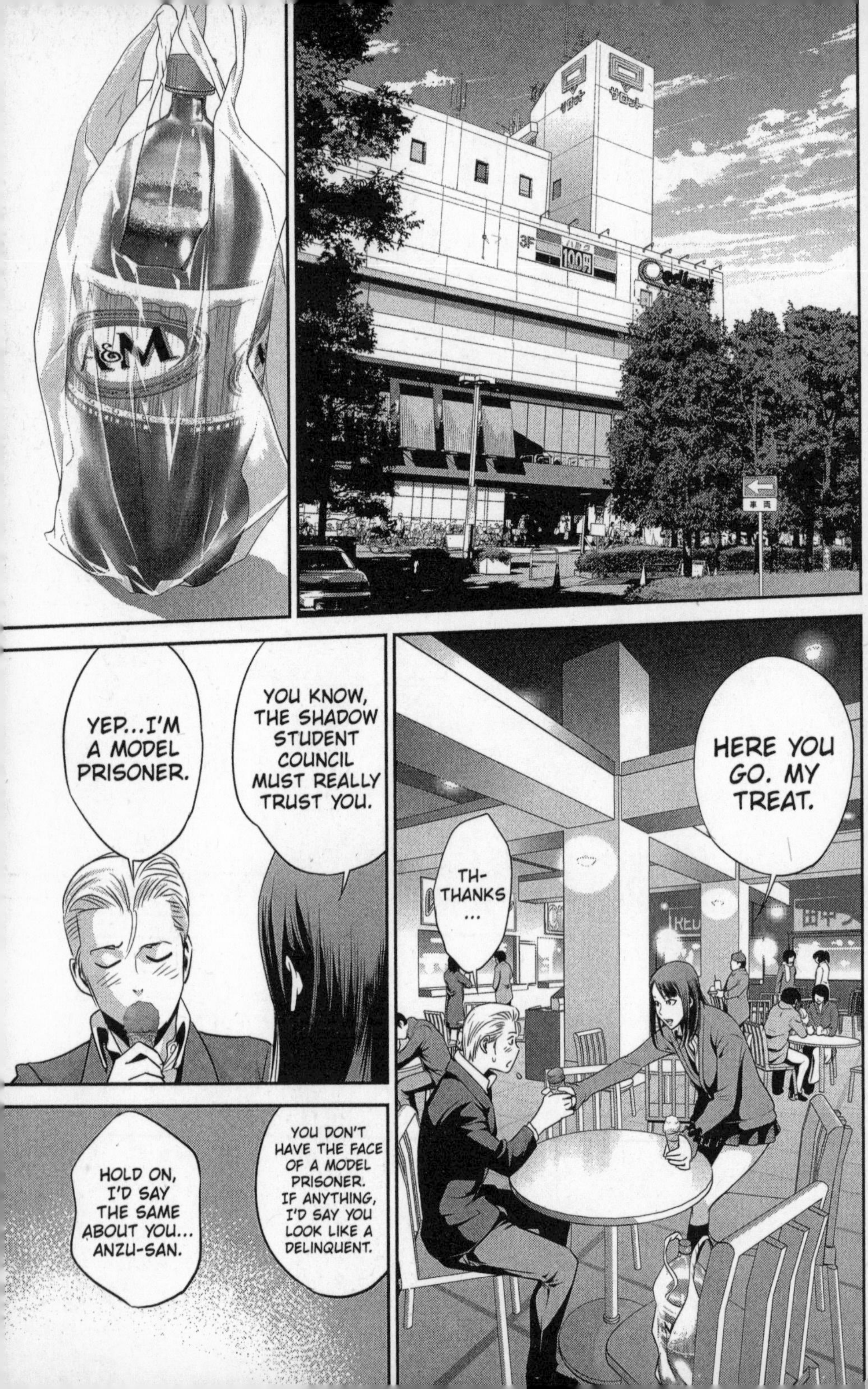
HERE YOU GO. MY TREAT.
TH-THANKS ...
YOU KNOW, THE SHADOW STUDENT COUNCIL MUST REALLY TRUST YOU.
YEP...I'M A MODEL PRISONER.
YOU DON'T HAVE THE FACE OF A MODEL PRISONER. IF ANYTHING, I'D SAY YOU LOOK LIKE A DELINQUENT.
HOLD ON, I'D SAY THE SAME ABOUT YOU... ANZU-SAN.

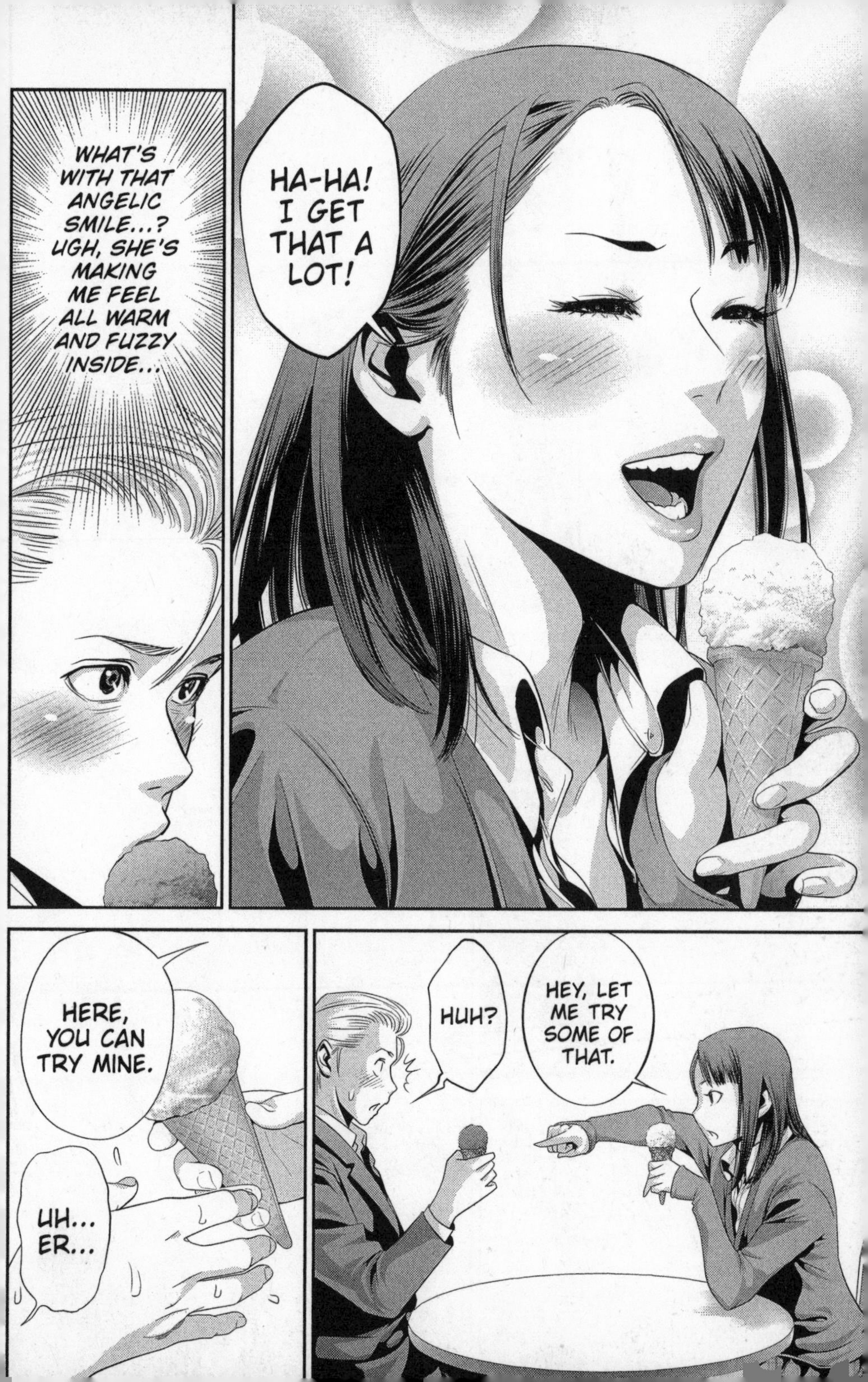
HA-HA! I GET THAT A LOT!
WHAT'S WITH THAT ANGELIC SMILE...? UGH, SHE'S MAKING ME FEEL ALL WARM AND FUZZY INSIDE...
HEY, LET ME TRY SOME OF THAT.
HUH?
HERE, YOU CAN TRY MINE.
UH... ER...

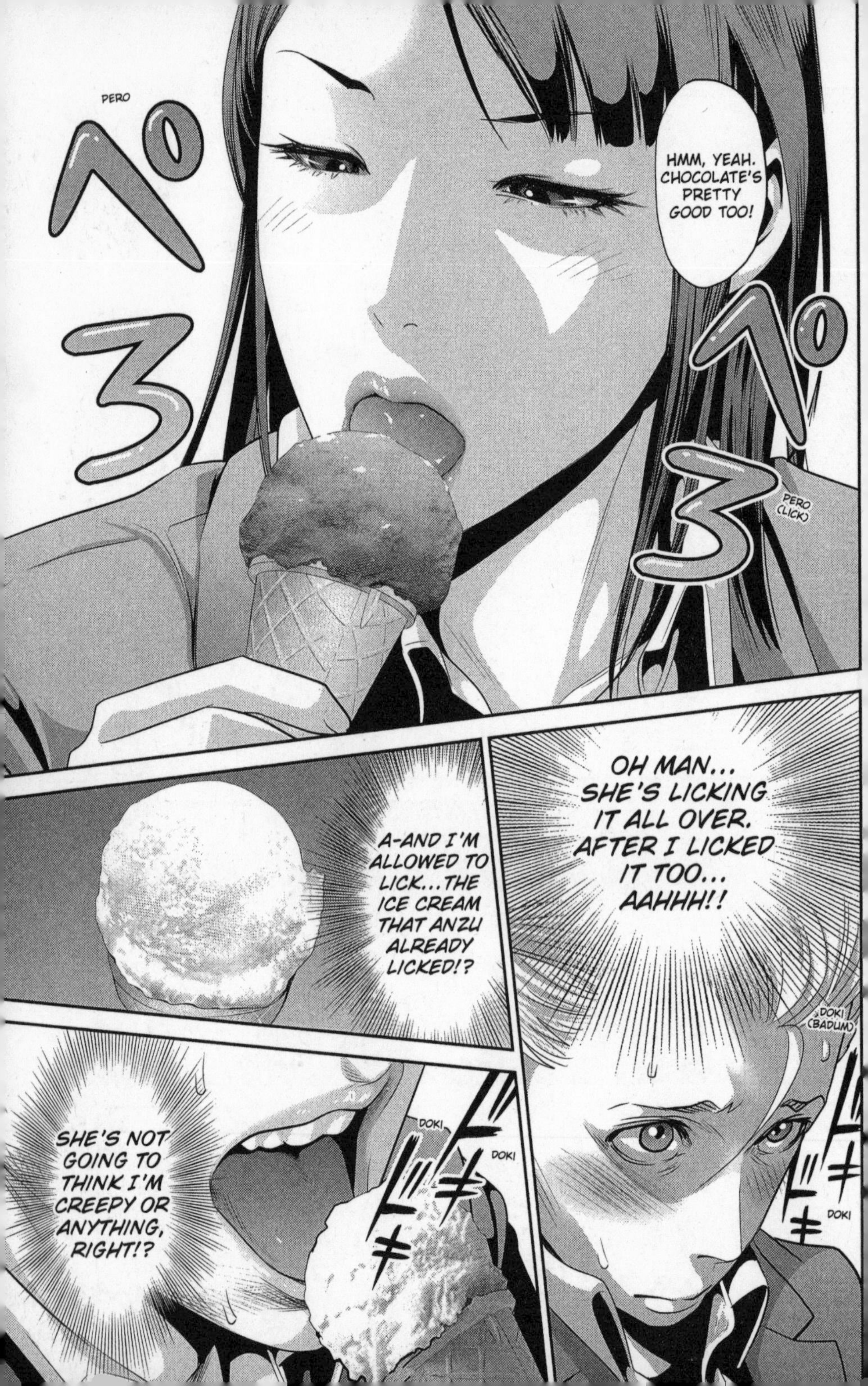
HMM, YEAH. CHOCOLATE'S PRETTY GOOD TOO!
PERO (LICK)
PERO
OH MAN... SHE'S LICKING IT ALL OVER. AFTER I LICKED IT TOO... AAHHH!!
A-AND I'M ALLOWED TO LICK...THE ICE CREAM THAT ANZU ALREADY LICKED!?
DOKI (BADUM)
DOKI
DOKI
DOKI
SHE'S NOT GOING TO THINK I'M CREEPY OR ANYTHING, RIGHT!?

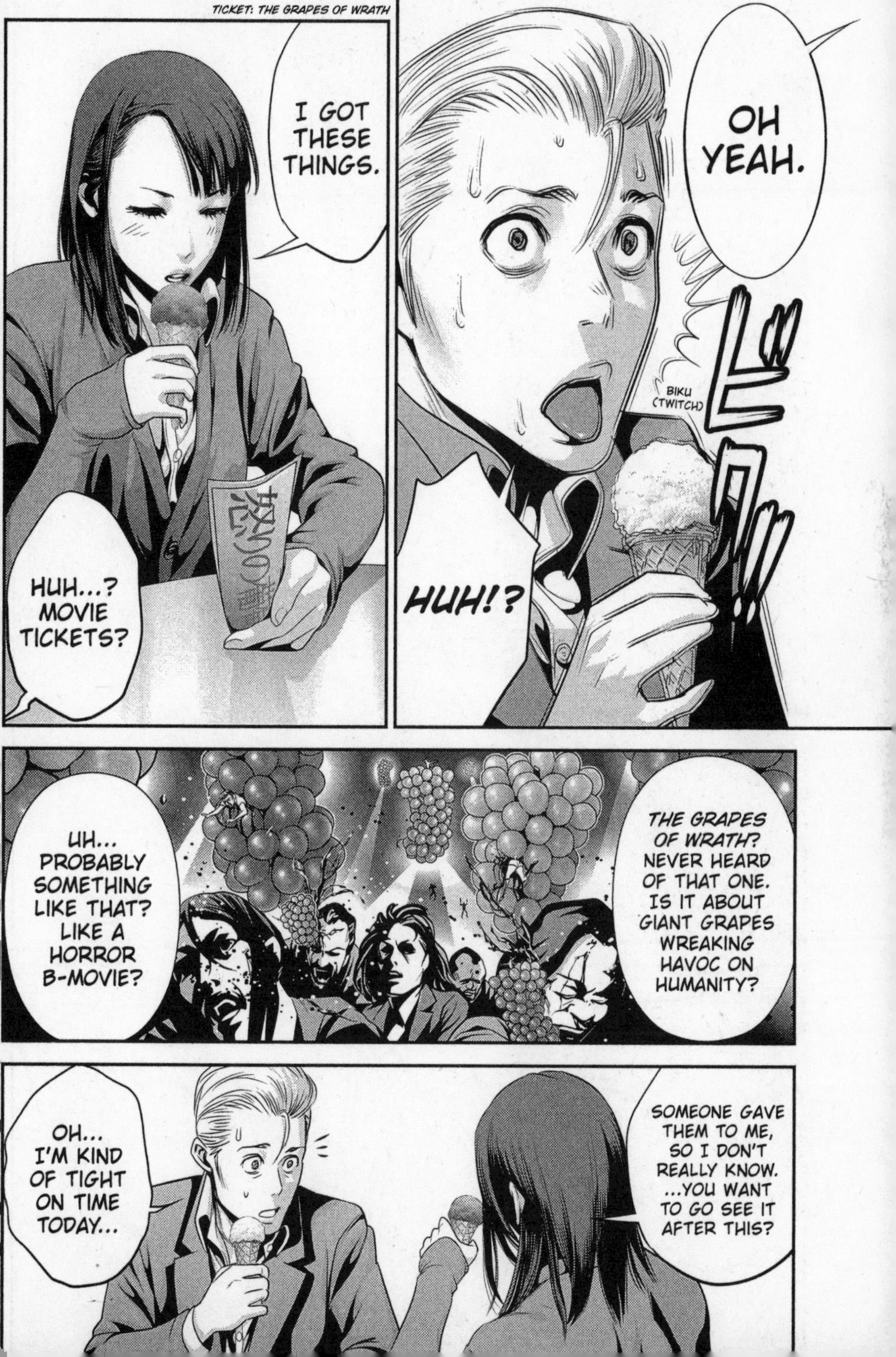
TICKET: THE GRAPES OF WRATH
OH YEAH.
BIKU (TWITCH)
HUH!?
I GOT THESE THINGS.
HUH...? MOVIE TICKETS?
THE GRAPES OF WRATH? NEVER HEARD OF THAT ONE. IS IT ABOUT GIANT GRAPES WREAKING HAVOC ON HUMANITY?
UH... PROBABLY SOMETHING LIKE THAT? LIKE A HORROR B-MOVIE?
SOMEONE GAVE THEM TO ME, SO I DON'T REALLY KNOW. ...YOU WANT TO GO SEE IT AFTER THIS?
OH... I'M KIND OF TIGHT ON TIME TODAY...

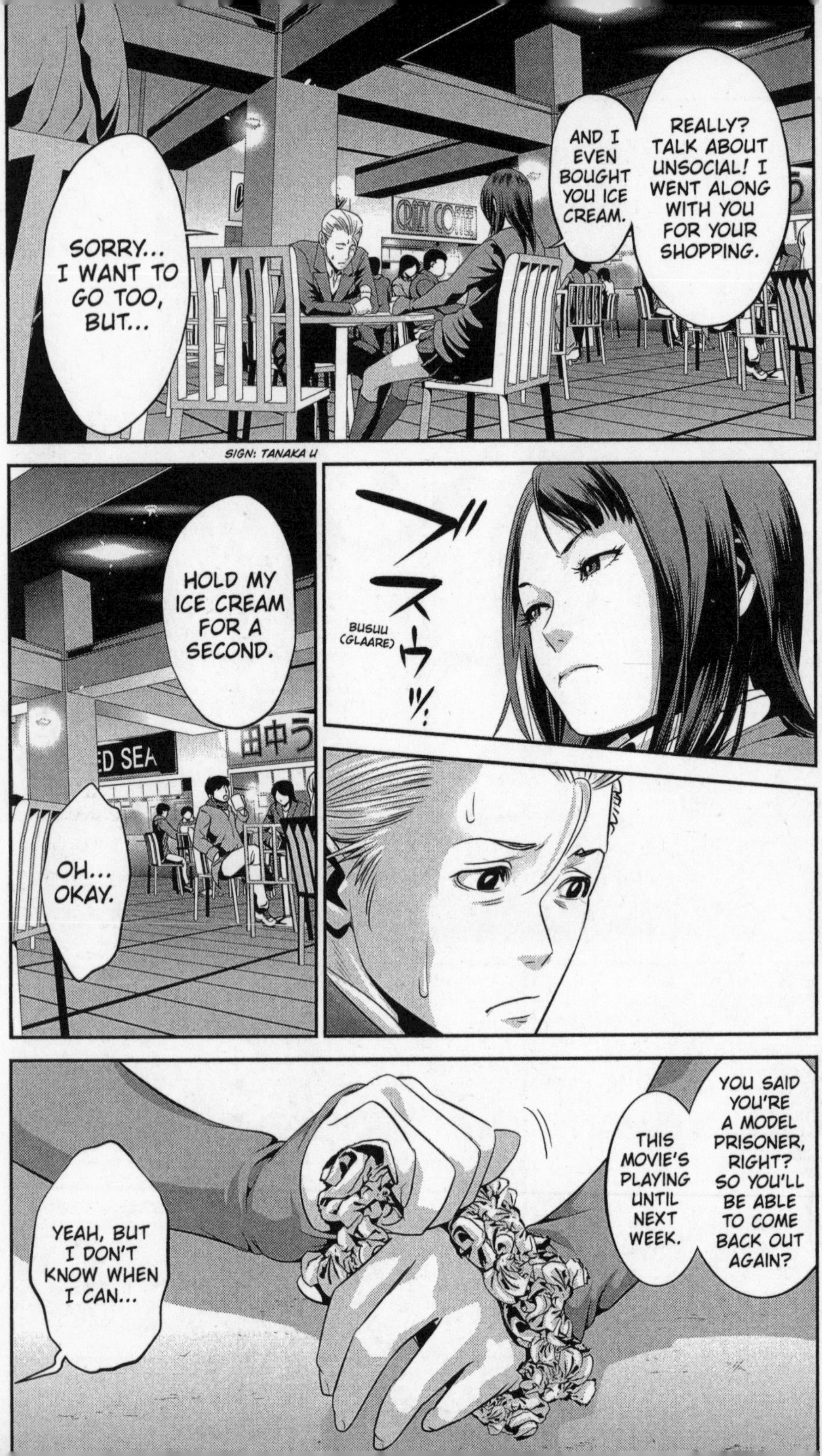
REALLY? TALK ABOUT UNSOCIAL! I WENT ALONG WITH YOU FOR YOUR SHOPPING.
AND I EVEN BOUGHT YOU ICE CREAM.
CRAZY COFFEE
SORRY... I WANT TO GO TOO, BUT...
SIGN: TANAKA U
BUSUU (GLAARE)
HOLD MY ICE CREAM FOR A SECOND.
ED SEA
田中う
OH... OKAY.
YOU SAID YOU'RE A MODEL PRISONER, RIGHT? SO YOU'LL BE ABLE TO COME BACK OUT AGAIN?
THIS MOVIE'S PLAYING UNTIL NEXT WEEK.
YEAH, BUT I DON'T KNOW WHEN I CAN...

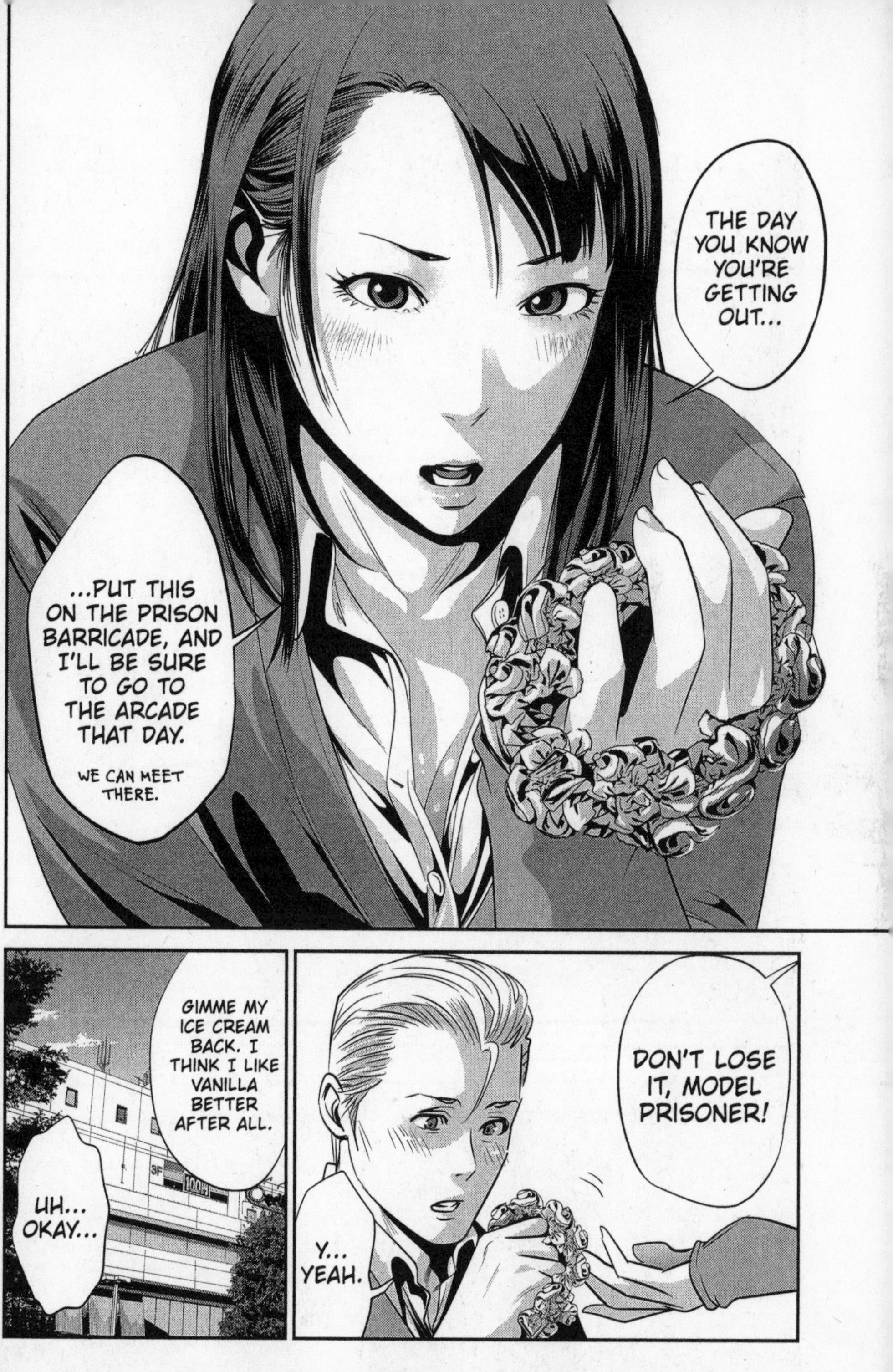
THE DAY YOU KNOW YOU'RE GETTING OUT...
...PUT THIS ON THE PRISON BARRICADE, AND I'LL BE SURE TO GO TO THE ARCADE THAT DAY.
WE CAN MEET THERE.
DON'T LOSE IT, MODEL PRISONER!
Y... YEAH.
GIMME MY ICE CREAM BACK. I THINK I LIKE VANILLA BETTER AFTER ALL.
UH... OKAY...
3F
100円

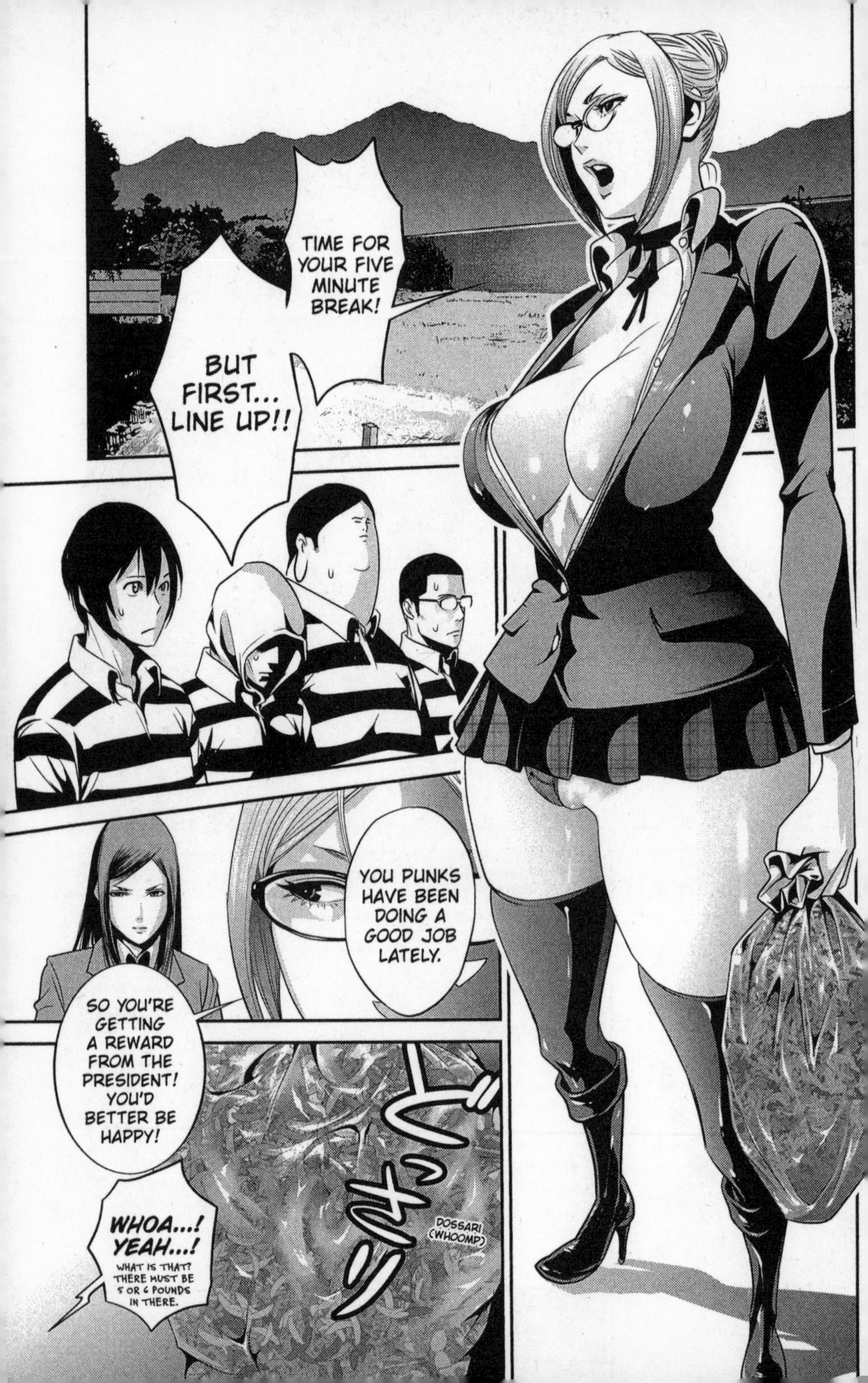
TIME FOR YOUR FIVE MINUTE BREAK!
BUT FIRST... LINE UP!!
YOU PUNKS HAVE BEEN DOING A GOOD JOB LATELY.
SO YOU'RE GETTING A REWARD FROM THE PRESIDENT! YOU'D BETTER BE HAPPY!
DOSSARI (WHOOMP)
WHOA...! YEAH...!
WHAT IS THAT? THERE MUST BE 5 OR 6 POUNDS IN THERE.

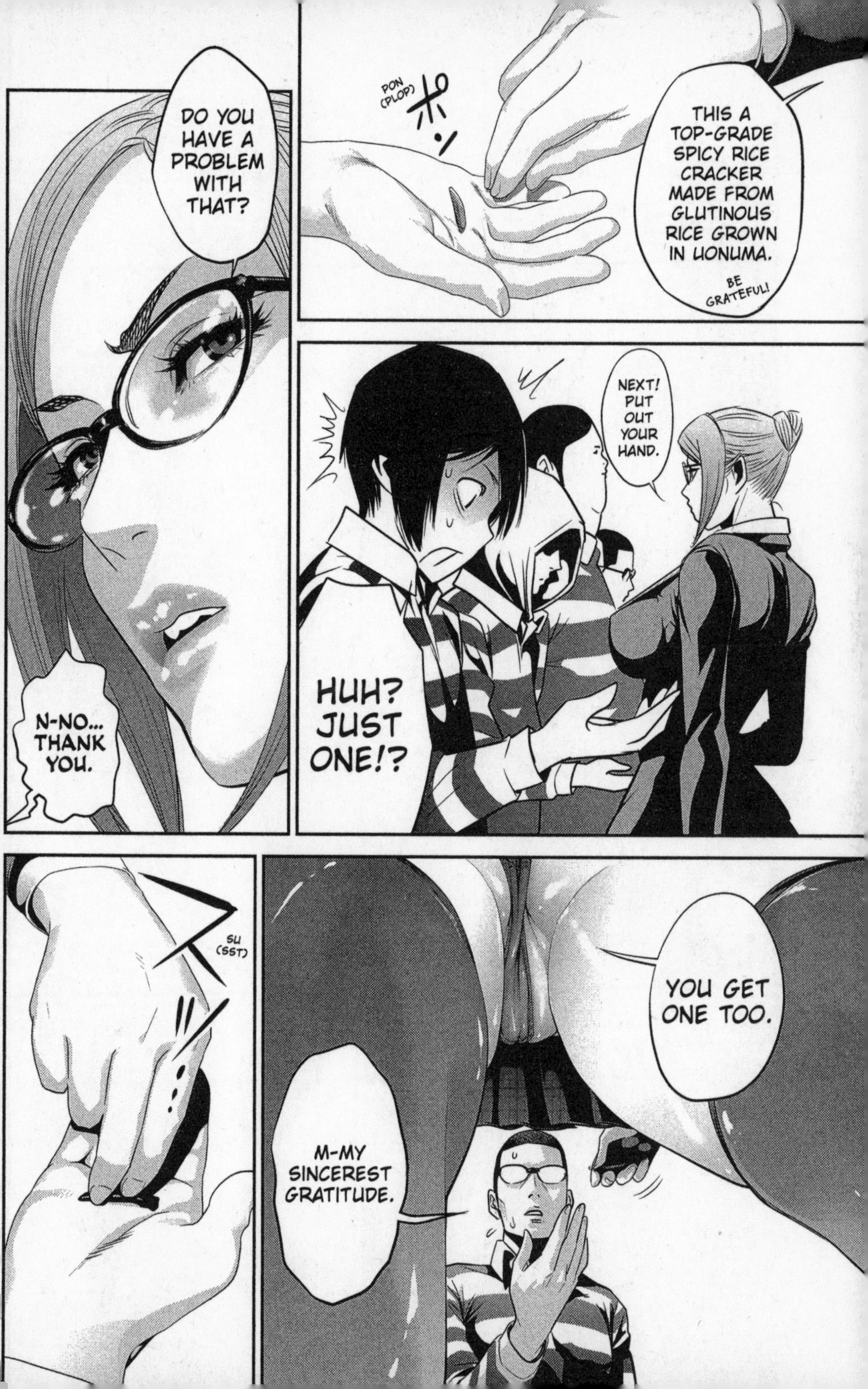
PON (PLOP)
THIS A TOP-GRADE SPICY RICE CRACKER MADE FROM GLUTINOUS RICE GROWN IN UONUMA.
BE GRATEFUL!
NEXT! PUT OUT YOUR HAND.
HUH? JUST ONE!?
DO YOU HAVE A PROBLEM WITH THAT?
N-NO... THANK YOU.
YOU GET ONE TOO.
M-MY SINCEREST GRATITUDE.
SU (SST)

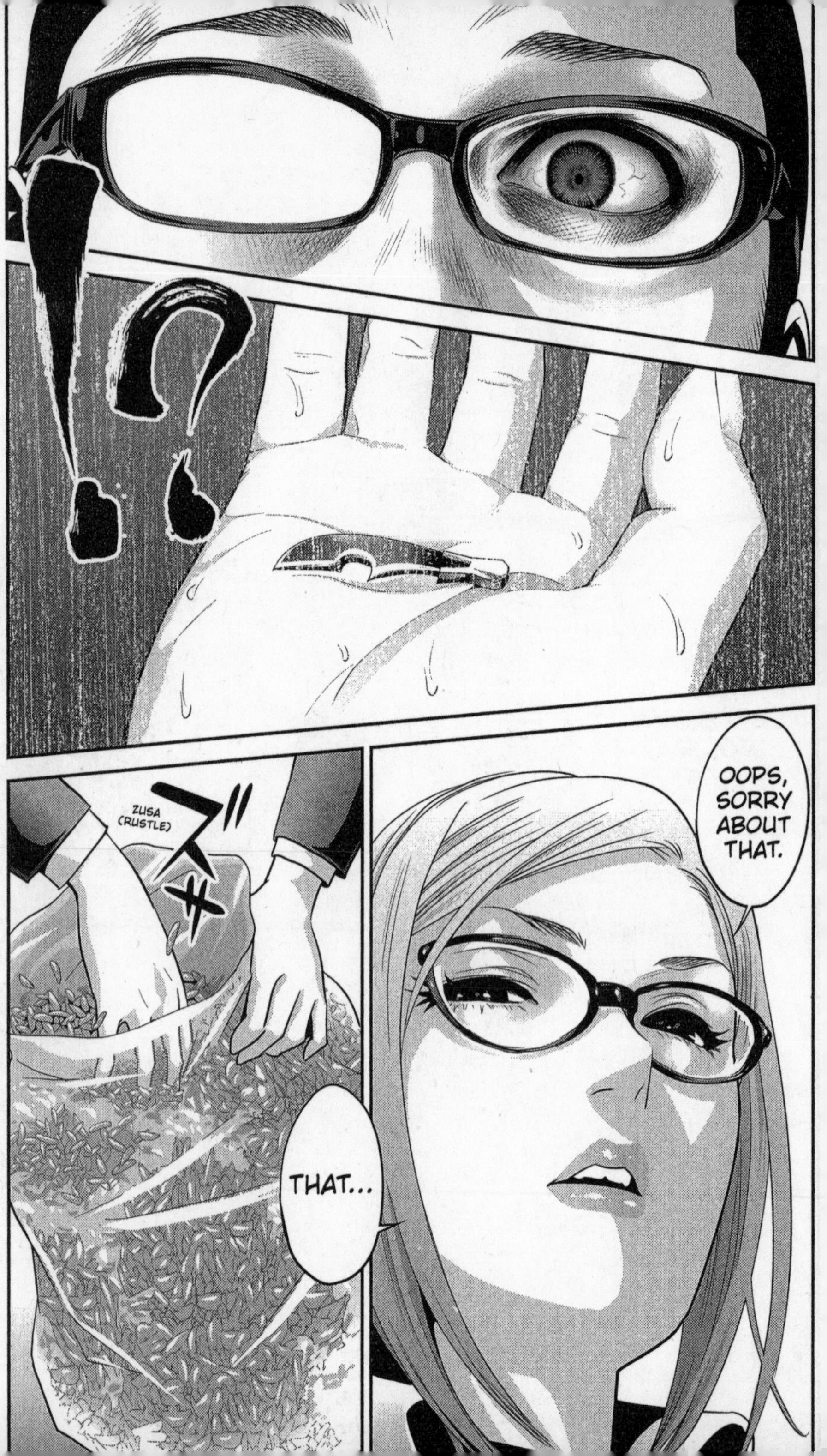
OOPS, SORRY ABOUT THAT.
THAT...
ZUSA (RUSTLE)

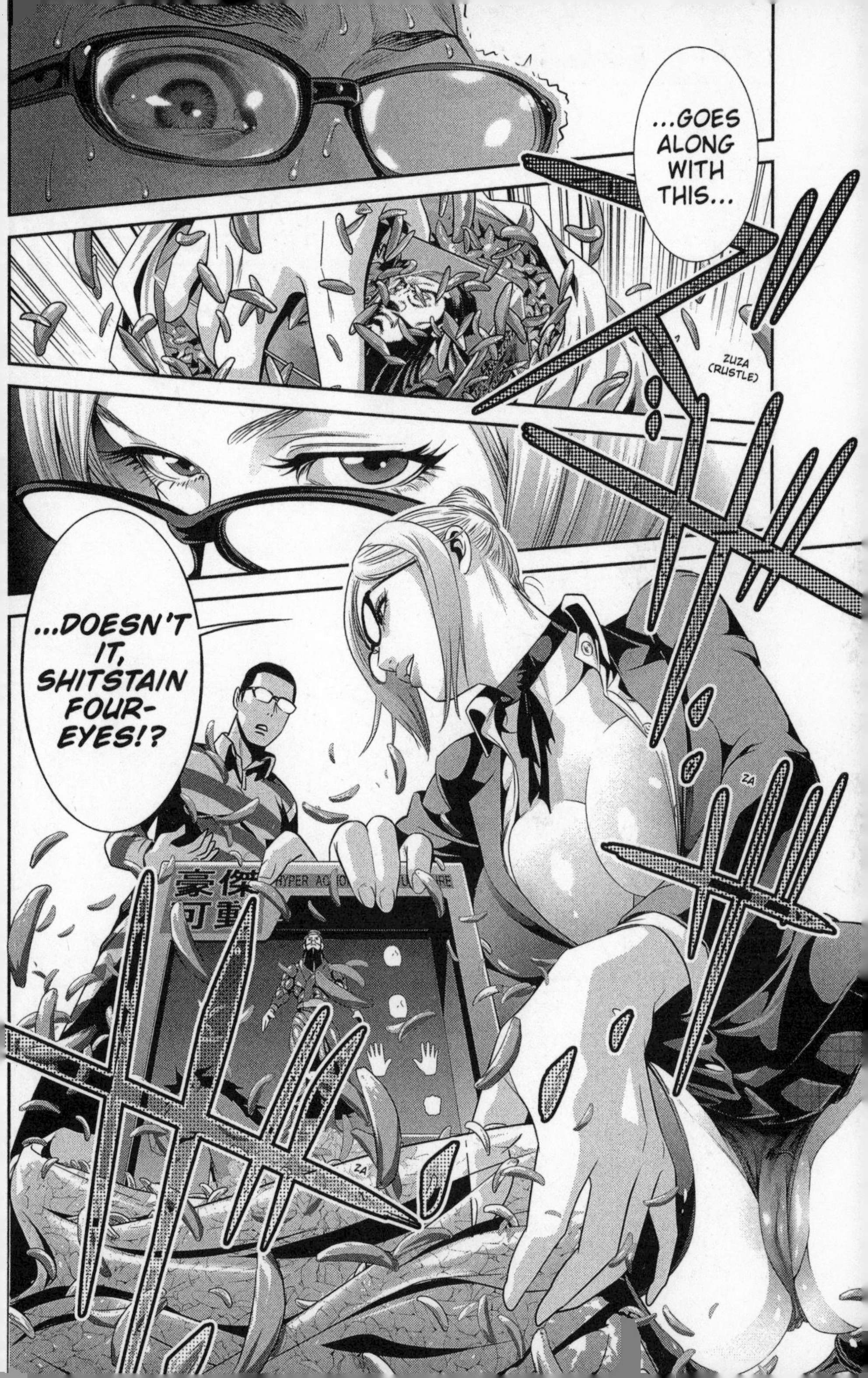
...GOES ALONG WITH THIS...
ZUZA (RUSTLE)
...DOESN'T IT, SHITSTAIN FOUR-EYES!?
ZA
ZA

CHAPTER 44: THE CLAIM

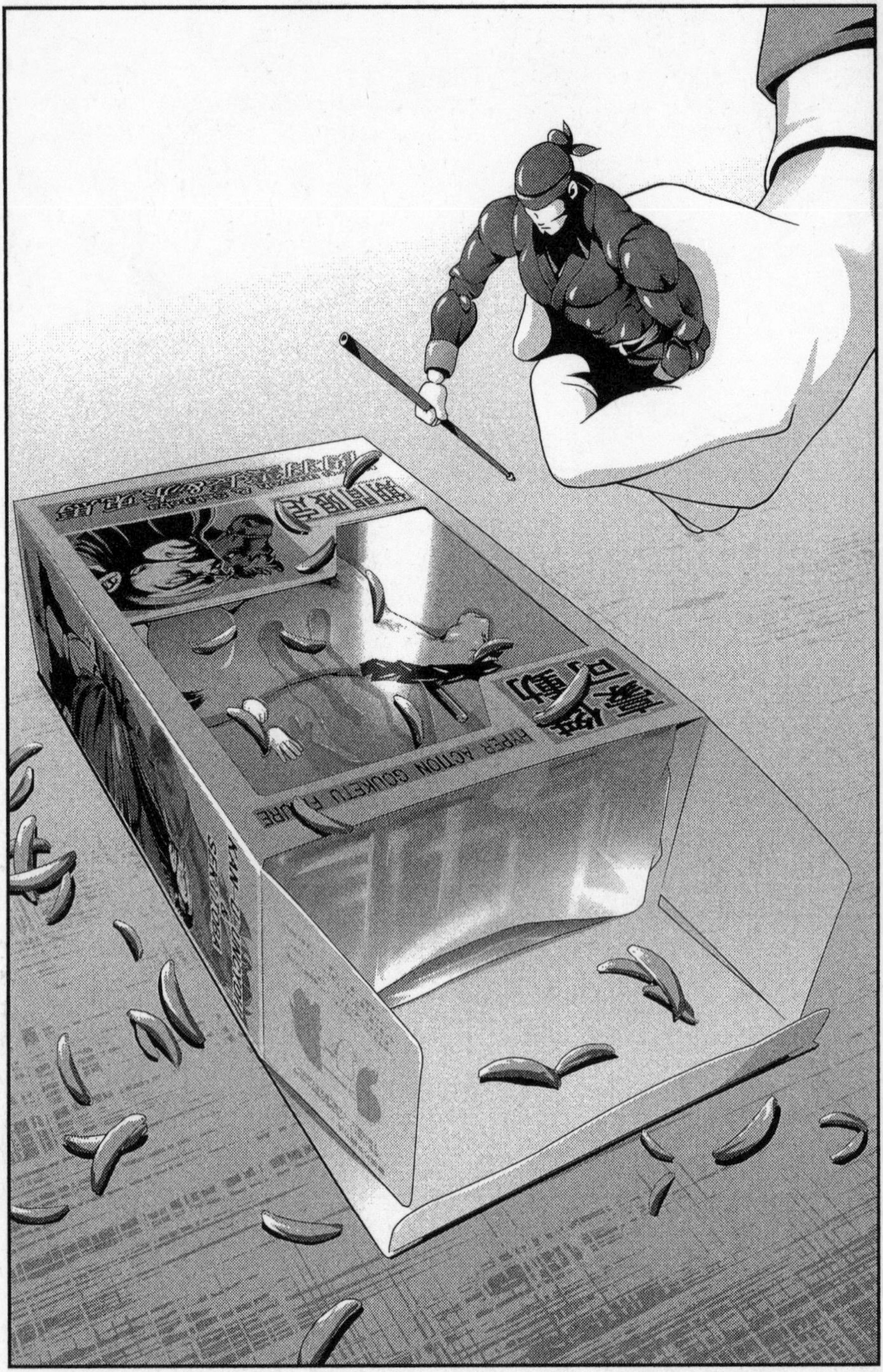

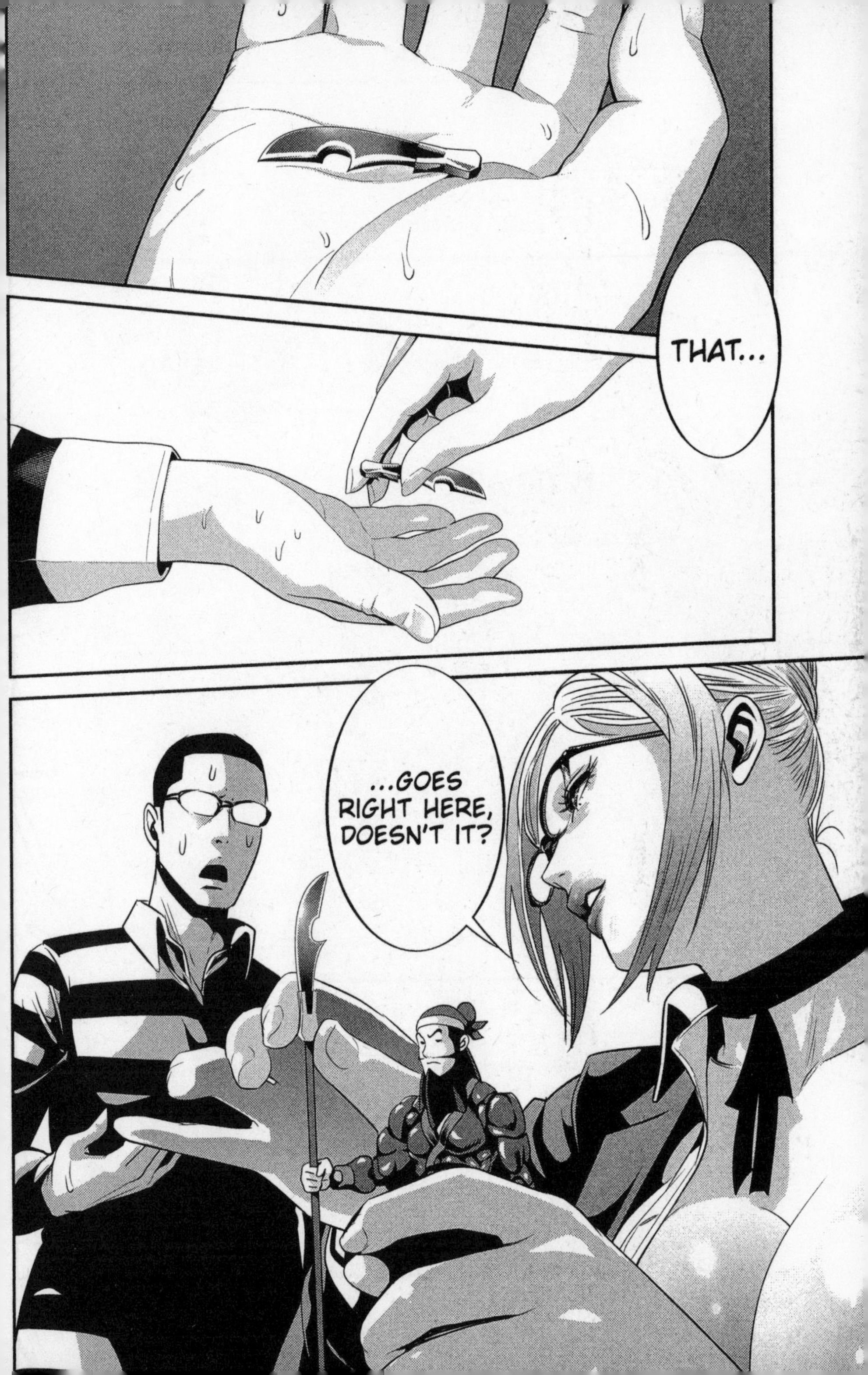
THAT...
...GOES RIGHT HERE, DOESN'T IT?

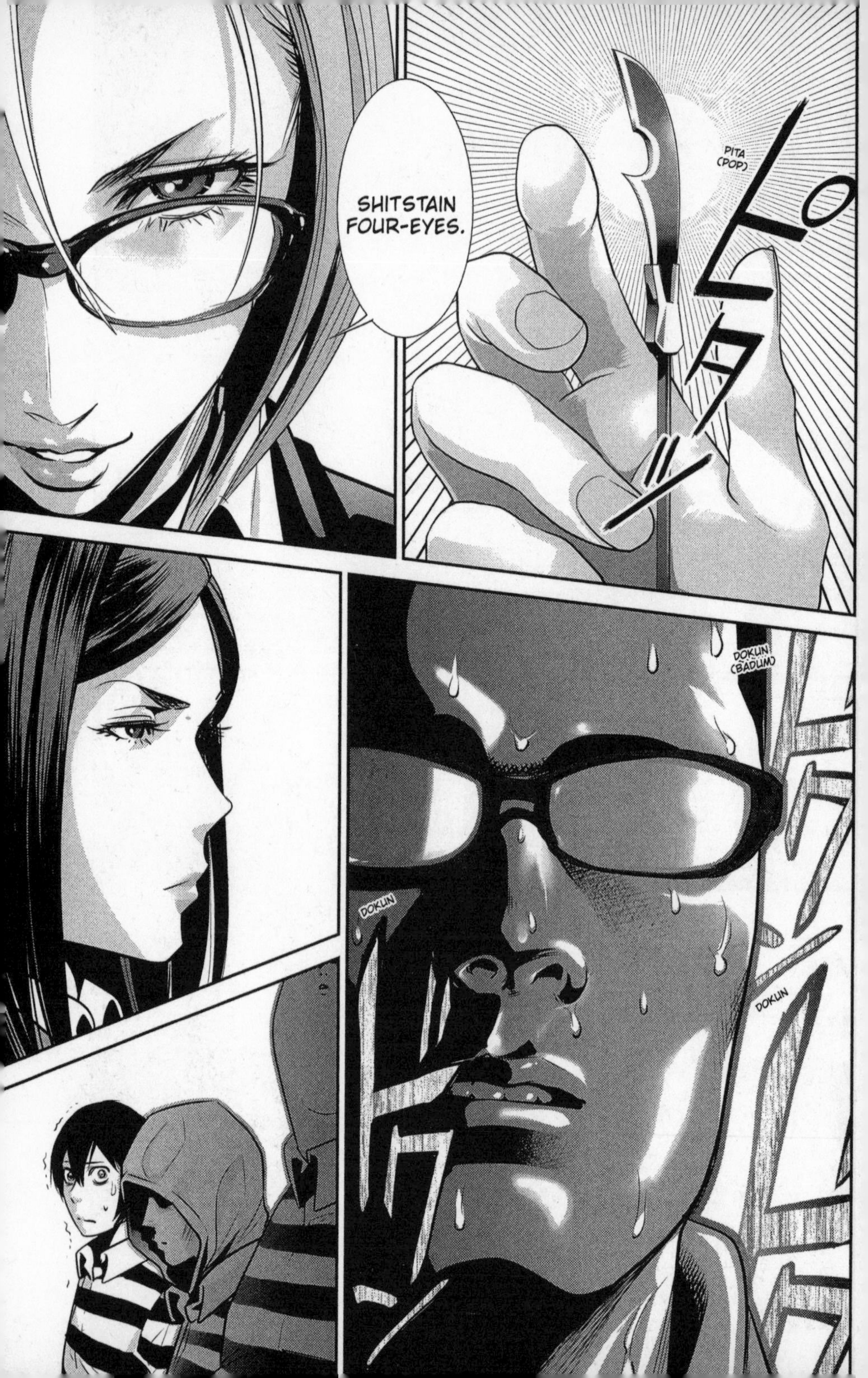
PITA (POP)
SHITSTAIN FOUR-EYES.
DOKUN (BADUM)
DOKUN
DOKUN

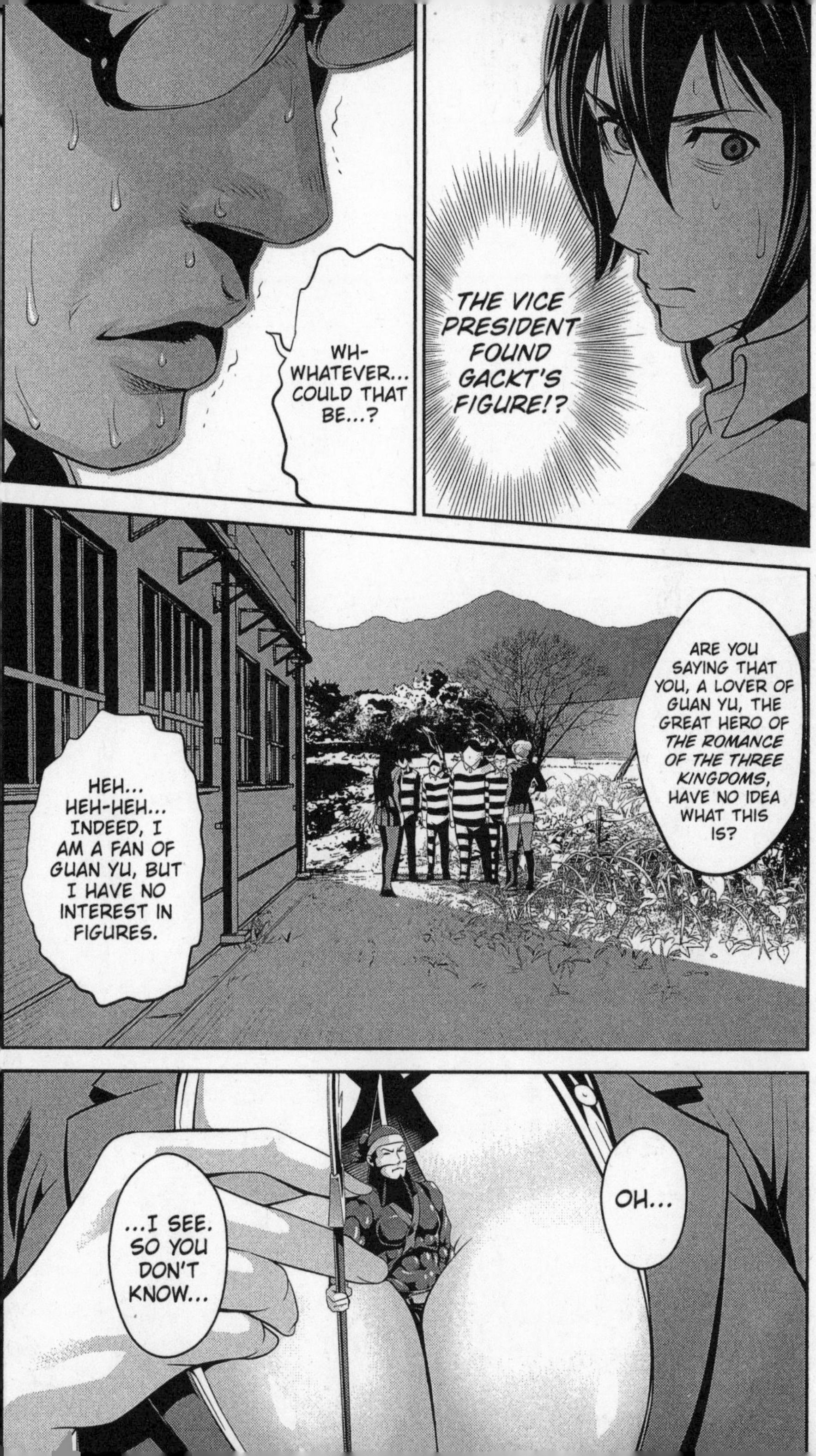
THE VICE PRESIDENT FOUND GACKT'S FIGURE!?
WH- WHATEVER... COULD THAT BE...?
ARE YOU SAYING THAT YOU, A LOVER OF GUAN YU, THE GREAT HERO OF *THE ROMANCE OF THE THREE KINGDOMS*, HAVE NO IDEA WHAT THIS IS?
HEH... HEH-HEH... INDEED, I AM A FAN OF GUAN YU, BUT I HAVE NO INTEREST IN FIGURES.
OH...
...I SEE. SO YOU DON'T KNOW...

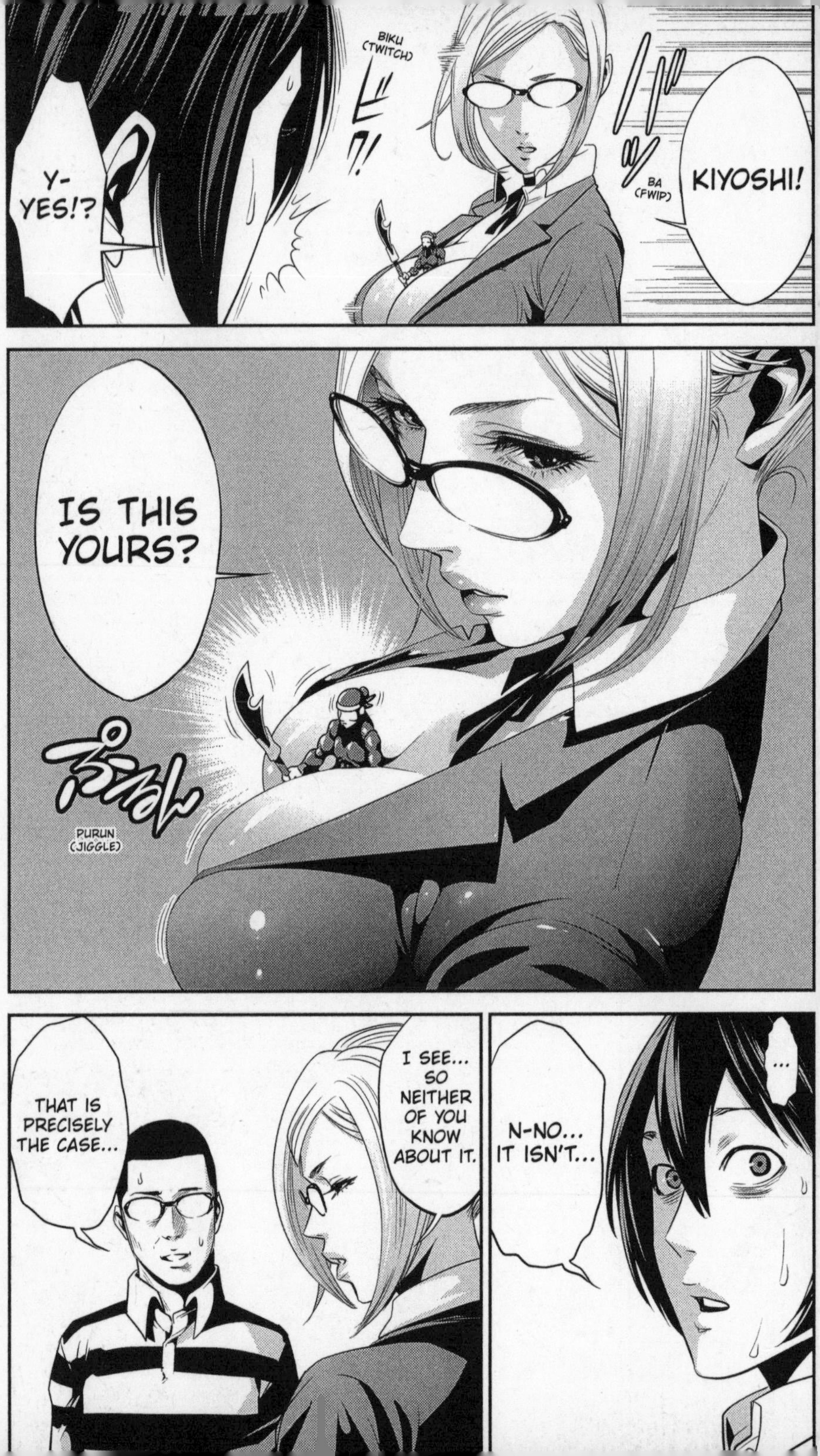
KIYOSHI!
BA (FWIP)
BIKU (TWITCH)
Y- YES!?
IS THIS YOURS?
PURUN (JIGGLE)
...
N-NO... IT ISN'T...
I SEE... SO NEITHER OF YOU KNOW ABOUT IT.
THAT IS PRECISELY THE CASE...

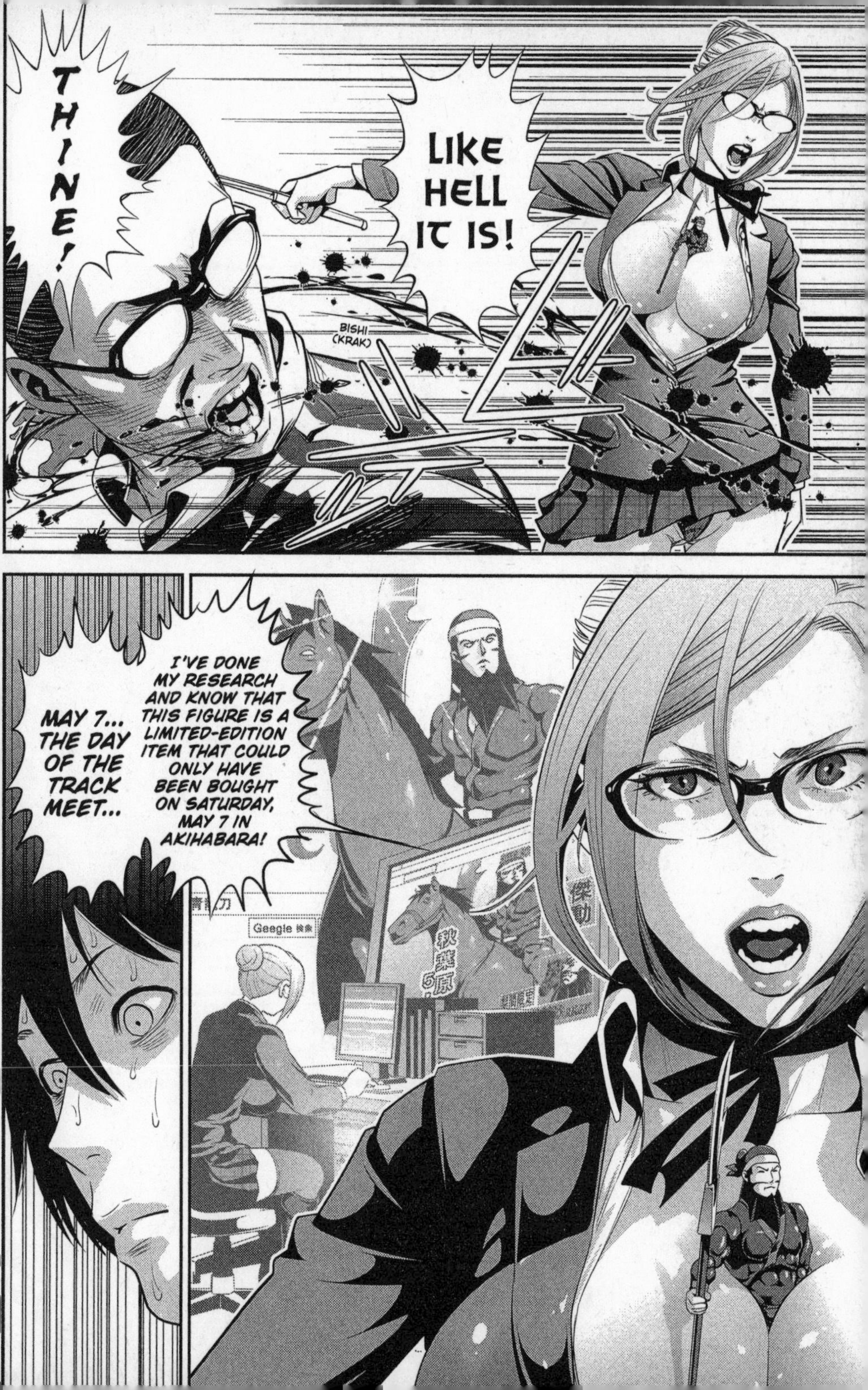
LIKE HELL IT IS!
BISHI (KRAK)
THINE!
I'VE DONE MY RESEARCH AND KNOW THAT THIS FIGURE IS A LIMITED-EDITION ITEM THAT COULD ONLY HAVE BEEN BOUGHT ON SATURDAY, MAY 7 IN AKIHABARA!
Geegle 検索
MAY 7... THE DAY OF THE TRACK MEET...

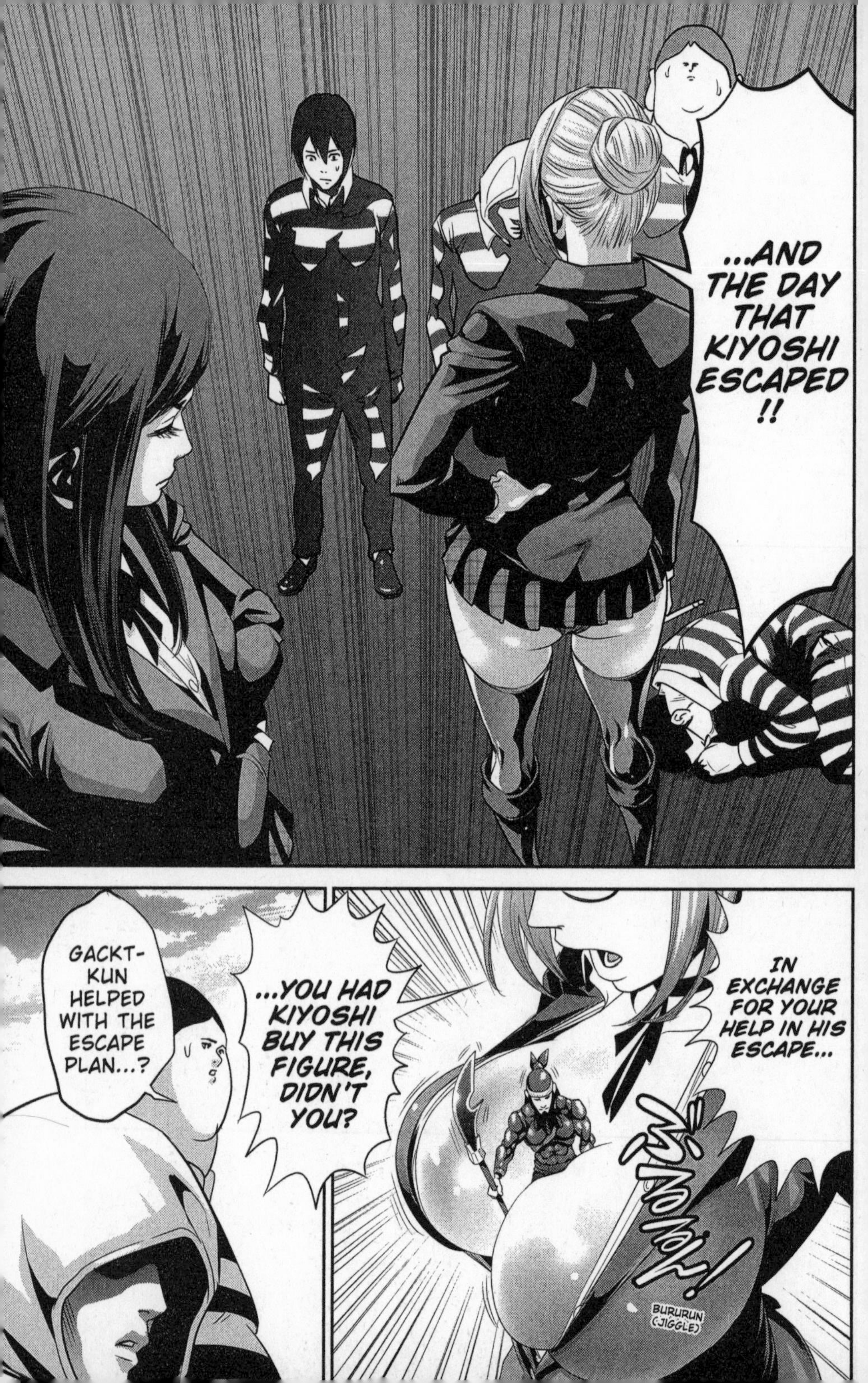
...AND THE DAY THAT KIYOSHI ESCAPED!!
IN EXCHANGE FOR YOUR HELP IN HIS ESCAPE...
BURURUN (JIGGLE)
...YOU HAD KIYOSHI BUY THIS FIGURE, DIDN'T YOU?
GACKT-KUN HELPED WITH THE ESCAPE PLAN...?

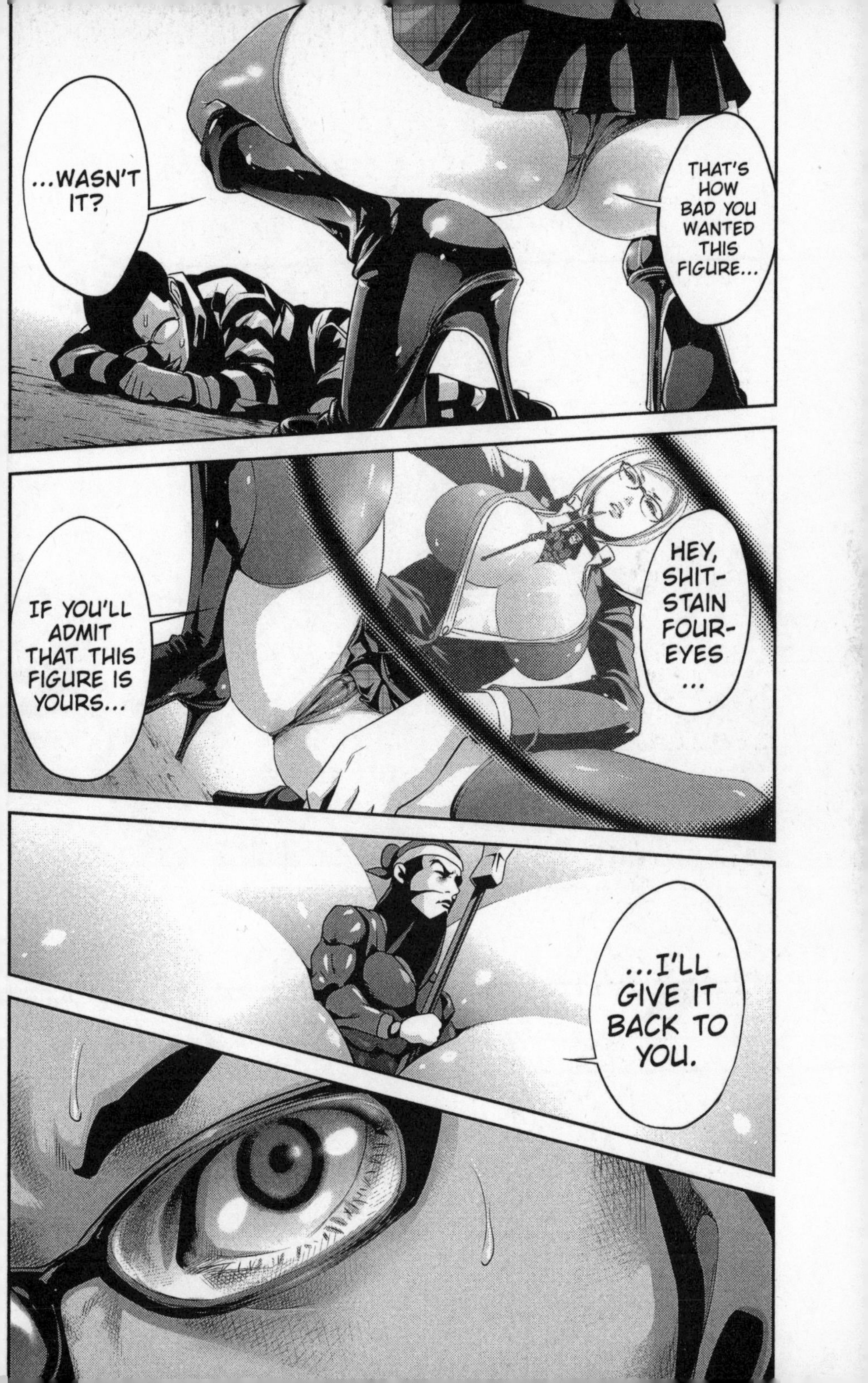
THAT'S HOW BAD YOU WANTED THIS FIGURE...
...WASN'T IT?
HEY, SHIT-STAIN FOUR-EYES ...
IF YOU'LL ADMIT THAT THIS FIGURE IS YOURS...
...I'LL GIVE IT BACK TO YOU.

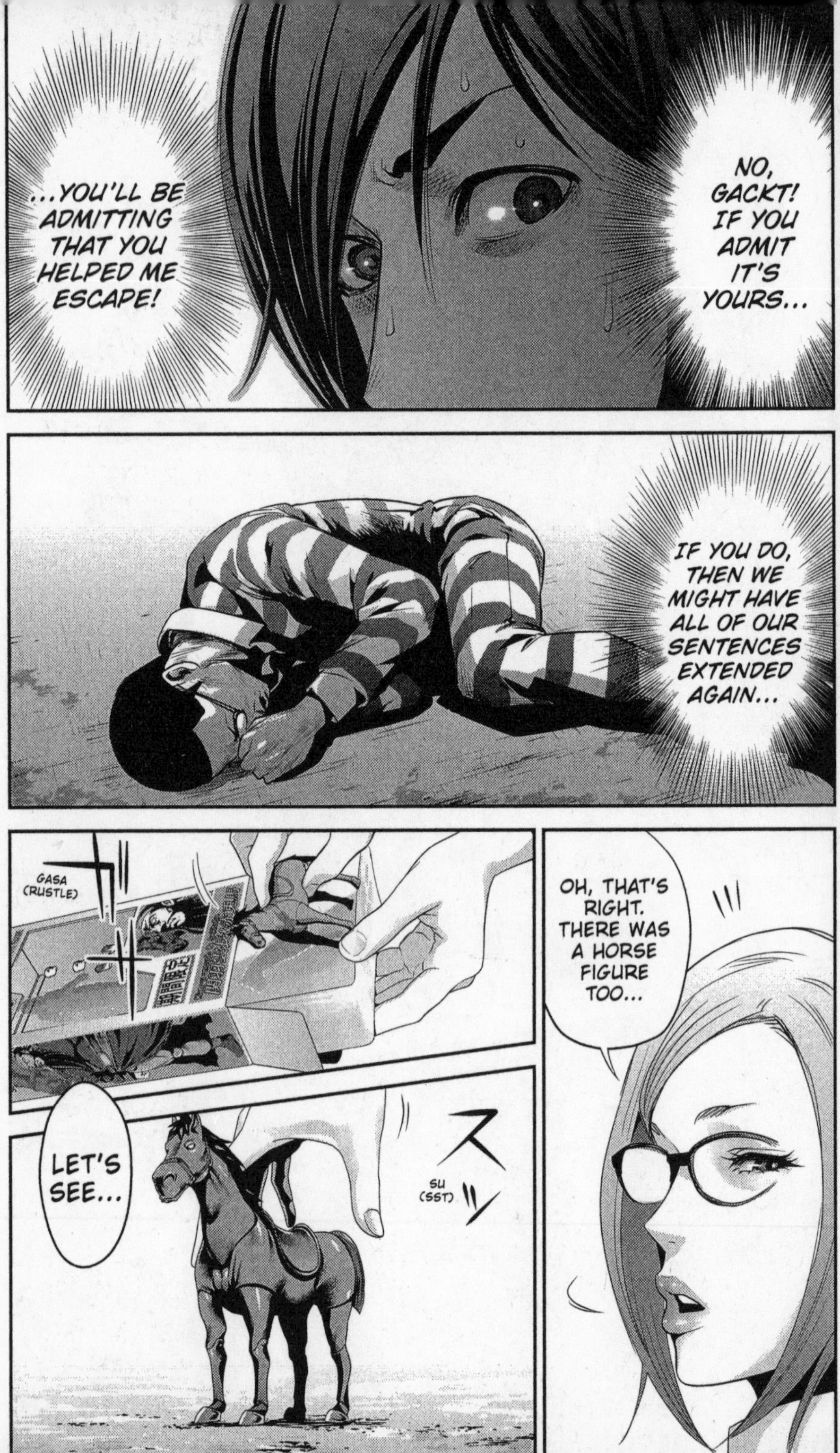
NO, GACKT! IF YOU ADMIT IT'S YOURS...
...YOU'LL BE ADMITTING THAT YOU HELPED ME ESCAPE!
IF YOU DO, THEN WE MIGHT HAVE ALL OF OUR SENTENCES EXTENDED AGAIN...
OH, THAT'S RIGHT. THERE WAS A HORSE FIGURE TOO...
GASA (RUSTLE)
LET'S SEE...
SU (SST)

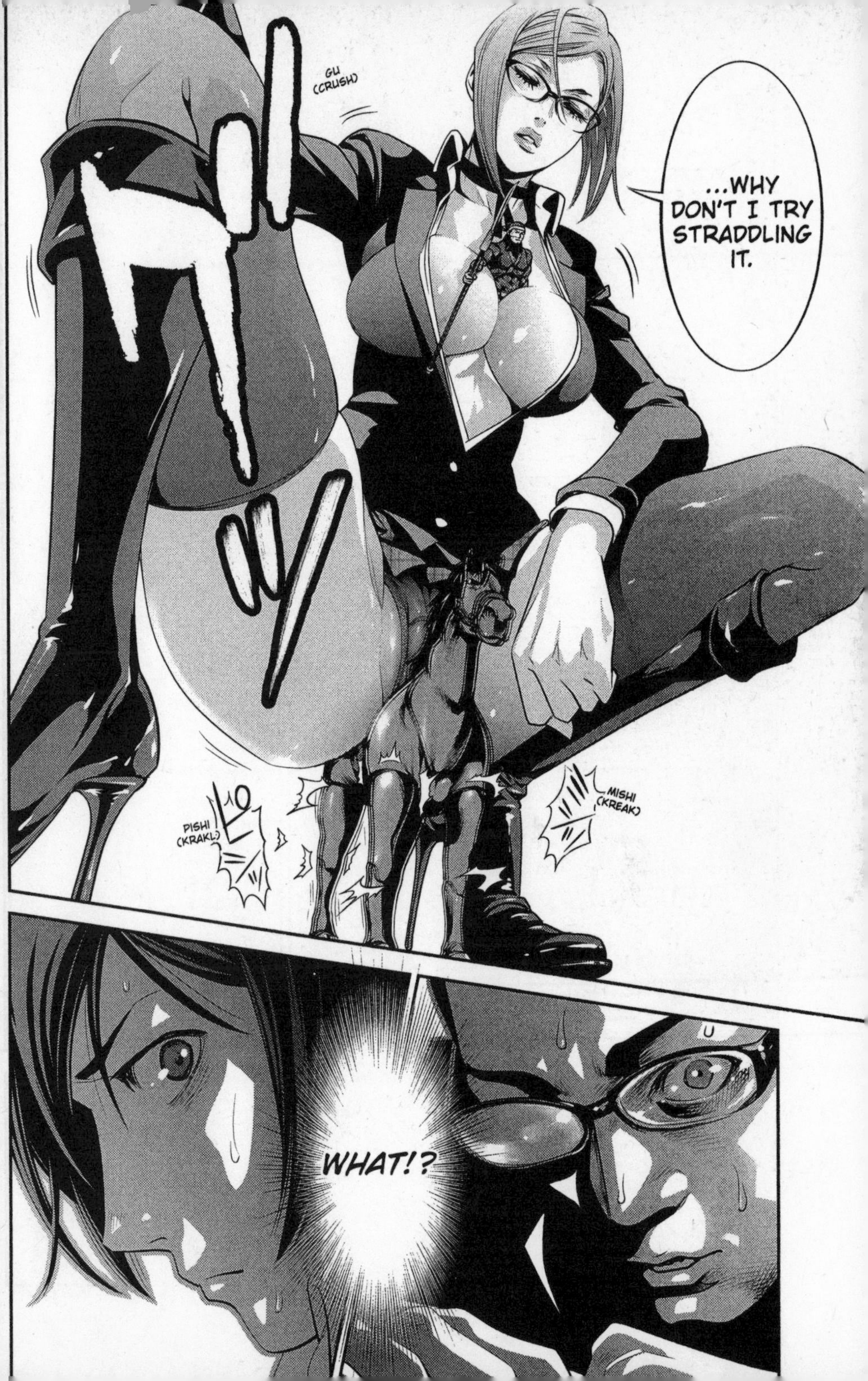
...WHY DON'T I TRY STRADDLING IT.
GU (CRUSH)
MISHI (KREAK)
PISHI (KRAKL)
WHAT!?

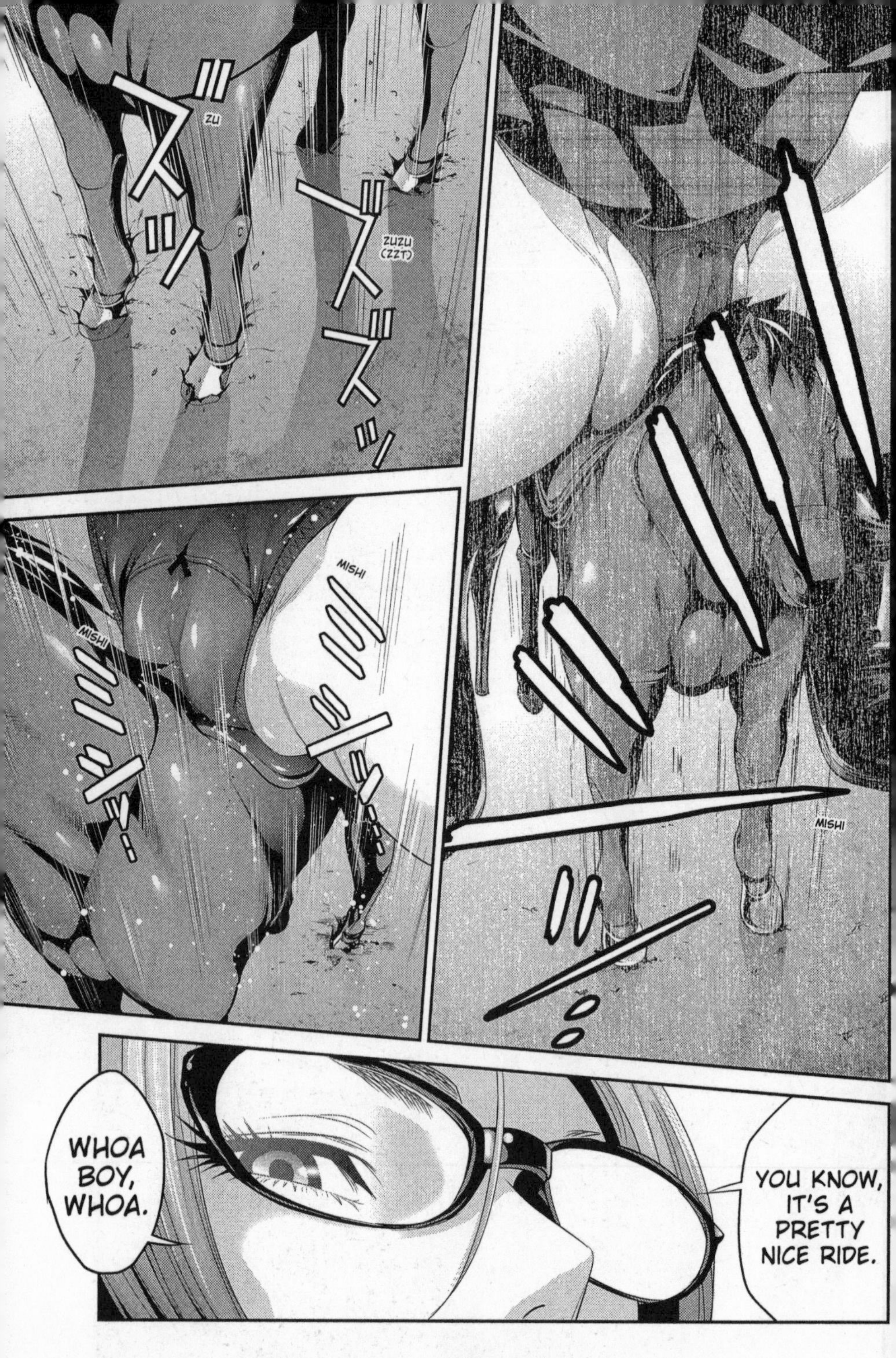
MISHI
ZU
ZUZU (ZZT)
MISHI
MISHI
YOU KNOW, IT'S A PRETTY NICE RIDE.
WHOA BOY, WHOA.

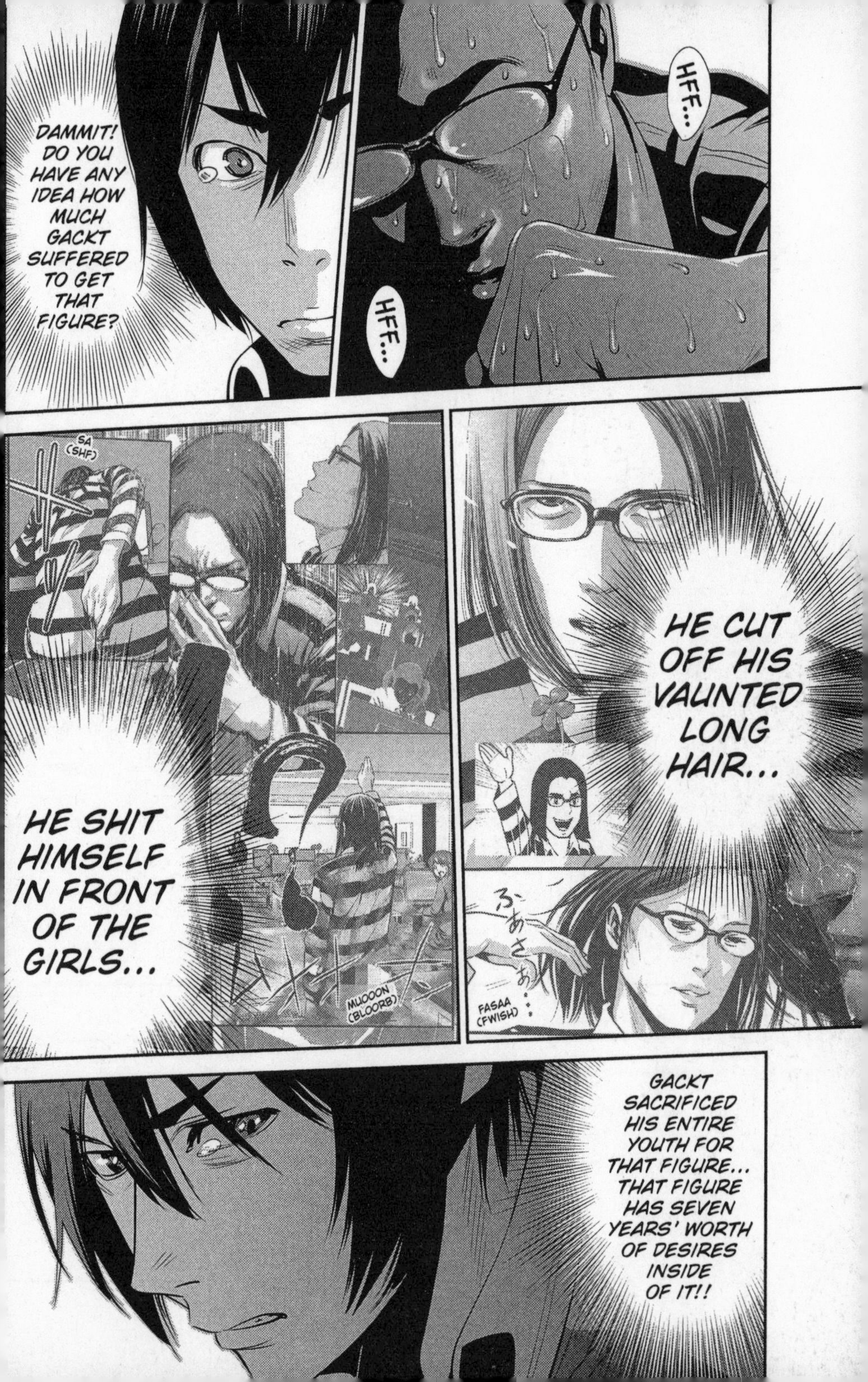
HFF...
HFF...
DAMMIT! DO YOU HAVE ANY IDEA HOW MUCH GACKT SUFFERED TO GET THAT FIGURE?
HE CUT OFF HIS VAUNTED LONG HAIR...
ふぁさぁ…
FASAA (FWISH)
SA (SHF)
HE SHIT HIMSELF IN FRONT OF THE GIRLS...
MUOOON (BLOORB)
GACKT SACRIFICED HIS ENTIRE YOUTH FOR THAT FIGURE... THAT FIGURE HAS SEVEN YEARS' WORTH OF DESIRES INSIDE OF IT!!

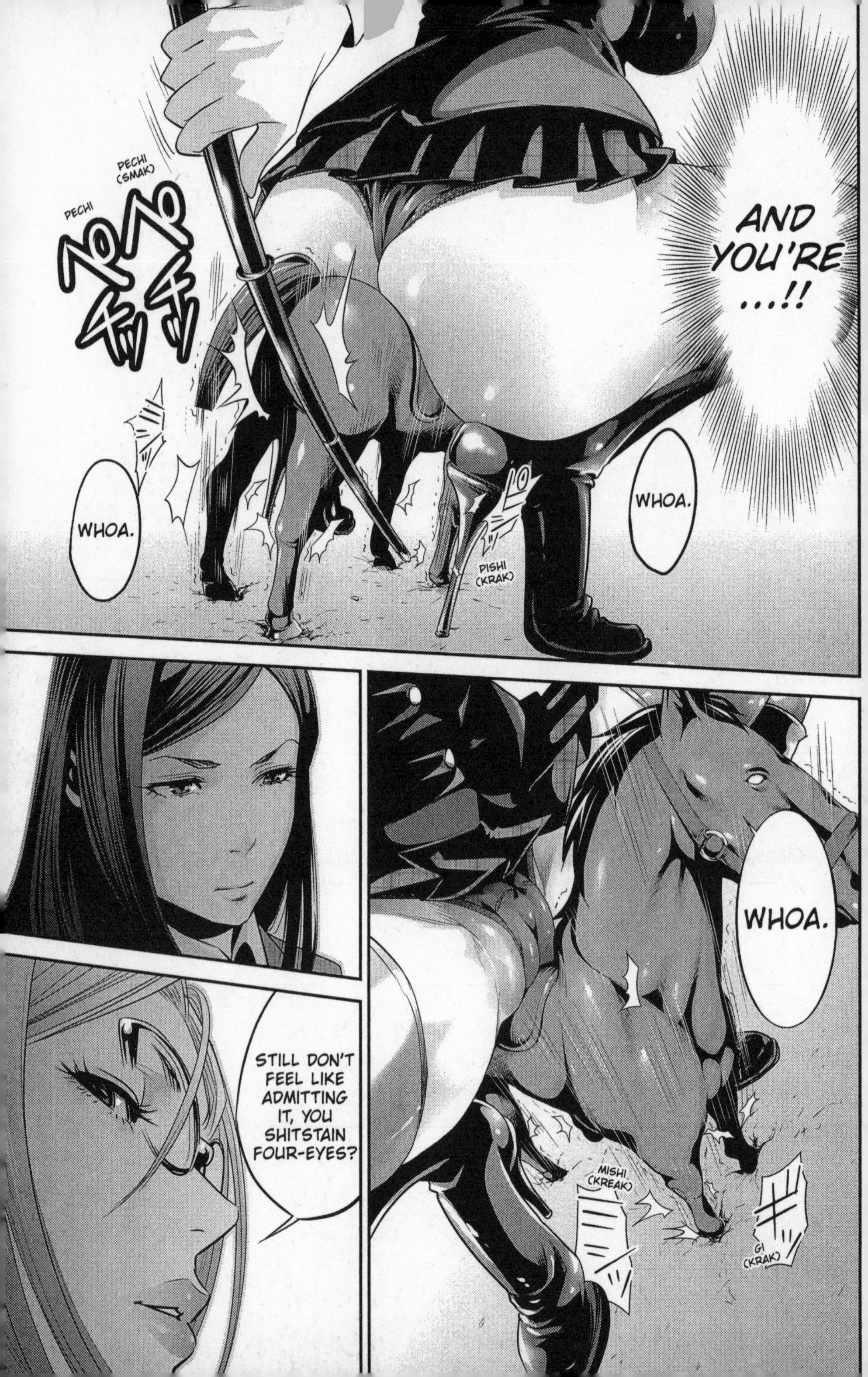
AND YOU'RE ...!!
WHOA.
PISHI (KRAK)
WHOA.
PECHI (SMAK)
PECHI
ペチペチ
WHOA.
MISHI (KREAK)
GI (KRAK)
STILL DON'T FEEL LIKE ADMITTING IT, YOU SHITSTAIN FOUR-EYES?

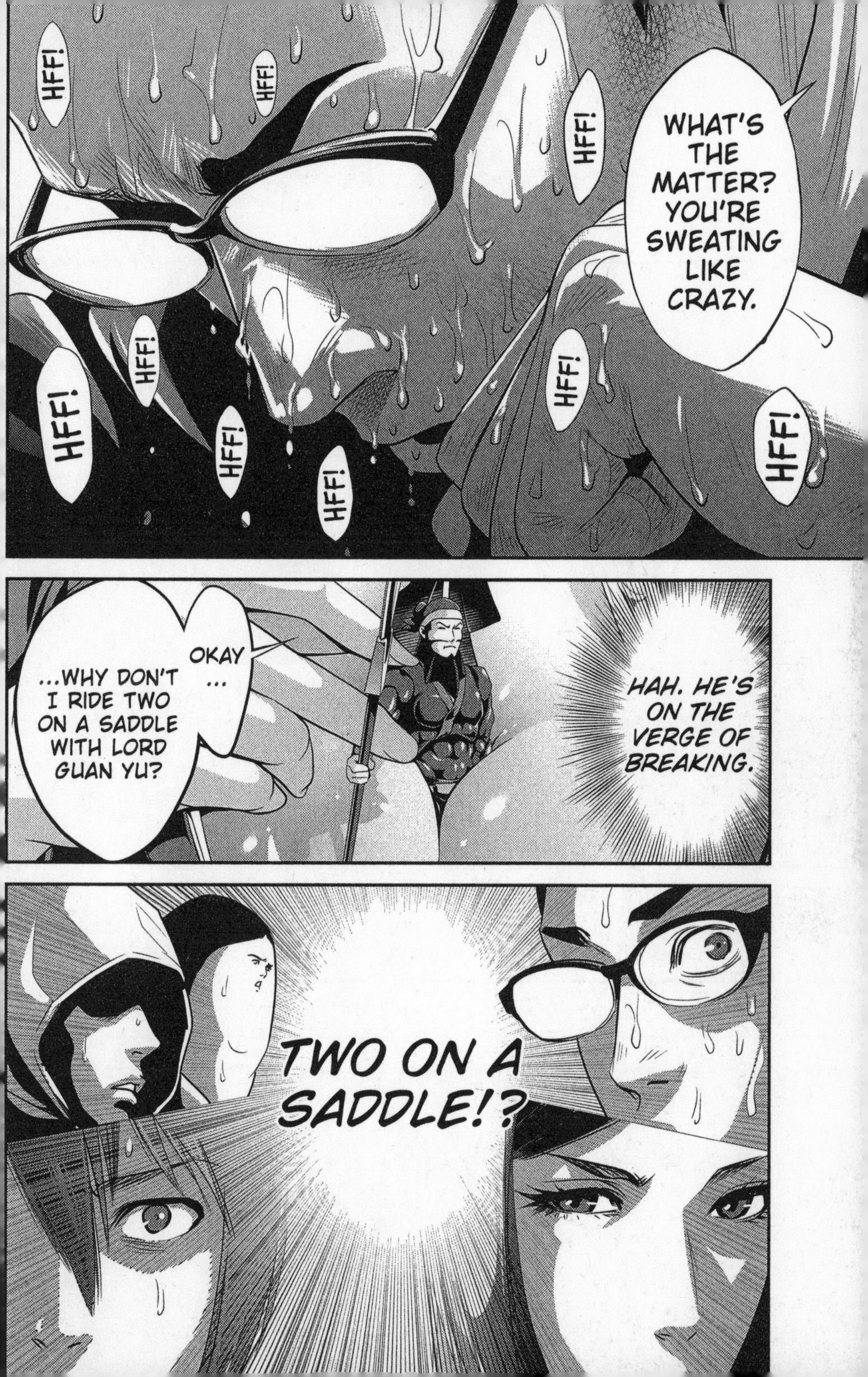
WHAT'S THE MATTER? YOU'RE SWEATING LIKE CRAZY.
HFF!
HFF!
HFF!
HFF!
HFF!
HFF!
HFF!
HFF!
HFF!
HAH. HE'S ON THE VERGE OF BREAKING.
OKAY ...
...WHY DON'T I RIDE TWO ON A SADDLE WITH LORD GUAN YU?
TWO ON A SADDLE!?

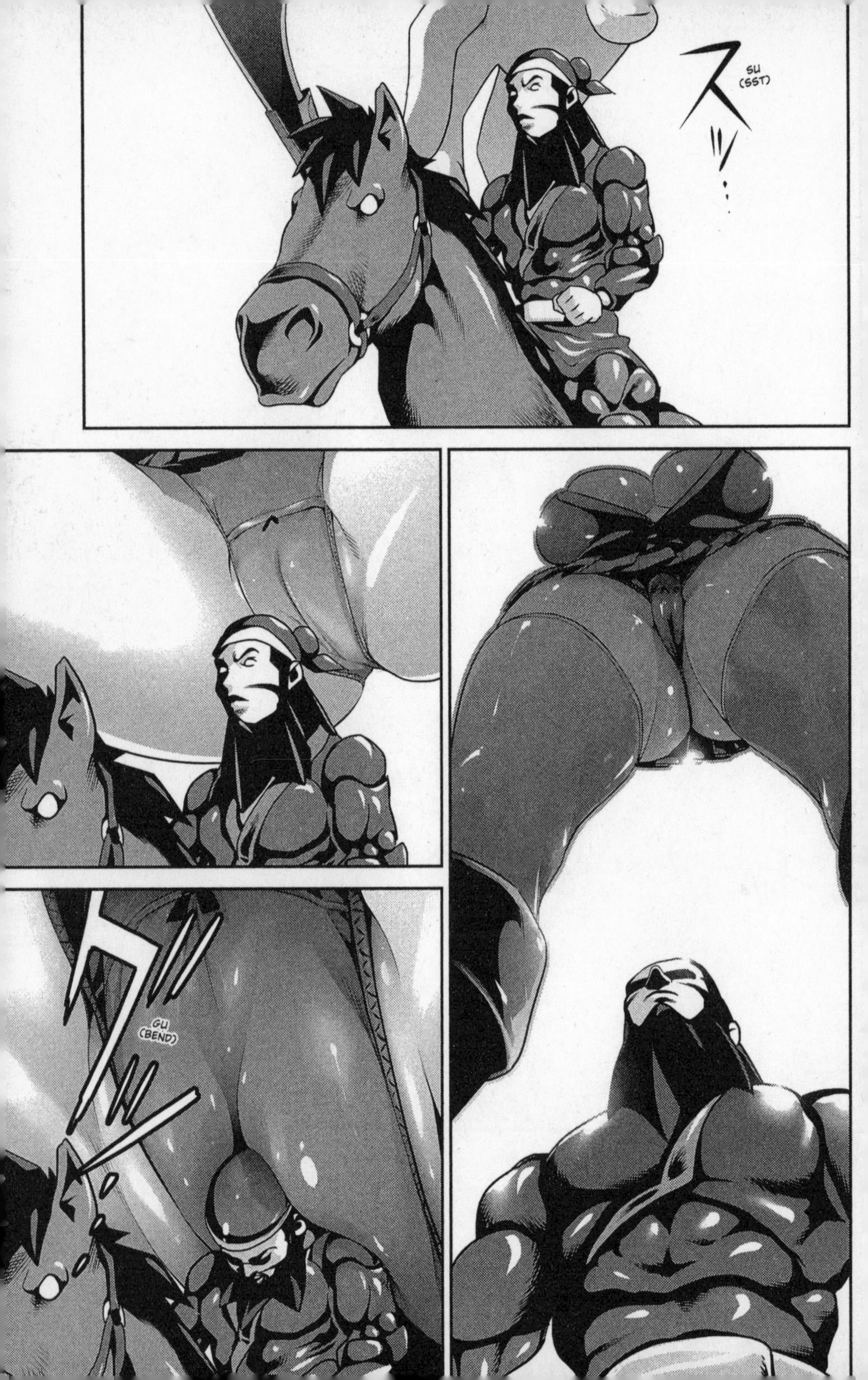
SU (SST)
GU (BEND)

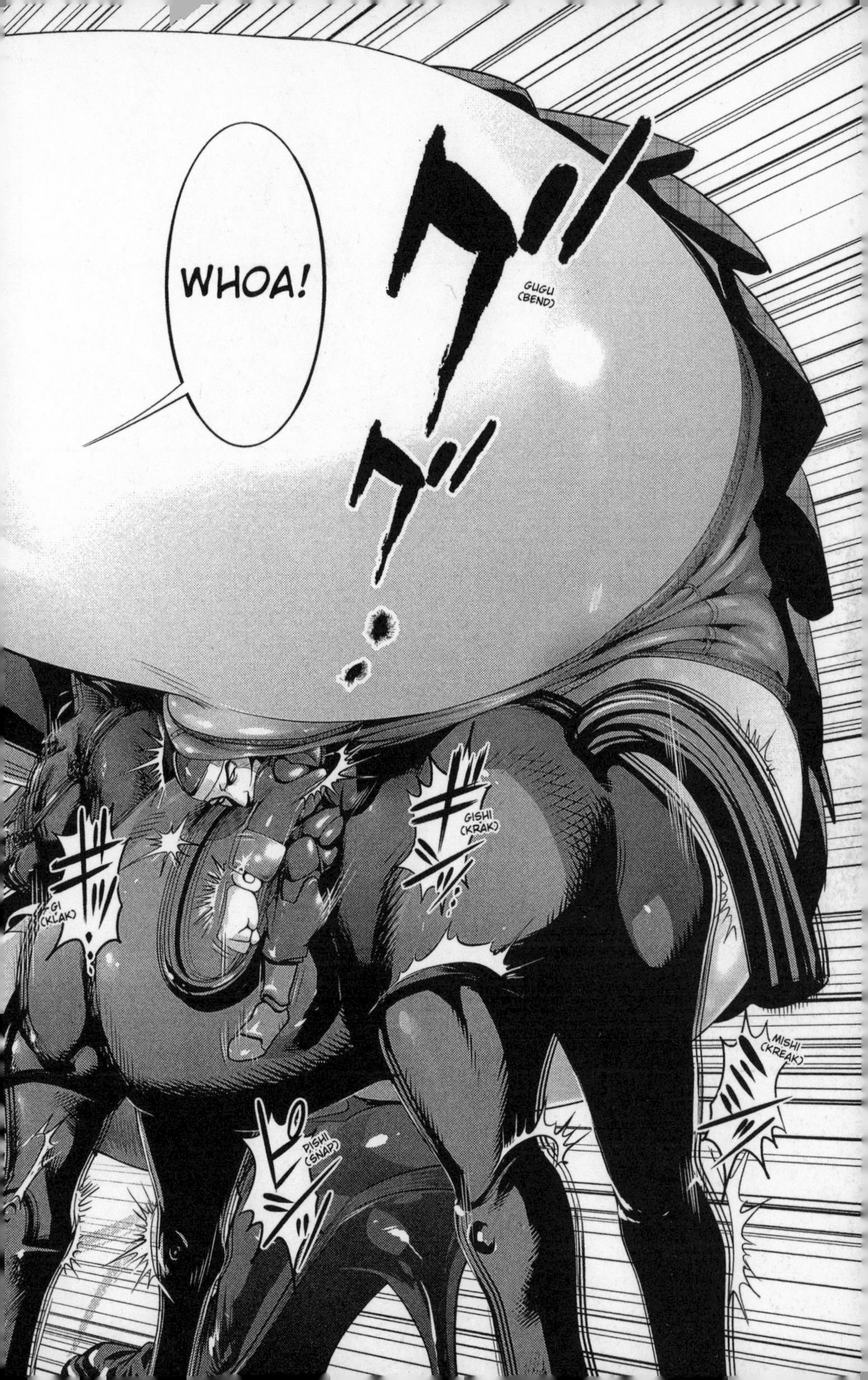
GUGU (BEND)
WHOA!
GISHI (KRAK)
GI (KLAK)
MISHI (KREAK)
PISHI (SNAP)

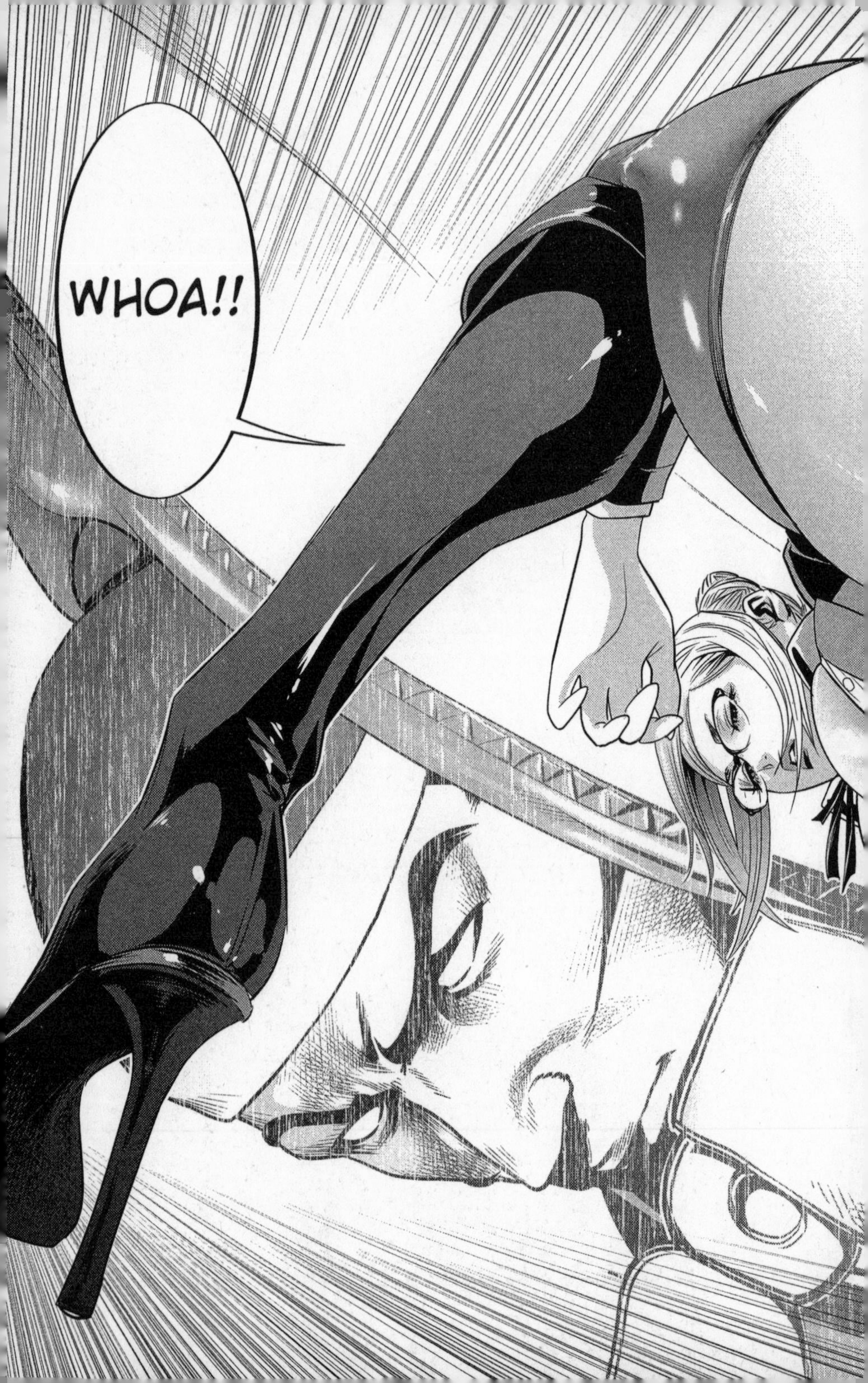
WHOA!!

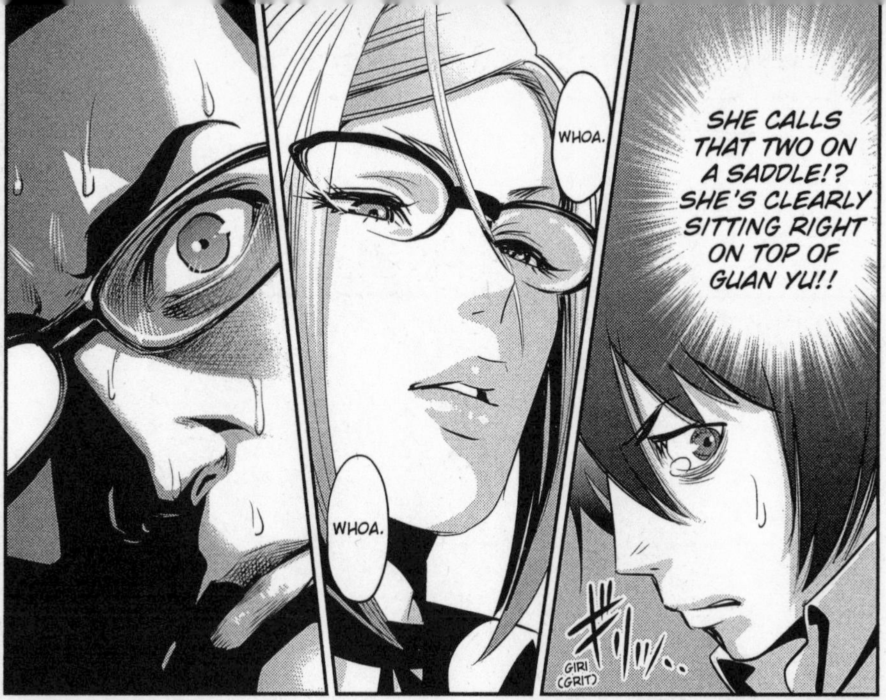
SHE CALLS THAT TWO ON A SADDLE!? SHE'S CLEARLY SITTING RIGHT ON TOP OF GUAN YU!!
GIRI (GRIT)
WHOA.
WHOA.

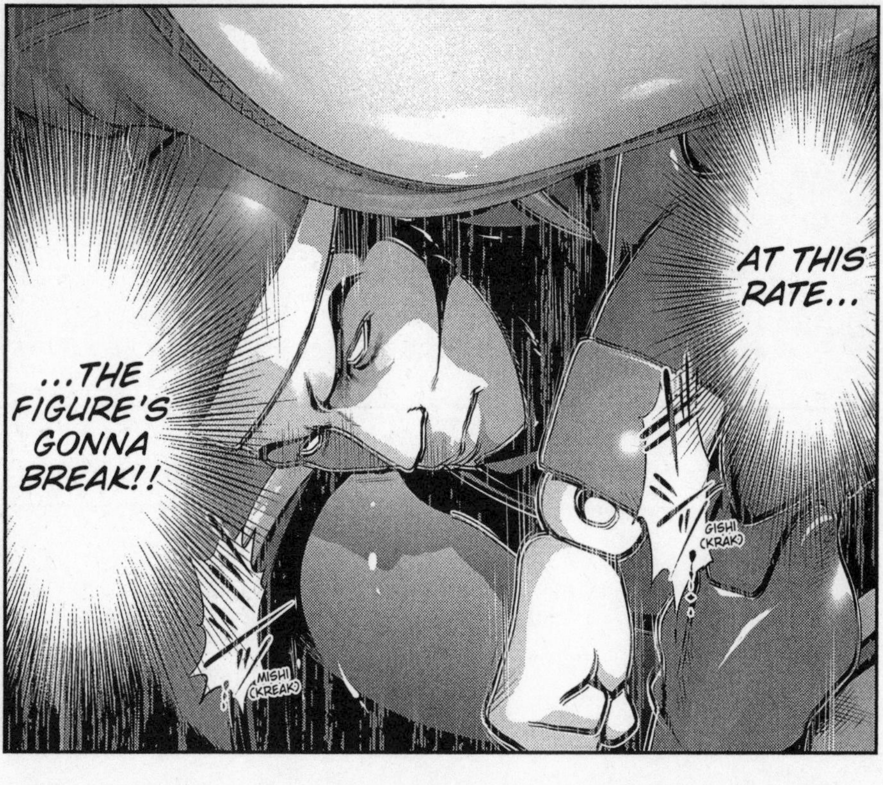
AT THIS RATE...
...THE FIGURE'S GONNA BREAK!!
GISHI (KRAK)
MISHI (KREAK)

CHAPTER 45: THE LONG GOODBYE

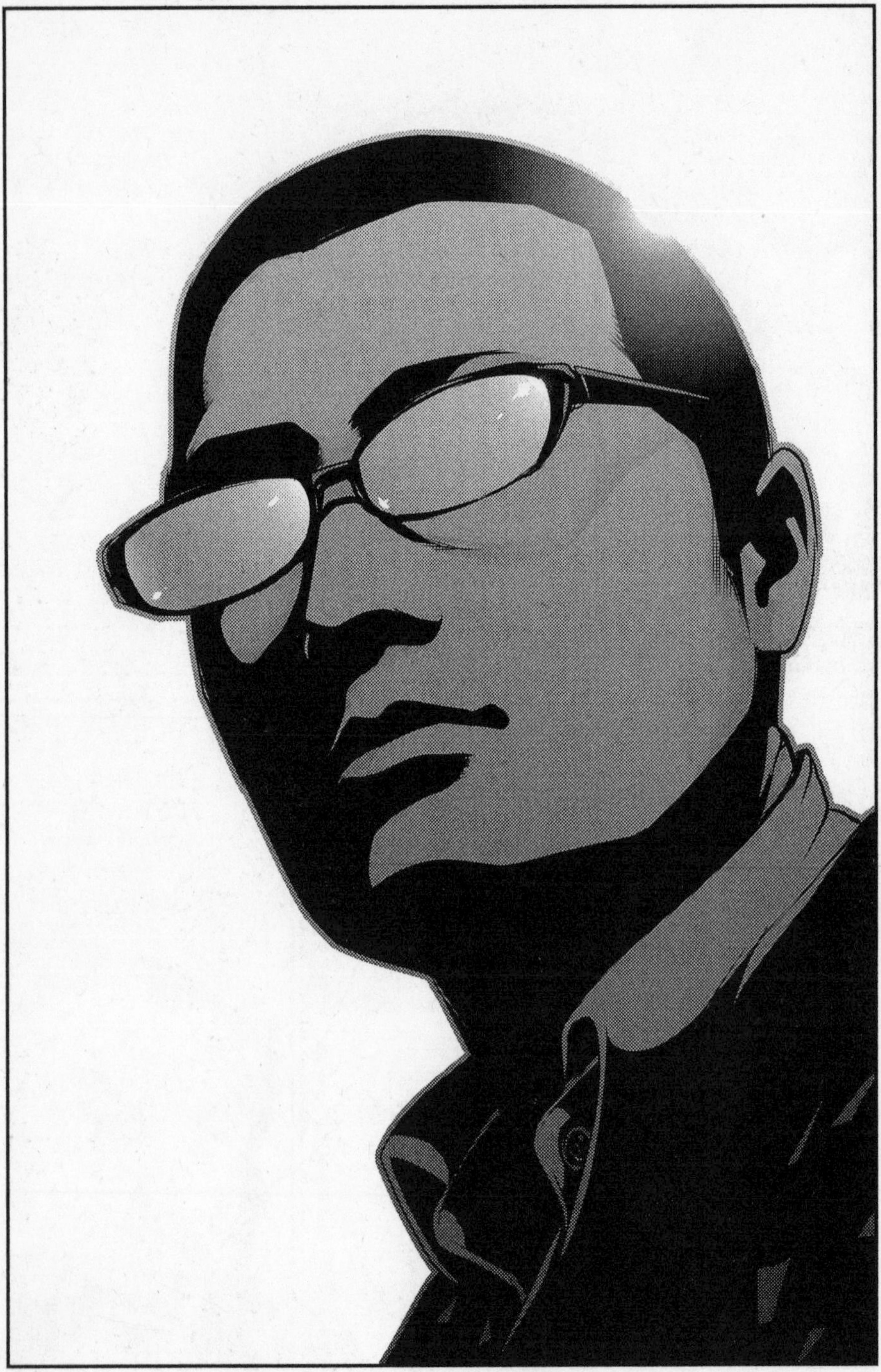

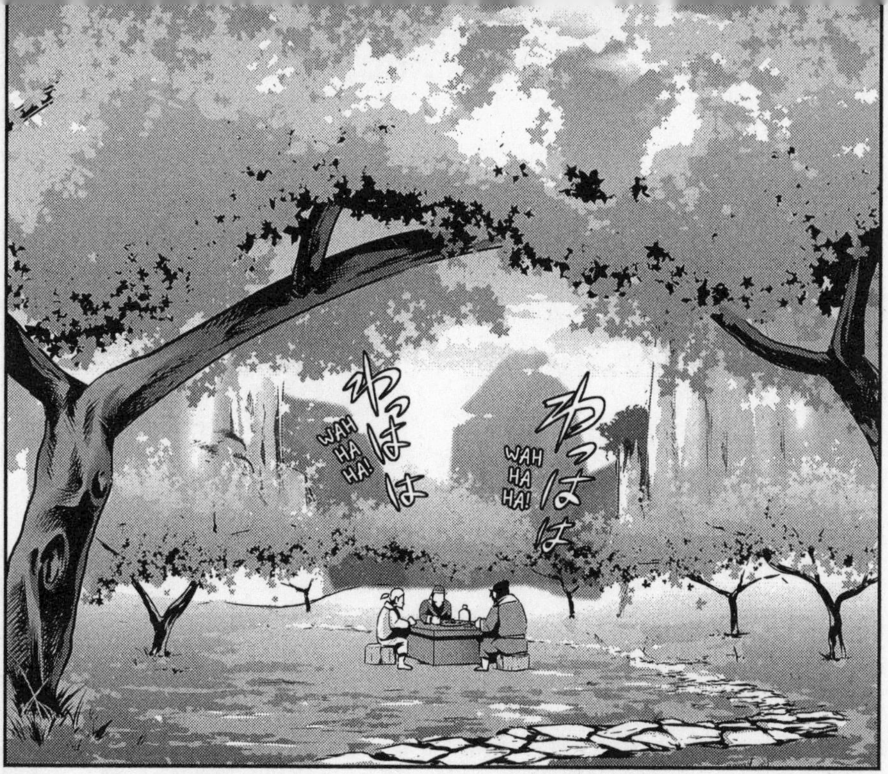
わっはは
WAH HA HA!
わっはは
WAH HA HA!
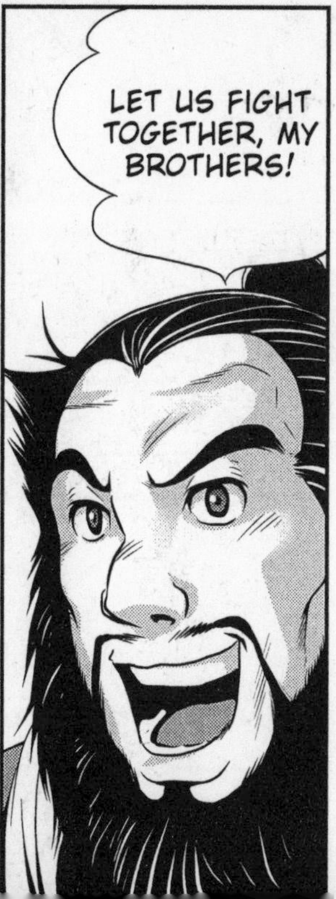
LET US FIGHT TOGETHER, MY BROTHERS!
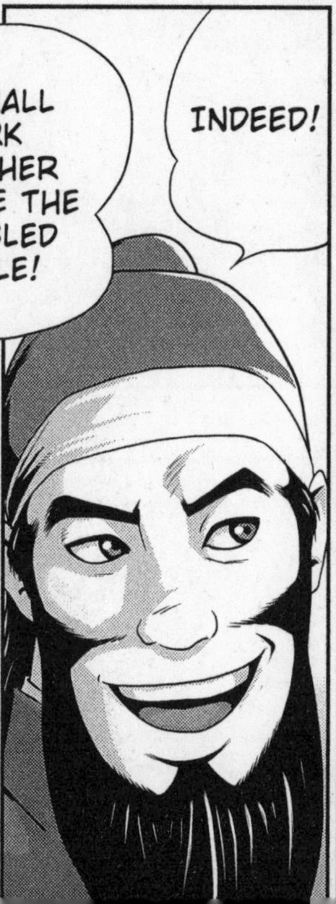
INDEED!
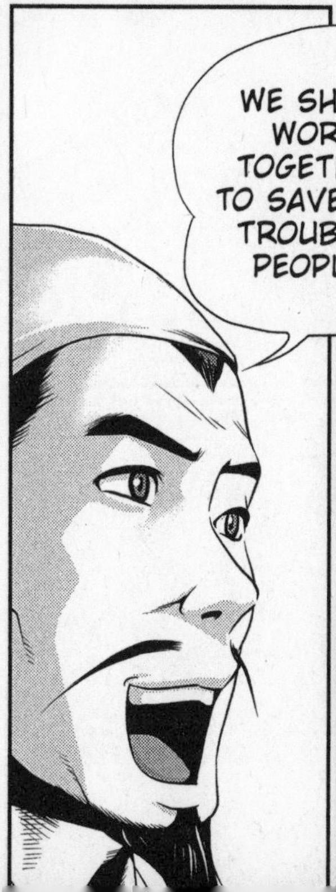
WE SHALL WORK TOGETHER TO SAVE THE TROUBLED PEOPLE!

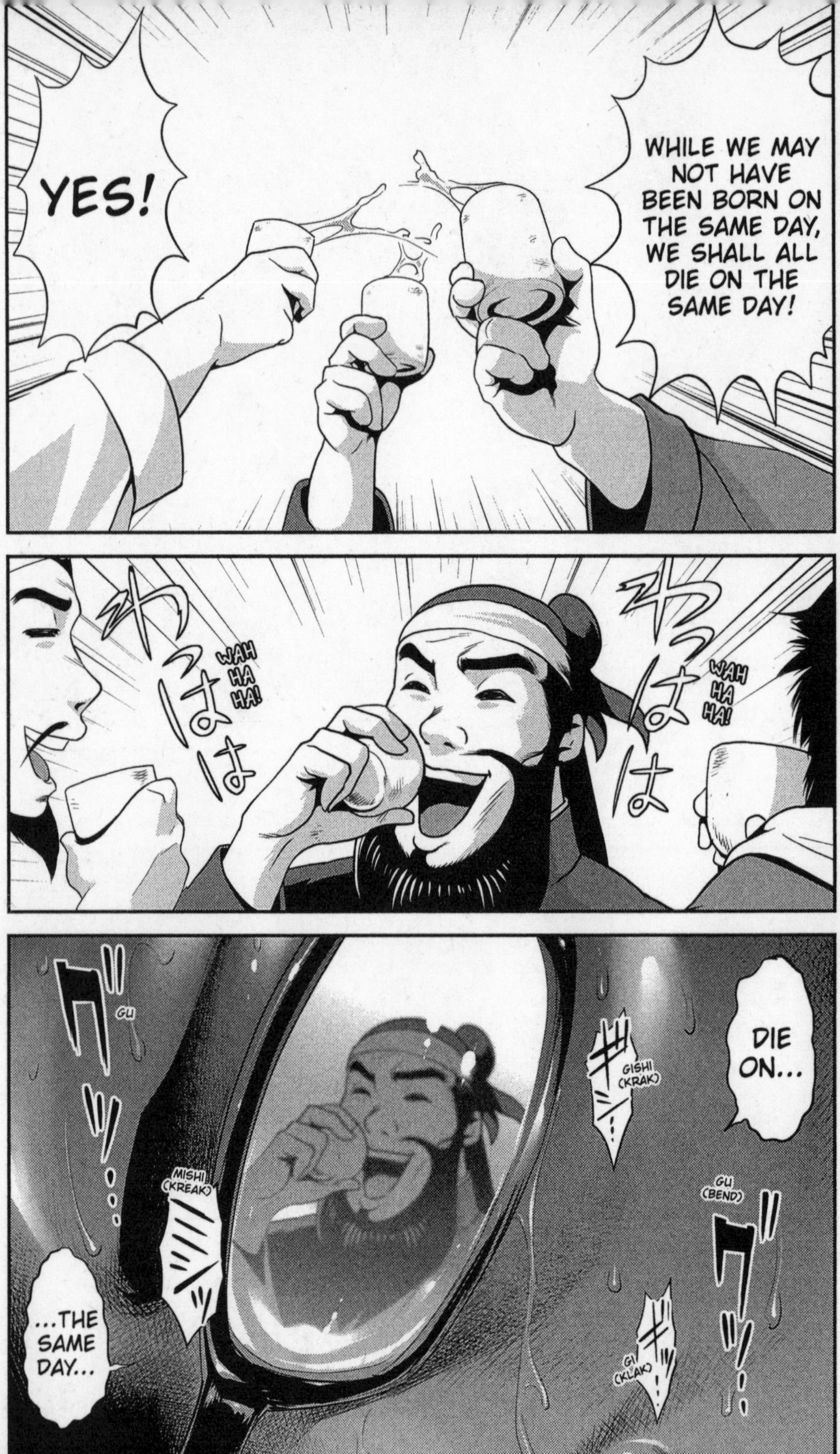
WHILE WE MAY NOT HAVE BEEN BORN ON THE SAME DAY, WE SHALL ALL DIE ON THE SAME DAY!
YES!
わっはは
WAH HA HA!
わっはは
WAH HA HA!
DIE ON...
GISHI (KRAK)
GU (BEND)
GI (KLAK)
MISHI (KREAK)
GU
...THE SAME DAY...

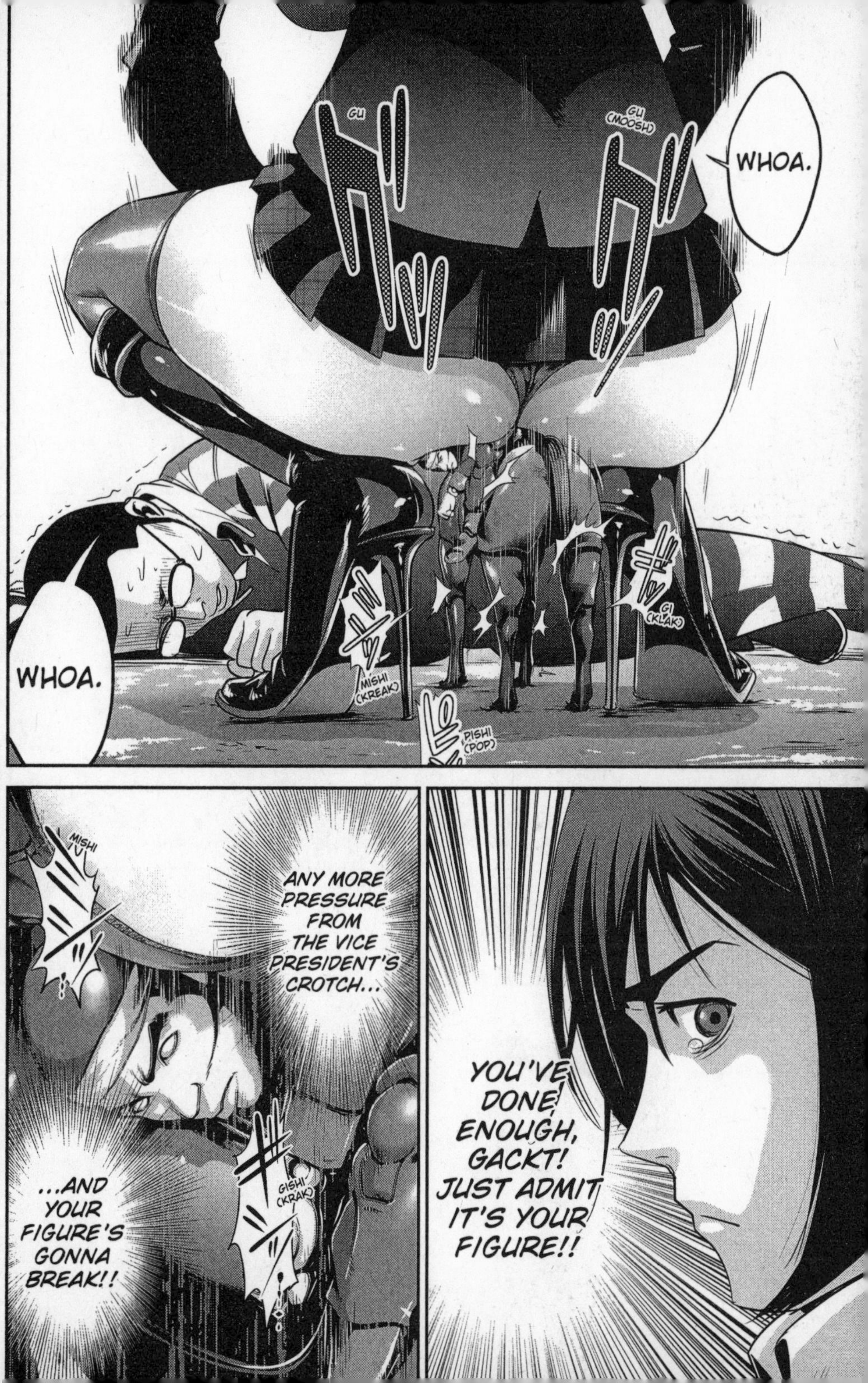
WHOA.
GU (MOOSH)
GU
GI (KLAK)
MISHI (KREAK)
WHOA.
PISHI (POP)
YOU'VE DONE ENOUGH, GACKT! JUST ADMIT IT'S YOUR FIGURE!!
MISHI
ANY MORE PRESSURE FROM THE VICE PRESIDENT'S CROTCH...
GISHI (KRAK)
...AND YOUR FIGURE'S GONNA BREAK!!

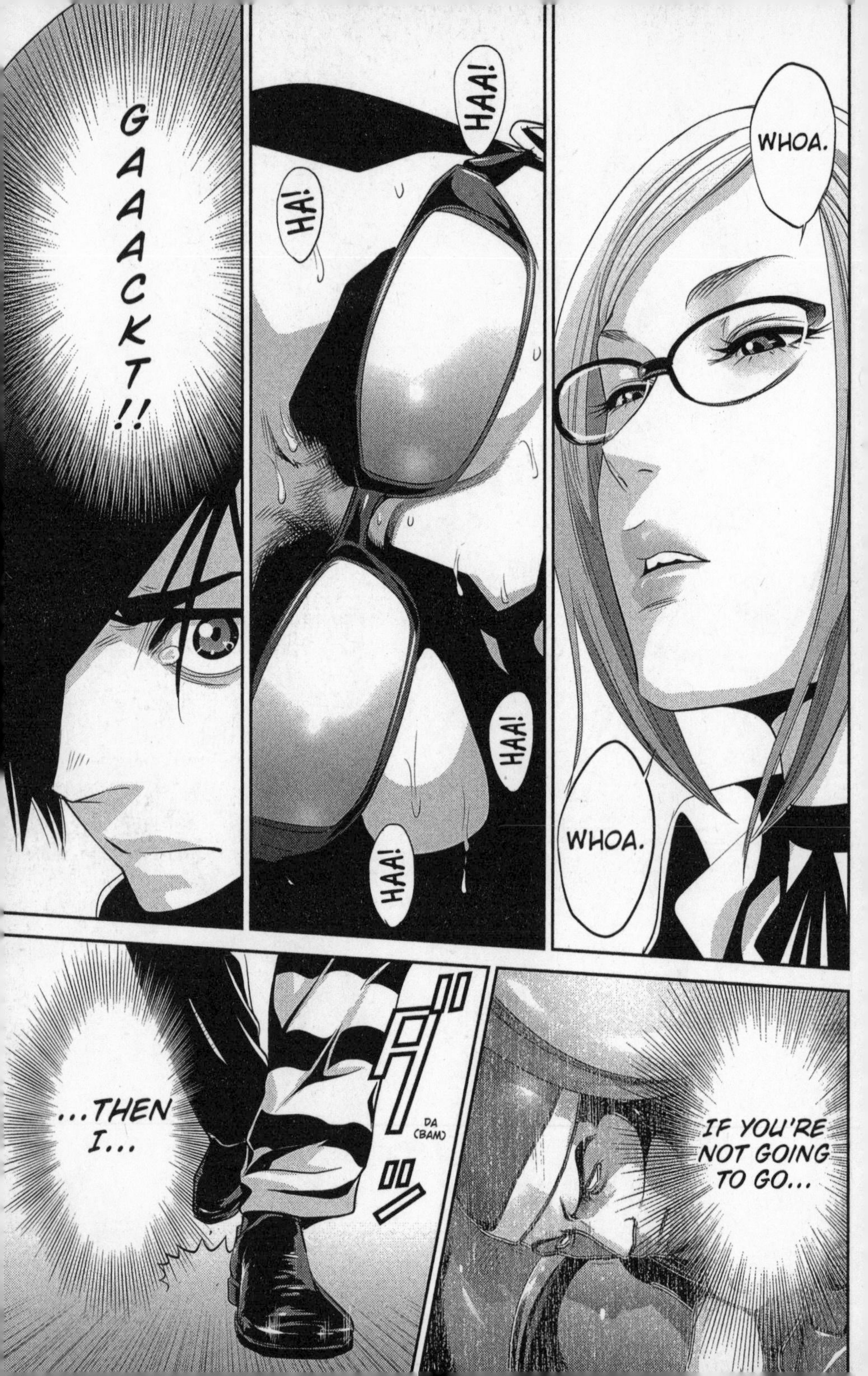
WHOA.
WHOA.
HAA!
HA!
HAA!
HAA!
GAAAACKT!!
IF YOU'RE NOT GOING TO GO...
DA (BAM)
...THEN I...

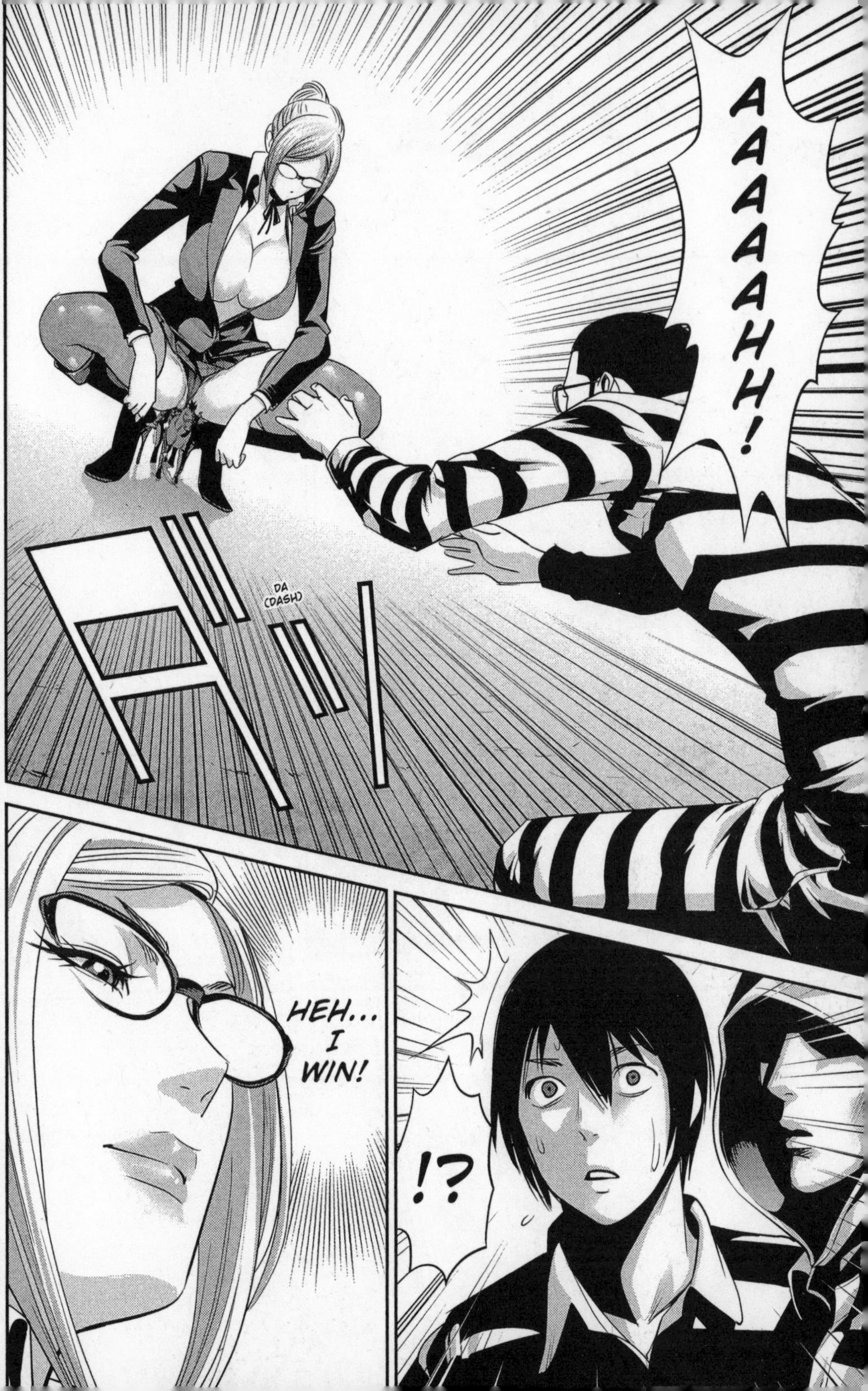
AAAAAHH!
DA (DASH)
!?
HEH... I WIN!

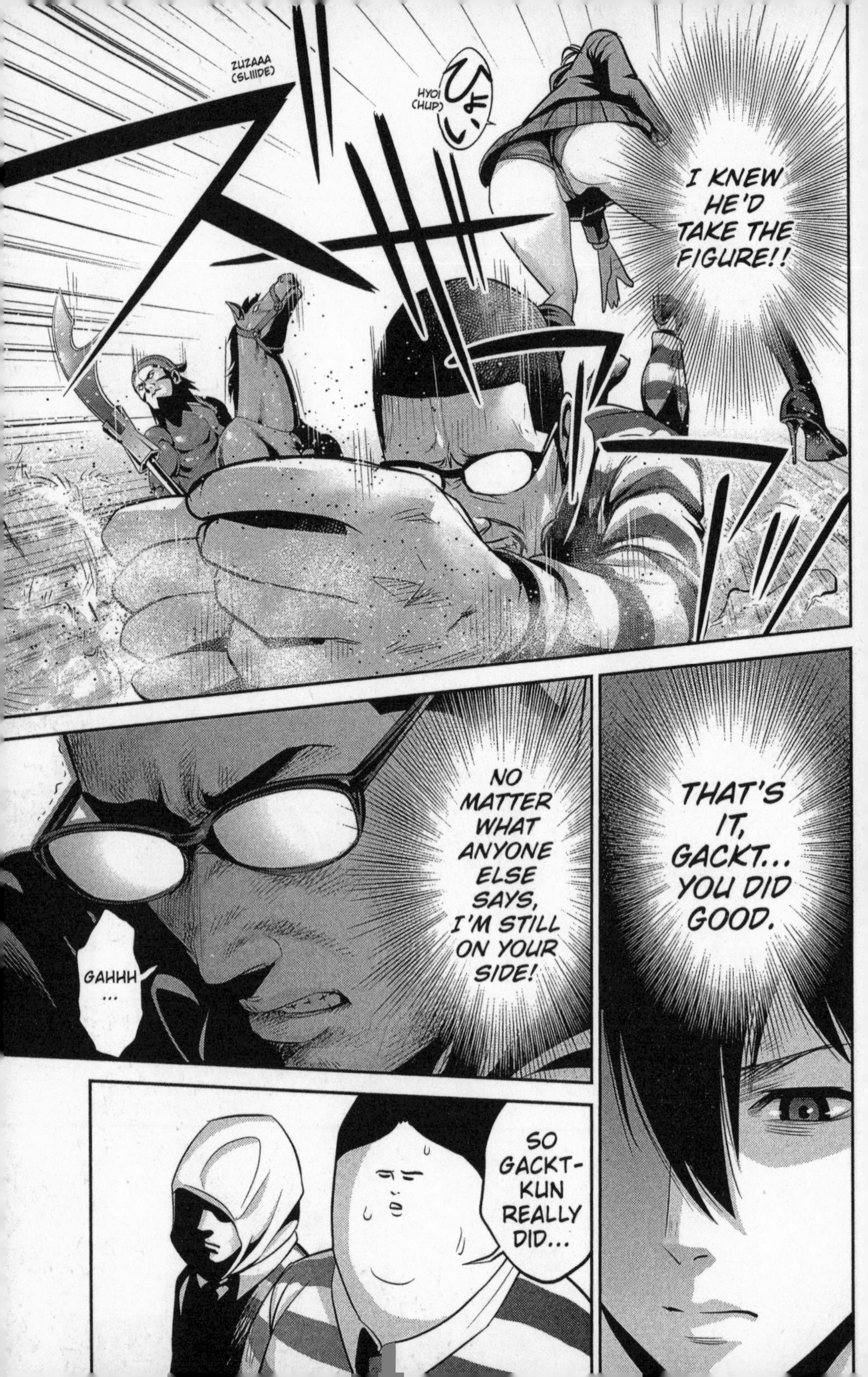
I KNEW HE'D TAKE THE FIGURE!!
ひょい
HYOI (HUP)
ZUZAAA (SLIIIDE)
THAT'S IT, GACKT... YOU DID GOOD.
NO MATTER WHAT ANYONE ELSE SAYS, I'M STILL ON YOUR SIDE!
GAHHH...
SO GACKT-KUN REALLY DID...

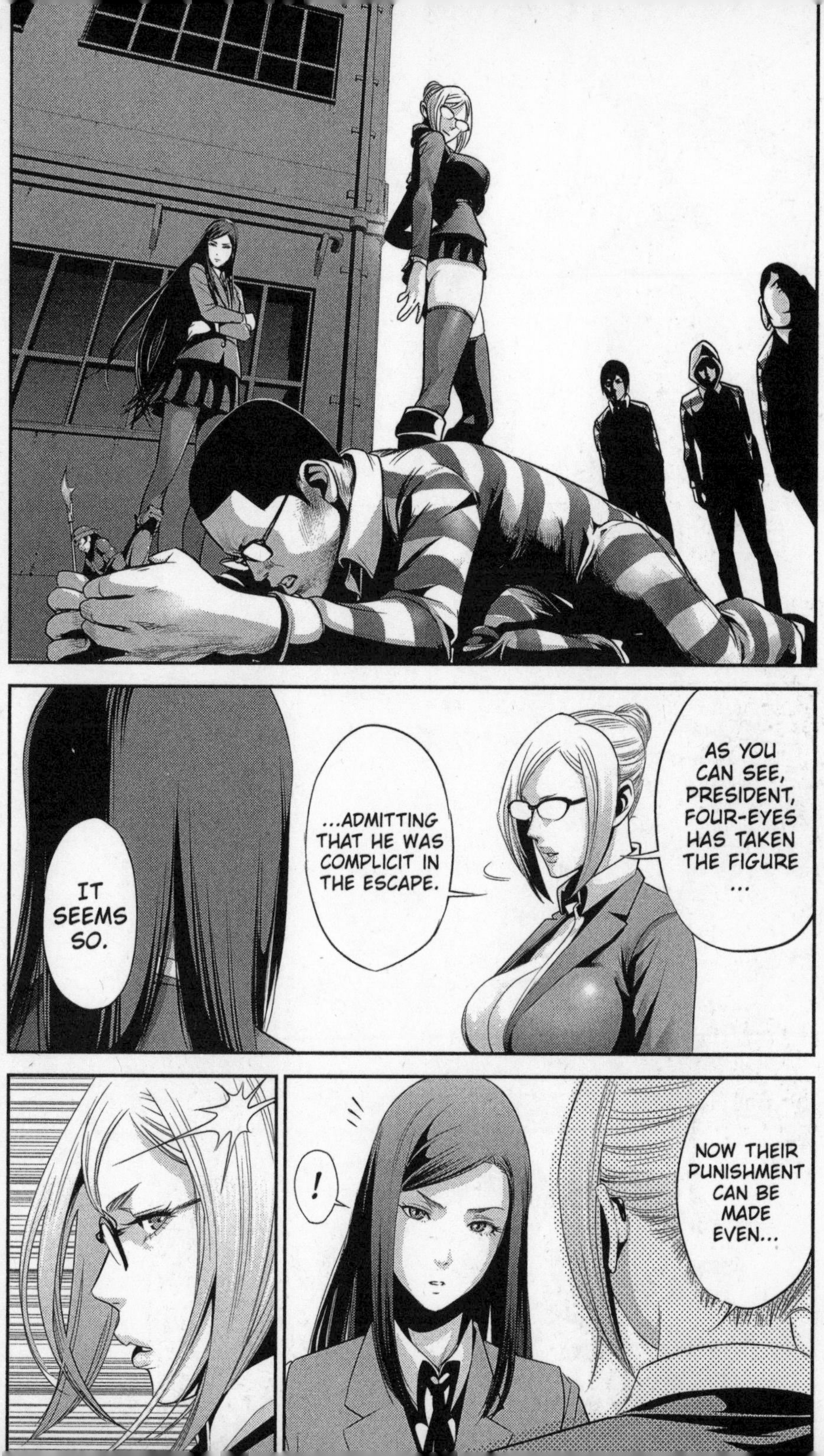
AS YOU CAN SEE, PRESIDENT, FOUR-EYES HAS TAKEN THE FIGURE ...
...ADMITTING THAT HE WAS COMPLICIT IN THE ESCAPE.
IT SEEMS SO.
NOW THEIR PUNISHMENT CAN BE MADE EVEN...
!

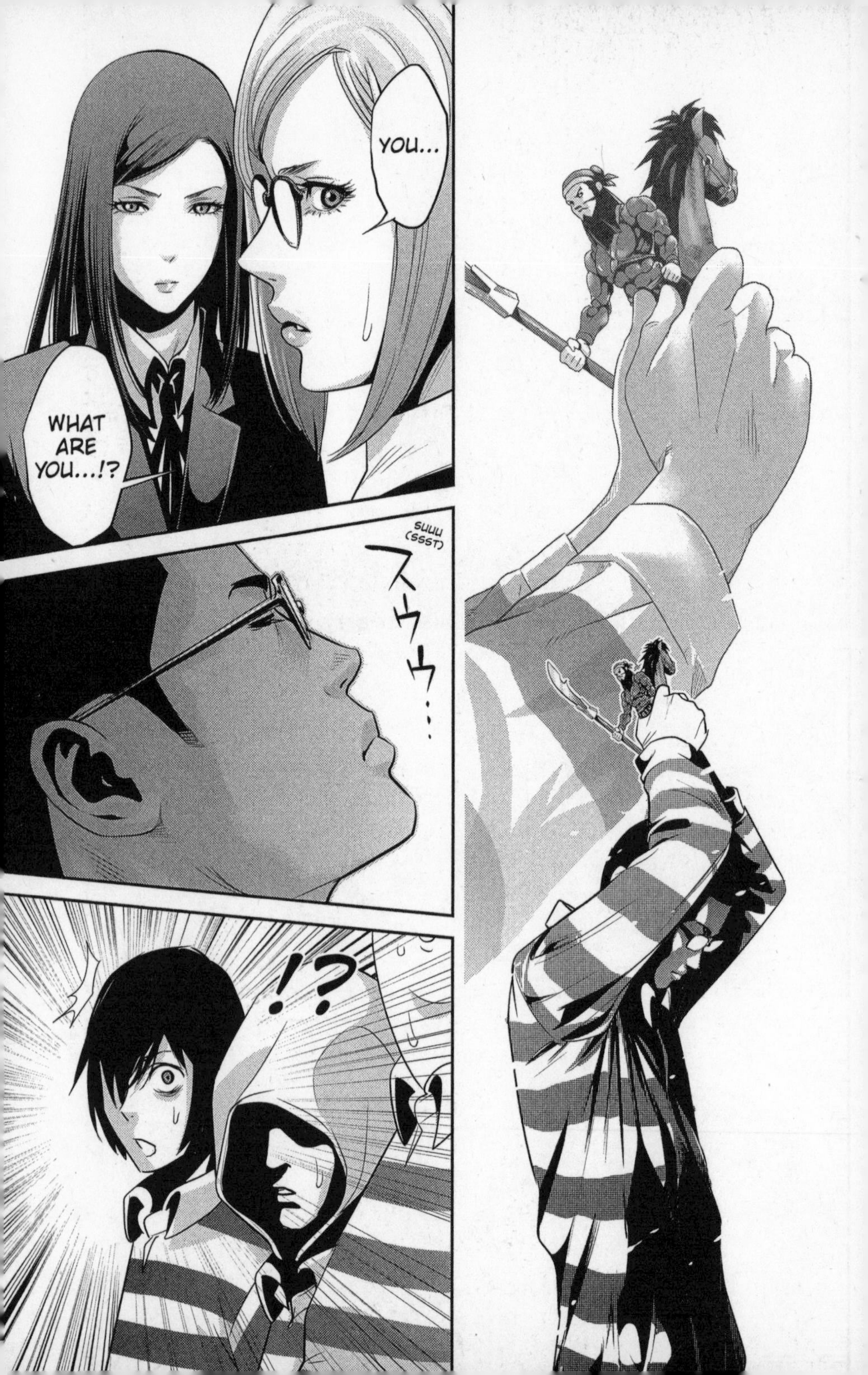
YOU...
WHAT ARE YOU...!?
SUUU (SSST)
スゥゥ…
!?

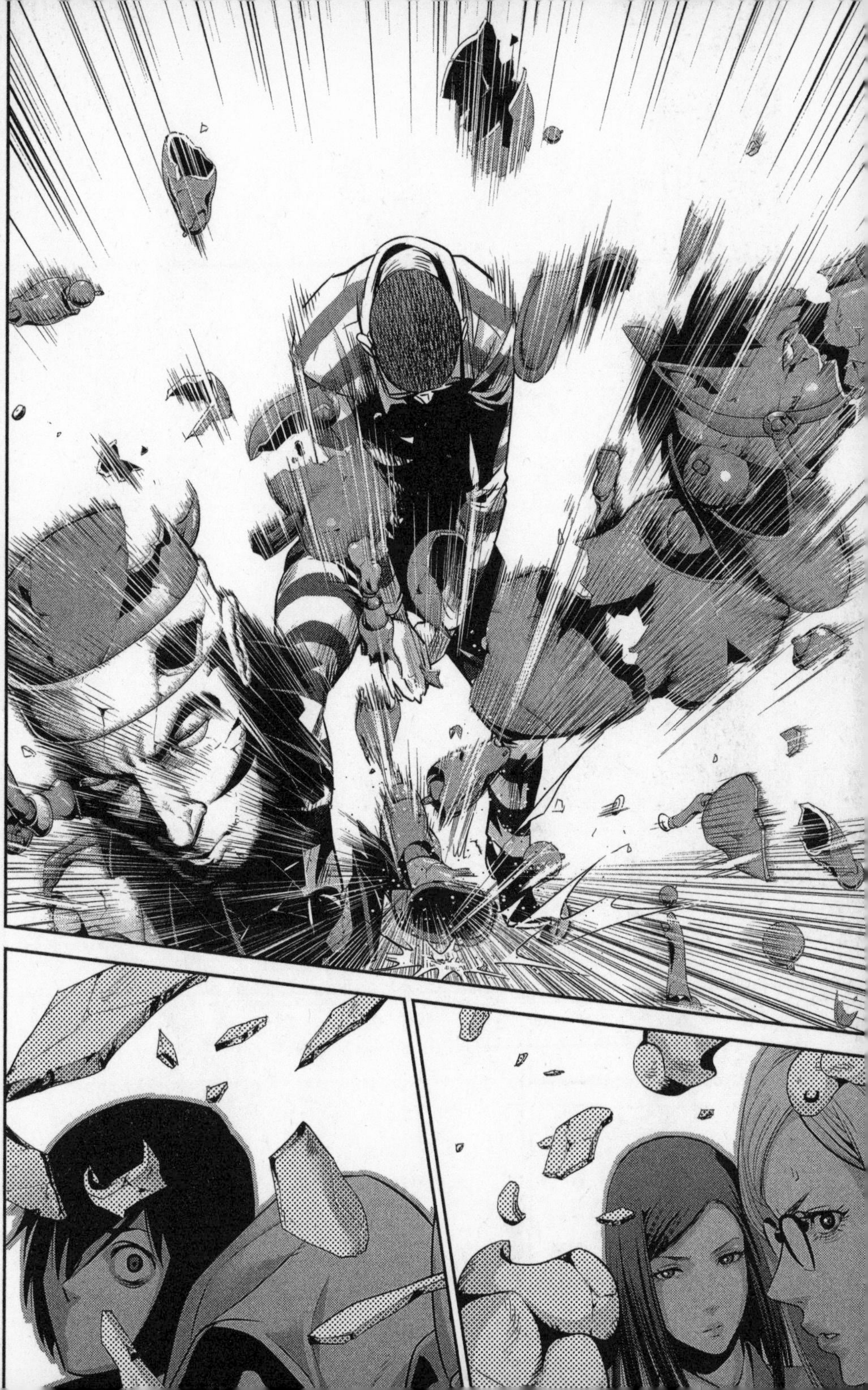

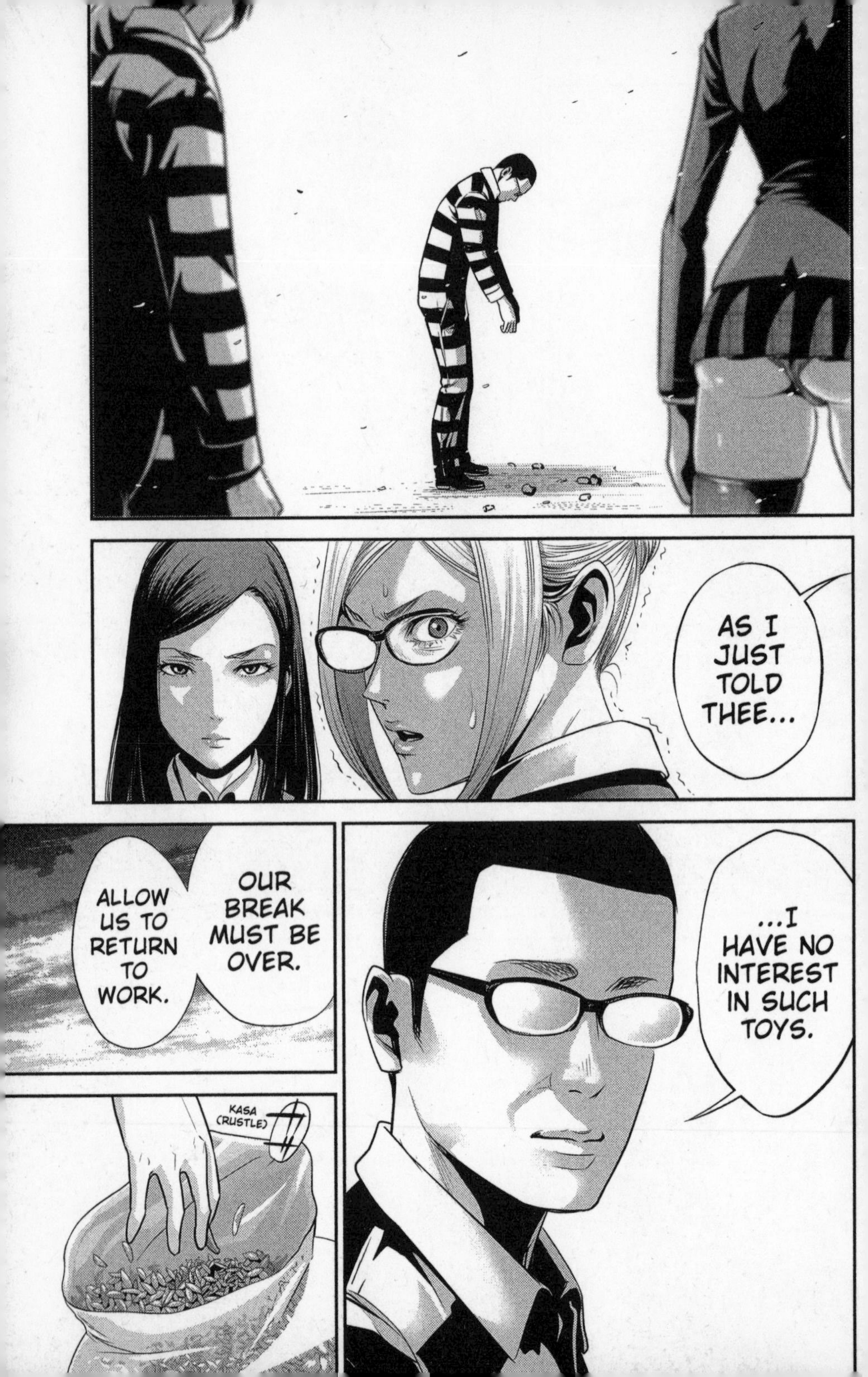
AS I JUST TOLD THEE...
...I HAVE NO INTEREST IN SUCH TOYS.
OUR BREAK MUST BE OVER.
ALLOW US TO RETURN TO WORK.
KASA (RUSTLE)

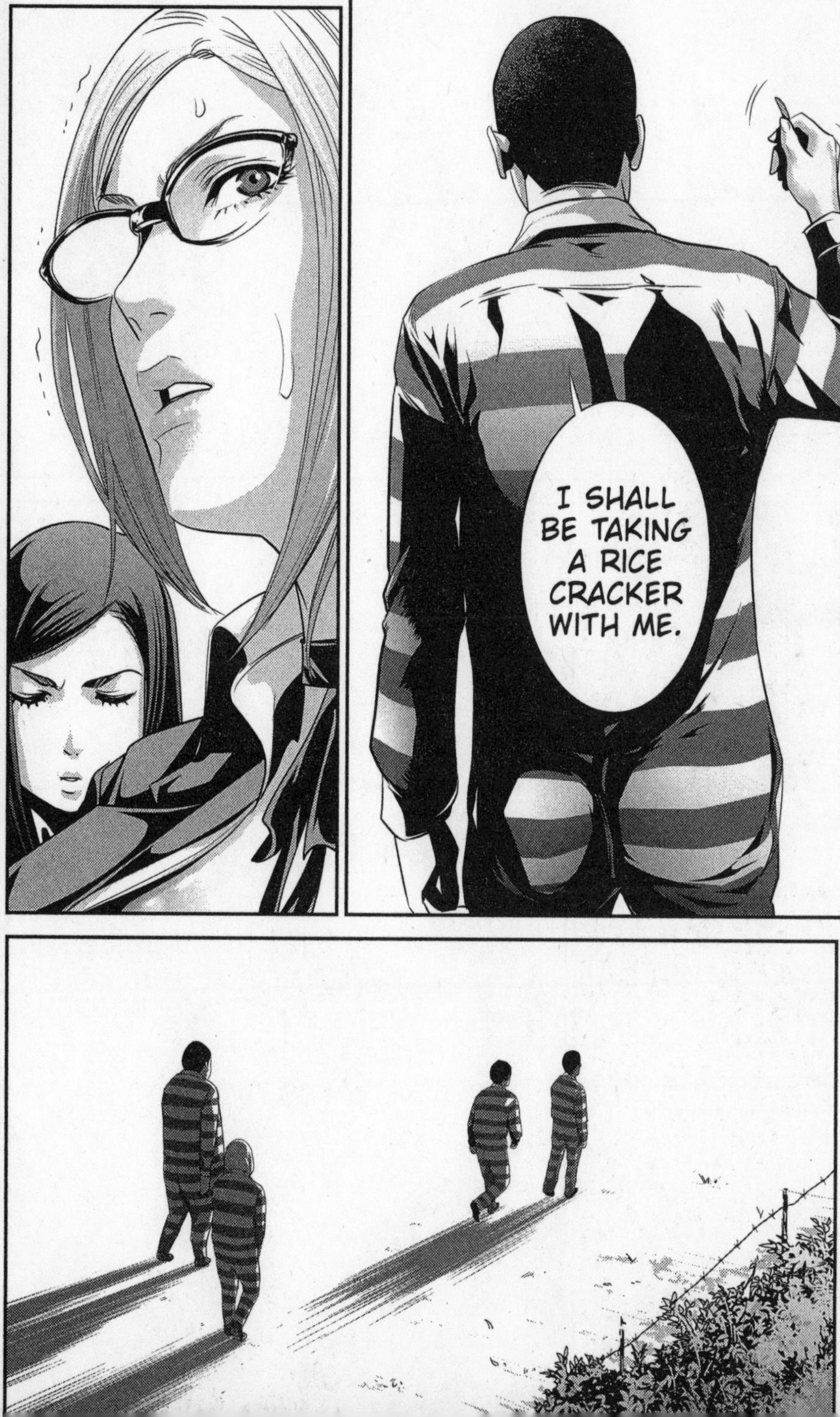
I SHALL BE TAKING A RICE CRACKER WITH ME.

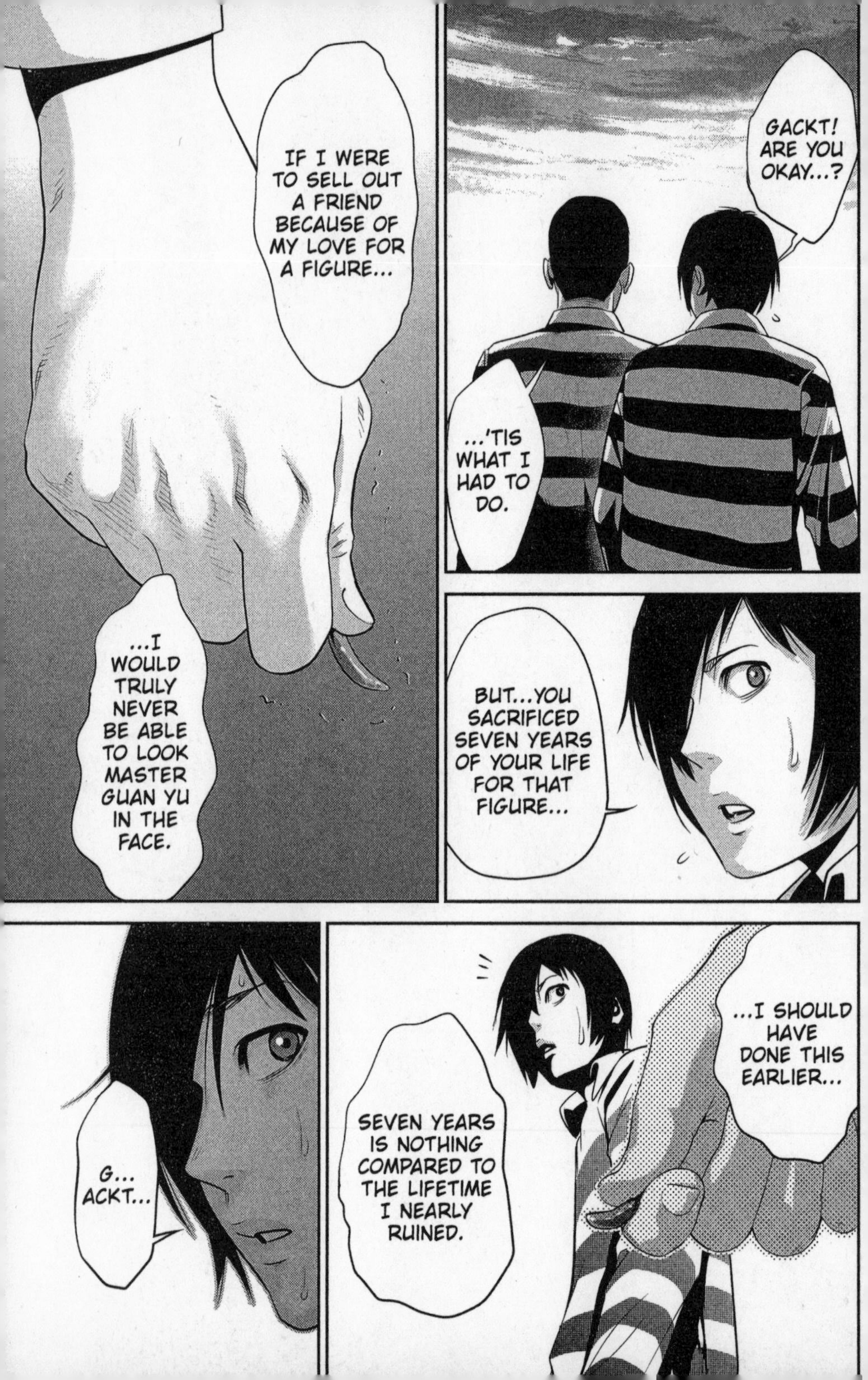
GACKT! ARE YOU OKAY...?
...'TIS WHAT I HAD TO DO.
BUT...YOU SACRIFICED SEVEN YEARS OF YOUR LIFE FOR THAT FIGURE...
IF I WERE TO SELL OUT A FRIEND BECAUSE OF MY LOVE FOR A FIGURE...
...I WOULD TRULY NEVER BE ABLE TO LOOK MASTER GUAN YU IN THE FACE.
...I SHOULD HAVE DONE THIS EARLIER...
SEVEN YEARS IS NOTHING COMPARED TO THE LIFETIME I NEARLY RUINED.
G... ACKT...

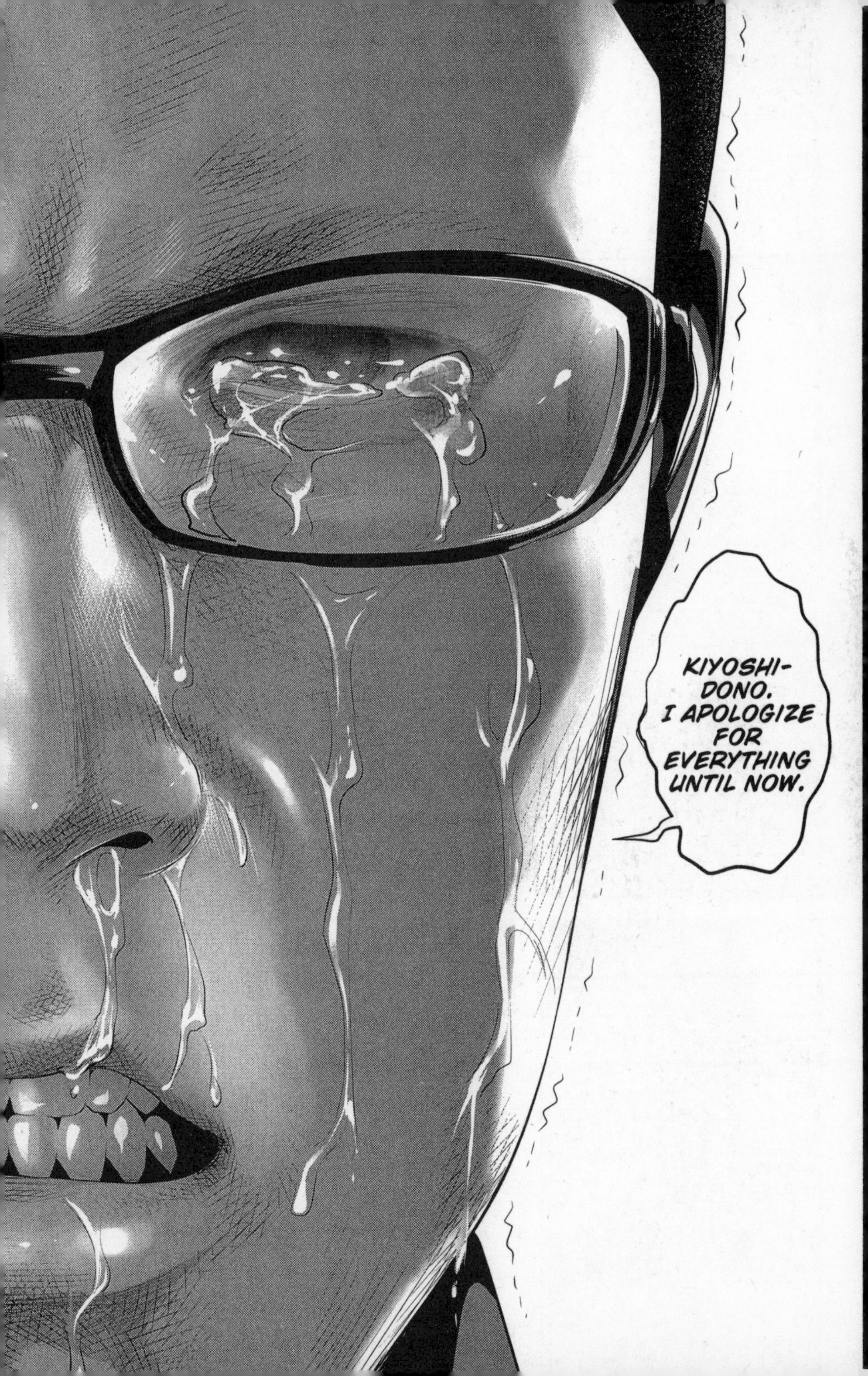
KIYOSHI-DONO. I APOLOGIZE FOR EVERYTHING UNTIL NOW.

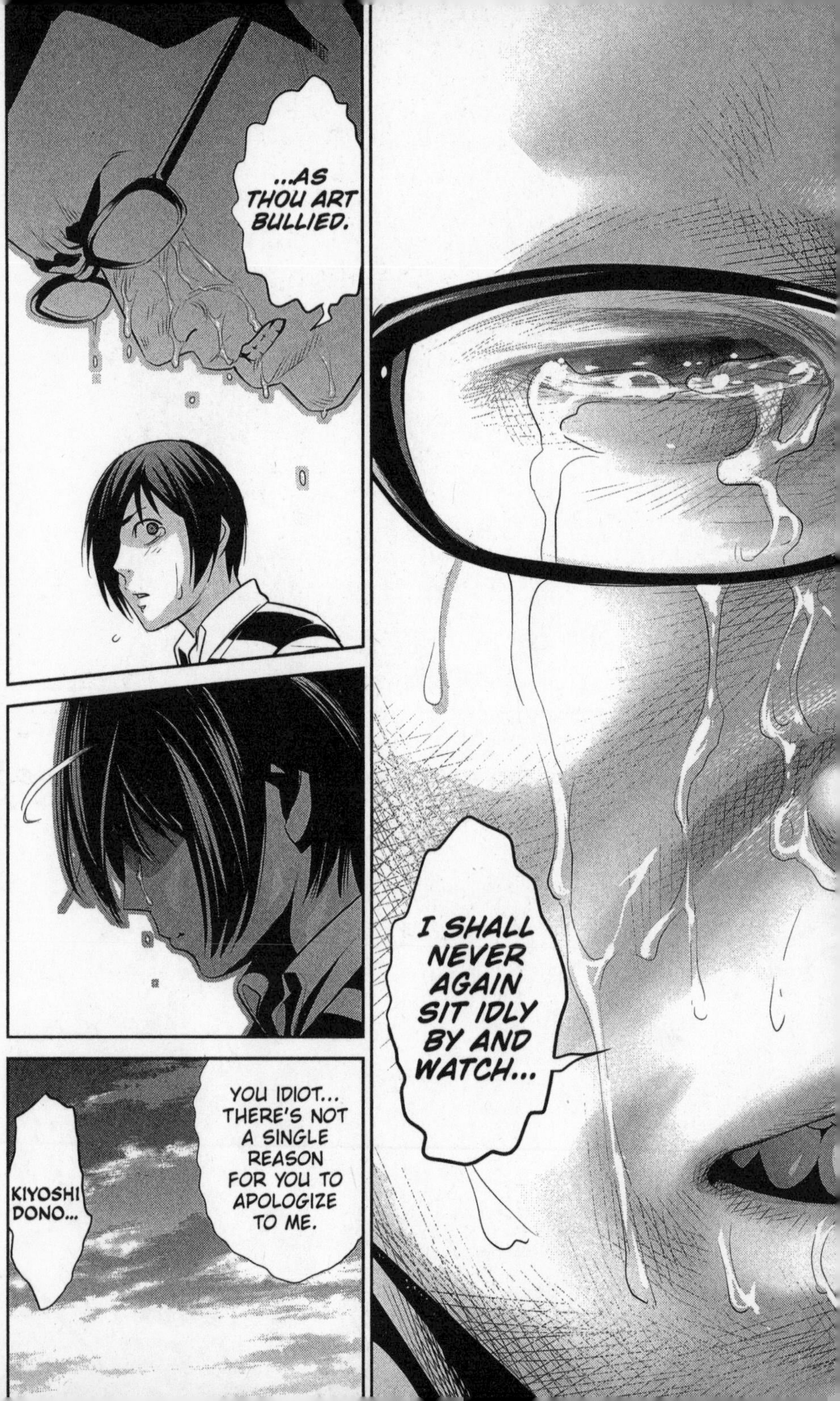
I SHALL NEVER AGAIN SIT IDLY BY AND WATCH...
...AS THOU ART BULLIED.
YOU IDIOT... THERE'S NOT A SINGLE REASON FOR YOU TO APOLOGIZE TO ME.
KIYOSHI DONO...

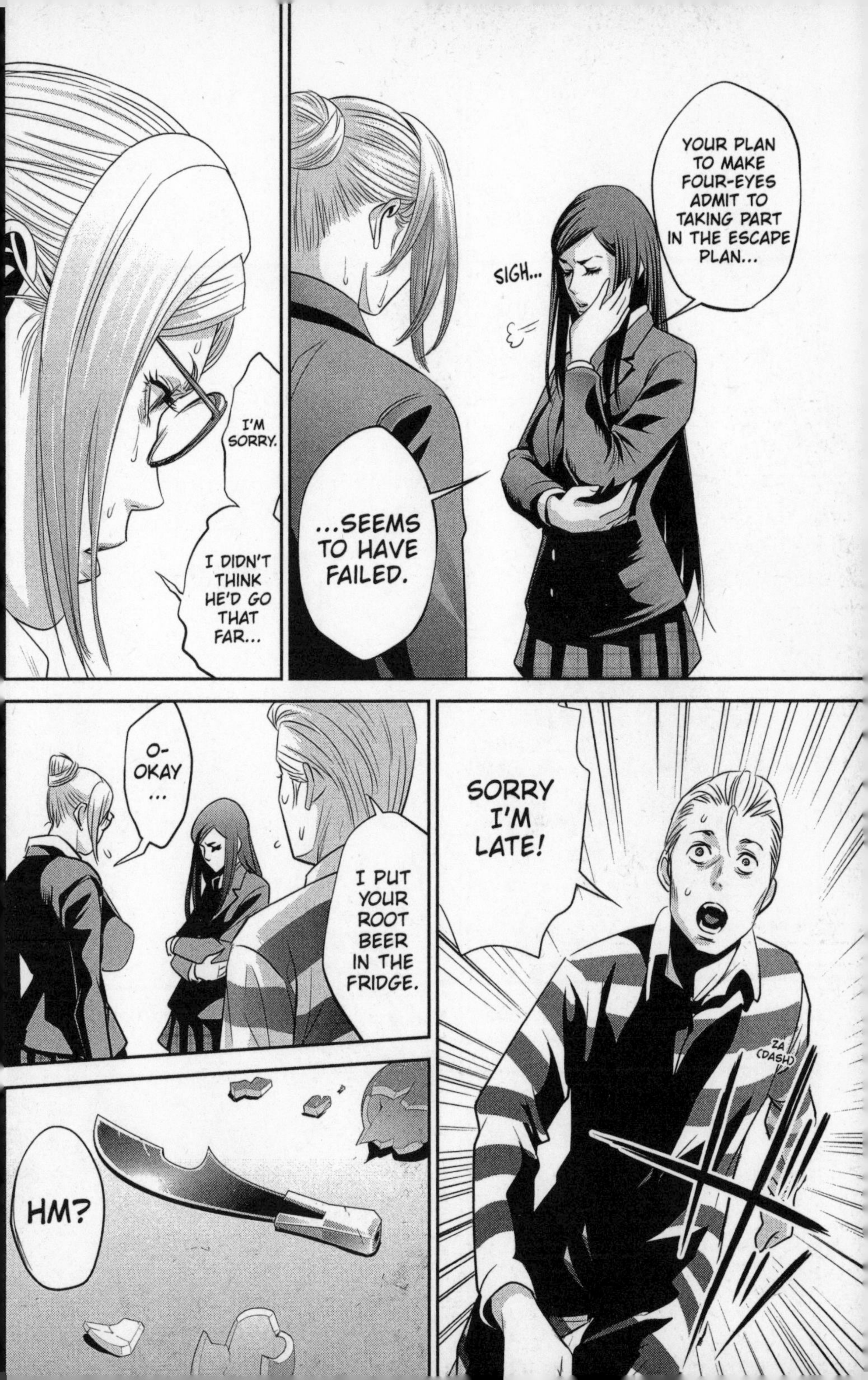
YOUR PLAN TO MAKE FOUR-EYES ADMIT TO TAKING PART IN THE ESCAPE PLAN...
SIGH...
...SEEMS TO HAVE FAILED.
I'M SORRY.
I DIDN'T THINK HE'D GO THAT FAR...
SORRY I'M LATE!
ZA (DASH)
I PUT YOUR ROOT BEER IN THE FRIDGE.
O-OKAY ...
HM?

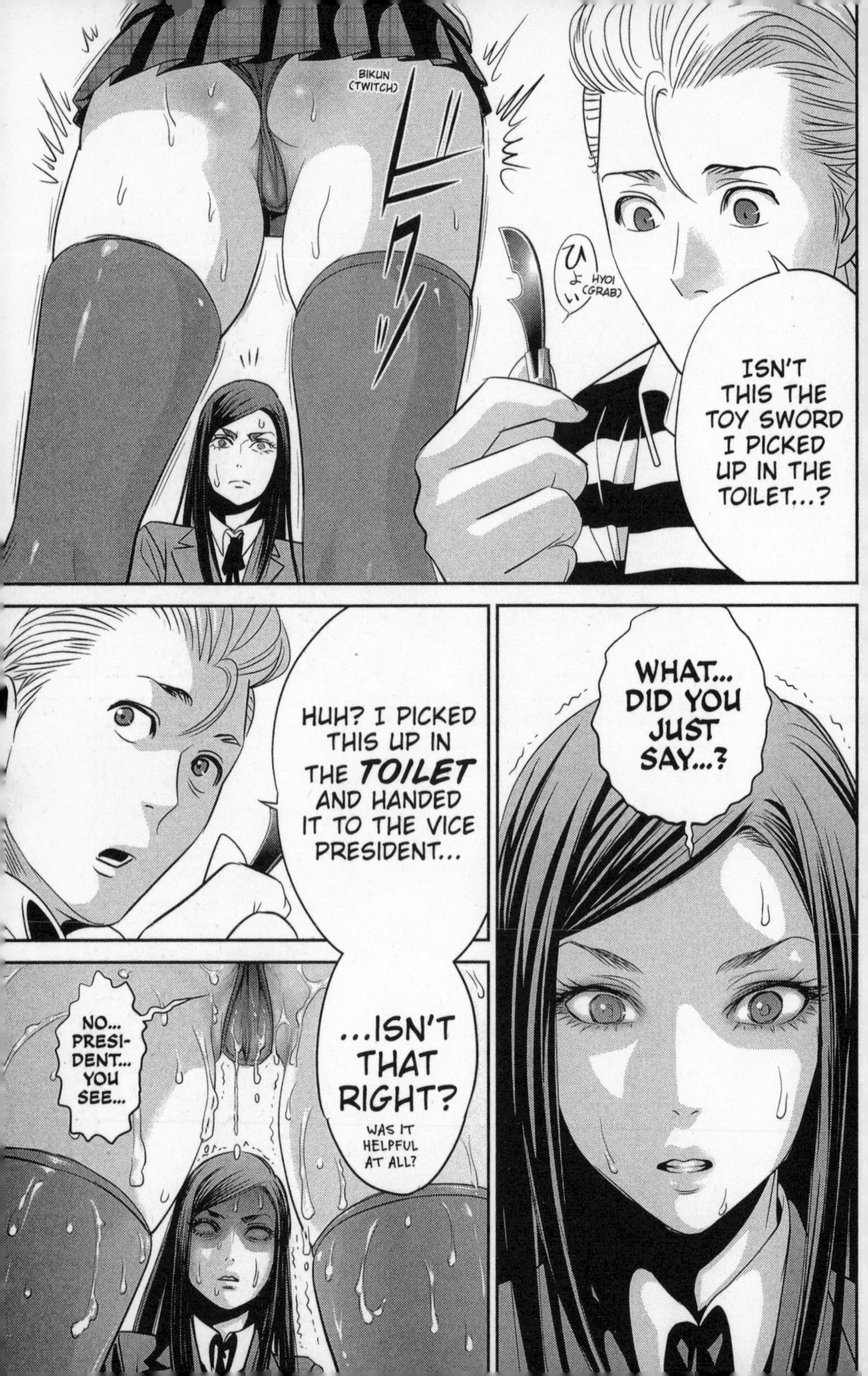
ISN'T THIS THE TOY SWORD I PICKED UP IN THE TOILET...?
ひょい
HYOI (GRAB)
BIKUN (TWITCH)
HUH? I PICKED THIS UP IN THE TOILET AND HANDED IT TO THE VICE PRESIDENT...
...ISN'T THAT RIGHT?
WAS IT HELPFUL AT ALL?
WHAT... DID YOU JUST SAY...?
NO... PRESIDENT... YOU SEE...

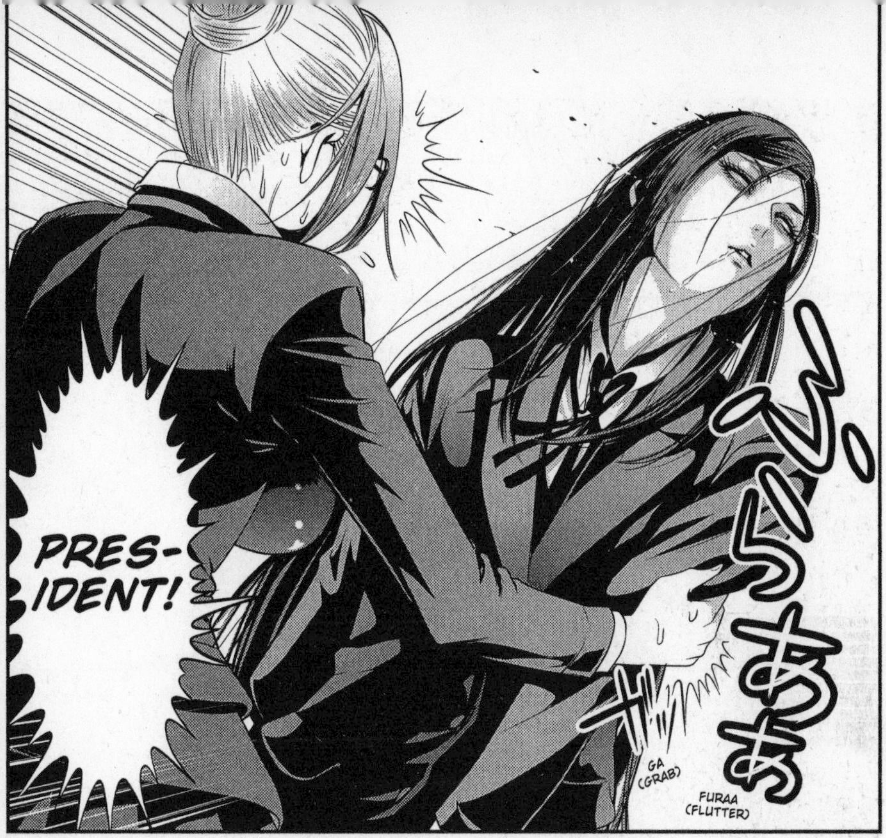
FURAA (FLUTTER)
GA (GRAB)
PRES-IDENT!
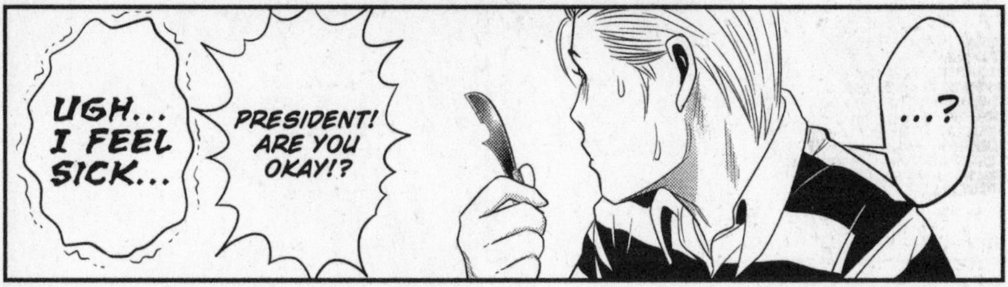
...?
PRESIDENT! ARE YOU OKAY!?
UGH... I FEEL SICK...
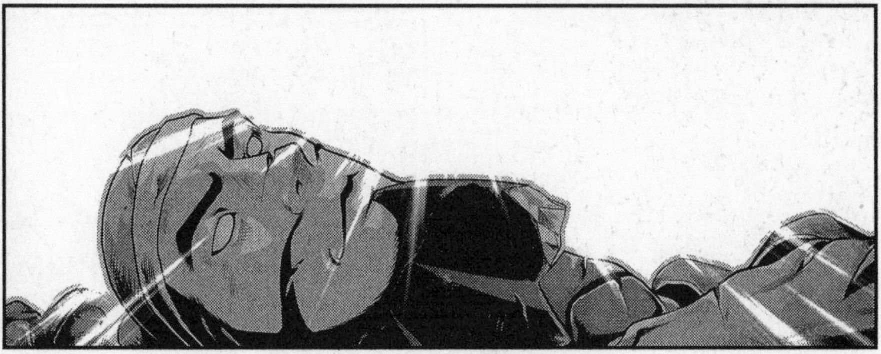

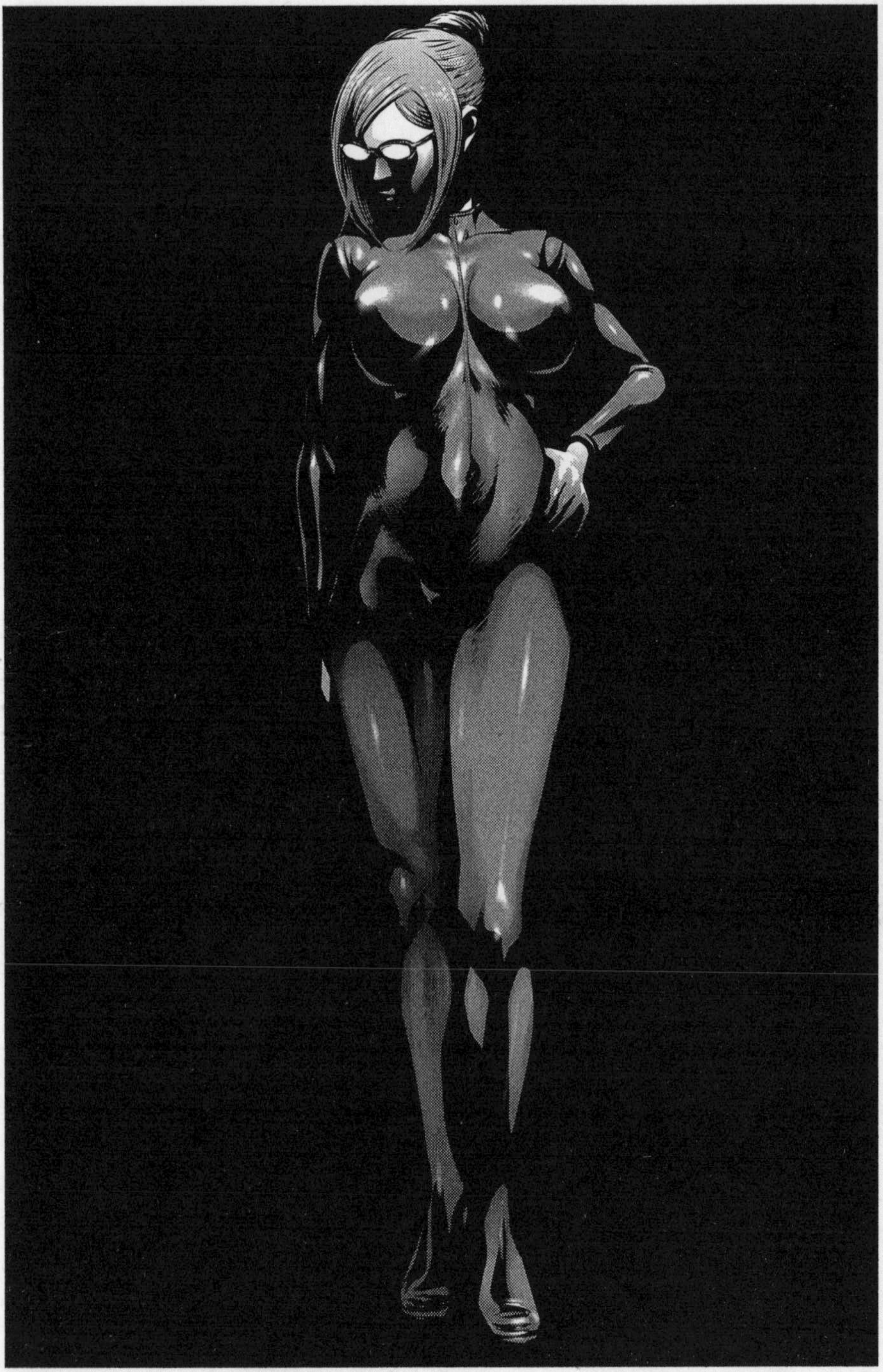

CHAPTER 46: BREATHLESS

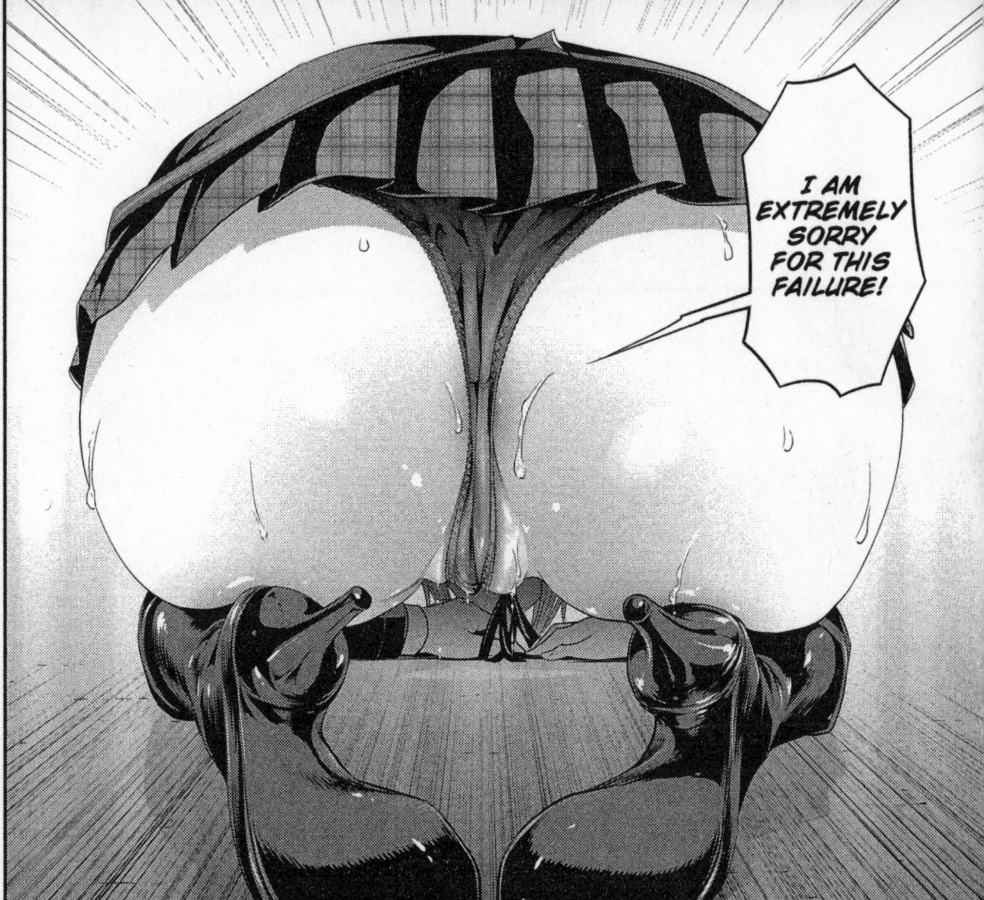
I AM EXTREMELY SORRY FOR THIS FAILURE!

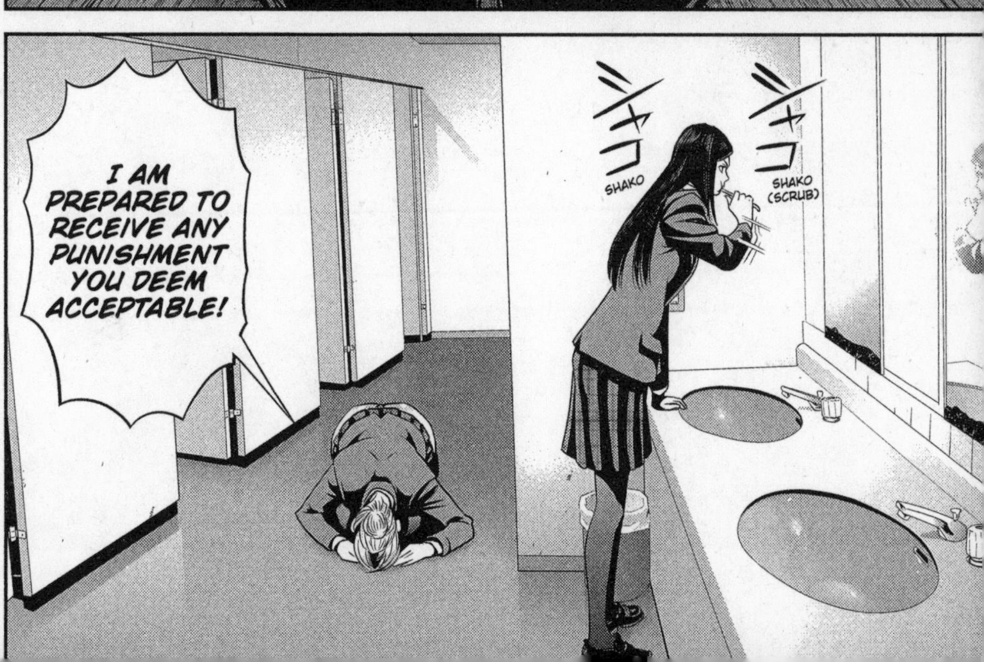
シャコ
SHAKO (SCRUB)
シャコ
SHAKO
I AM PREPARED TO RECEIVE ANY PUNISHMENT YOU DEEM ACCEPTABLE!

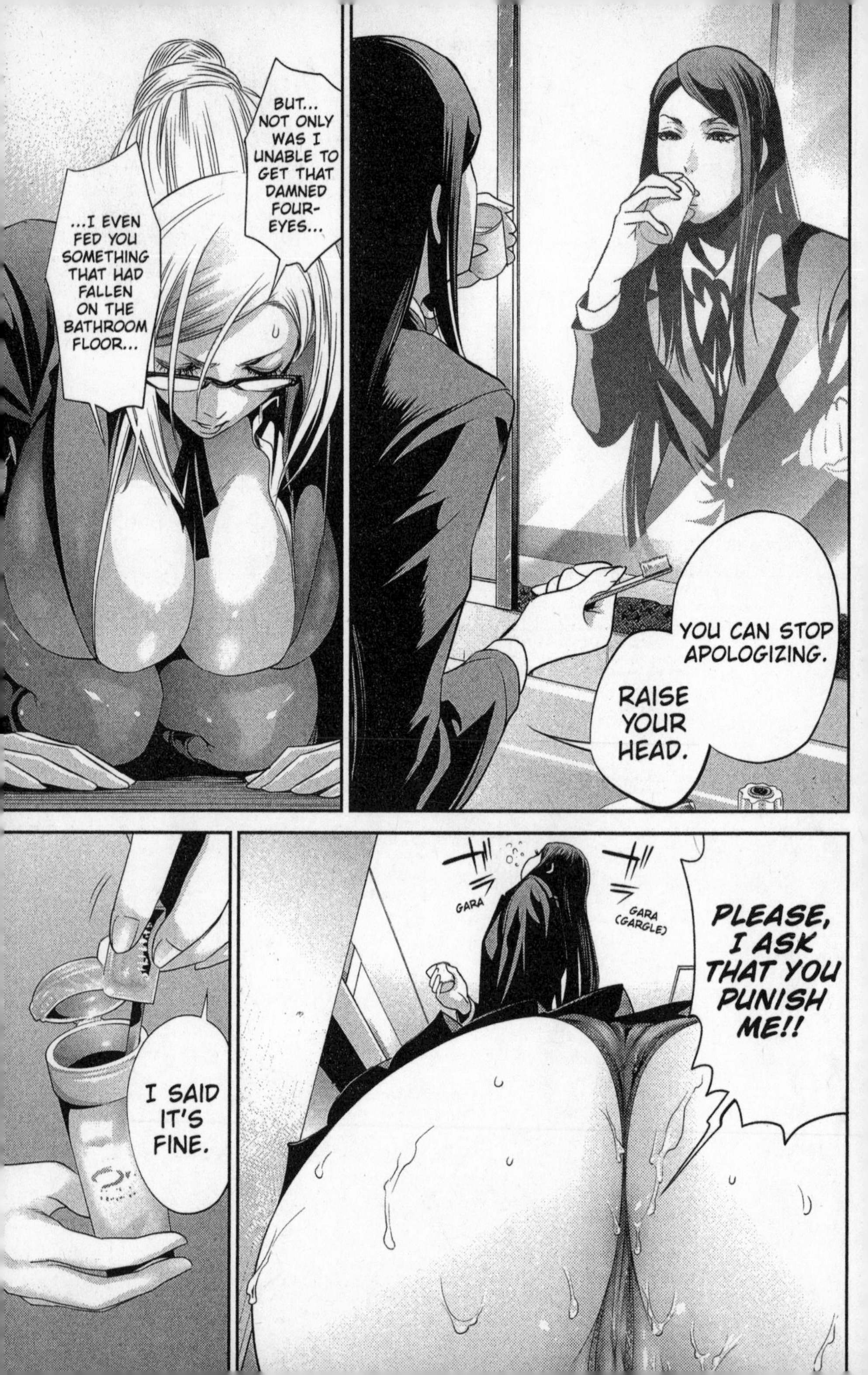
YOU CAN STOP APOLOGIZING.
RAISE YOUR HEAD.
BUT... NOT ONLY WAS I UNABLE TO GET THAT DAMNED FOUR-EYES...
...I EVEN FED YOU SOMETHING THAT HAD FALLEN ON THE BATHROOM FLOOR...
PLEASE, I ASK THAT YOU PUNISH ME!!
GARA (GARGLE)
GARA
I SAID IT'S FINE.

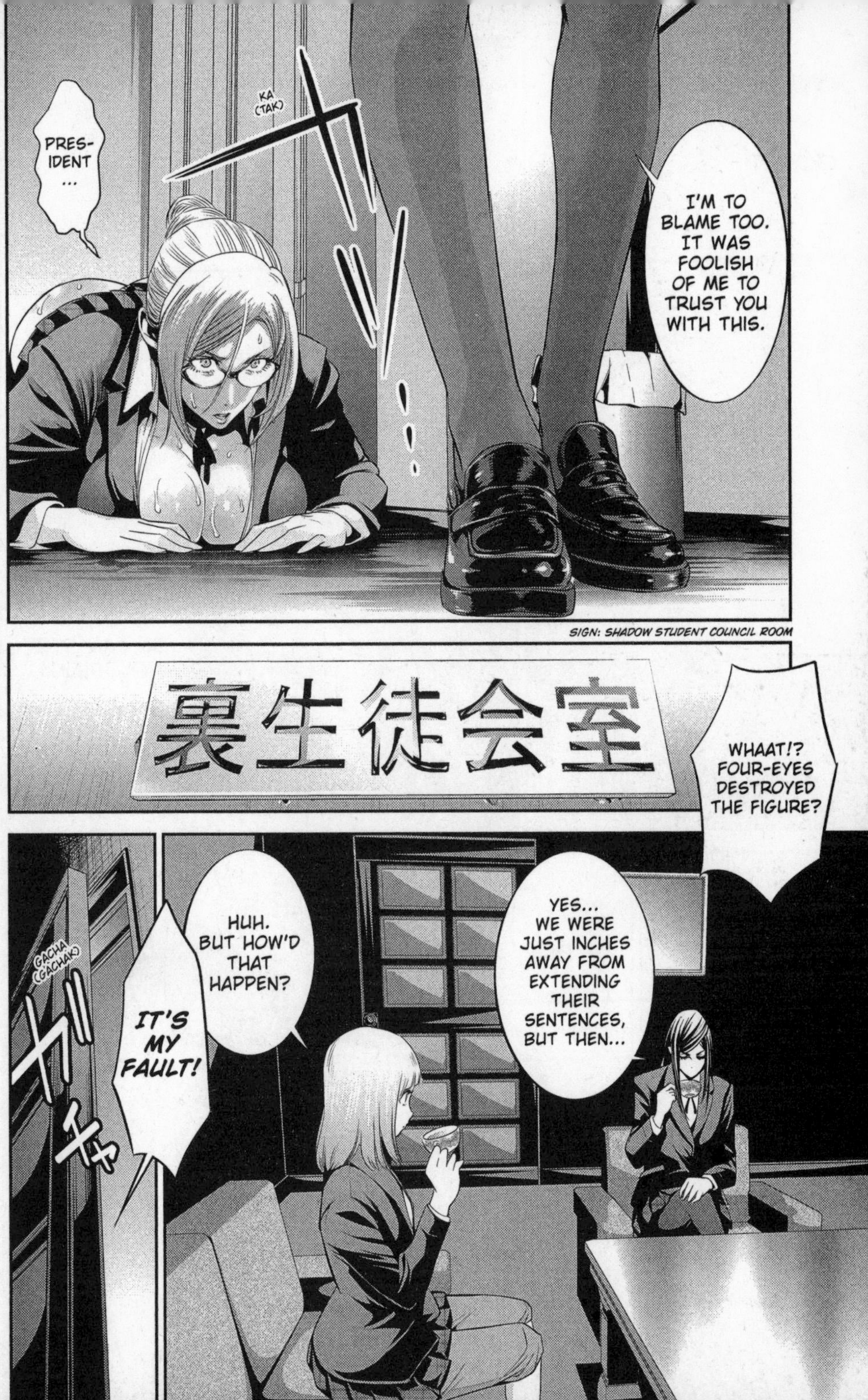
I'M TO BLAME TOO. IT WAS FOOLISH OF ME TO TRUST YOU WITH THIS.
KA (TAK)
PRES-IDENT ...
SIGN: SHADOW STUDENT COUNCIL ROOM
裏生徒会室
WHAAT!? FOUR-EYES DESTROYED THE FIGURE?
YES... WE WERE JUST INCHES AWAY FROM EXTENDING THEIR SENTENCES, BUT THEN...
HUH. BUT HOW'D THAT HAPPEN?
IT'S MY FAULT!
GACHA (GACHAK)

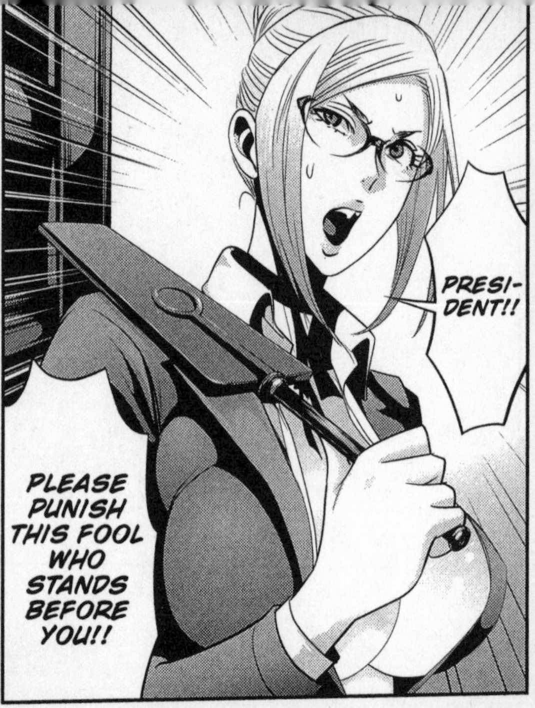
PRESI-DENT!!
PLEASE PUNISH THIS FOOL WHO STANDS BEFORE YOU!!
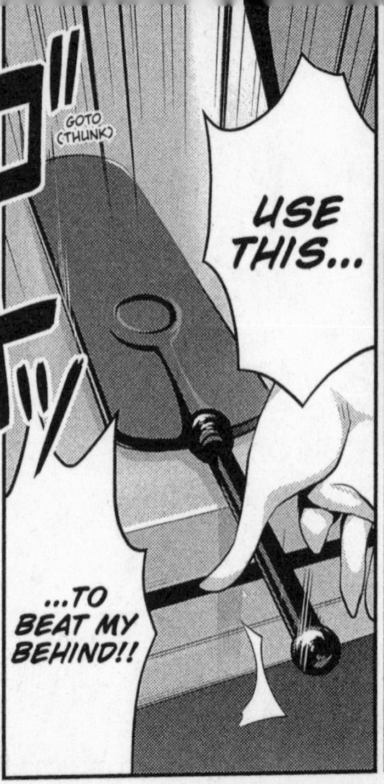
GOTO (THUNK)
USE THIS...
...TO BEAT MY BEHIND!!
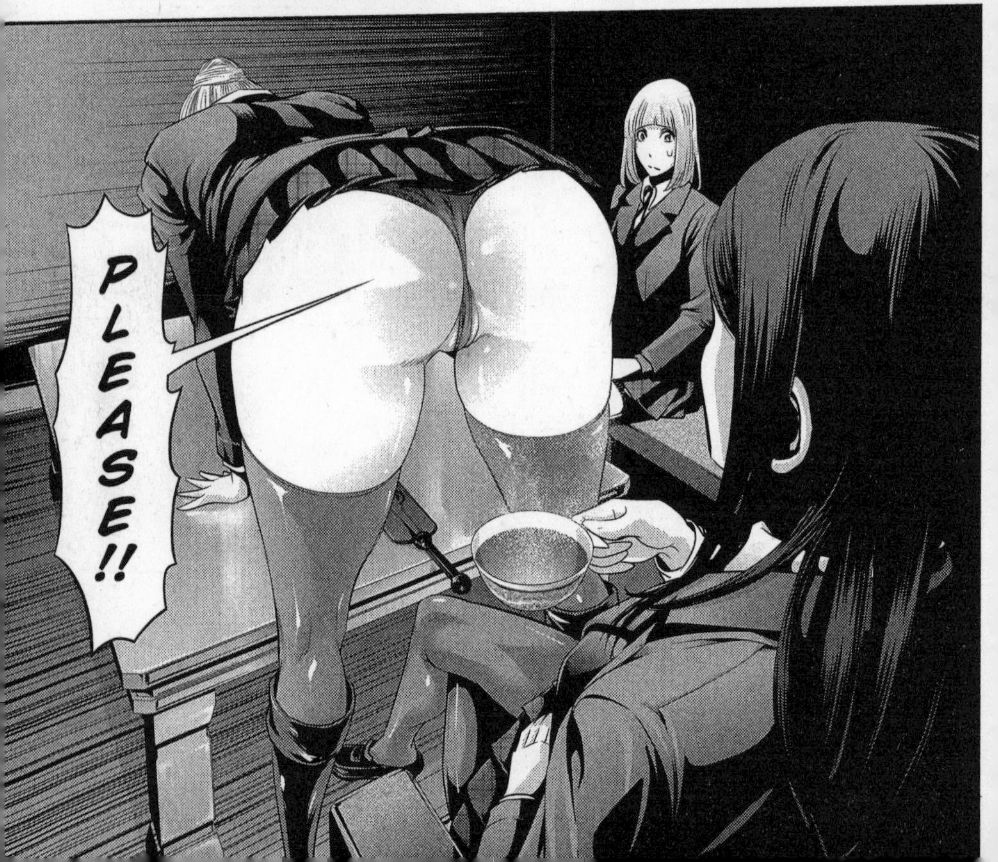
PLEASE!!

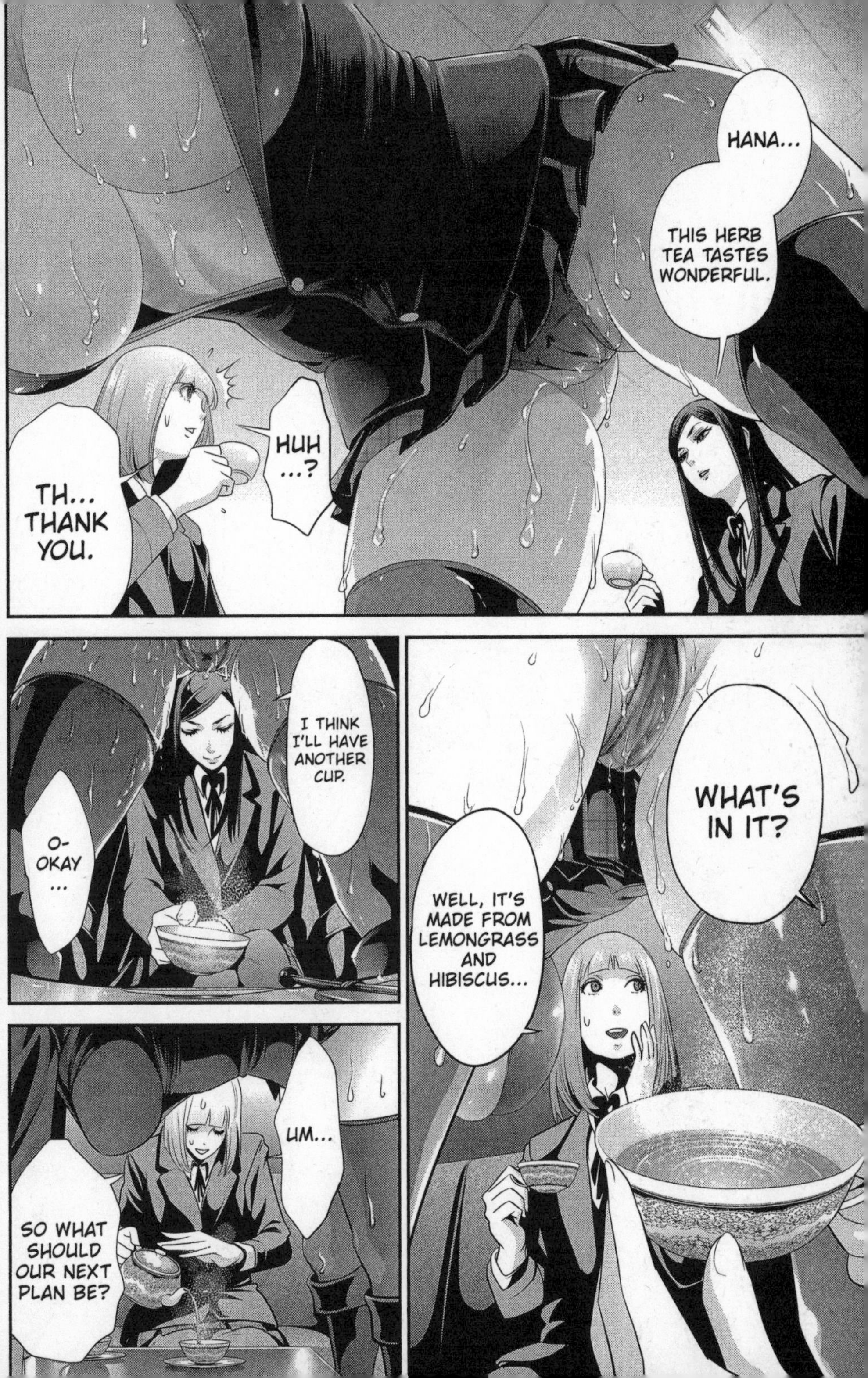
HANA...
THIS HERB TEA TASTES WONDERFUL.
HUH ...?
TH... THANK YOU.
WHAT'S IN IT?
WELL, IT'S MADE FROM LEMONGRASS AND HIBISCUS...
I THINK I'LL HAVE ANOTHER CUP.
O-OKAY ...
UM...
SO WHAT SHOULD OUR NEXT PLAN BE?

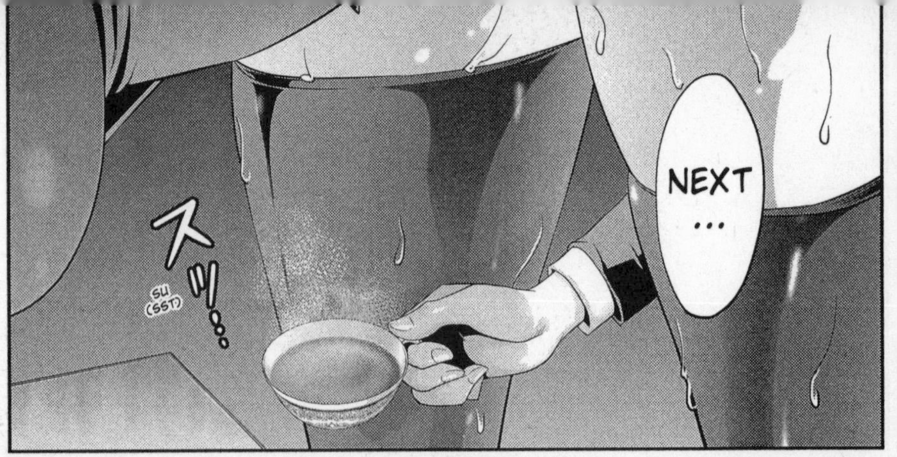
NEXT ...
スッ...
SU (SST)
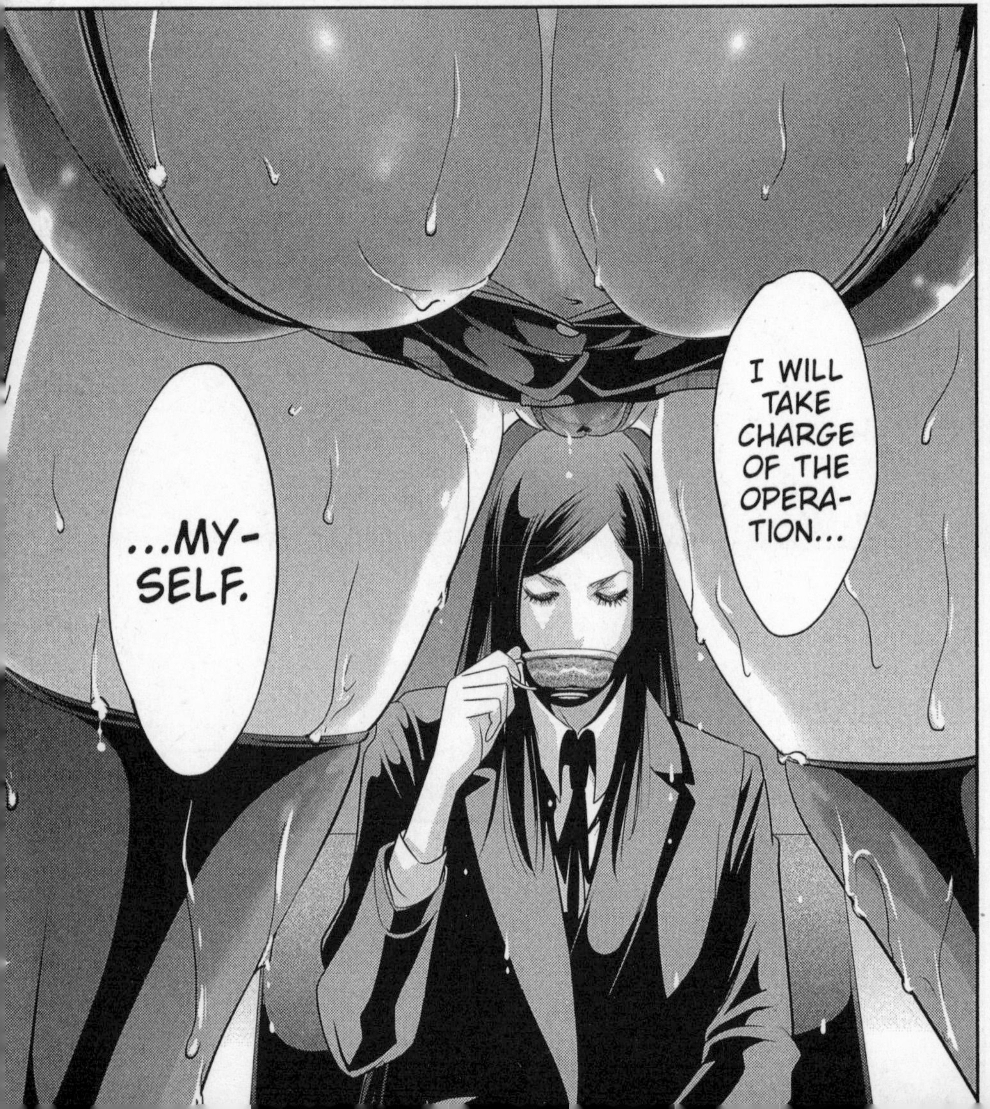
I WILL TAKE CHARGE OF THE OPERATION...
...MY-SELF.

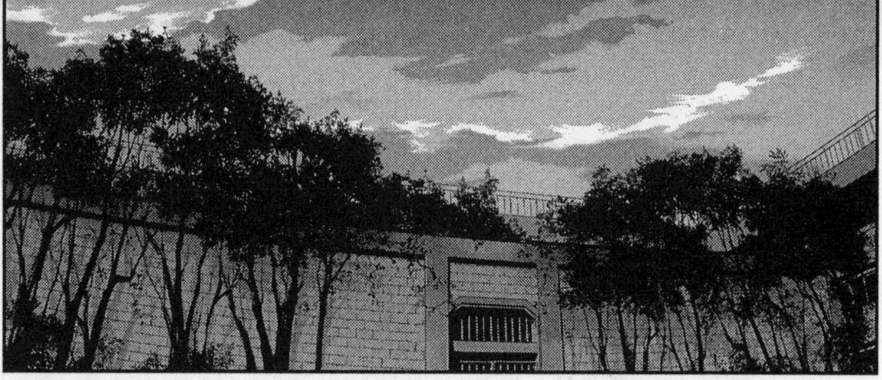
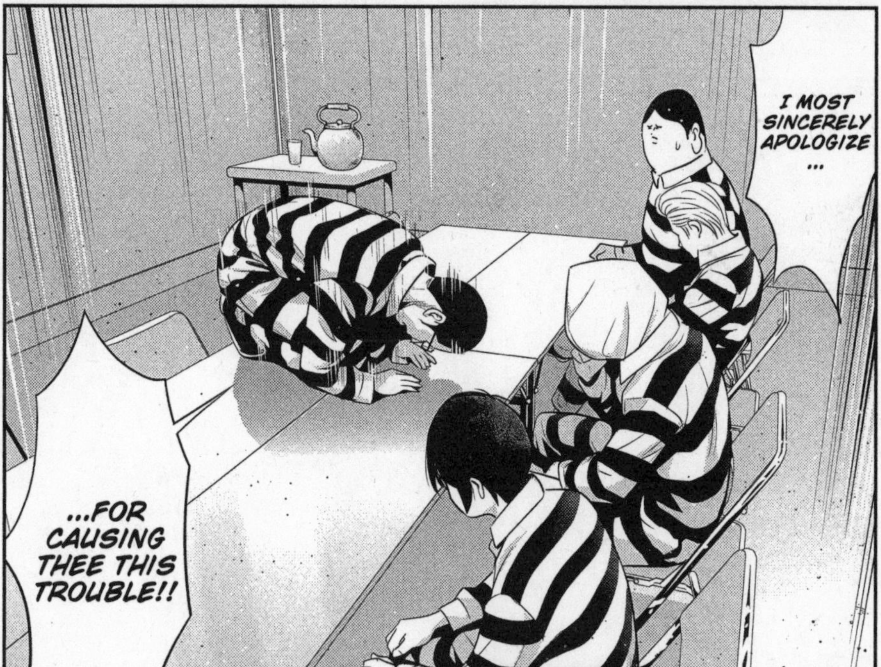
I MOST SINCERELY APOLOGIZE...
...FOR CAUSING THEE THIS TROUBLE!!
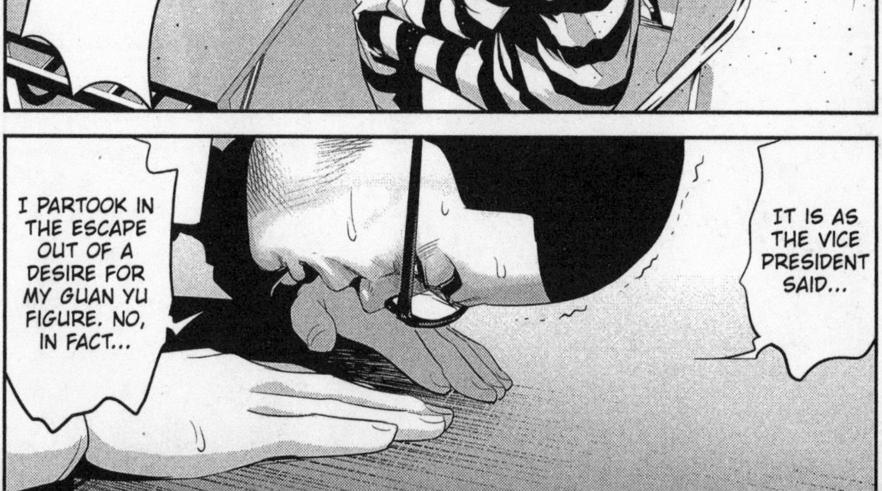
IT IS AS THE VICE PRESIDENT SAID...
I PARTOOK IN THE ESCAPE OUT OF A DESIRE FOR MY GUAN YU FIGURE. NO, IN FACT...

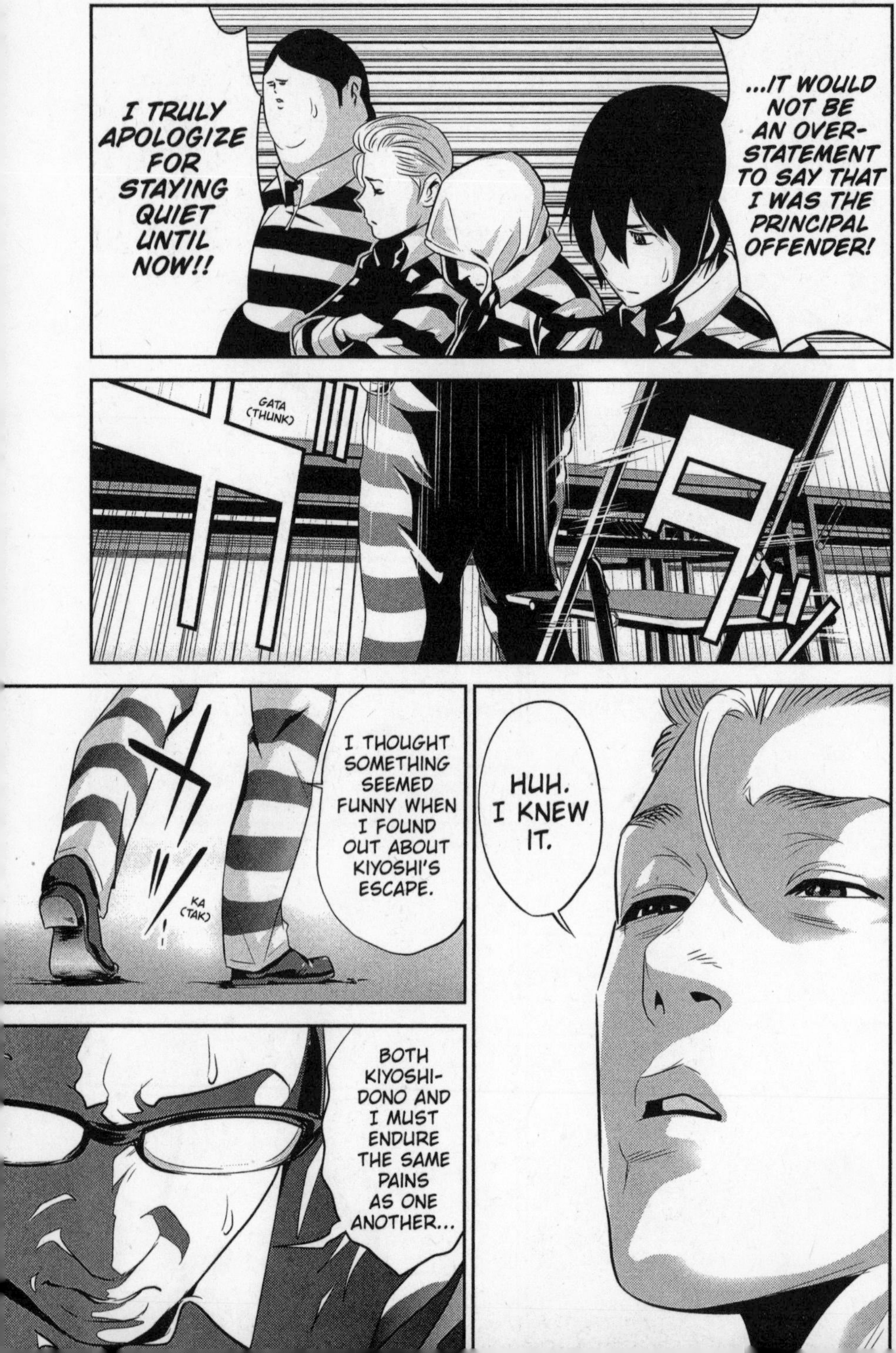
...IT WOULD NOT BE AN OVER-STATEMENT TO SAY THAT I WAS THE PRINCIPAL OFFENDER!
I TRULY APOLOGIZE FOR STAYING QUIET UNTIL NOW!!
GATA (THUNK)
HUH. I KNEW IT.
I THOUGHT SOMETHING SEEMED FUNNY WHEN I FOUND OUT ABOUT KIYOSHI'S ESCAPE.
KA (TAK)
BOTH KIYOSHI-DONO AND I MUST ENDURE THE SAME PAINS AS ONE ANOTHER...

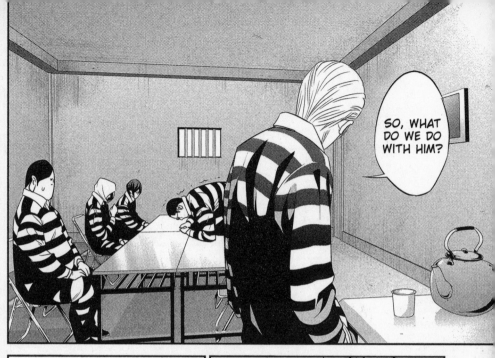

SO, WHAT DO WE DO WITH HIM?

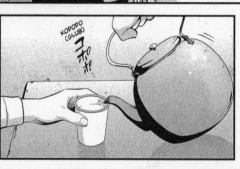

KOPODO (GLUB)

...ANY-THING.

I'M NOT DOING...

-KOFF-

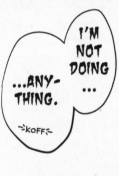

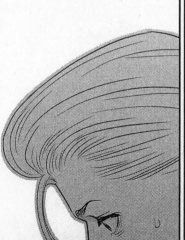

WE'VE GOT A TRAITOR ON OUR HANDS.

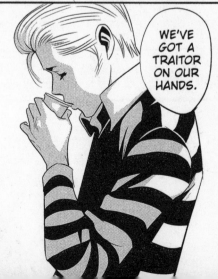

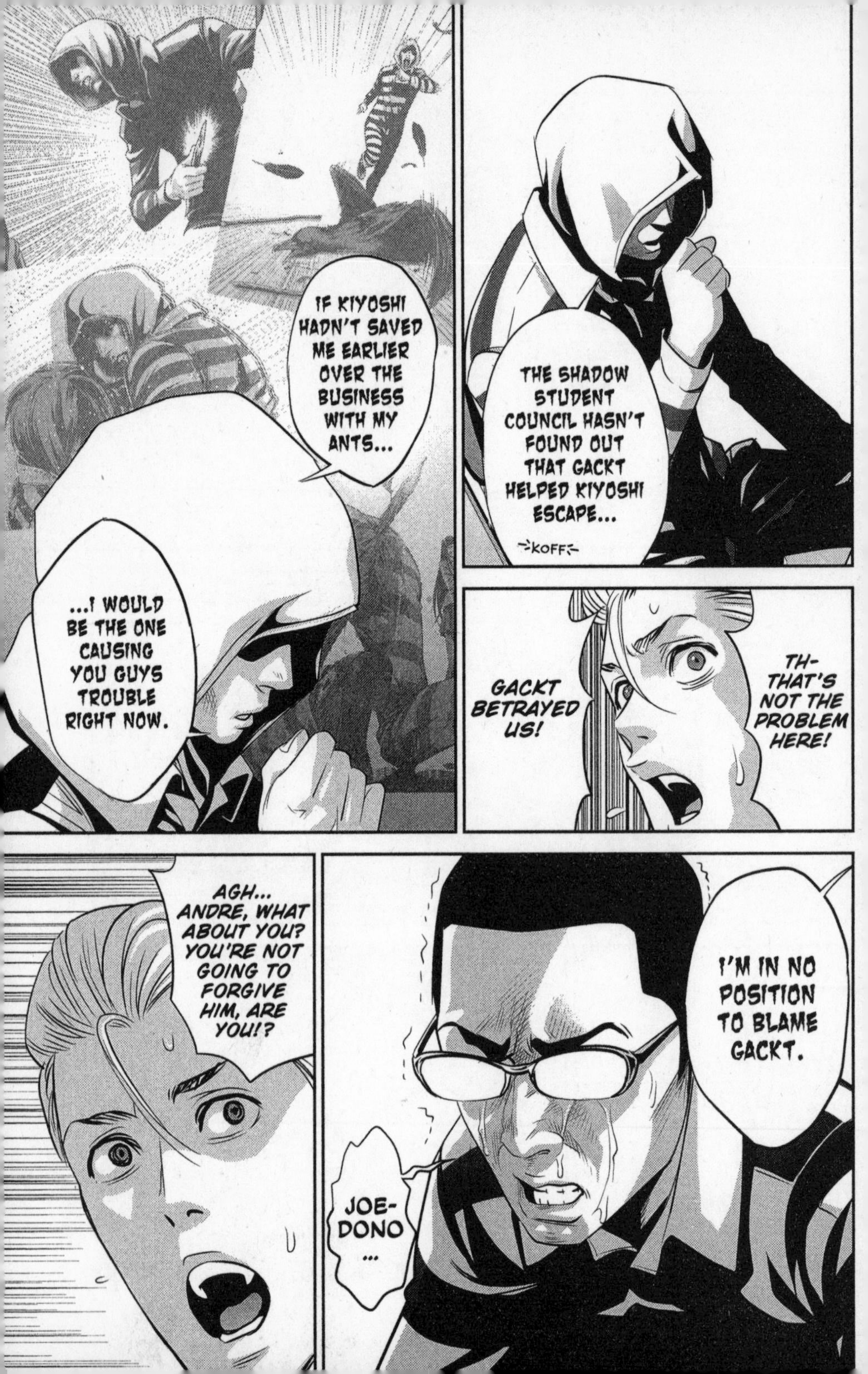
IF KIYOSHI HADN'T SAVED ME EARLIER OVER THE BUSINESS WITH MY ANTS...
...I WOULD BE THE ONE CAUSING YOU GUYS TROUBLE RIGHT NOW.
THE SHADOW STUDENT COUNCIL HASN'T FOUND OUT THAT GACKT HELPED KIYOSHI ESCAPE...
KOFF
GACKT BETRAYED US!
TH-THAT'S NOT THE PROBLEM HERE!
AGH... ANDRE, WHAT ABOUT YOU? YOU'RE NOT GOING TO FORGIVE HIM, ARE YOU!?
I'M IN NO POSITION TO BLAME GACKT.
JOE-DONO...

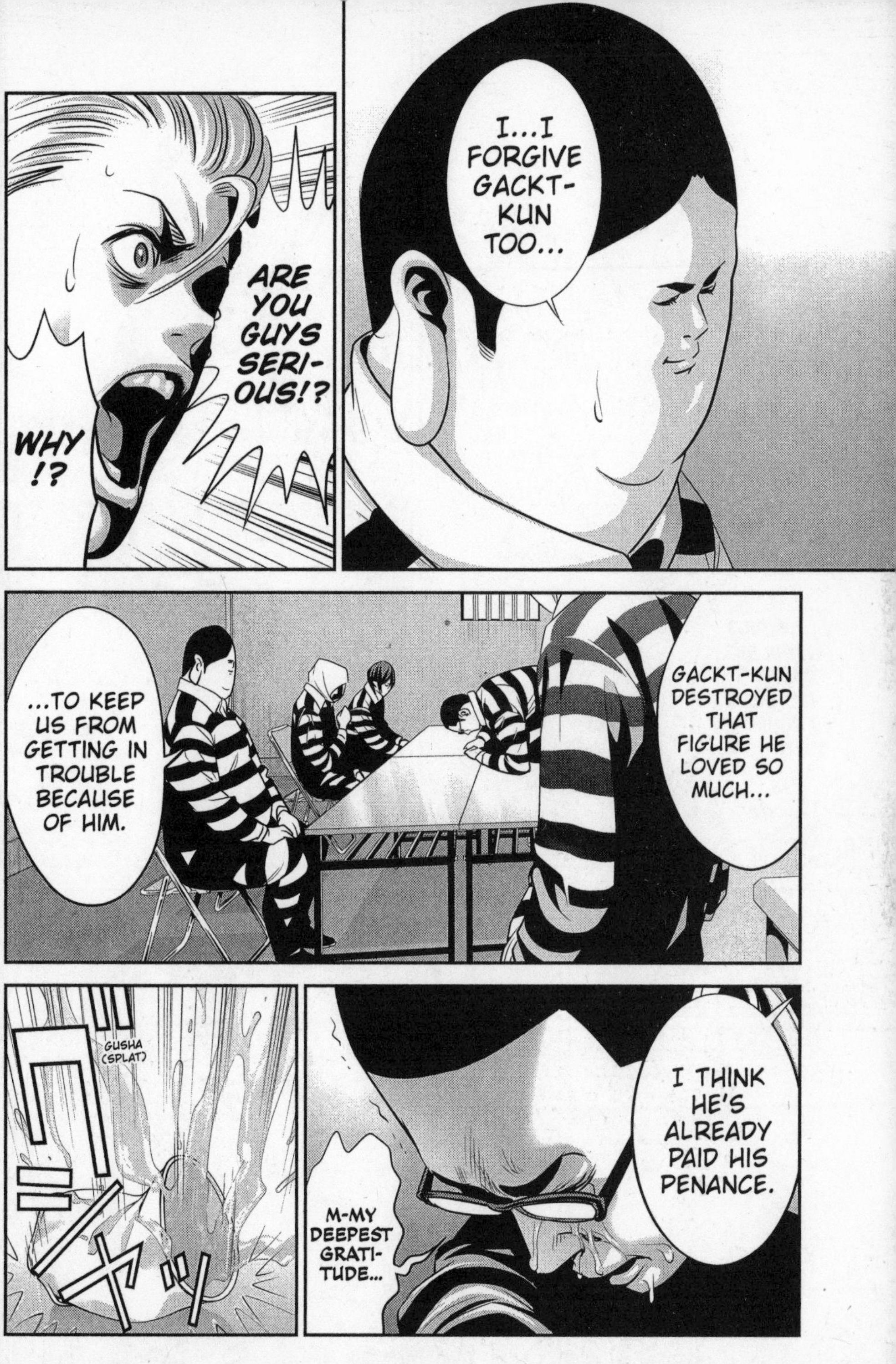
I...I FORGIVE GACKT-KUN TOO...
ARE YOU GUYS SERIOUS!?
WHY!?
GACKT-KUN DESTROYED THAT FIGURE HE LOVED SO MUCH...
...TO KEEP US FROM GETTING IN TROUBLE BECAUSE OF HIM.
I THINK HE'S ALREADY PAID HIS PENANCE.
M-MY DEEPEST GRATITUDE...
GUSHA (SPLAT)

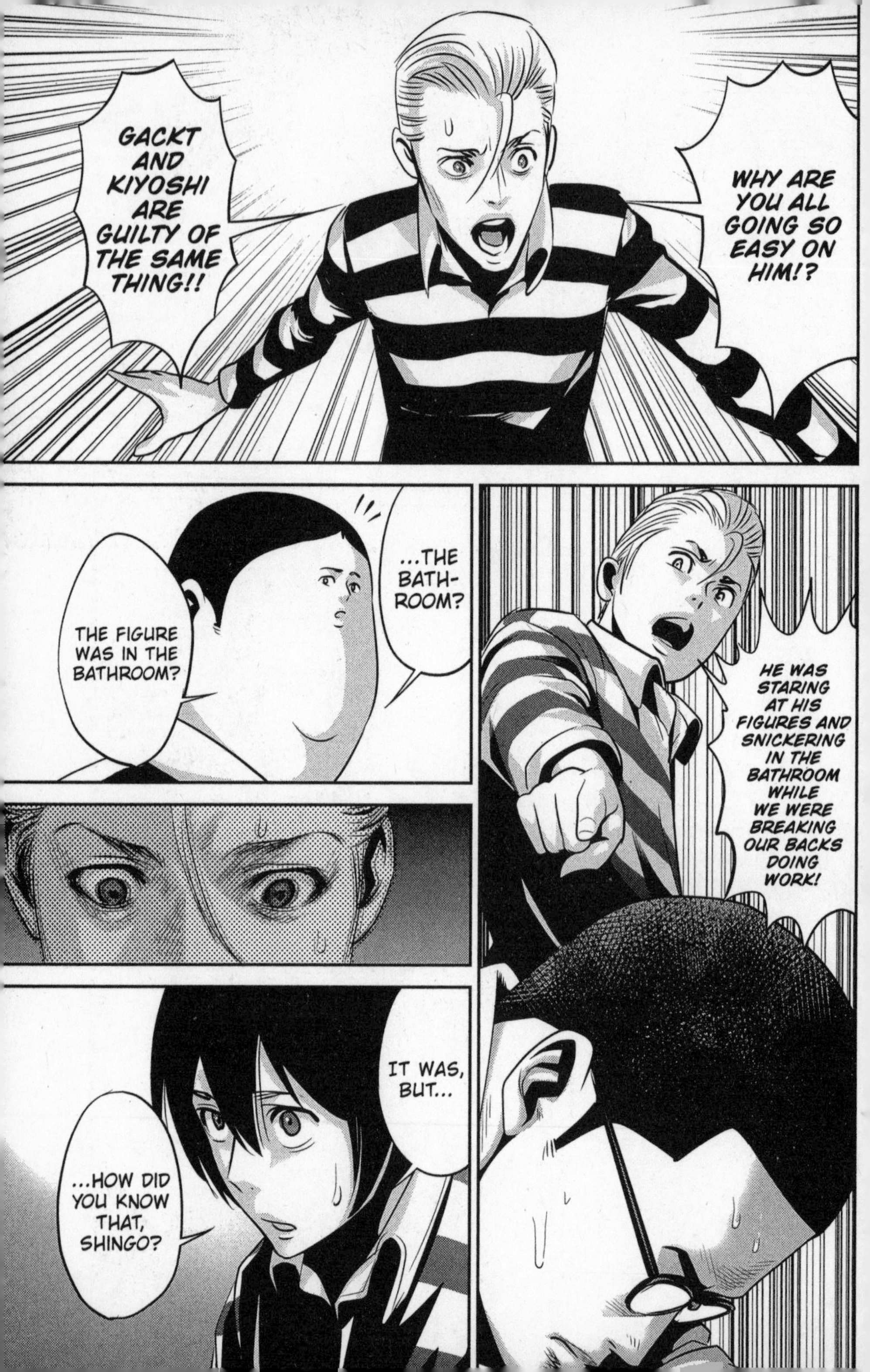
WHY ARE YOU ALL GOING SO EASY ON HIM!?
GACKT AND KIYOSHI ARE GUILTY OF THE SAME THING!!
HE WAS STARING AT HIS FIGURES AND SNICKERING IN THE BATHROOM WHILE WE WERE BREAKING OUR BACKS DOING WORK!
...THE BATH-ROOM?
THE FIGURE WAS IN THE BATHROOM?
IT WAS, BUT...
...HOW DID YOU KNOW THAT, SHINGO?

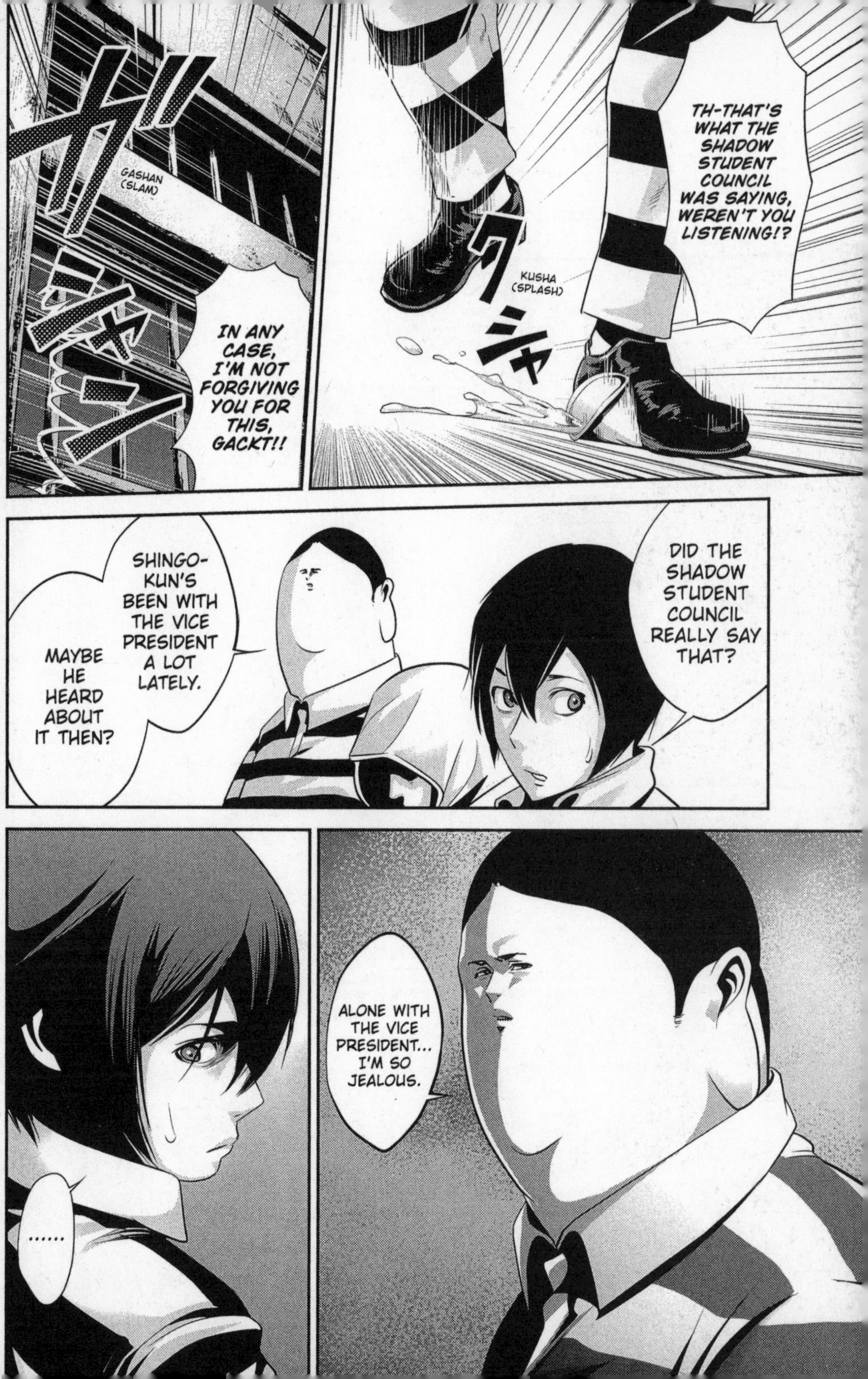
TH-THAT'S WHAT THE SHADOW STUDENT COUNCIL WAS SAYING, WEREN'T YOU LISTENING!?
KUSHA (SPLASH)
IN ANY CASE, I'M NOT FORGIVING YOU FOR THIS, GACKT!!
GASHAN (SLAM)
DID THE SHADOW STUDENT COUNCIL REALLY SAY THAT?
SHINGO-KUN'S BEEN WITH THE VICE PRESIDENT A LOT LATELY.
MAYBE HE HEARD ABOUT IT THEN?
ALONE WITH THE VICE PRESIDENT... I'M SO JEALOUS.
......

裏生徒会室

SIGN: SHADOW STUDENT COUNCIL ROOM

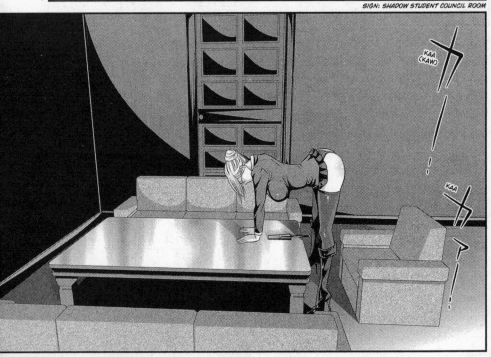

KAA
(KAW)

KAA

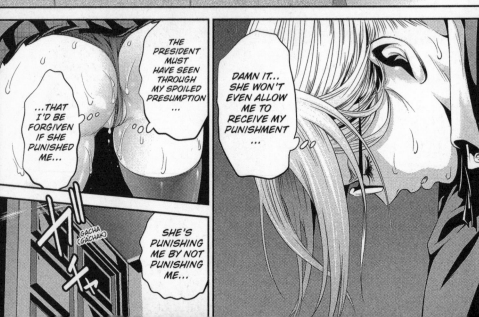

THE PRESIDENT MUST HAVE SEEN THROUGH MY SPOILED PRESUMPTION...

...THAT I'D BE FORGIVEN IF SHE PUNISHED ME...

DAMN IT... SHE WON'T EVEN ALLOW ME TO RECEIVE MY PUNISHMENT...

GACHA GACHAK

SHE'S PUNISHING ME BY NOT PUNISHING ME...

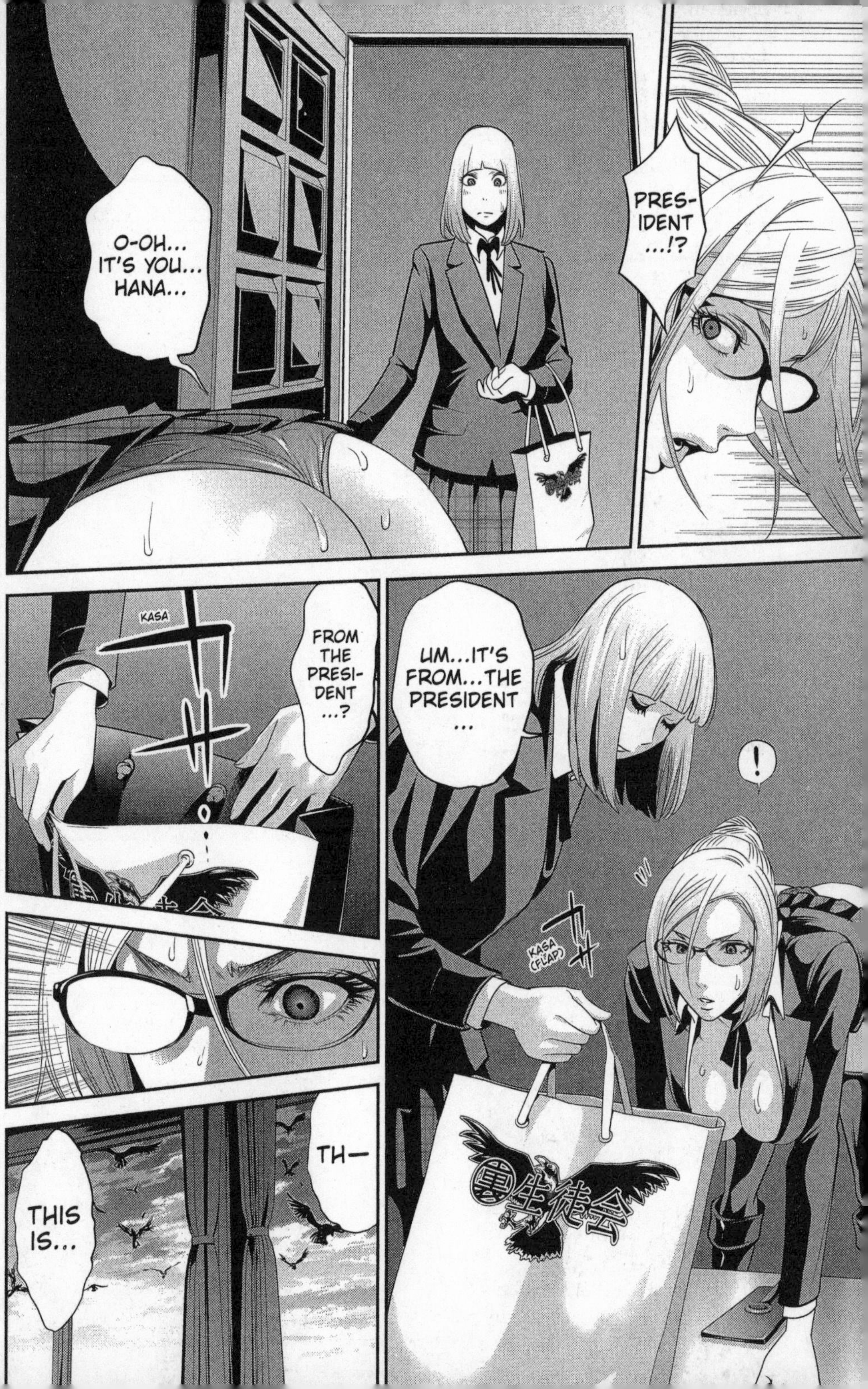
PRES-
IDENT
...!?
O-OH...
IT'S YOU...
HANA...
UM...IT'S
FROM...THE
PRESIDENT
...
!
KASA
(FLAP)
裏生徒会
FROM
THE
PRESI-
DENT
...?
KASA
TH—
THIS
IS...

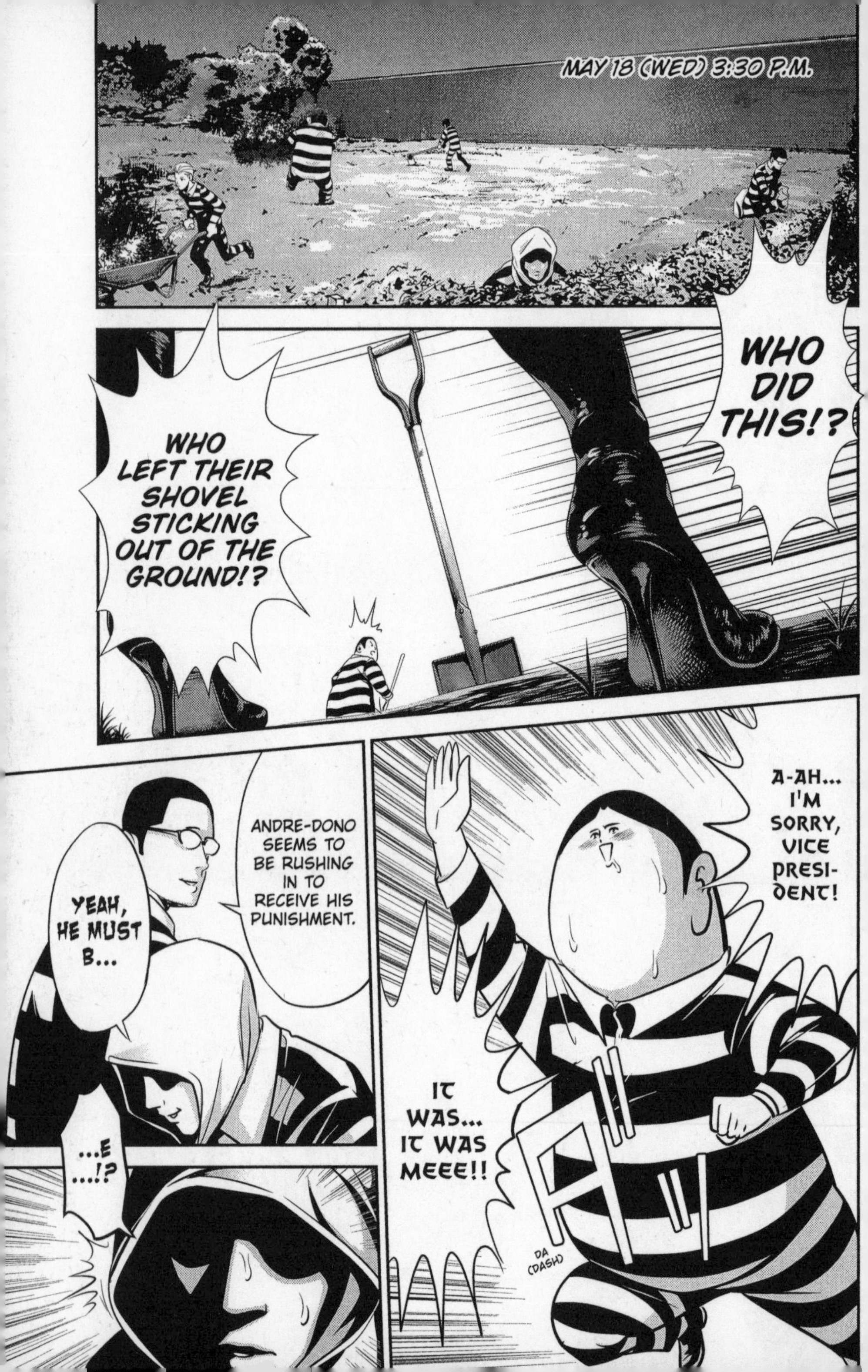
MAY 18 (WED) 3:30 P.M.
WHO DID THIS!?
WHO LEFT THEIR SHOVEL STICKING OUT OF THE GROUND!?
A-AH... I'M SORRY, VICE PRESIDENT!
IT WAS... IT WAS MEEE!!
DA (DASH)
ANDRE-DONO SEEMS TO BE RUSHING IN TO RECEIVE HIS PUNISHMENT.
YEAH, HE MUST B...
...E ...!?

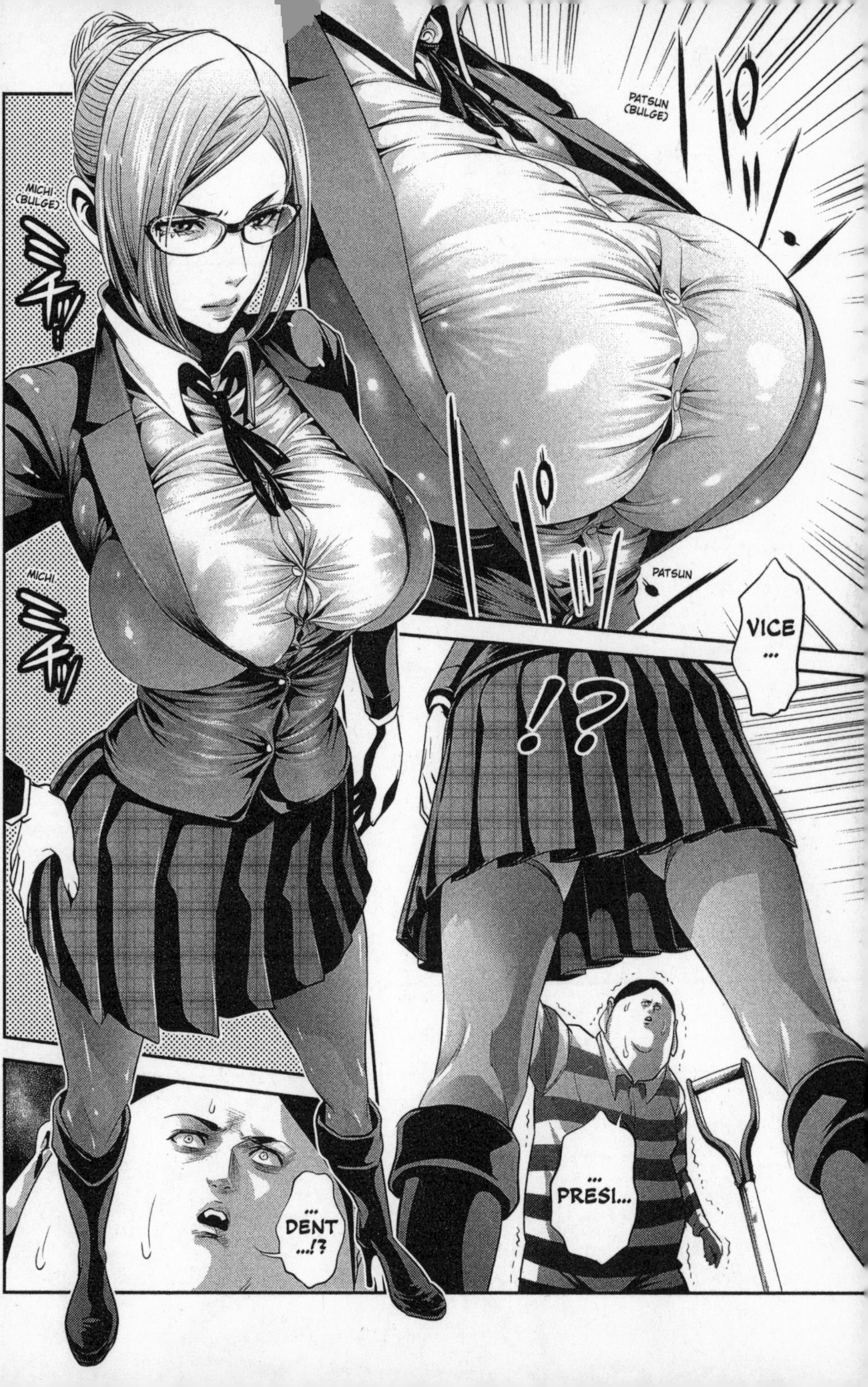
PATSUN (BULGE)
PATSUN
VICE ...
!?
MICHI (BULGE)
MICHI
... PRESI...
... DENT ...!?

CHAPTER 47: DIARY OF THE DEAD

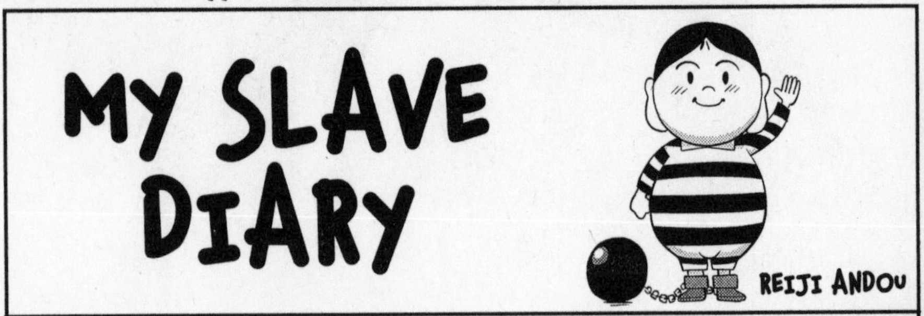
MY SLAVE DIARY
REIJI ANDOU

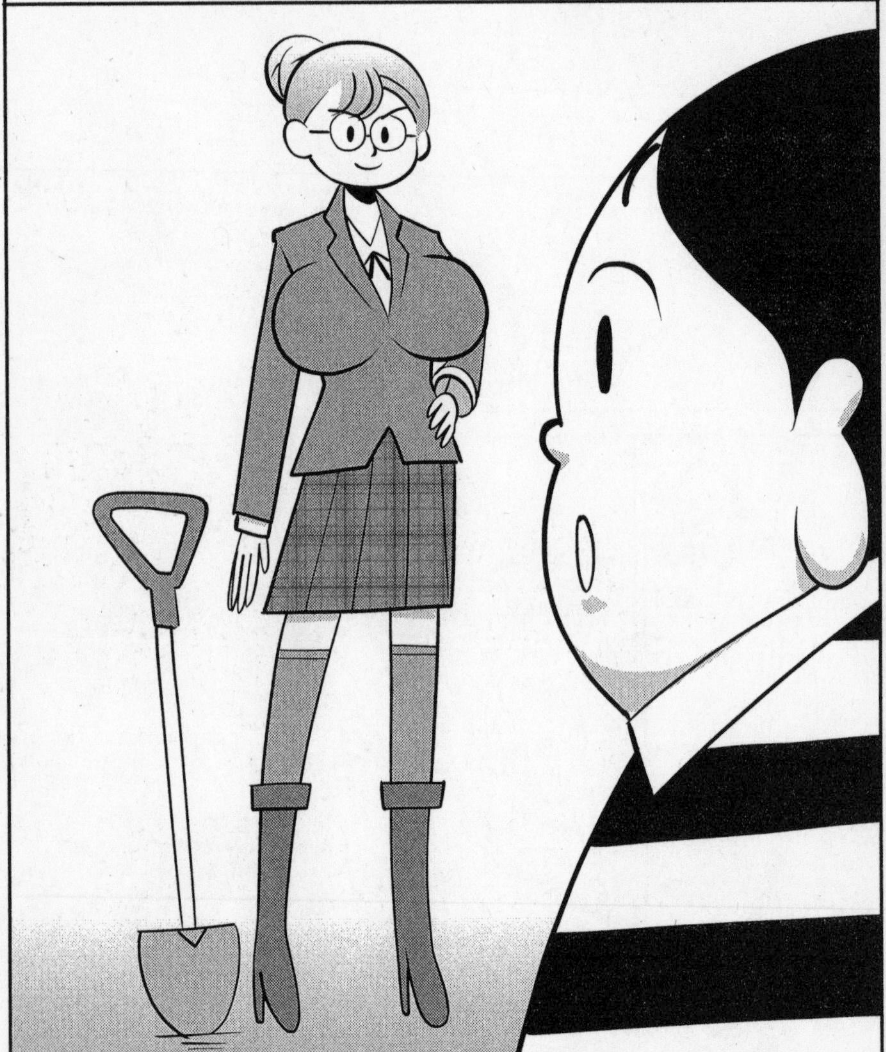

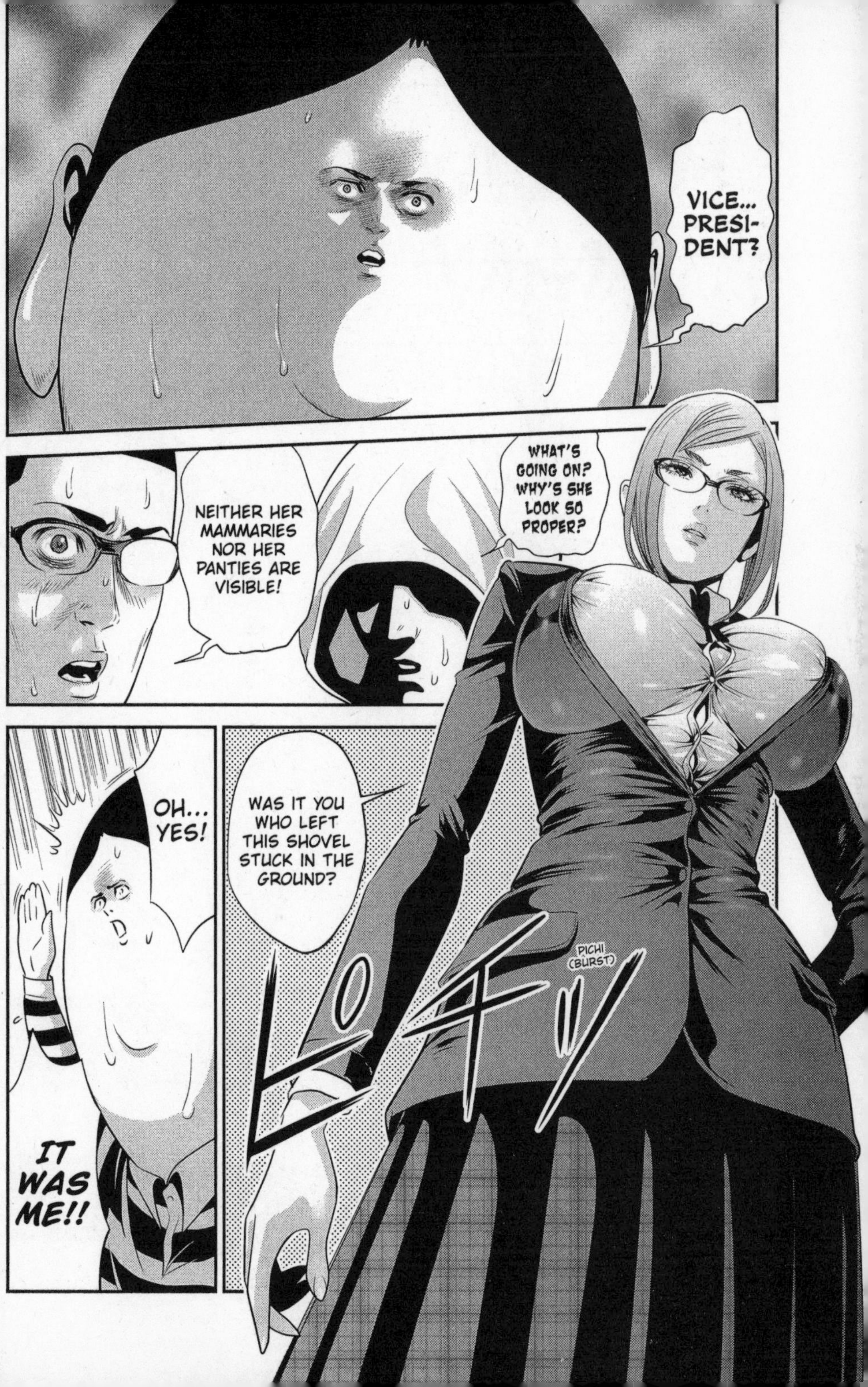
VICE... PRESIDENT?
WHAT'S GOING ON? WHY'S SHE LOOK SO PROPER?
NEITHER HER MAMMARIES NOR HER PANTIES ARE VISIBLE!
WAS IT YOU WHO LEFT THIS SHOVEL STUCK IN THE GROUND?
PICHI (BURST)
OH... YES!
IT WAS ME!!

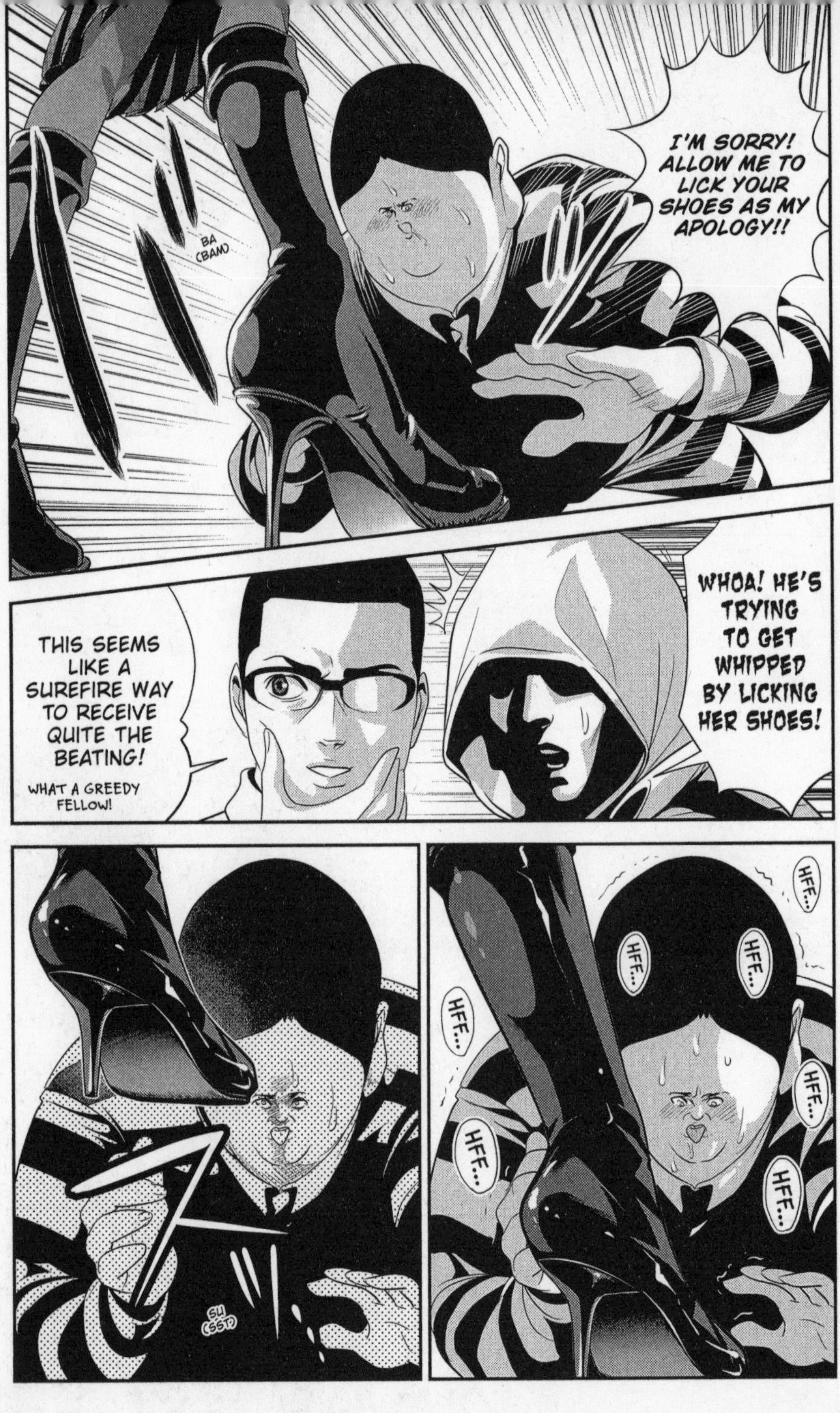
I'M SORRY! ALLOW ME TO LICK YOUR SHOES AS MY APOLOGY!!
BA (BAM)
WHOA! HE'S TRYING TO GET WHIPPED BY LICKING HER SHOES!
THIS SEEMS LIKE A SUREFIRE WAY TO RECEIVE QUITE THE BEATING!
WHAT A GREEDY FELLOW!
HFF...
HFF...
HFF...
HFF...
HFF...
HFF...
SU (SST)

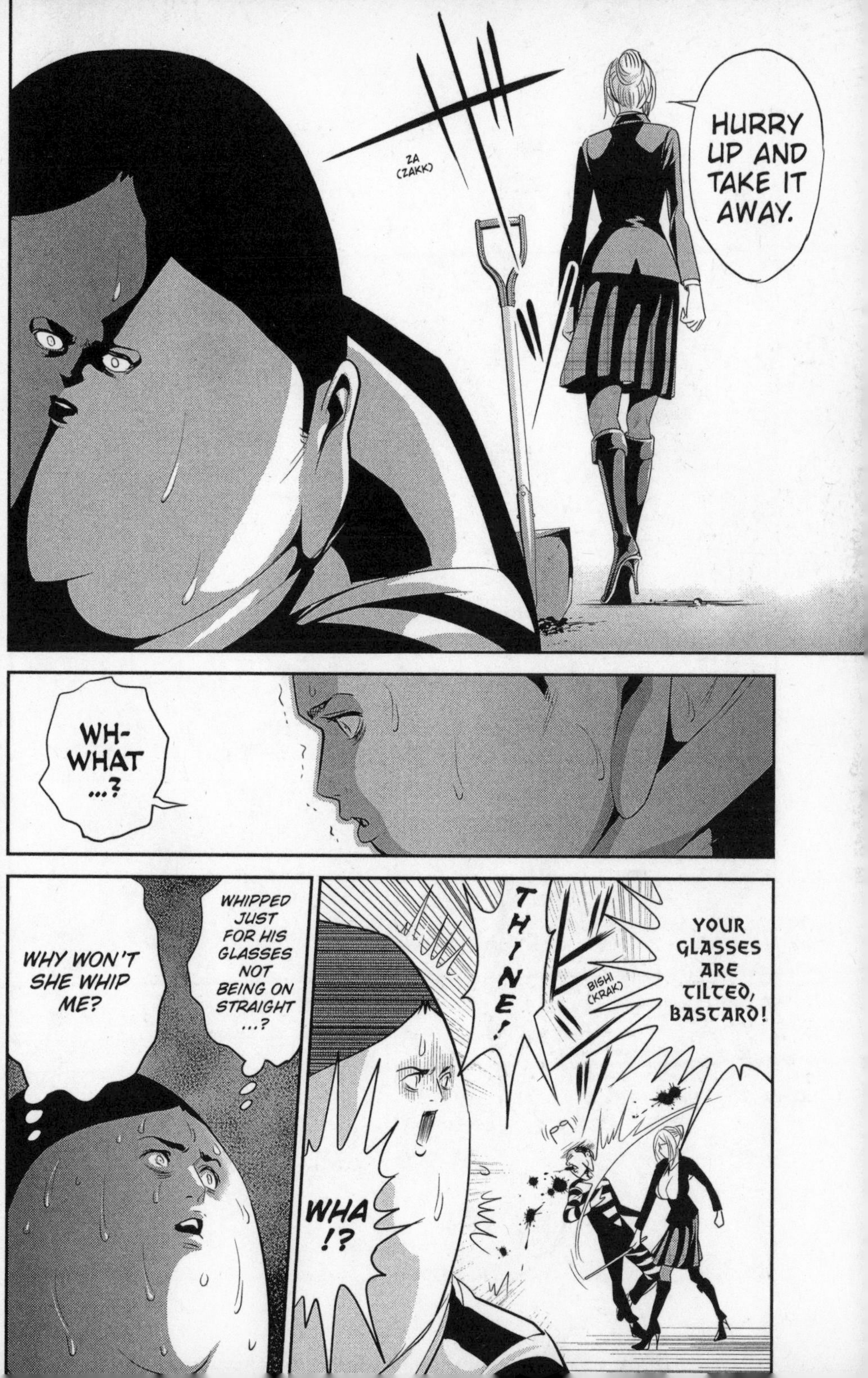
HURRY UP AND TAKE IT AWAY.
ZA (ZAKK)
WH-WHAT ...?
YOUR GLASSES ARE TILTED, BASTARD!
THINE!
BISHI (KRAK)
WHA !?
WHIPPED JUST FOR HIS GLASSES NOT BEING ON STRAIGHT ...?
WHY WON'T SHE WHIP ME?

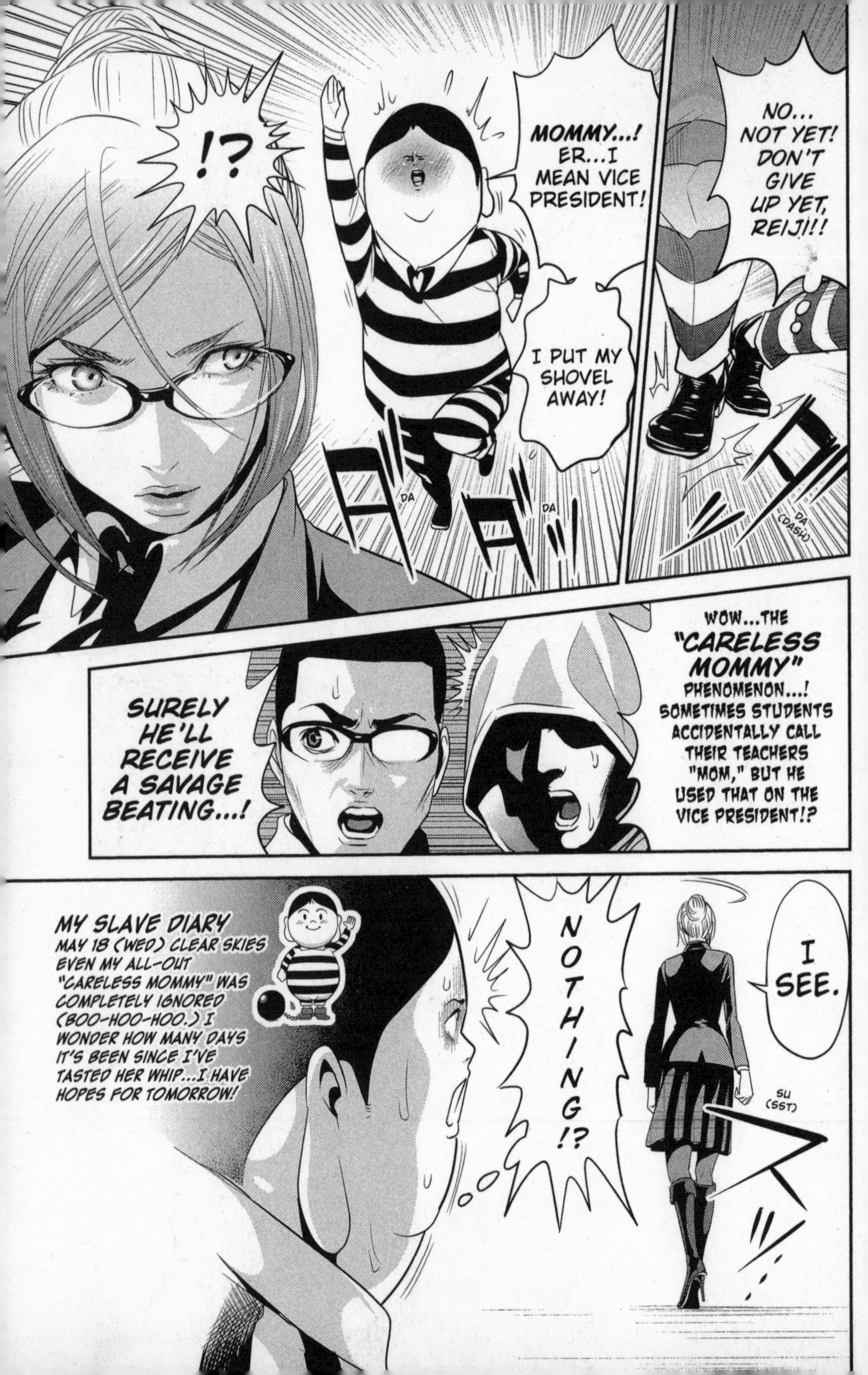
NO... NOT YET! DON'T GIVE UP YET, REIJI!!
DA (DASH)
MOMMY...! ER...I MEAN VICE PRESIDENT!
I PUT MY SHOVEL AWAY!
DA
DA
!?
WOW...THE "CARELESS MOMMY" PHENOMENON...! SOMETIMES STUDENTS ACCIDENTALLY CALL THEIR TEACHERS "MOM," BUT HE USED THAT ON THE VICE PRESIDENT!?
SURELY HE'LL RECEIVE A SAVAGE BEATING...!
I SEE.
SU (SST)
NOTHING!?
MY SLAVE DIARY
MAY 18 (WED) CLEAR SKIES
EVEN MY ALL-OUT "CARELESS MOMMY" WAS COMPLETELY IGNORED (BOO-HOO-HOO.) I WONDER HOW MANY DAYS IT'S BEEN SINCE I'VE TASTED HER WHIP...I HAVE HOPES FOR TOMORROW!

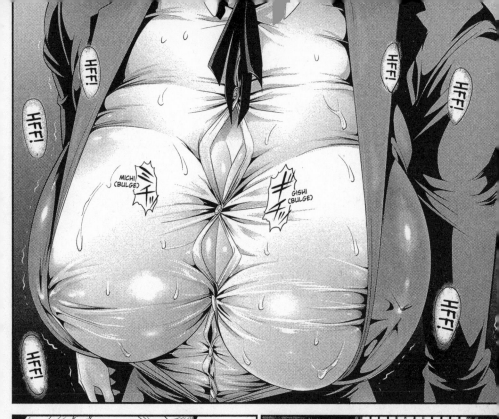

MICHI
(BULGE)

GISHI
(BULGE)

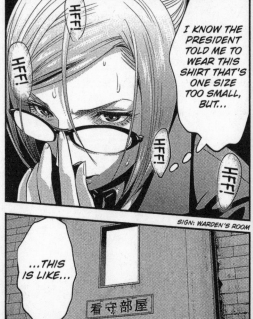

HFF!

HFF!

HFF!

HFF!

I KNOW THE PRESIDENT TOLD ME TO WEAR THIS SHIRT THAT'S ONE SIZE TOO SMALL, BUT...

...THIS IS LIKE...

SIGN: WARDEN'S ROOM

看守部屋

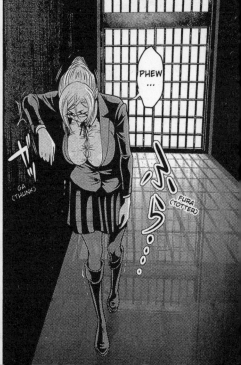

PHEW...

GA
(THUNK)

FURA
(TOTTER)

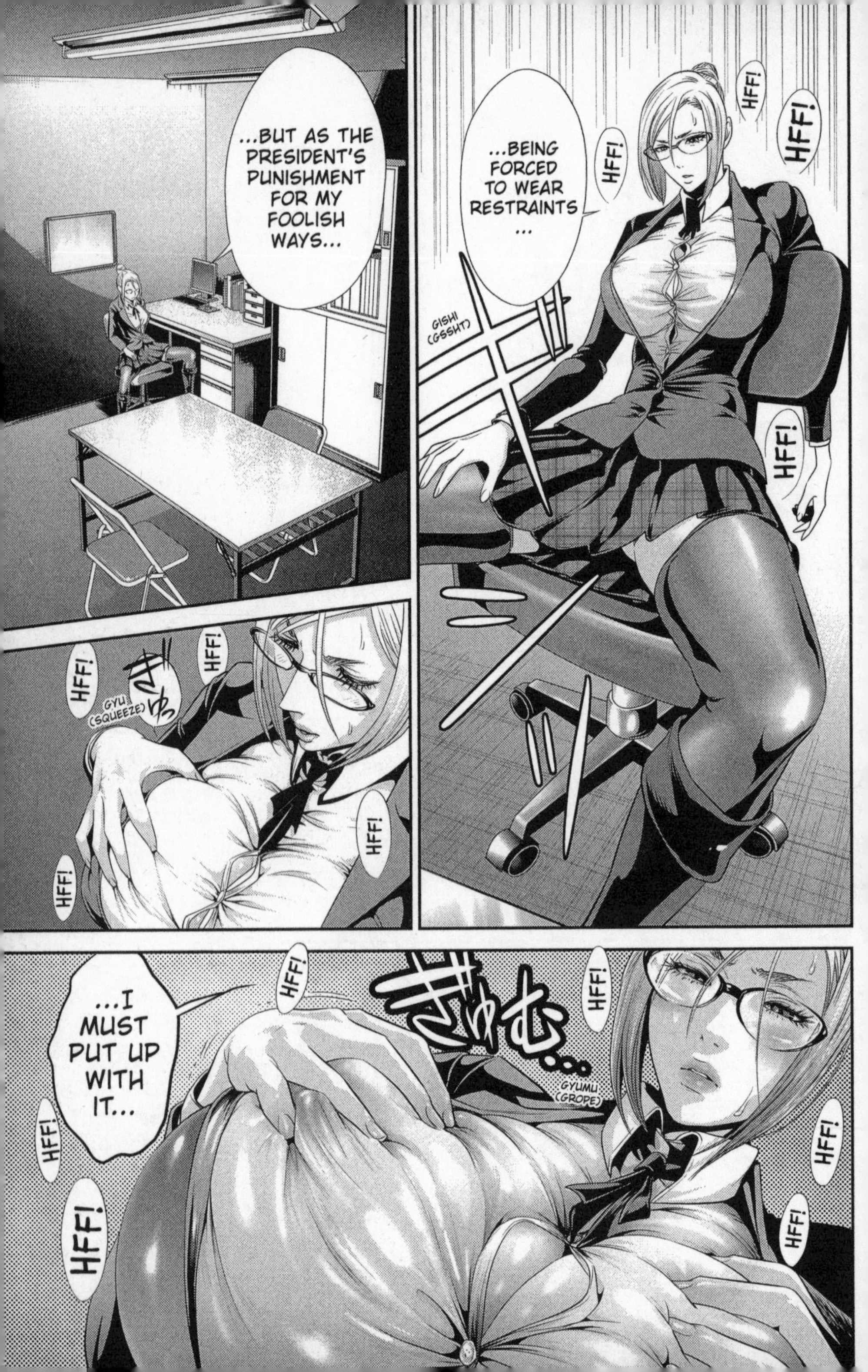

HFF!
HFF!
HFF!
...BEING FORCED TO WEAR RESTRAINTS ...
GISHI (GSSHT)
HFF!
...BUT AS THE PRESIDENT'S PUNISHMENT FOR MY FOOLISH WAYS...
HFF!
HFF!
GYU (SQUEEZE)
HFF!
HFF!
HFF!
HFF!
GYUMU (GROPE)
...I MUST PUT UP WITH IT...
HFF!
HFF!
HFF!
HFF!
HFF!

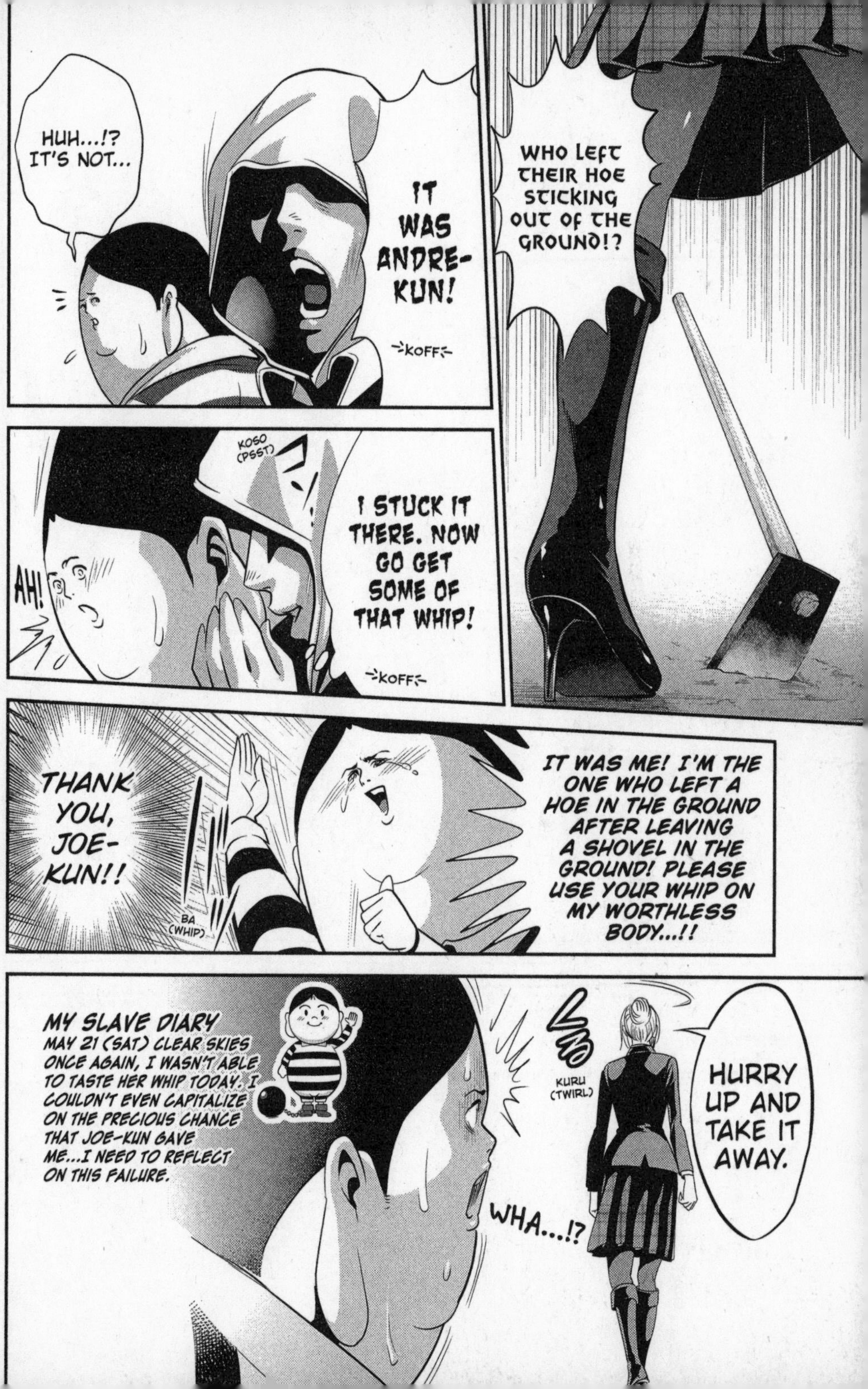
WHO LEFT THEIR HOE STICKING OUT OF THE GROUND!?
IT WAS ANDRE-KUN!
KOFF
HUH...!? IT'S NOT...
KOSO (PSST)
I STUCK IT THERE. NOW GO GET SOME OF THAT WHIP!
KOFF
AH!
IT WAS ME! I'M THE ONE WHO LEFT A HOE IN THE GROUND AFTER LEAVING A SHOVEL IN THE GROUND! PLEASE USE YOUR WHIP ON MY WORTHLESS BODY...!!
THANK YOU, JOE-KUN!!
BA (WHIP)
HURRY UP AND TAKE IT AWAY.
KURU (TWIRL)
WHA...!?
MY SLAVE DIARY
MAY 21 (SAT) CLEAR SKIES
ONCE AGAIN, I WASN'T ABLE TO TASTE HER WHIP TODAY. I COULDN'T EVEN CAPITALIZE ON THE PRECIOUS CHANCE THAT JOE-KUN GAVE ME...I NEED TO REFLECT ON THIS FAILURE.

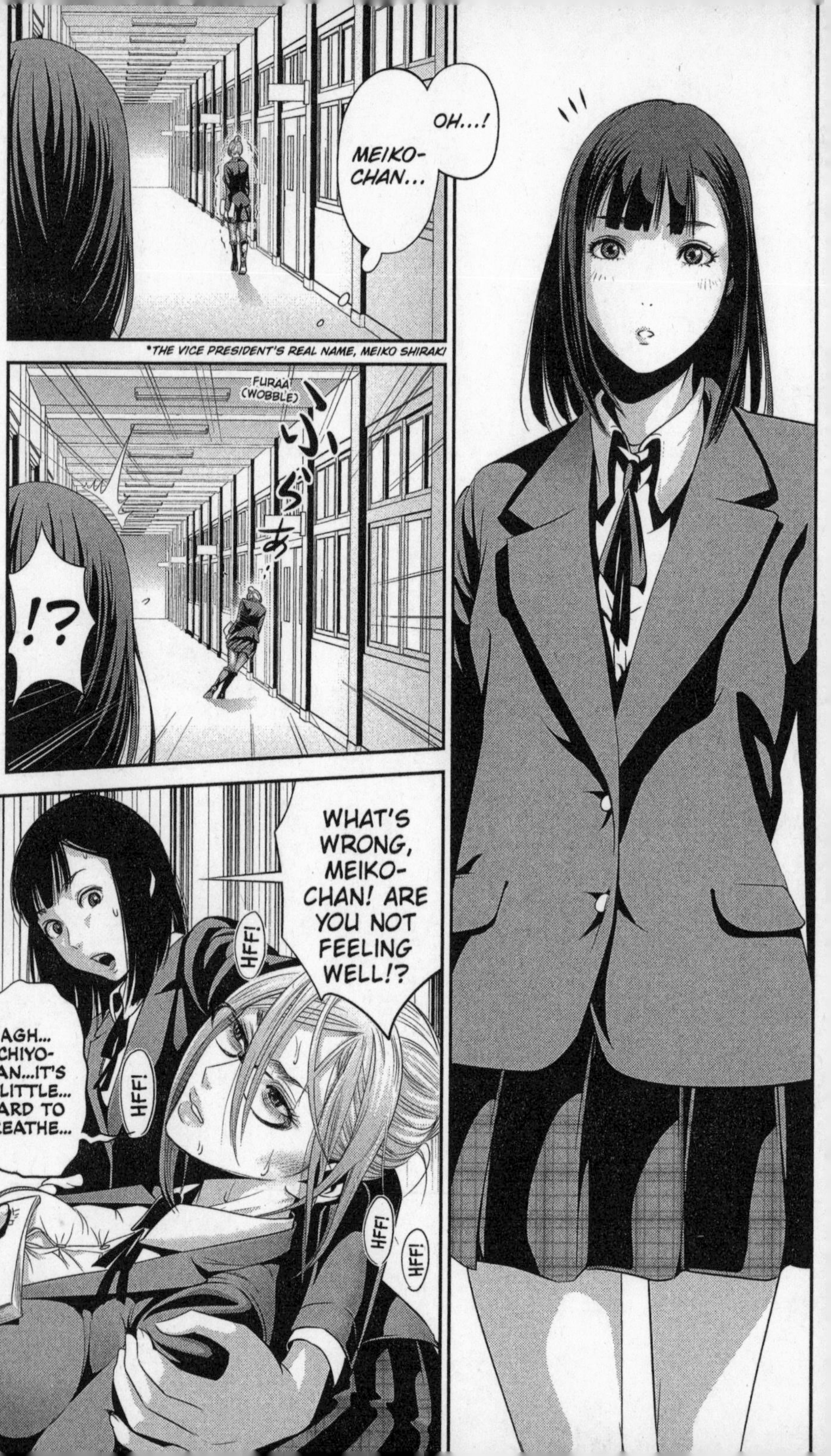
OH...!
MEIKO-CHAN...
*THE VICE PRESIDENT'S REAL NAME, MEIKO SHIRAKI
FURAA! (WOBBLE)
ふらぁ
!?
WHAT'S WRONG, MEIKO-CHAN! ARE YOU NOT FEELING WELL!?
HFF!
AGH... CHIYO-SAN...IT'S A LITTLE... HARD TO BREATHE...
HFF!
HFF!
HFF!

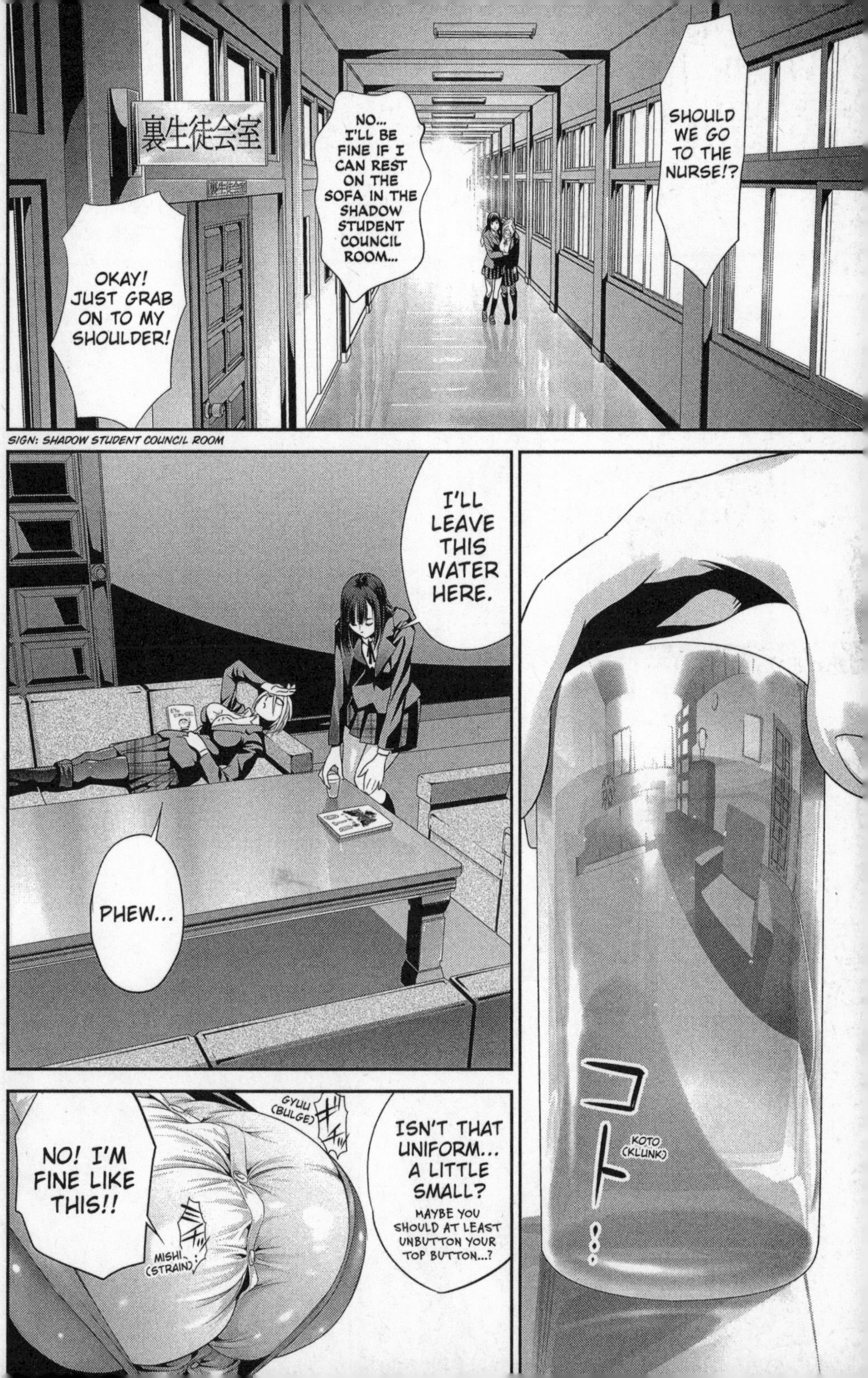
SHOULD WE GO TO THE NURSE!?
NO... I'LL BE FINE IF I CAN REST ON THE SOFA IN THE SHADOW STUDENT COUNCIL ROOM...
裏生徒会室
OKAY! JUST GRAB ON TO MY SHOULDER!
SIGN: SHADOW STUDENT COUNCIL ROOM
コト!!
KOTO (KLUNK)
I'LL LEAVE THIS WATER HERE.
PHEW...
ISN'T THAT UNIFORM... A LITTLE SMALL?
MAYBE YOU SHOULD AT LEAST UNBUTTON YOUR TOP BUTTON...?
GYUU (BULGE)
NO! I'M FINE LIKE THIS!!
MISHI (STRAIN)

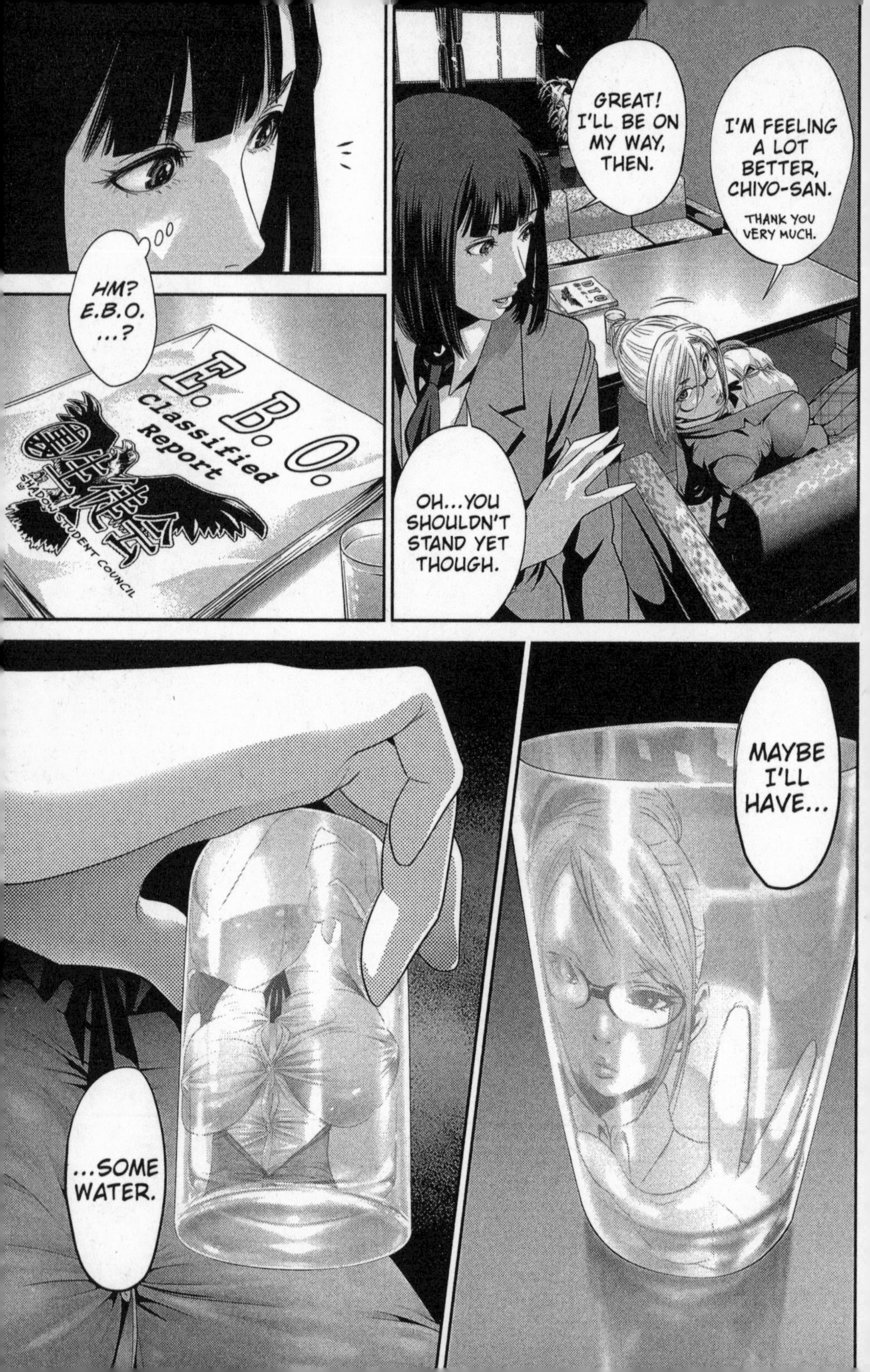
I'M FEELING A LOT BETTER, CHIYO-SAN.
THANK YOU VERY MUCH.
GREAT! I'LL BE ON MY WAY, THEN.
OH...YOU SHOULDN'T STAND YET THOUGH.
HM? E.B.O. ...?
E.B.O.
Classified Report
SHADOW STUDENT COUNCIL
MAYBE I'LL HAVE...
...SOME WATER.

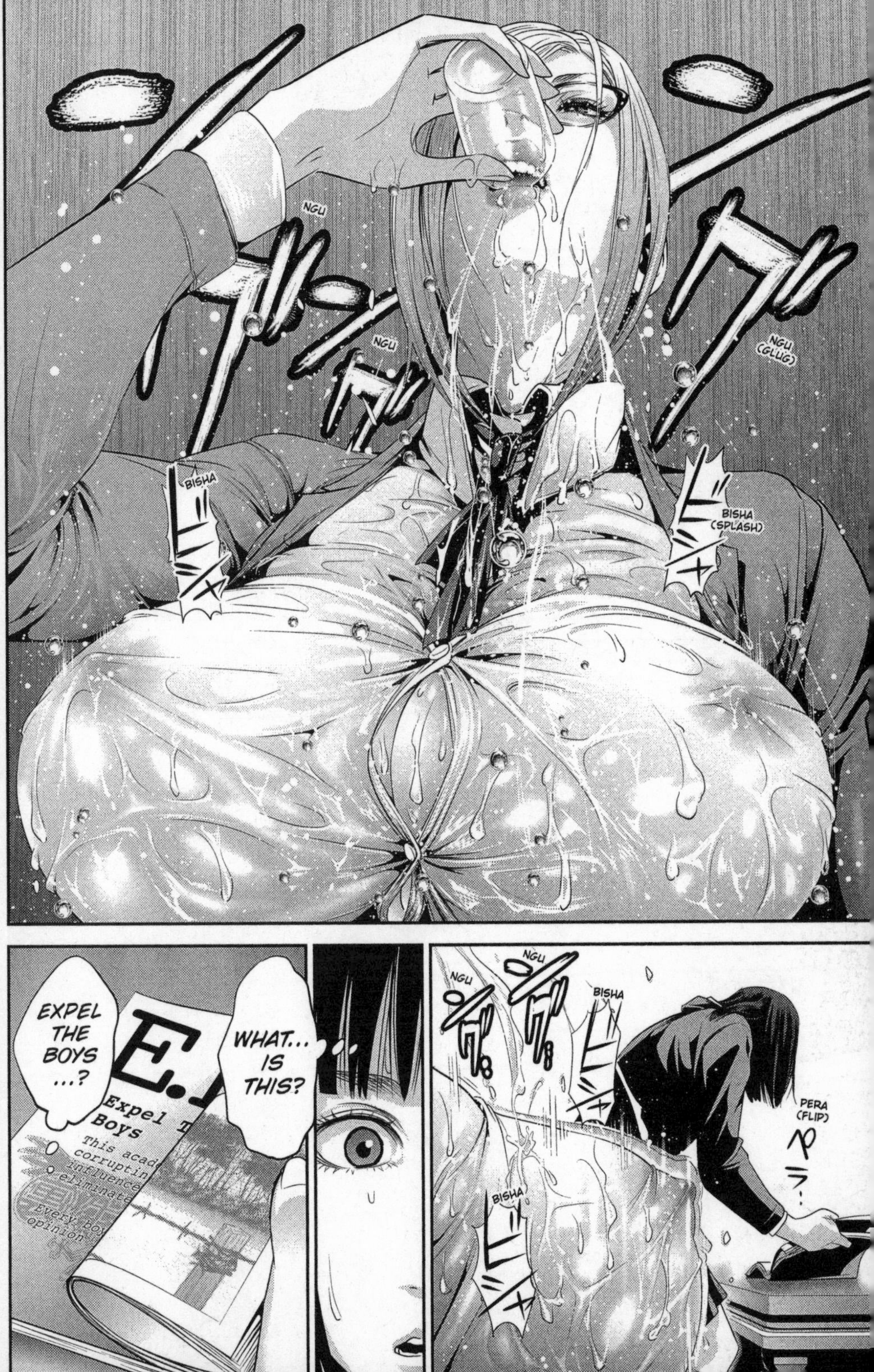
NGU (GLUG)
NGU
NGU
BISHA (SPLASH)
BISHA
NGU
NGU
BISHA
PERA (FLIP)
BISHA
WHAT... IS THIS?
EXPEL THE BOYS ...?
Expel
Boys

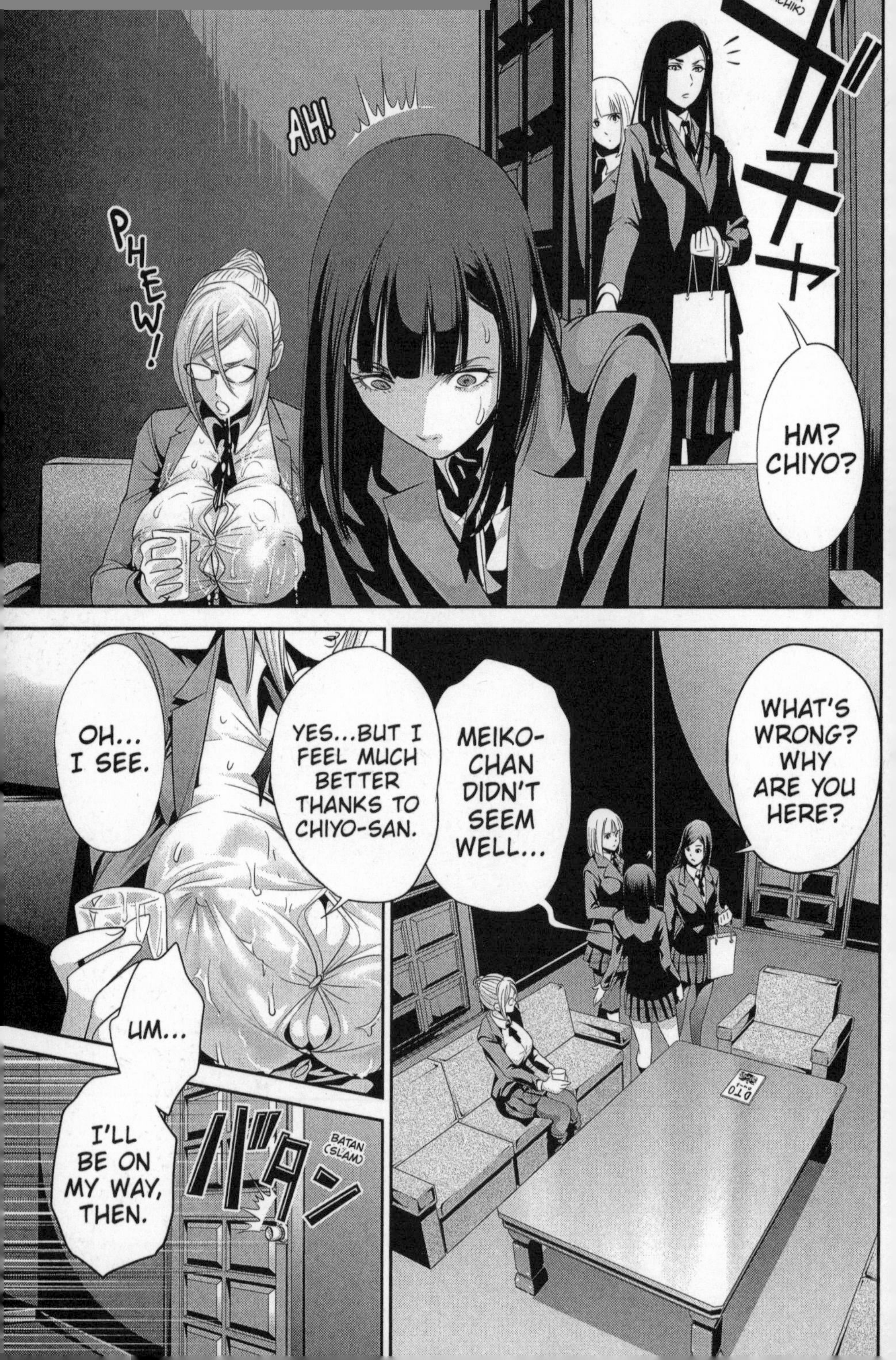
ガチャ
GACHA (GACHIK)
HM? CHIYO?
AH!
PHEW!
WHAT'S WRONG? WHY ARE YOU HERE?
MEIKO-CHAN DIDN'T SEEM WELL...
YES...BUT I FEEL MUCH BETTER THANKS TO CHIYO-SAN.
OH... I SEE.
UM...
バタン
BATAN (SLAM)
I'LL BE ON MY WAY, THEN.

MY SLAVE DIARY

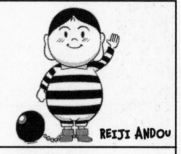

REIJI ANDOU

MY SLAVE DIARY
MAY 24 (TUE) CLEAR SKIES
I CAN'T STAND IT ANY LONGER...
GIVE ME YOUR WHIP.
I'M AT MY LIMIT...BAD-MOUTH ME.
I CAN'T TAKE ANY MORE...
SCORN ME.

WHY WILL YOU NOT
DO ANYTHING TO ME?
I DON'T UNDERSTAND...
EVERYONE ELSE IS
BEING PUNISHED...

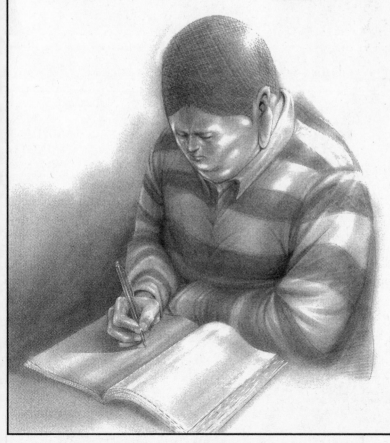

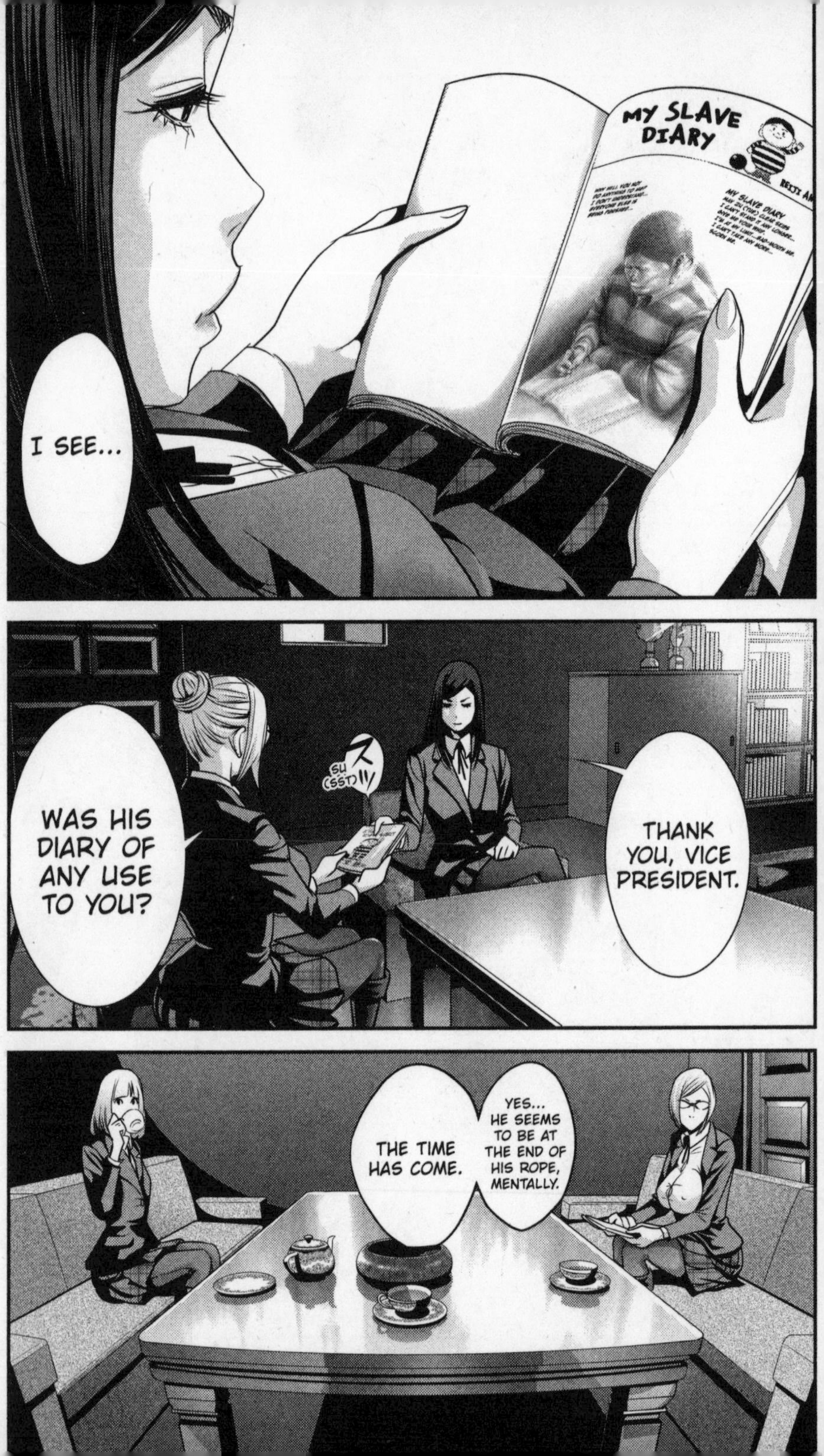
MY SLAVE DIARY
I SEE...
THANK YOU, VICE PRESIDENT.
SU (SST)
WAS HIS DIARY OF ANY USE TO YOU?
YES... HE SEEMS TO BE AT THE END OF HIS ROPE, MENTALLY.
THE TIME HAS COME.

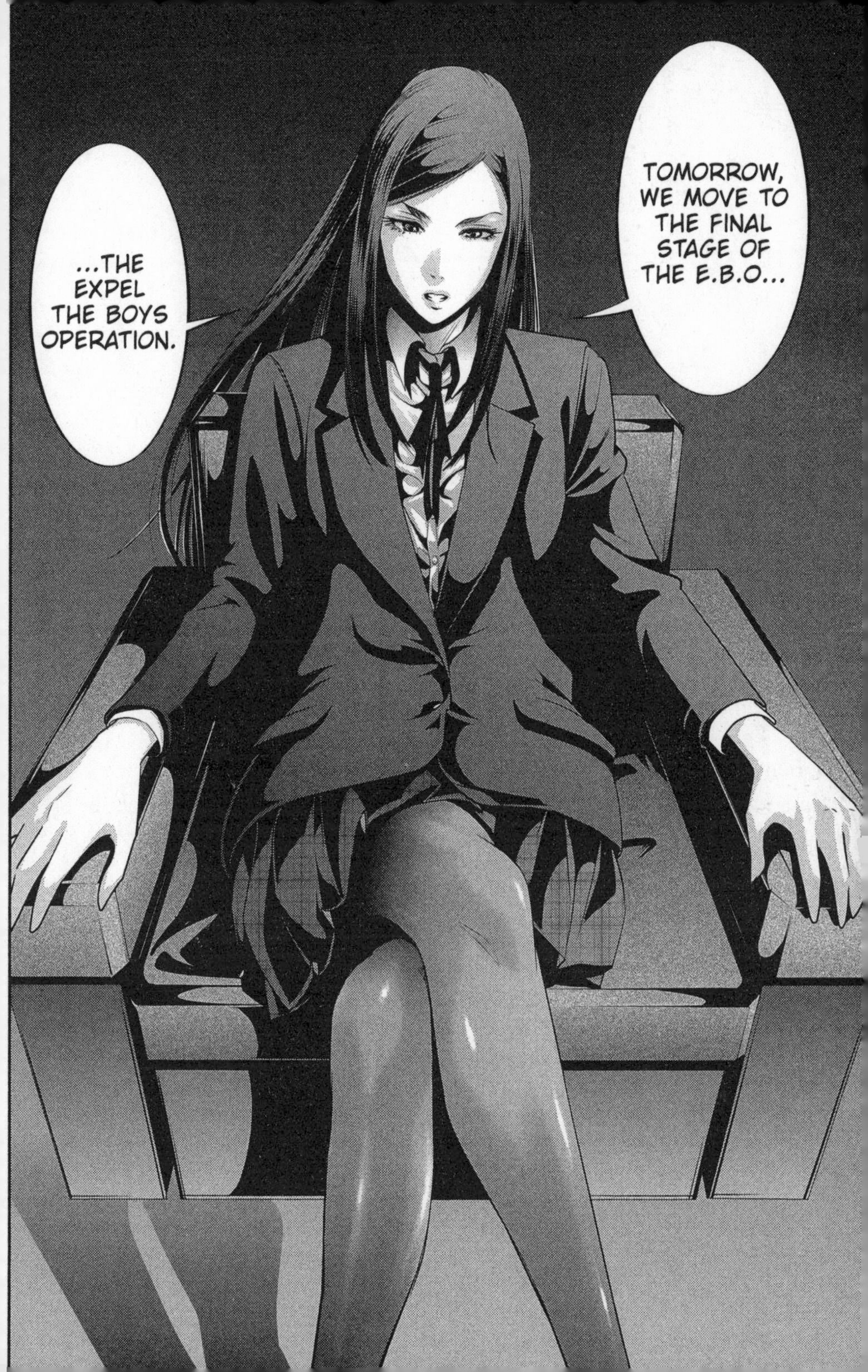
TOMORROW, WE MOVE TO THE FINAL STAGE OF THE E.B.O...
...THE EXPEL THE BOYS OPERATION.

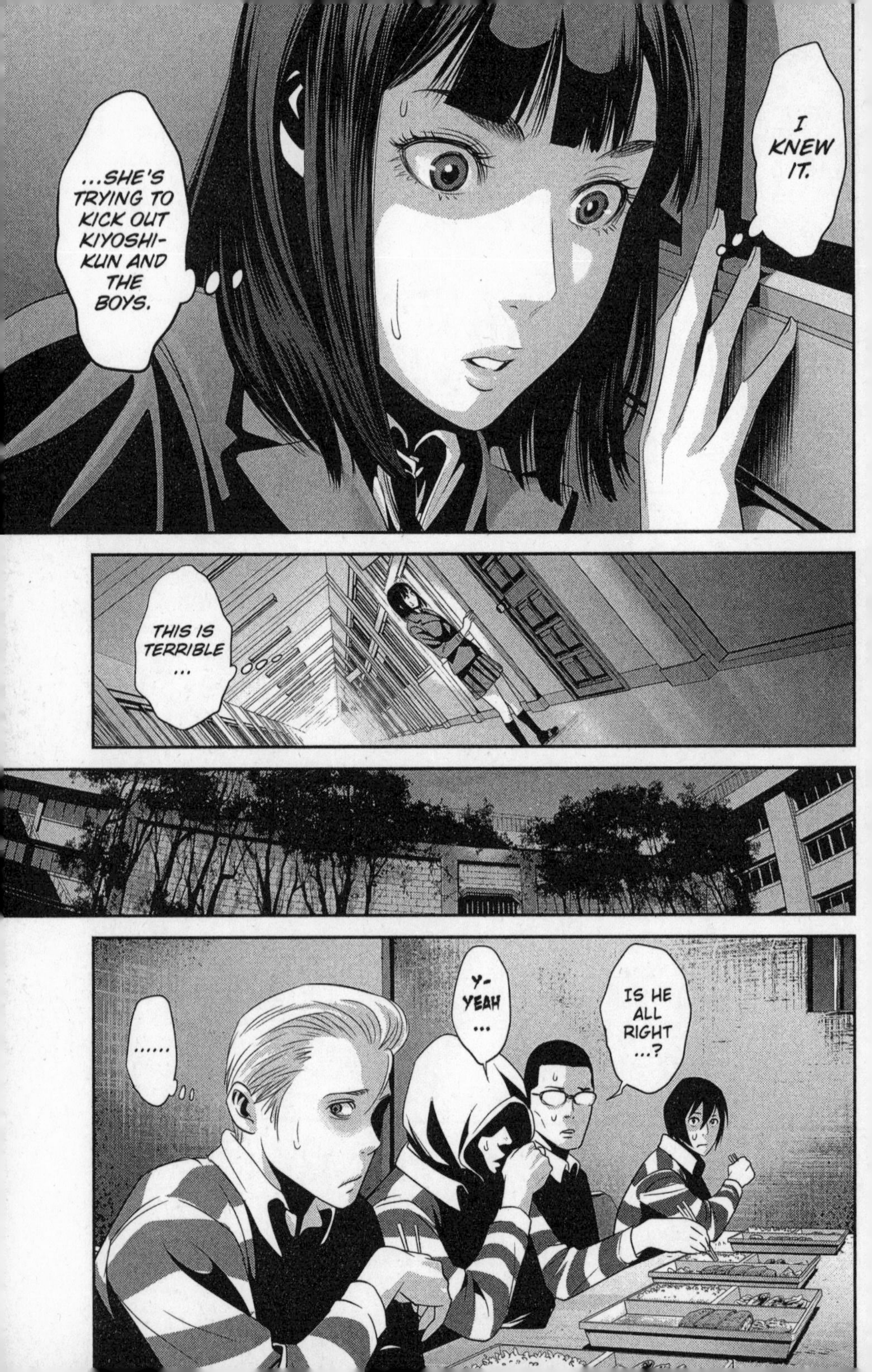
I KNEW IT.
...SHE'S TRYING TO KICK OUT KIYOSHI-KUN AND THE BOYS.
THIS IS TERRIBLE...
IS HE ALL RIGHT...?
Y-YEAH...
......

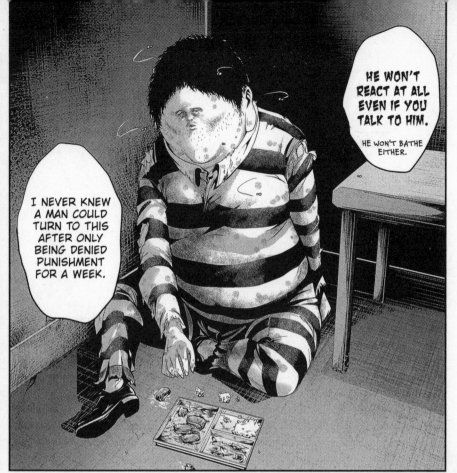

HE WON'T REACT AT ALL EVEN IF YOU TALK TO HIM.

HE WON'T BATHE EITHER.

I NEVER KNEW A MAN COULD TURN TO THIS AFTER ONLY BEING DENIED PUNISHMENT FOR A WEEK.

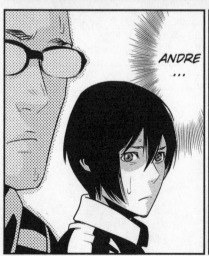

ANDRE...

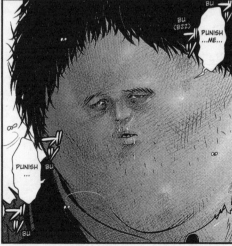

BU

BU (BZZ)

PUNISH ...ME...

PUNISH ...

BU

BU

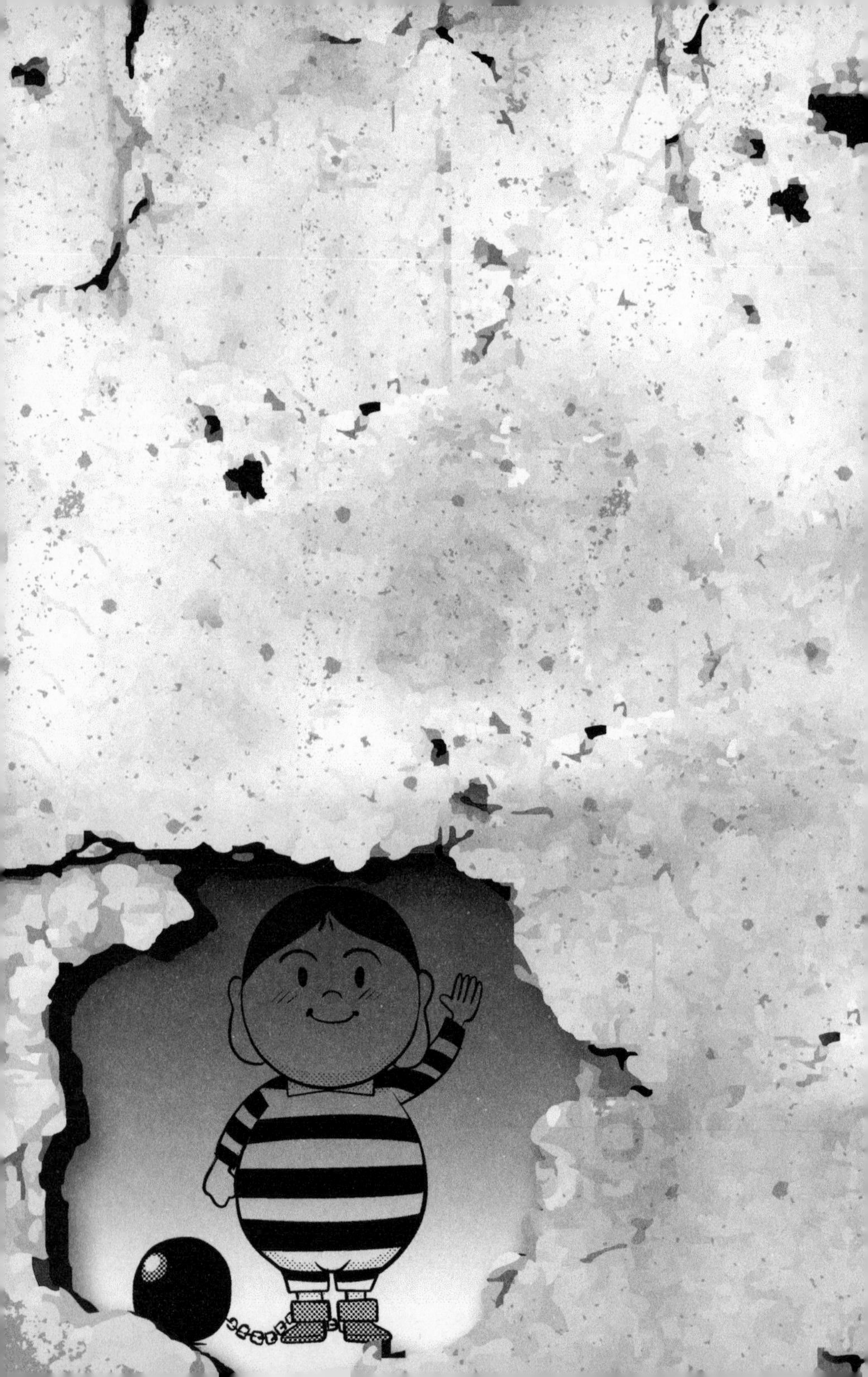

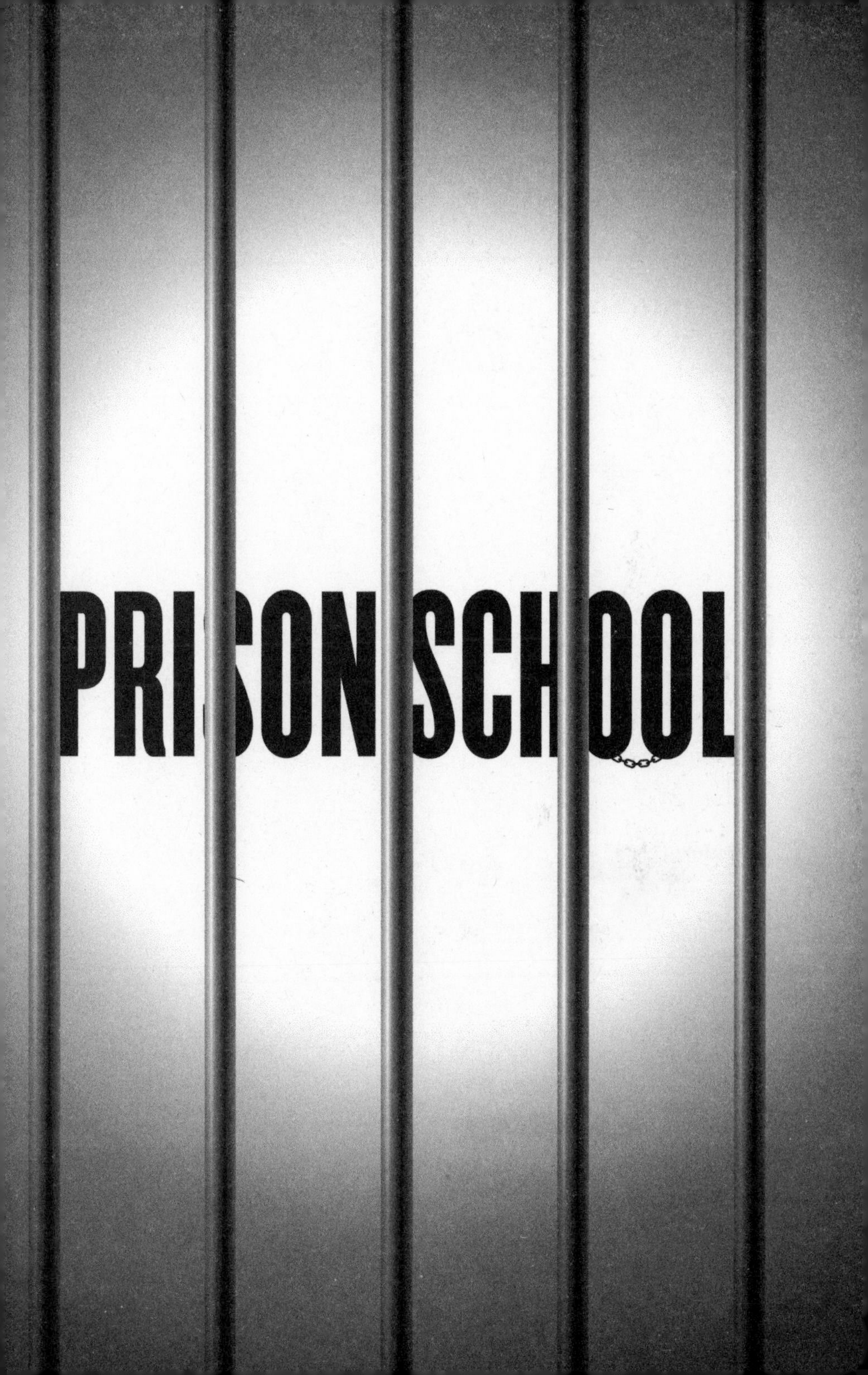
PRISON SCHOOL

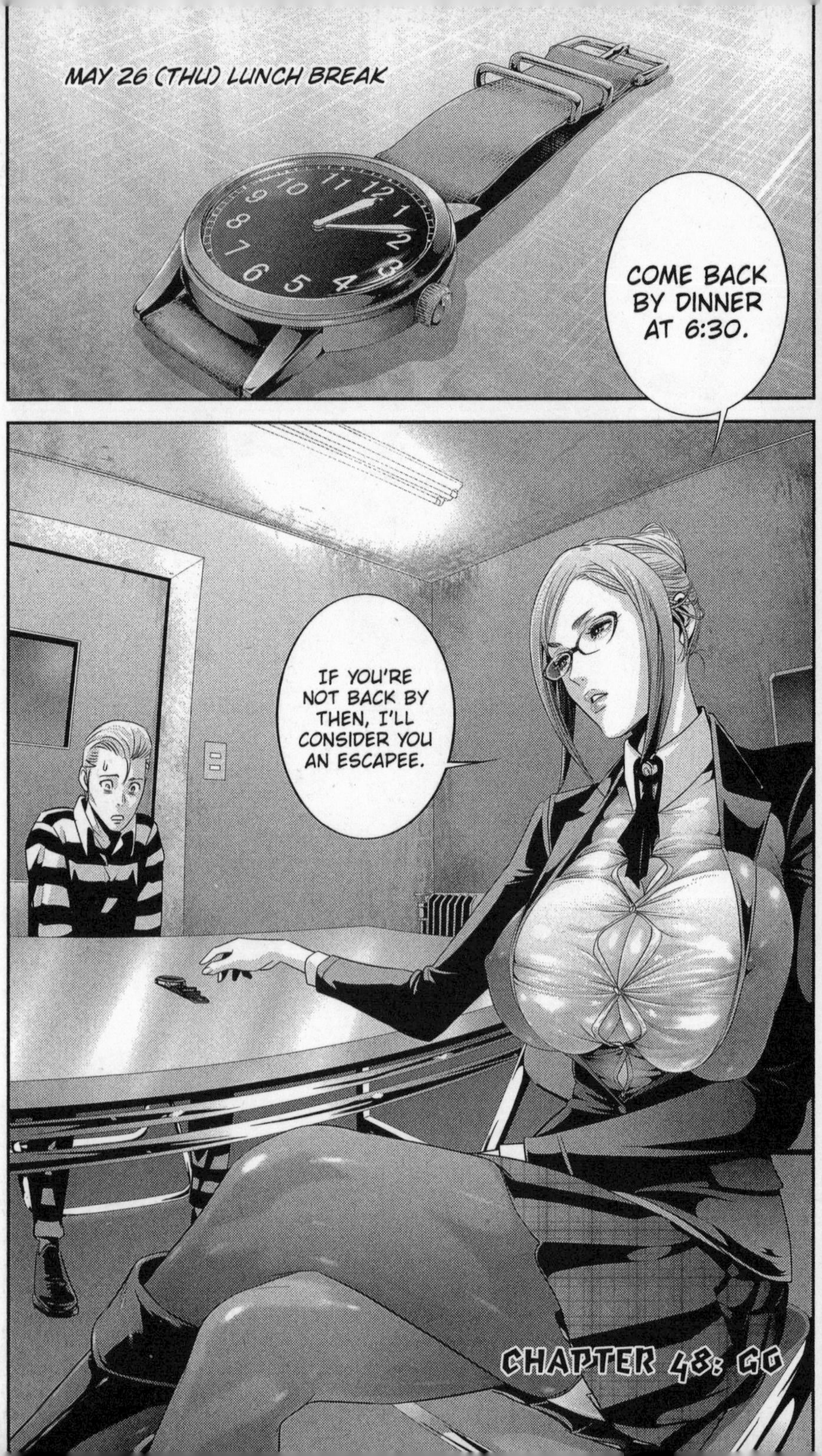
MAY 26 (THU) LUNCH BREAK
COME BACK BY DINNER AT 6:30.
IF YOU'RE NOT BACK BY THEN, I'LL CONSIDER YOU AN ESCAPEE.
CHAPTER 48: GG

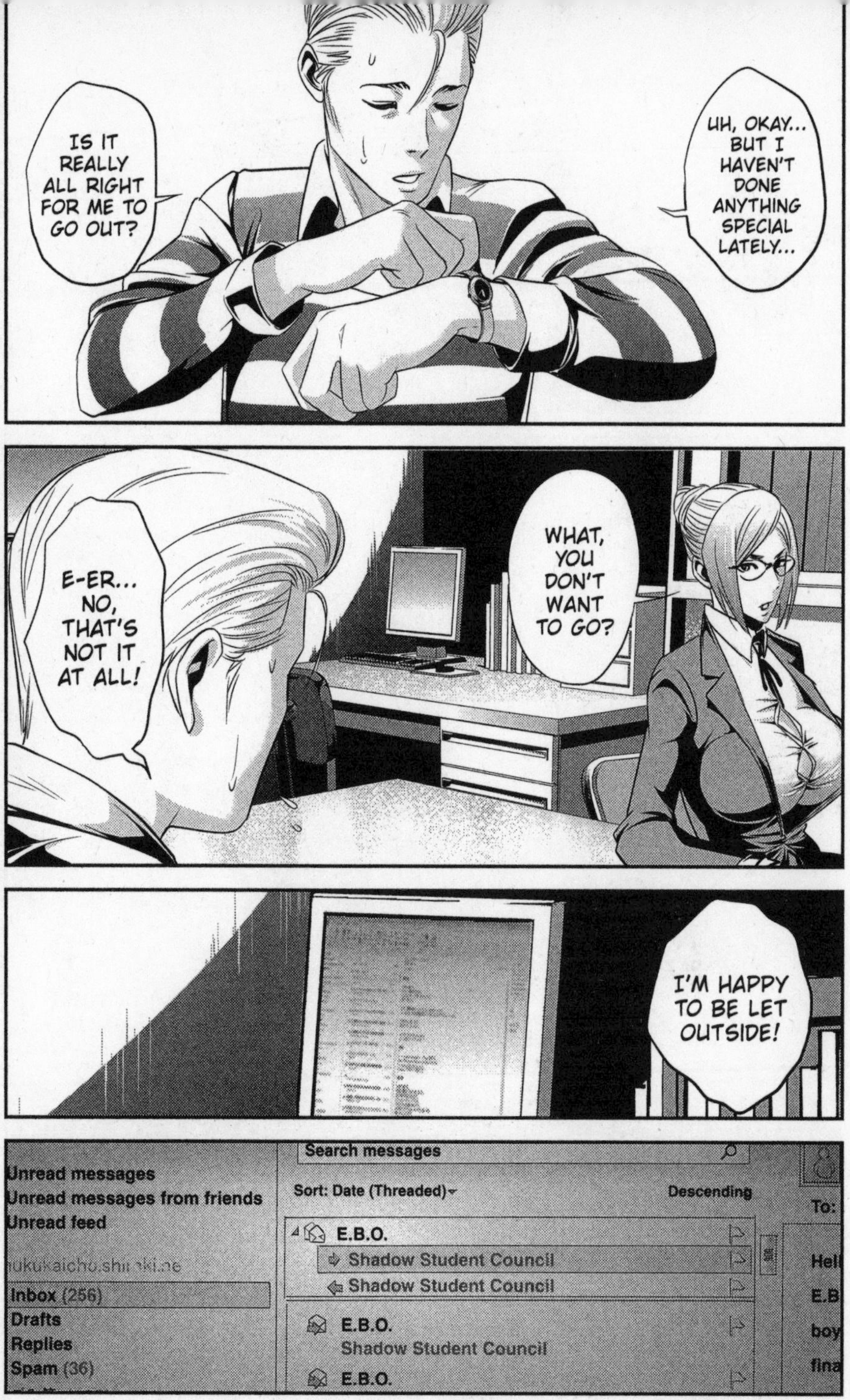
UH, OKAY... BUT I HAVEN'T DONE ANYTHING SPECIAL LATELY...
IS IT REALLY ALL RIGHT FOR ME TO GO OUT?
WHAT, YOU DON'T WANT TO GO?
E-ER... NO, THAT'S NOT IT AT ALL!
I'M HAPPY TO BE LET OUTSIDE!
Search messages
Unread messages
Unread messages from friends
Unread feed
Inbox (256)
Drafts
Replies
Spam (36)
Sort: Date (Threaded)
Descending
E.B.O.
Shadow Student Council
Shadow Student Council
E.B.O.
Shadow Student Council
E.B.O.
To:

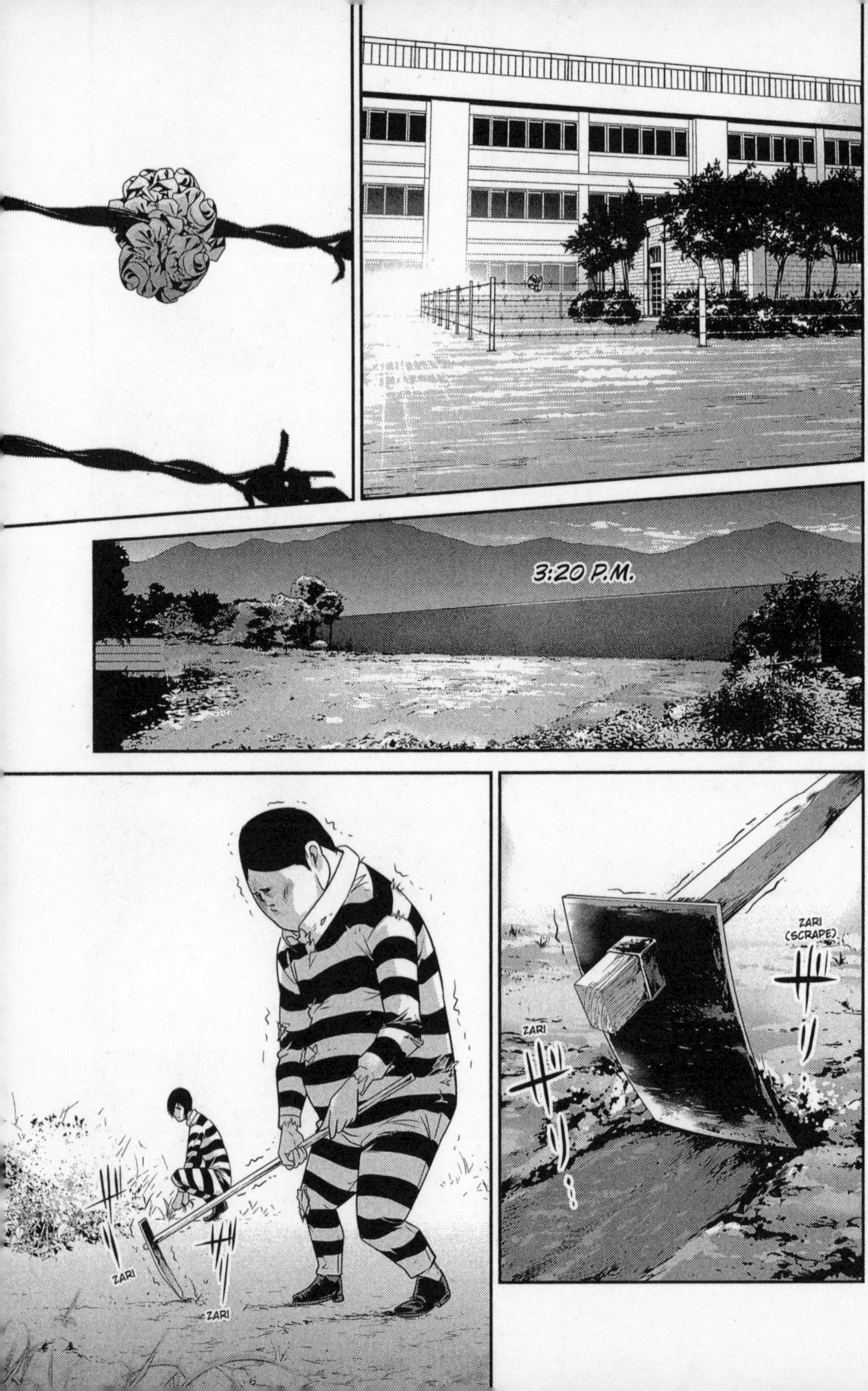
3:20 P.M.
ZARI (SCRAPE)
ZARI
ZARI
ZARI

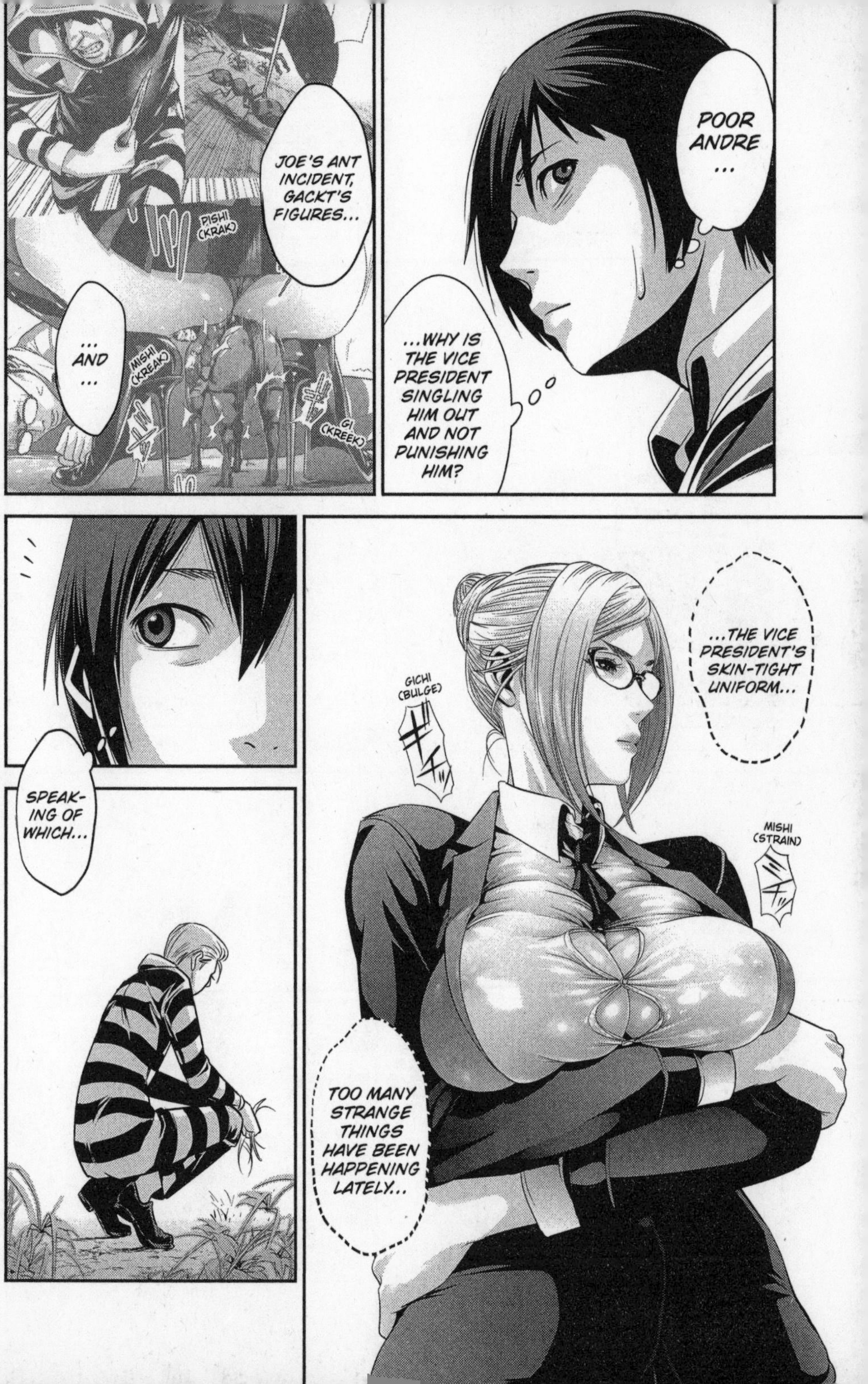
POOR ANDRE ...
...WHY IS THE VICE PRESIDENT SINGLING HIM OUT AND NOT PUNISHING HIM?
JOE'S ANT INCIDENT, GACKT'S FIGURES...
PISHI (KRAK)
... AND ...
MISHI (KREAK)
GI (KREEK)
...THE VICE PRESIDENT'S SKIN-TIGHT UNIFORM...
GICHI (BULGE)
MISHI (STRAIN)
TOO MANY STRANGE THINGS HAVE BEEN HAPPENING LATELY...
SPEAK-ING OF WHICH...

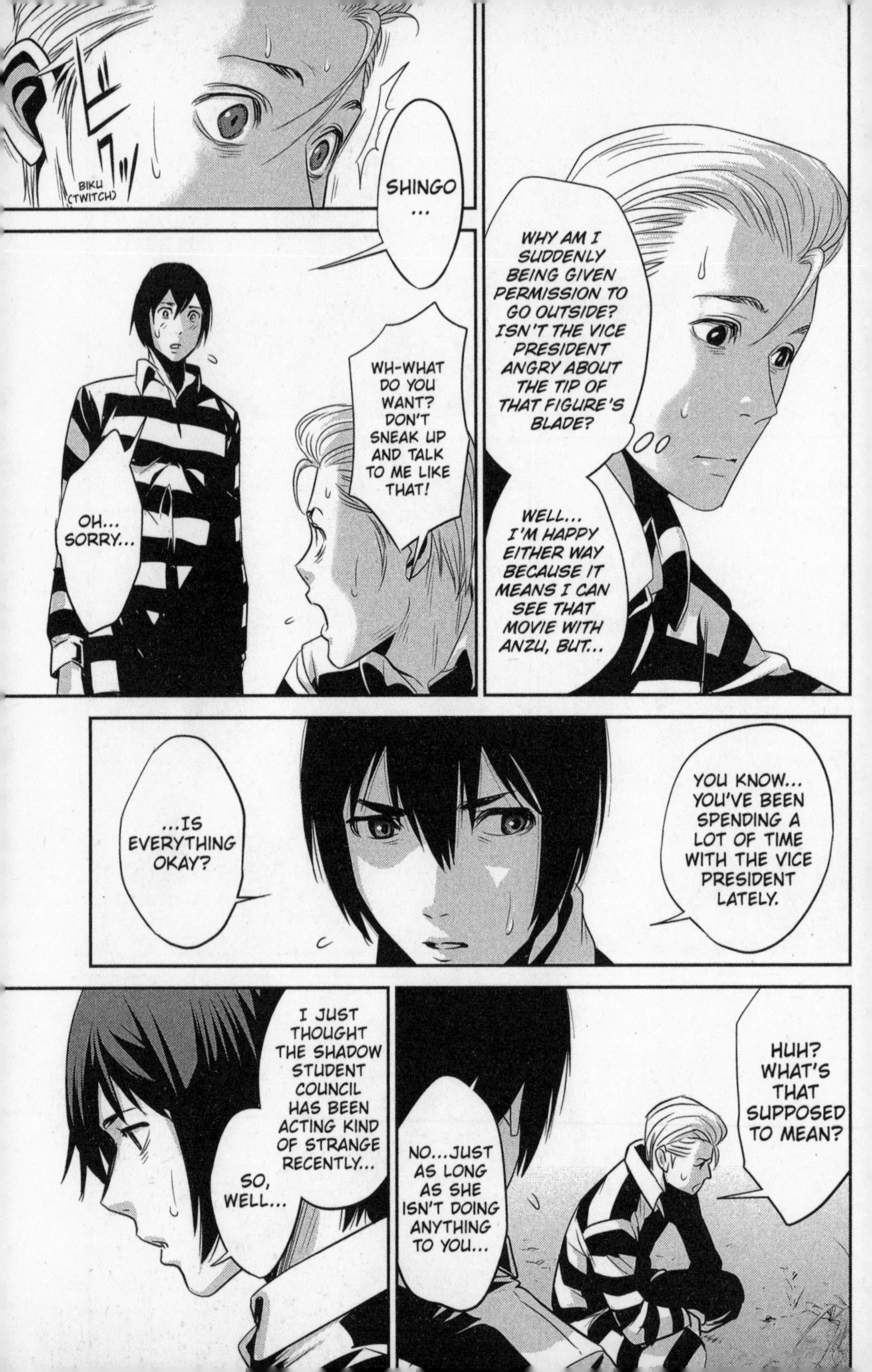
WHY AM I SUDDENLY BEING GIVEN PERMISSION TO GO OUTSIDE? ISN'T THE VICE PRESIDENT ANGRY ABOUT THE TIP OF THAT FIGURE'S BLADE?
WELL... I'M HAPPY EITHER WAY BECAUSE IT MEANS I CAN SEE THAT MOVIE WITH ANZU, BUT...
BIKU (TWITCH)
SHINGO ...
WH-WHAT DO YOU WANT? DON'T SNEAK UP AND TALK TO ME LIKE THAT!
OH... SORRY...
YOU KNOW... YOU'VE BEEN SPENDING A LOT OF TIME WITH THE VICE PRESIDENT LATELY.
...IS EVERYTHING OKAY?
HUH? WHAT'S THAT SUPPOSED TO MEAN?
NO...JUST AS LONG AS SHE ISN'T DOING ANYTHING TO YOU...
I JUST THOUGHT THE SHADOW STUDENT COUNCIL HAS BEEN ACTING KIND OF STRANGE RECENTLY...
SO, WELL...

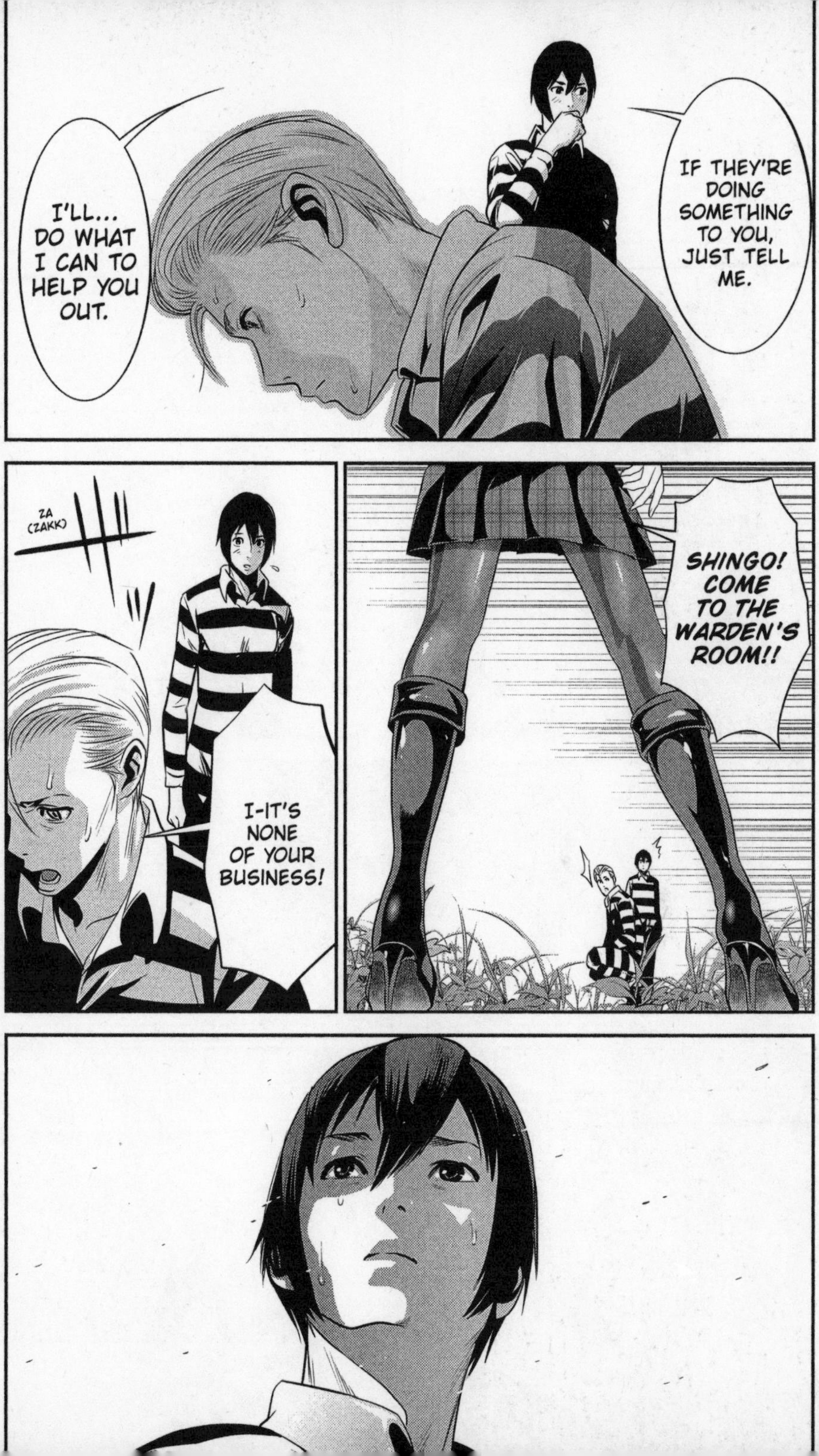
IF THEY'RE DOING SOMETHING TO YOU, JUST TELL ME.
I'LL... DO WHAT I CAN TO HELP YOU OUT.
SHINGO! COME TO THE WARDEN'S ROOM!!
ZA (ZAKK)
I-IT'S NONE OF YOUR BUSINESS!

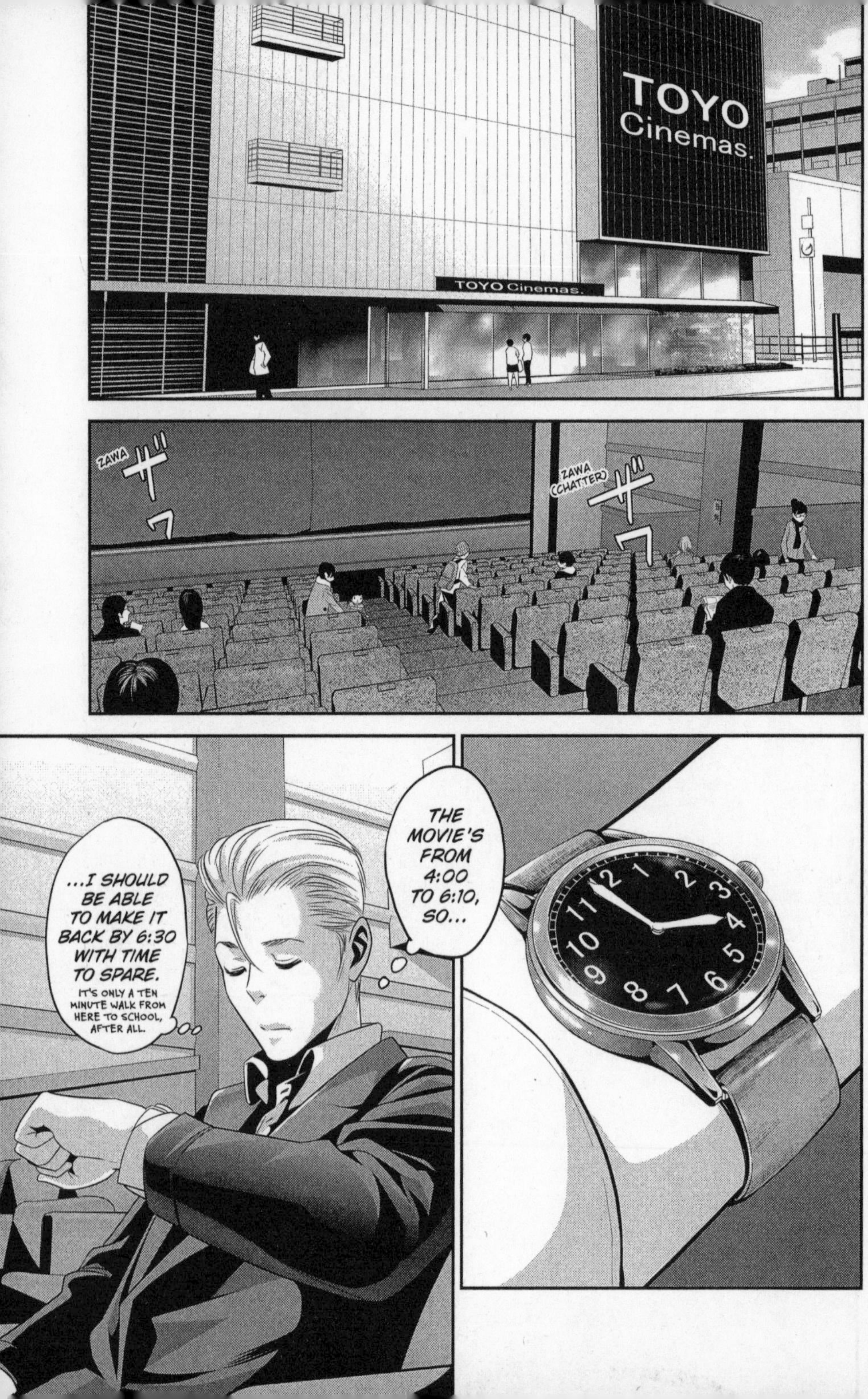
TOYO Cinemas.
TOYO Cinemas.
ZAWA (CHATTER)
ザワ
ZAWA
ザワ
THE MOVIE'S FROM 4:00 TO 6:10, SO...
...I SHOULD BE ABLE TO MAKE IT BACK BY 6:30 WITH TIME TO SPARE.
IT'S ONLY A TEN MINUTE WALK FROM HERE TO SCHOOL, AFTER ALL.

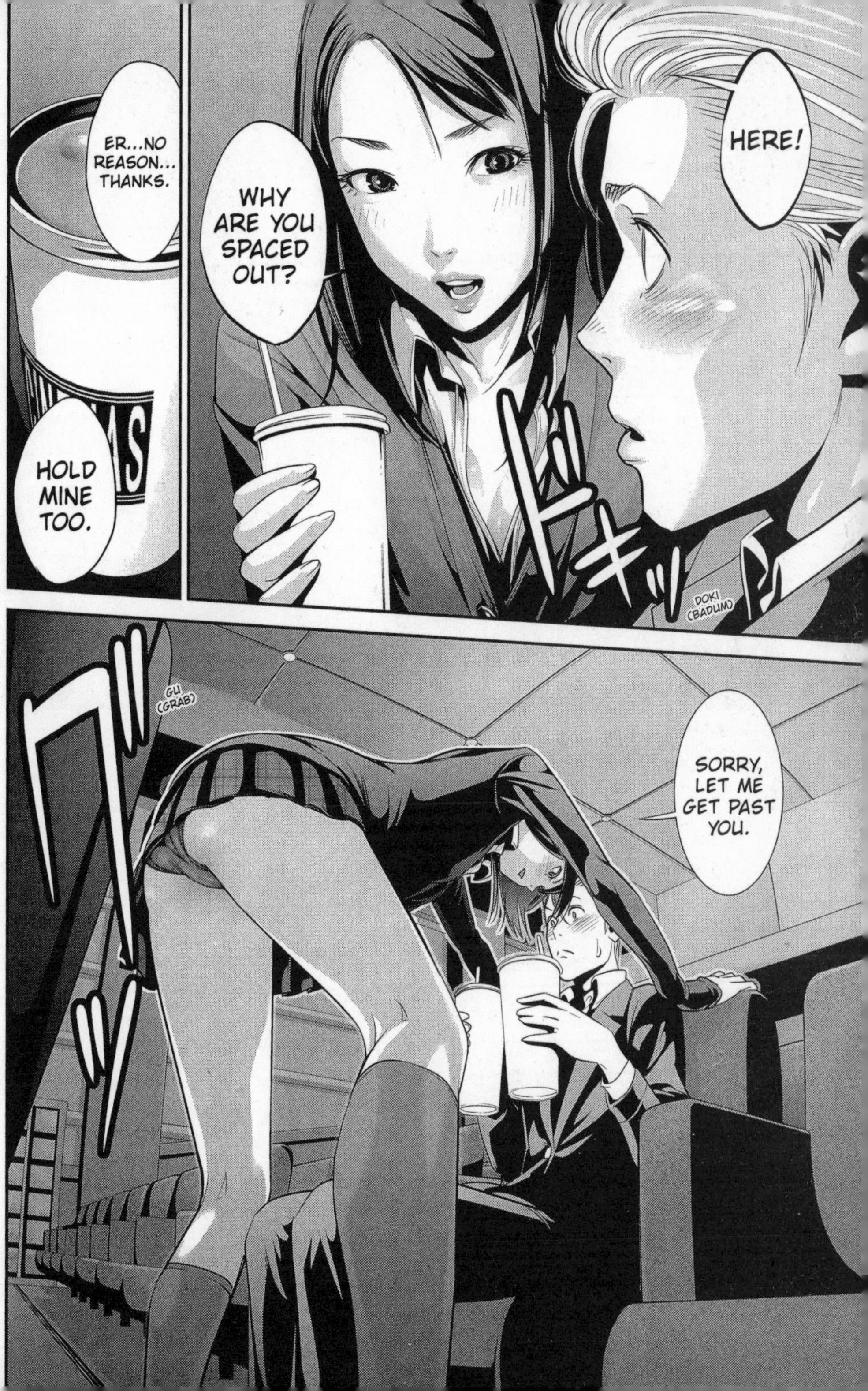
HERE!
WHY ARE YOU SPACED OUT?
DOKI (BADUM)
ER...NO REASON... THANKS.
HOLD MINE TOO.
SORRY, LET ME GET PAST YOU.
GU (GRAB)

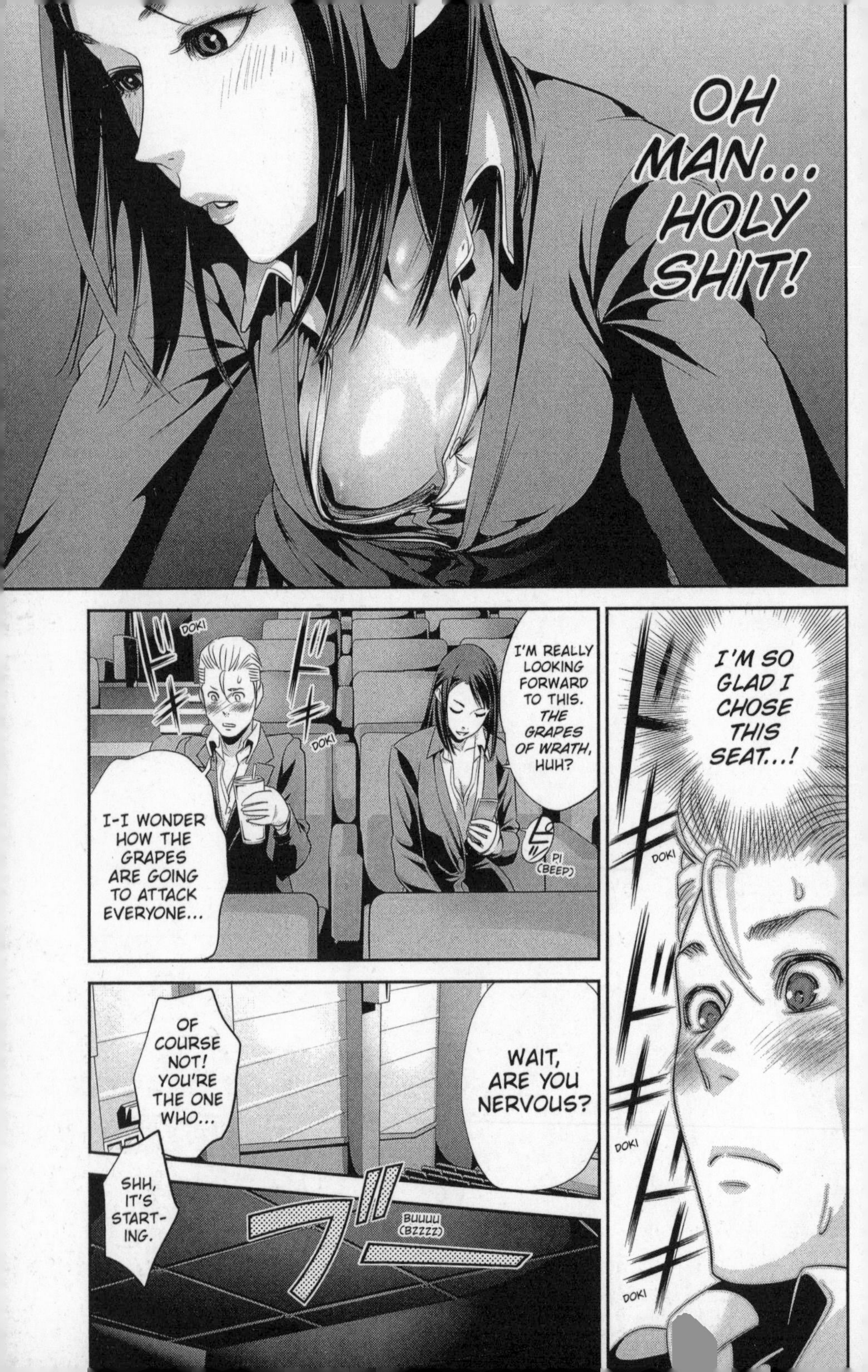
OH MAN... HOLY SHIT!
I'M SO GLAD I CHOSE THIS SEAT...!
DOKI
DOKI
DOKI
DOKI
I'M REALLY LOOKING FORWARD TO THIS. *THE GRAPES OF WRATH*, HUH?
DOKI
PI (BEEP)
I-I WONDER HOW THE GRAPES ARE GOING TO ATTACK EVERYONE...
WAIT, ARE YOU NERVOUS?
OF COURSE NOT! YOU'RE THE ONE WHO...
SHH, IT'S START-ING.
BUUUU (BZZZZ)

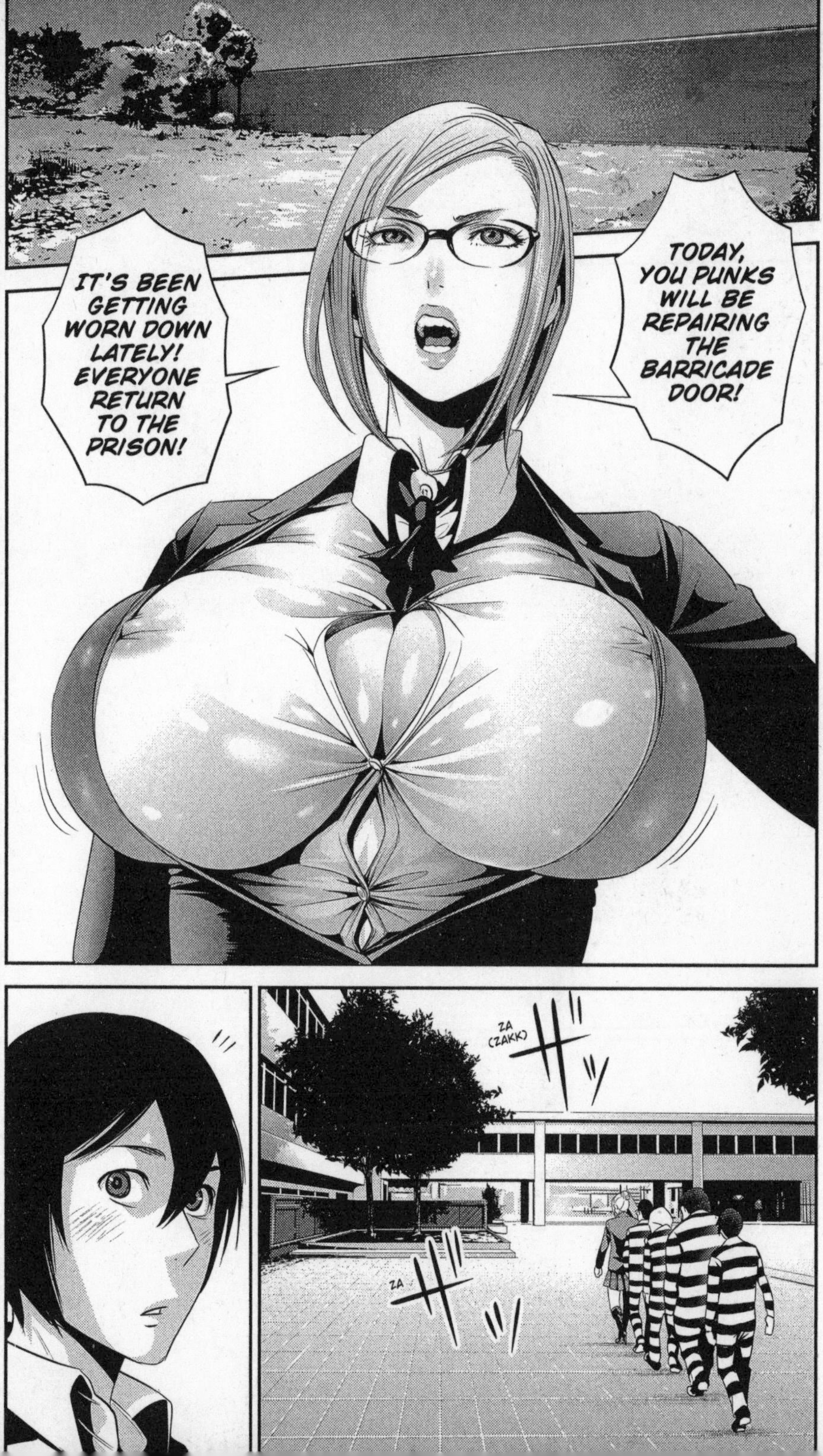
TODAY, YOU PUNKS WILL BE REPAIRING THE BARRICADE DOOR!
IT'S BEEN GETTING WORN DOWN LATELY! EVERYONE RETURN TO THE PRISON!
ZA (ZAKK)
ZA

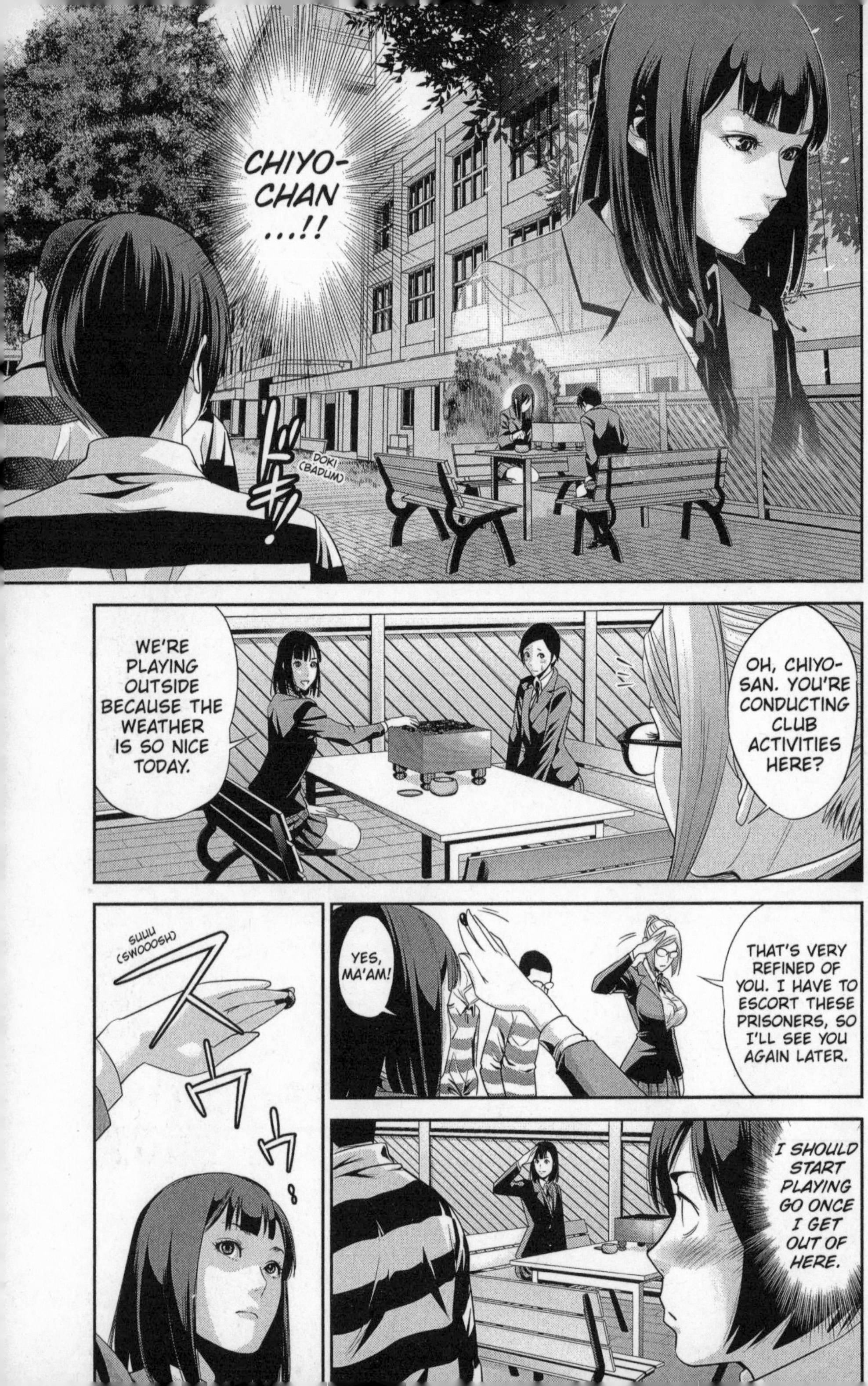
CHIYO-CHAN ...!!
DOKI (BADUM)
OH, CHIYO-SAN. YOU'RE CONDUCTING CLUB ACTIVITIES HERE?
WE'RE PLAYING OUTSIDE BECAUSE THE WEATHER IS SO NICE TODAY.
THAT'S VERY REFINED OF YOU. I HAVE TO ESCORT THESE PRISONERS, SO I'LL SEE YOU AGAIN LATER.
YES, MA'AM!
SUUU (SWOOOSH)
I SHOULD START PLAYING GO ONCE I GET OUT OF HERE.

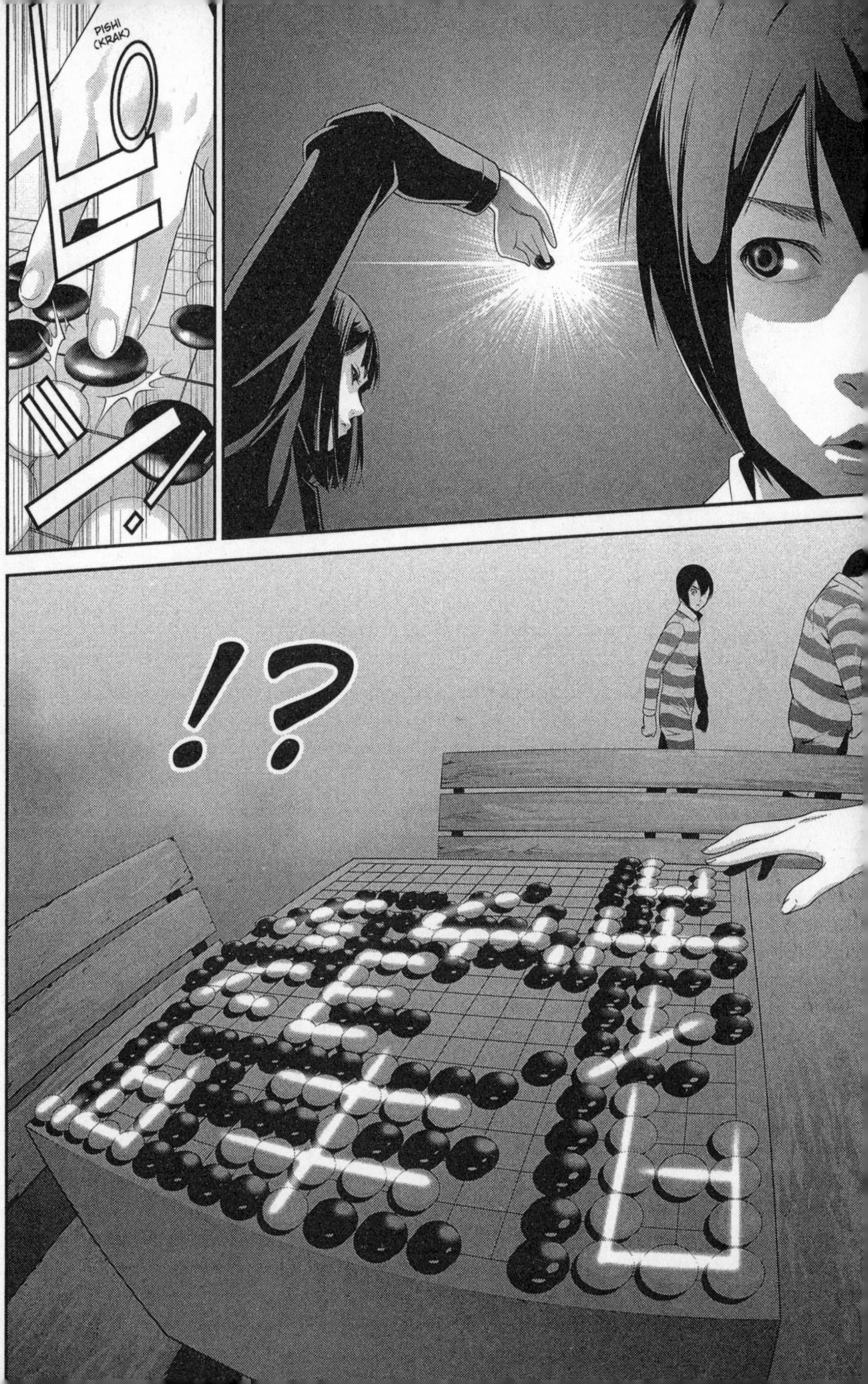
PISHI
(KRAK)
!?

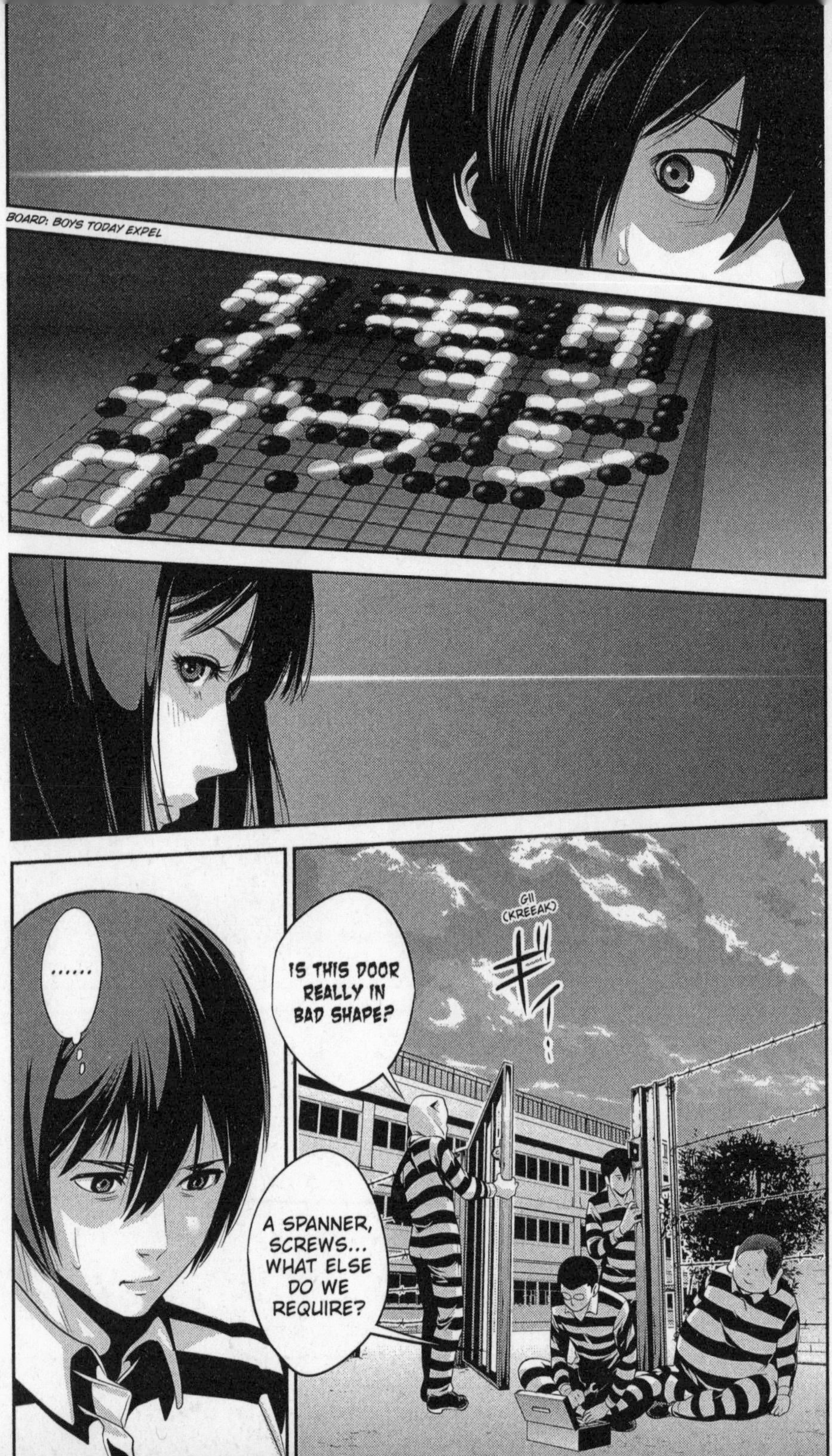
BOARD: BOYS TODAY EXPEL
GII (KREEAK)
IS THIS DOOR REALLY IN BAD SHAPE?
A SPANNER, SCREWS... WHAT ELSE DO WE REQUIRE?
......

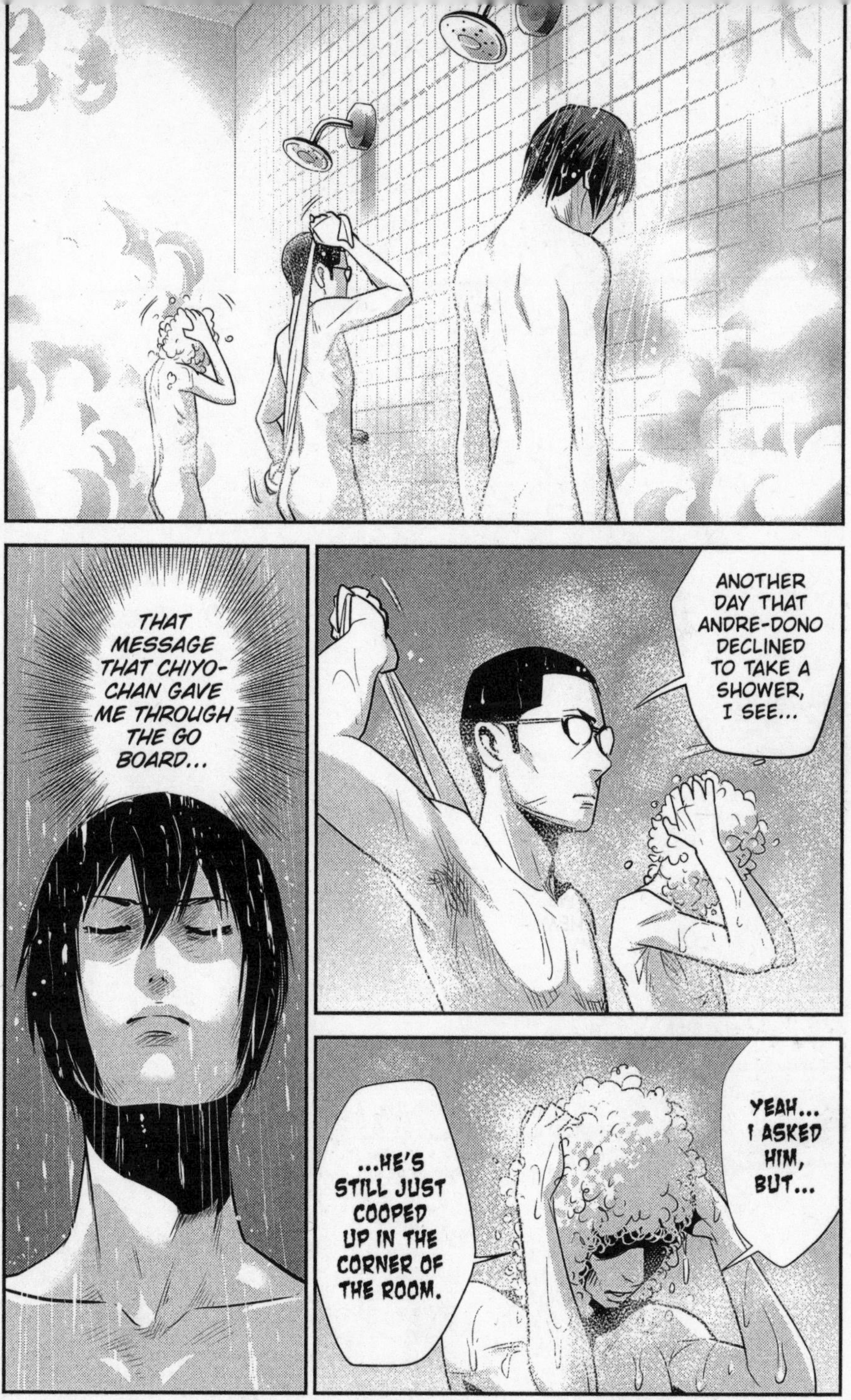
ANOTHER DAY THAT ANDRE-DONO DECLINED TO TAKE A SHOWER, I SEE...
YEAH... I ASKED HIM, BUT...
...HE'S STILL JUST COOPED UP IN THE CORNER OF THE ROOM.
THAT MESSAGE THAT CHIYO-CHAN GAVE ME THROUGH THE GO BOARD...

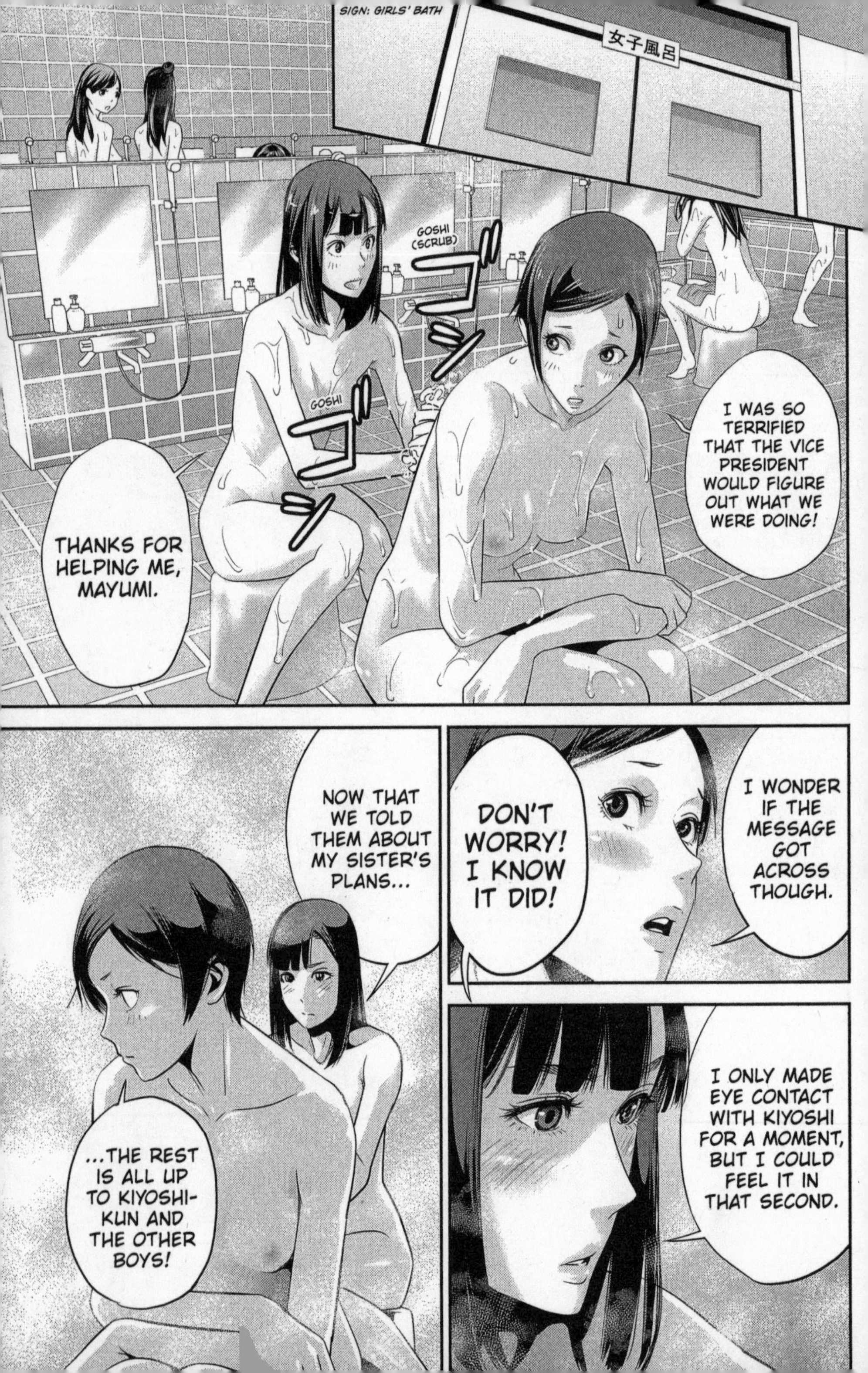
SIGN: GIRLS' BATH
女子風呂
I WAS SO TERRIFIED THAT THE VICE PRESIDENT WOULD FIGURE OUT WHAT WE WERE DOING!
GOSHI (SCRUB)
GOSHI
THANKS FOR HELPING ME, MAYUMI.
I WONDER IF THE MESSAGE GOT ACROSS THOUGH.
DON'T WORRY! I KNOW IT DID!
I ONLY MADE EYE CONTACT WITH KIYOSHI FOR A MOMENT, BUT I COULD FEEL IT IN THAT SECOND.
NOW THAT WE TOLD THEM ABOUT MY SISTER'S PLANS...
...THE REST IS ALL UP TO KIYOSHI-KUN AND THE OTHER BOYS!

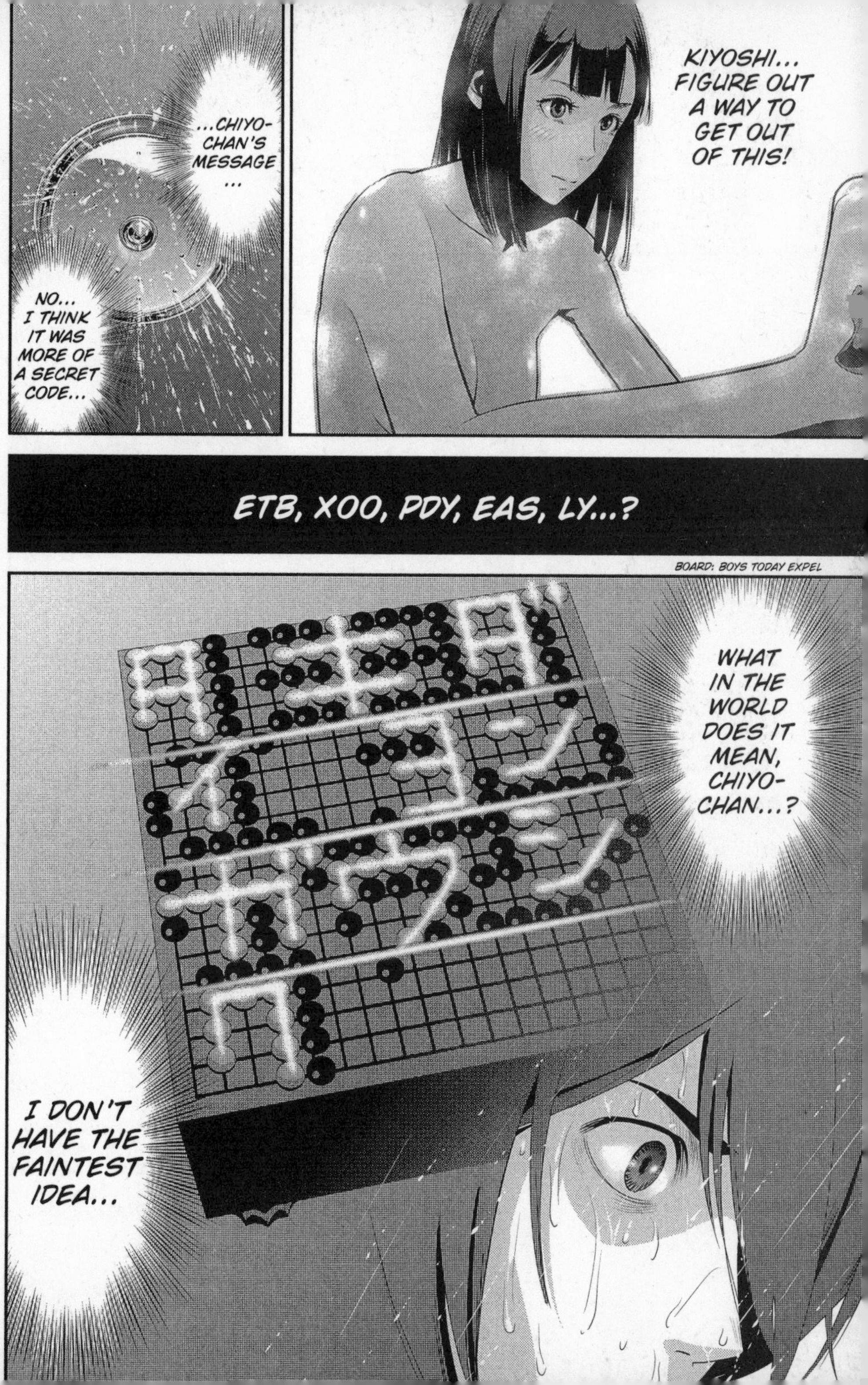
KIYOSHI... FIGURE OUT A WAY TO GET OUT OF THIS!
...CHIYO-CHAN'S MESSAGE ...
NO... I THINK IT WAS MORE OF A SECRET CODE...
ETB, XOO, PDY, EAS, LY...?
BOARD: BOYS TODAY EXPEL
WHAT IN THE WORLD DOES IT MEAN, CHIYO-CHAN...?
I DON'T HAVE THE FAINTEST IDEA...

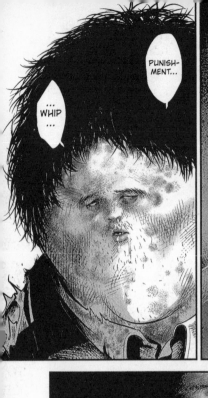

... WHIP ...

PUNISH-
MENT...

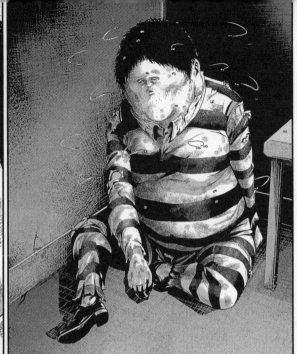

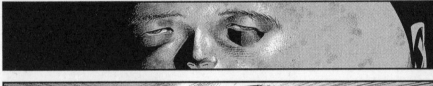

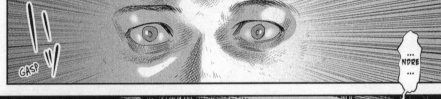

GASP

...NDRE
...

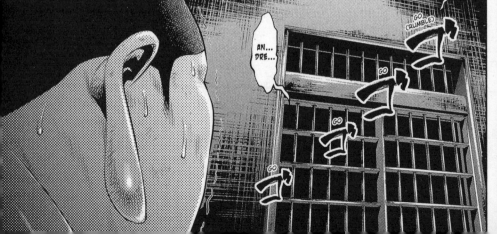

AN...
DRE...

GO
(RUMBLE)

GO

GO

GO

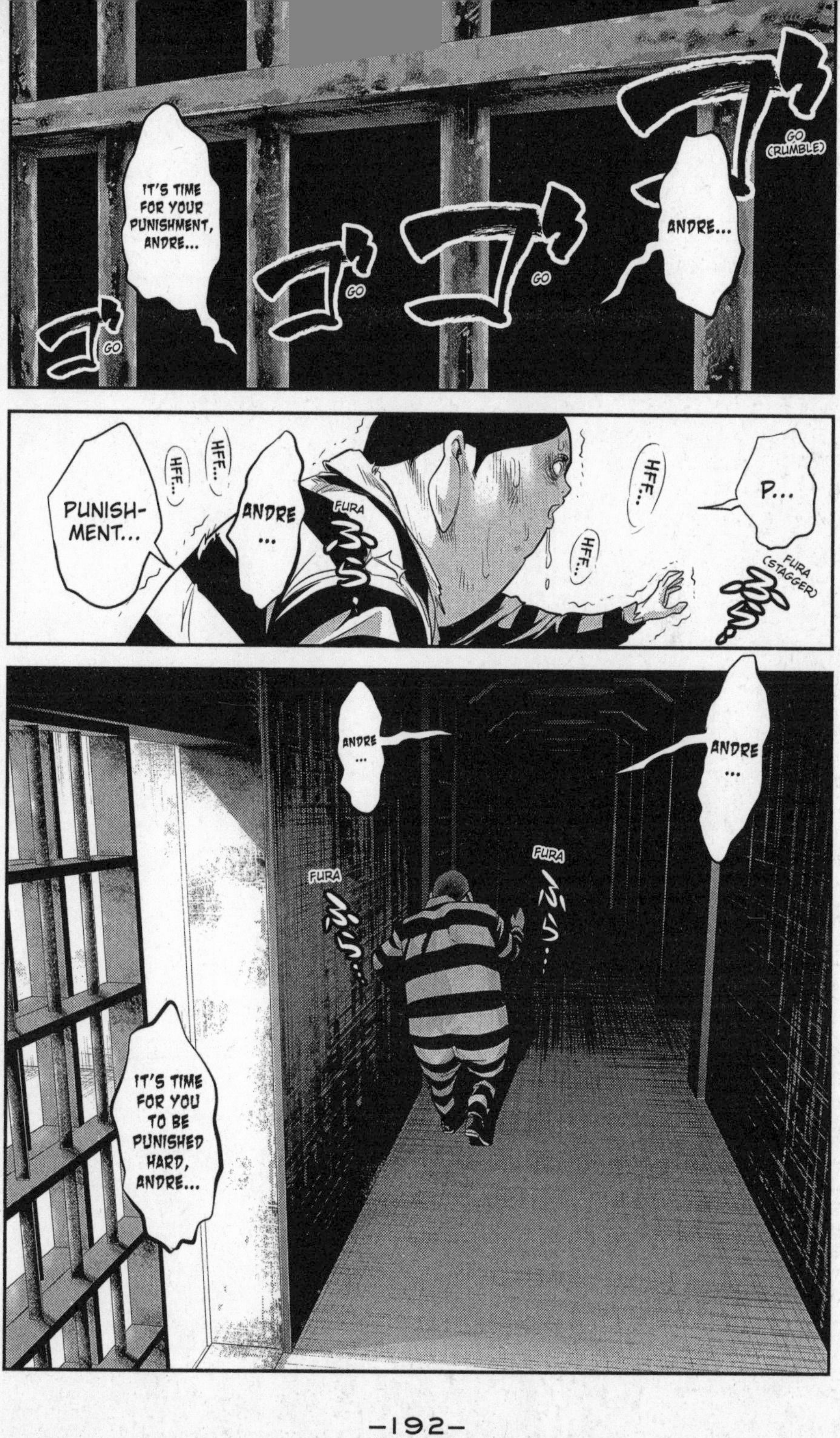
GO (RUMBLE)
ANDRE...
GO
GO
IT'S TIME FOR YOUR PUNISHMENT, ANDRE...
GO
P...
FURA (STAGGER)
HFF...
HFF...
FURA
ANDRE ...
HFF...
HFF...
PUNISHMENT...
ANDRE ...
ANDRE ...
FURA
FURA
IT'S TIME FOR YOU TO BE PUNISHED HARD, ANDRE...

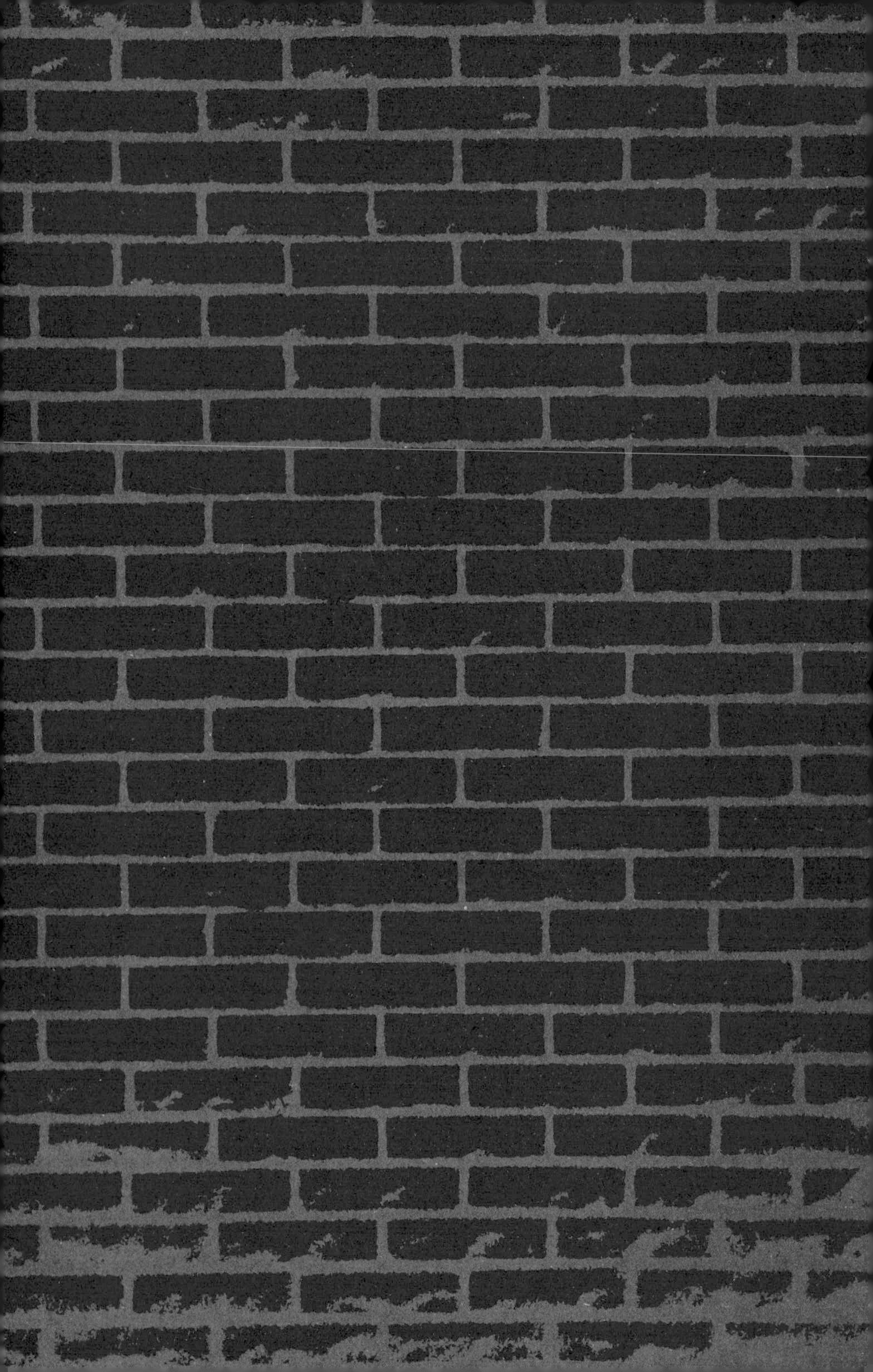

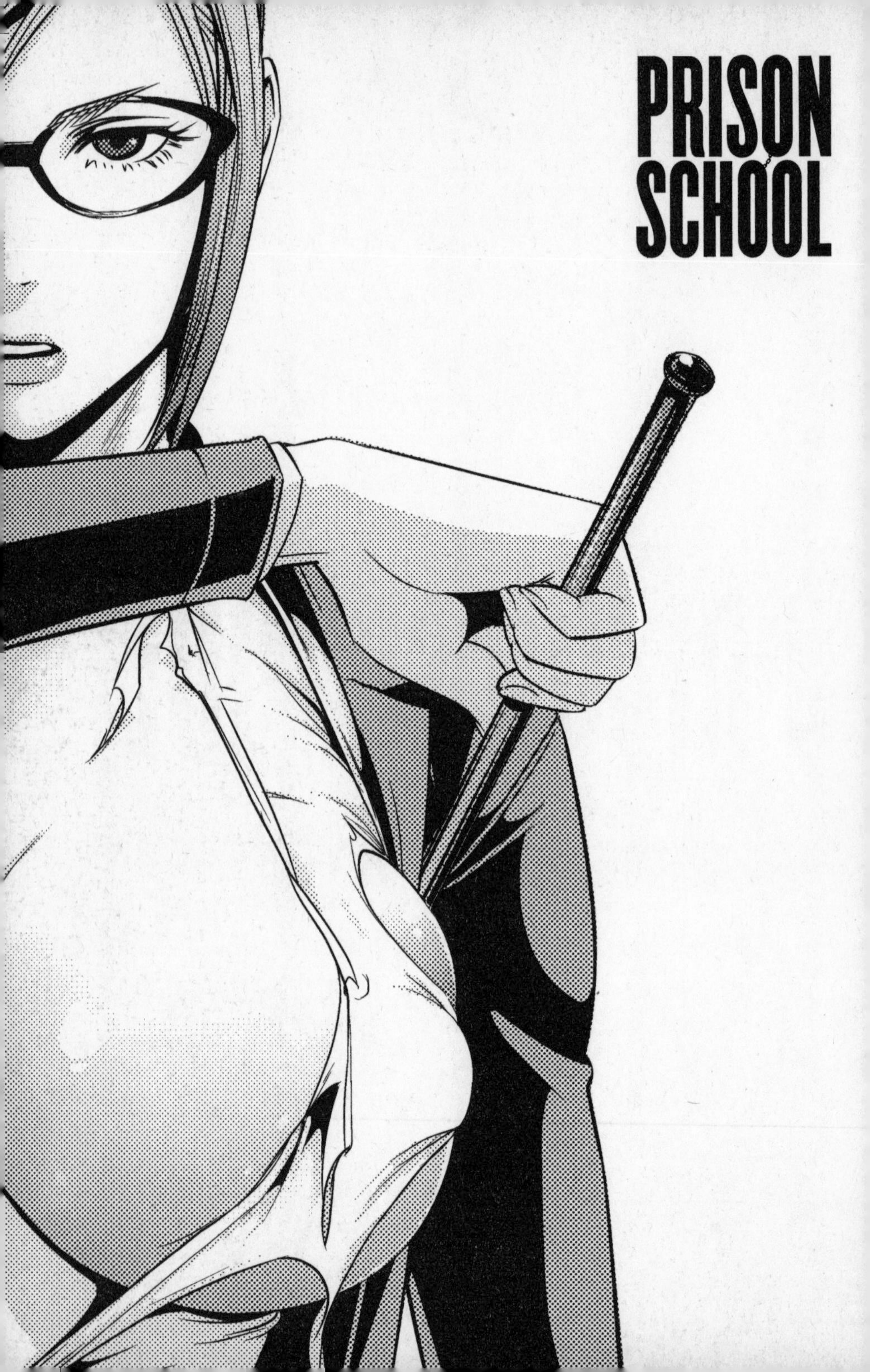
PRISON
SCHOOL

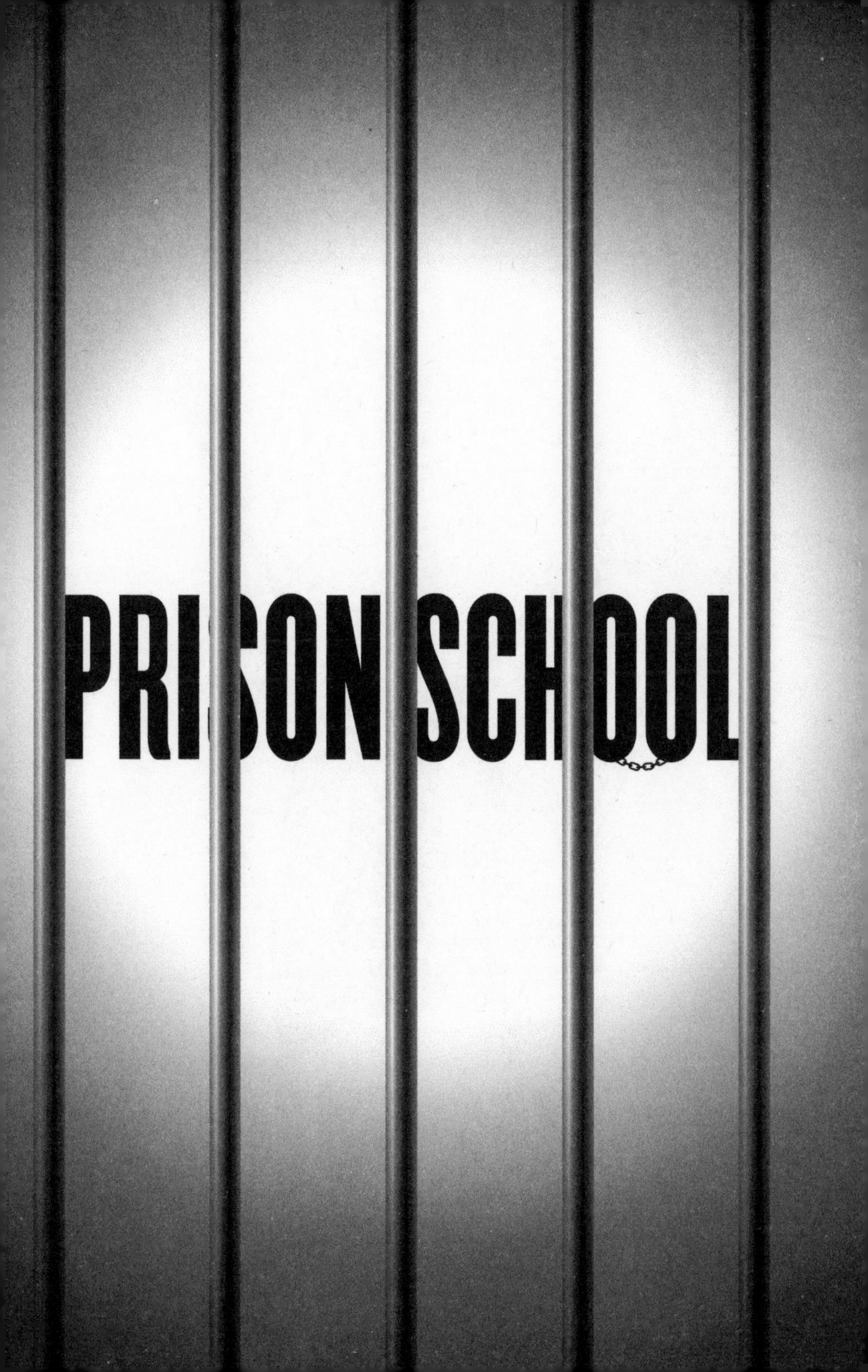
PRISON SCHOOL

CHAPTER 49: PHONE

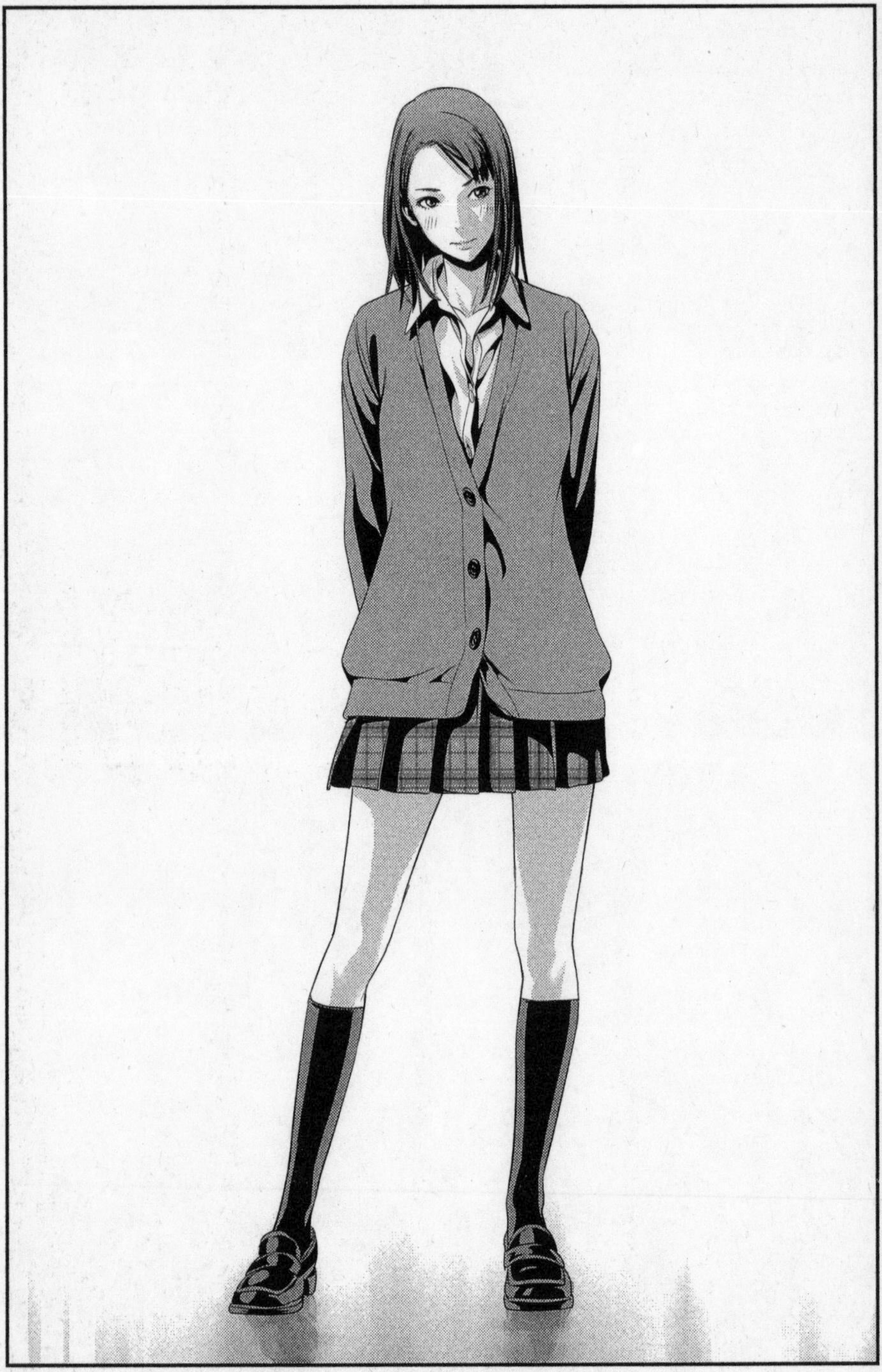

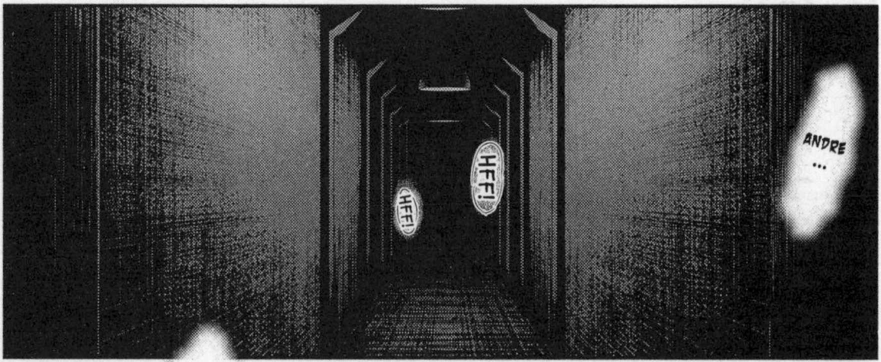
ANDRE ...
HFF!
HFF!

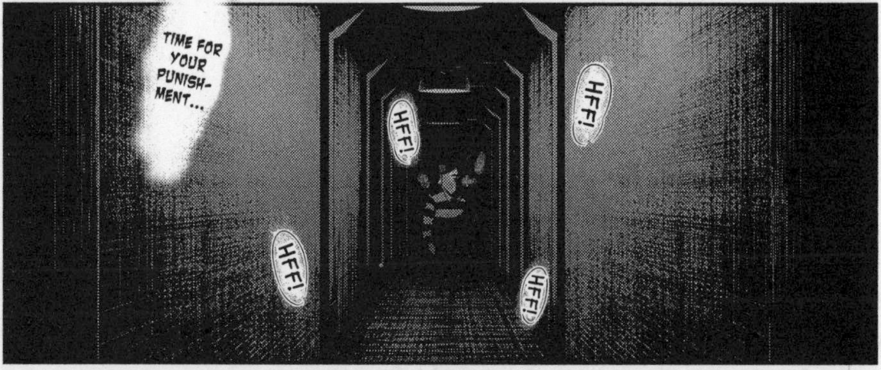
HFF!
HFF!
TIME FOR YOUR PUNISH-MENT...
HFF!
HFF!

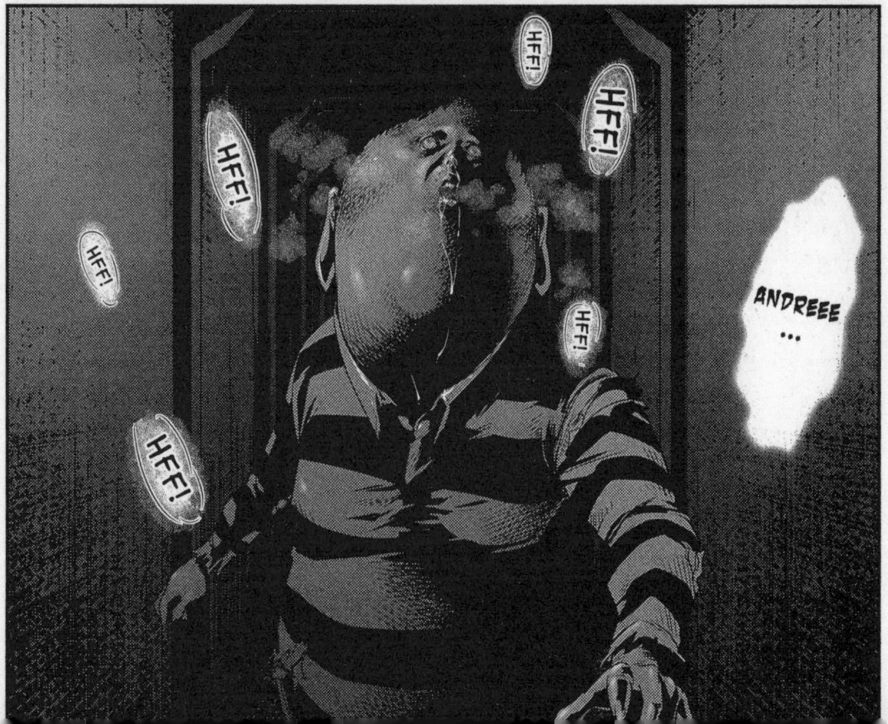
HFF!
HFF!
ANDREEE ...
HFF!
HFF!
HFF!
HFF!

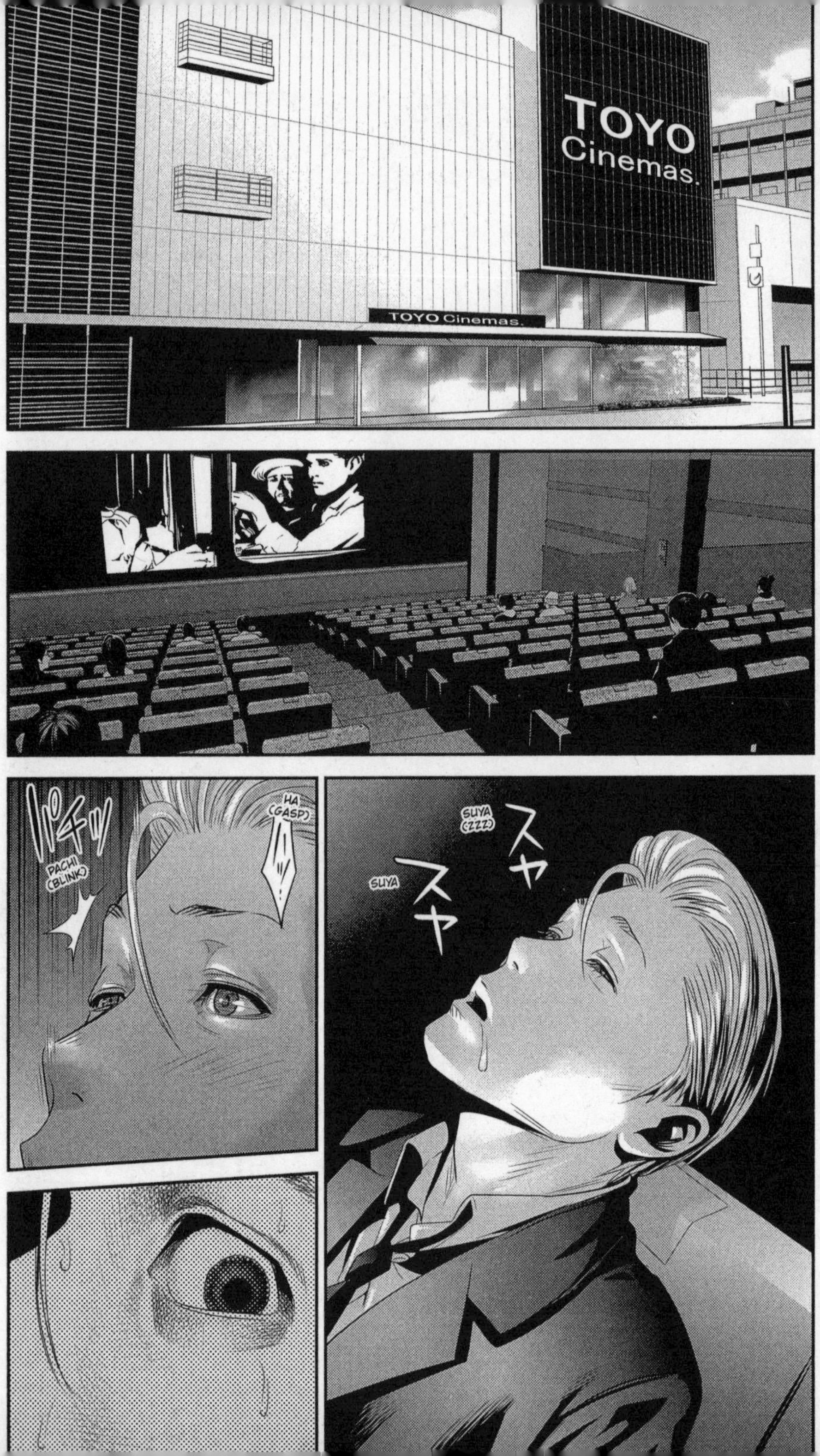
TOYO Cinemas.
TOYO Cinemas.
スヤ
SUYA (ZZZ)
スヤ
SUYA
HA (GASP)
パチッ
PACHI (BLINK)

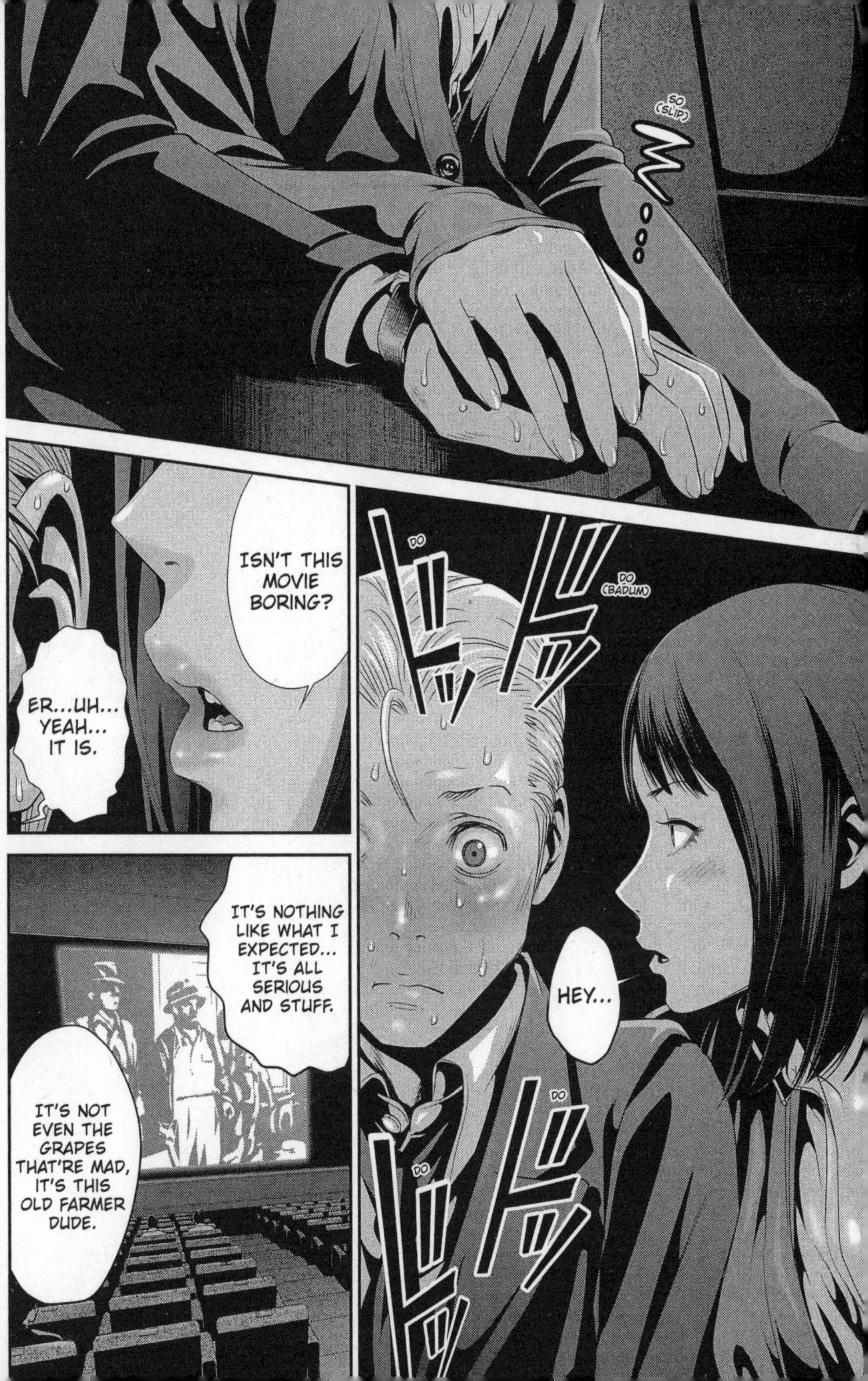
SO (SLIP)
DO
DO (BADUM)
HEY...
DO
DO
ISN'T THIS MOVIE BORING?
ER...UH... YEAH... IT IS.
IT'S NOTHING LIKE WHAT I EXPECTED... IT'S ALL SERIOUS AND STUFF.
IT'S NOT EVEN THE GRAPES THAT'RE MAD, IT'S THIS OLD FARMER DUDE.

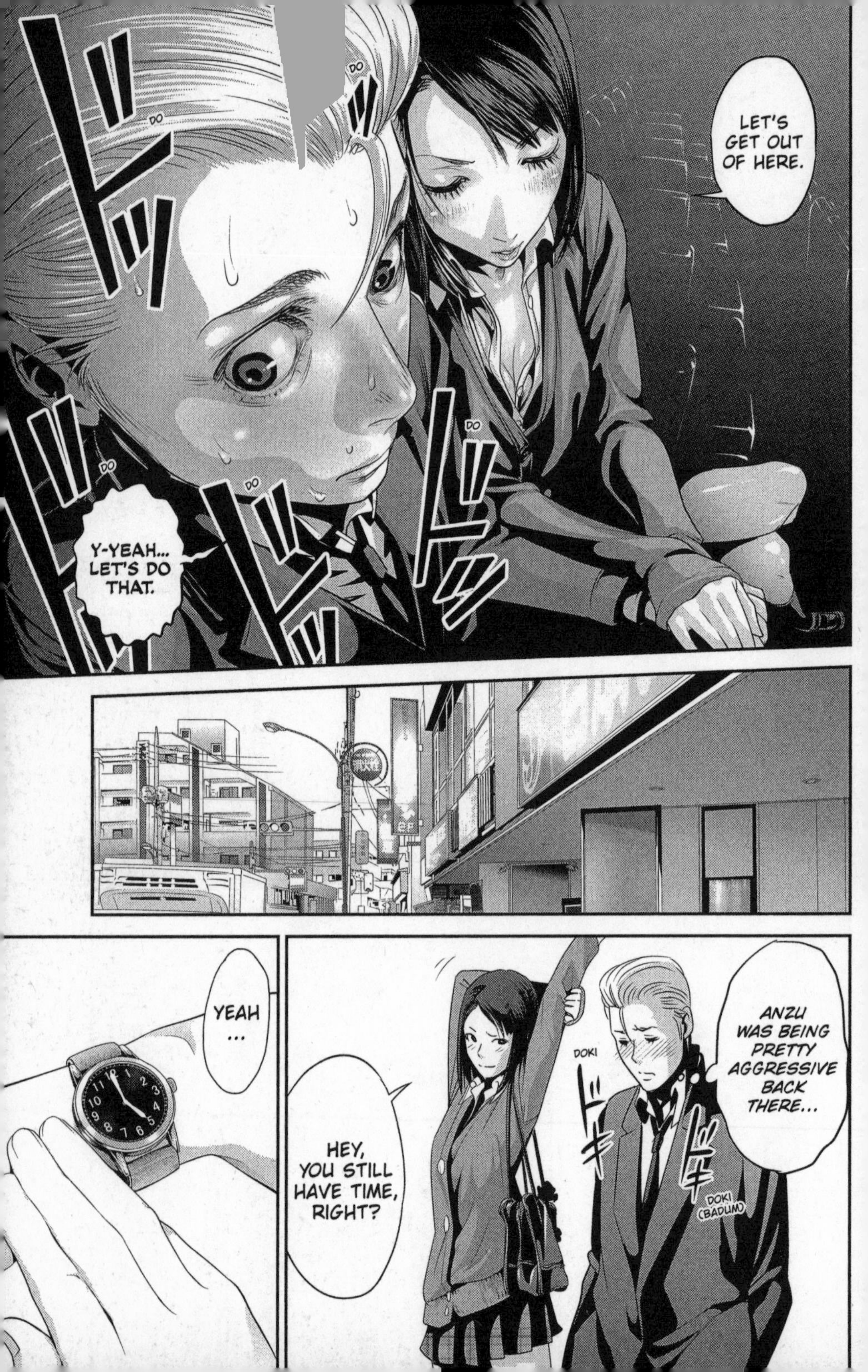
LET'S GET OUT OF HERE.
DO
DO
DO
DO
DO
Y-YEAH... LET'S DO THAT.
ANZU WAS BEING PRETTY AGGRESSIVE BACK THERE...
DOKI
DOKI (BADUM)
HEY, YOU STILL HAVE TIME, RIGHT?
YEAH ...

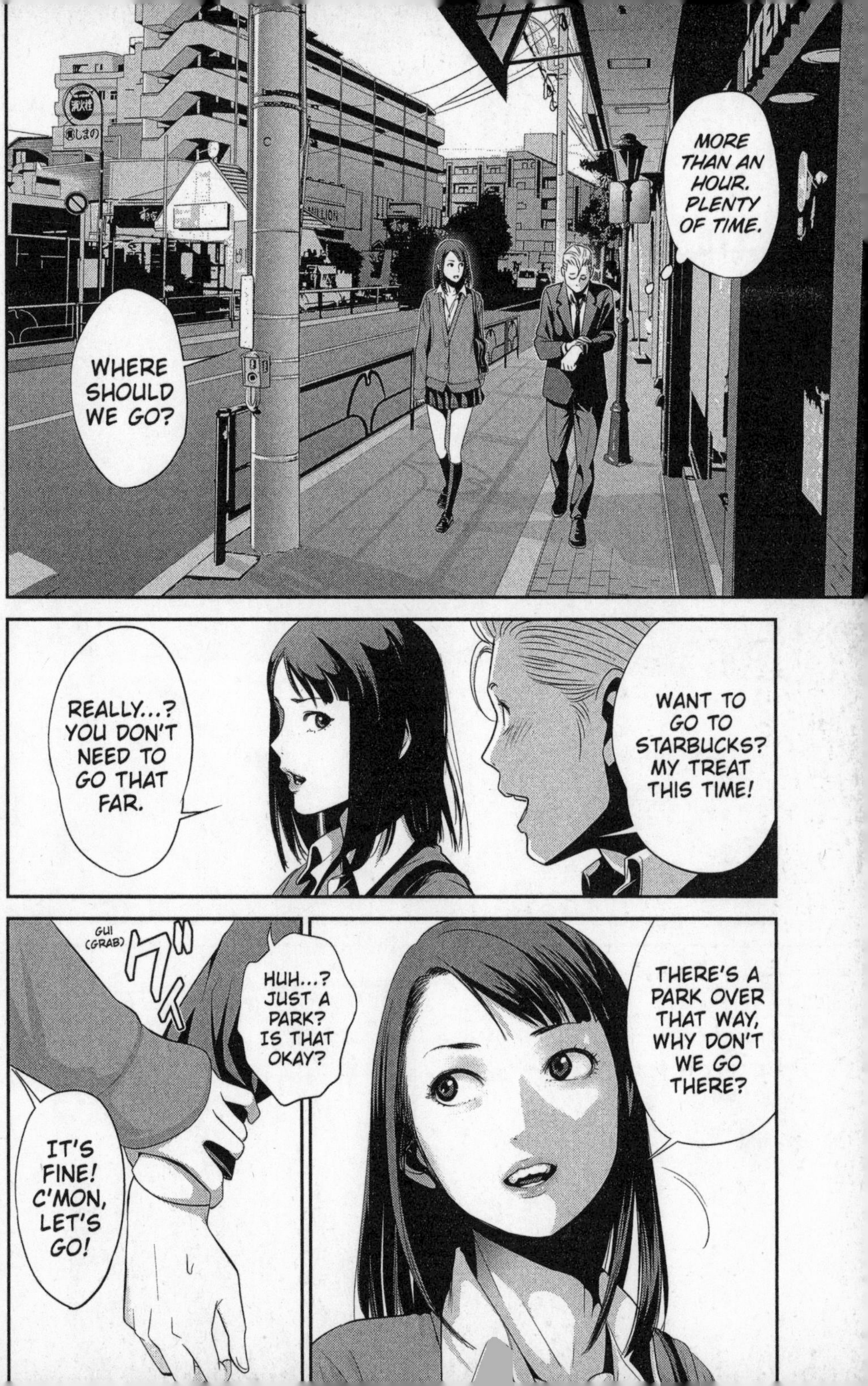
MORE THAN AN HOUR. PLENTY OF TIME.
WHERE SHOULD WE GO?
WANT TO GO TO STARBUCKS? MY TREAT THIS TIME!
REALLY...? YOU DON'T NEED TO GO THAT FAR.
THERE'S A PARK OVER THAT WAY, WHY DON'T WE GO THERE?
HUH...? JUST A PARK? IS THAT OKAY?
GUI (GRAB)
IT'S FINE! C'MON, LET'S GO!

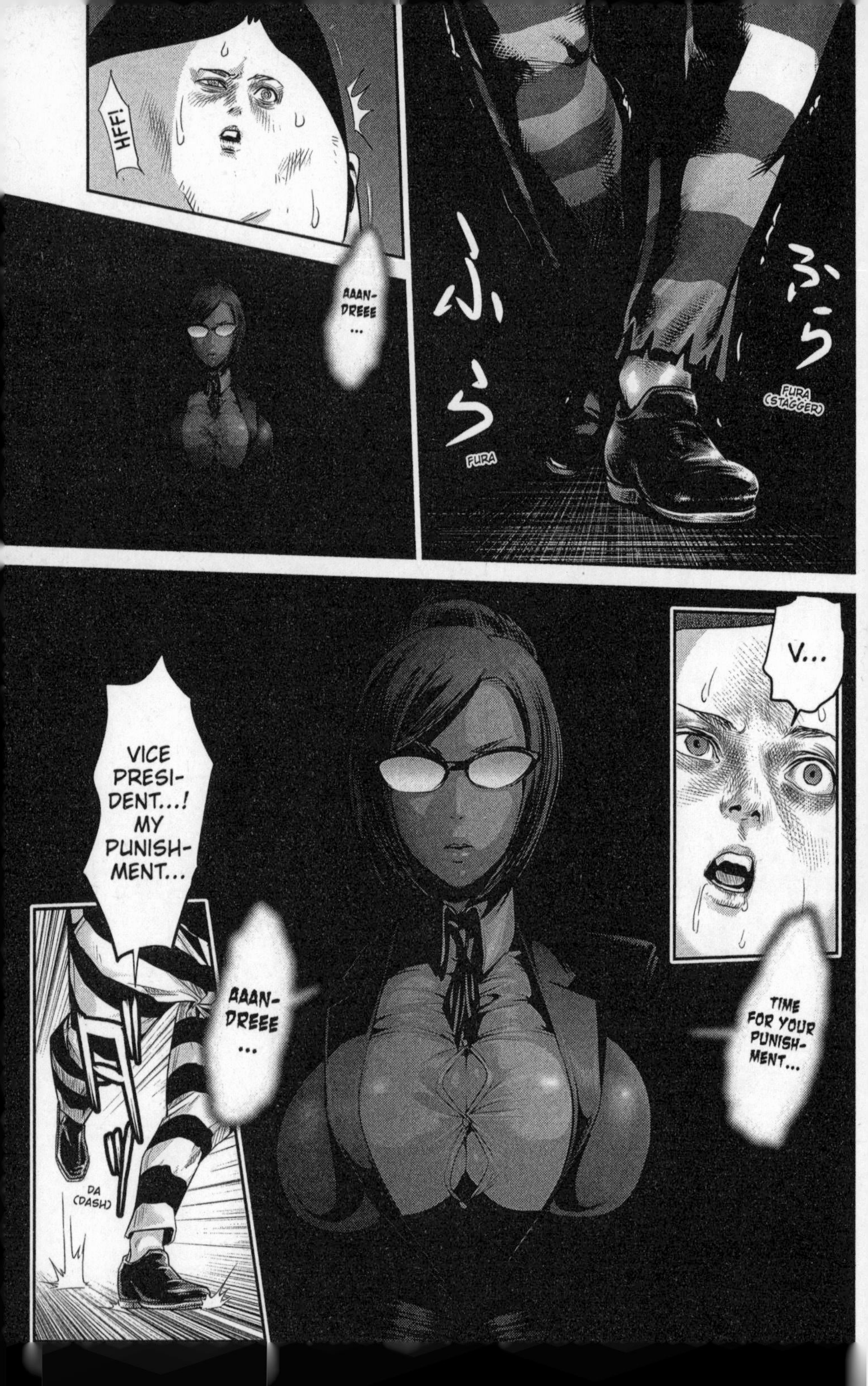
ふら
FURA (STAGGER)
ふら
FURA
HFF!
AAAN-DREEE...
V...
TIME FOR YOUR PUNISHMENT...
AAAN-DREEE...
VICE PRESIDENT...! MY PUNISHMENT...
DA (DASH)

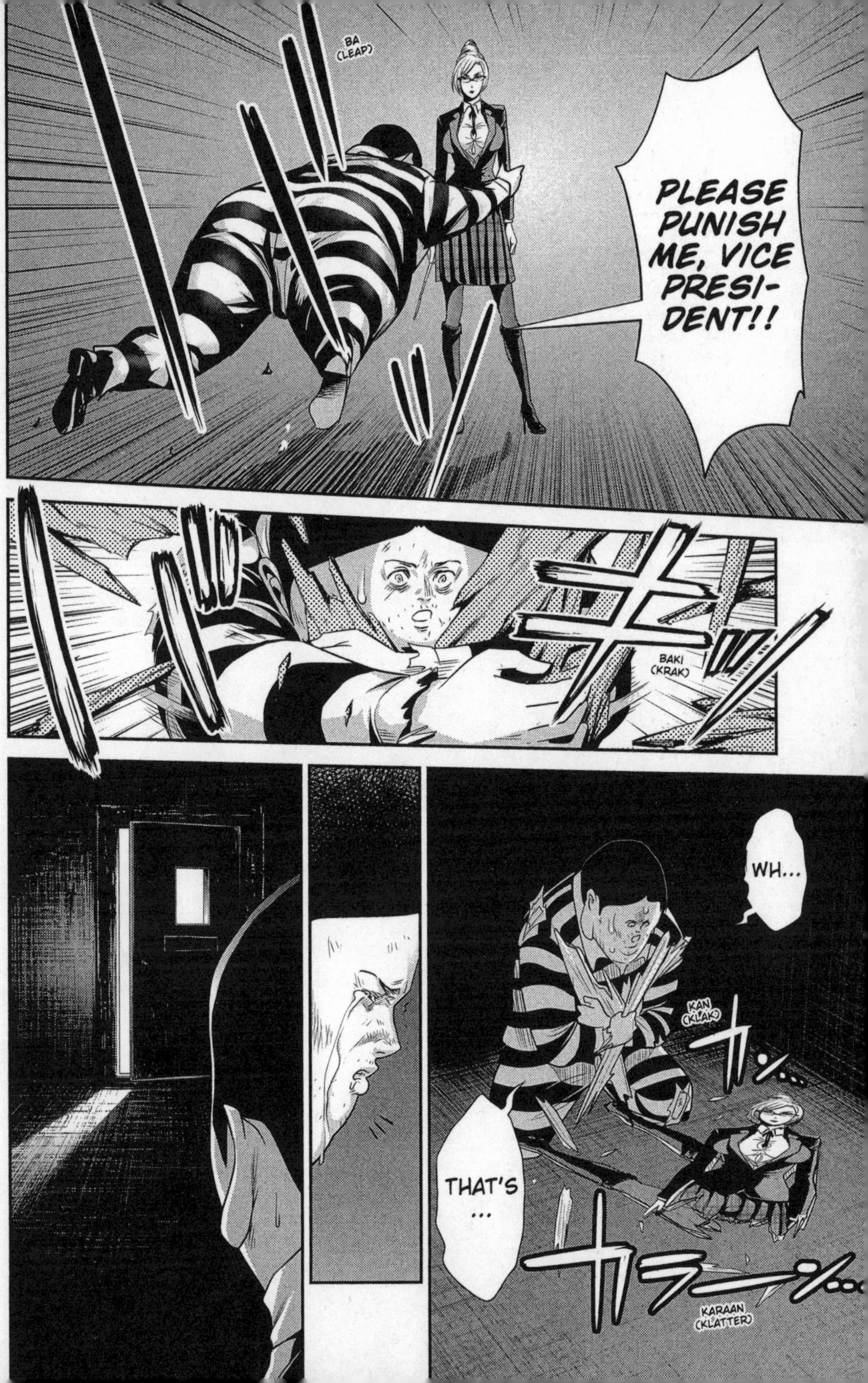
BA (LEAP)
PLEASE PUNISH ME, VICE PRESIDENT!!
BAKI (KRAK)
WH...
KAN (KLAK)
THAT'S ...
KARAAN (KLATTER)

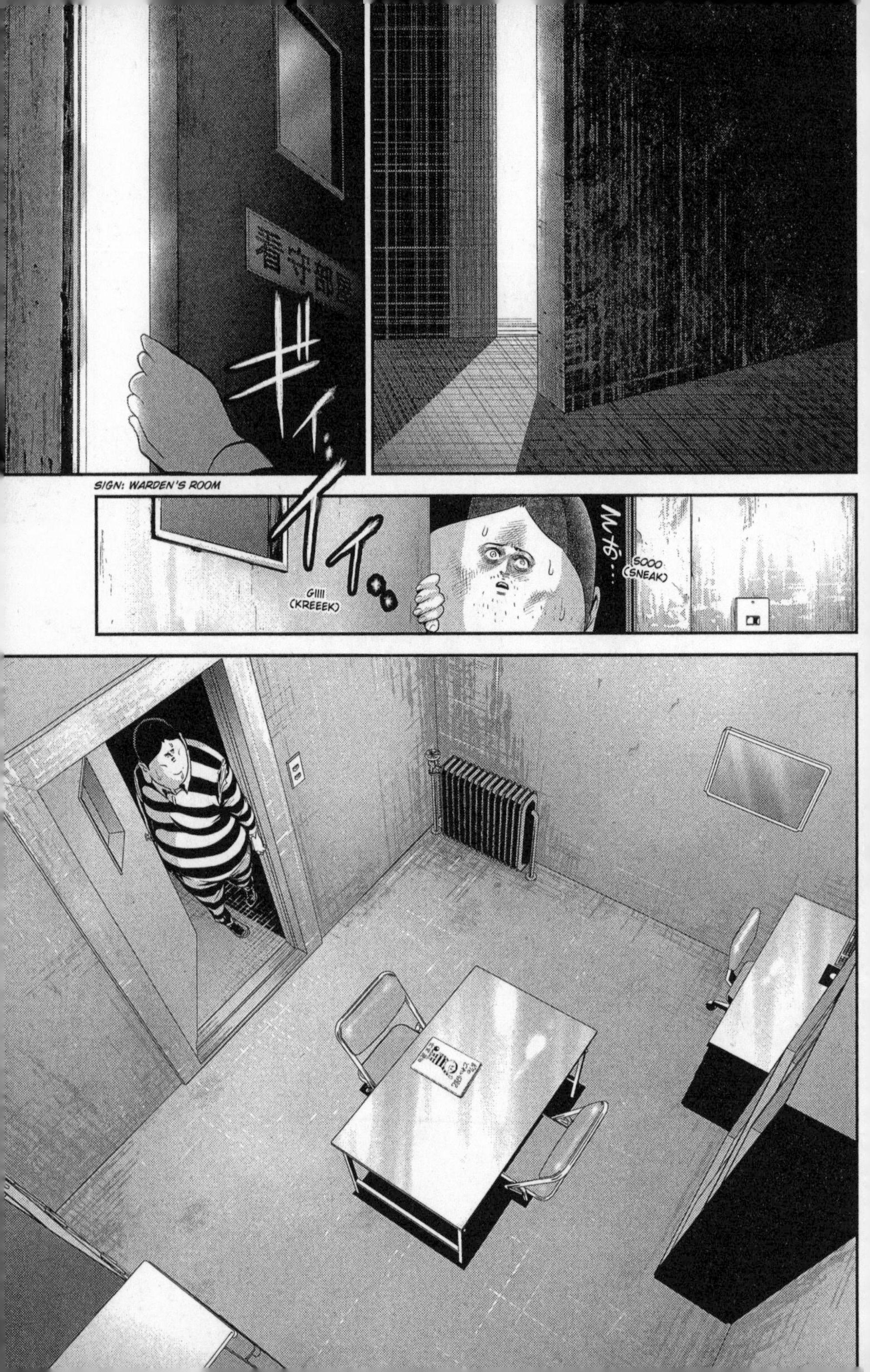
看守部屋
SIGN: WARDEN'S ROOM
ギィ…ィ…
そぉ…
SOOO (SNEAK)
GIIII (KREEEK)

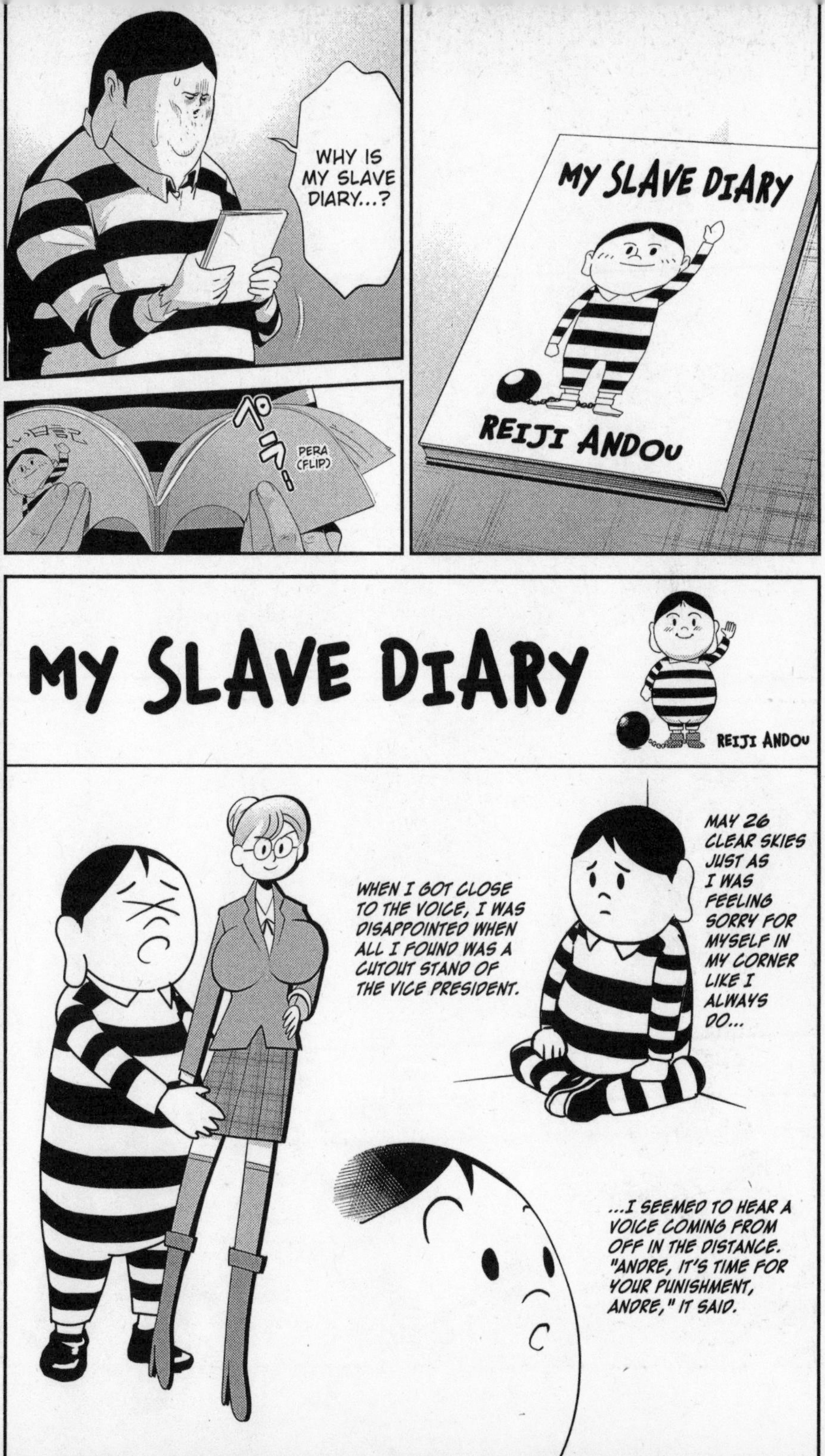
MY SLAVE DIARY
REIJI ANDOU
WHY IS MY SLAVE DIARY...?
PERA (FLIP)
MY SLAVE DIARY
REIJI ANDOU
MAY 26 CLEAR SKIES JUST AS I WAS FEELING SORRY FOR MYSELF IN MY CORNER LIKE I ALWAYS DO...
...I SEEMED TO HEAR A VOICE COMING FROM OFF IN THE DISTANCE. "ANDRE, IT'S TIME FOR YOUR PUNISHMENT, ANDRE," IT SAID.
WHEN I GOT CLOSE TO THE VOICE, I WAS DISAPPOINTED WHEN ALL I FOUND WAS A CUTOUT STAND OF THE VICE PRESIDENT.

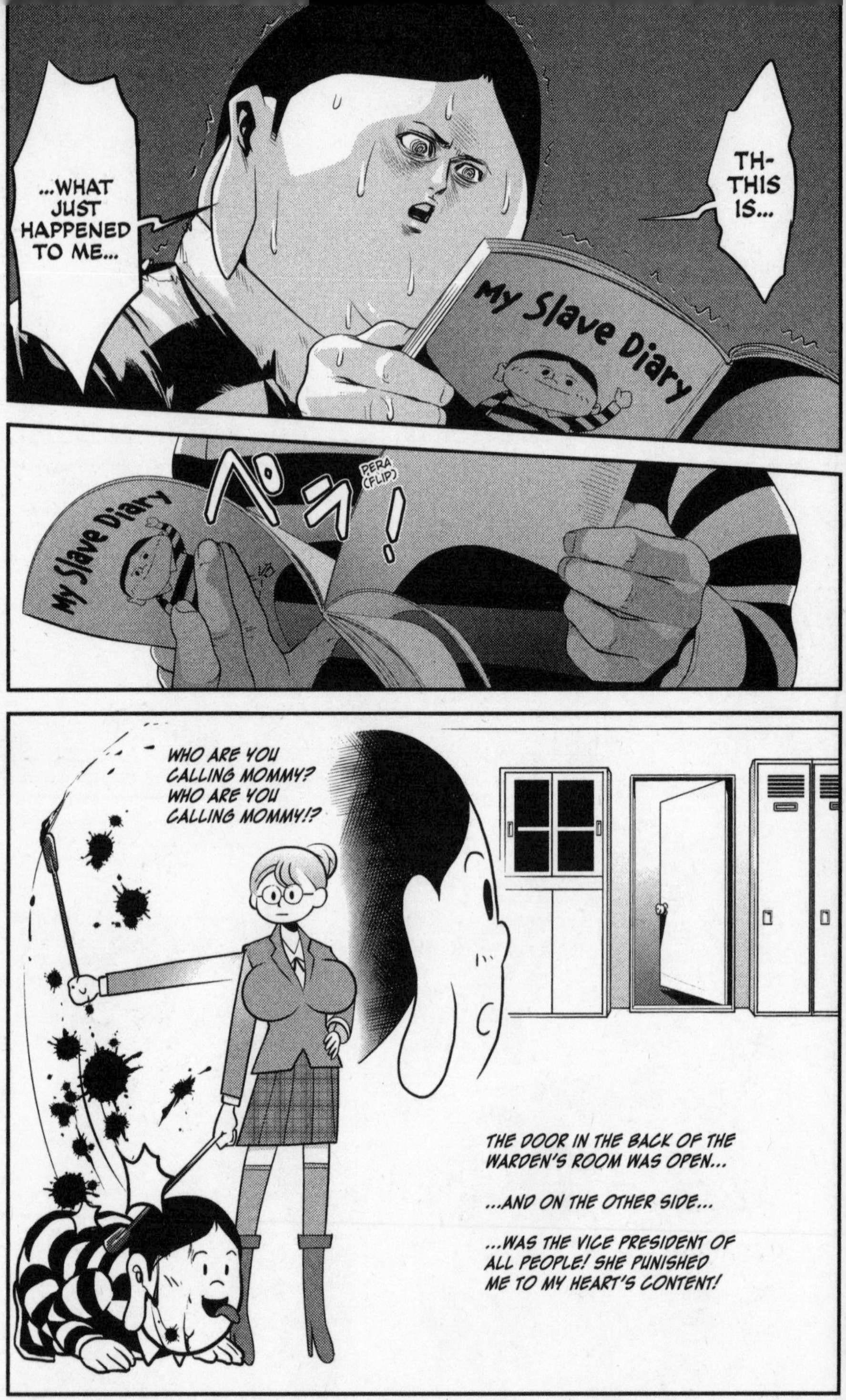
TH- THIS IS...
...WHAT JUST HAPPENED TO ME...
My Slave Diary
PERA (FLIP)
My Slave Diary
WHO ARE YOU CALLING MOMMY? WHO ARE YOU CALLING MOMMY!?
THE DOOR IN THE BACK OF THE WARDEN'S ROOM WAS OPEN...
...AND ON THE OTHER SIDE...
...WAS THE VICE PRESIDENT OF ALL PEOPLE! SHE PUNISHED ME TO MY HEART'S CONTENT!

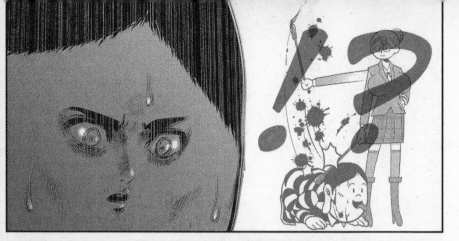

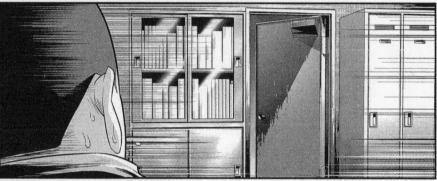

IF I
PASS
THROUGH
IT...

GACHA
(GACHIK)

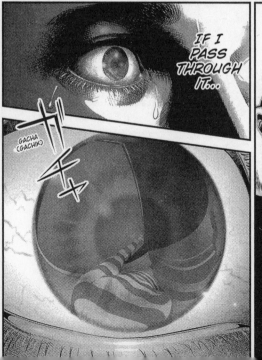

THAT
DOOR...

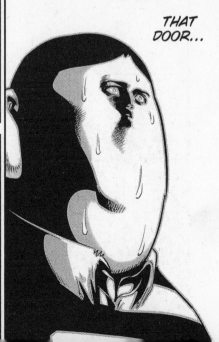

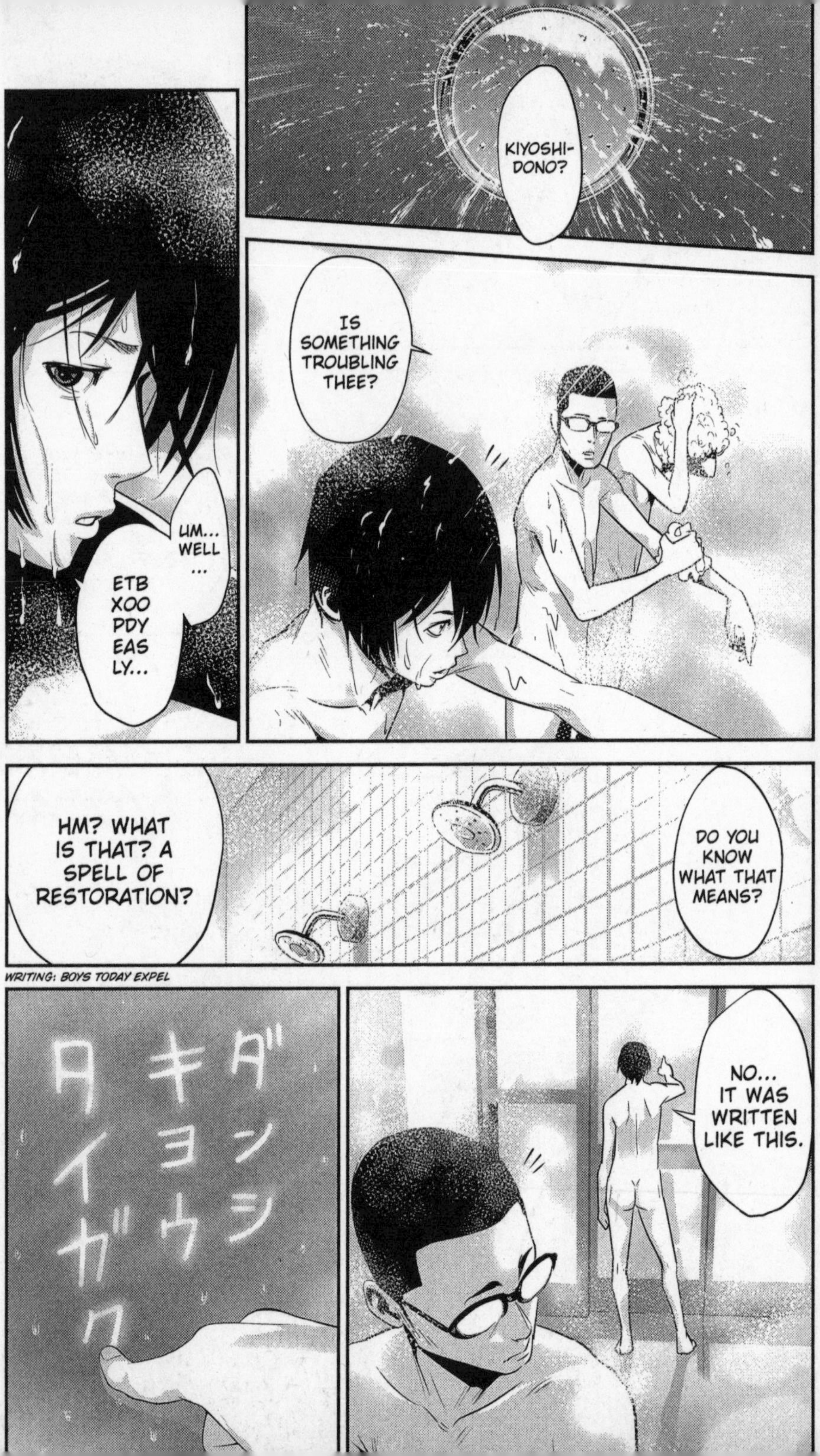
KIYOSHI-DONO?
IS SOMETHING TROUBLING THEE?
UM... WELL...
ETB XOO PDY EAS LY...
DO YOU KNOW WHAT THAT MEANS?
HM? WHAT IS THAT? A SPELL OF RESTORATION?
WRITING: BOYS TODAY EXPEL
NO... IT WAS WRITTEN LIKE THIS.
ダンシ
キヨウ
タイガク

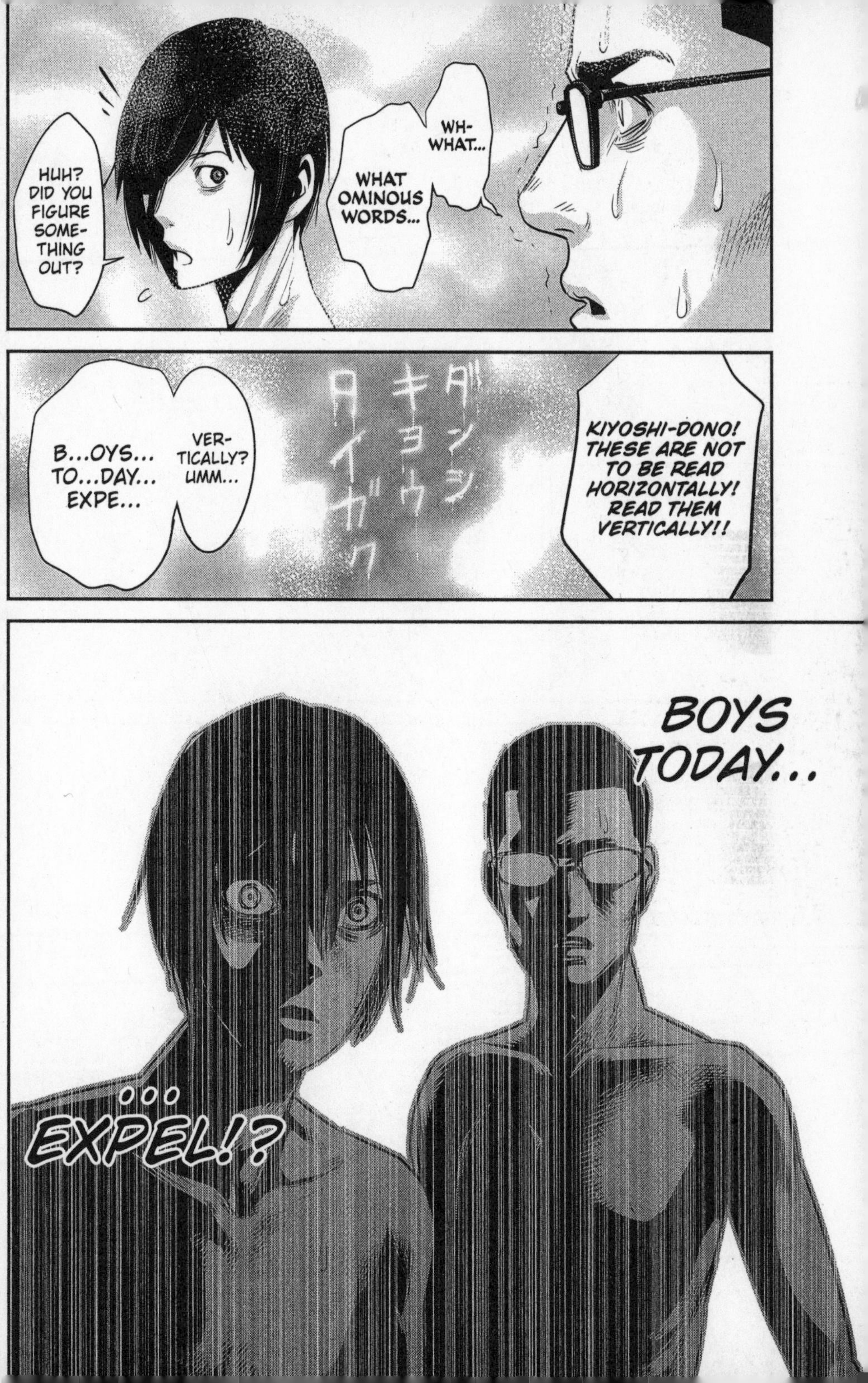
WH-WHAT...
WHAT OMINOUS WORDS...
HUH? DID YOU FIGURE SOME-THING OUT?
KIYOSHI-DONO! THESE ARE NOT TO BE READ HORIZONTALLY! READ THEM VERTICALLY!!
ダンシ
キョウ
タイガク
VER-TICALLY? UMM...
B...OYS... TO...DAY... EXPE...
BOYS TODAY...
...EXPEL!?

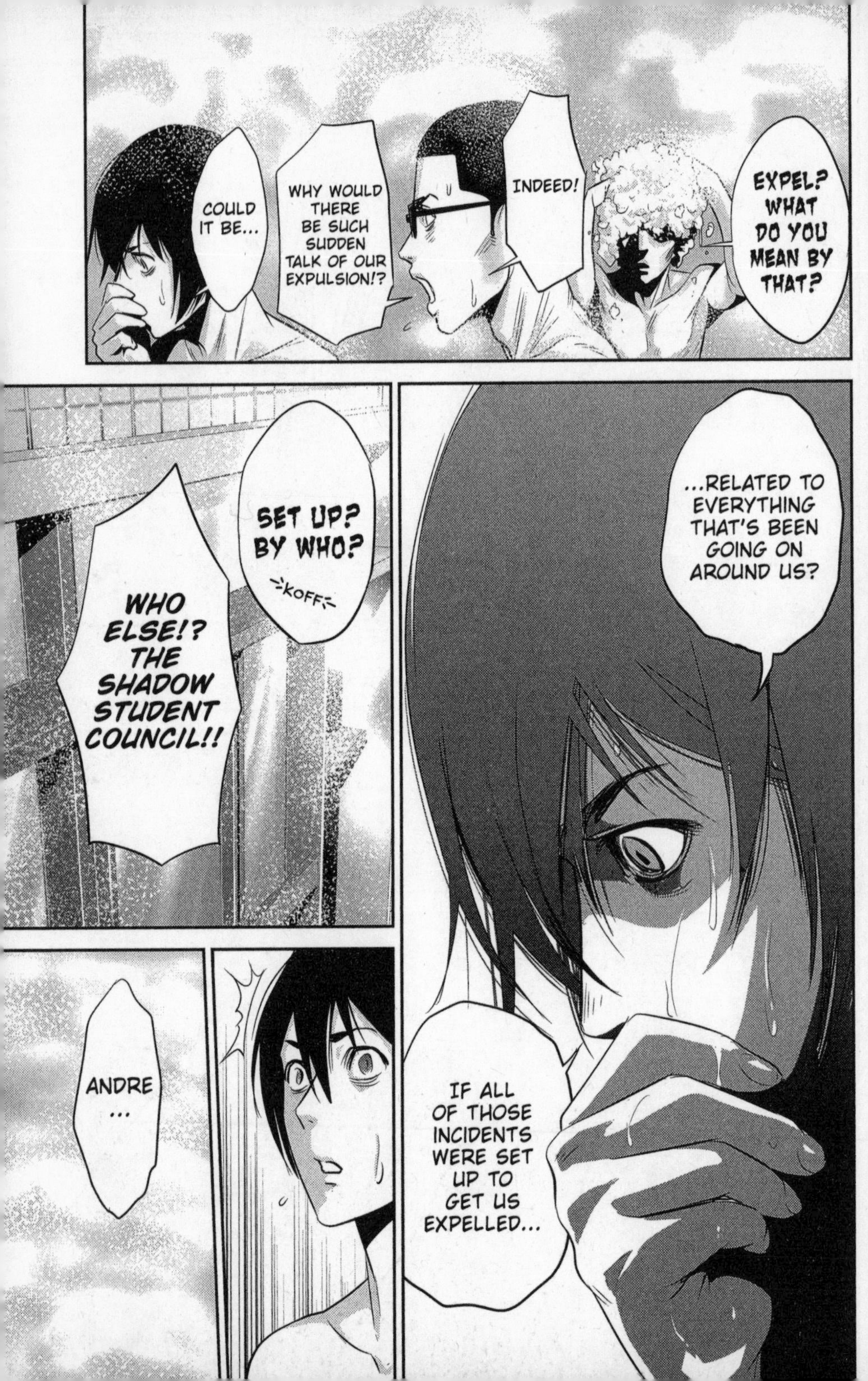
EXPEL? WHAT DO YOU MEAN BY THAT?
INDEED!
WHY WOULD THERE BE SUCH SUDDEN TALK OF OUR EXPULSION!?
COULD IT BE...
...RELATED TO EVERYTHING THAT'S BEEN GOING ON AROUND US?
IF ALL OF THOSE INCIDENTS WERE SET UP TO GET US EXPELLED...
SET UP? BY WHO?
KOFF
WHO ELSE!? THE SHADOW STUDENT COUNCIL!!
ANDRE...

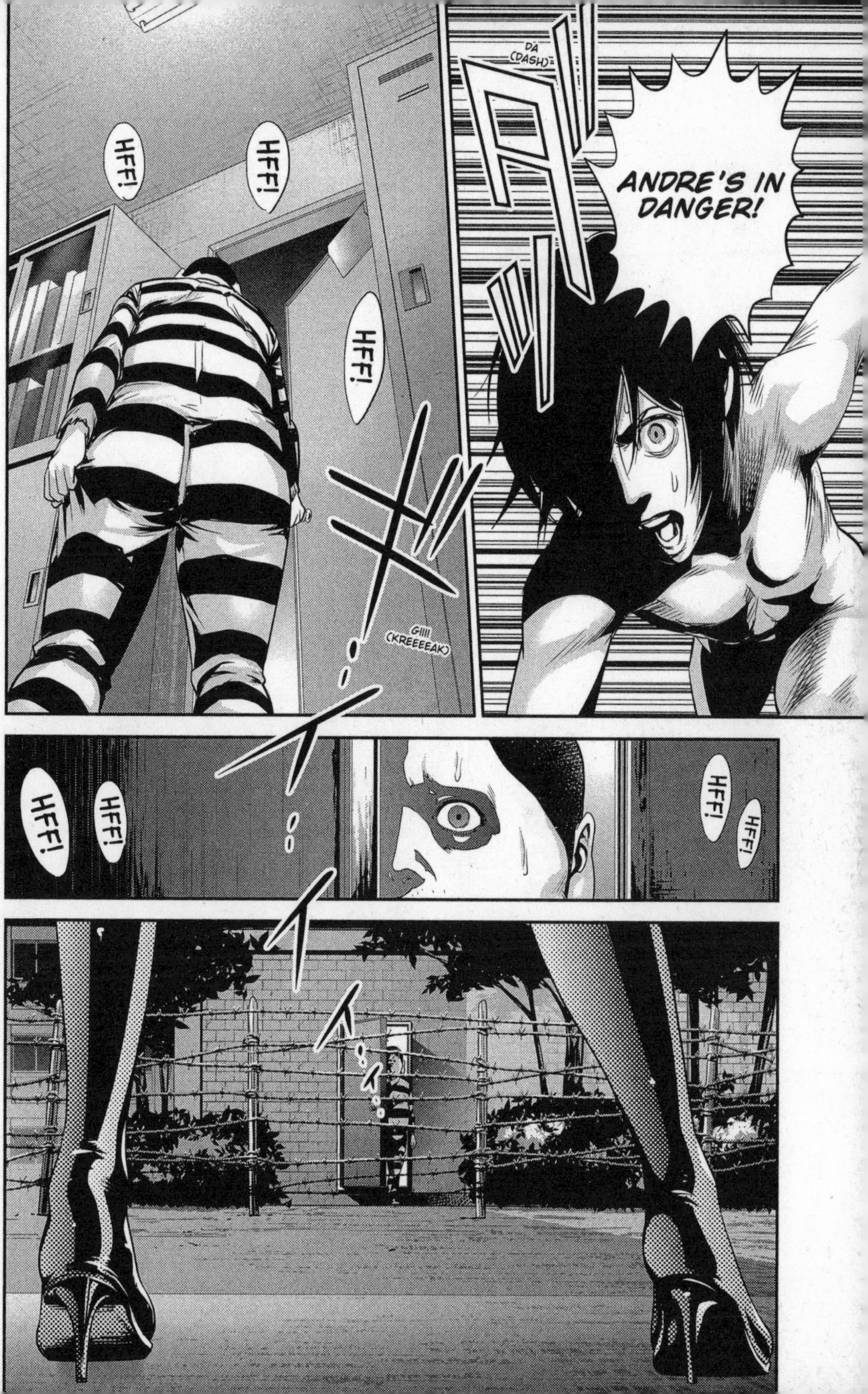
DA (DASH)
ANDRE'S IN DANGER!
HFF!
HFF!
HFF!
GIII (KREEEEAK)
HFF!
HFF!
HFF!
HFF!

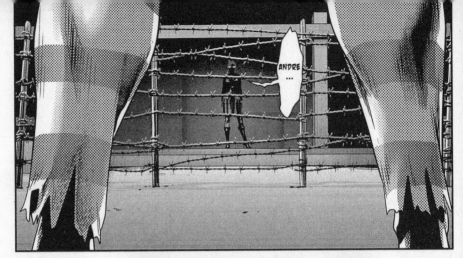

ANDRE
...

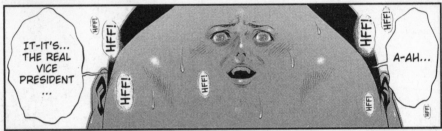

IT-IT'S...
THE REAL
VICE
PRESIDENT
...

HFF!

HFF!

HFF!

HFF!

HFF!

HFF!

HFF!

A-AH...

HFF!

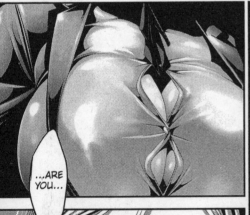

...ARE
YOU...

WHO...

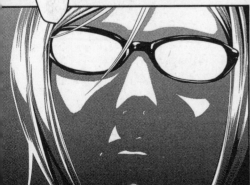

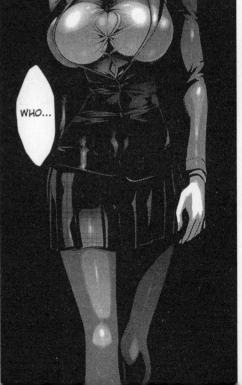

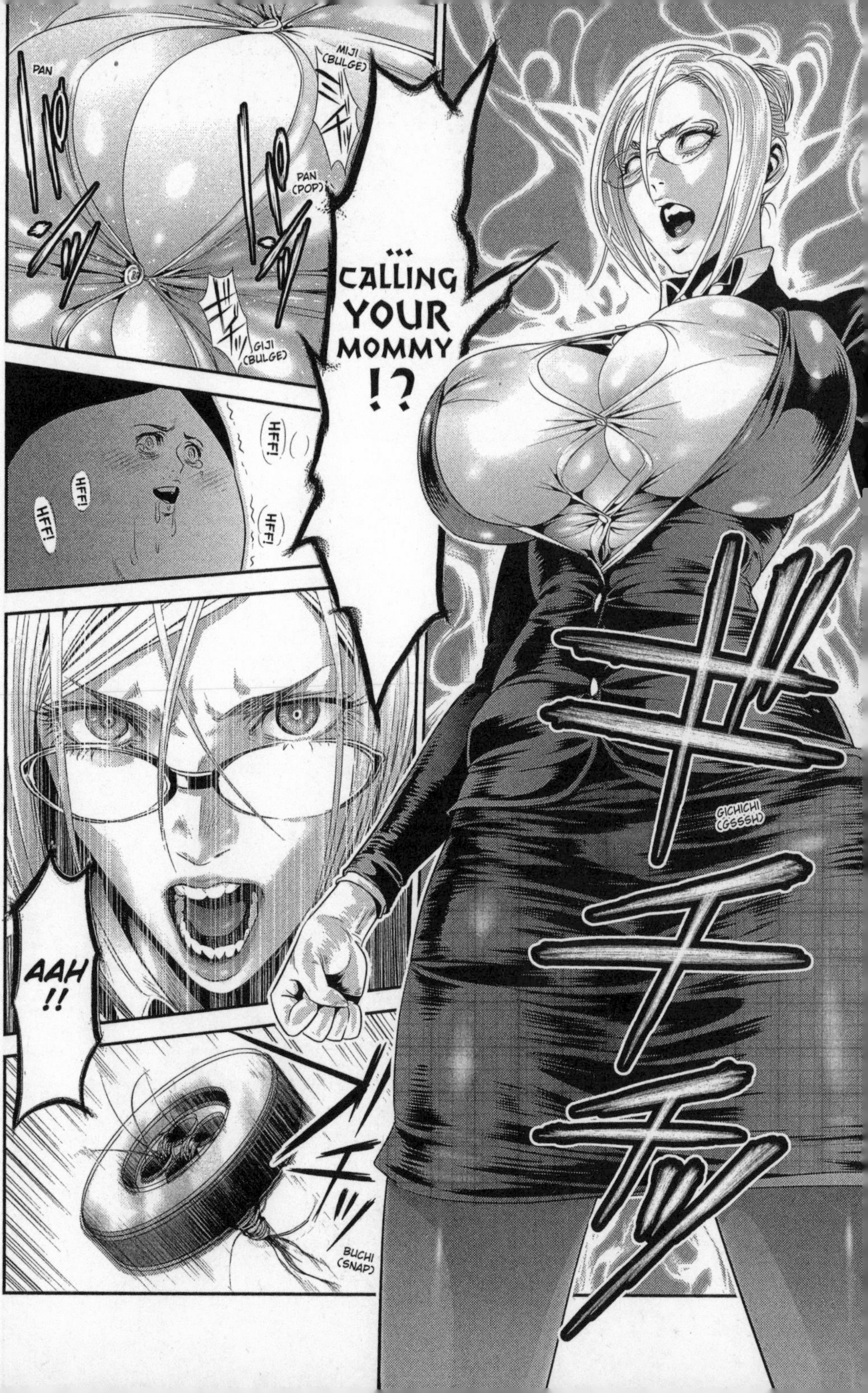
...CALLING YOUR MOMMY!?
GICHICHI (GSSSH)
PAN
MIJI (BULGE)
PAN (POP)
GIJI (BULGE)
HFF!
HFF!
HFF!
HFF!
AAH!!
BUCHI (SNAP)

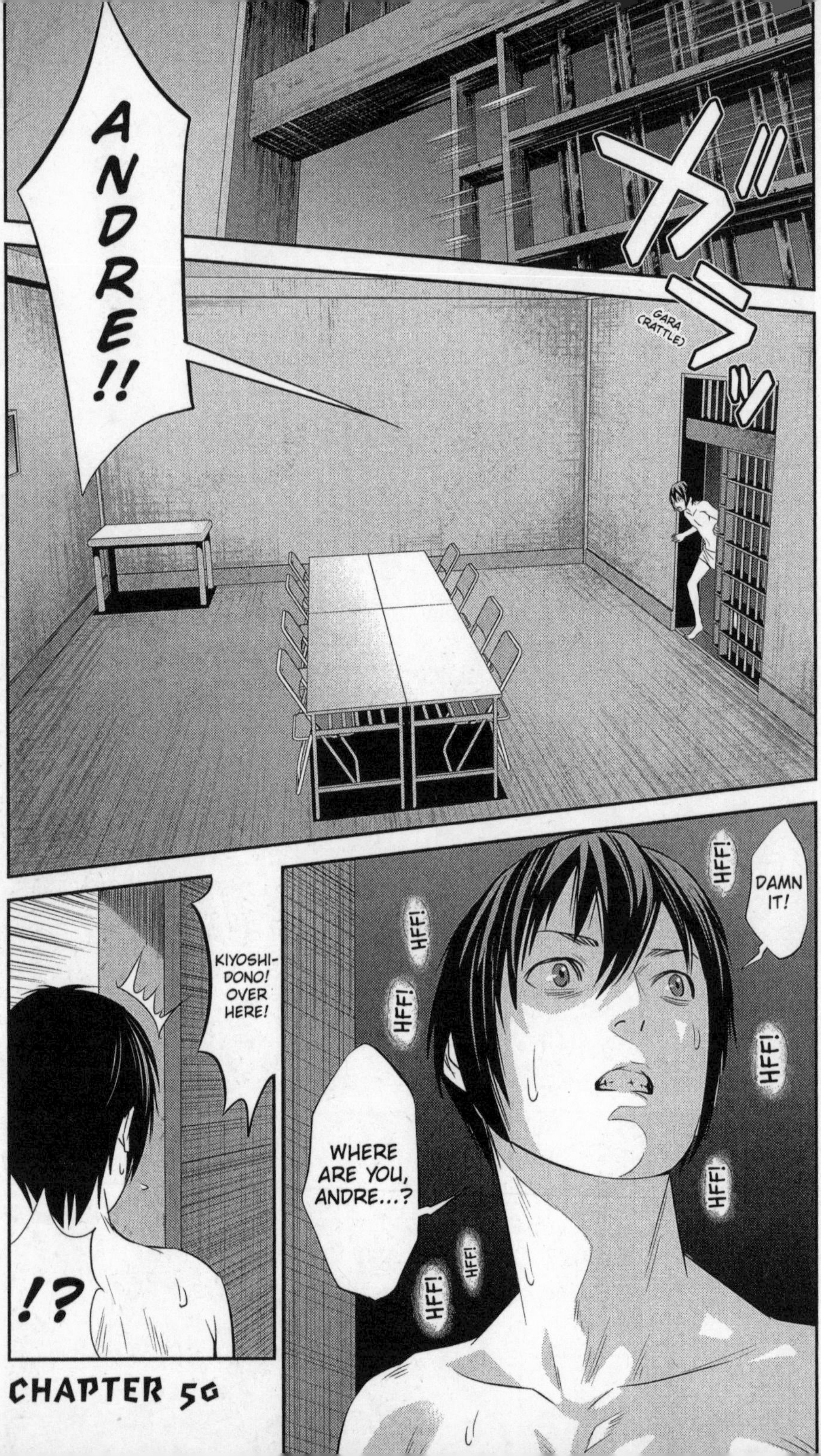
ANDRE!!
ガラッ
GARA (RATTLE)
DAMN IT!
HFF! HFF! HFF!
HFF! HFF!
WHERE ARE YOU, ANDRE...?
HFF! HFF!
KIYOSHI-DONO! OVER HERE!
!?

CHAPTER 56

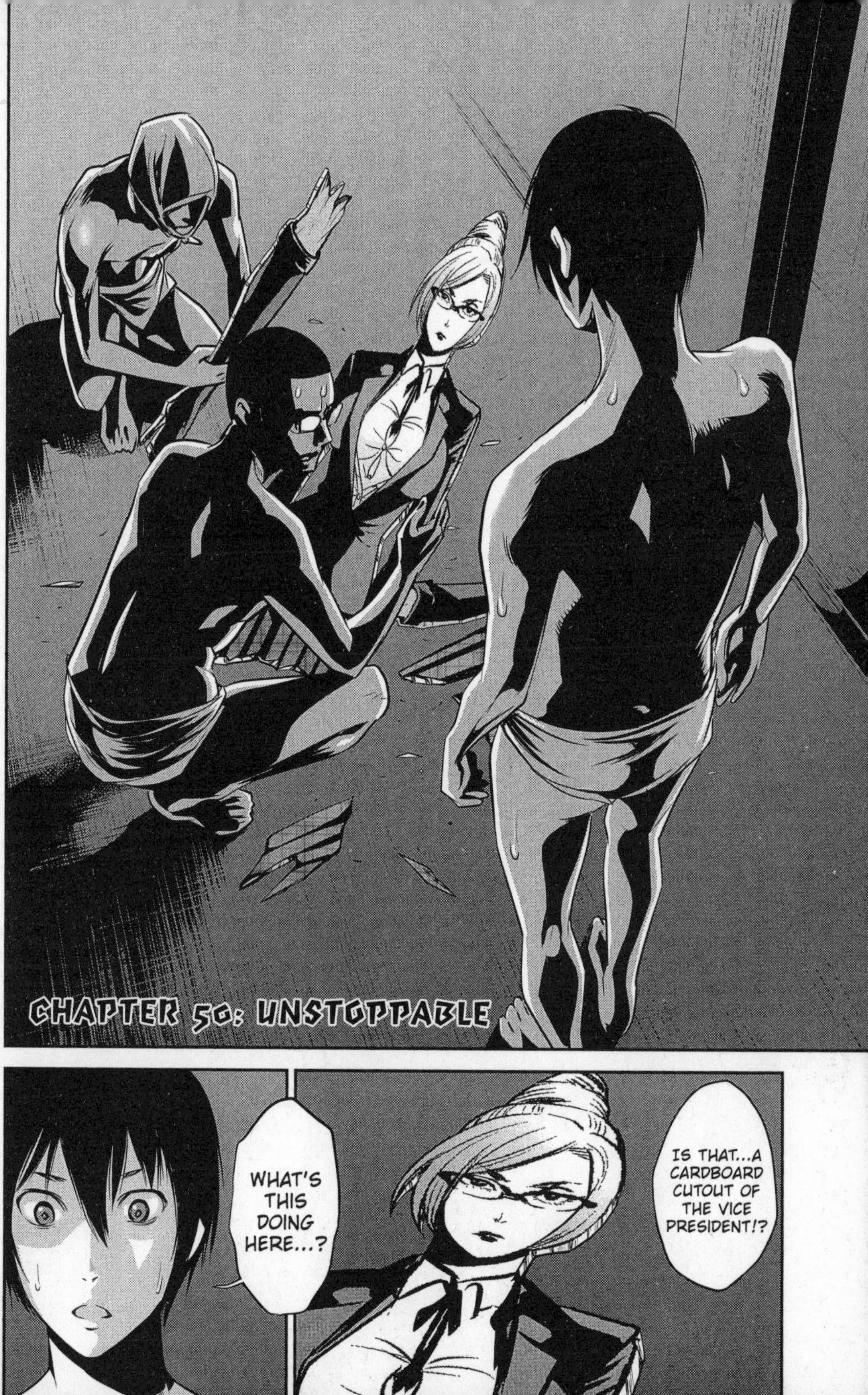
CHAPTER 50: UNSTOPPABLE
IS THAT...A CARDBOARD CUTOUT OF THE VICE PRESIDENT!?
WHAT'S THIS DOING HERE...?

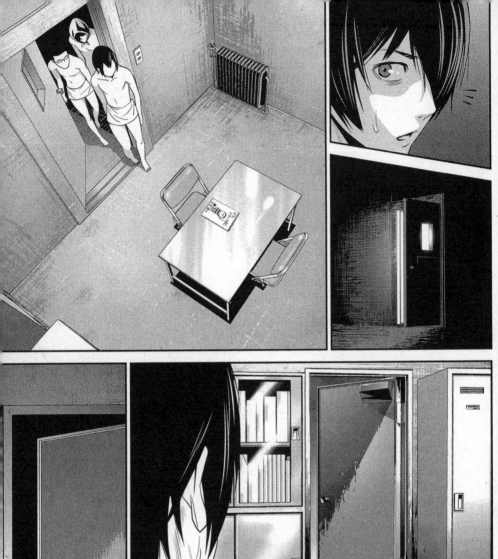

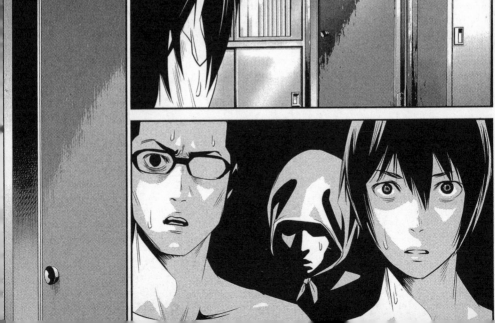

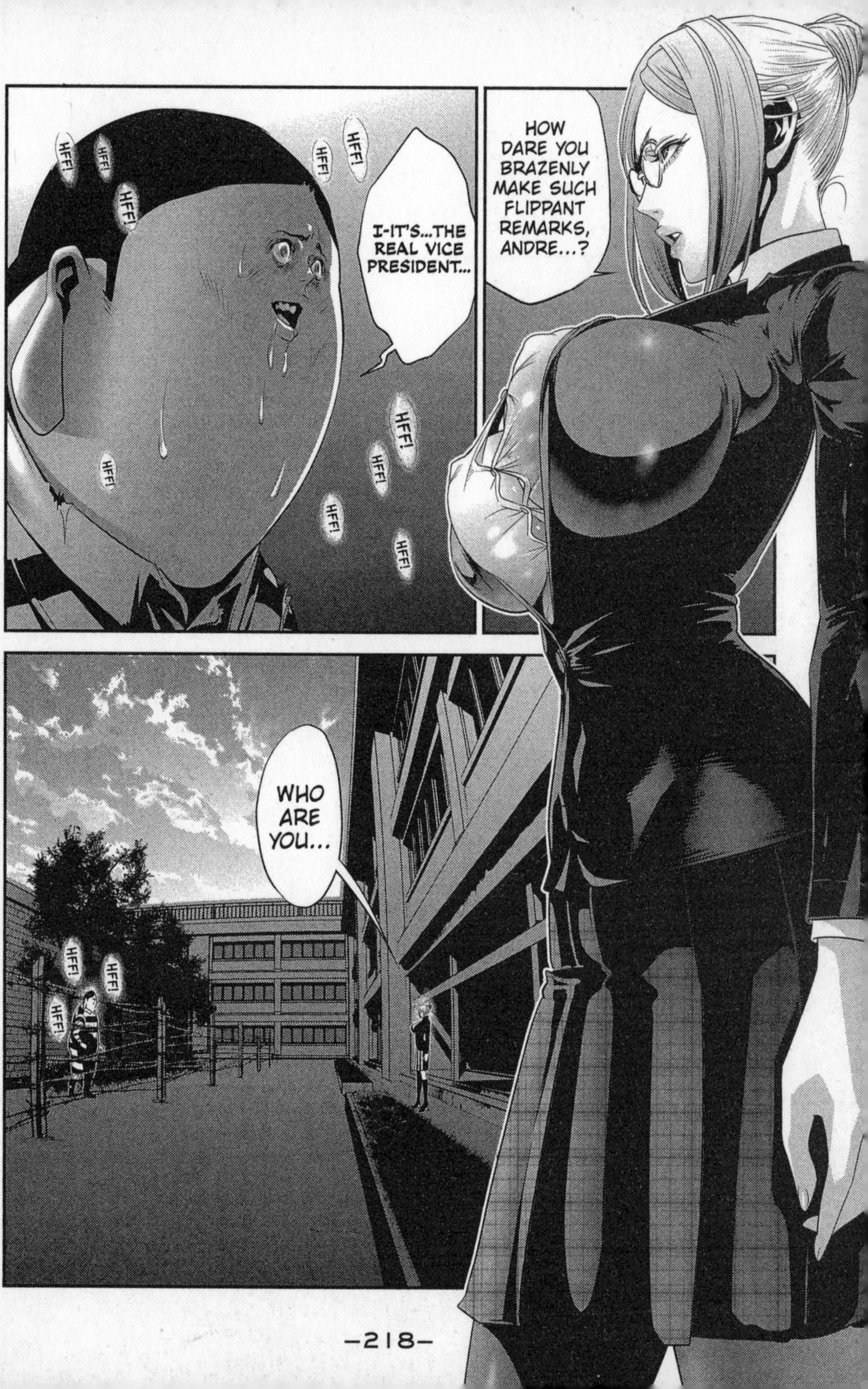
HOW DARE YOU BRAZENLY MAKE SUCH FLIPPANT REMARKS, ANDRE...?
HFF!
HFF!
HFF!
HFF!
HFF!
I-IT'S...THE REAL VICE PRESIDENT...
HFF!
HFF!
HFF!
HFF!
HFF!
WHO ARE YOU...
HFF!
HFF!
HFF!

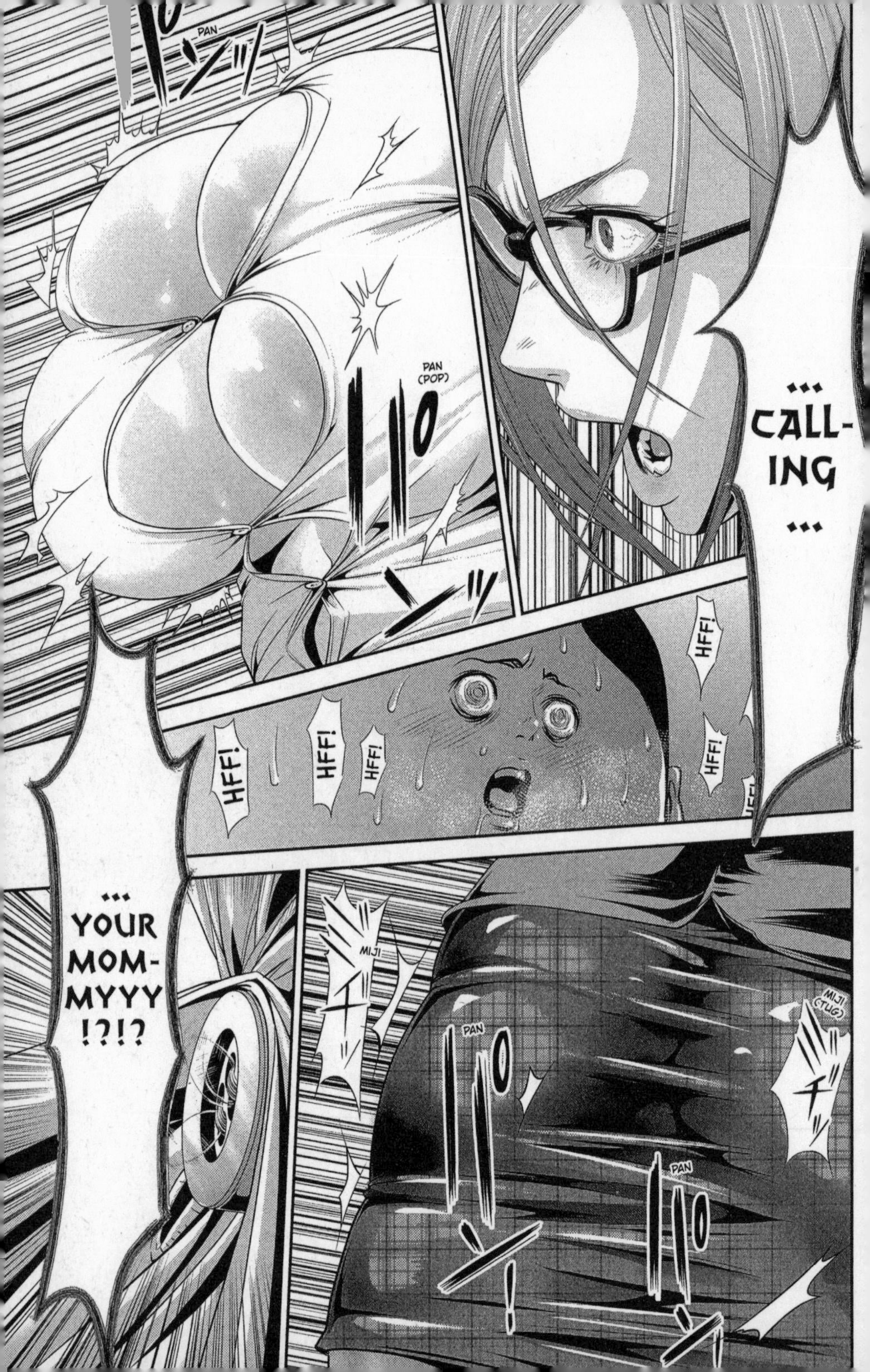
PAN
PAN (POP)
... CALLING ...
HFF!
HFF!
HFF!
HFF!
HFF!
MIJI (TUG)
PAN
MIJI
PAN
... YOUR MOM-MYYY !?!?

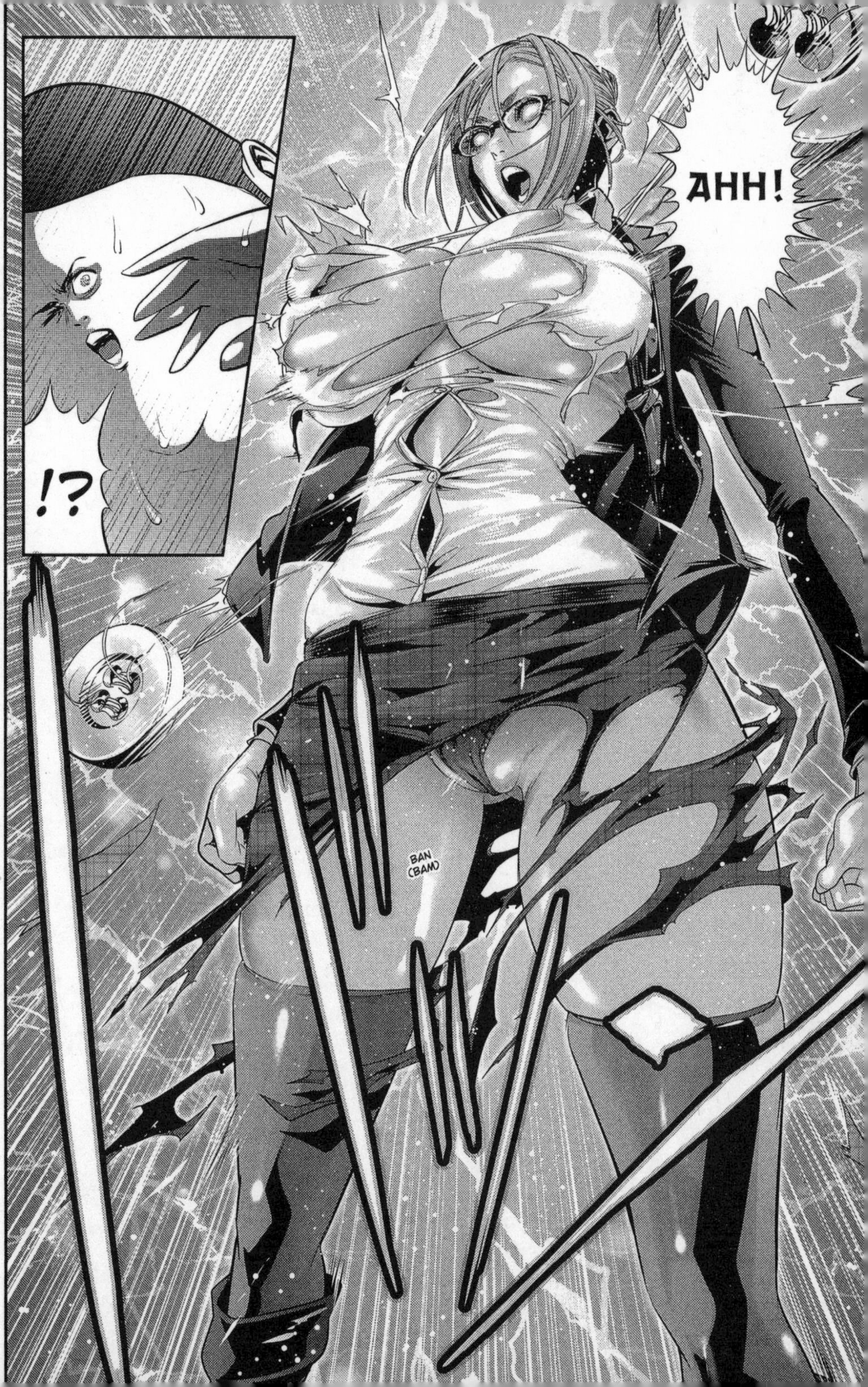
AHH!
!?
BAN
(BAM)

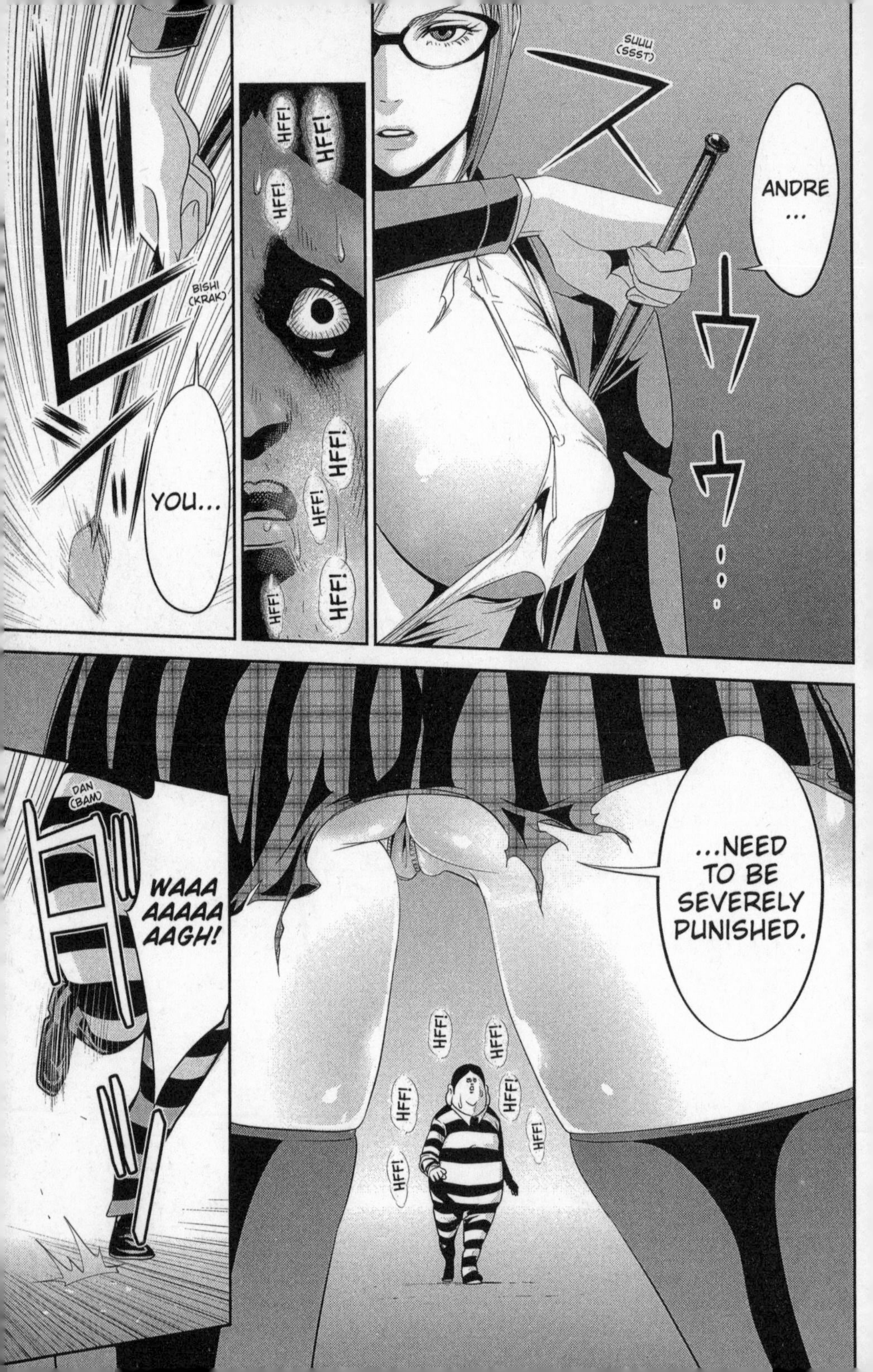
SUUU (SSST)
ANDRE ...
HFF!
HFF!
HFF!
HFF!
HFF!
HFF!
HFF!
BISHI (KRAK)
YOU...
...NEED TO BE SEVERELY PUNISHED.
HFF!
HFF!
HFF!
HFF!
HFF!
HFF!
DAN (BAM)
WAAA AAAAA AAGH!

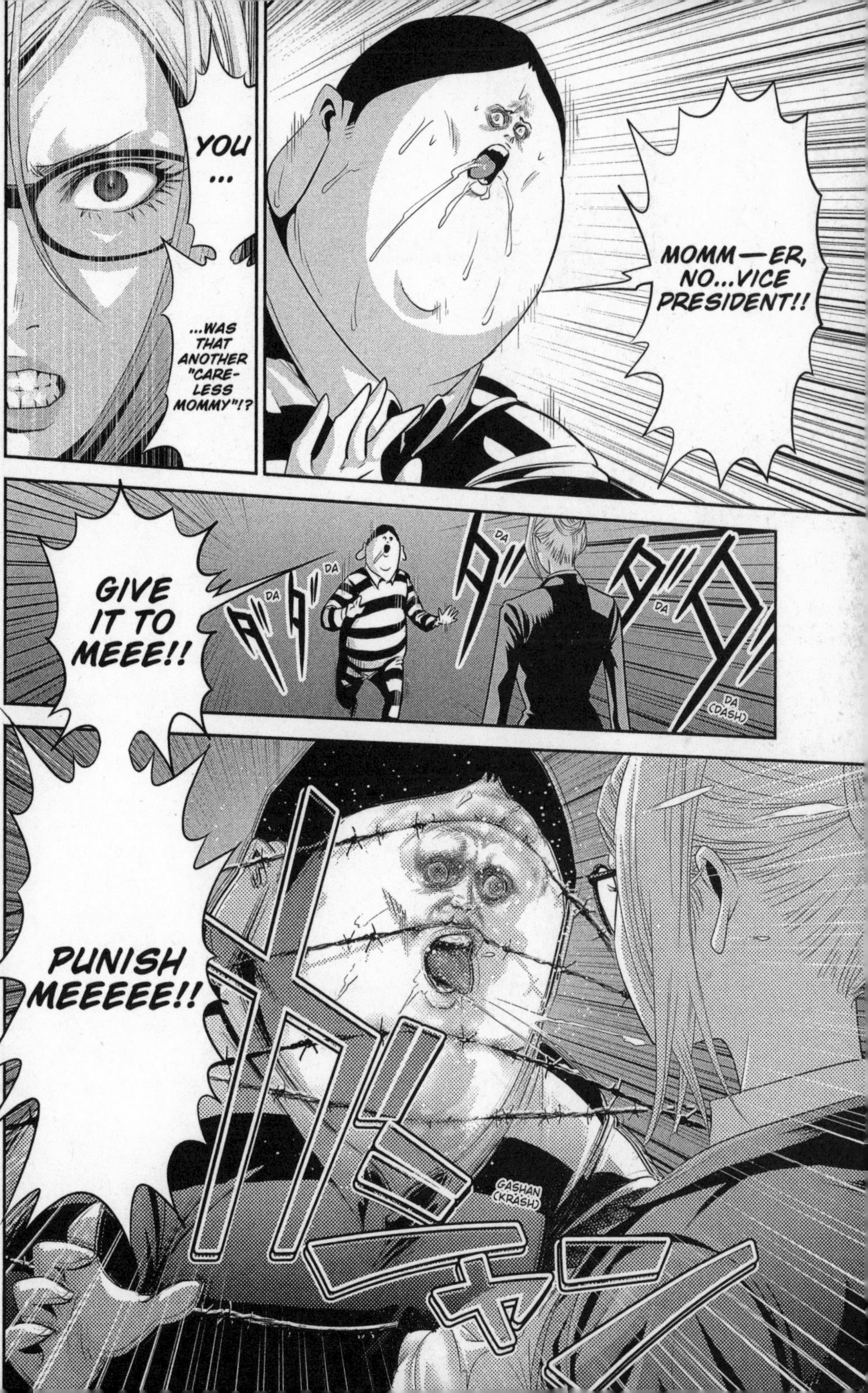
MOMM—ER, NO...VICE PRESIDENT!!
YOU...
...WAS THAT ANOTHER "CARE-LESS MOMMY"!?
DA
DA
DA
DA (DASH)
GIVE IT TO MEEE!!
PUNISH MEEEEE!!
GASHAN (KRASH)

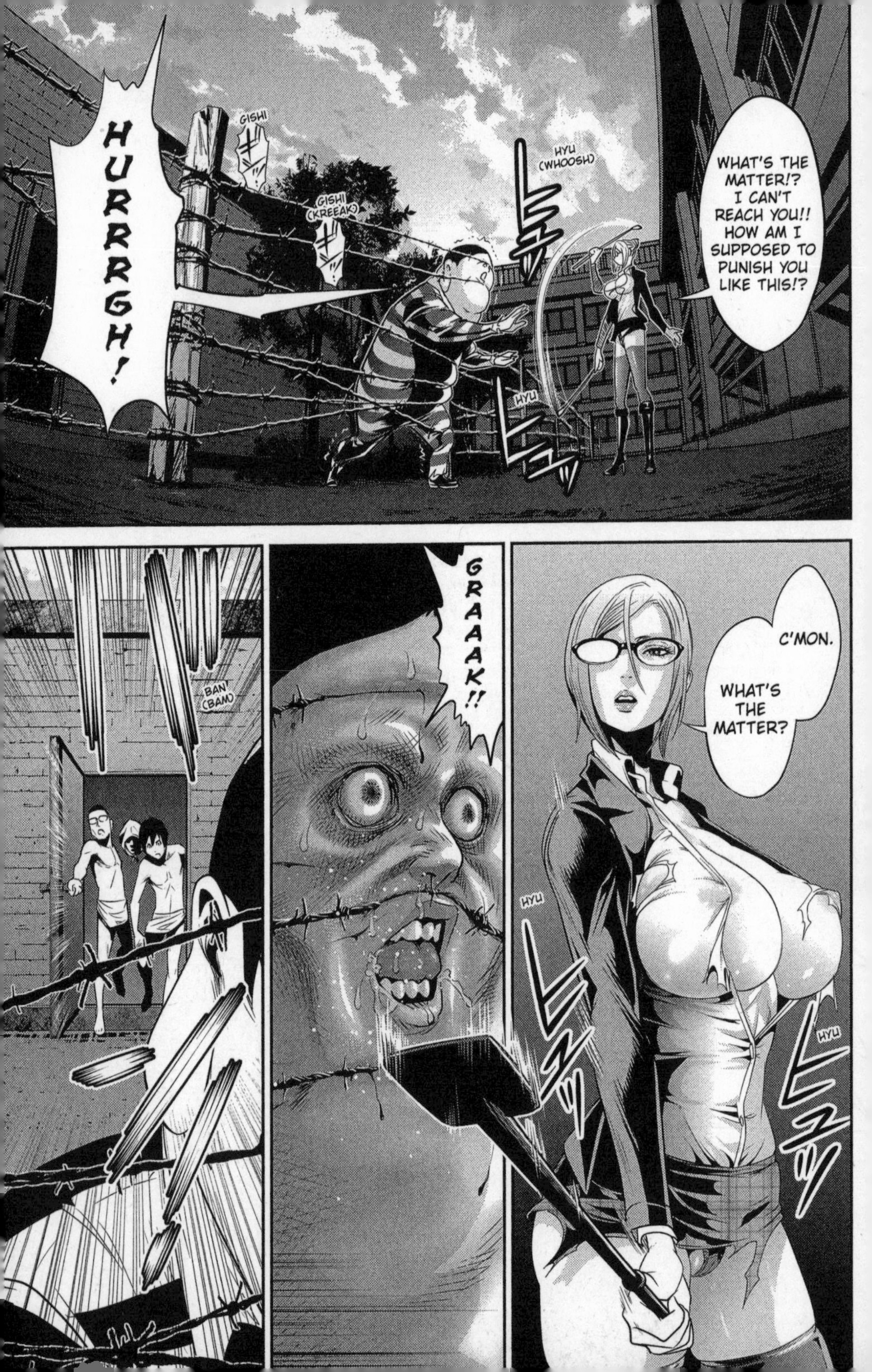
WHAT'S THE MATTER!? I CAN'T REACH YOU!! HOW AM I SUPPOSED TO PUNISH YOU LIKE THIS!?
HYU (WHOOSH)
GISHI (KREEAK)
GISHI
HURRRGH!
HYU
C'MON.
WHAT'S THE MATTER?
HYU
HYU
GRAAAK!!
BAN (BAM)

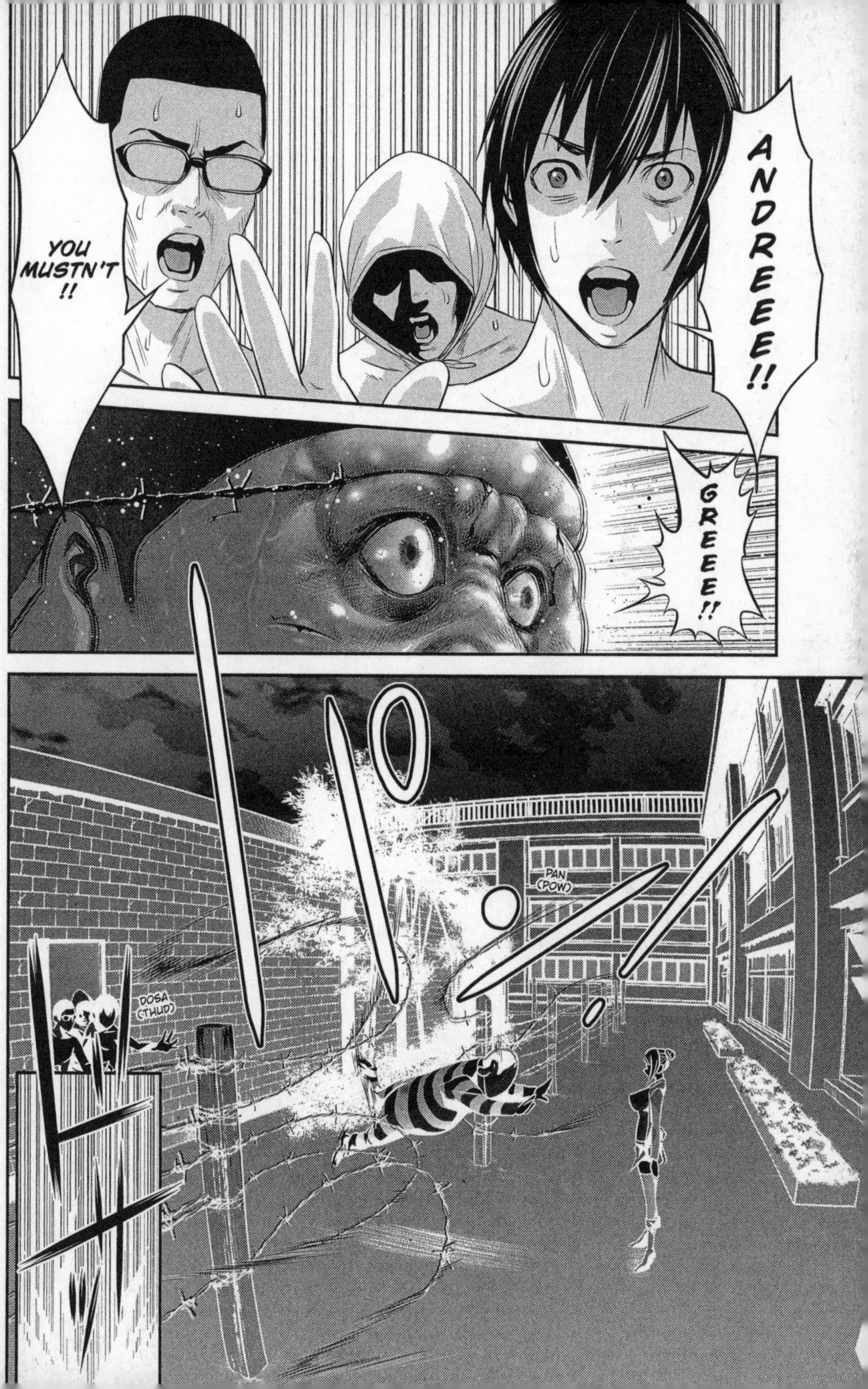
ANDREEE!!
YOU MUSTN'T !!
GREEE!!
PAN (POW)
DOSA (THUD)

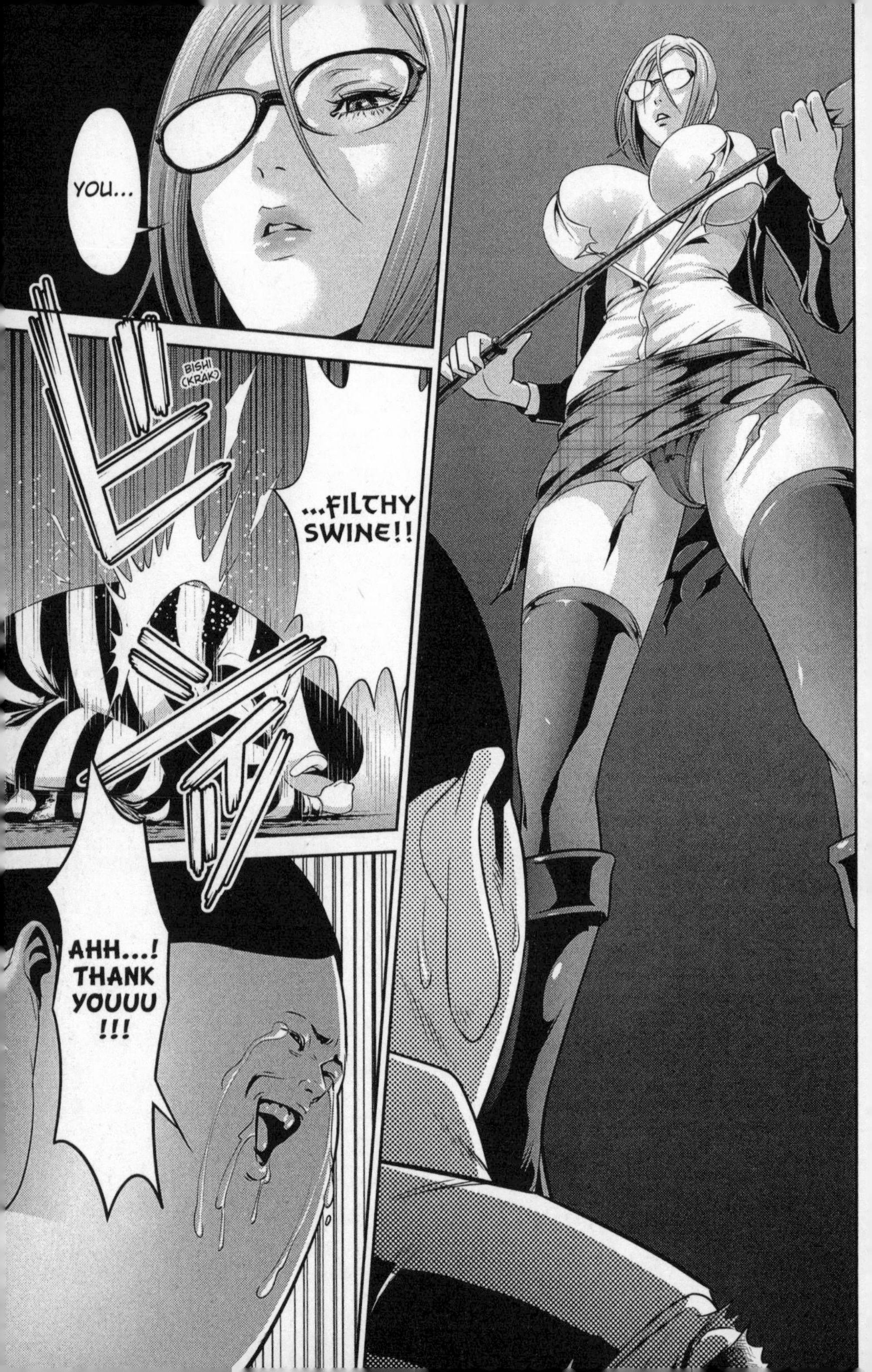
YOU...
BISHI (KRAK)
...FILTHY SWINE!!
AHH...! THANK YOUUU !!!

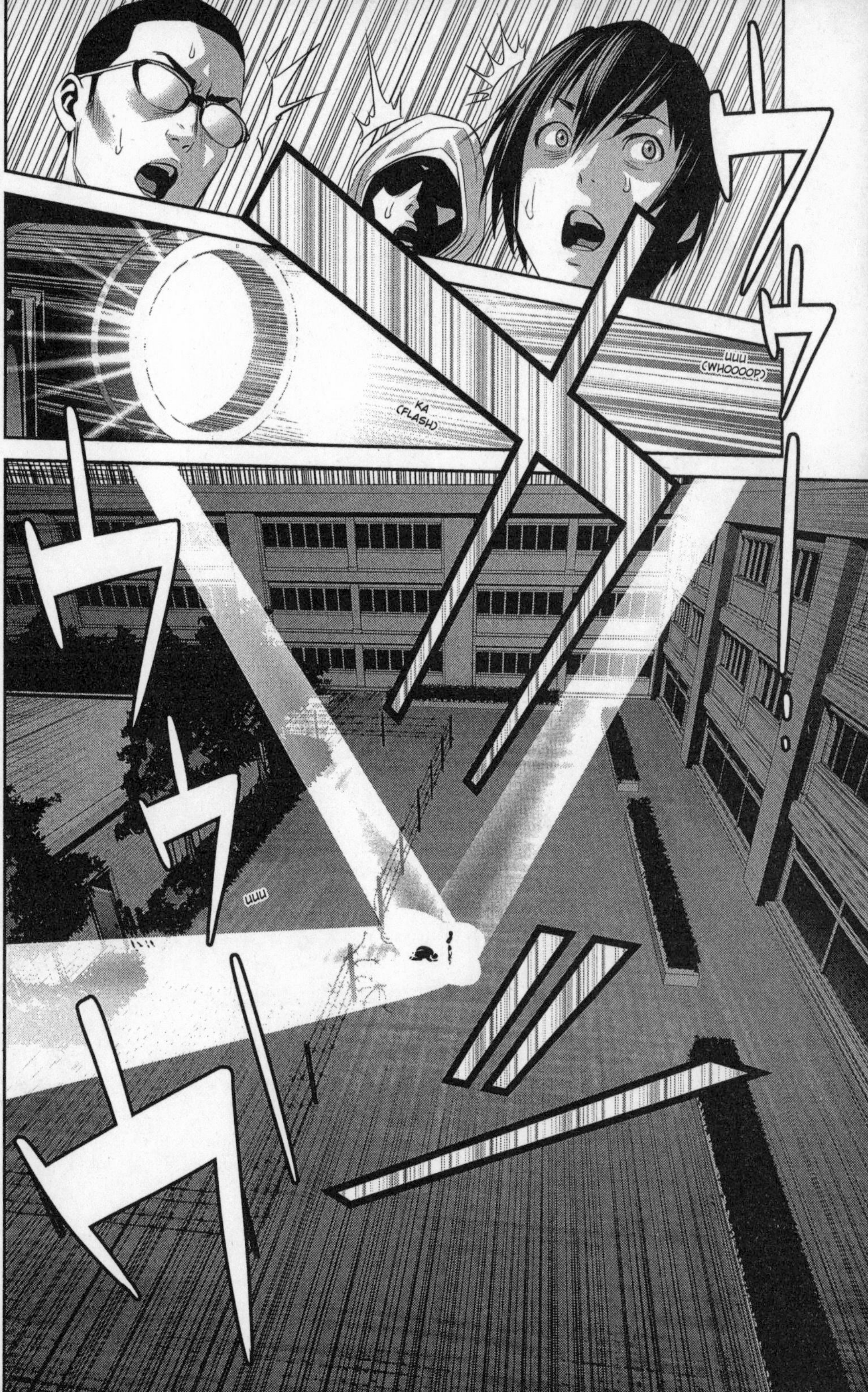

UUU (WHOOOOP)
KA (FLASH)
UUU

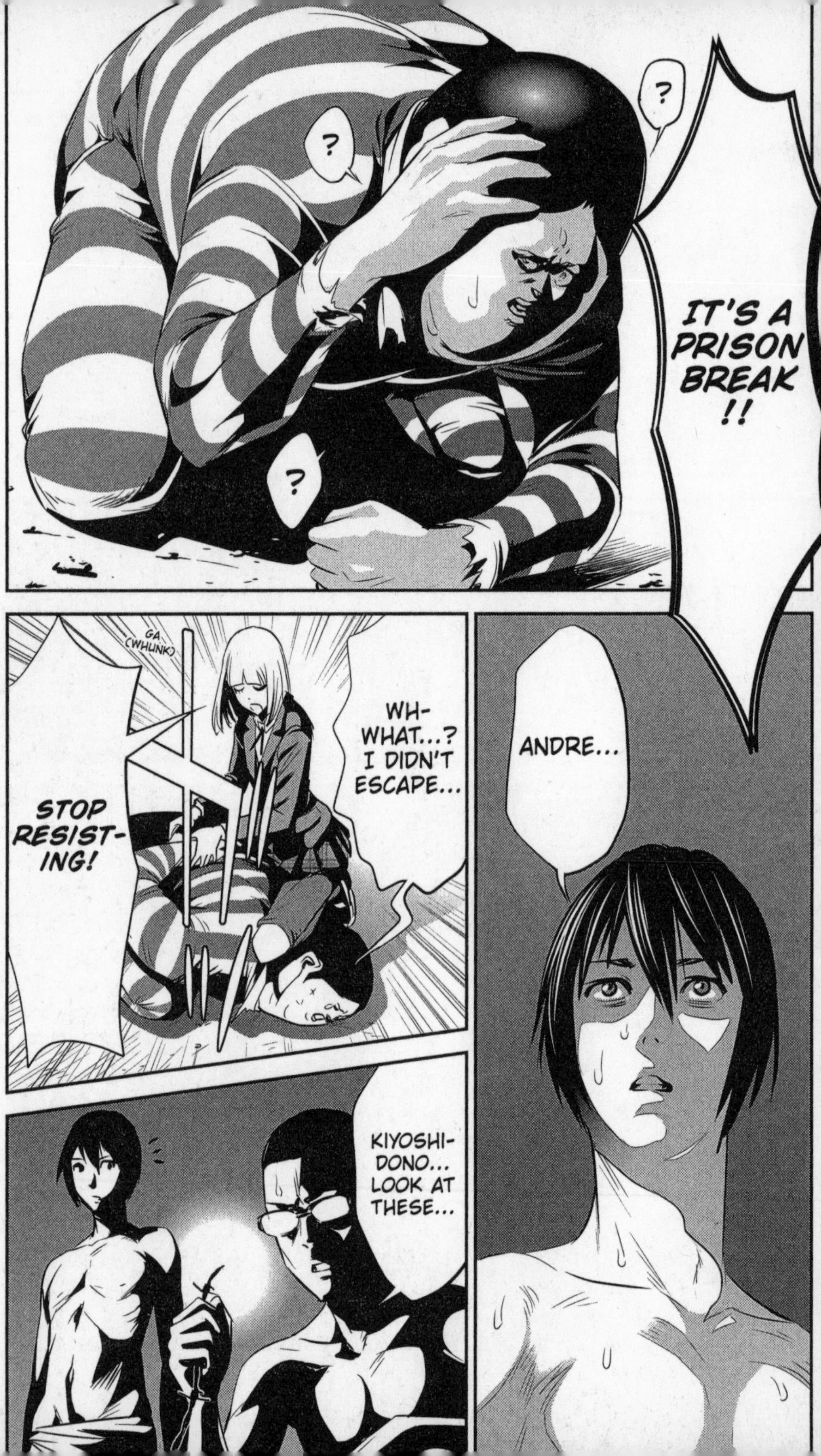
?
IT'S A PRISON BREAK!!
?
?
ANDRE...
WH-WHAT...? I DIDN'T ESCAPE...
GA (WHUNK)
STOP RESISTING!
KIYOSHI-DONO... LOOK AT THESE...

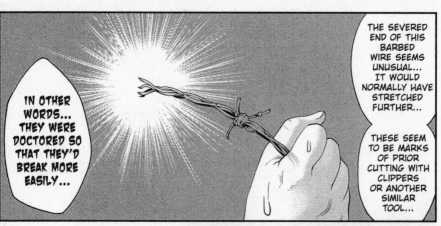

THE SEVERED END OF THIS BARBED WIRE SEEMS UNUSUAL... IT WOULD NORMALLY HAVE STRETCHED FURTHER...

THESE SEEM TO BE MARKS OF PRIOR CUTTING WITH CLIPPERS OR ANOTHER SIMILAR TOOL...

IN OTHER WORDS... THEY WERE DOCTORED SO THAT THEY'D BREAK MORE EASILY...

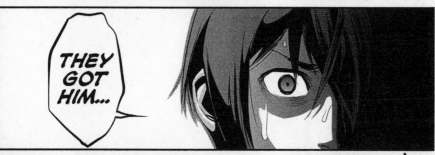

THEY GOT HIM...

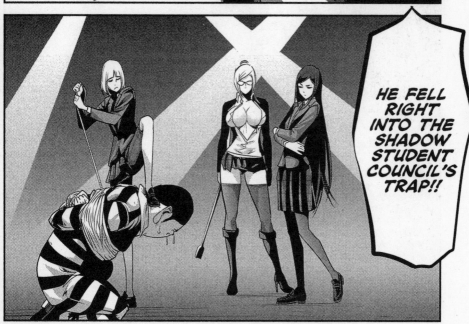

HE FELL RIGHT INTO THE SHADOW STUDENT COUNCIL'S TRAP!!

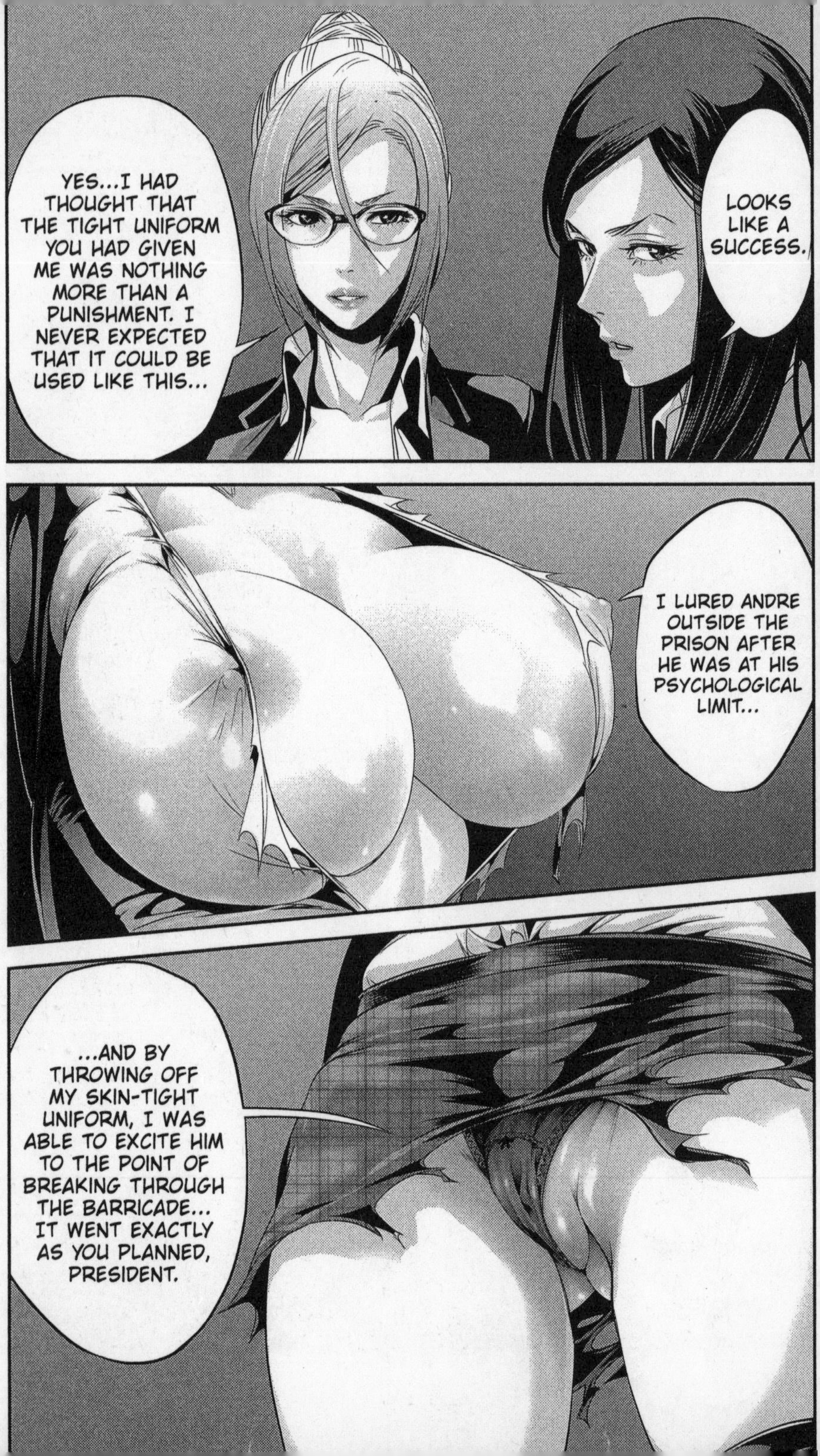
LOOKS LIKE A SUCCESS.
YES...I HAD THOUGHT THAT THE TIGHT UNIFORM YOU HAD GIVEN ME WAS NOTHING MORE THAN A PUNISHMENT. I NEVER EXPECTED THAT IT COULD BE USED LIKE THIS...
I LURED ANDRE OUTSIDE THE PRISON AFTER HE WAS AT HIS PSYCHOLOGICAL LIMIT...
...AND BY THROWING OFF MY SKIN-TIGHT UNIFORM, I WAS ABLE TO EXCITE HIM TO THE POINT OF BREAKING THROUGH THE BARRICADE... IT WENT EXACTLY AS YOU PLANNED, PRESIDENT.

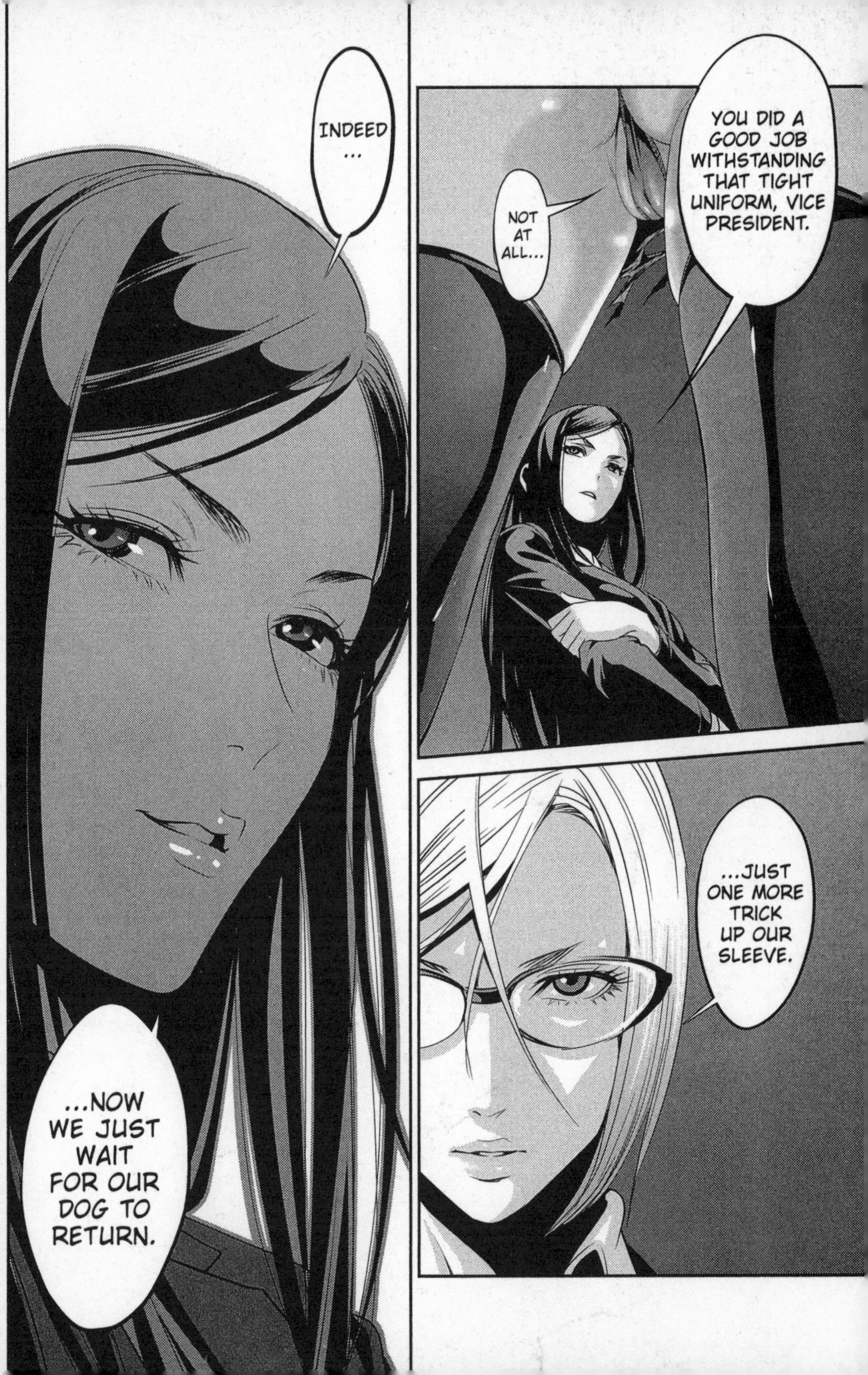
YOU DID A GOOD JOB WITHSTANDING THAT TIGHT UNIFORM, VICE PRESIDENT.
NOT AT ALL...
...JUST ONE MORE TRICK UP OUR SLEEVE.
INDEED...
...NOW WE JUST WAIT FOR OUR DOG TO RETURN.

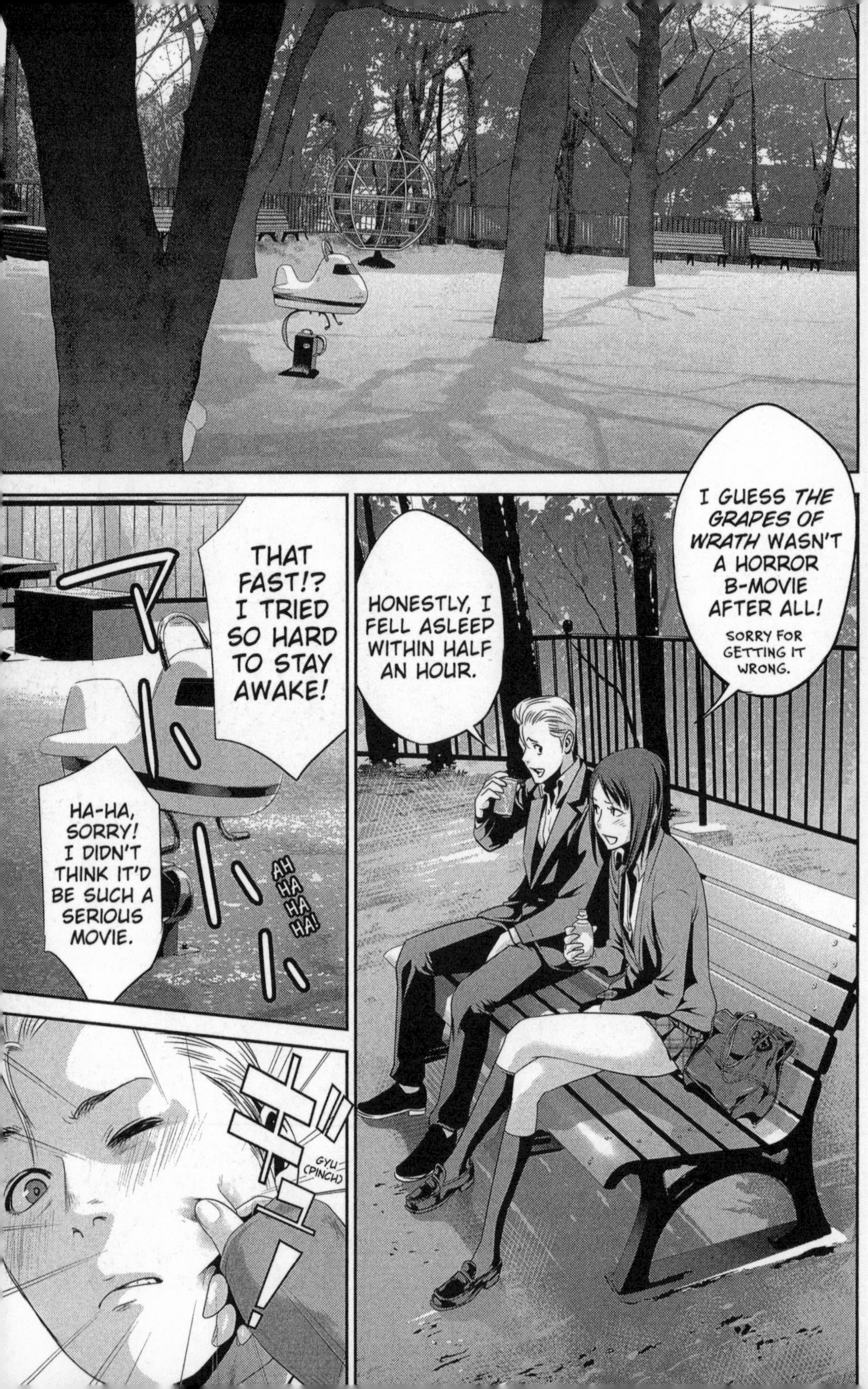
I GUESS *THE GRAPES OF WRATH* WASN'T A HORROR B-MOVIE AFTER ALL!
SORRY FOR GETTING IT WRONG.
HONESTLY, I FELL ASLEEP WITHIN HALF AN HOUR.
THAT FAST!? I TRIED SO HARD TO STAY AWAKE!
HA-HA, SORRY! I DIDN'T THINK IT'D BE SUCH A SERIOUS MOVIE.
AH HA HA HA!
GYU (PINCH)

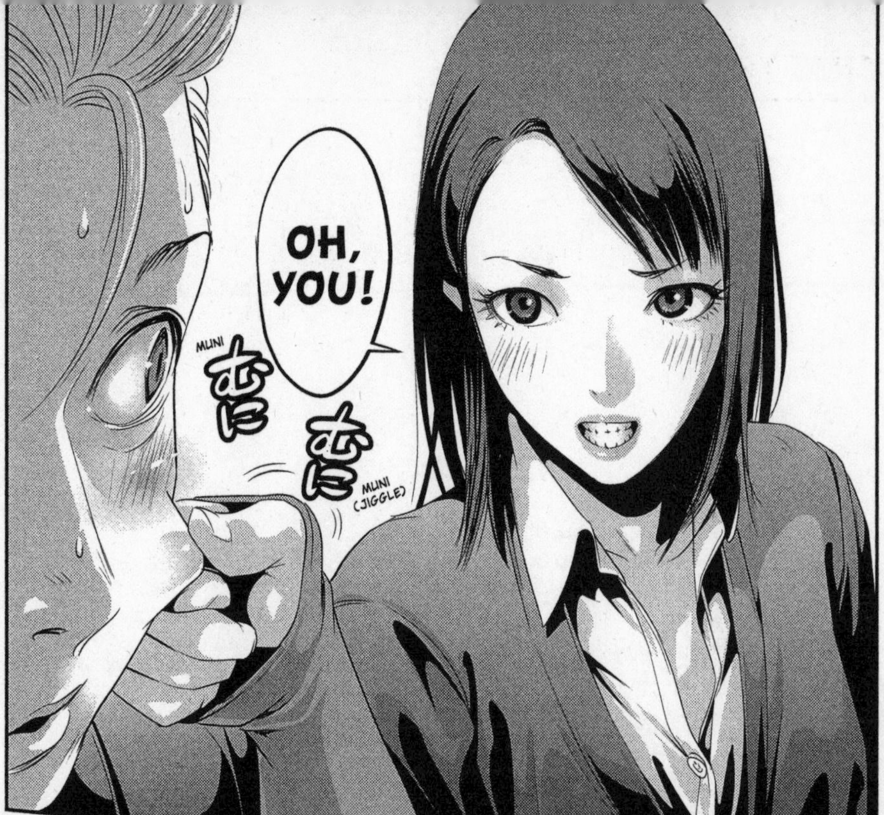
OH, YOU!
MUNI
むに
むに
MUNI (JIGGLE)

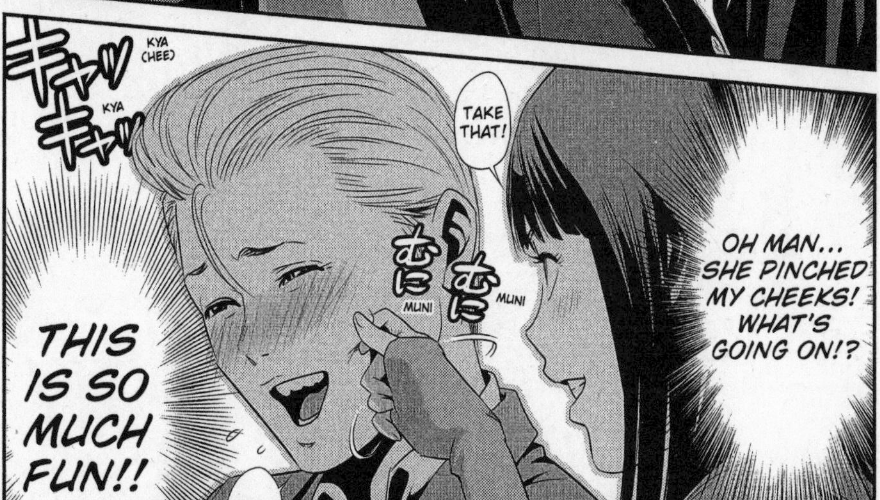
OH MAN... SHE PINCHED MY CHEEKS! WHAT'S GOING ON!?
TAKE THAT!
むに
MUNI
むに
MUNI
KYA (CHEE)
キャッ
KYA
キャッ
THIS IS SO MUCH FUN!!
AW, STOP IT!!

CHAPTER 51

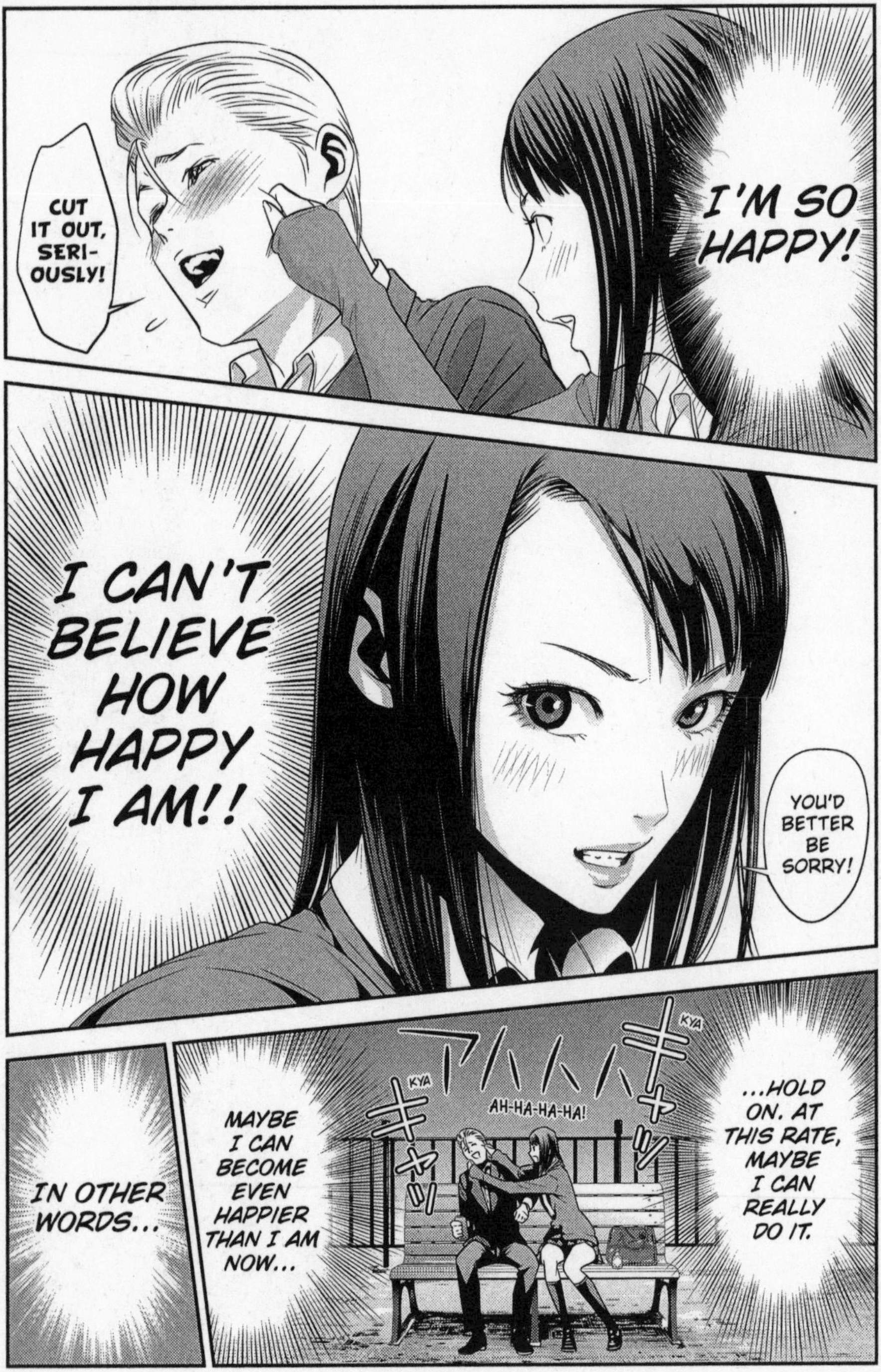
I'M SO HAPPY!
CUT IT OUT, SERI-OUSLY!
YOU'D BETTER BE SORRY!
I CAN'T BELIEVE HOW HAPPY I AM!!
...HOLD ON. AT THIS RATE, MAYBE I CAN REALLY DO IT.
キャッ
KYA
アハハハ
AH-HA-HA-HA!
キャッ
KYA
MAYBE I CAN BECOME EVEN HAPPIER THAN I AM NOW...
IN OTHER WORDS...

CHAPTER 51: TALK TO HER

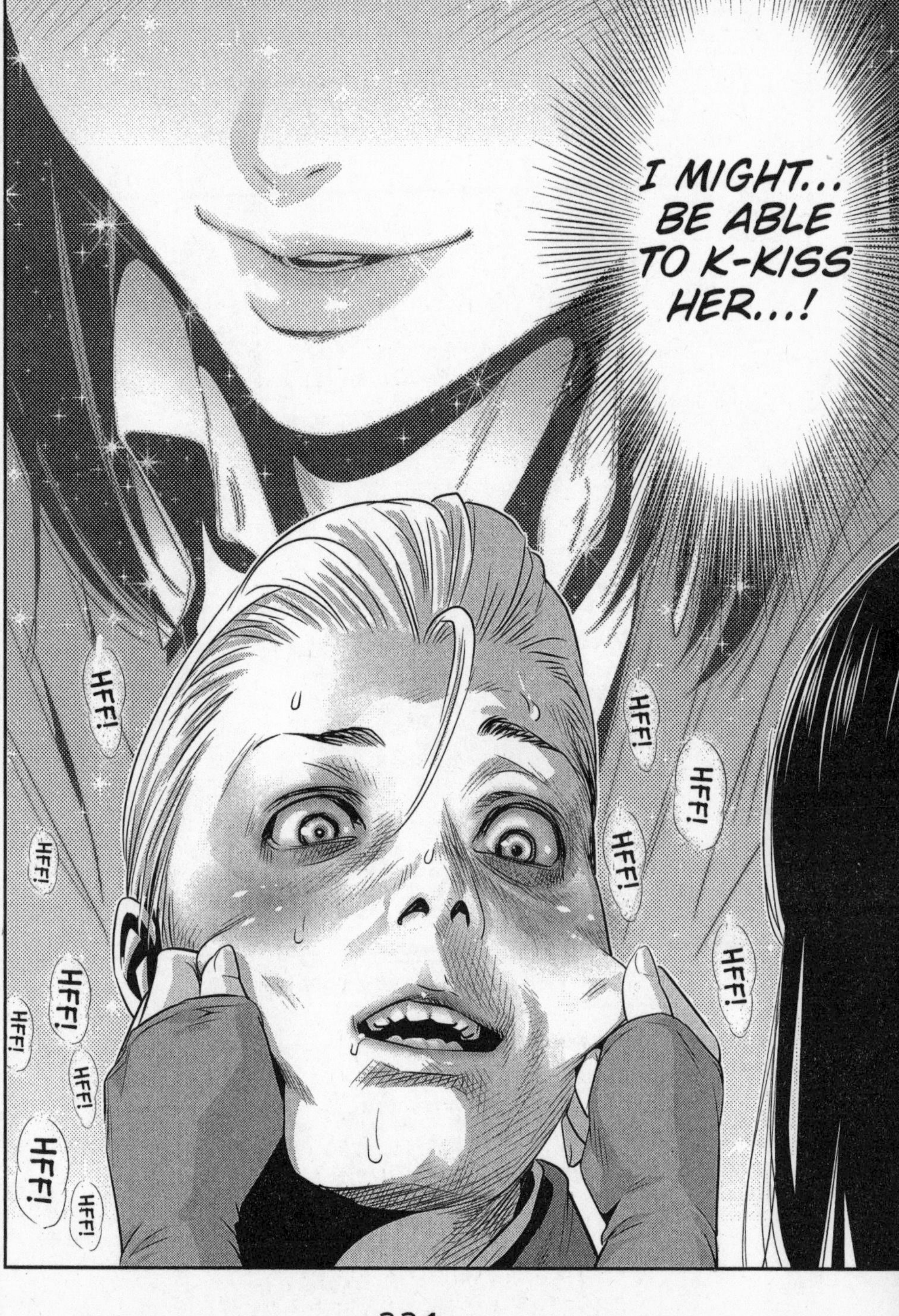
I MIGHT... BE ABLE TO K-KISS HER...!
HFF!
HFF!
HFF!
HFF!
HFF!
HFF!
HFF!
HFF!
HFF!
HFF!
HFF!

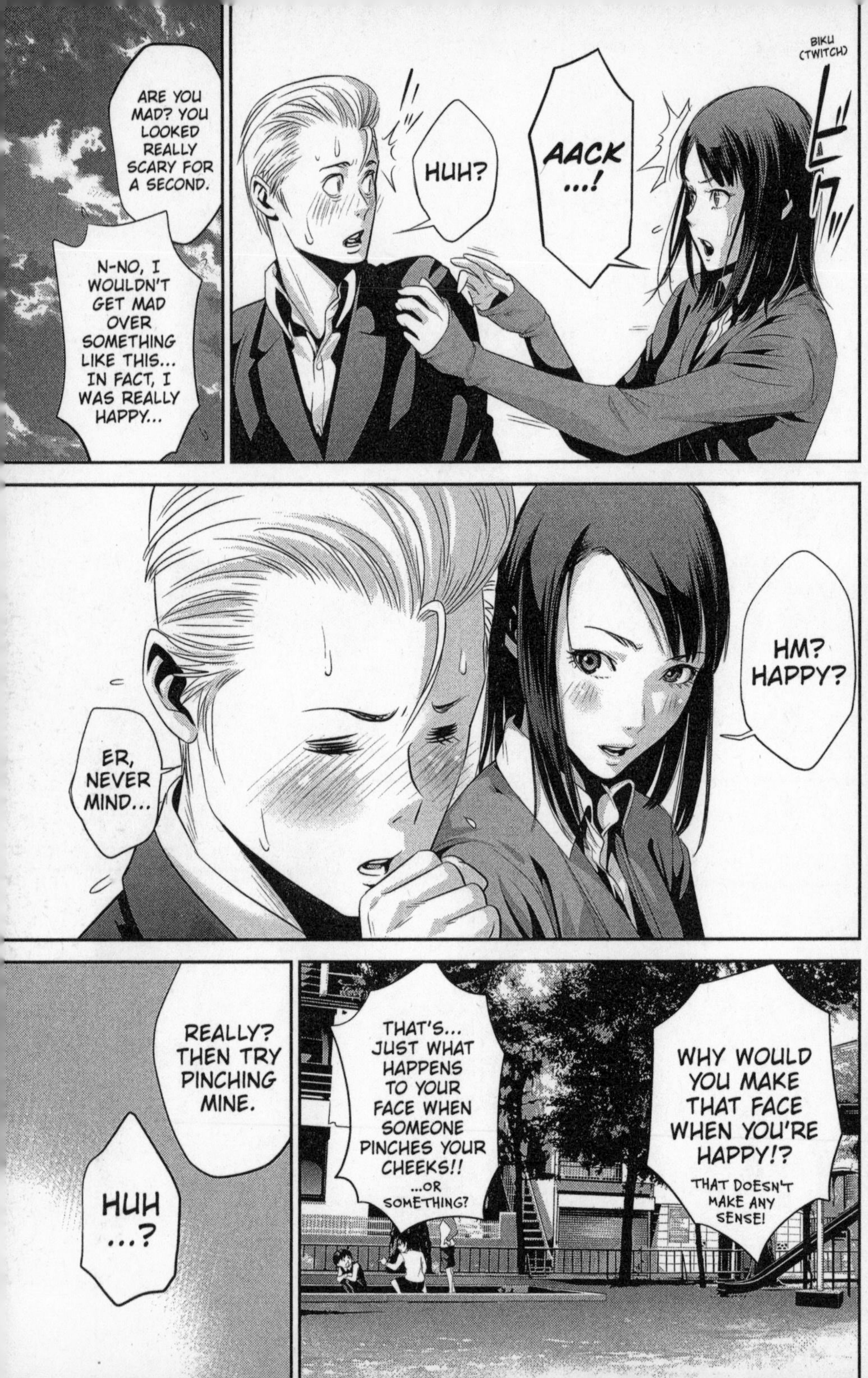
BIKU (TWITCH)
AACK ...!
HUH?
ARE YOU MAD? YOU LOOKED REALLY SCARY FOR A SECOND.
N-NO, I WOULDN'T GET MAD OVER SOMETHING LIKE THIS... IN FACT, I WAS REALLY HAPPY...
HM? HAPPY?
ER, NEVER MIND...
WHY WOULD YOU MAKE THAT FACE WHEN YOU'RE HAPPY!?
THAT DOESN'T MAKE ANY SENSE!
THAT'S... JUST WHAT HAPPENS TO YOUR FACE WHEN SOMEONE PINCHES YOUR CHEEKS!!
...OR SOMETHING?
REALLY? THEN TRY PINCHING MINE.
HUH ...?

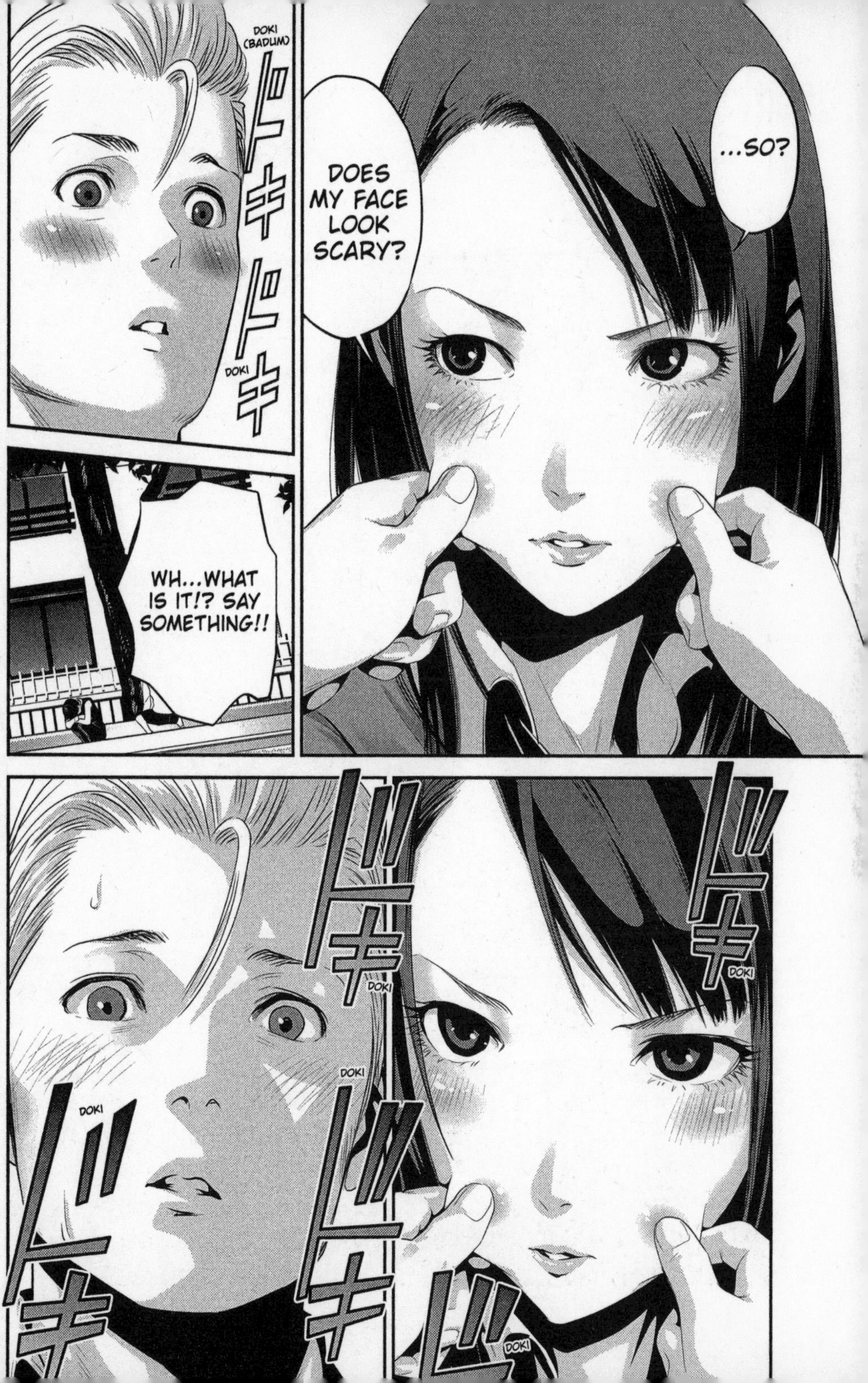
...SO?
DOES MY FACE LOOK SCARY?
DOKI (BADUM)
DOKI
WH...WHAT IS IT!? SAY SOMETHING!!
DOKI
DOKI
DOKI
DOKI
DOKI

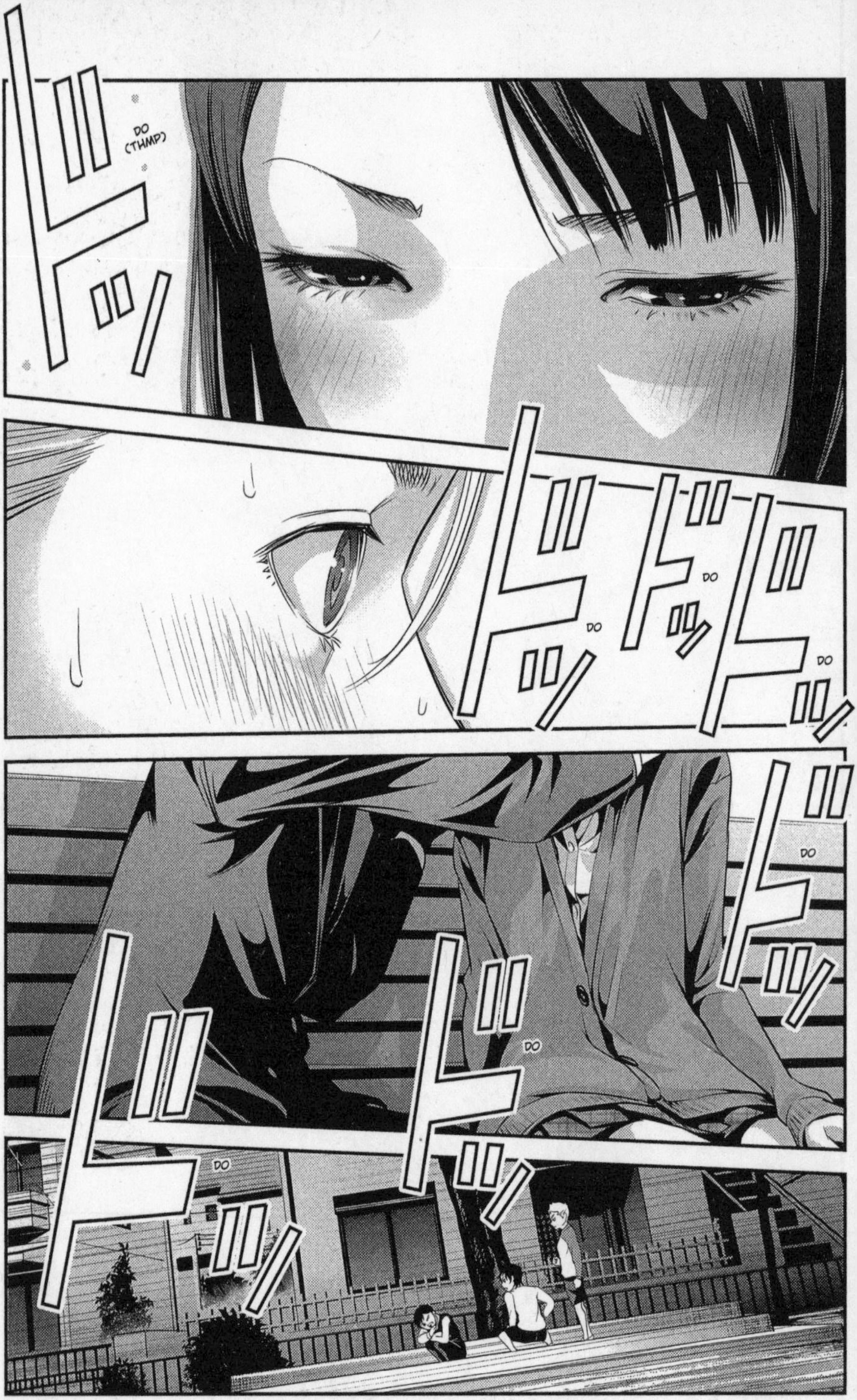
DO (THMP)
DO
DO
DO
DO
DO
DO

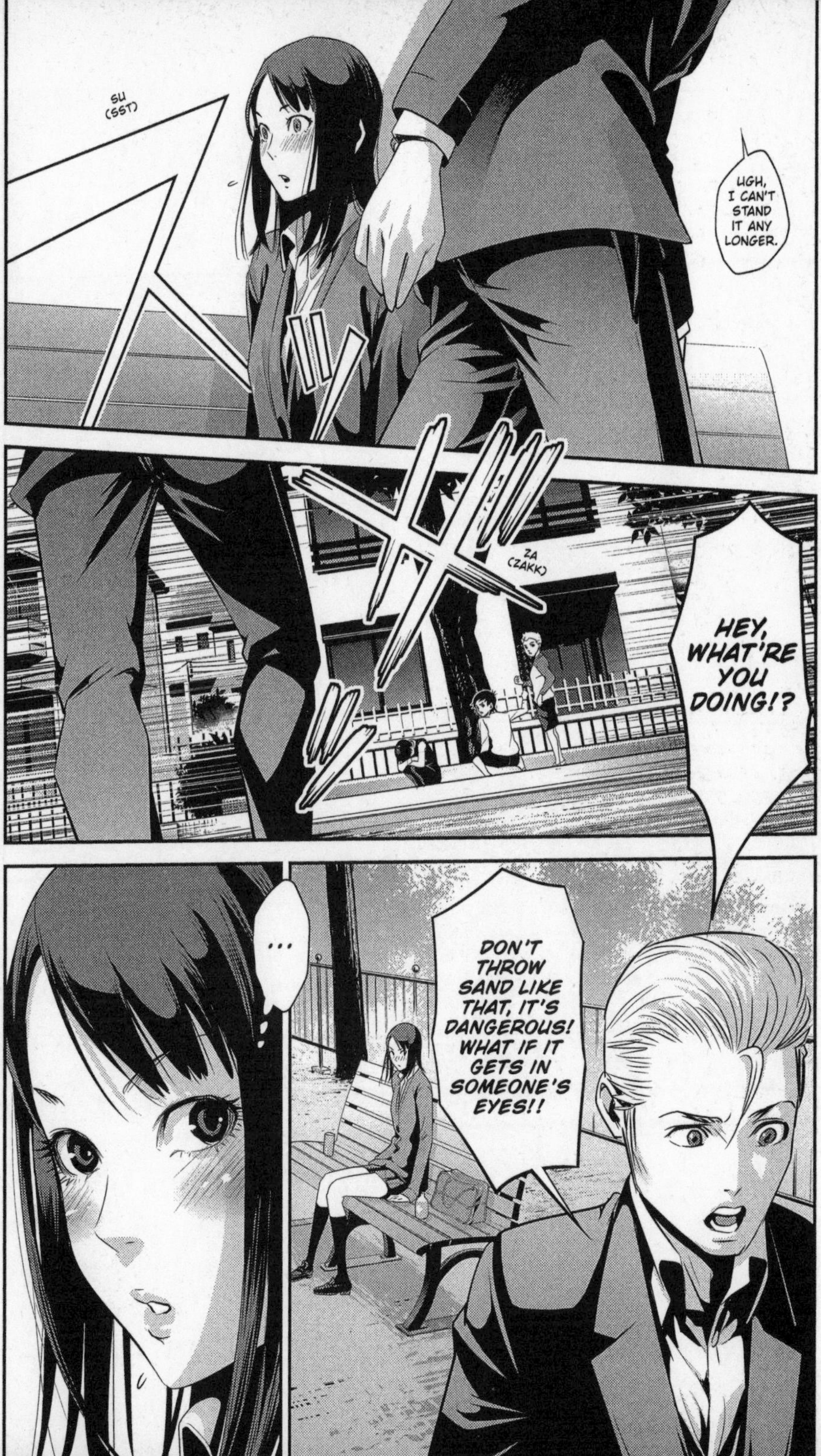
UGH, I CAN'T STAND IT ANY LONGER.
SU (SST)
ZA (ZAKK)
HEY, WHAT'RE YOU DOING!?
DON'T THROW SAND LIKE THAT, IT'S DANGEROUS! WHAT IF IT GETS IN SOMEONE'S EYES!!
...

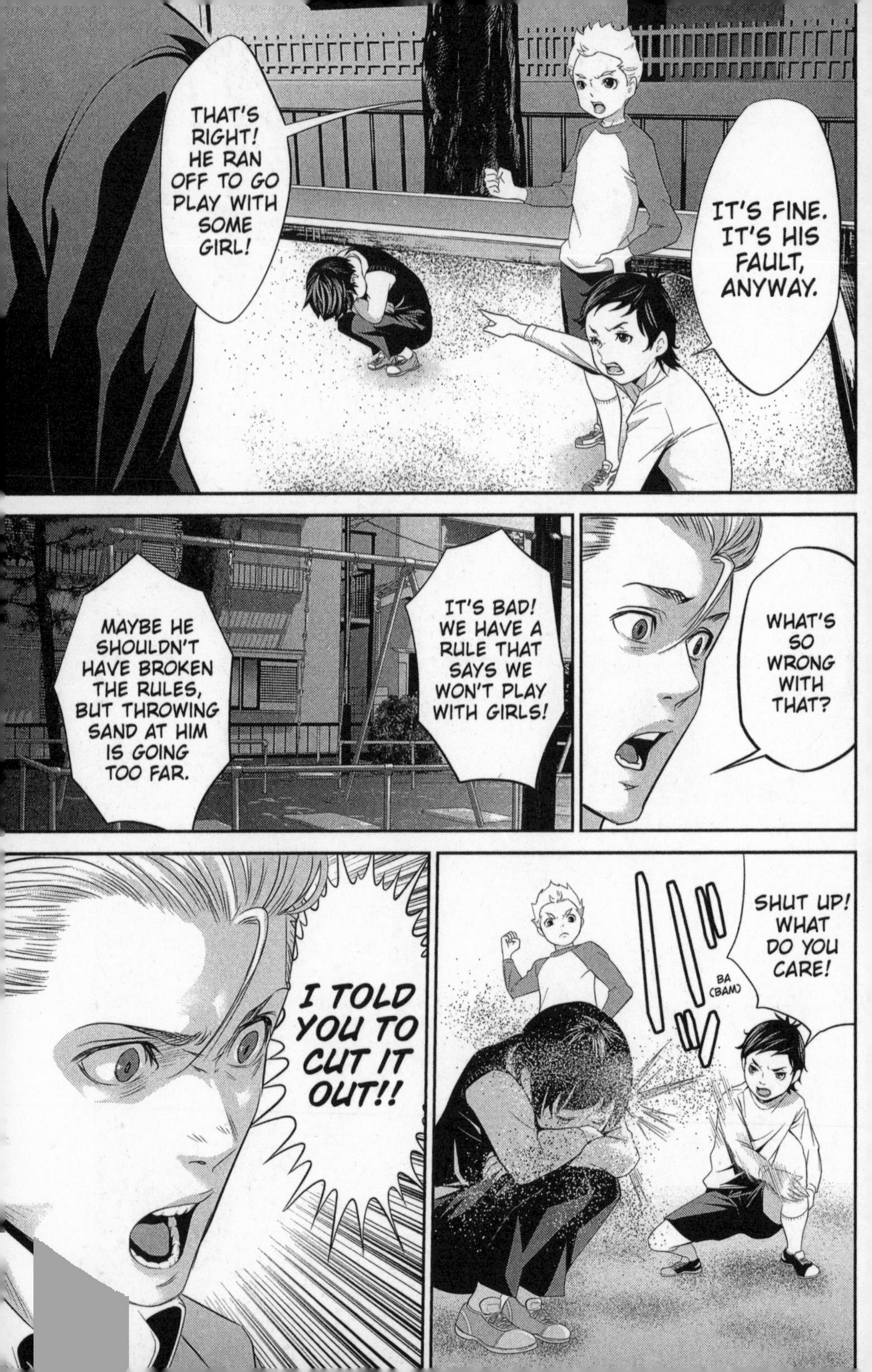
IT'S FINE. IT'S HIS FAULT, ANYWAY.
THAT'S RIGHT! HE RAN OFF TO GO PLAY WITH SOME GIRL!
WHAT'S SO WRONG WITH THAT?
IT'S BAD! WE HAVE A RULE THAT SAYS WE WON'T PLAY WITH GIRLS!
MAYBE HE SHOULDN'T HAVE BROKEN THE RULES, BUT THROWING SAND AT HIM IS GOING TOO FAR.
SHUT UP! WHAT DO YOU CARE!
BA (BAM)
I TOLD YOU TO CUT IT OUT!!

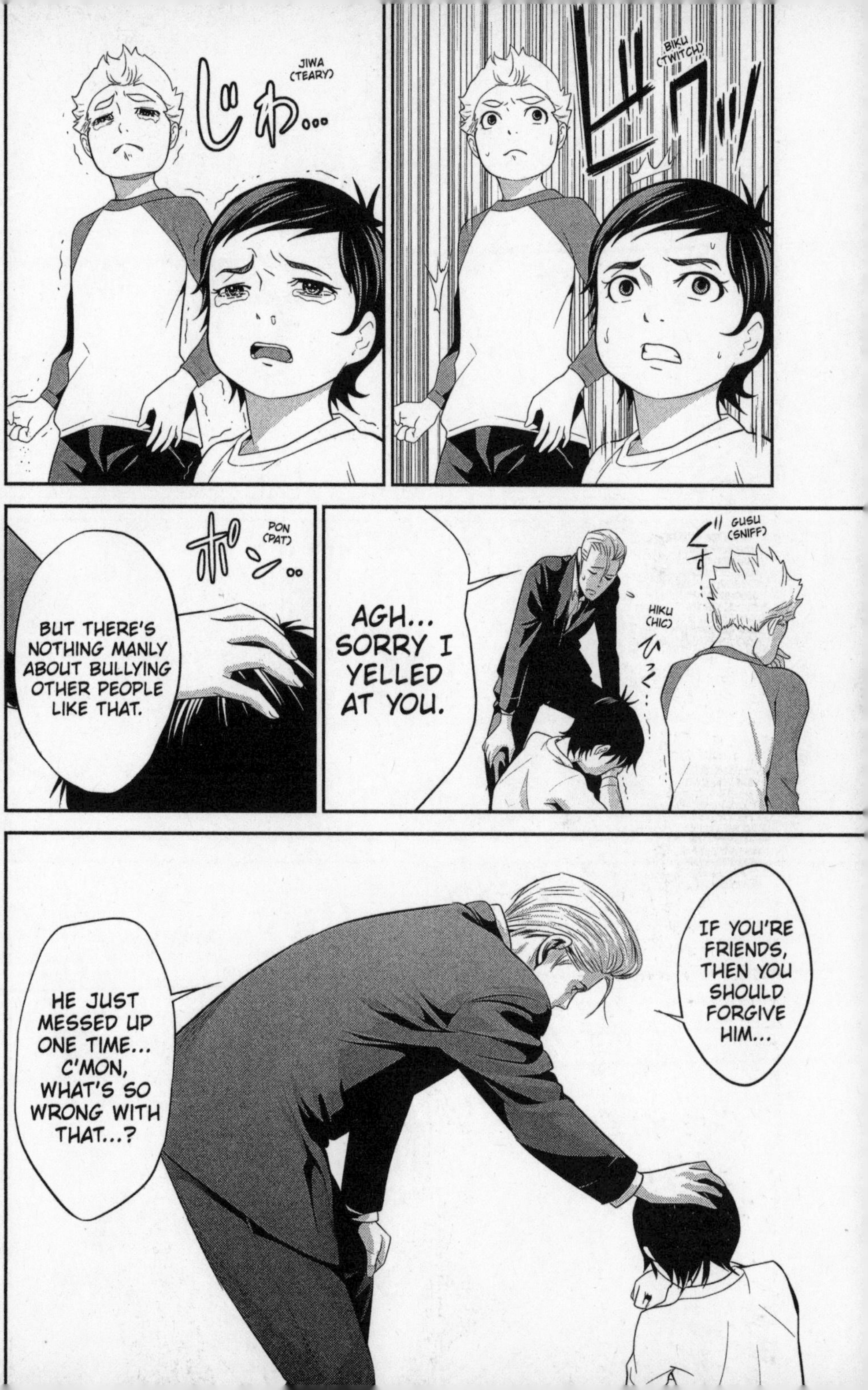
BIKU (TWITCH)
ビクッ
JIWA (TEARY)
じわ…
AGH... SORRY I YELLED AT YOU.
GUSU (SNIFF)
HIKU (HIC)
PON (PAT)
BUT THERE'S NOTHING MANLY ABOUT BULLYING OTHER PEOPLE LIKE THAT.
IF YOU'RE FRIENDS, THEN YOU SHOULD FORGIVE HIM...
HE JUST MESSED UP ONE TIME... C'MON, WHAT'S SO WRONG WITH THAT...?

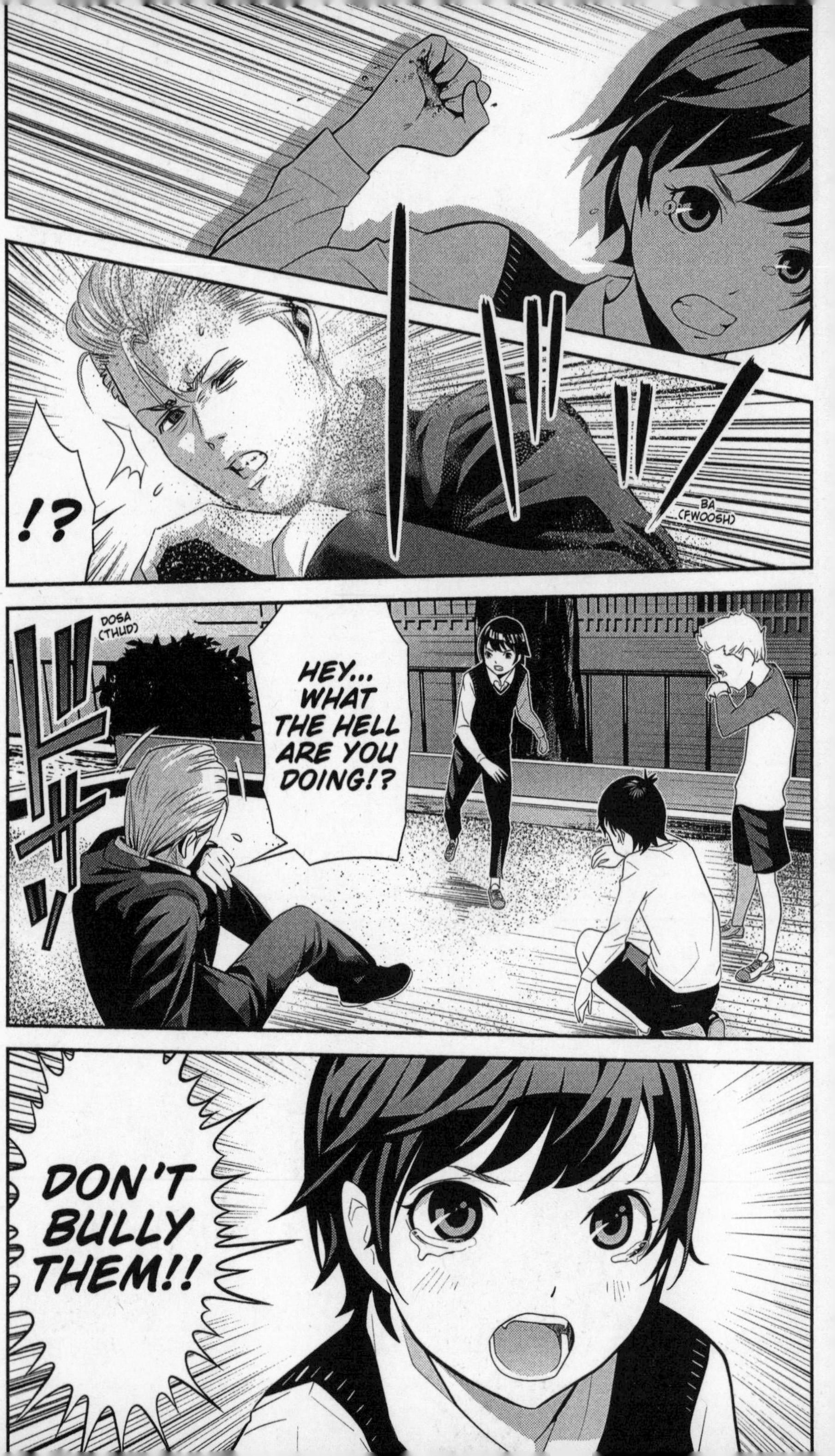
!?
BA (FWOOSH)
HEY... WHAT THE HELL ARE YOU DOING!?
DOSA (THUD)
DON'T BULLY THEM!!

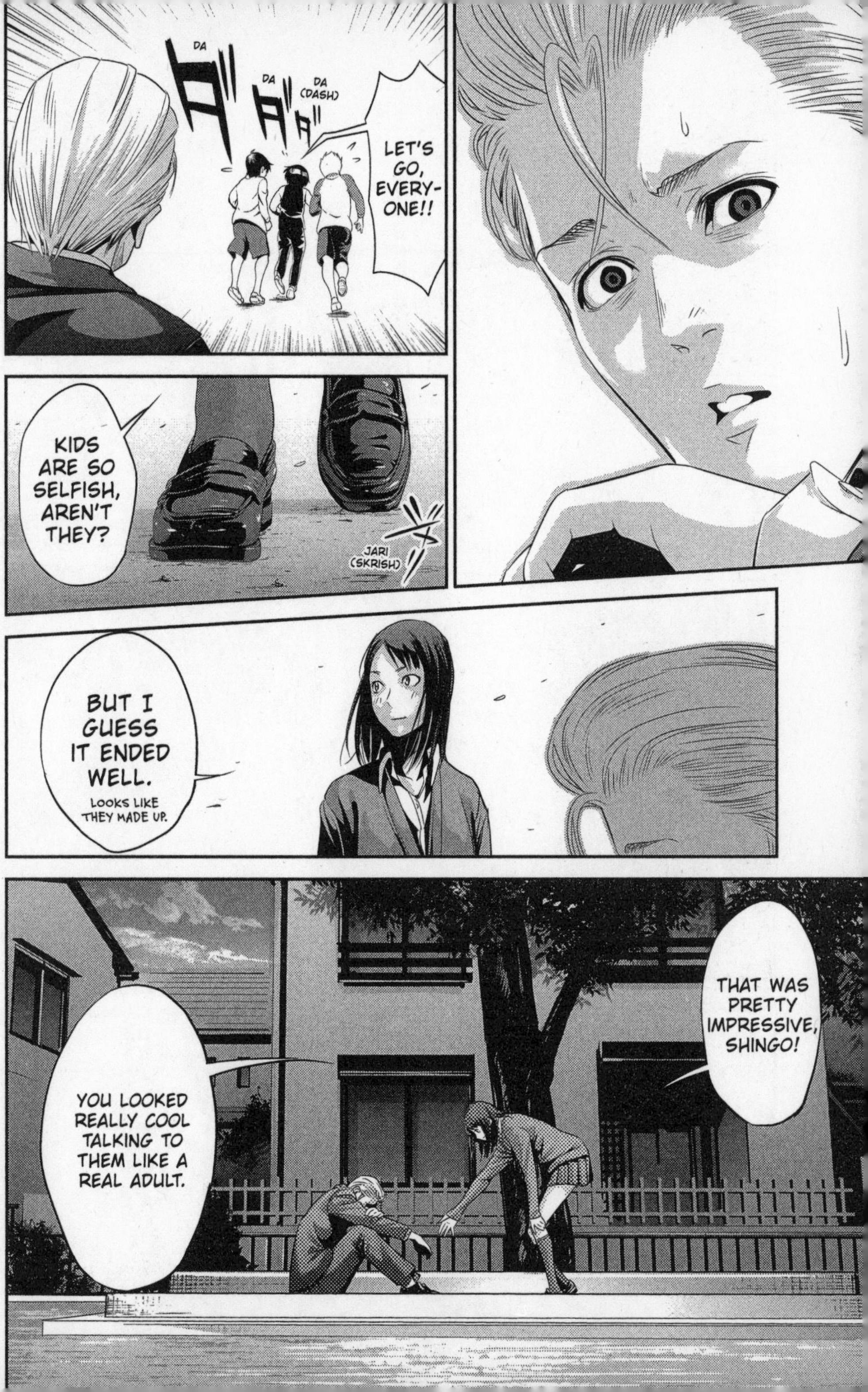
LET'S GO, EVERY-ONE!!
DA DA DA (DASH)
KIDS ARE SO SELFISH, AREN'T THEY?
JARI (SKRISH)
BUT I GUESS IT ENDED WELL.
LOOKS LIKE THEY MADE UP.
THAT WAS PRETTY IMPRESSIVE, SHINGO!
YOU LOOKED REALLY COOL TALKING TO THEM LIKE A REAL ADULT.

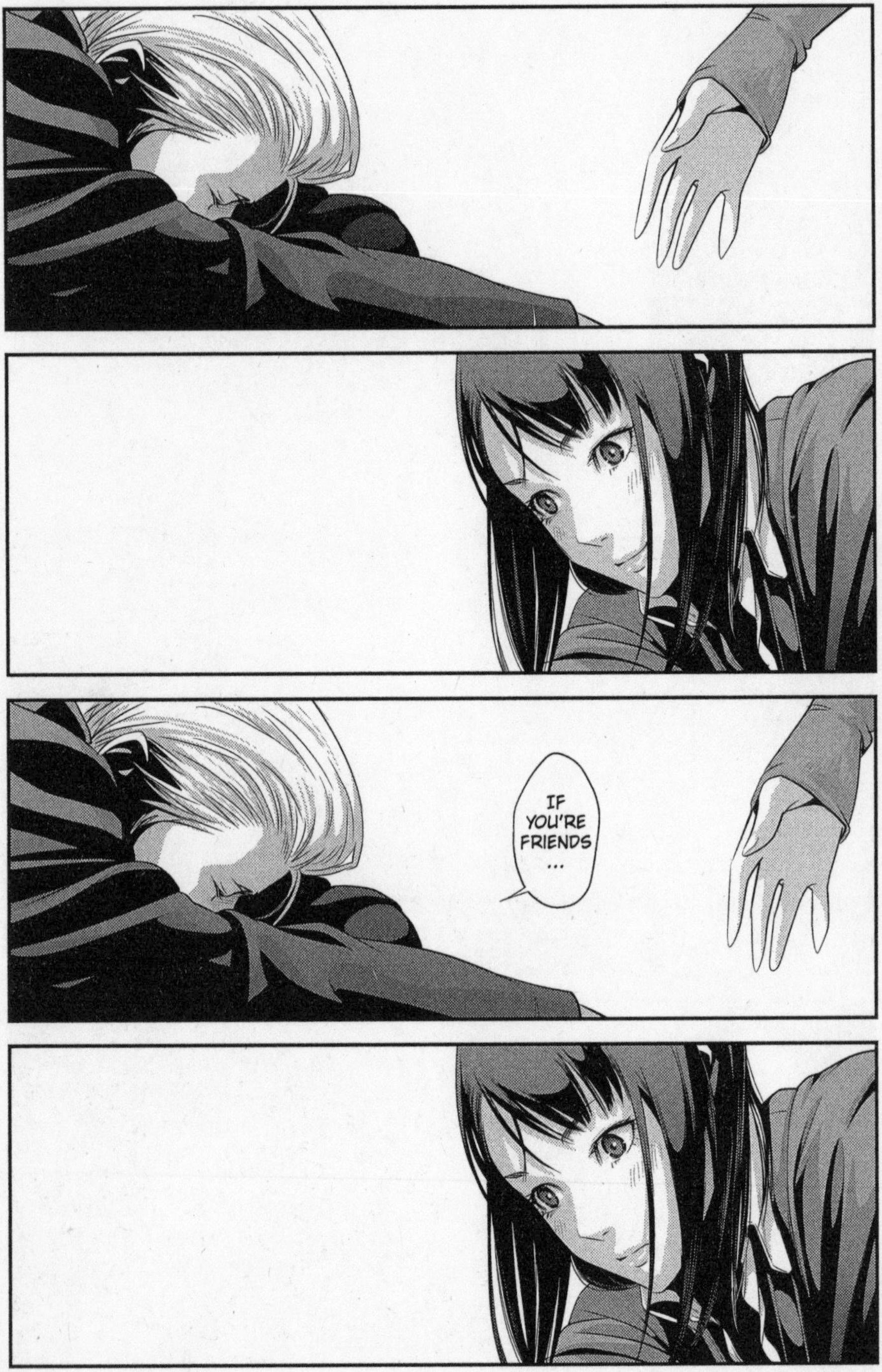
IF YOU'RE FRIENDS ...

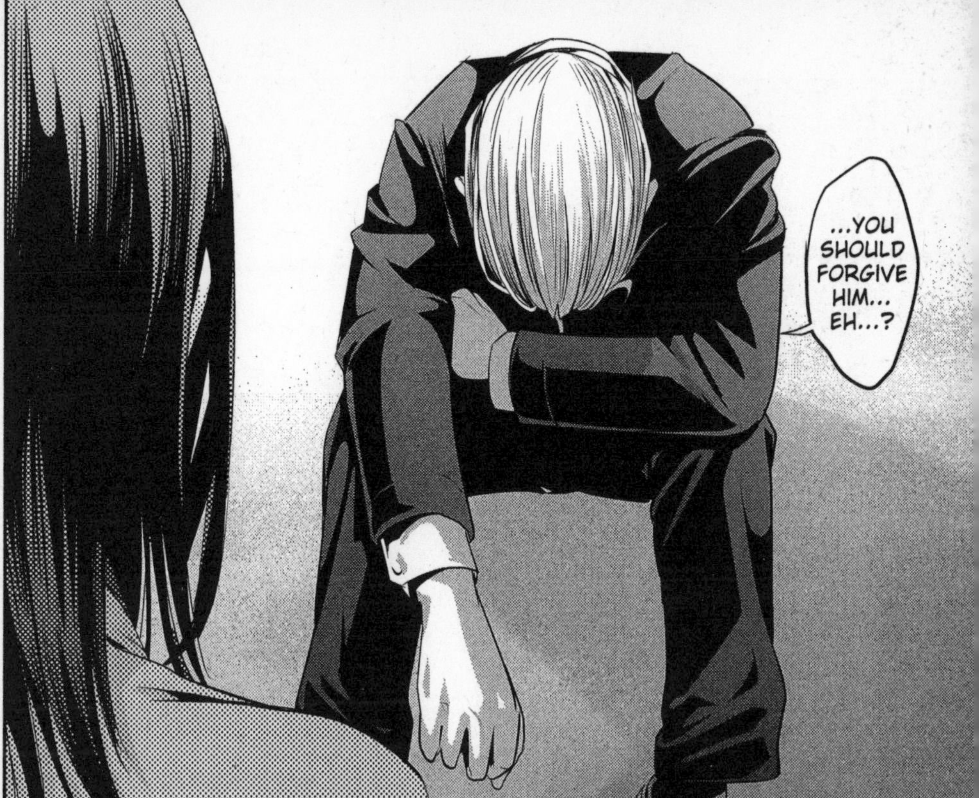
...YOU SHOULD FORGIVE HIM... EH...?

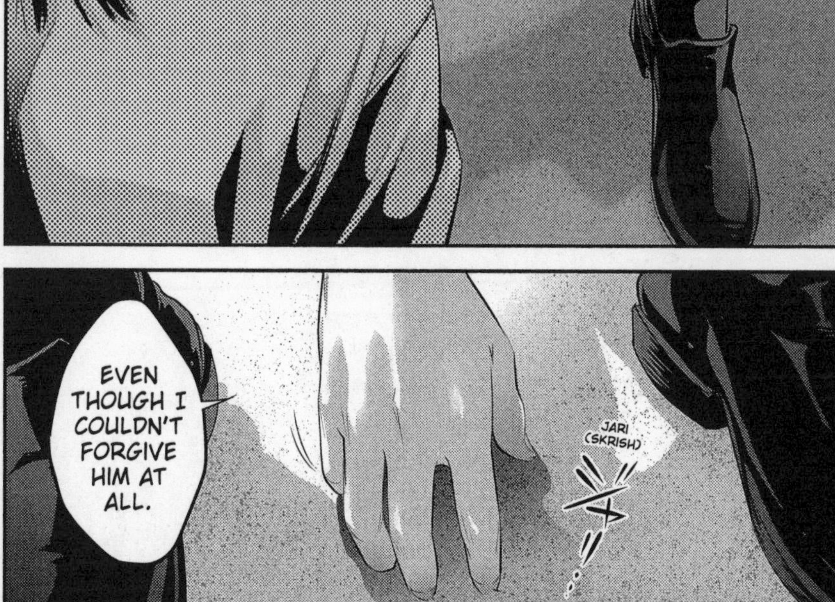
JARI (SKRISH)
EVEN THOUGH I COULDN'T FORGIVE HIM AT ALL.

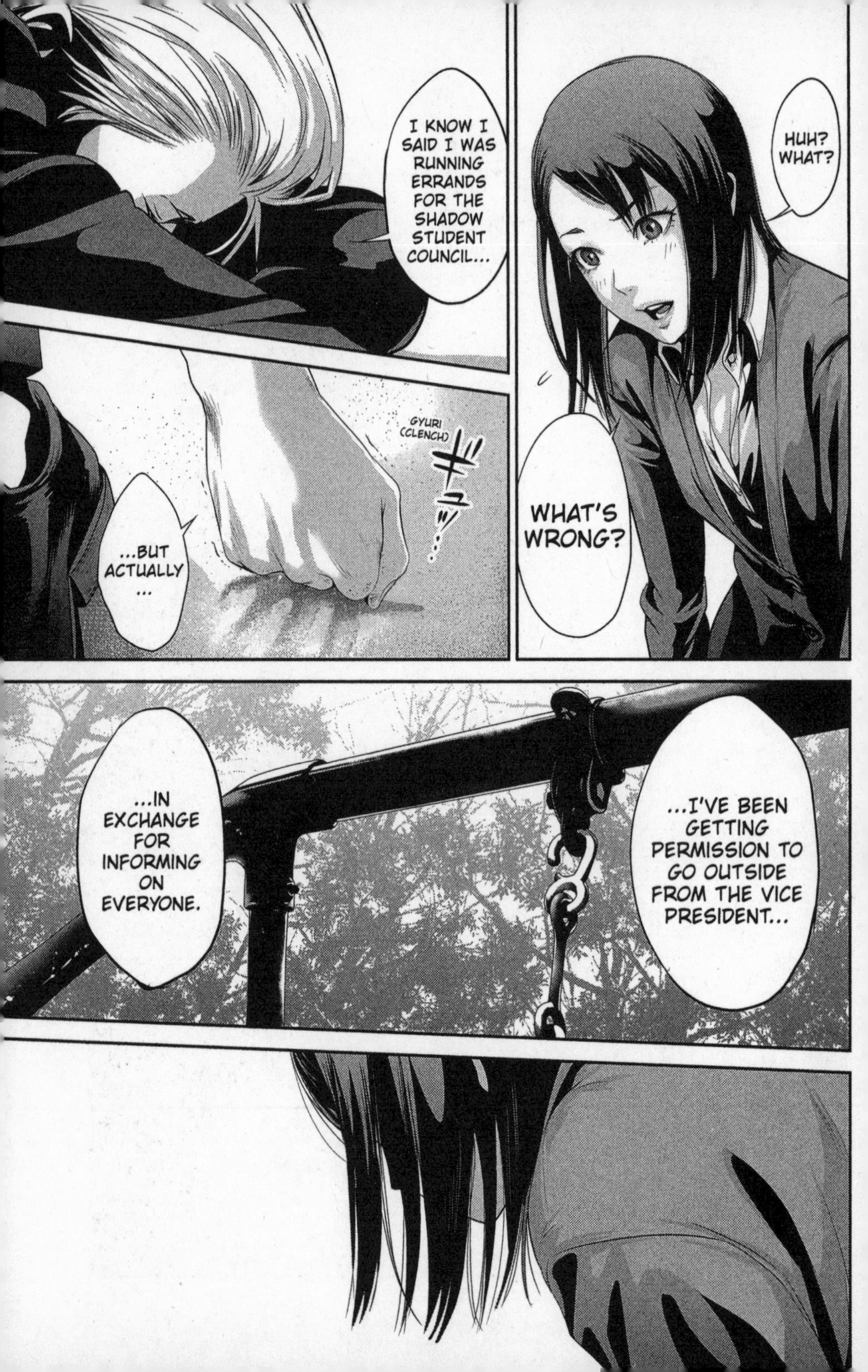
HUH? WHAT?
WHAT'S WRONG?
I KNOW I SAID I WAS RUNNING ERRANDS FOR THE SHADOW STUDENT COUNCIL...
GYURI (CLENCH)
...BUT ACTUALLY ...
...I'VE BEEN GETTING PERMISSION TO GO OUTSIDE FROM THE VICE PRESIDENT...
...IN EXCHANGE FOR INFORMING ON EVERYONE.

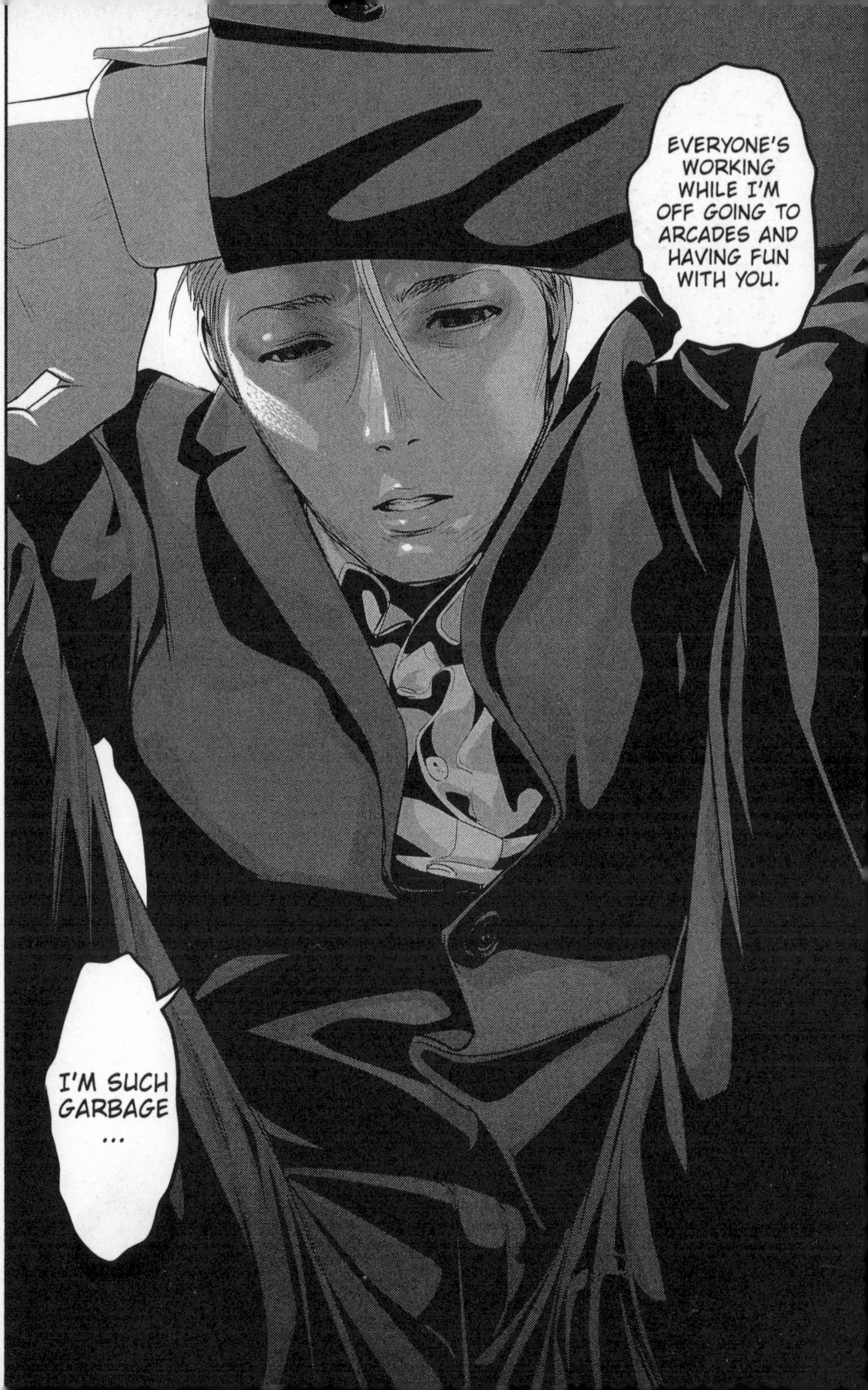
EVERYONE'S WORKING WHILE I'M OFF GOING TO ARCADES AND HAVING FUN WITH YOU.
I'M SUCH GARBAGE ...

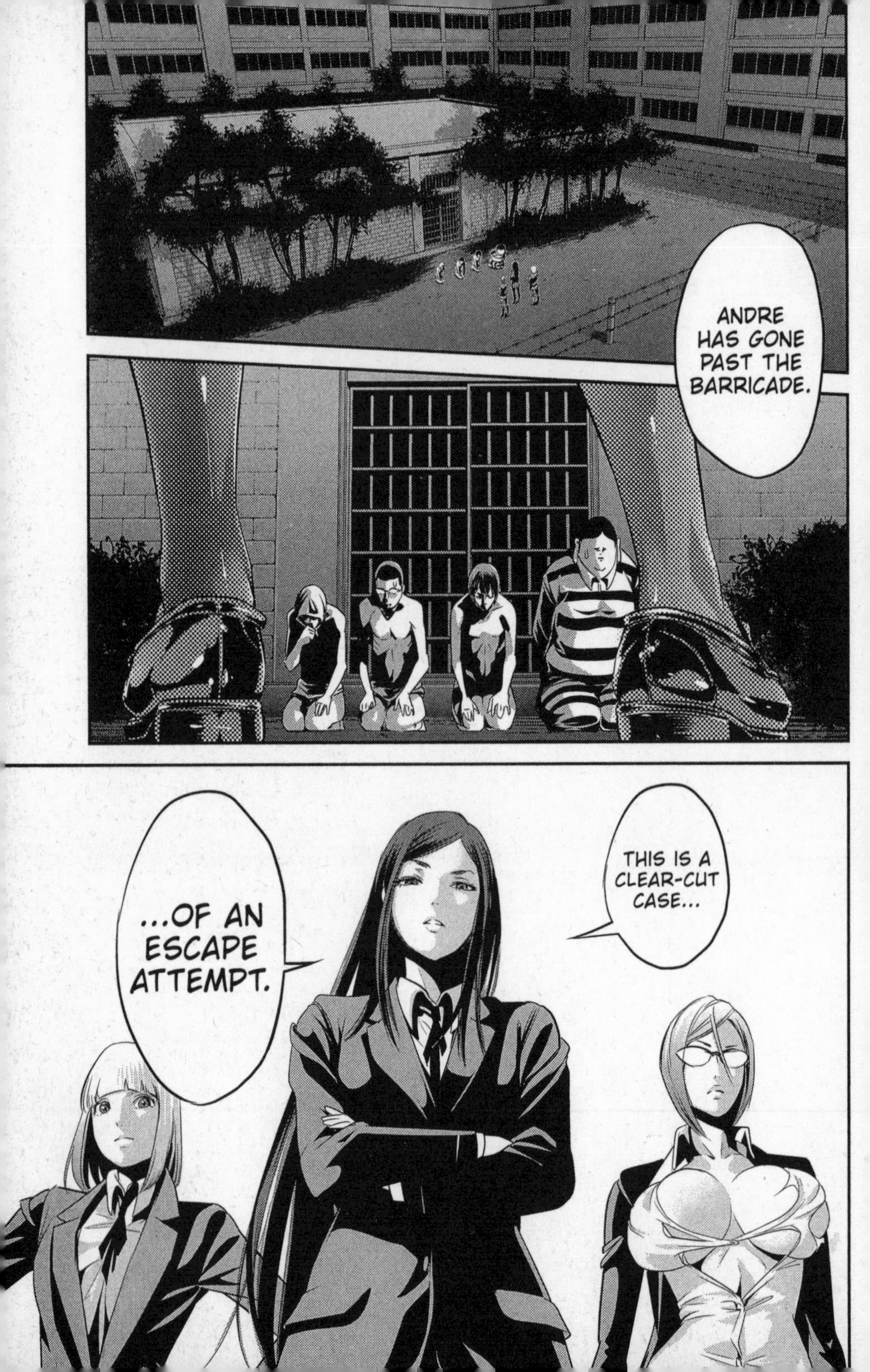
ANDRE HAS GONE PAST THE BARRICADE.
THIS IS A CLEAR-CUT CASE...
...OF AN ESCAPE ATTEMPT.

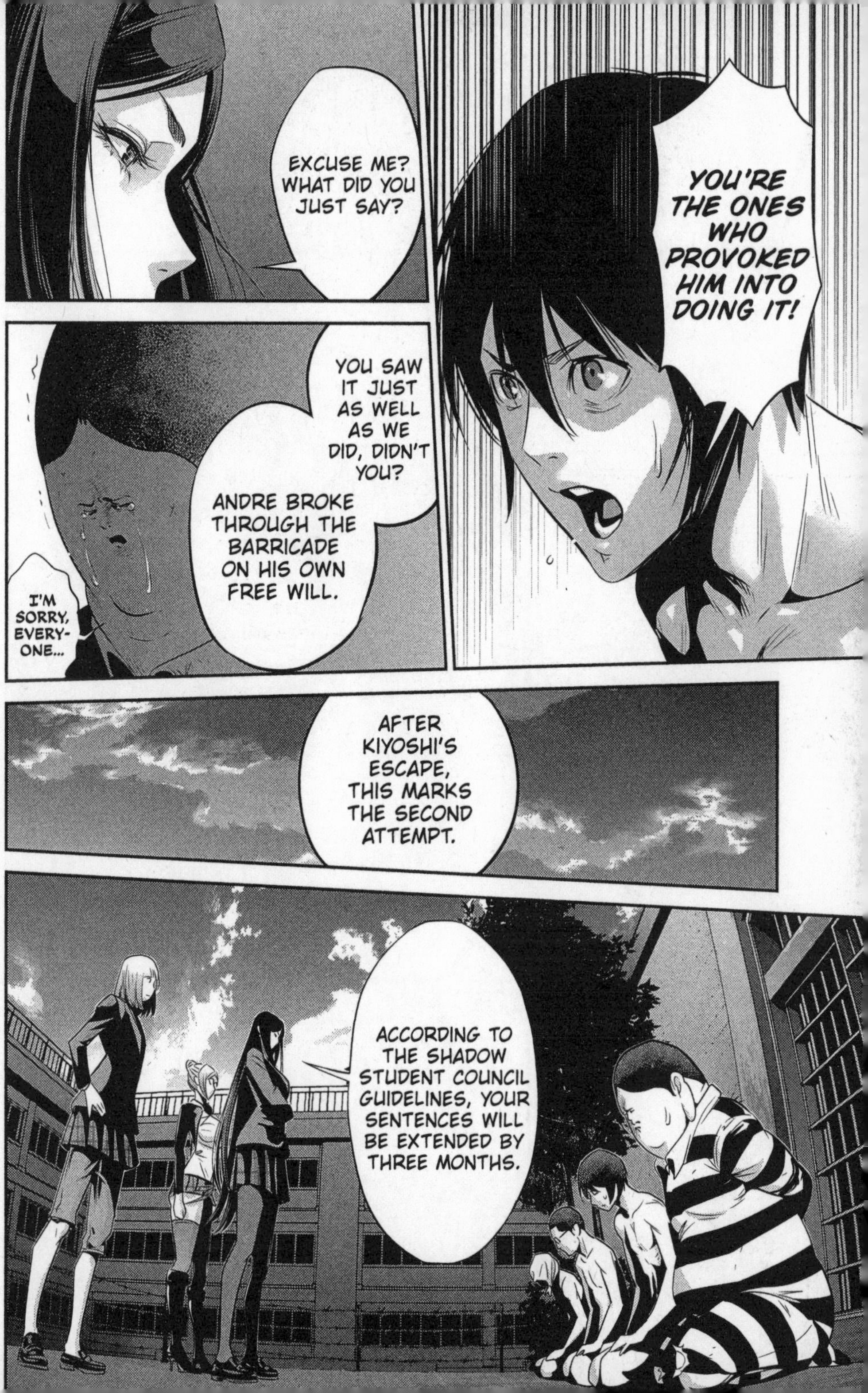
YOU'RE THE ONES WHO PROVOKED HIM INTO DOING IT!
EXCUSE ME? WHAT DID YOU JUST SAY?
YOU SAW IT JUST AS WELL AS WE DID, DIDN'T YOU?
ANDRE BROKE THROUGH THE BARRICADE ON HIS OWN FREE WILL.
I'M SORRY, EVERY-ONE...
AFTER KIYOSHI'S ESCAPE, THIS MARKS THE SECOND ATTEMPT.
ACCORDING TO THE SHADOW STUDENT COUNCIL GUIDELINES, YOUR SENTENCES WILL BE EXTENDED BY THREE MONTHS.

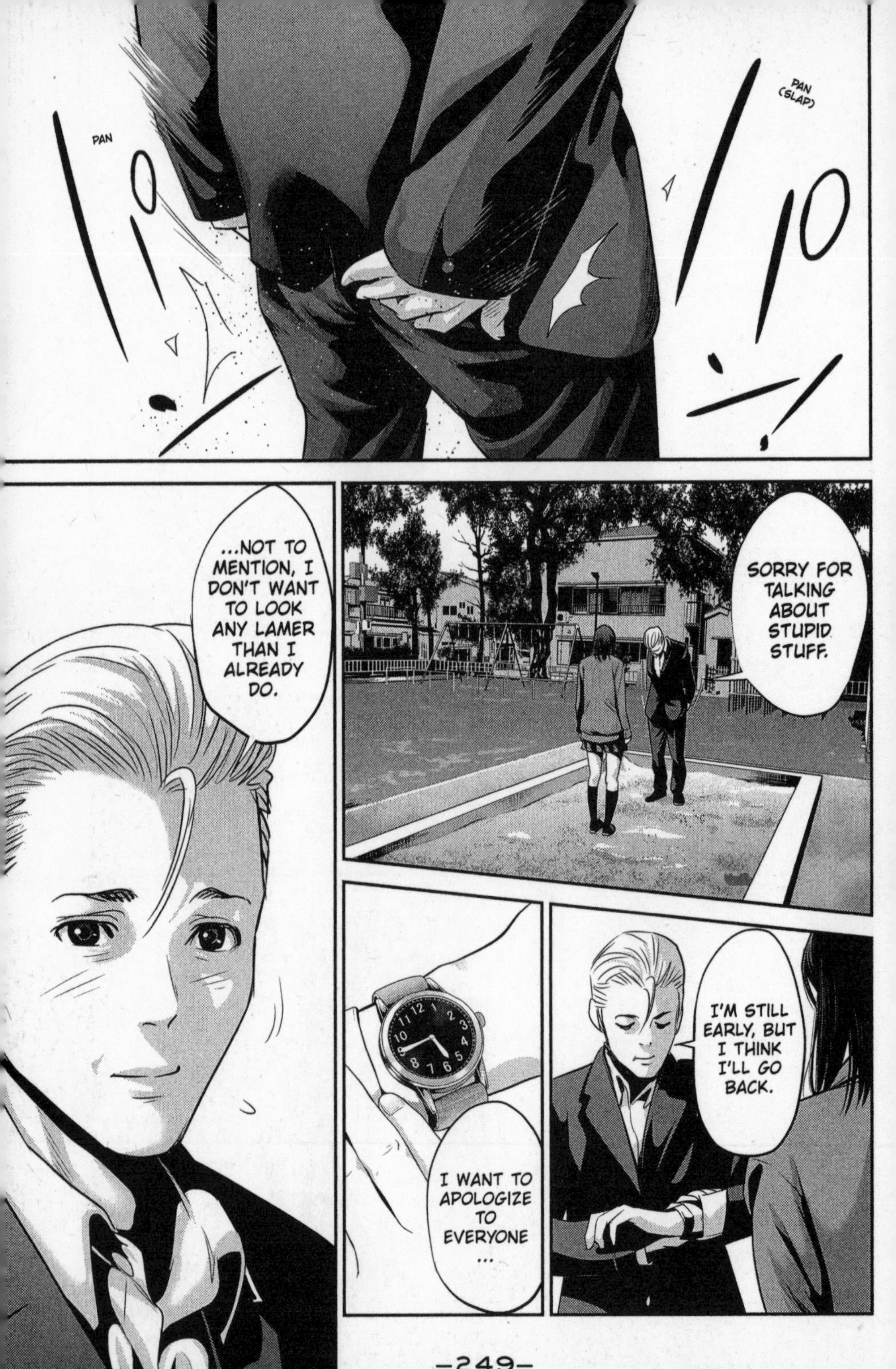
PAN (SLAP)
PAN
SORRY FOR TALKING ABOUT STUPID STUFF.
I'M STILL EARLY, BUT I THINK I'LL GO BACK.
I WANT TO APOLOGIZE TO EVERYONE ...
...NOT TO MENTION, I DON'T WANT TO LOOK ANY LAMER THAN I ALREADY DO.

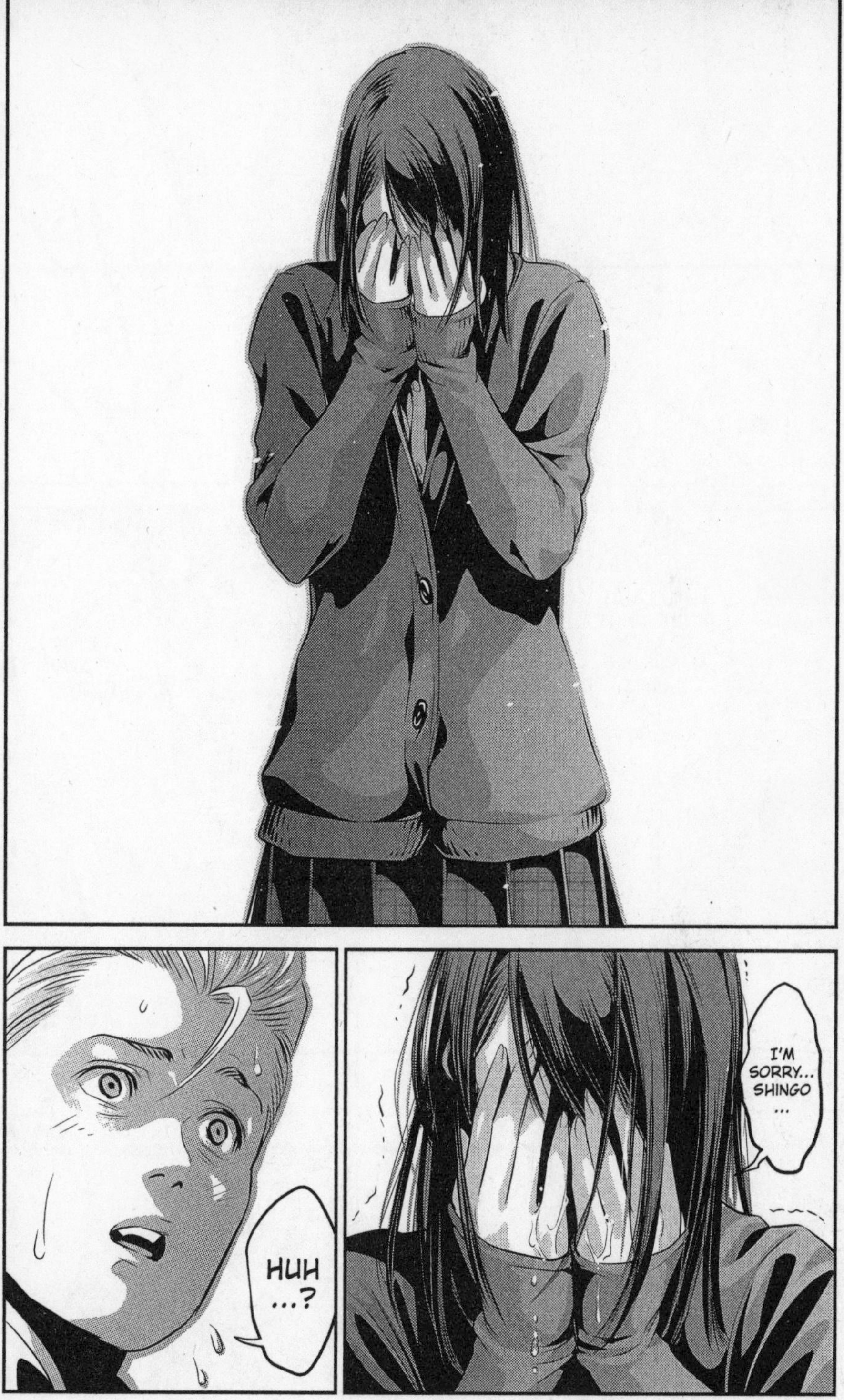
I'M SORRY... SHINGO ...
HUH ...?

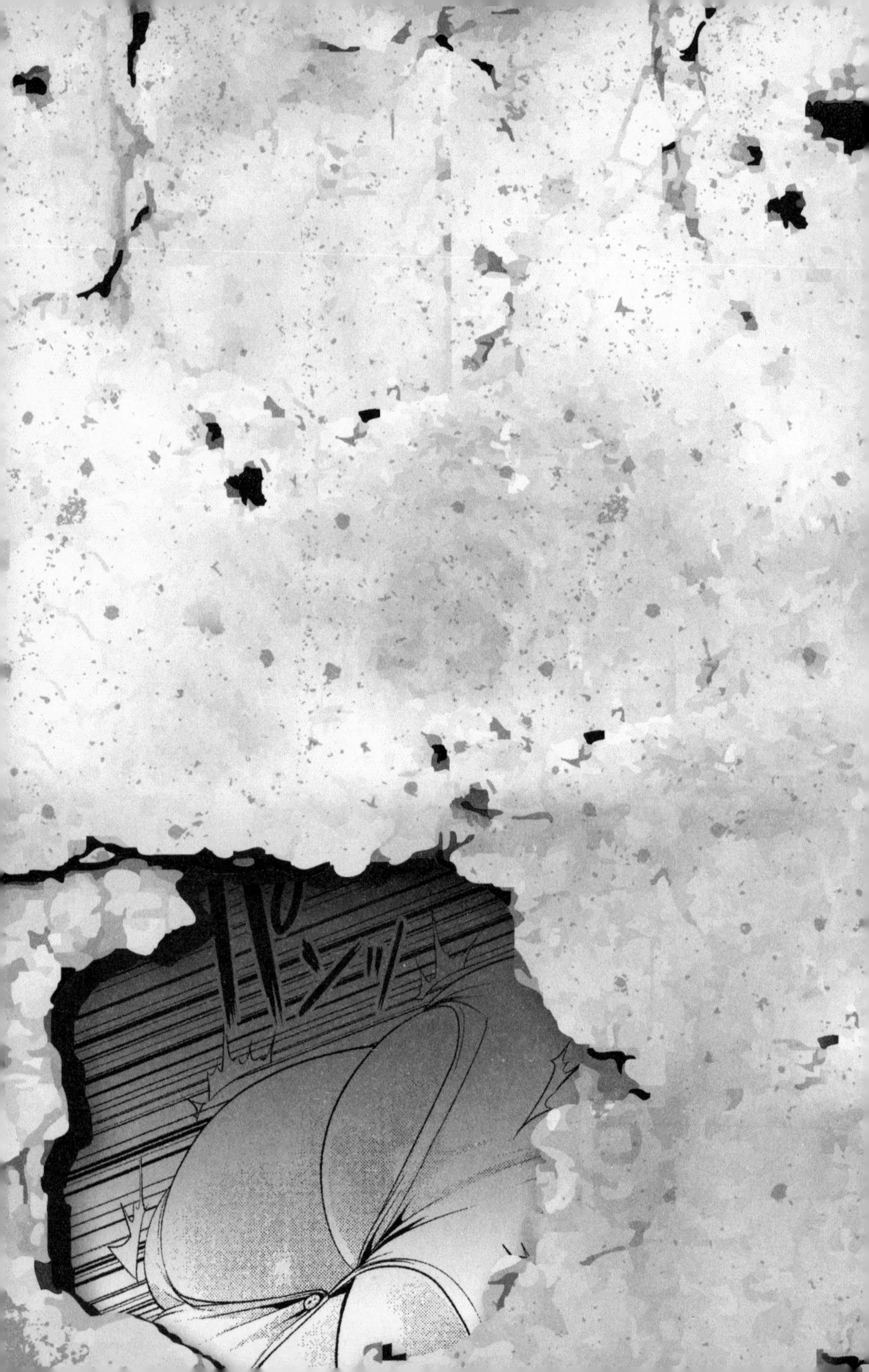
パッ!

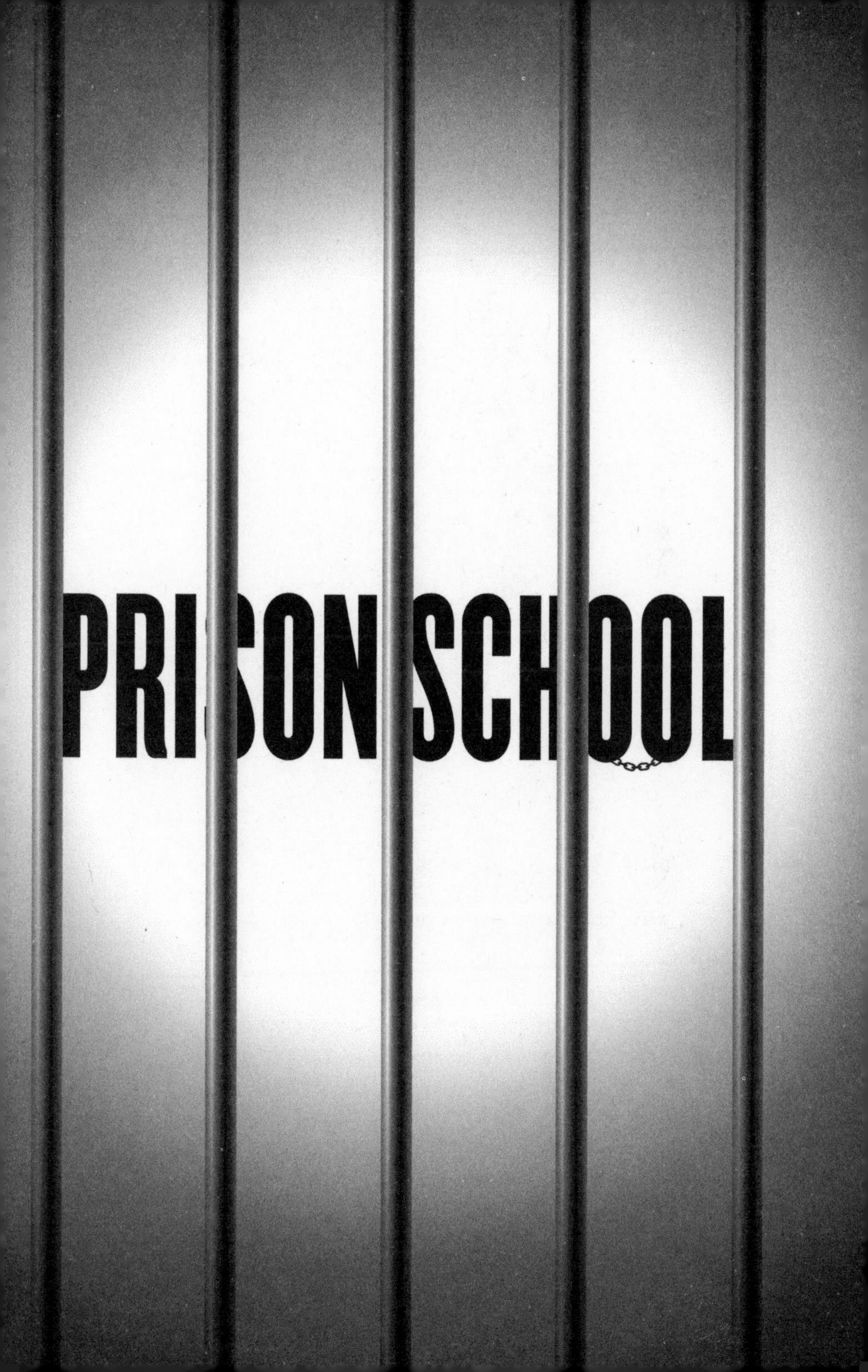
PRISON SCHOOL

CHAPTER 52

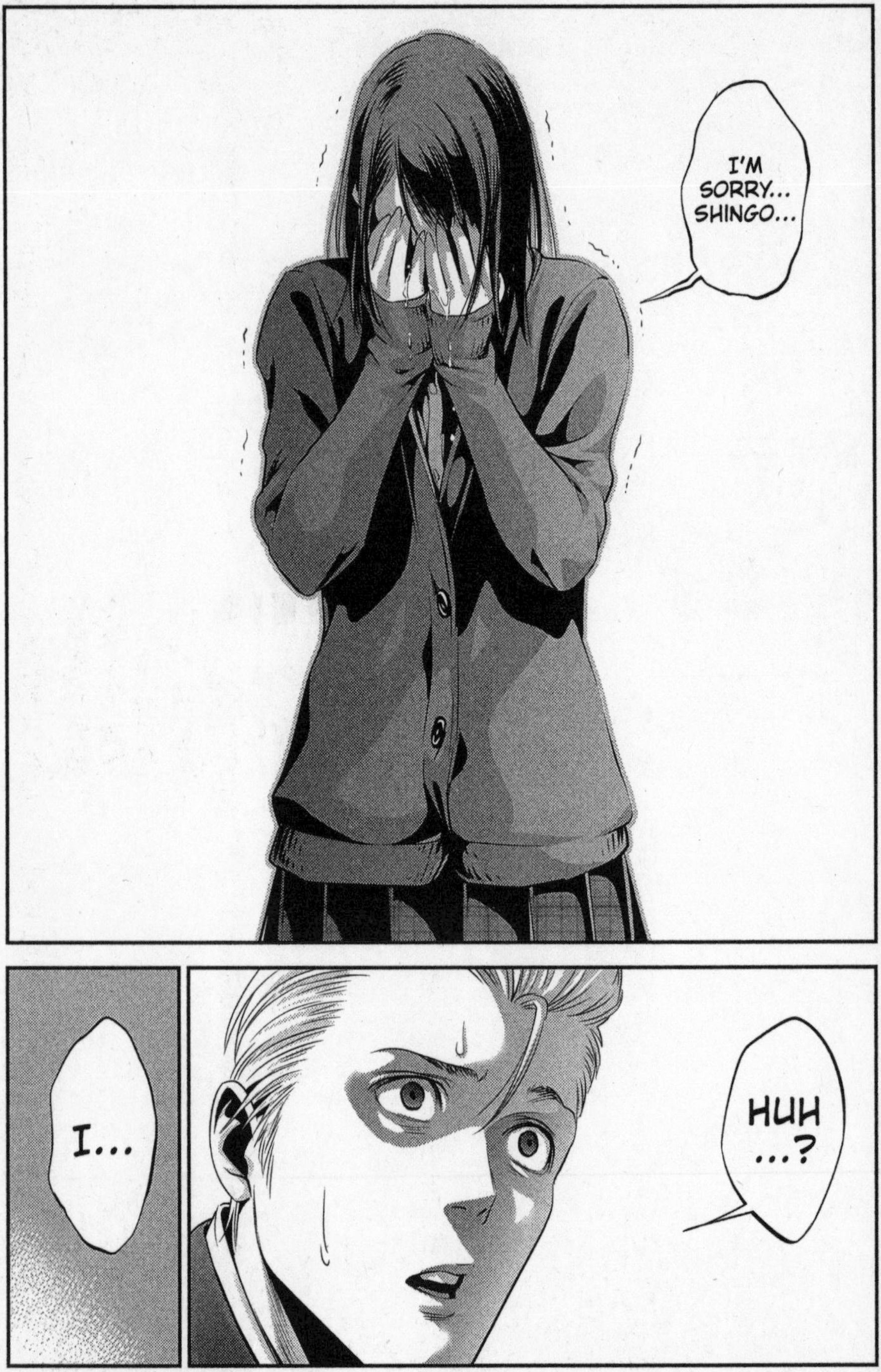
I'M SORRY... SHINGO...
HUH ...?
I...

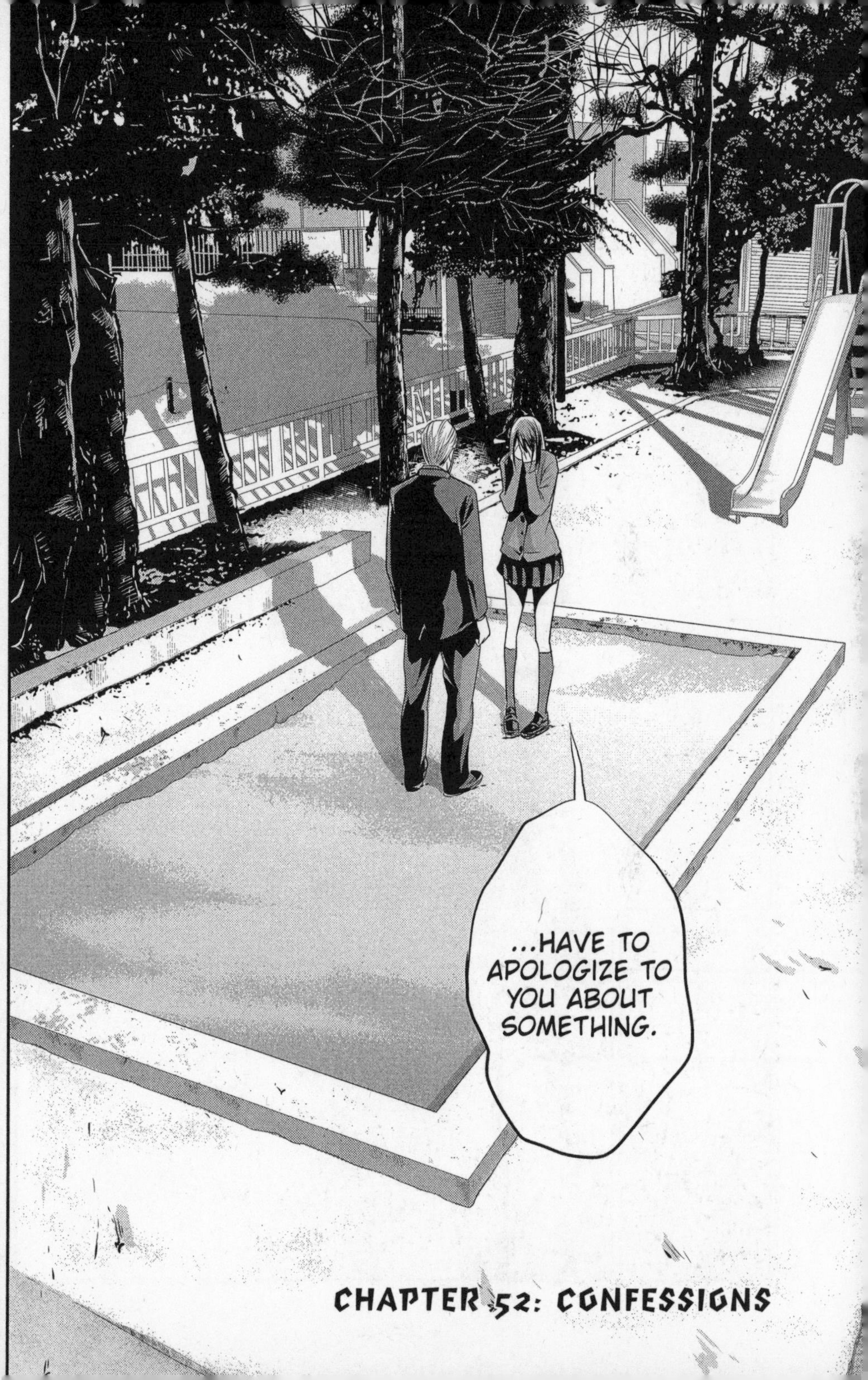
...HAVE TO APOLOGIZE TO YOU ABOUT SOMETHING.
CHAPTER 52: CONFESSIONS

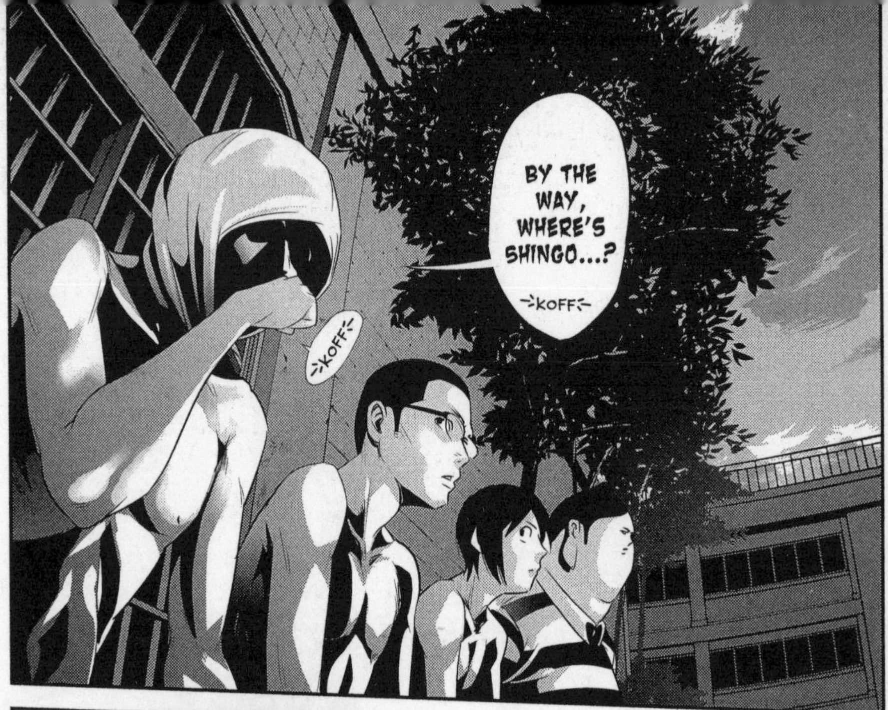
BY THE WAY, WHERE'S SHINGO...?
-KOFF-
-KOFF-

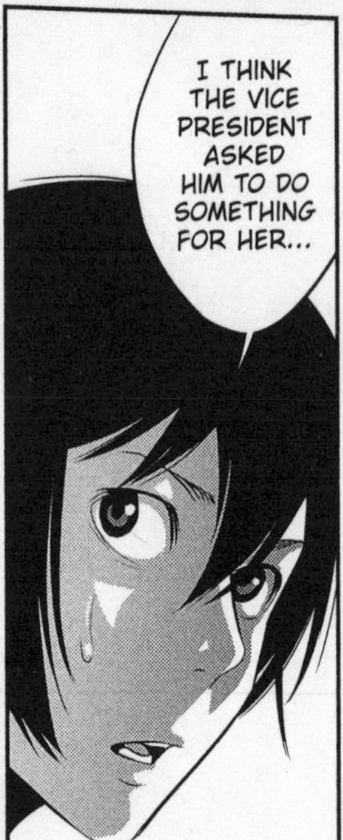
I THINK THE VICE PRESIDENT ASKED HIM TO DO SOMETHING FOR HER...

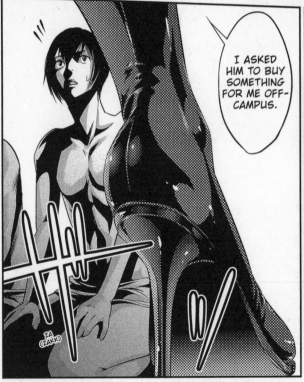

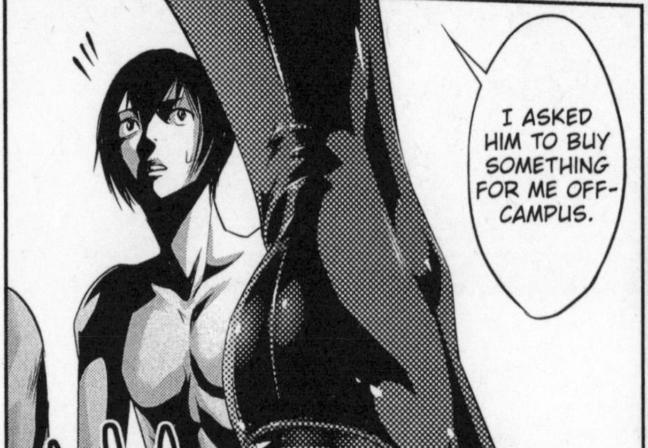
I ASKED HIM TO BUY SOMETHING FOR ME OFF-CAMPUS.
ZA (ZAKK)

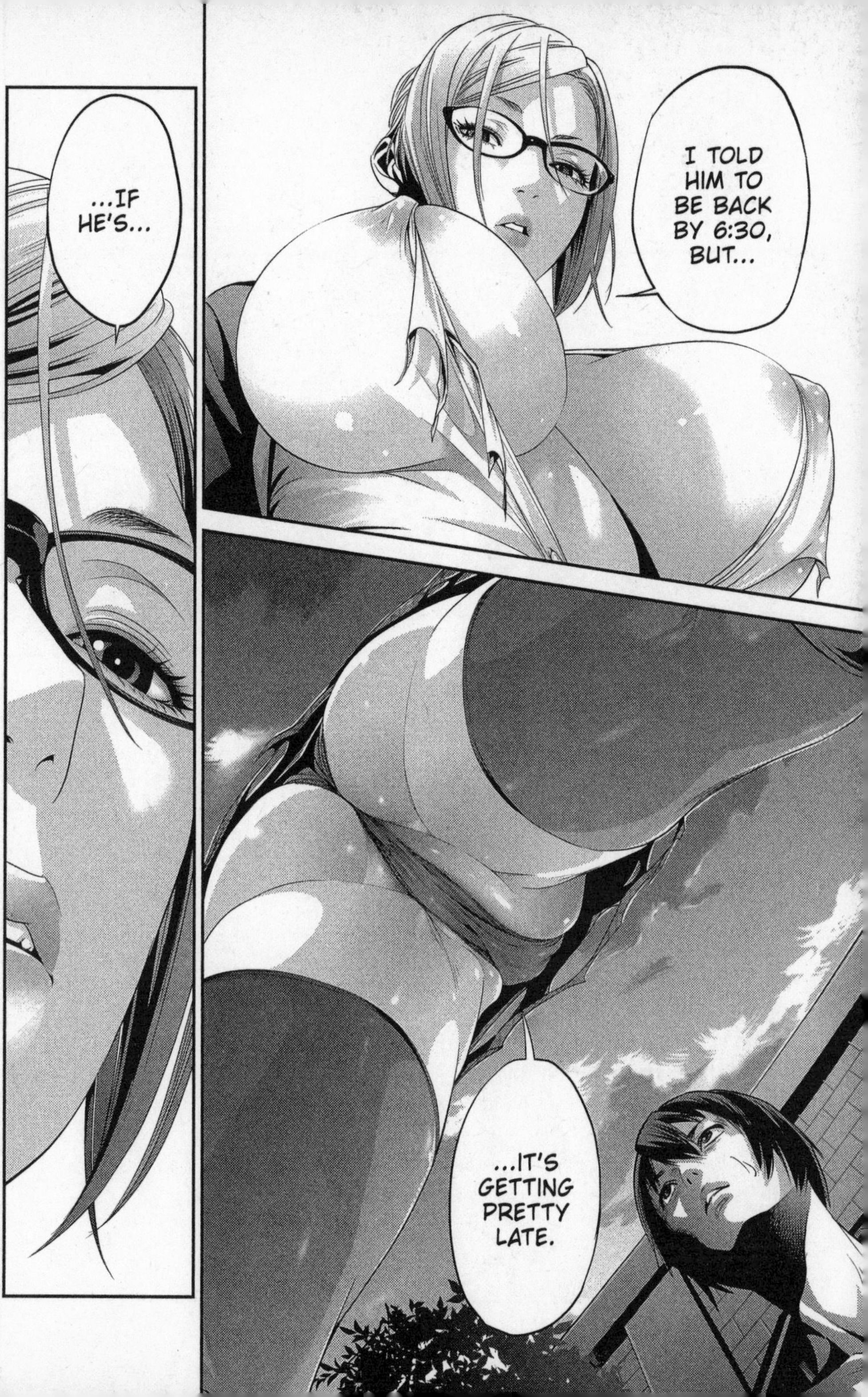
I TOLD HIM TO BE BACK BY 6:30, BUT...
...IT'S GETTING PRETTY LATE.
...IF HE'S...

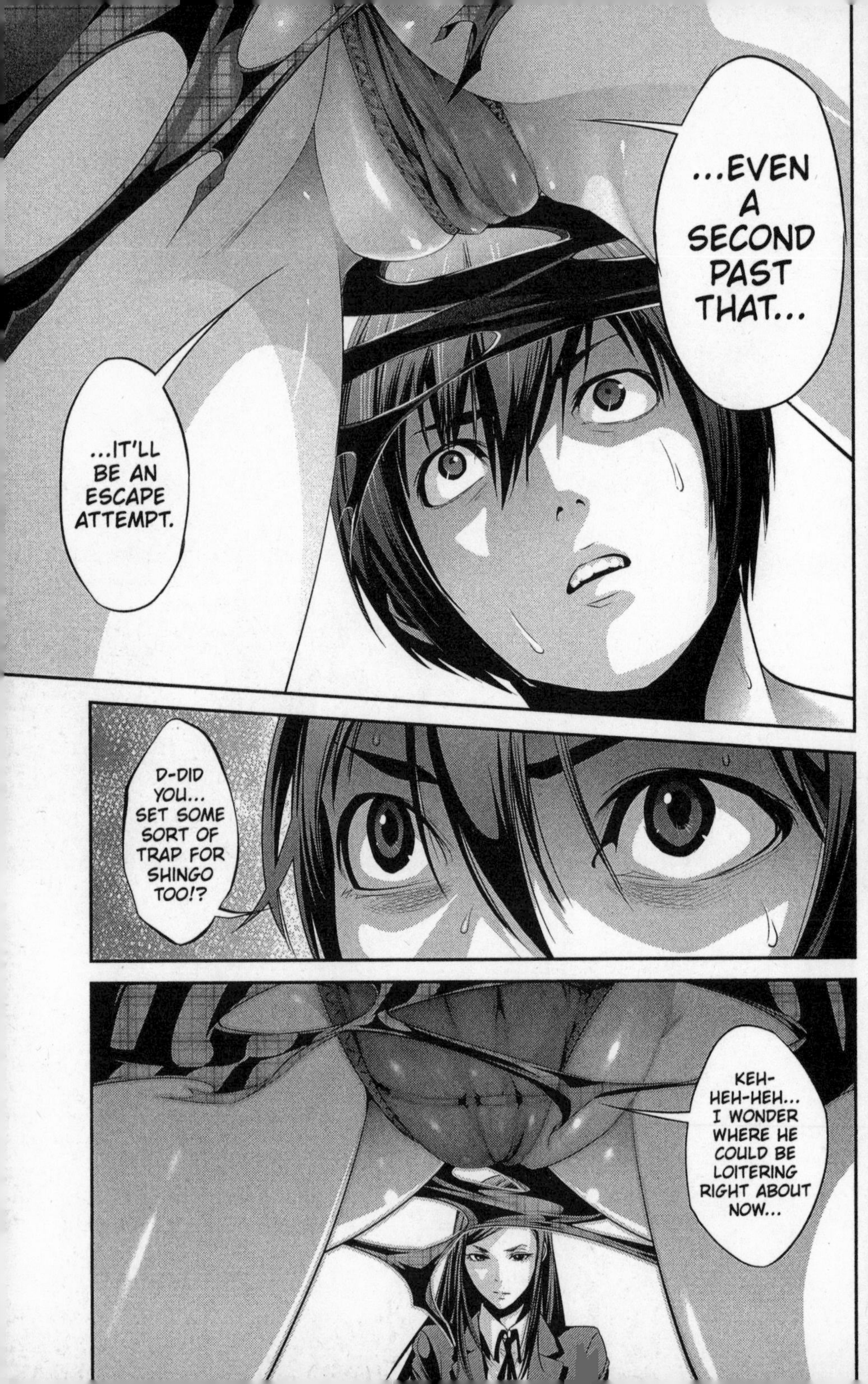
...EVEN A SECOND PAST THAT...
...IT'LL BE AN ESCAPE ATTEMPT.
D-DID YOU... SET SOME SORT OF TRAP FOR SHINGO TOO!?
KEH-HEH-HEH... I WONDER WHERE HE COULD BE LOITERING RIGHT ABOUT NOW...

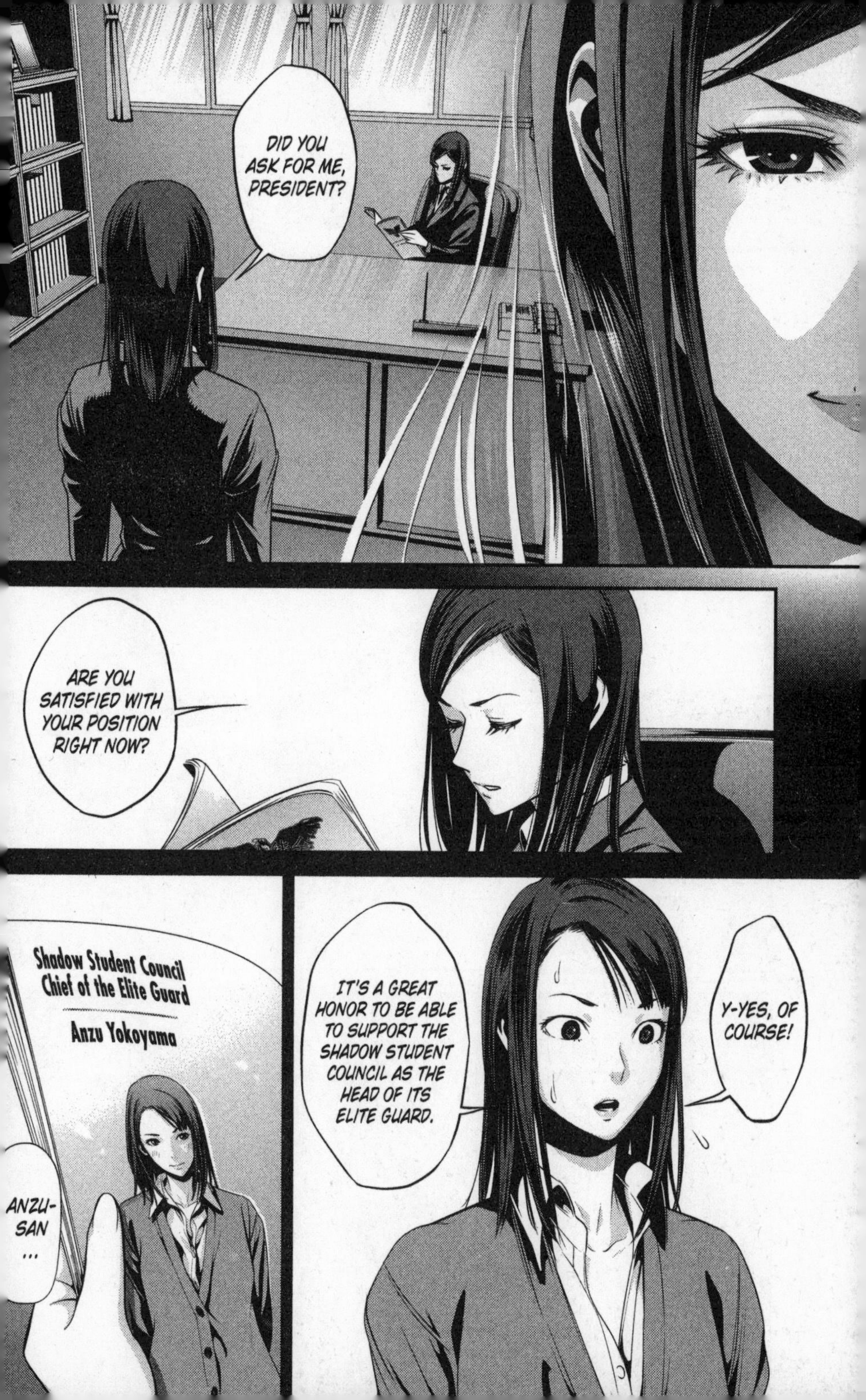
DID YOU ASK FOR ME, PRESIDENT?
ARE YOU SATISFIED WITH YOUR POSITION RIGHT NOW?
Y-YES, OF COURSE!
IT'S A GREAT HONOR TO BE ABLE TO SUPPORT THE SHADOW STUDENT COUNCIL AS THE HEAD OF ITS ELITE GUARD.
Shadow Student Council Chief of the Elite Guard
Anzu Yokoyama
ANZU-SAN...

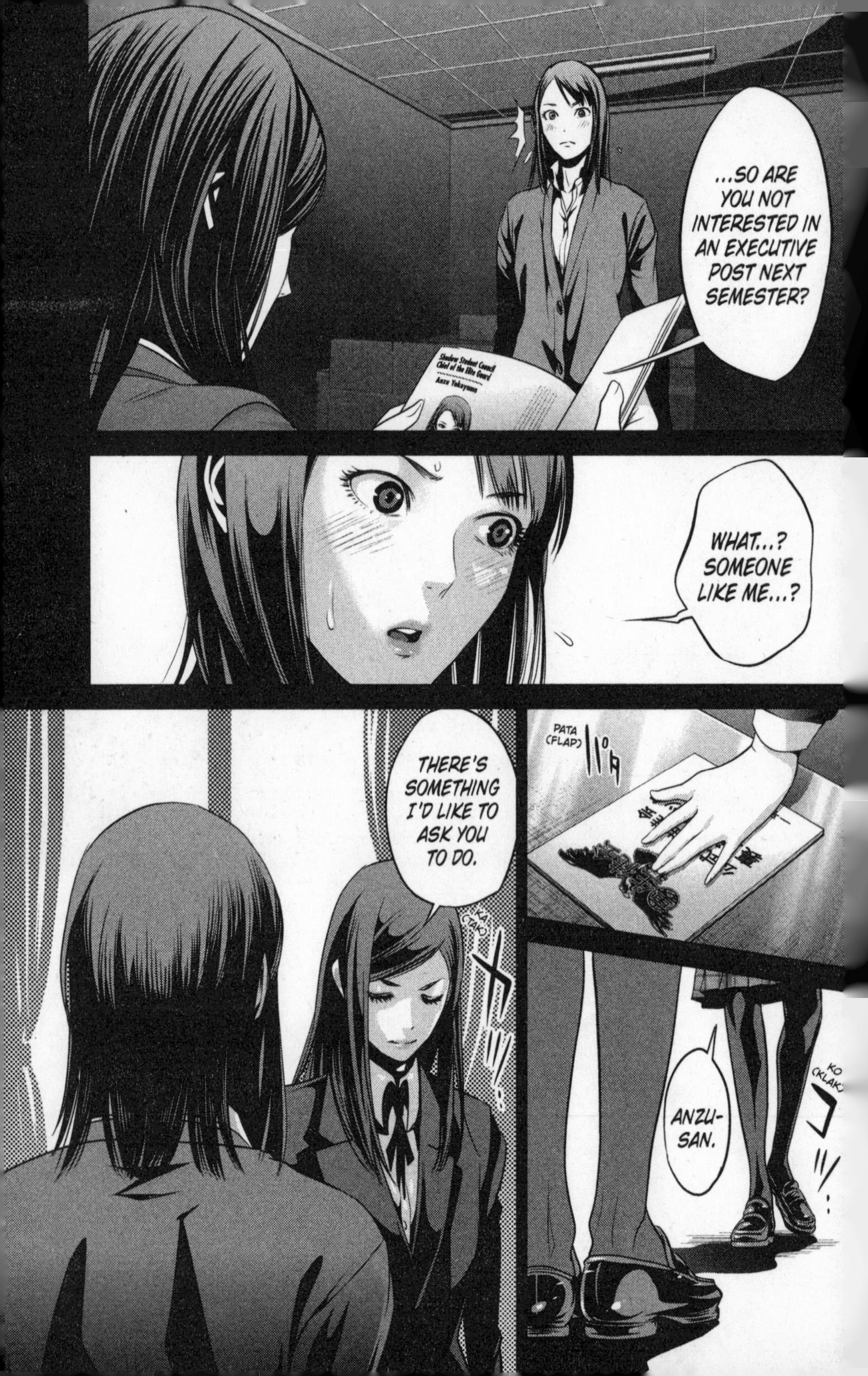
...SO ARE YOU NOT INTERESTED IN AN EXECUTIVE POST NEXT SEMESTER?
Shadow Student Council Chief of the Elite Guard
Anzu Yokoyama
WHAT...? SOMEONE LIKE ME...?
PATA (FLAP)
ANZU-SAN.
KO (KLAK)
THERE'S SOMETHING I'D LIKE TO ASK YOU TO DO.
KA (TAK)

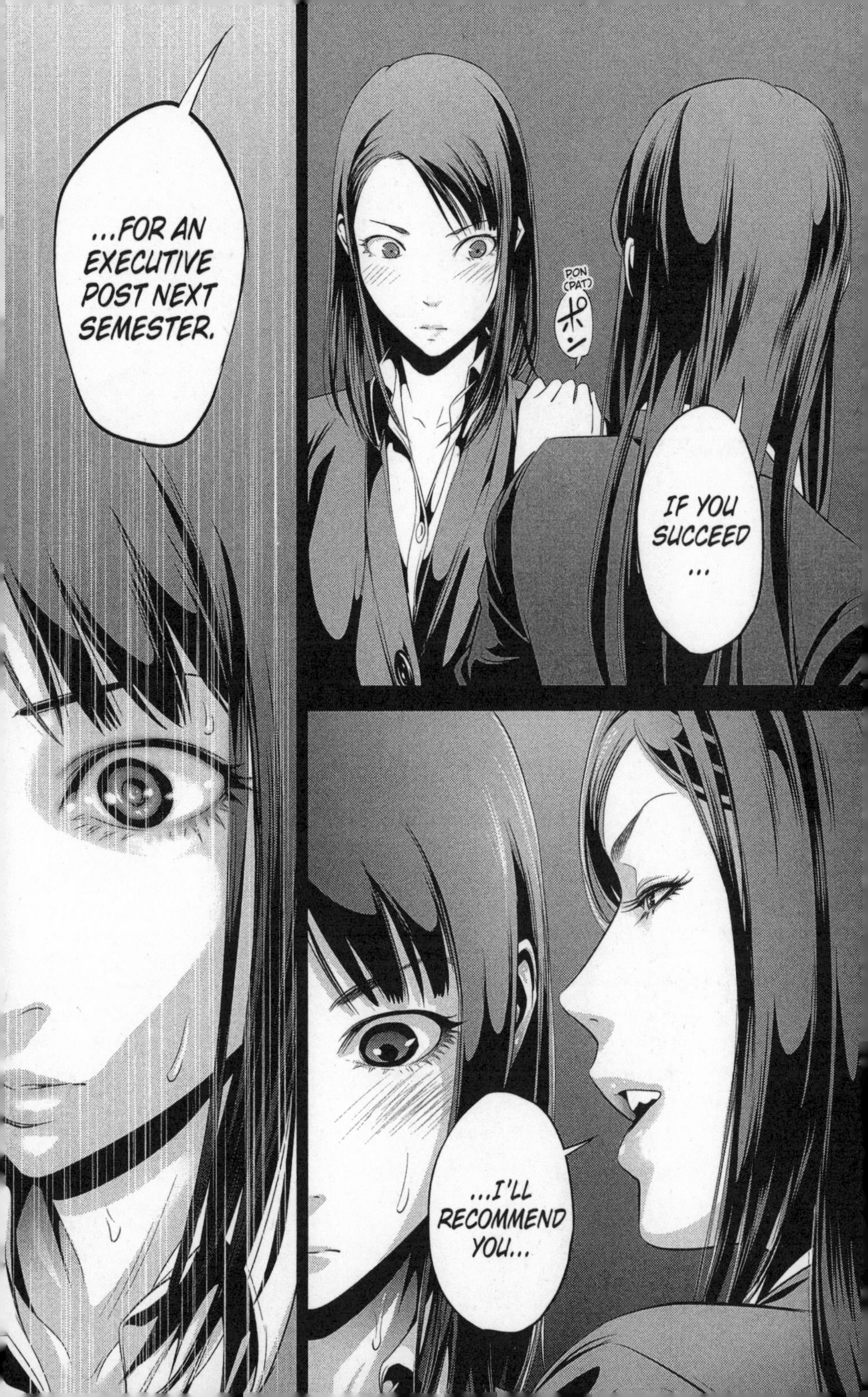
PON (PAT)
ポン
IF YOU SUCCEED...
...I'LL RECOMMEND YOU...
...FOR AN EXECUTIVE POST NEXT SEMESTER.

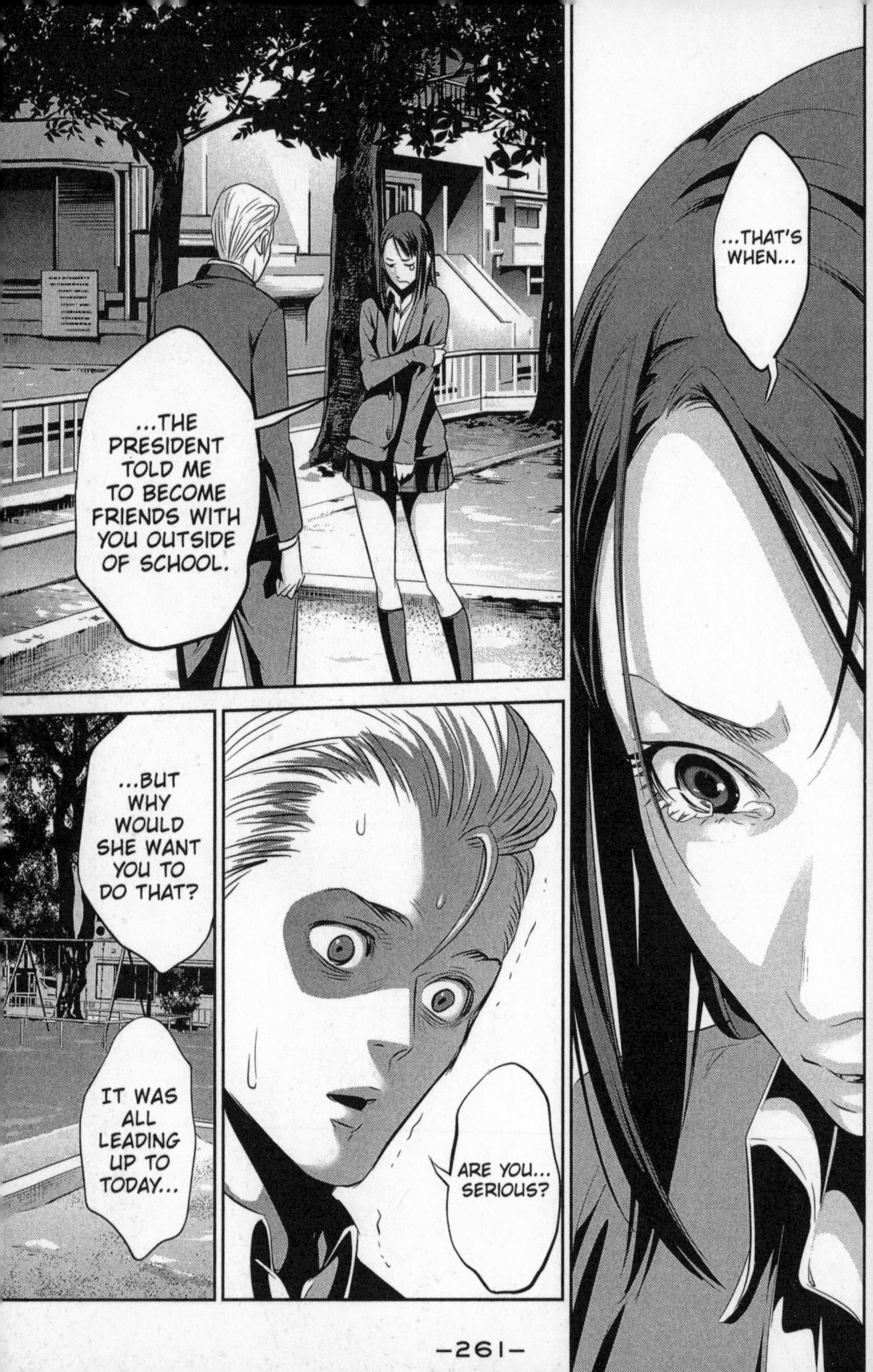
...THAT'S WHEN...
...THE PRESIDENT TOLD ME TO BECOME FRIENDS WITH YOU OUTSIDE OF SCHOOL.
ARE YOU... SERIOUS?
...BUT WHY WOULD SHE WANT YOU TO DO THAT?
IT WAS ALL LEADING UP TO TODAY...

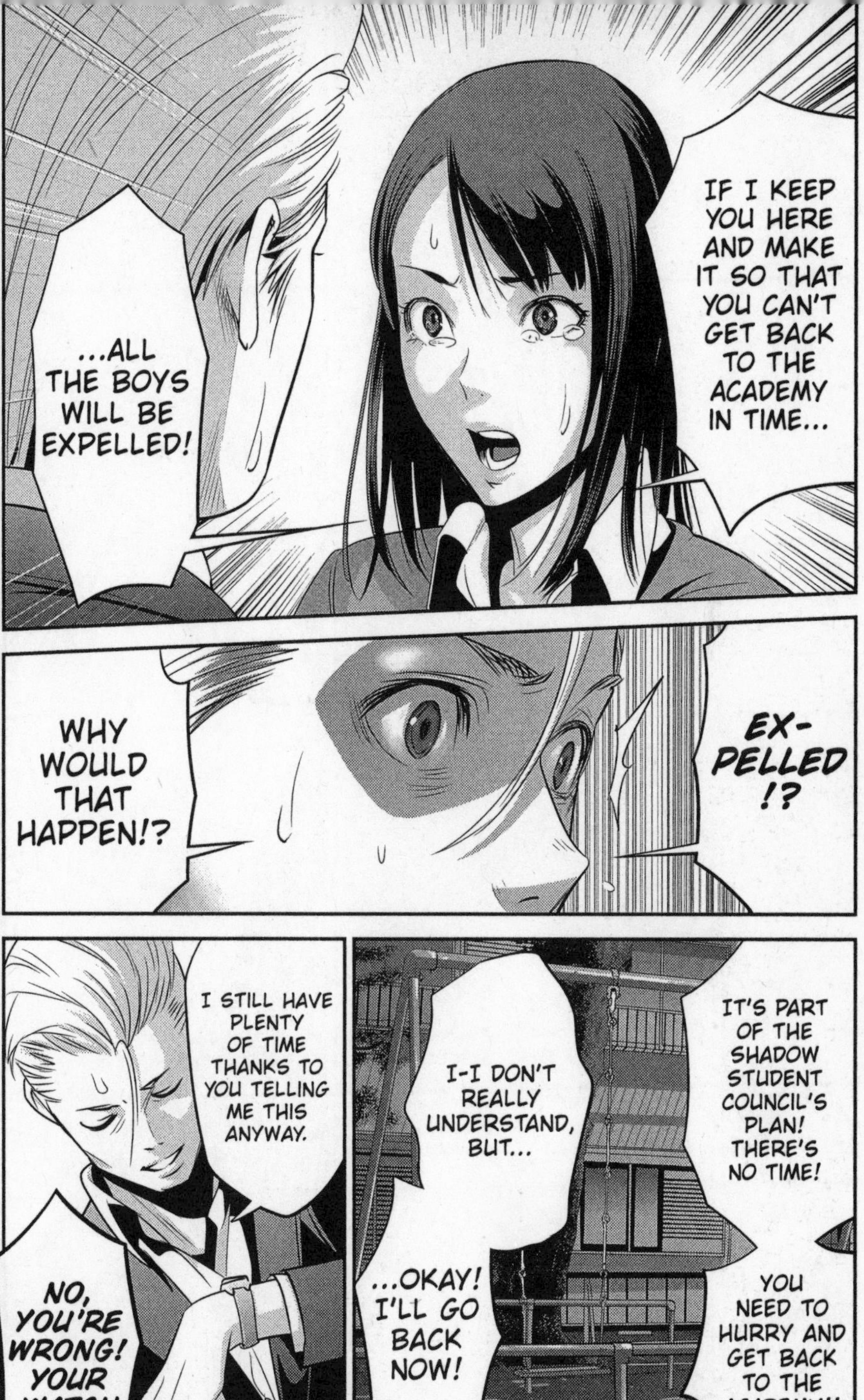
IF I KEEP YOU HERE AND MAKE IT SO THAT YOU CAN'T GET BACK TO THE ACADEMY IN TIME...
...ALL THE BOYS WILL BE EXPELLED!
EX-PELLED!?
WHY WOULD THAT HAPPEN!?
IT'S PART OF THE SHADOW STUDENT COUNCIL'S PLAN! THERE'S NO TIME!
YOU NEED TO HURRY AND GET BACK TO THE ACADEMY!!
I-I DON'T REALLY UNDERSTAND, BUT...
...OKAY! I'LL GO BACK NOW!
I STILL HAVE PLENTY OF TIME THANKS TO YOU TELLING ME THIS ANYWAY.
NO, YOU'RE WRONG! YOUR WATCH ...

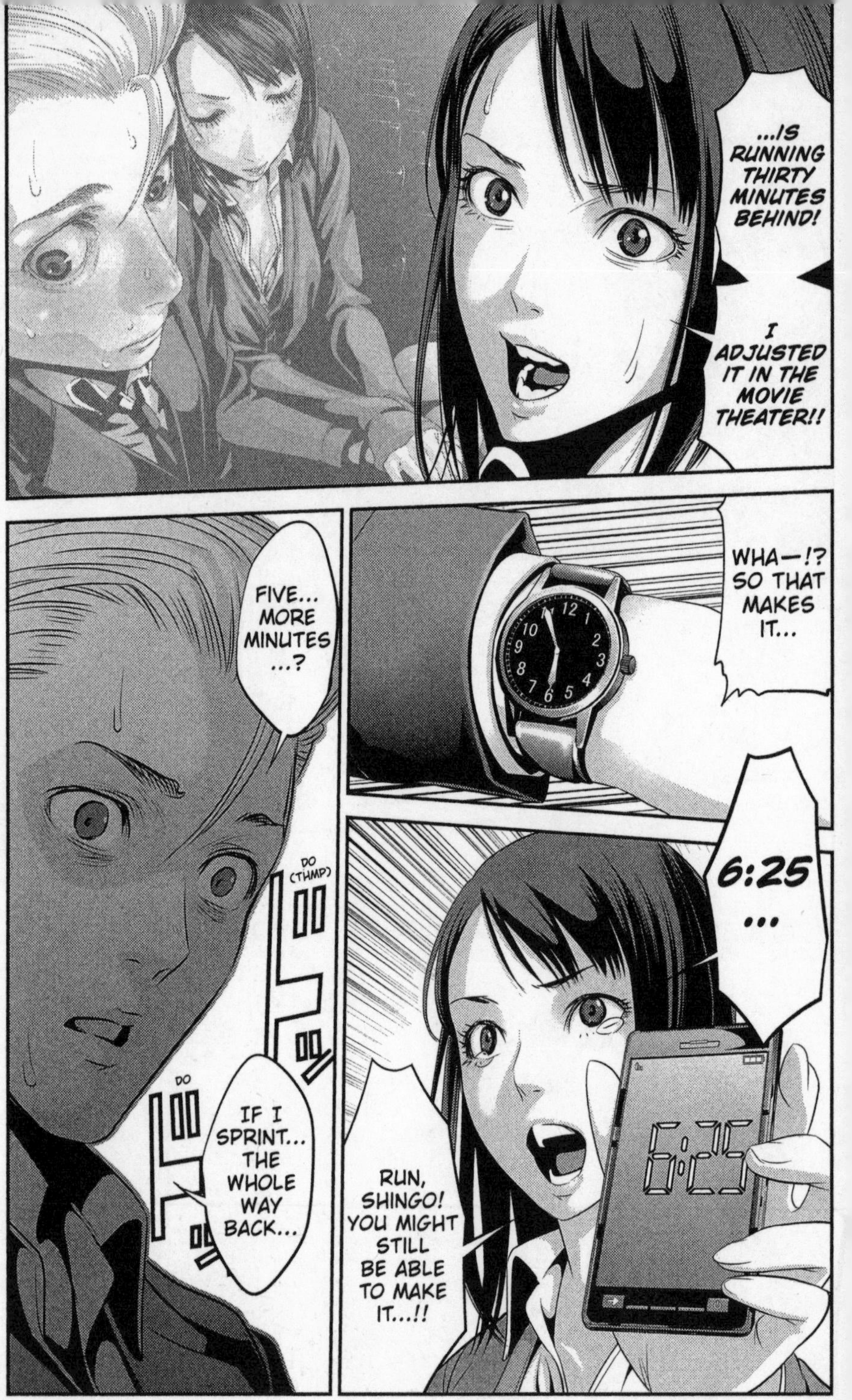
...IS RUNNING THIRTY MINUTES BEHIND!
I ADJUSTED IT IN THE MOVIE THEATER!!
WHA—!? SO THAT MAKES IT...
6:25 ...
RUN, SHINGO! YOU MIGHT STILL BE ABLE TO MAKE IT...!!
FIVE... MORE MINUTES ...?
DO (THMP)
DO
IF I SPRINT... THE WHOLE WAY BACK...

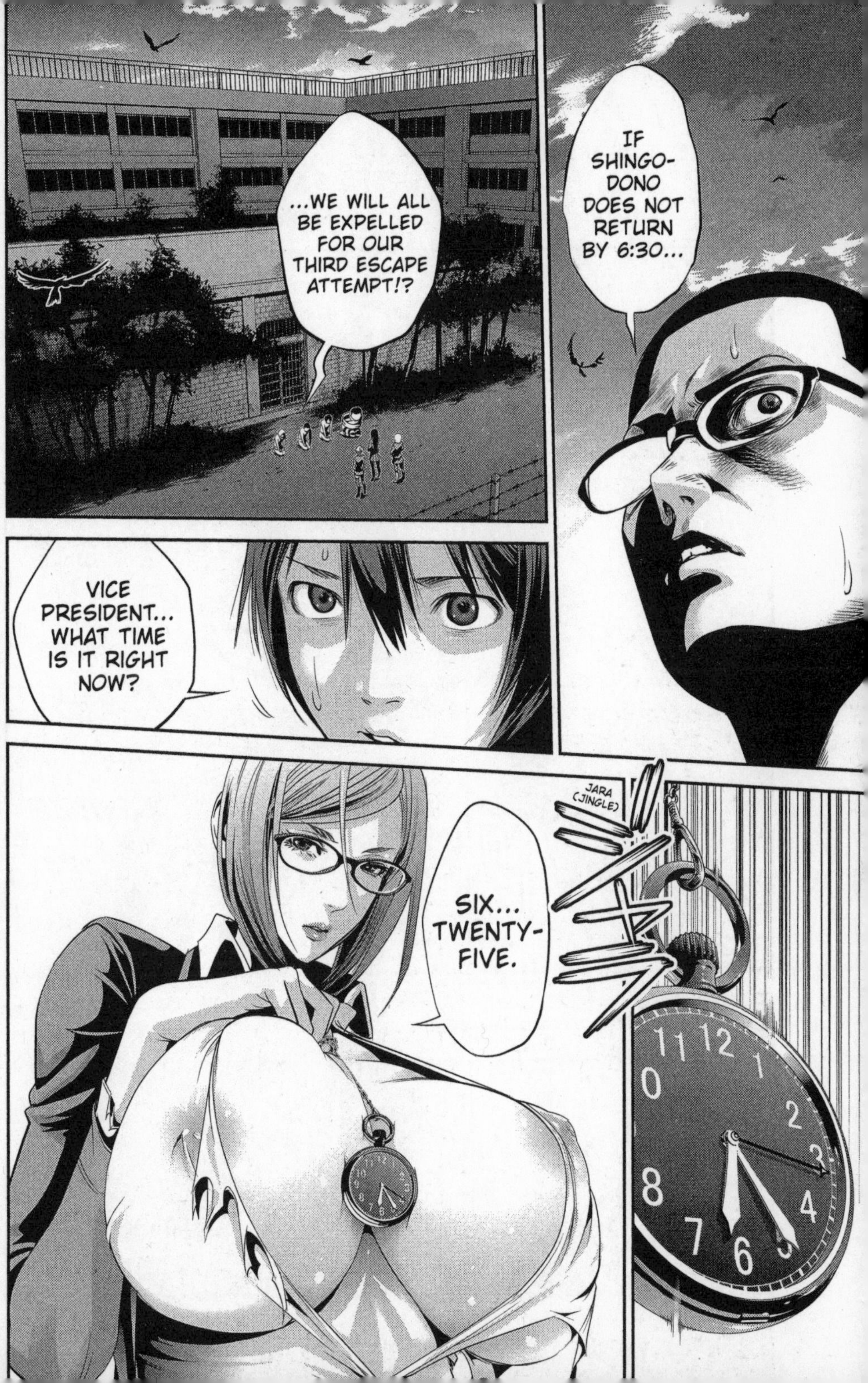
IF SHINGO-DONO DOES NOT RETURN BY 6:30...
...WE WILL ALL BE EXPELLED FOR OUR THIRD ESCAPE ATTEMPT!?
VICE PRESIDENT... WHAT TIME IS IT RIGHT NOW?
JARA (JINGLE)
SIX... TWENTY-FIVE.

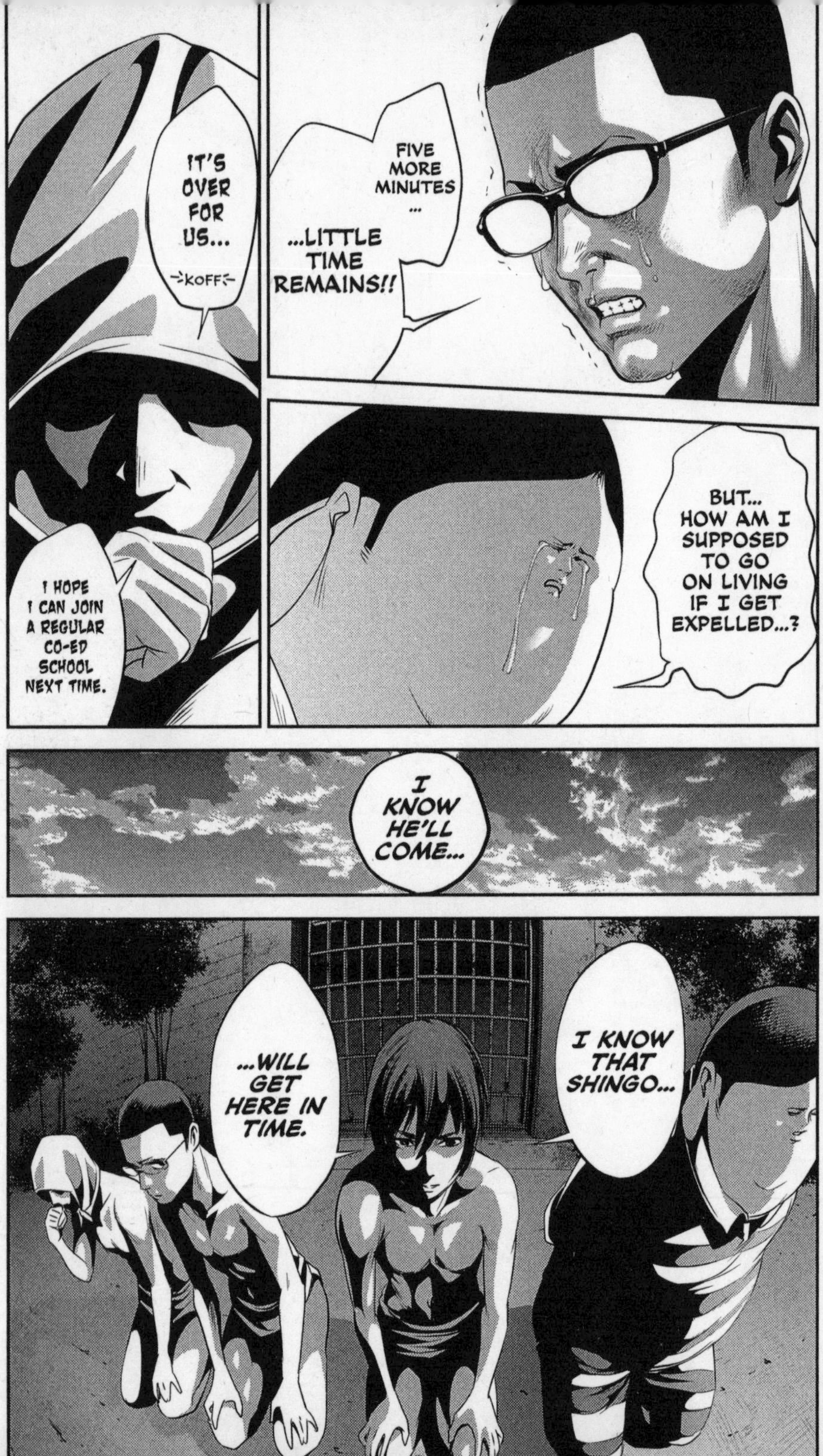
FIVE MORE MINUTES ... ...LITTLE TIME REMAINS!!
BUT... HOW AM I SUPPOSED TO GO ON LIVING IF I GET EXPELLED...?
IT'S OVER FOR US... KOFF
I HOPE I CAN JOIN A REGULAR CO-ED SCHOOL NEXT TIME.
I KNOW HE'LL COME...
I KNOW THAT SHINGO...
...WILL GET HERE IN TIME.

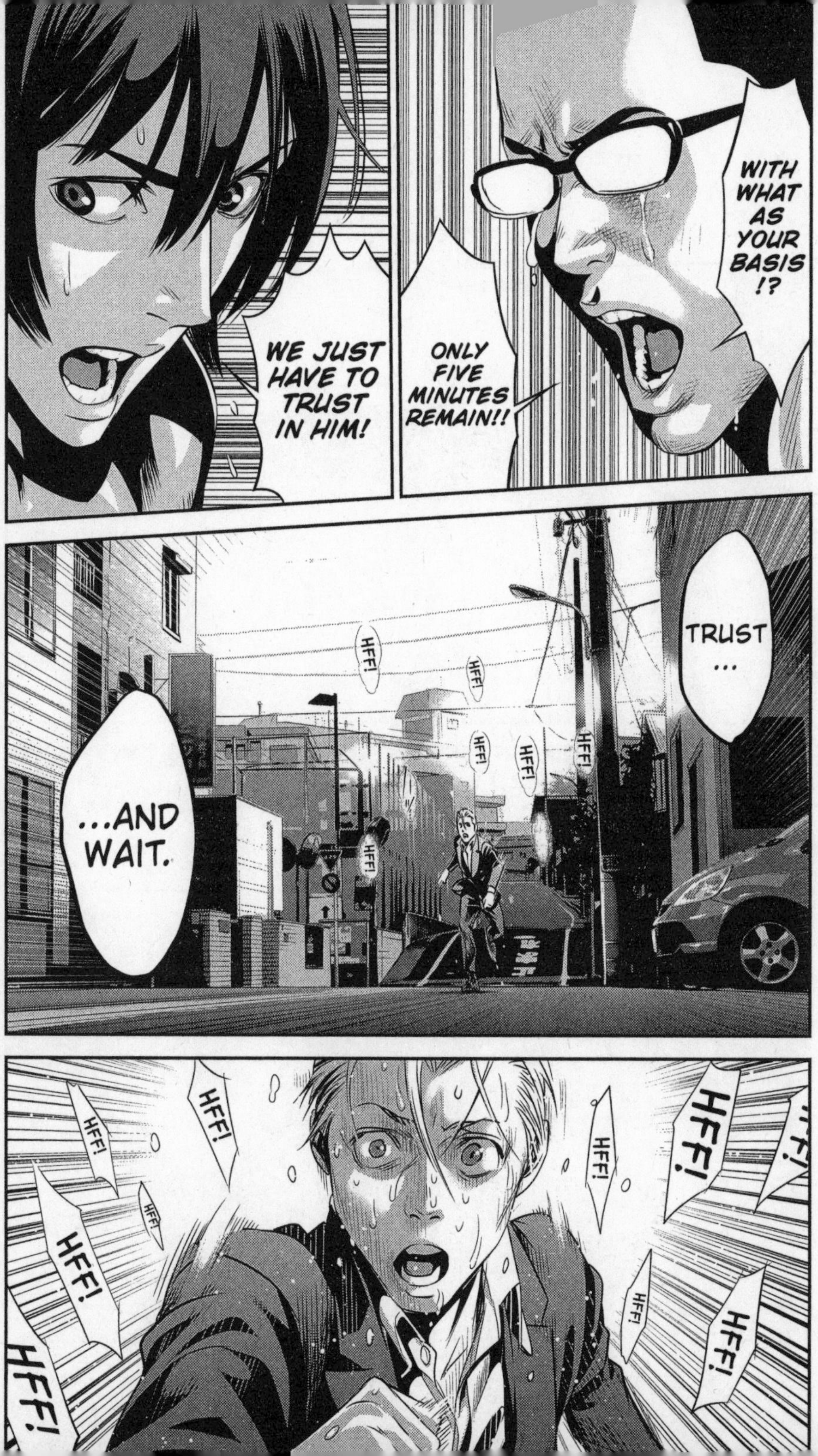
WITH WHAT AS YOUR BASIS!?
ONLY FIVE MINUTES REMAIN!!
WE JUST HAVE TO TRUST IN HIM!
TRUST ...
HFF!
HFF!
HFF!
HFF!
HFF!
HFF!
...AND WAIT.
HFF!
HFF!
HFF!
HFF!
HFF!
HFF!
HFF!
HFF!
HFF!
HFF!
HFF!

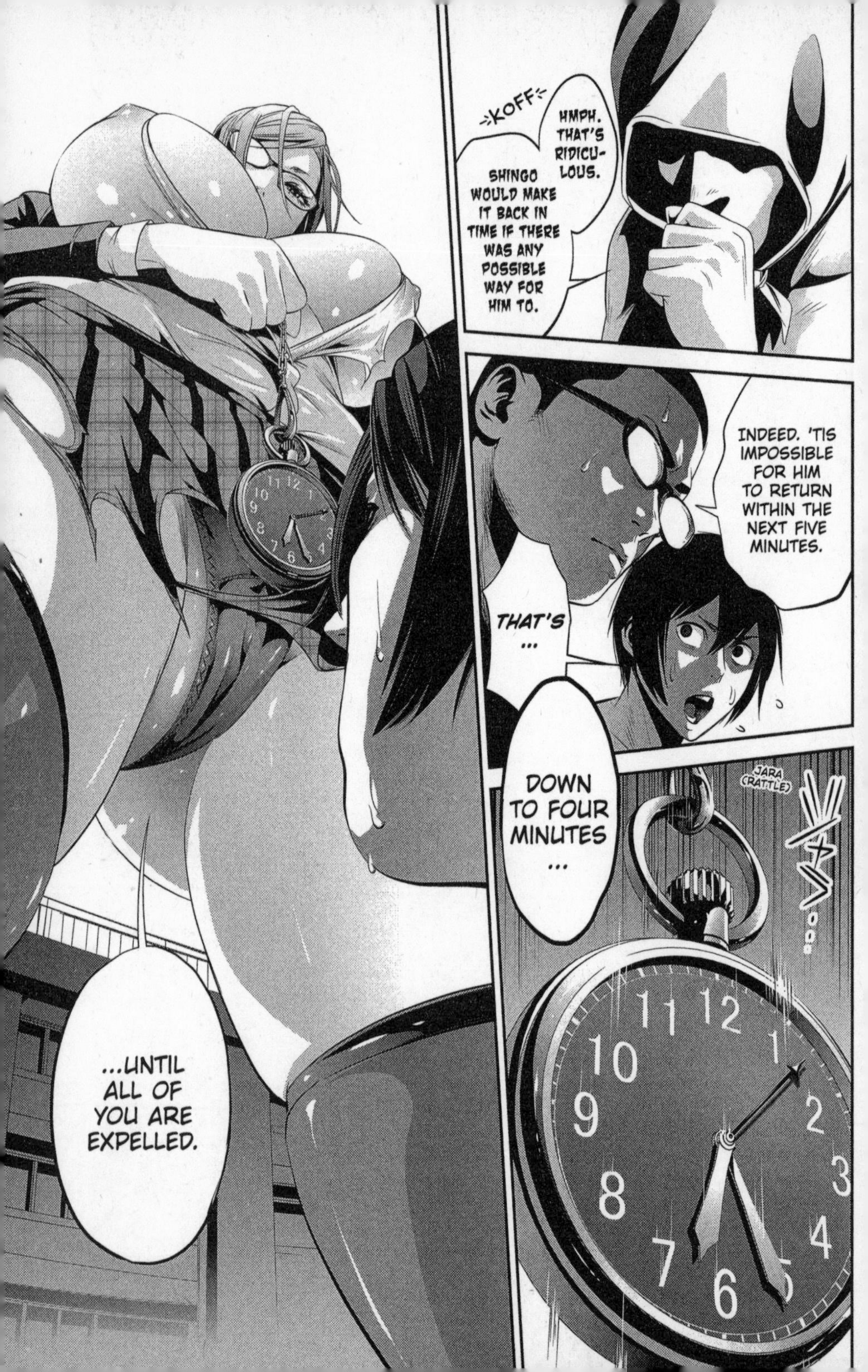

HMPH. THAT'S RIDICULOUS.
-KOFF-
SHINGO WOULD MAKE IT BACK IN TIME IF THERE WAS ANY POSSIBLE WAY FOR HIM TO.
INDEED. 'TIS IMPOSSIBLE FOR HIM TO RETURN WITHIN THE NEXT FIVE MINUTES.
THAT'S ...
JARA (RATTLE)
DOWN TO FOUR MINUTES ...
...UNTIL ALL OF YOU ARE EXPELLED.

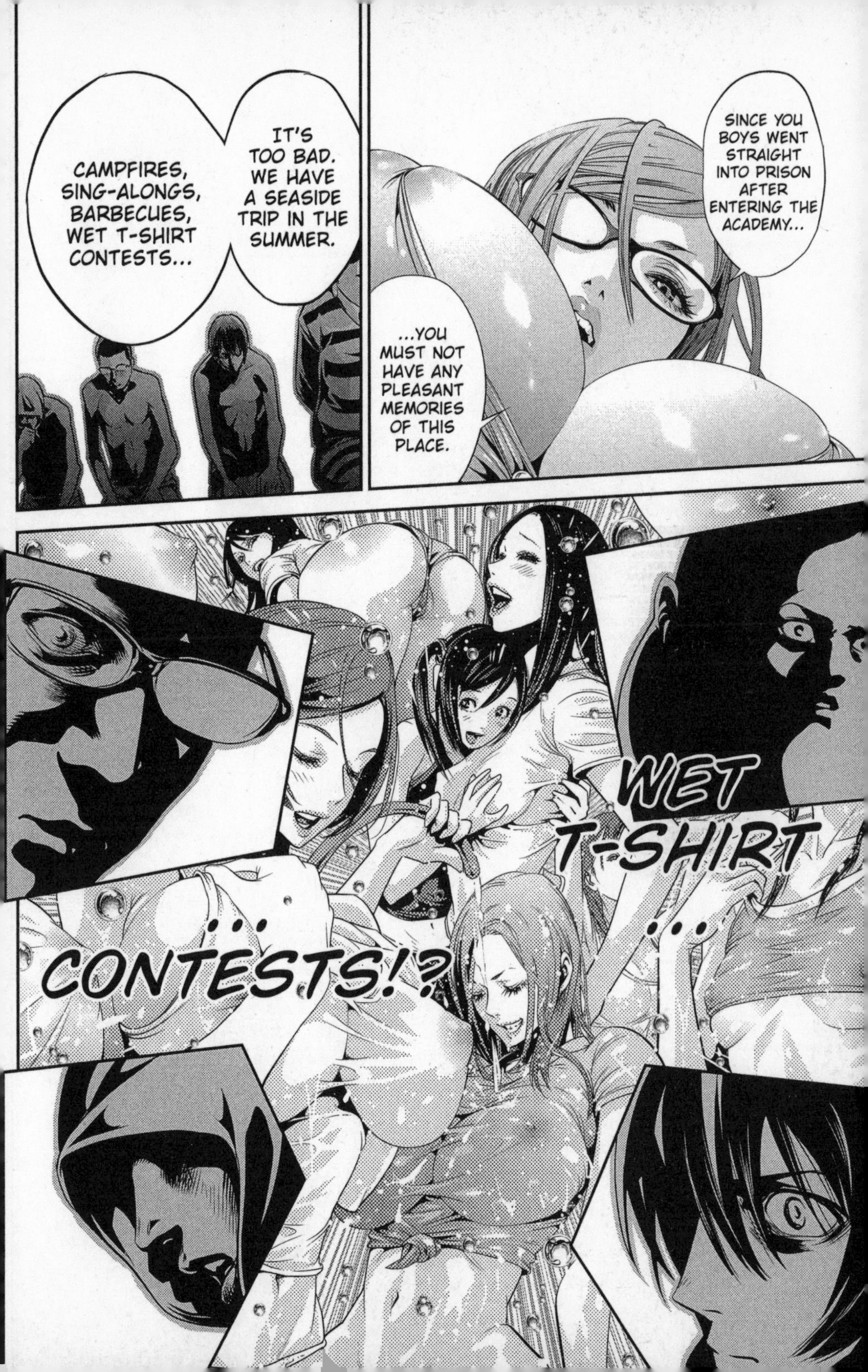
SINCE YOU BOYS WENT STRAIGHT INTO PRISON AFTER ENTERING THE ACADEMY...
...YOU MUST NOT HAVE ANY PLEASANT MEMORIES OF THIS PLACE.
IT'S TOO BAD. WE HAVE A SEASIDE TRIP IN THE SUMMER.
CAMPFIRES, SING-ALONGS, BARBECUES, WET T-SHIRT CONTESTS...
WET T-SHIRT
...
...
CONTESTS!?

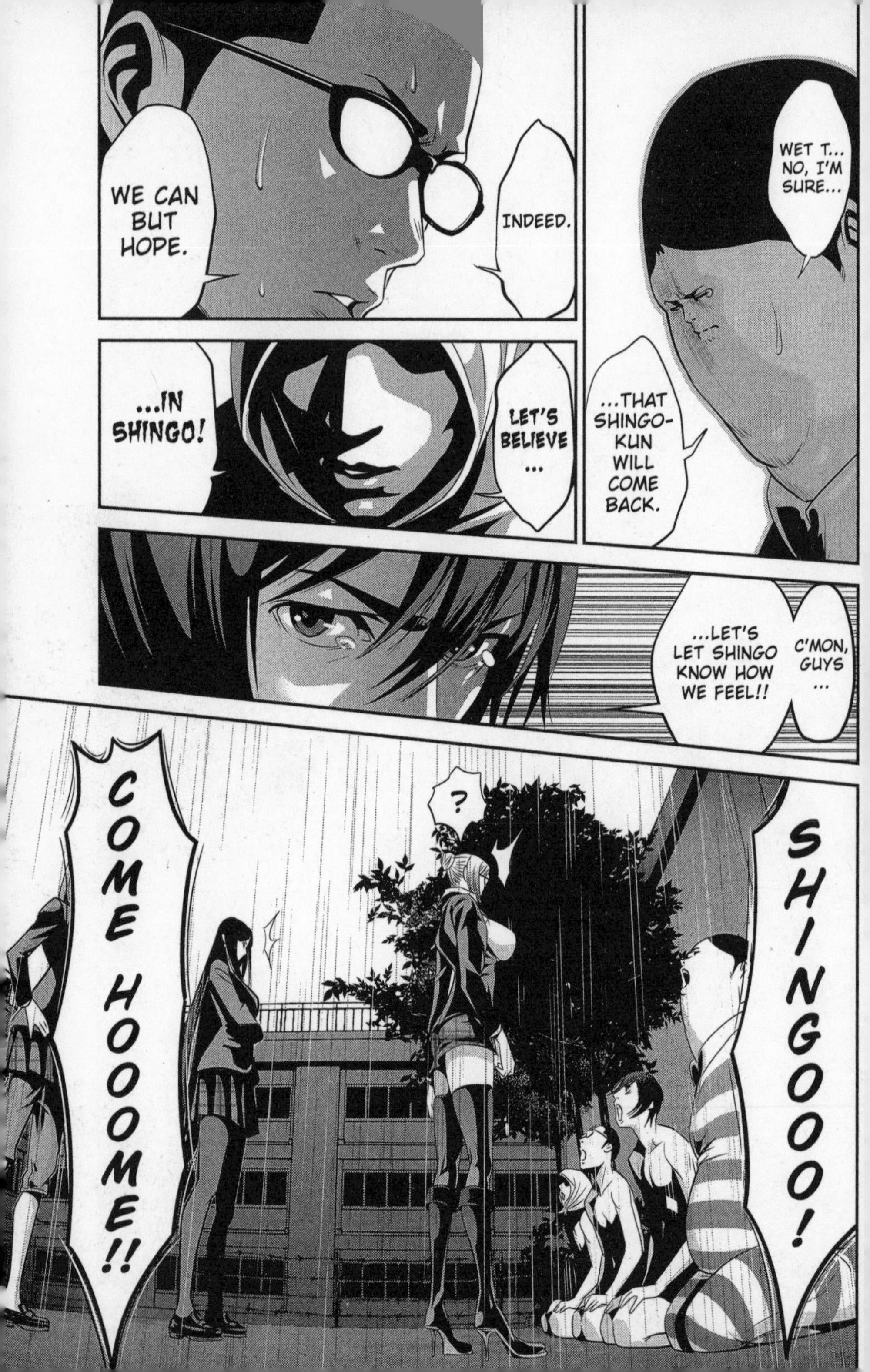
WET T... NO, I'M SURE...
...THAT SHINGO-KUN WILL COME BACK.
INDEED.
WE CAN BUT HOPE.
LET'S BELIEVE ...
...IN SHINGO!
C'MON, GUYS ...
...LET'S LET SHINGO KNOW HOW WE FEEL!!
SHINGOOOO!
?
COME HOOOOME!!

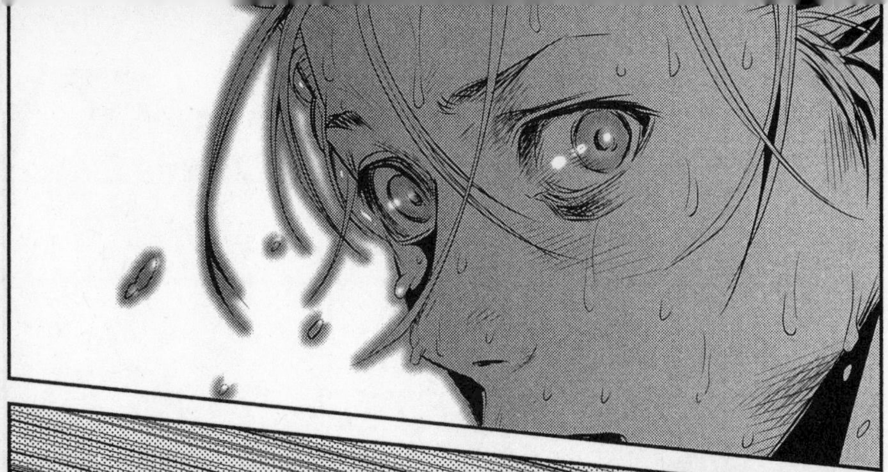

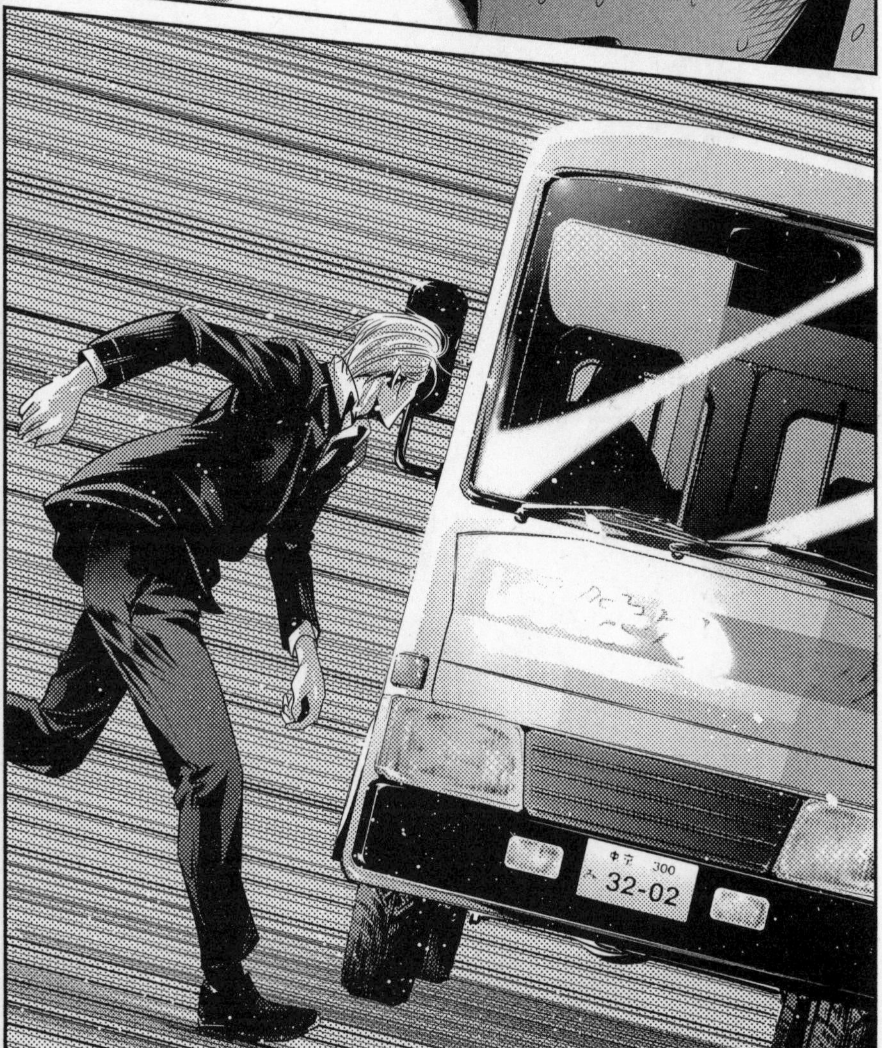
300
32-02

CHAPTER 53: BURIED

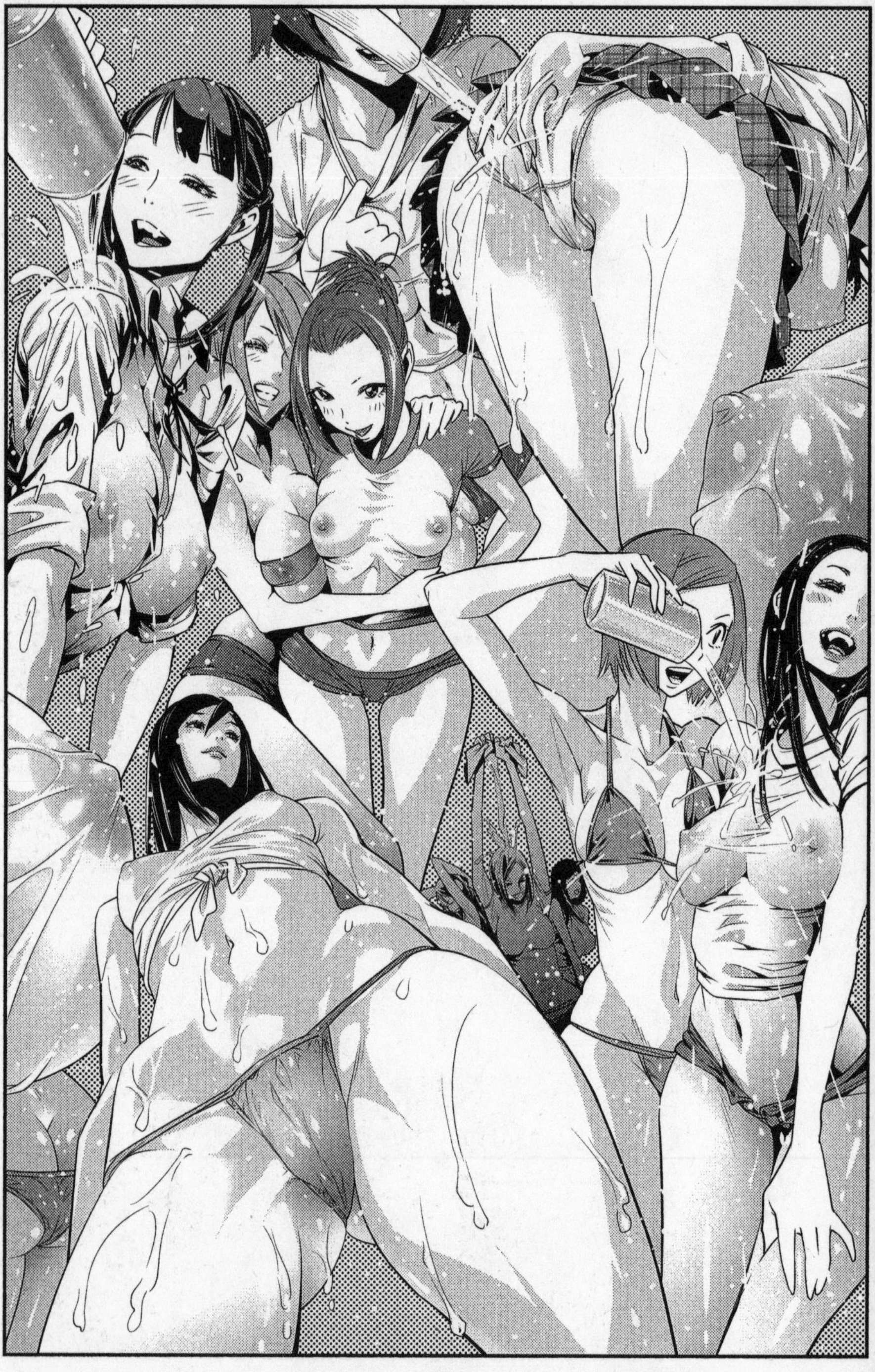

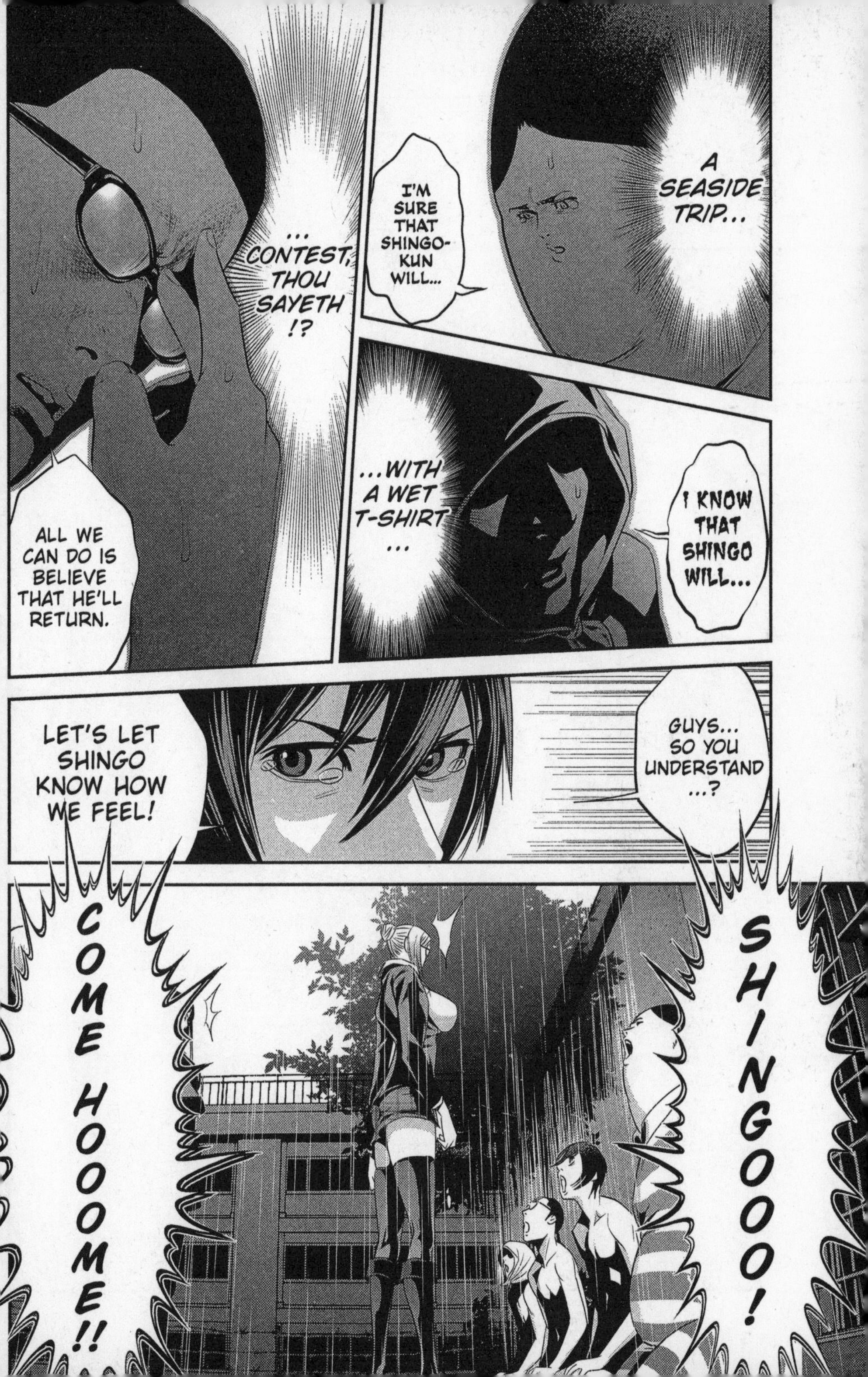
A SEASIDE TRIP...
I'M SURE THAT SHINGO-KUN WILL...
I KNOW THAT SHINGO WILL...
...WITH A WET T-SHIRT...
...CONTEST, THOU SAYETH!?
ALL WE CAN DO IS BELIEVE THAT HE'LL RETURN.
GUYS... SO YOU UNDERSTAND...?
LET'S LET SHINGO KNOW HOW WE FEEL!
SHINGOOOO!
COME HOOOOME!!

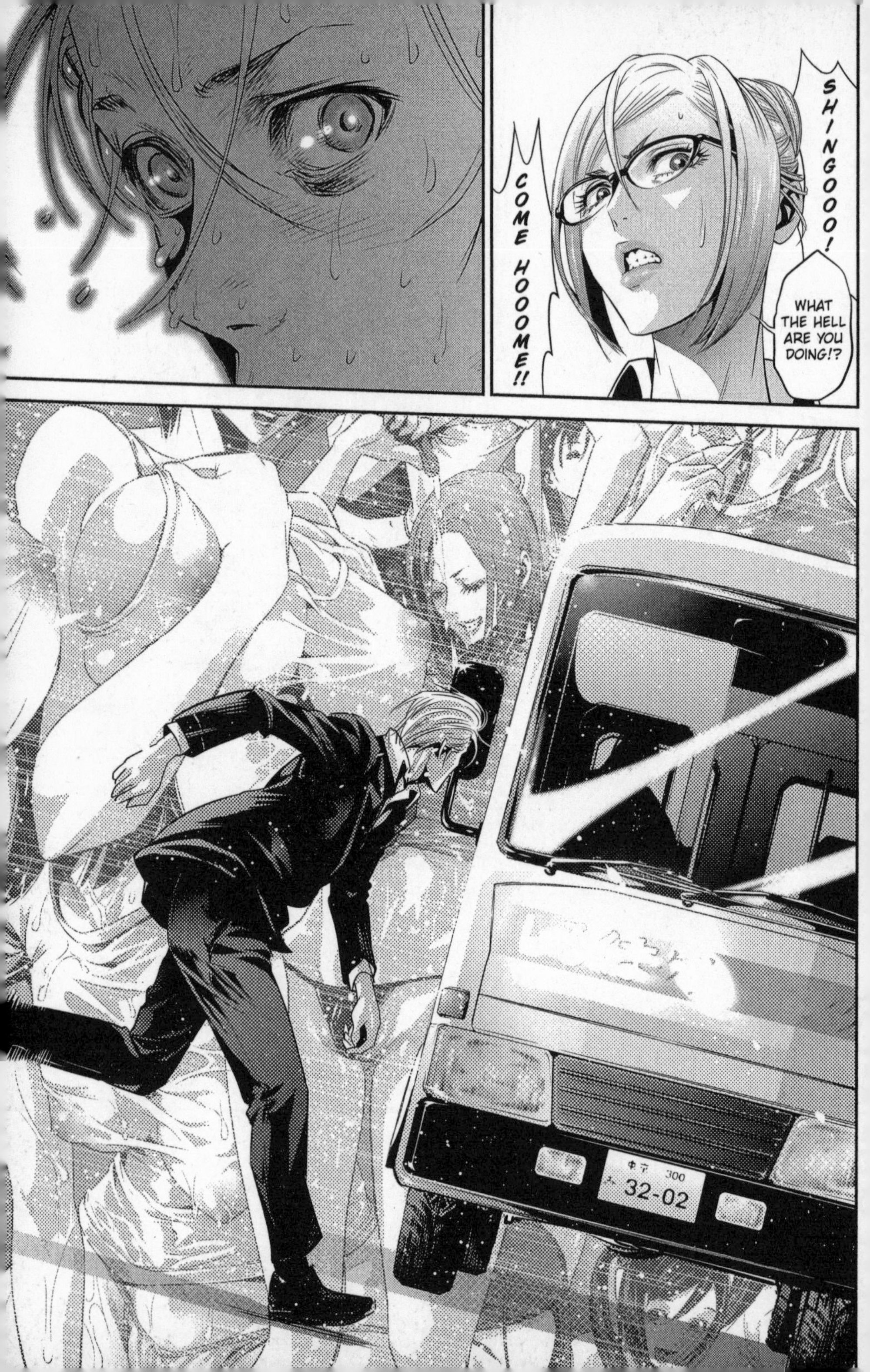
SHINGOOOO!
WHAT THE HELL ARE YOU DOING!?
COME HOOOOME!!
300
32-02

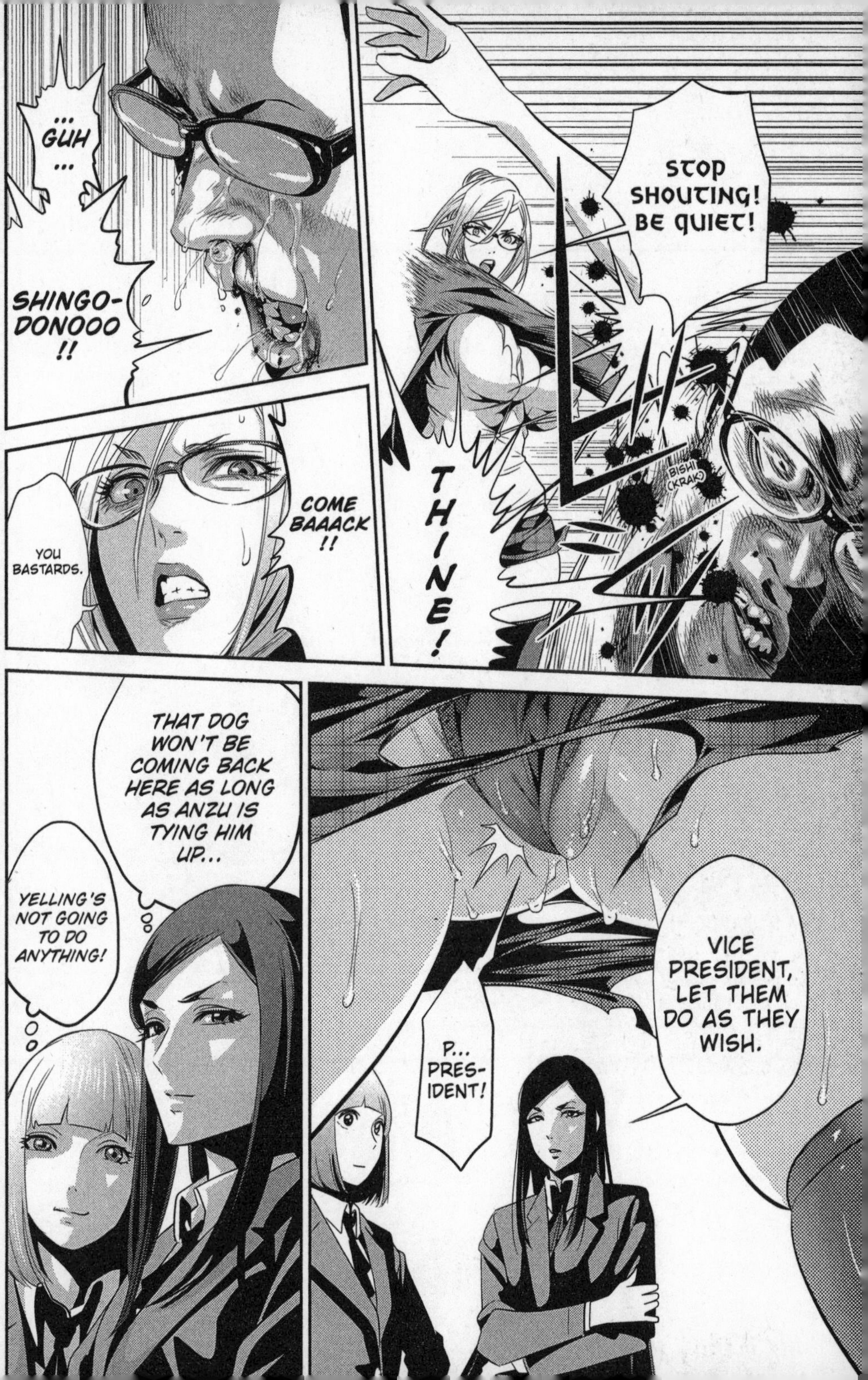
STOP SHOUTING! BE QUIET!
THINE!
BISHI (KRAK)
... GUH ...
SHINGO-DONOOO !!
COME BAAACK !!
YOU BASTARDS.
VICE PRESIDENT, LET THEM DO AS THEY WISH.
P... PRES-IDENT!
THAT DOG WON'T BE COMING BACK HERE AS LONG AS ANZU IS TYING HIM UP...
YELLING'S NOT GOING TO DO ANYTHING!

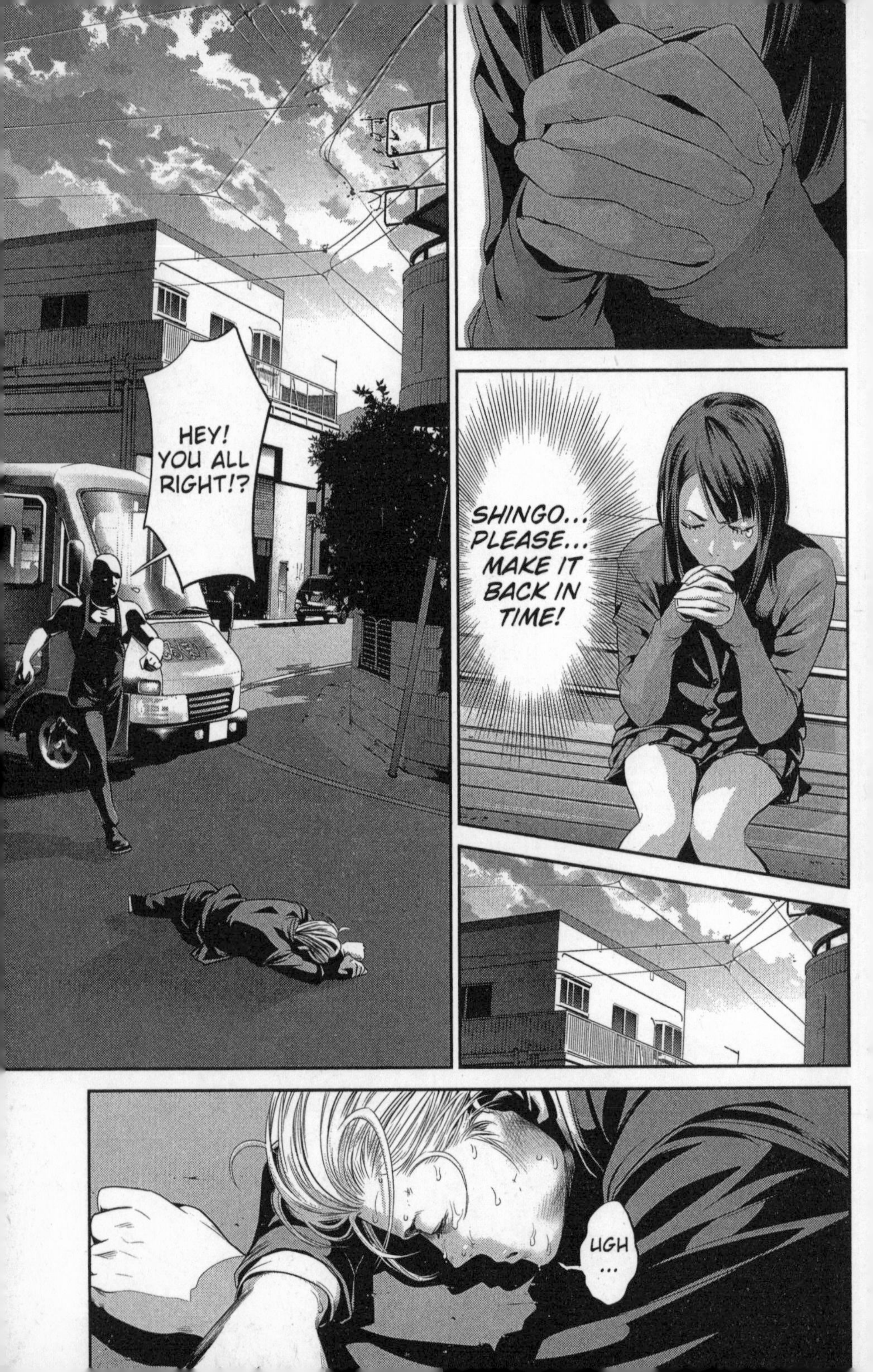
SHINGO... PLEASE... MAKE IT BACK IN TIME!
HEY! YOU ALL RIGHT!?
UGH ...

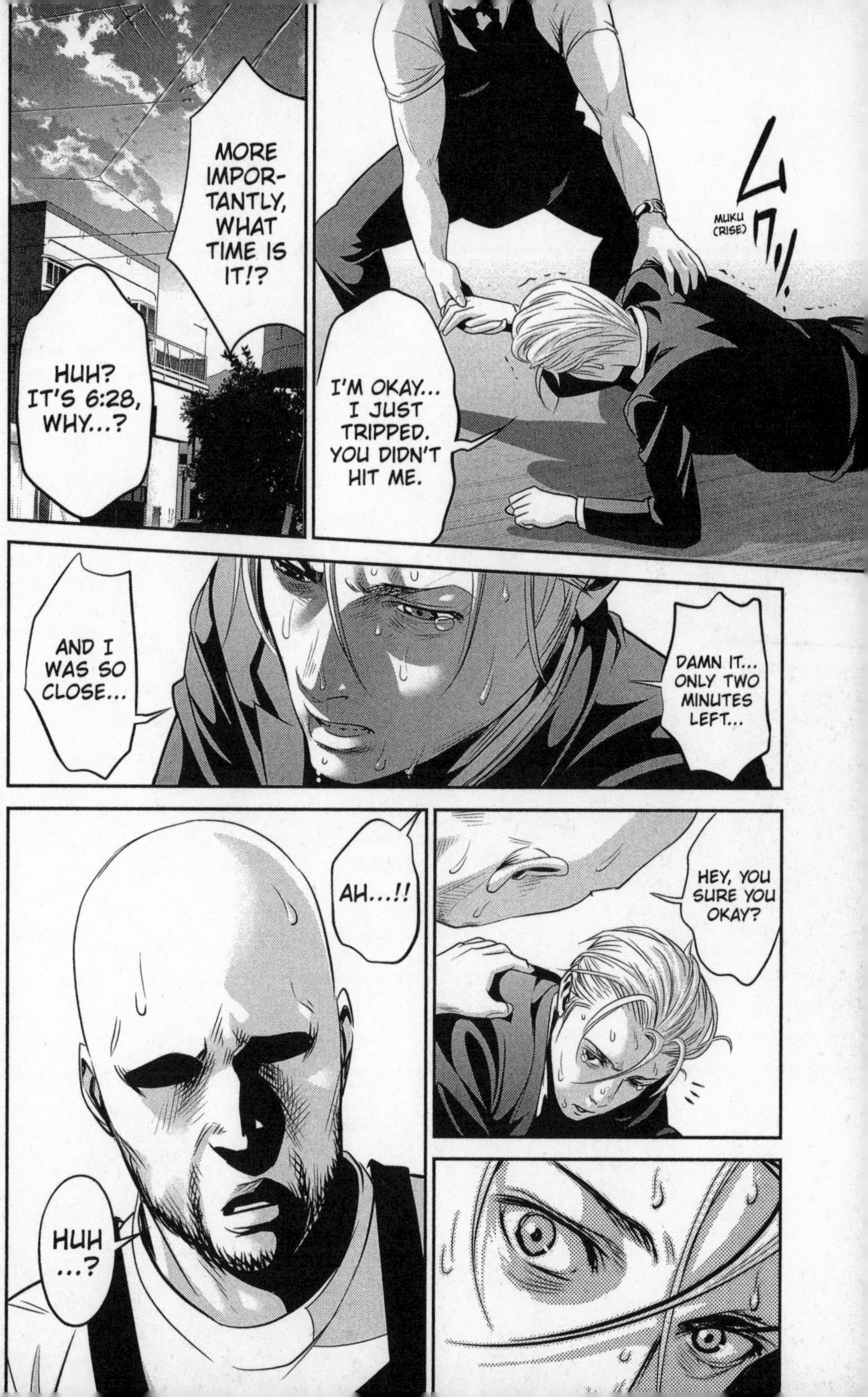
MUKU (RISE)
I'M OKAY... I JUST TRIPPED. YOU DIDN'T HIT ME.
MORE IMPORTANTLY, WHAT TIME IS IT!?
HUH? IT'S 6:28, WHY...?
DAMN IT... ONLY TWO MINUTES LEFT...
AND I WAS SO CLOSE...
HEY, YOU SURE YOU OKAY?
AH...!!
HUH ...?

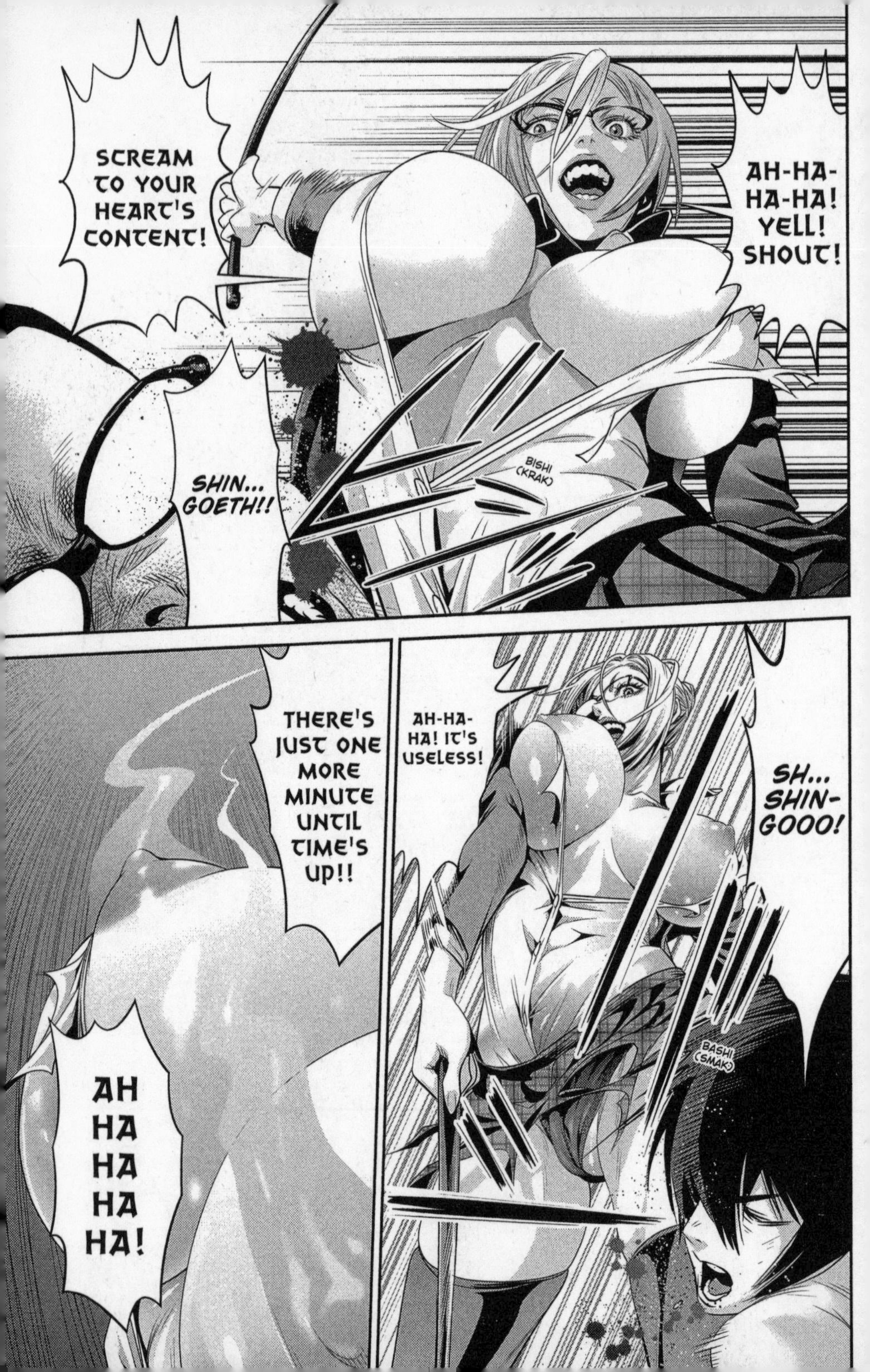
AH-HA-HA-HA! YELL! SHOUT!
SCREAM TO YOUR HEART'S CONTENT!
BISHI (KRAK)
SHIN... GOETH!!
SH... SHIN-GOOO!
AH-HA-HA! IT'S USELESS!
BASHI (SMAK)
THERE'S JUST ONE MORE MINUTE UNTIL TIME'S UP!!
AH HA HA HA HA HA!

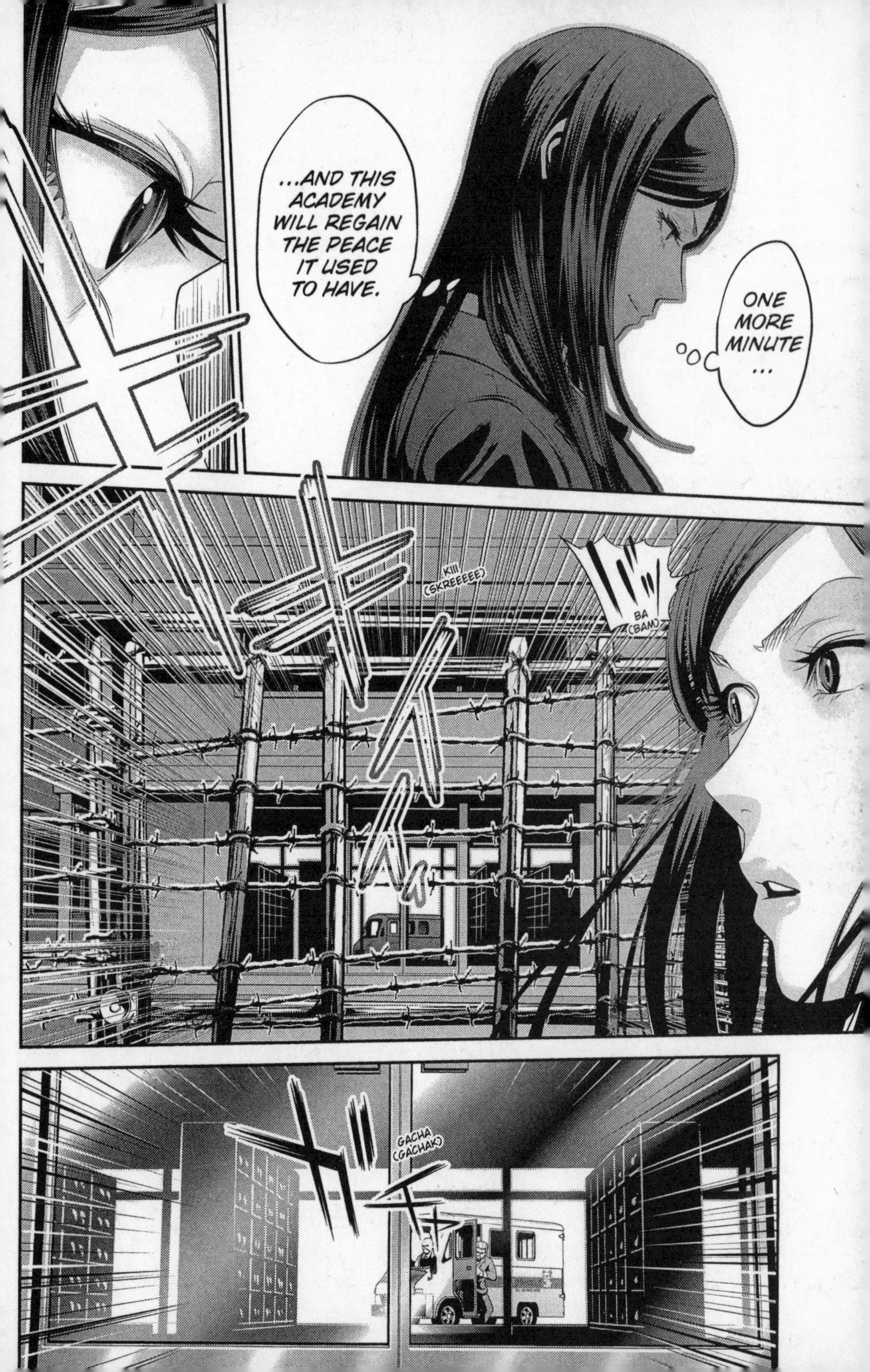
ONE MORE MINUTE ...
...AND THIS ACADEMY WILL REGAIN THE PEACE IT USED TO HAVE.
BA (BAM)
KIII (SKREEEEE)
GACHA (GACHAK)

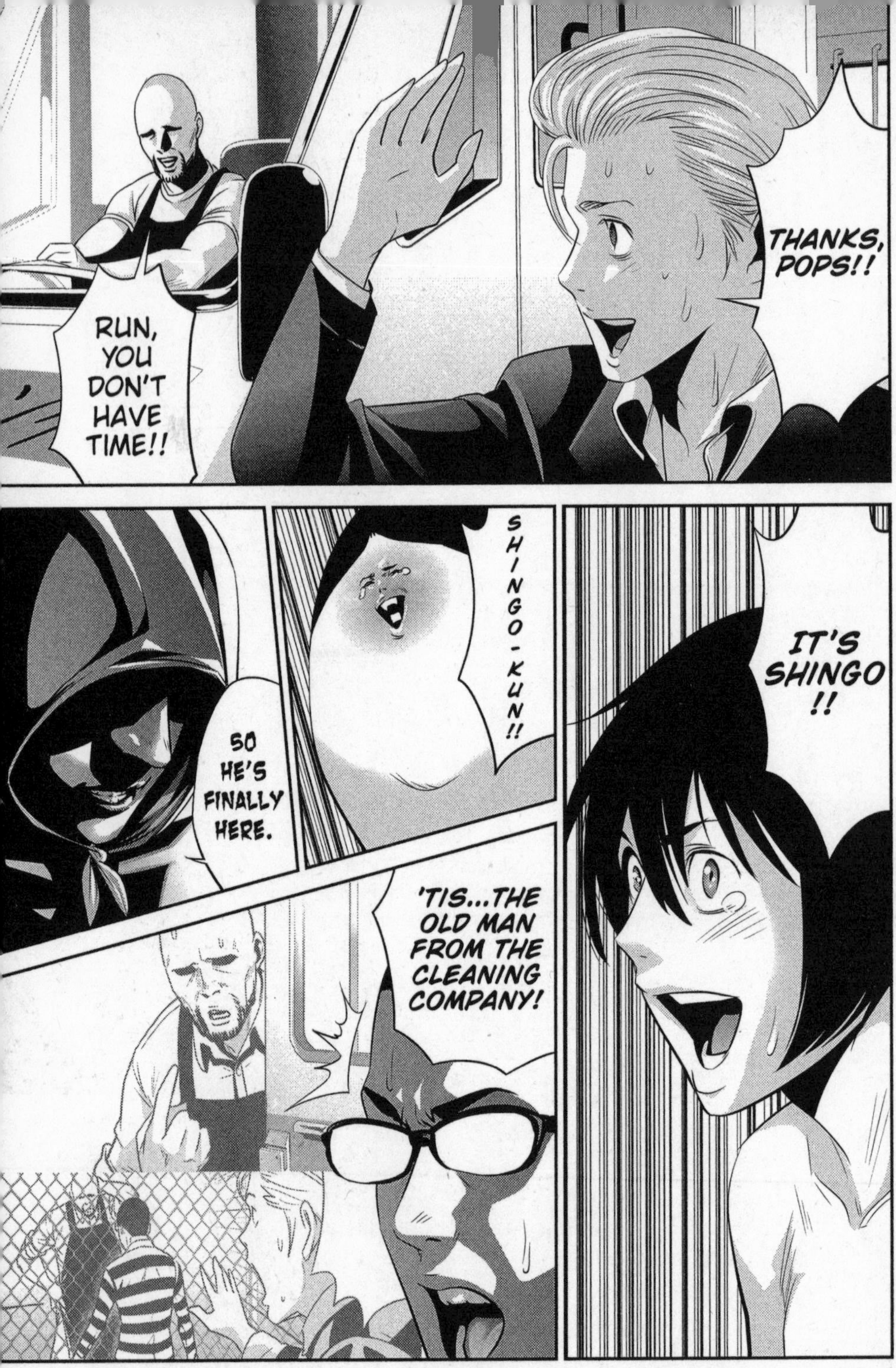
THANKS, POPS!!
RUN, YOU DON'T HAVE TIME!!
IT'S SHINGO!!
SHINGO-KUN!!
SO HE'S FINALLY HERE.
'TIS...THE OLD MAN FROM THE CLEANING COMPANY!

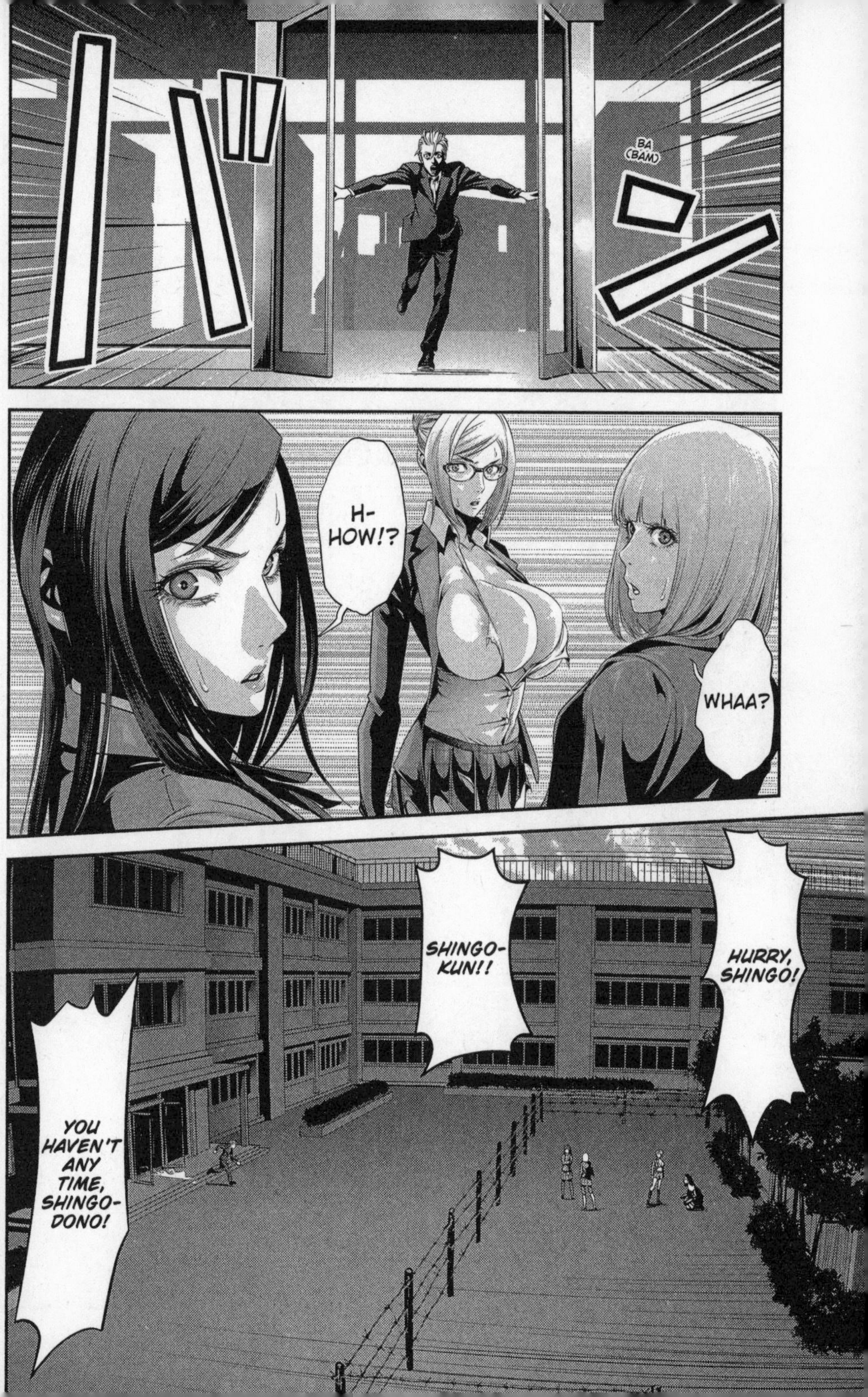
BA (BAM)
WHAA?
H-HOW!?
HURRY, SHINGO!
SHINGO-KUN!!
YOU HAVEN'T ANY TIME, SHINGO-DONO!

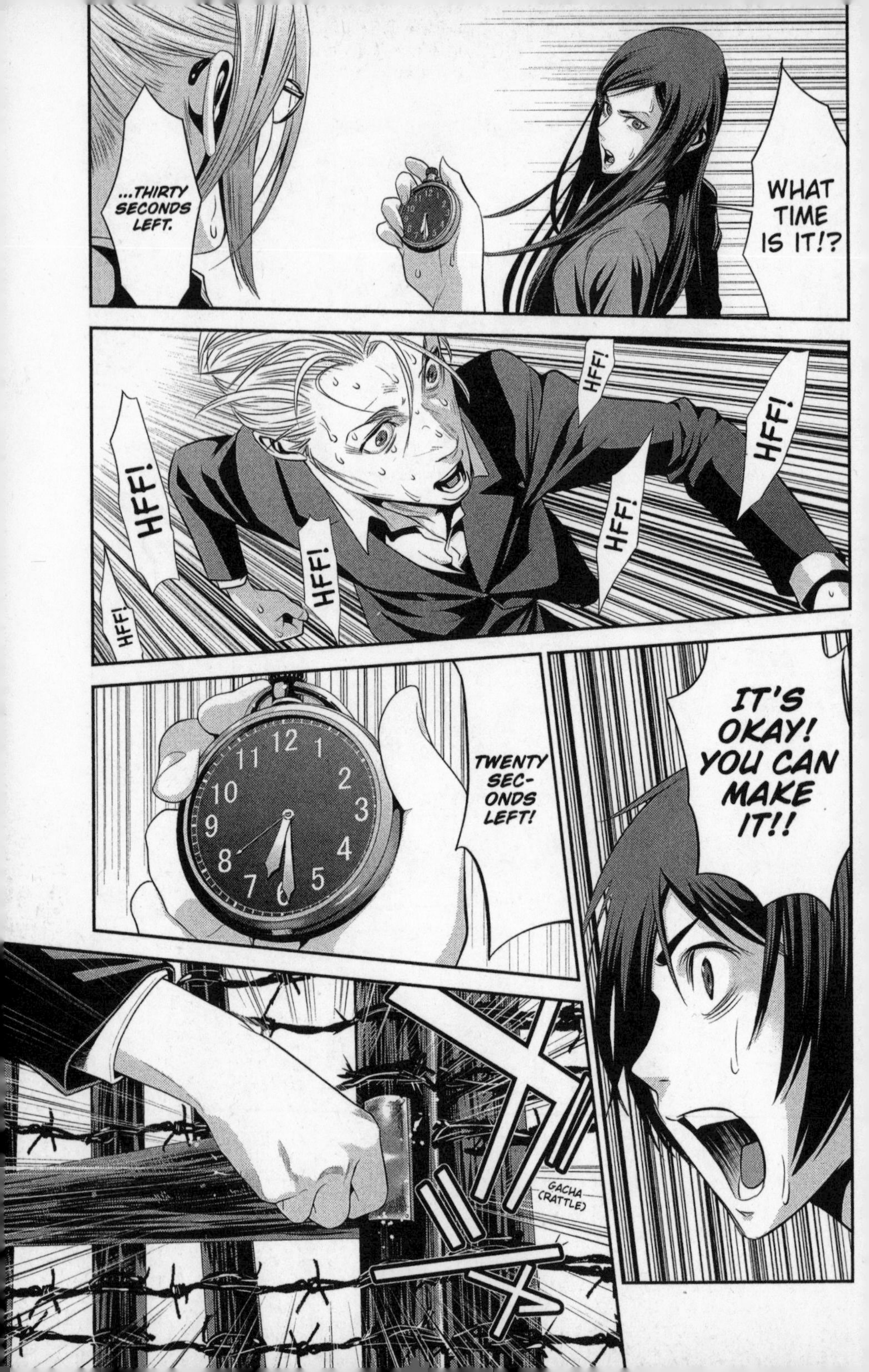
WHAT TIME IS IT!?
...THIRTY SECONDS LEFT.
HFF!
HFF!
HFF!
HFF!
HFF!
HFF!
IT'S OKAY! YOU CAN MAKE IT!!
TWENTY SEC- ONDS LEFT!
GACHA (RATTLE)

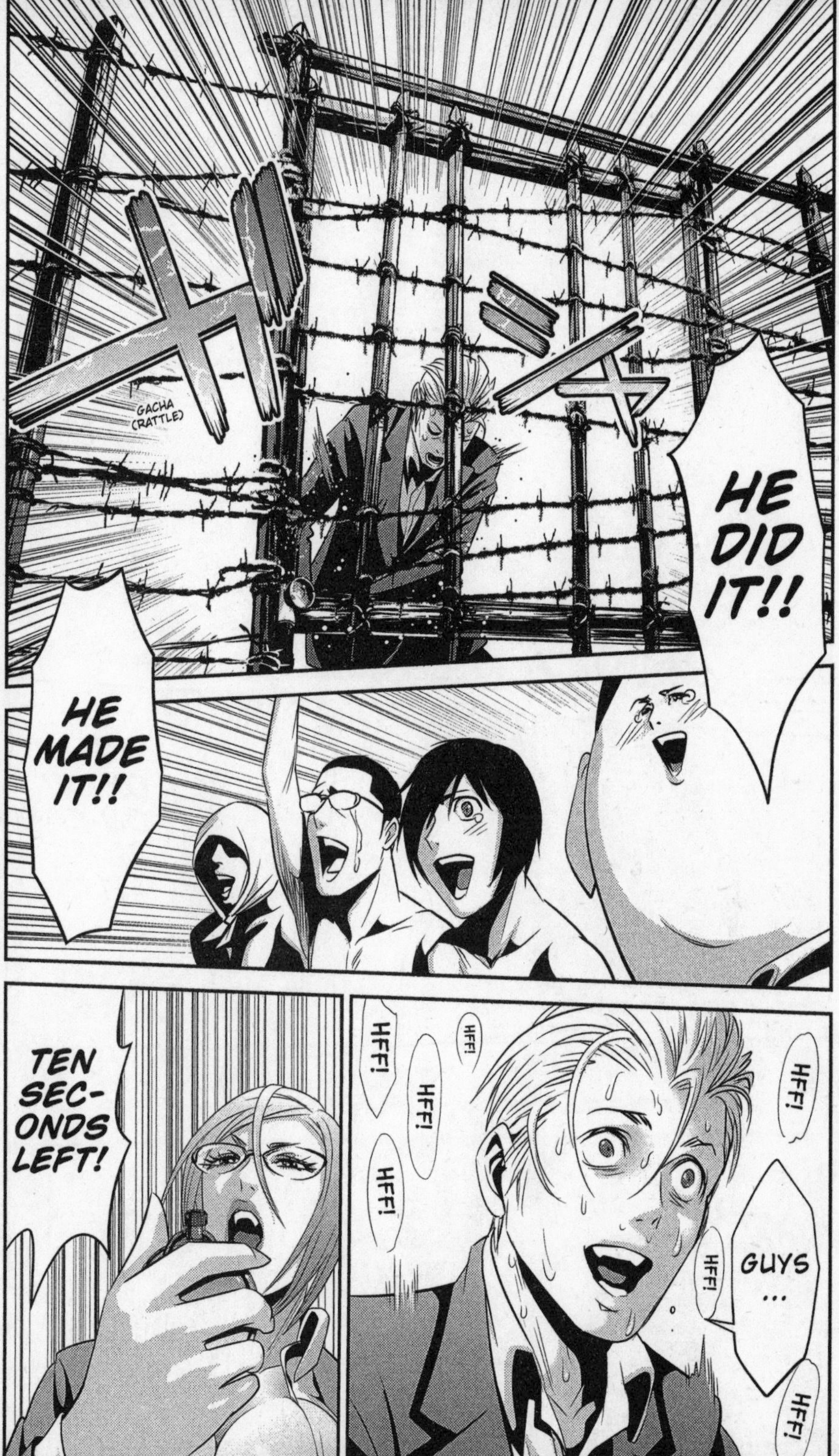

GACHA (RATTLE)
HE DID IT!!
HE MADE IT!!
HFF!
HFF!
HFF!
HFF!
HFF!
GUYS ...
HFF!
TEN SEC-ONDS LEFT!

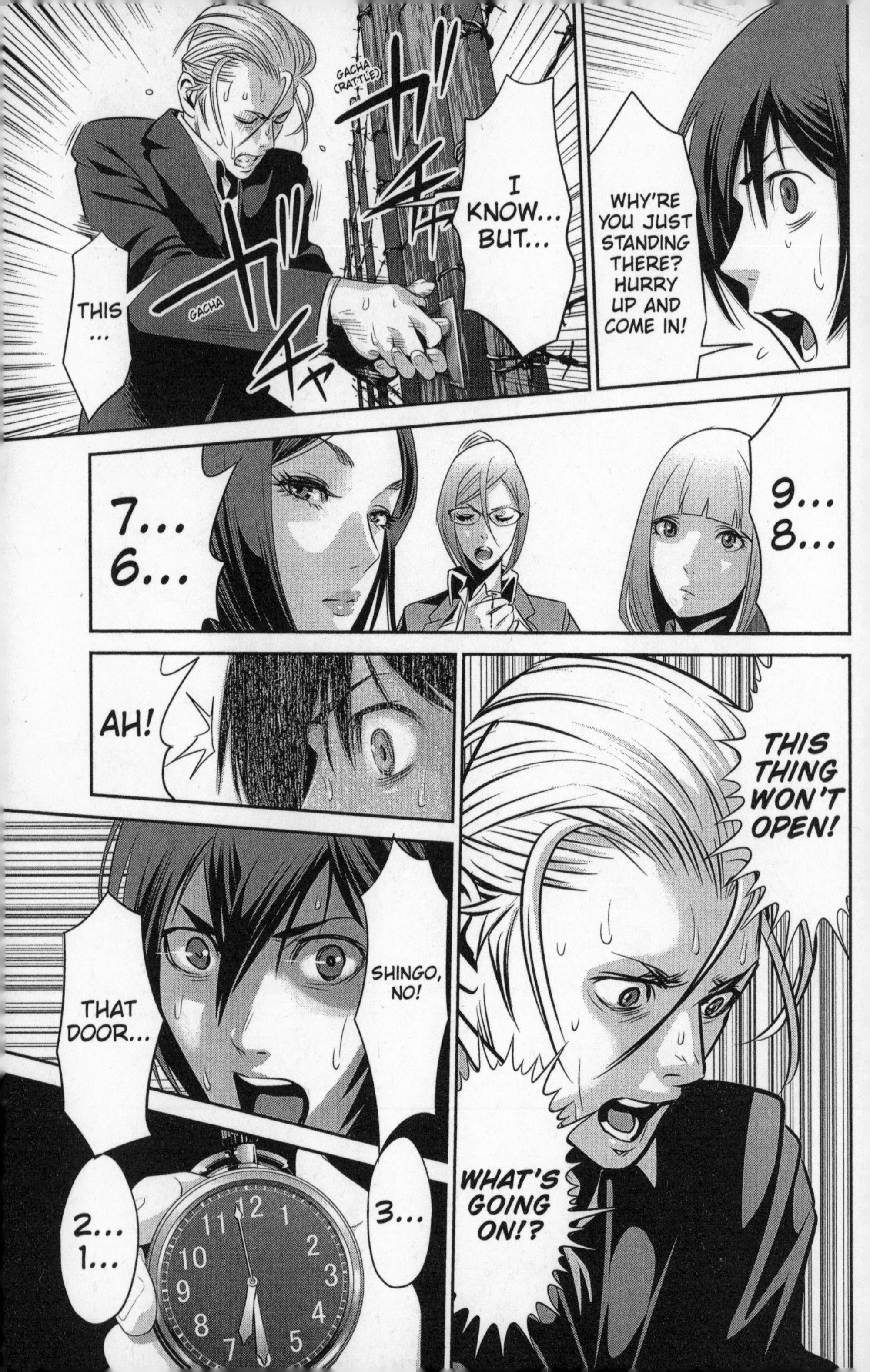
WHY'RE YOU JUST STANDING THERE? HURRY UP AND COME IN!
I KNOW... BUT...
GACHA (RATTLE)
GACHA
THIS ...
9... 8...
7... 6...
THIS THING WON'T OPEN!
WHAT'S GOING ON!?
AH!
SHINGO, NO!
THAT DOOR...
3...
2... 1...

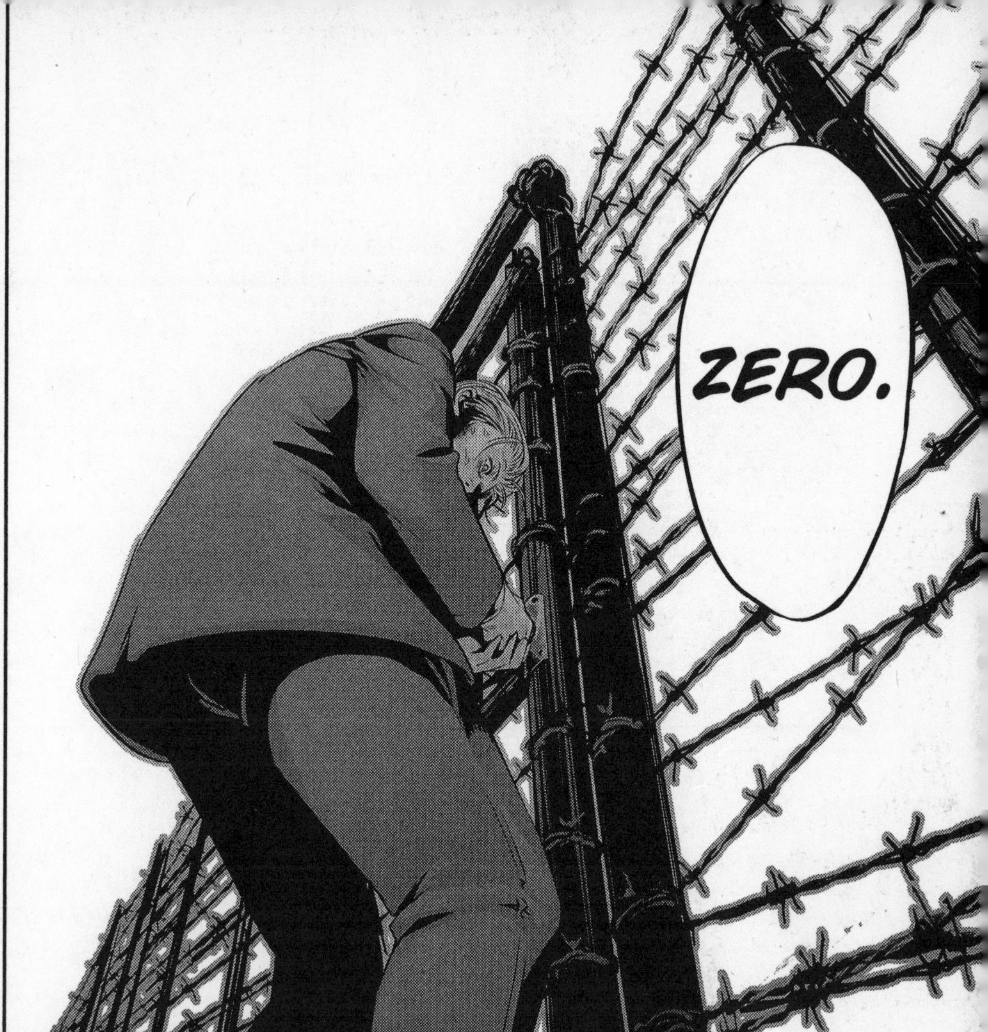
ZERO.

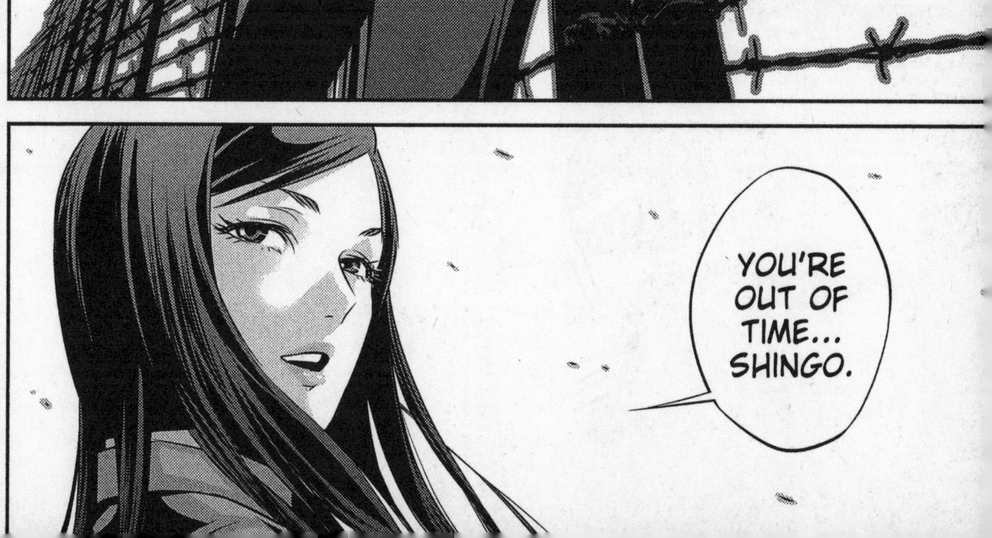
YOU'RE OUT OF TIME... SHINGO.

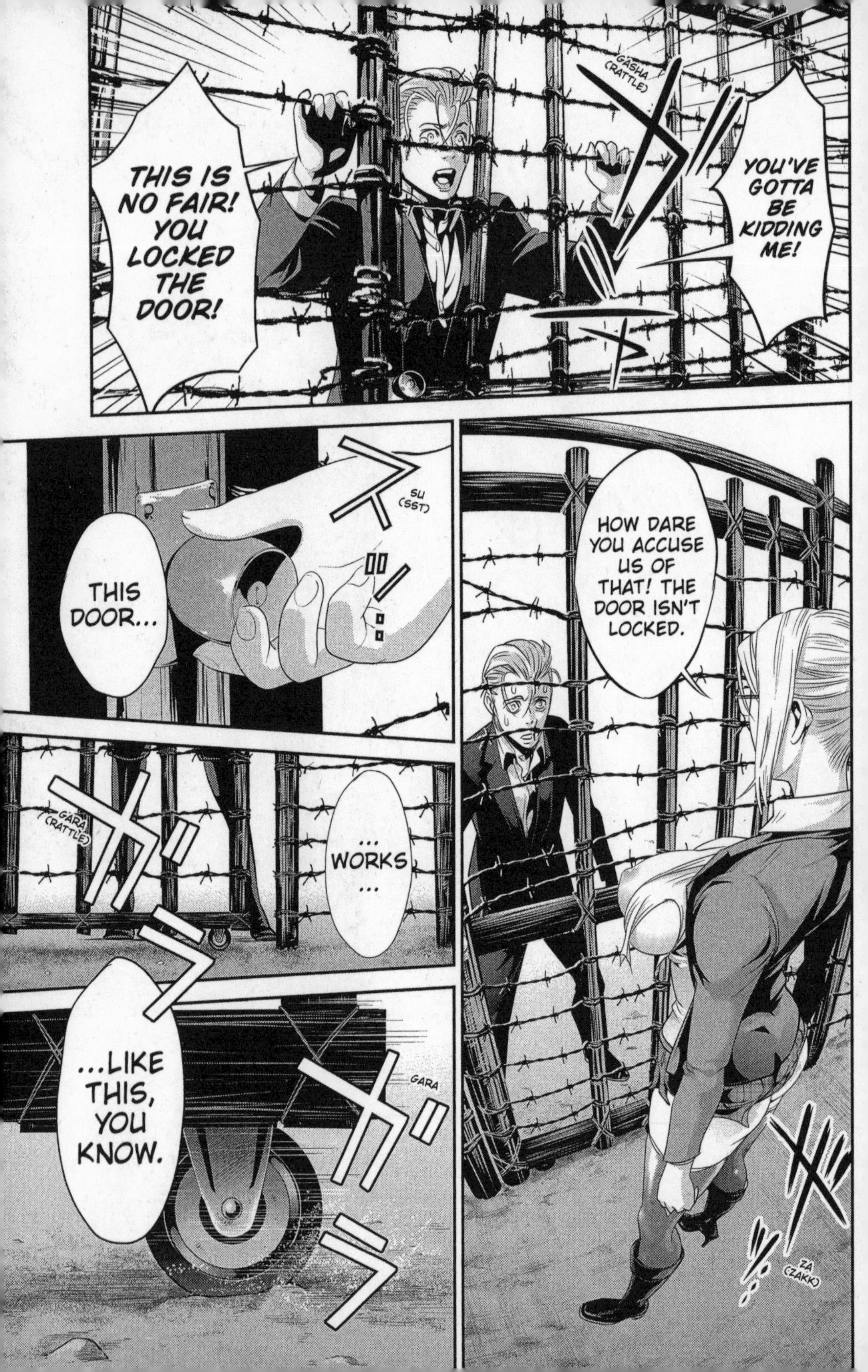
YOU'VE GOTTA BE KIDDING ME!
GASHA (RATTLE)
THIS IS NO FAIR! YOU LOCKED THE DOOR!
HOW DARE YOU ACCUSE US OF THAT! THE DOOR ISN'T LOCKED.
ZA (ZAKK)
SU (SST)
THIS DOOR...
GARA (RATTLE)
... WORKS ...
GARA
...LIKE THIS, YOU KNOW.

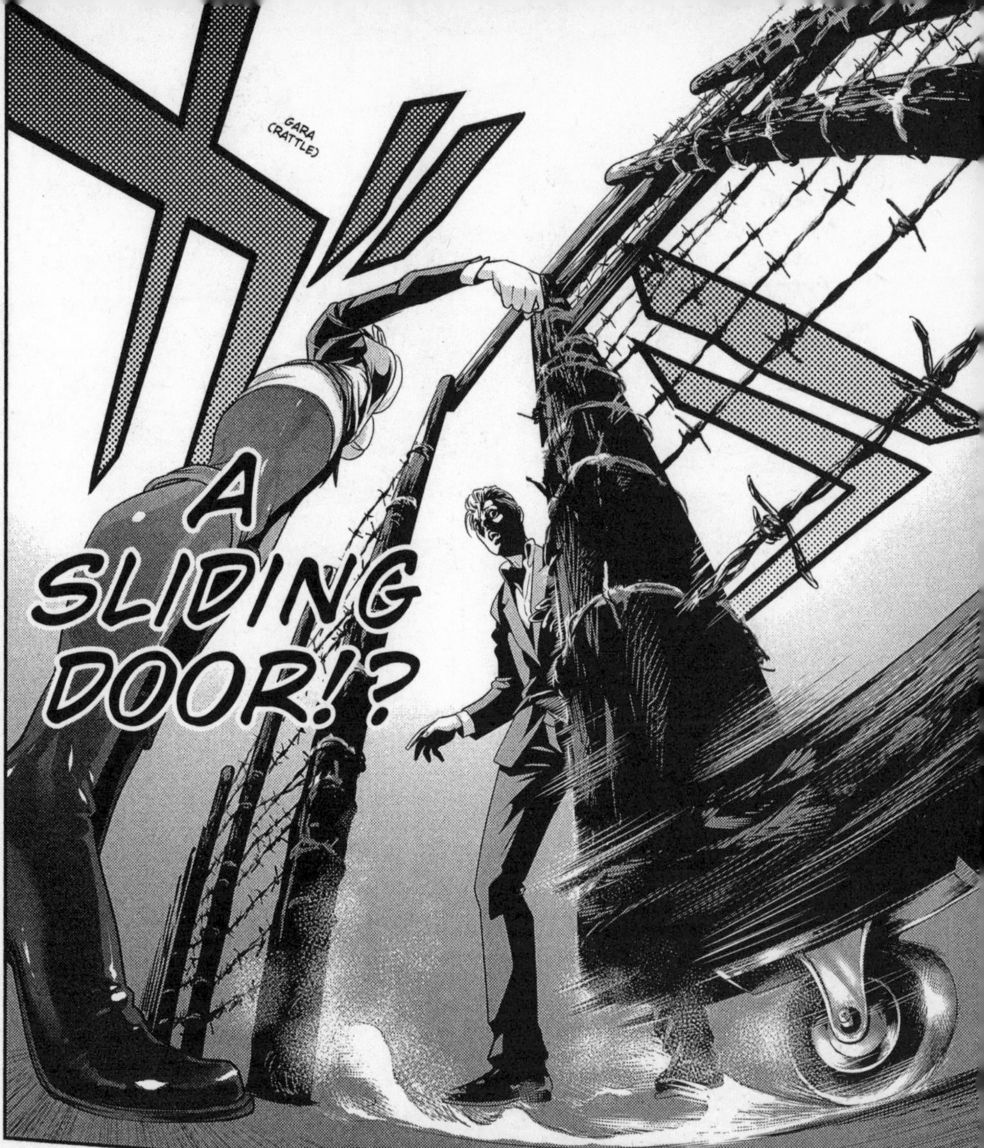
GARA (RATTLE)
A SLIDING DOOR!?
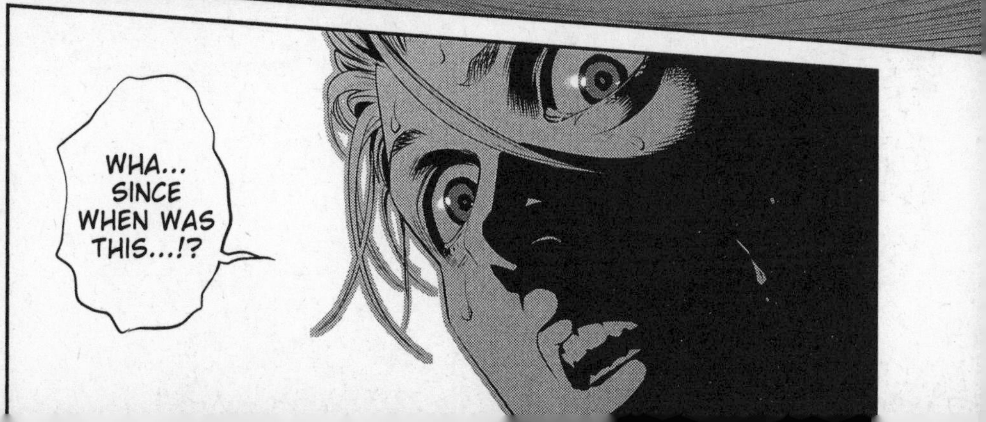
WHA... SINCE WHEN WAS THIS...!?

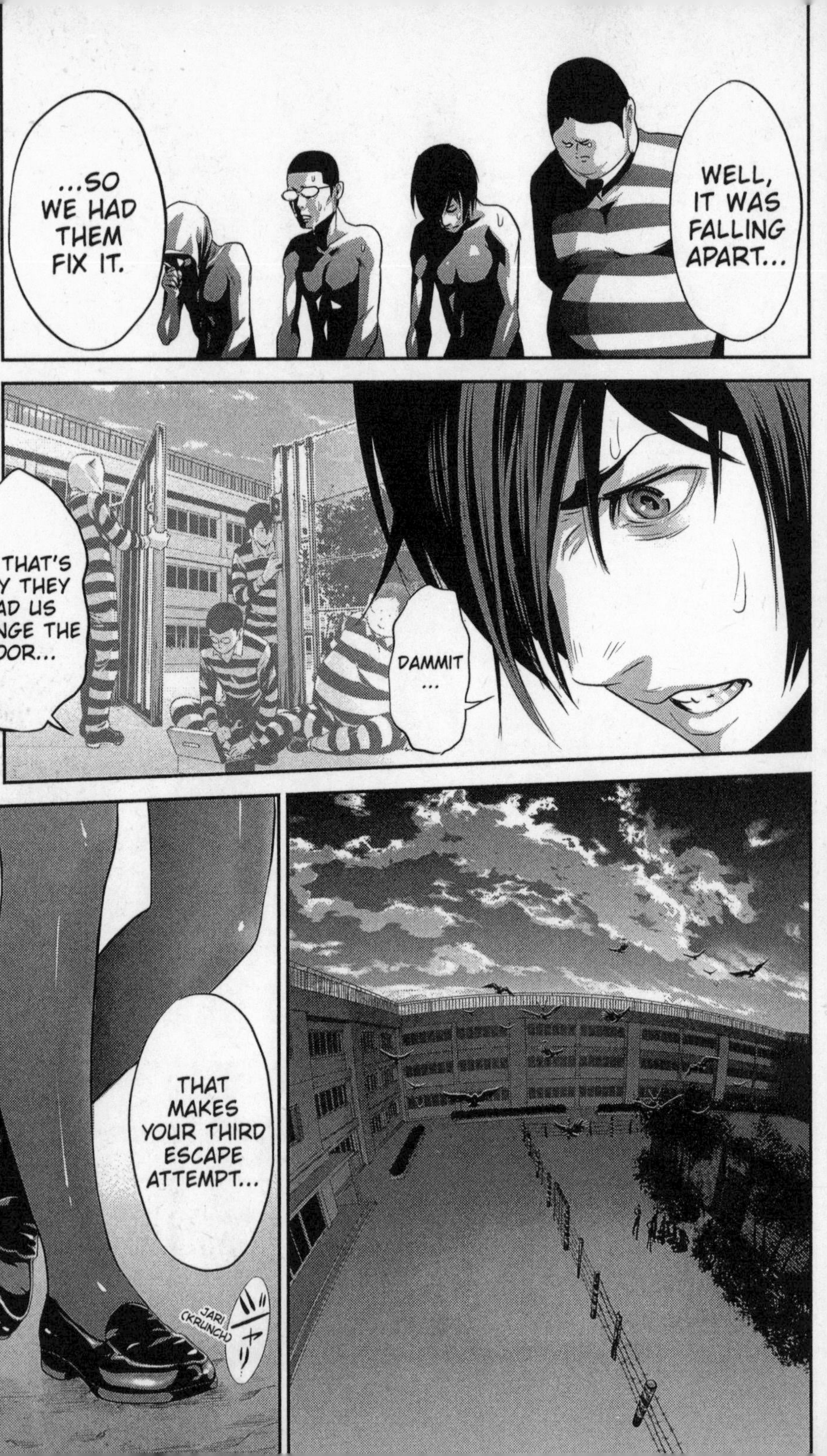
WELL, IT WAS FALLING APART...
...SO WE HAD THEM FIX IT.
DAMMIT ...
SO THAT'S WHY THEY HAD US CHANGE THE DOOR...
THAT MAKES YOUR THIRD ESCAPE ATTEMPT...
JARI (KRUNCH)

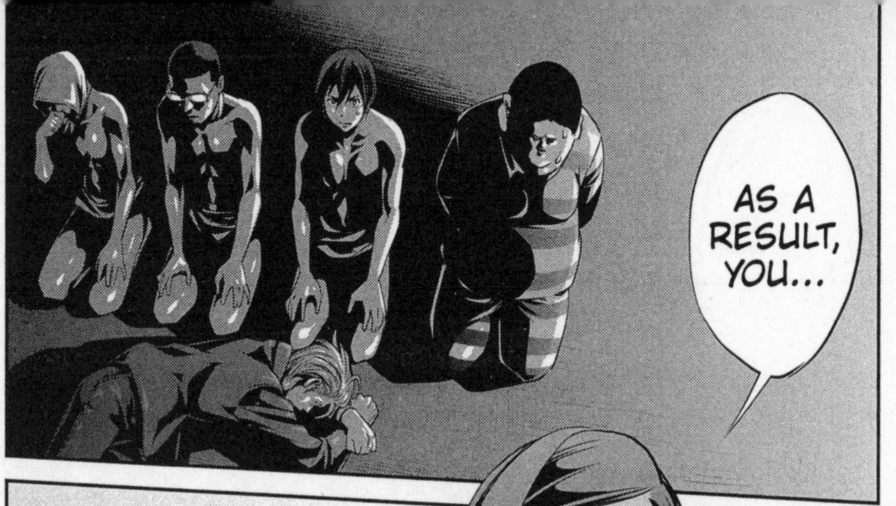
AS A RESULT, YOU...

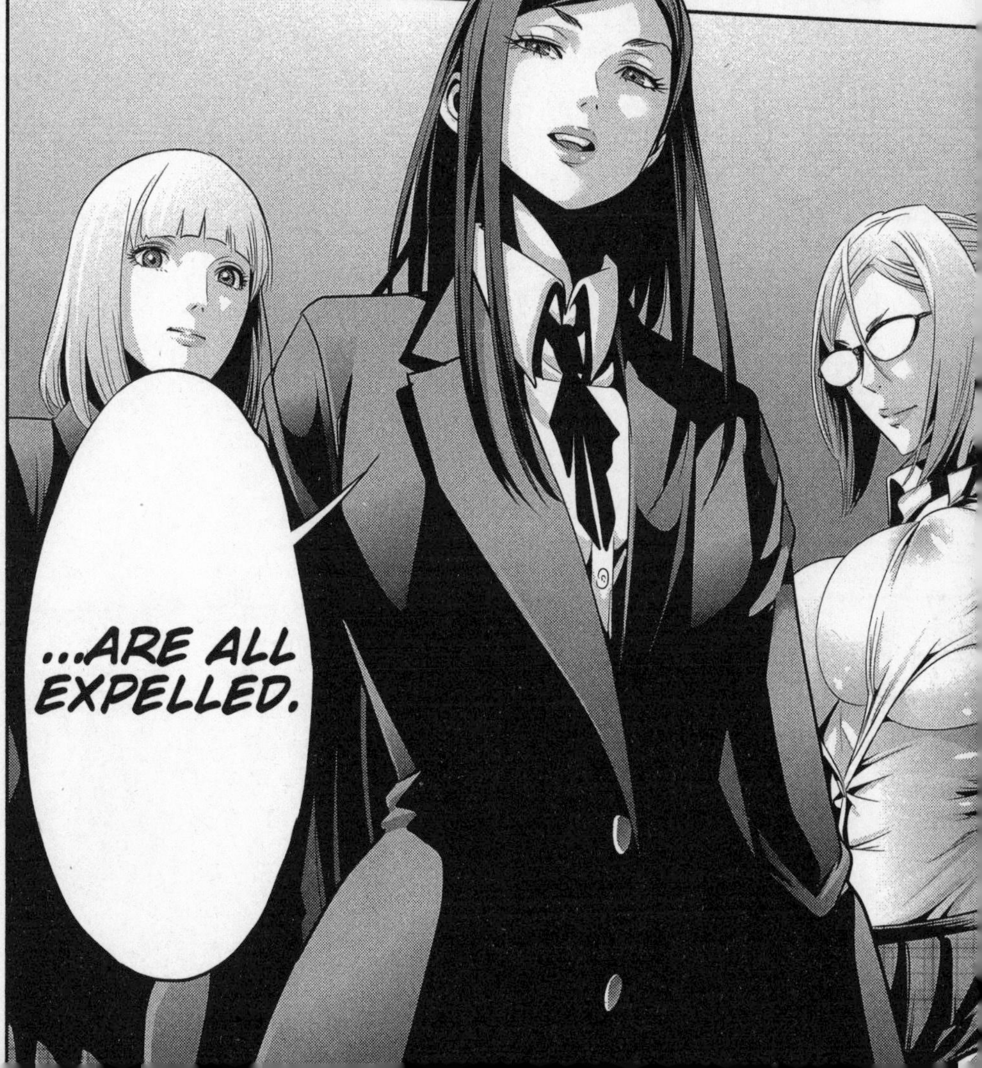
...ARE ALL EXPELLED.

CHAPTER 54: BRING IT ON!

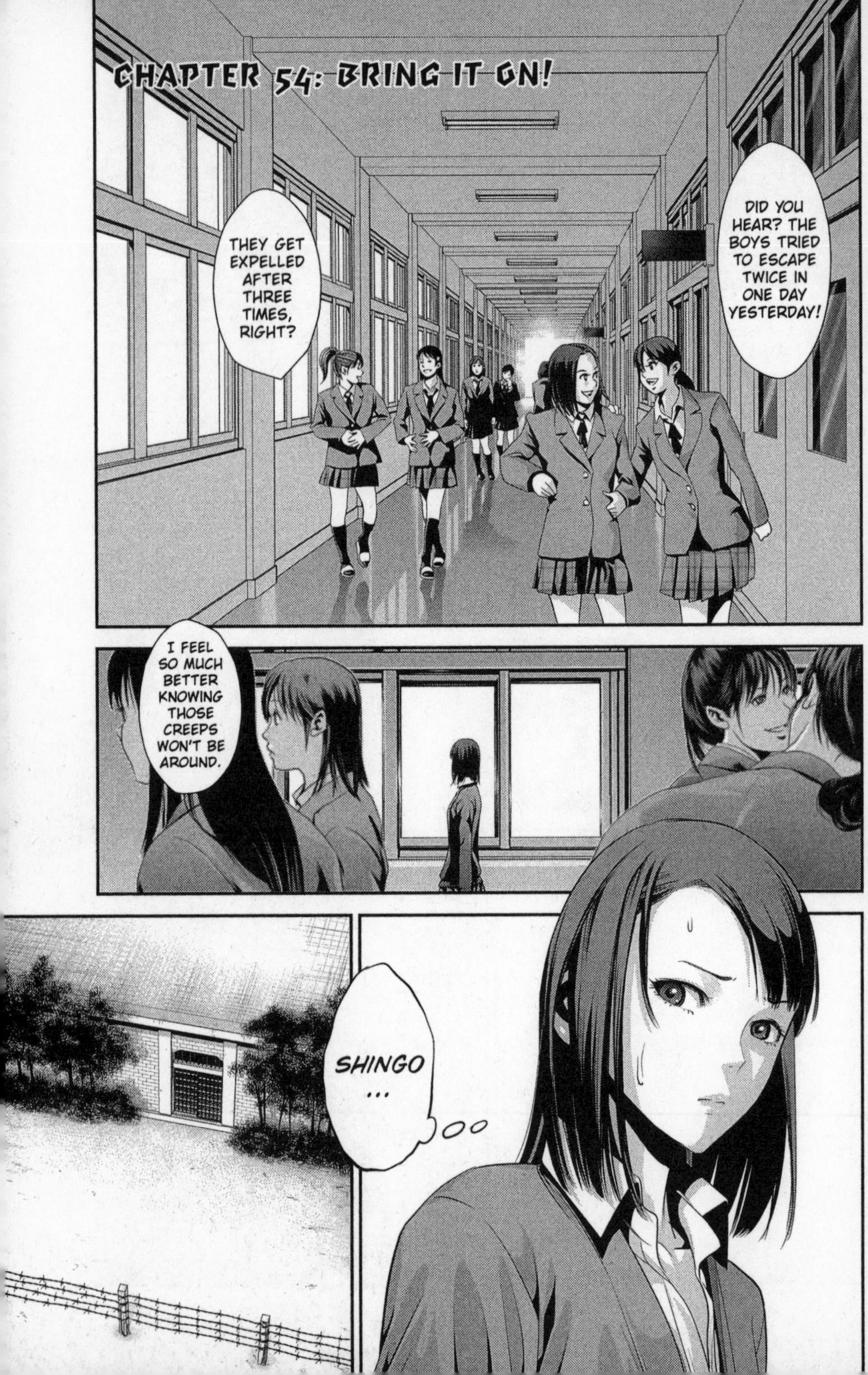
DID YOU HEAR? THE BOYS TRIED TO ESCAPE TWICE IN ONE DAY YESTERDAY!
THEY GET EXPELLED AFTER THREE TIMES, RIGHT?
I FEEL SO MUCH BETTER KNOWING THOSE CREEPS WON'T BE AROUND.
SHINGO ...

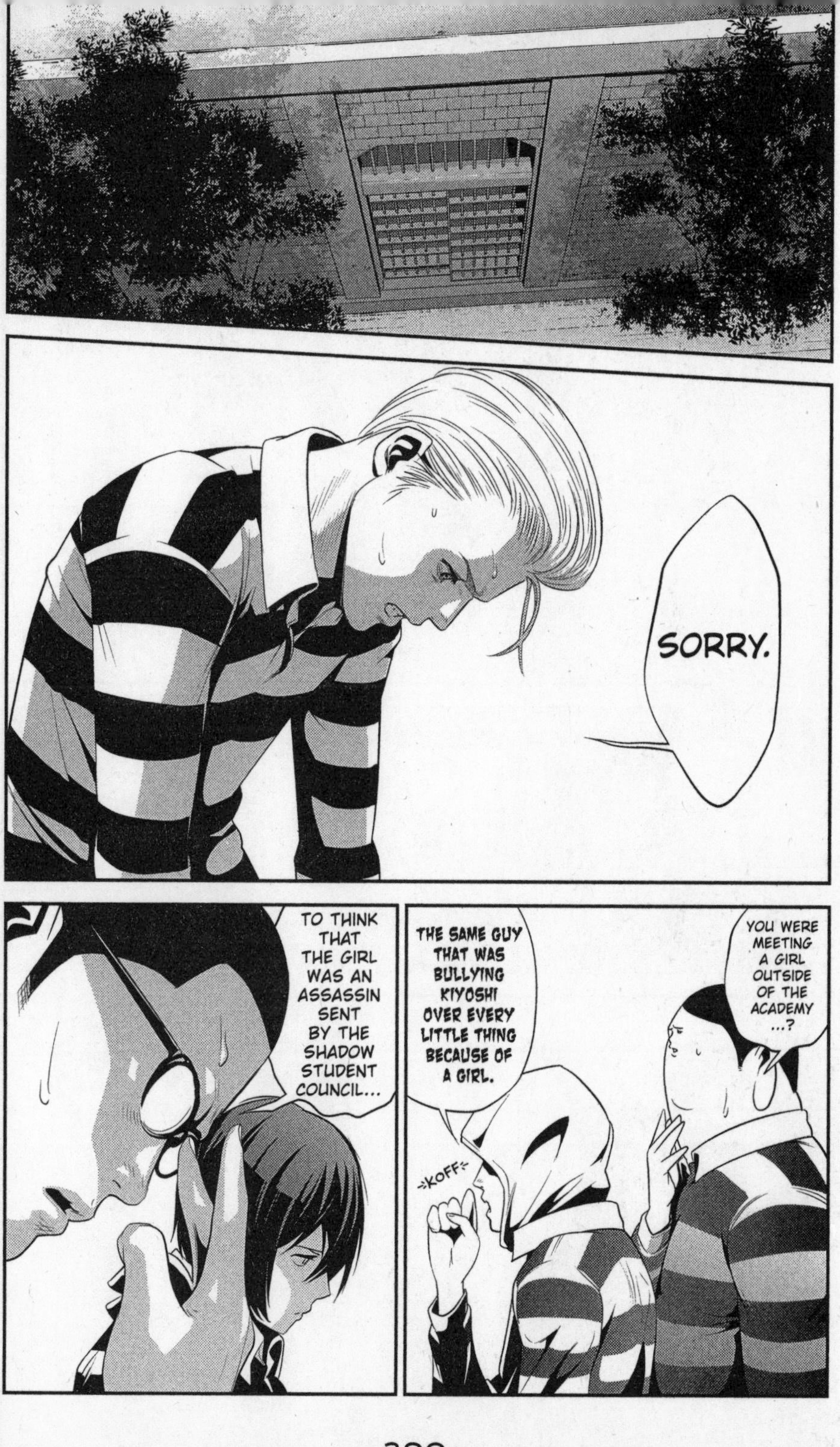
SORRY.
YOU WERE MEETING A GIRL OUTSIDE OF THE ACADEMY ...?
THE SAME GUY THAT WAS BULLYING KIYOSHI OVER EVERY LITTLE THING BECAUSE OF A GIRL.
KOFF
TO THINK THAT THE GIRL WAS AN ASSASSIN SENT BY THE SHADOW STUDENT COUNCIL...

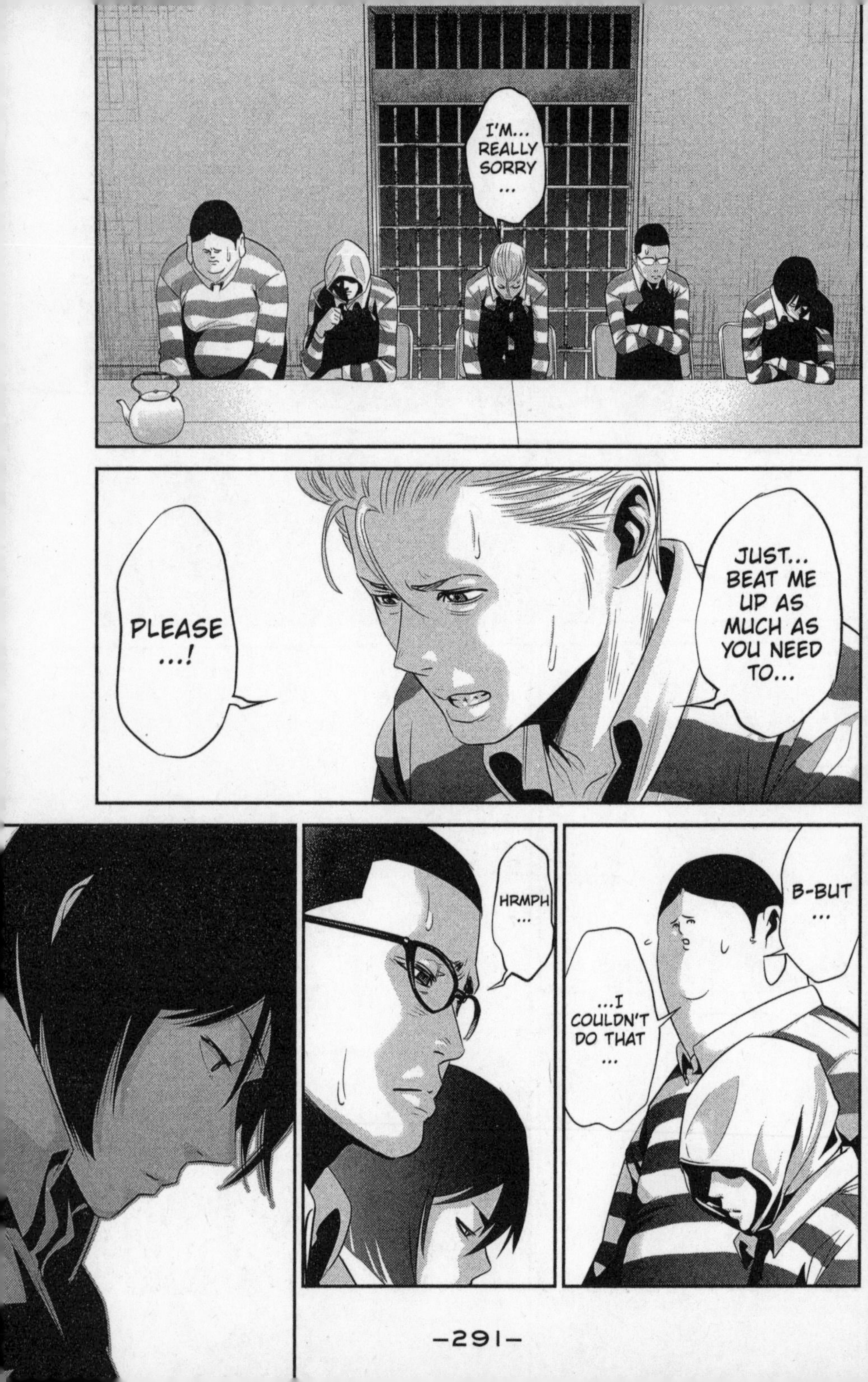
I'M... REALLY SORRY ...
JUST... BEAT ME UP AS MUCH AS YOU NEED TO...
PLEASE ...!
B-BUT ...
...I COULDN'T DO THAT ...
HRMPH ...

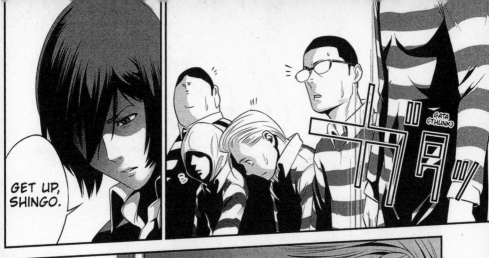

GATA (THUNK)
GET UP, SHINGO.
REMEMBER HOW YOU HIT ME WHEN THEY FOUND OUT I ESCAPED?
KIYOSHI-DONO... VIOLENCE IS NOT...
YEAH... GET ME BACK AS HARD AS YOU WANT.
GIRI (GRIP)
THEN I WON'T HOLD BACK...

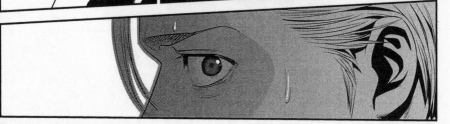

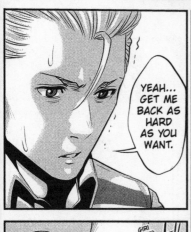

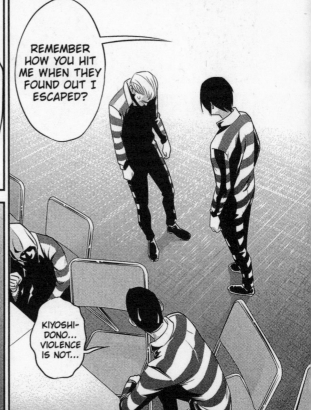

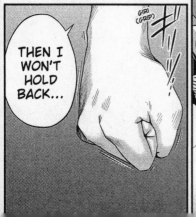

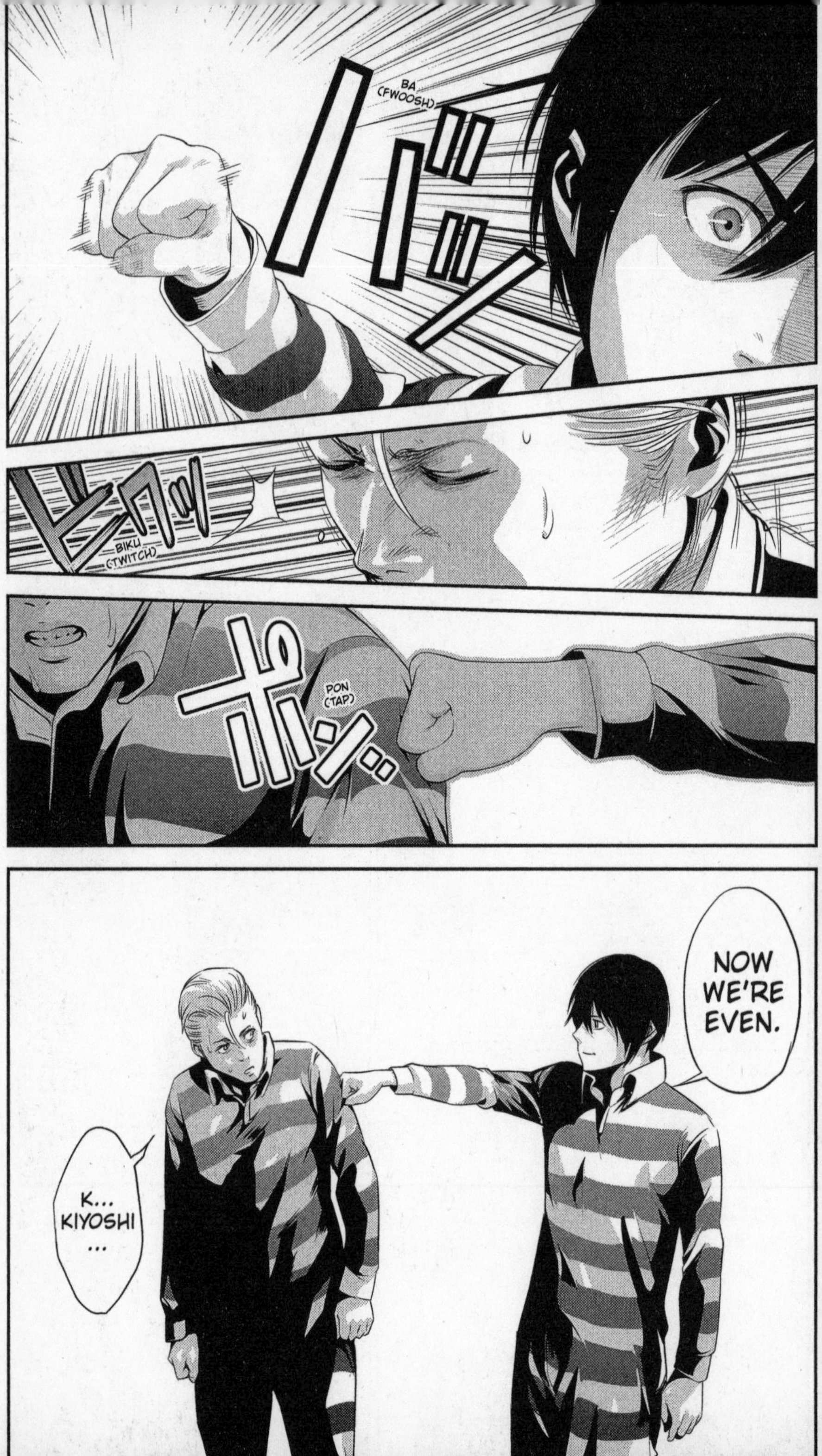
BA (FWOOSH)
BIKU (TWITCH)
PON (TAP)
NOW WE'RE EVEN.
K... KIYOSHI ...

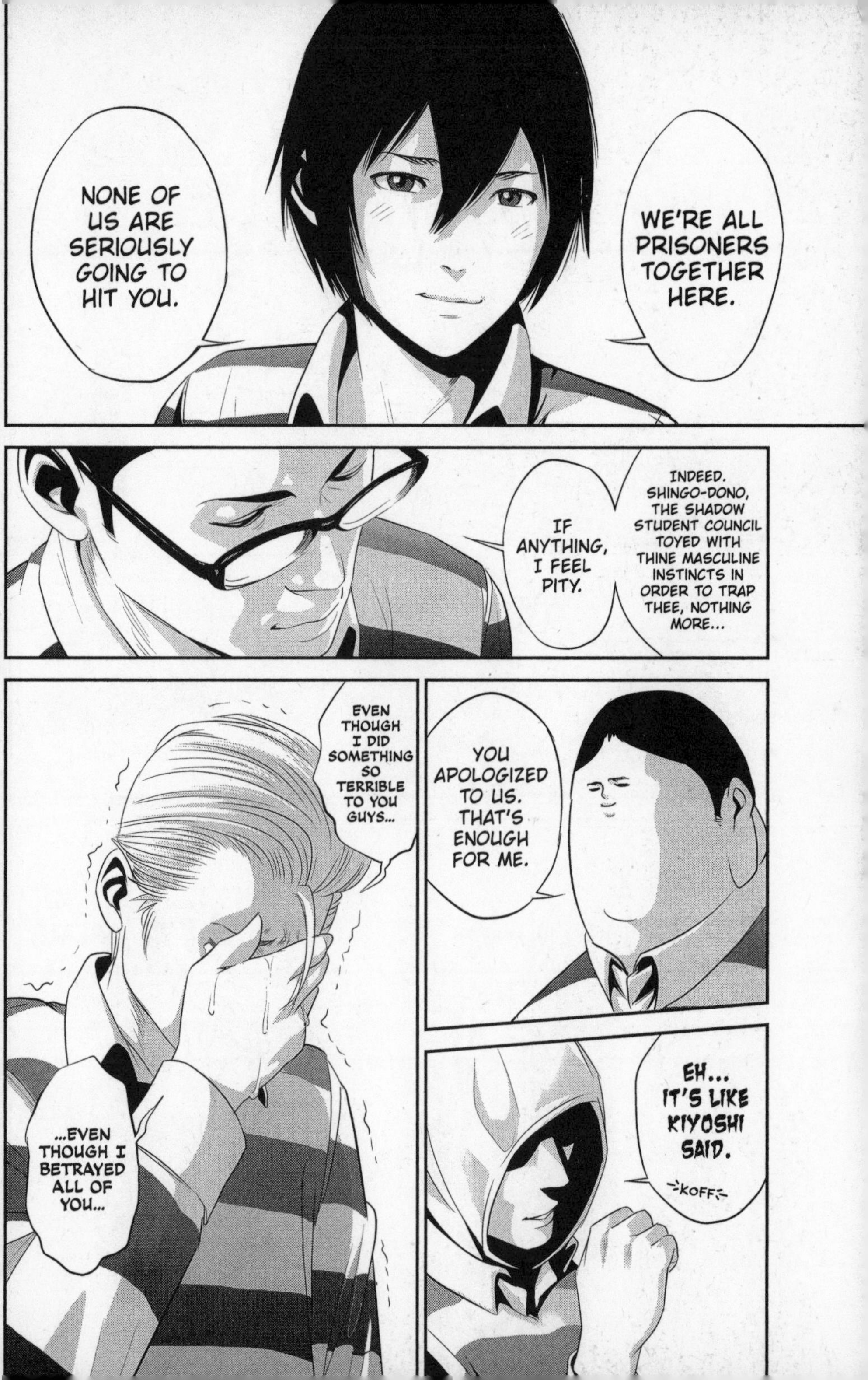
WE'RE ALL PRISONERS TOGETHER HERE.
NONE OF US ARE SERIOUSLY GOING TO HIT YOU.
INDEED. SHINGO-DONO, THE SHADOW STUDENT COUNCIL TOYED WITH THINE MASCULINE INSTINCTS IN ORDER TO TRAP THEE, NOTHING MORE...
IF ANYTHING, I FEEL PITY.
YOU APOLOGIZED TO US. THAT'S ENOUGH FOR ME.
EH... IT'S LIKE KIYOSHI SAID.
KOFF
EVEN THOUGH I DID SOMETHING SO TERRIBLE TO YOU GUYS...
...EVEN THOUGH I BETRAYED ALL OF YOU...

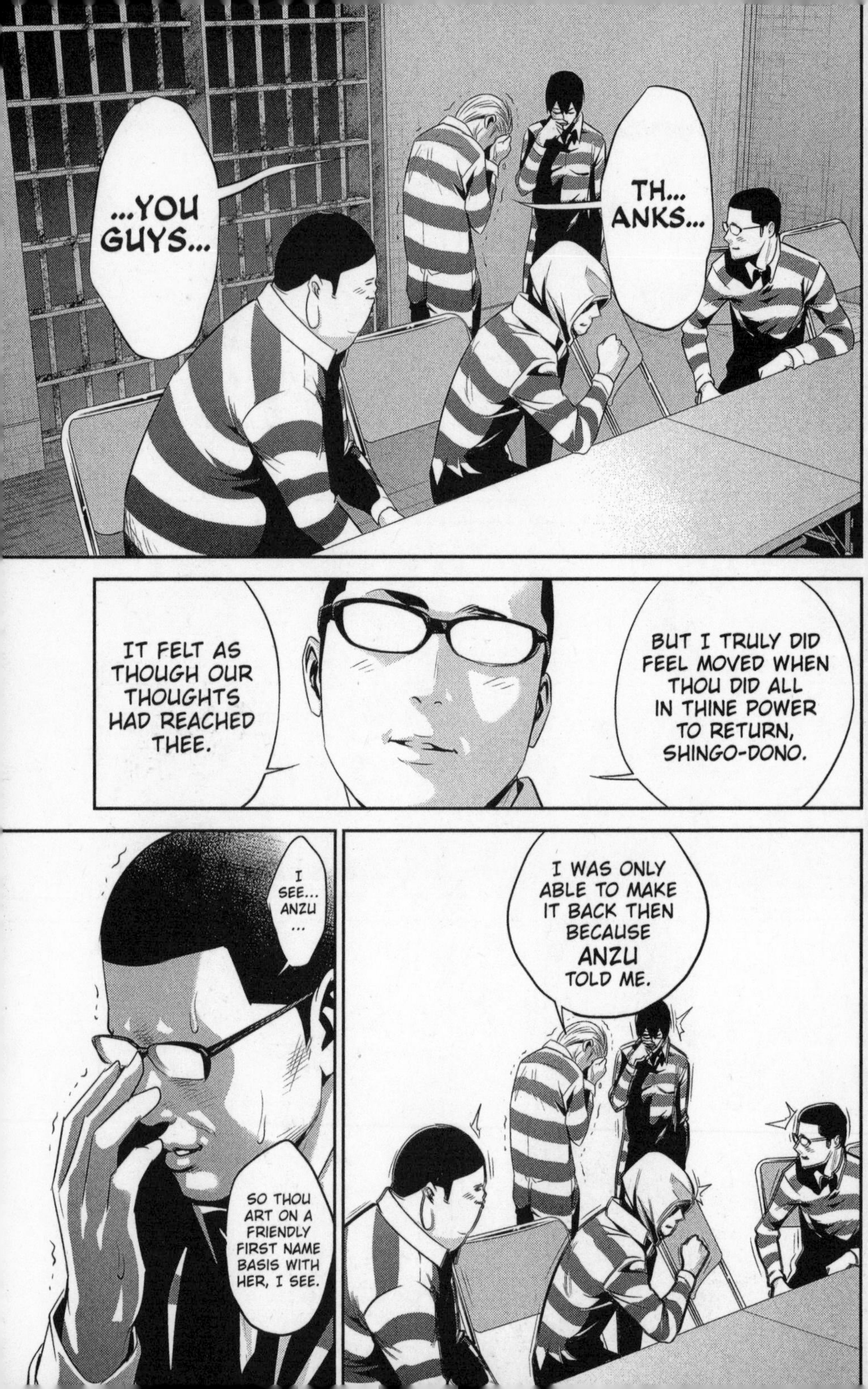
TH... ANKS...
...YOU GUYS...
BUT I TRULY DID FEEL MOVED WHEN THOU DID ALL IN THINE POWER TO RETURN, SHINGO-DONO.
IT FELT AS THOUGH OUR THOUGHTS HAD REACHED THEE.
I WAS ONLY ABLE TO MAKE IT BACK THEN BECAUSE ANZU TOLD ME.
I SEE... ANZU ...
SO THOU ART ON A FRIENDLY FIRST NAME BASIS WITH HER, I SEE.

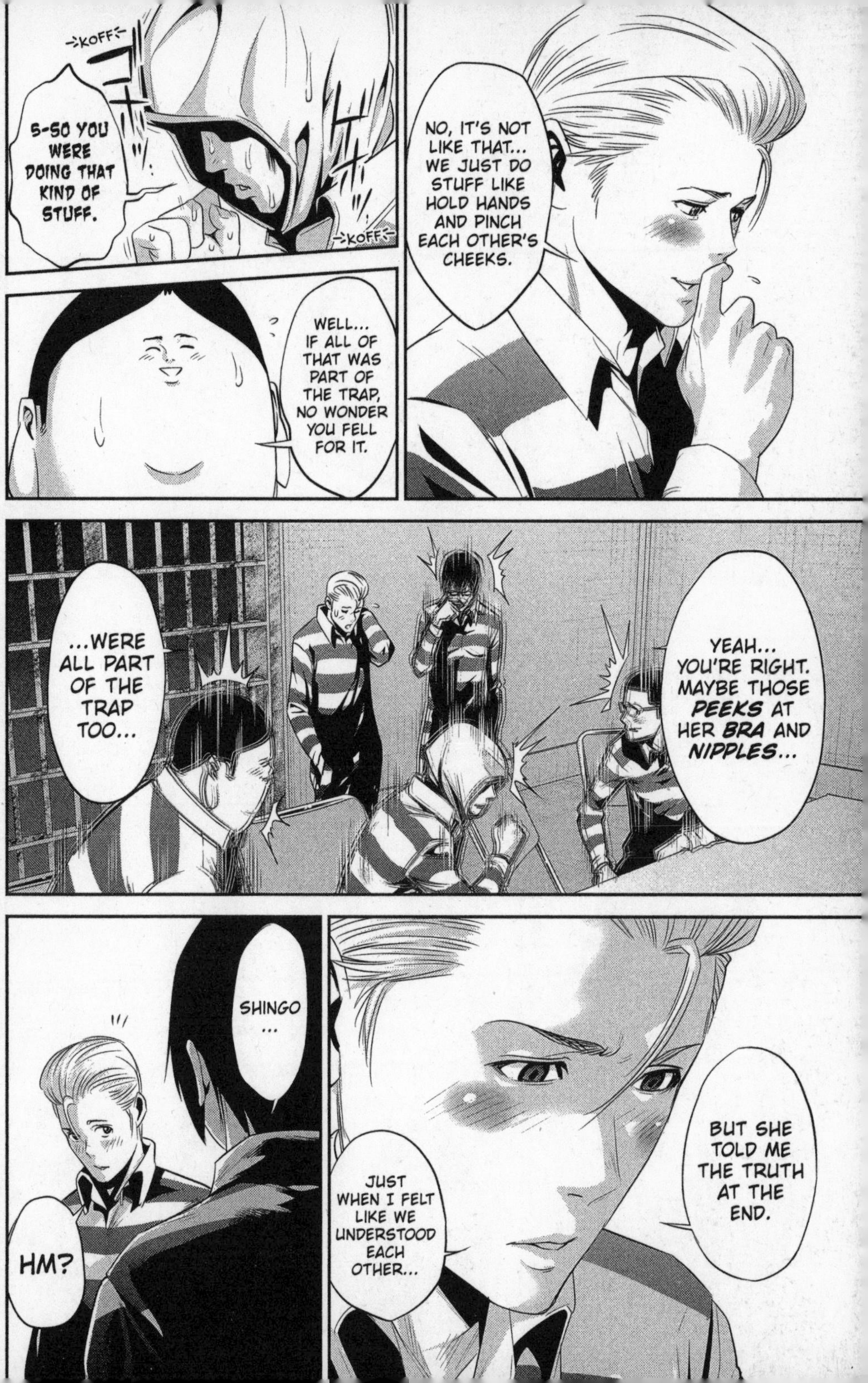
KOFF
S-SO YOU WERE DOING THAT KIND OF STUFF.
KOFF
NO, IT'S NOT LIKE THAT... WE JUST DO STUFF LIKE HOLD HANDS AND PINCH EACH OTHER'S CHEEKS.
WELL... IF ALL OF THAT WAS PART OF THE TRAP, NO WONDER YOU FELL FOR IT.
YEAH... YOU'RE RIGHT. MAYBE THOSE PEEKS AT HER BRA AND NIPPLES...
...WERE ALL PART OF THE TRAP TOO...
BUT SHE TOLD ME THE TRUTH AT THE END.
JUST WHEN I FELT LIKE WE UNDERSTOOD EACH OTHER...
SHINGO ...
HM?

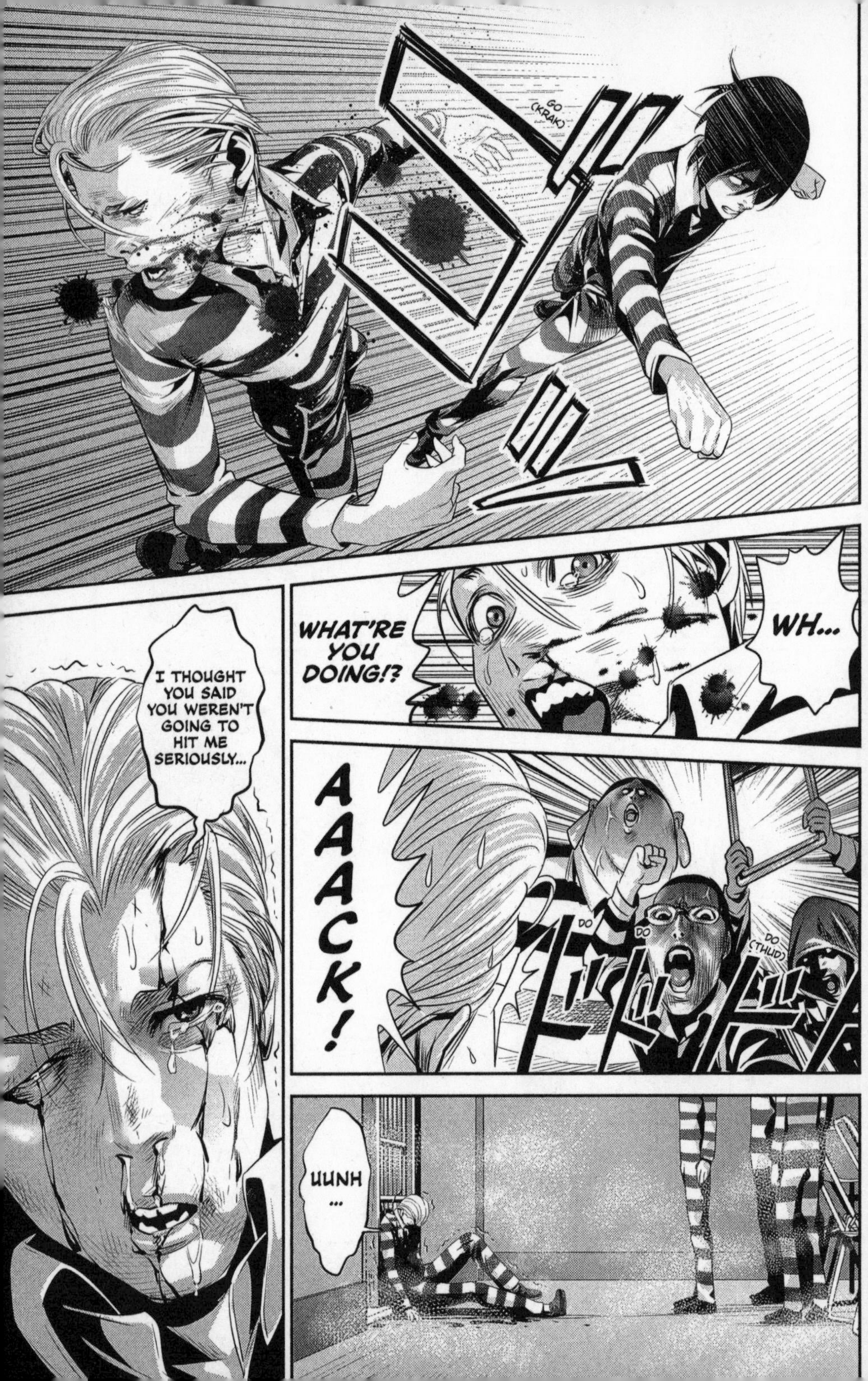
GO (KRAK)
WH...
WHAT'RE YOU DOING!?
AAACK!
DO
DO
DO (THUD)
UUNH ...
I THOUGHT YOU SAID YOU WEREN'T GOING TO HIT ME SERIOUSLY...

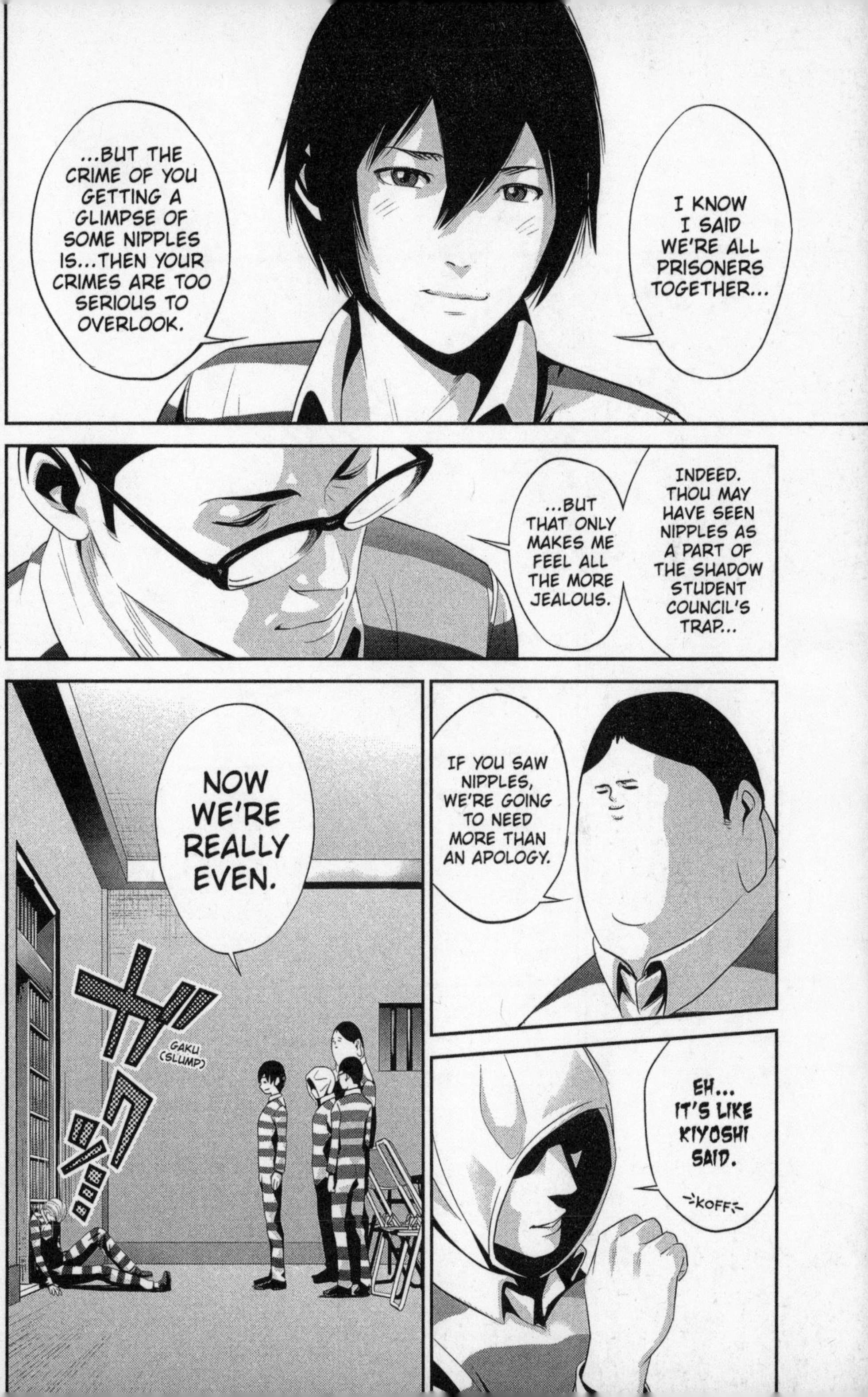
I KNOW I SAID WE'RE ALL PRISONERS TOGETHER...
...BUT THE CRIME OF YOU GETTING A GLIMPSE OF SOME NIPPLES IS...THEN YOUR CRIMES ARE TOO SERIOUS TO OVERLOOK.
INDEED. THOU MAY HAVE SEEN NIPPLES AS A PART OF THE SHADOW STUDENT COUNCIL'S TRAP...
...BUT THAT ONLY MAKES ME FEEL ALL THE MORE JEALOUS.
IF YOU SAW NIPPLES, WE'RE GOING TO NEED MORE THAN AN APOLOGY.
EH... IT'S LIKE KIYOSHI SAID.
KOFF
NOW WE'RE REALLY EVEN.
GAKU (SLUMP)

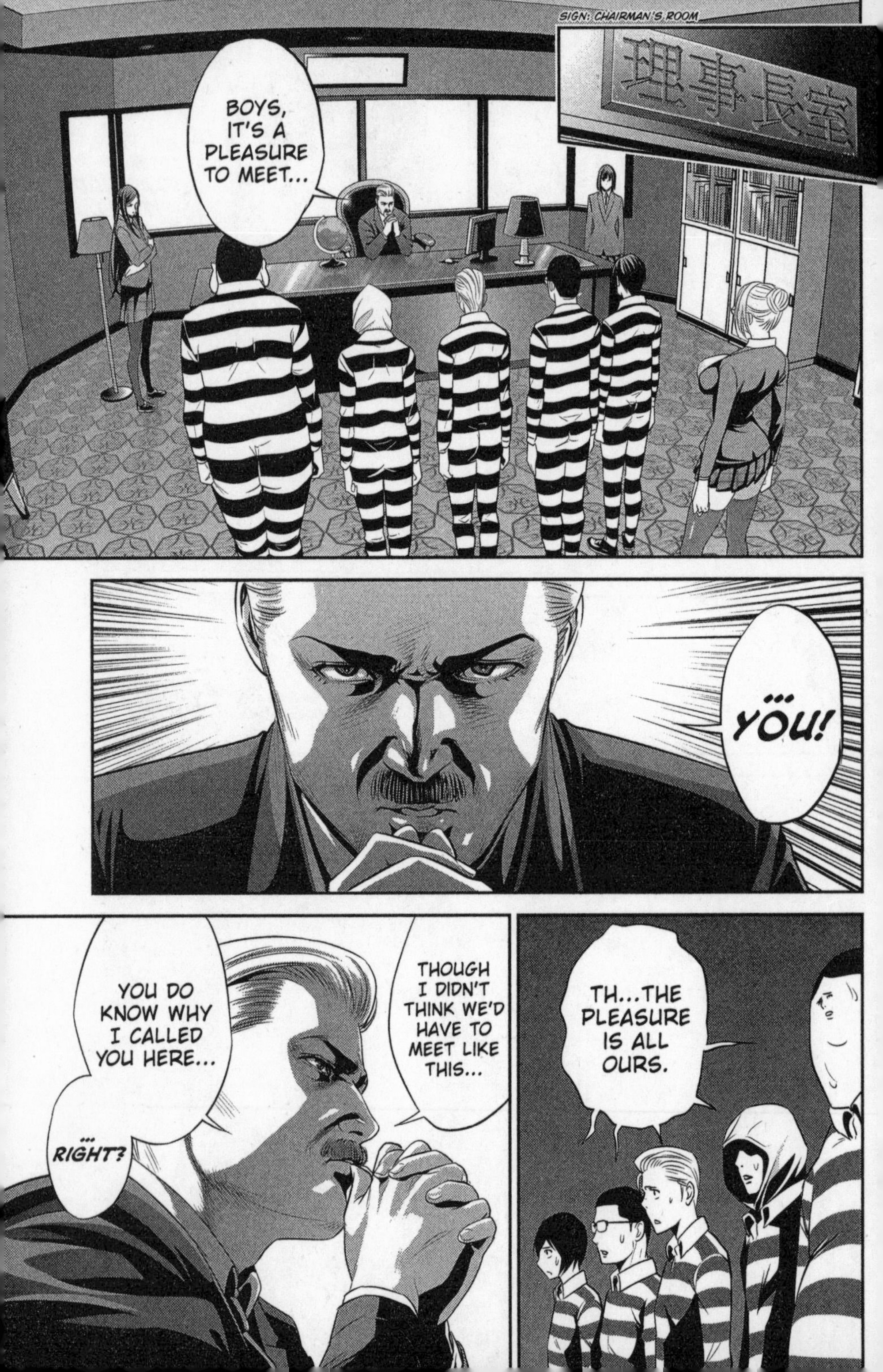
SIGN: CHAIRMAN'S ROOM
理事長室
BOYS, IT'S A PLEASURE TO MEET...
...YOU!
TH...THE PLEASURE IS ALL OURS.
THOUGH I DIDN'T THINK WE'D HAVE TO MEET LIKE THIS...
YOU DO KNOW WHY I CALLED YOU HERE...
...RIGHT?

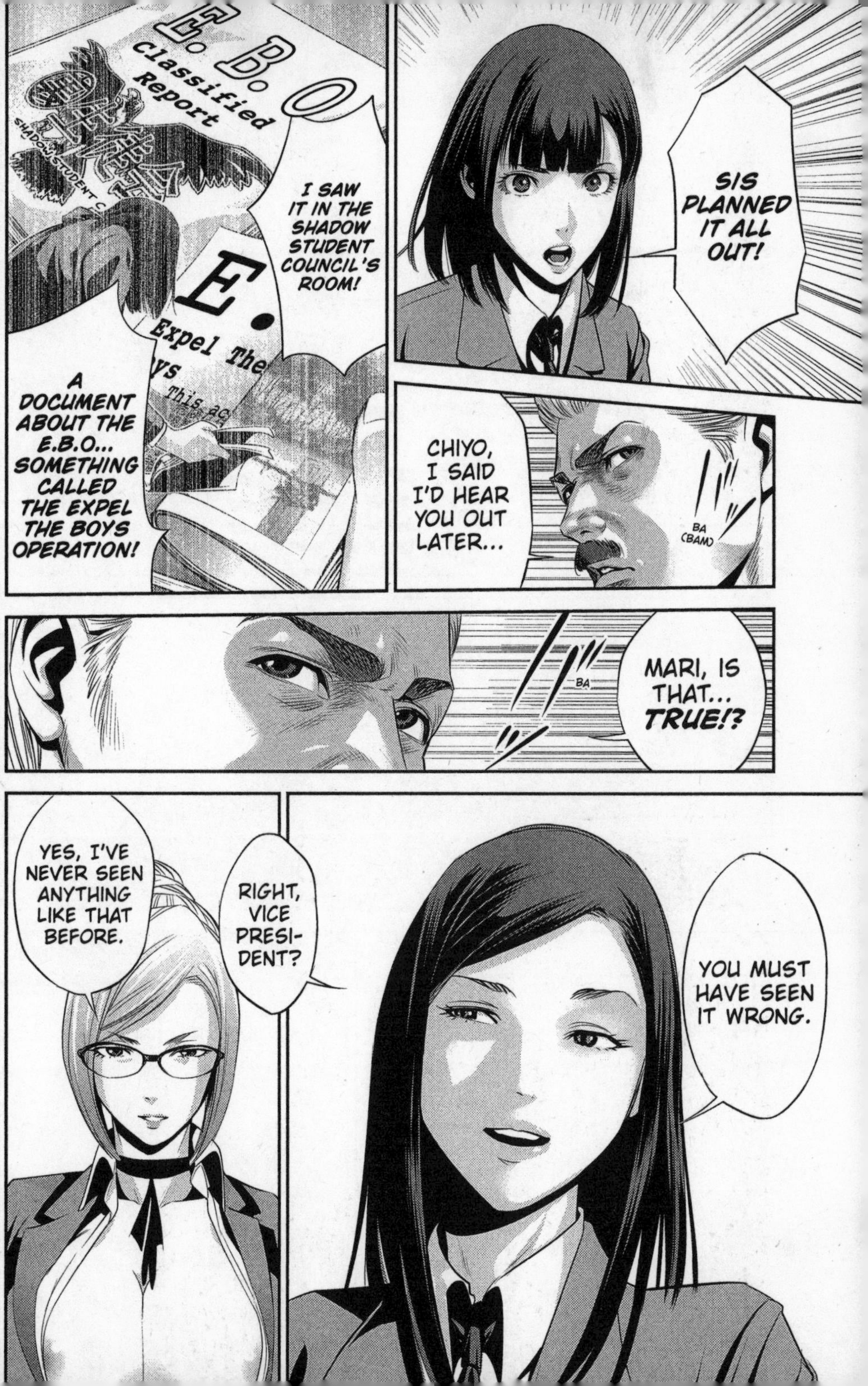
SIS PLANNED IT ALL OUT!
E.B.O Classified Report
SHADOW STUDENT C
E. Expel The
ys
This ac
I SAW IT IN THE SHADOW STUDENT COUNCIL'S ROOM!
A DOCUMENT ABOUT THE E.B.O... SOMETHING CALLED THE EXPEL THE BOYS OPERATION!
CHIYO, I SAID I'D HEAR YOU OUT LATER...
BA (BAM)
BA
MARI, IS THAT... *TRUE!?*
YOU MUST HAVE SEEN IT WRONG.
RIGHT, VICE PRESIDENT?
YES, I'VE NEVER SEEN ANYTHING LIKE THAT BEFORE.

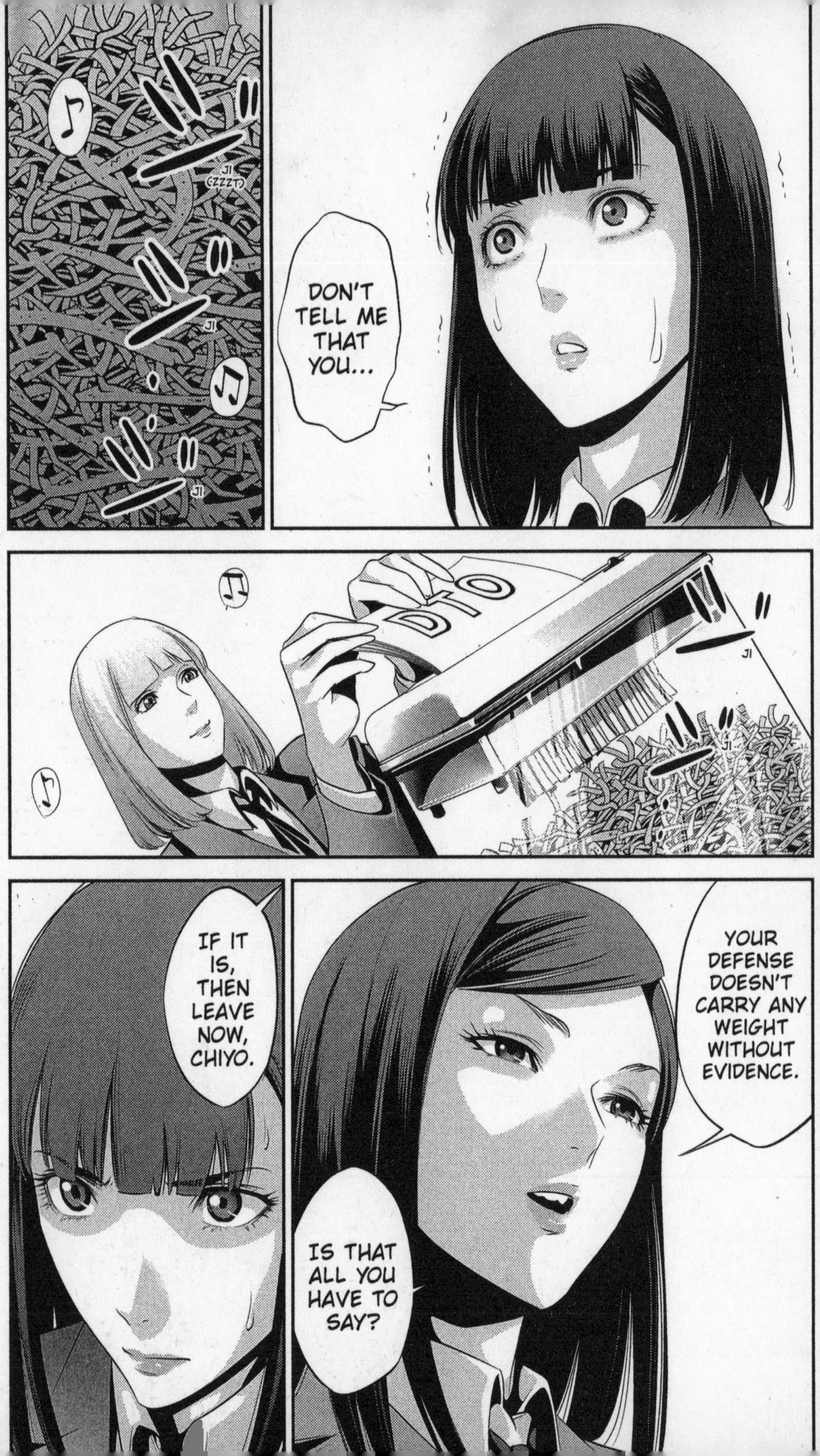
DON'T TELL ME THAT YOU...
JI (ZZZT)
JI
JI
JI
JI
YOUR DEFENSE DOESN'T CARRY ANY WEIGHT WITHOUT EVIDENCE.
IS THAT ALL YOU HAVE TO SAY?
IF IT IS, THEN LEAVE NOW, CHIYO.

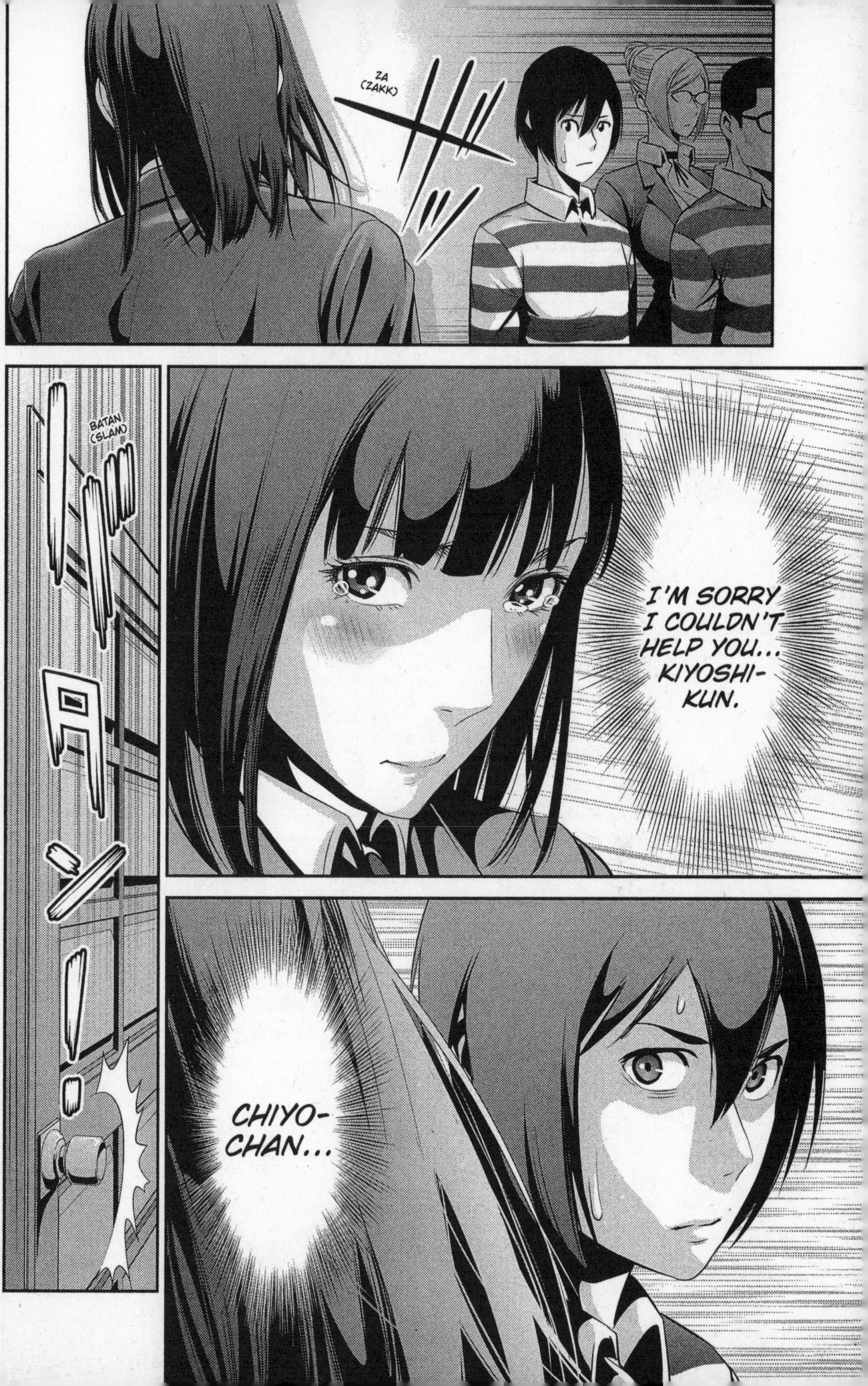
ZA (ZAKK)
I'M SORRY I COULDN'T HELP YOU... KIYOSHI-KUN.
CHIYO-CHAN...
BATAN (SLAM)

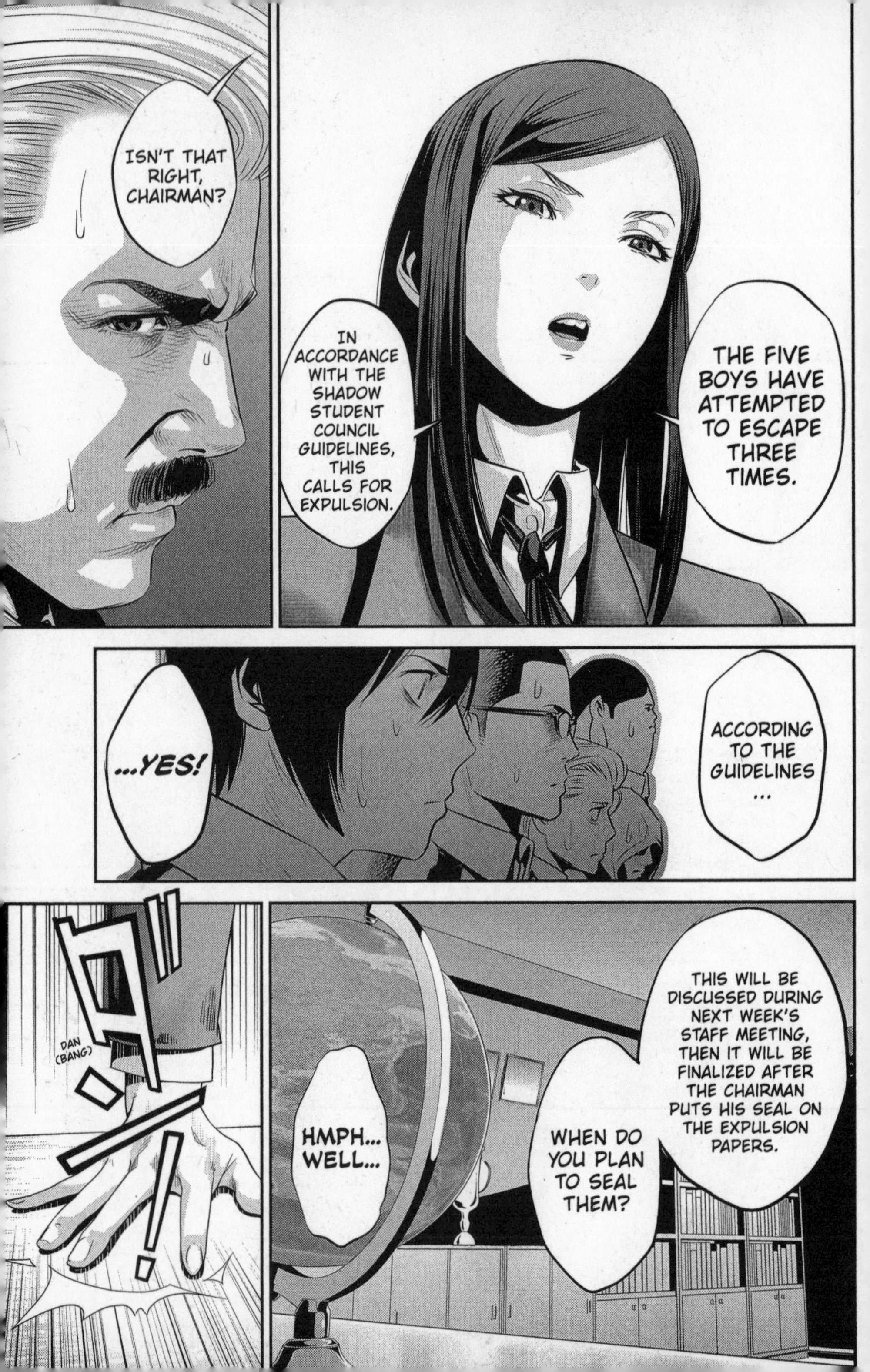
THE FIVE BOYS HAVE ATTEMPTED TO ESCAPE THREE TIMES.
IN ACCORDANCE WITH THE SHADOW STUDENT COUNCIL GUIDELINES, THIS CALLS FOR EXPULSION.
ISN'T THAT RIGHT, CHAIRMAN?
ACCORDING TO THE GUIDELINES ...
...YES!
THIS WILL BE DISCUSSED DURING NEXT WEEK'S STAFF MEETING, THEN IT WILL BE FINALIZED AFTER THE CHAIRMAN PUTS HIS SEAL ON THE EXPULSION PAPERS.
WHEN DO YOU PLAN TO SEAL THEM?
HMPH... WELL...
DAN (BANG)

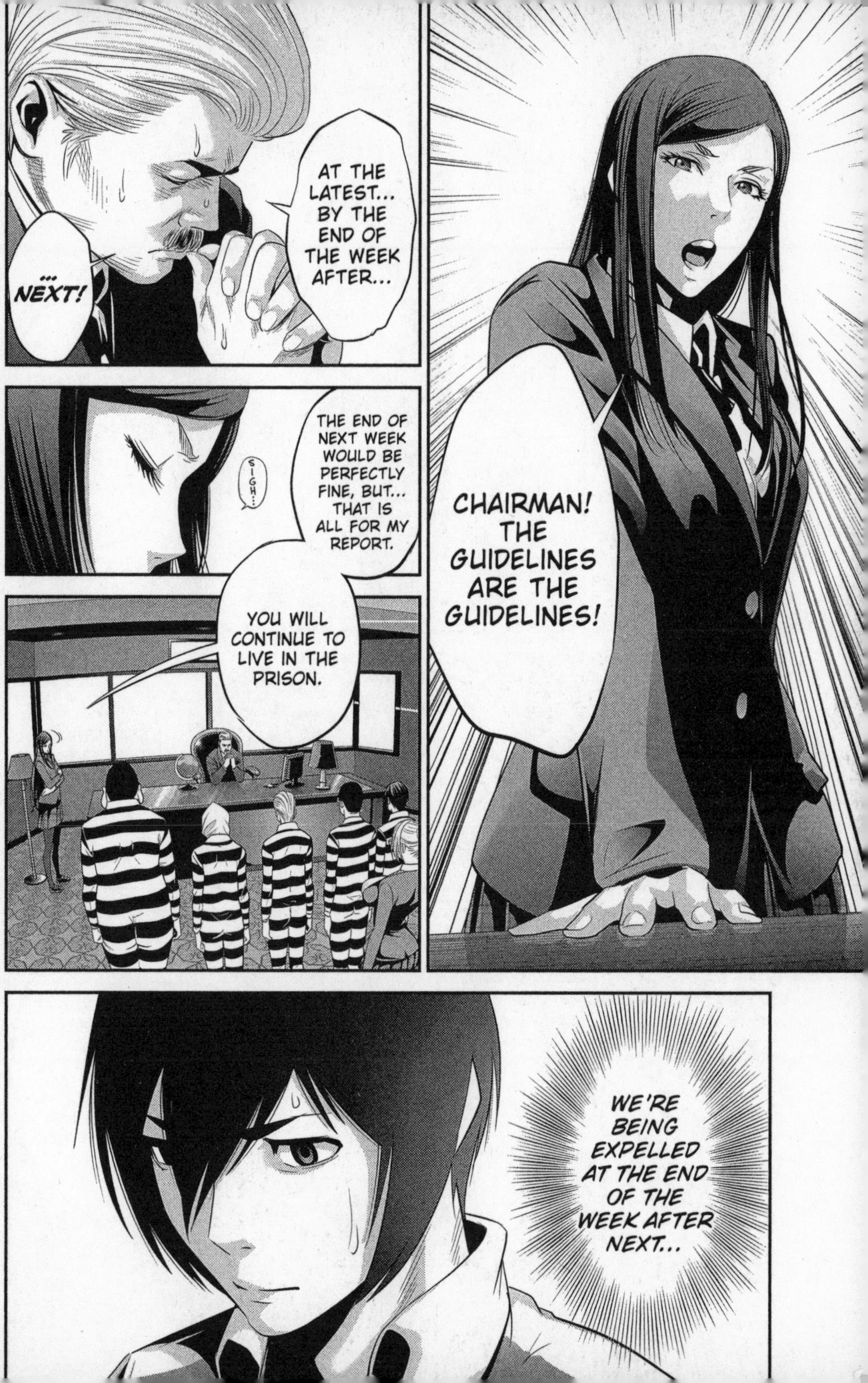
CHAIRMAN! THE GUIDELINES ARE THE GUIDELINES!
AT THE LATEST... BY THE END OF THE WEEK AFTER...
...NEXT!
THE END OF NEXT WEEK WOULD BE PERFECTLY FINE, BUT... THAT IS ALL FOR MY REPORT.
SIGH...
YOU WILL CONTINUE TO LIVE IN THE PRISON.
WE'RE BEING EXPELLED AT THE END OF THE WEEK AFTER NEXT...

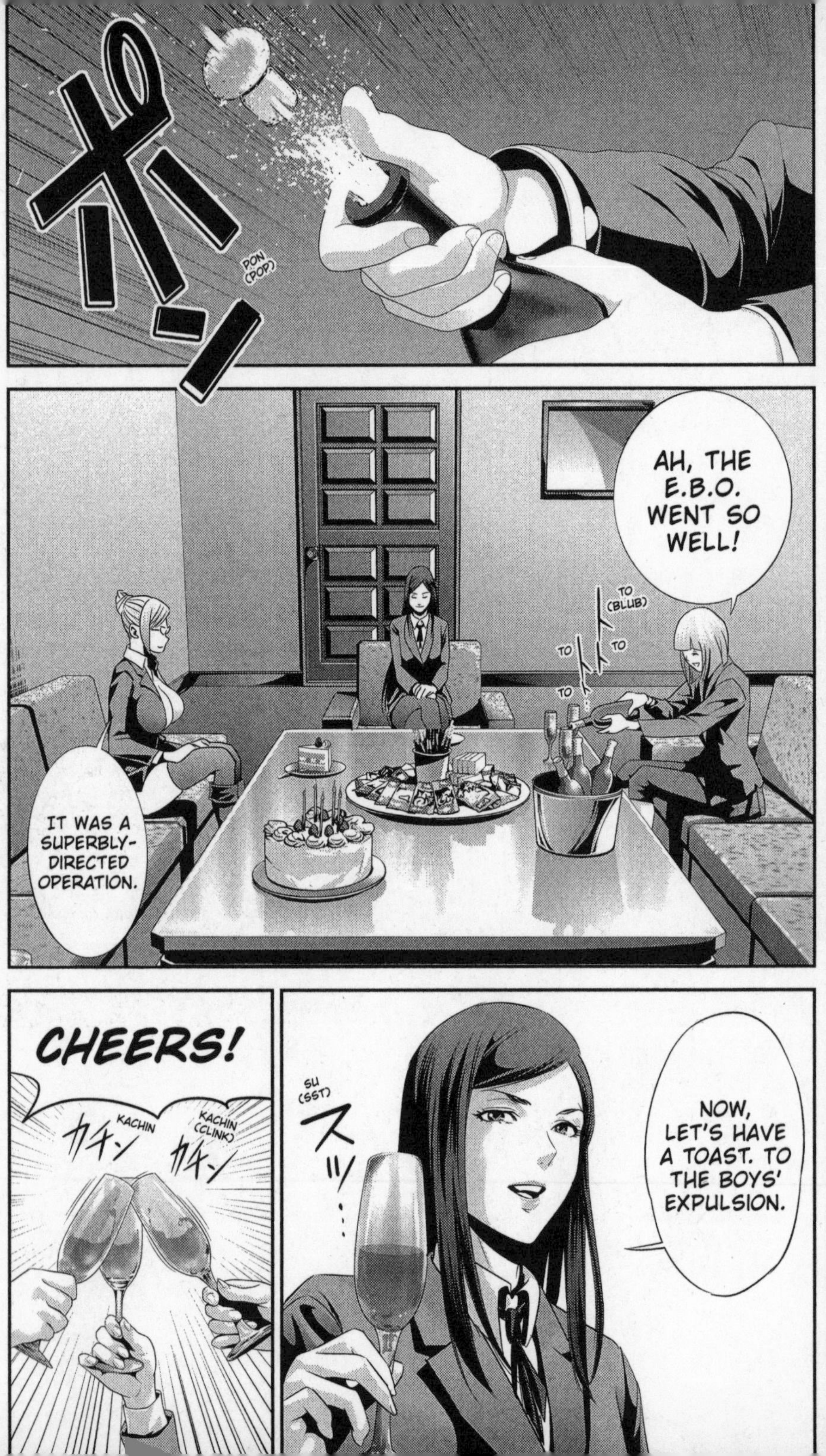
PON (POP)
AH, THE E.B.O. WENT SO WELL!
TO (BLUB)
TO
TO
TO
IT WAS A SUPERBLY-DIRECTED OPERATION.
SU (SST)
NOW, LET'S HAVE A TOAST. TO THE BOYS' EXPULSION.
CHEERS!
KACHIN (CLINK)
KACHIN

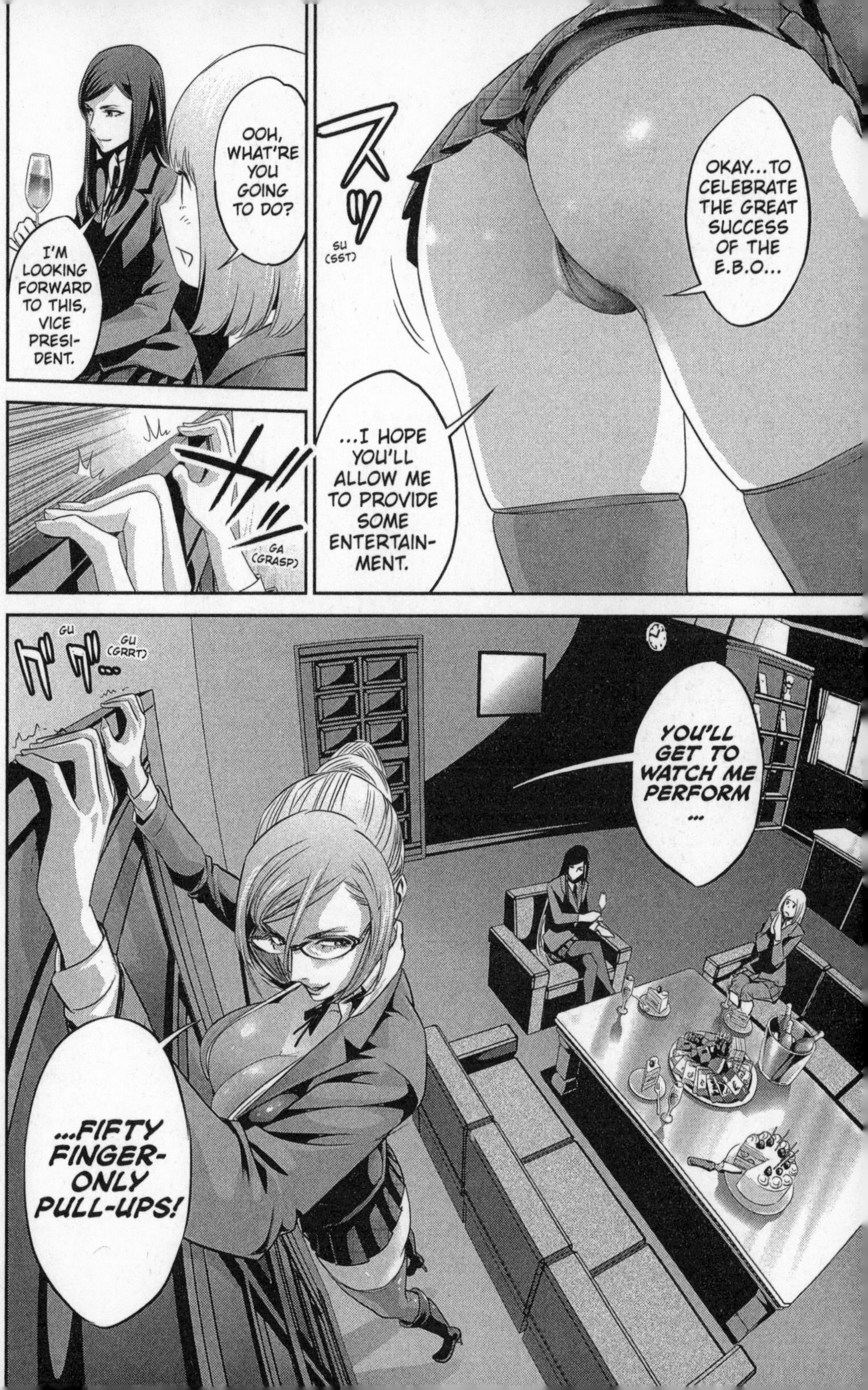

OKAY...TO CELEBRATE THE GREAT SUCCESS OF THE E.B.O...
SU (SST)
...I HOPE YOU'LL ALLOW ME TO PROVIDE SOME ENTERTAINMENT.
OOH, WHAT'RE YOU GOING TO DO?
I'M LOOKING FORWARD TO THIS, VICE PRESIDENT.
GA (GRASP)
GU GU (GRRT)
YOU'LL GET TO WATCH ME PERFORM...
...FIFTY FINGER-ONLY PULL-UPS!

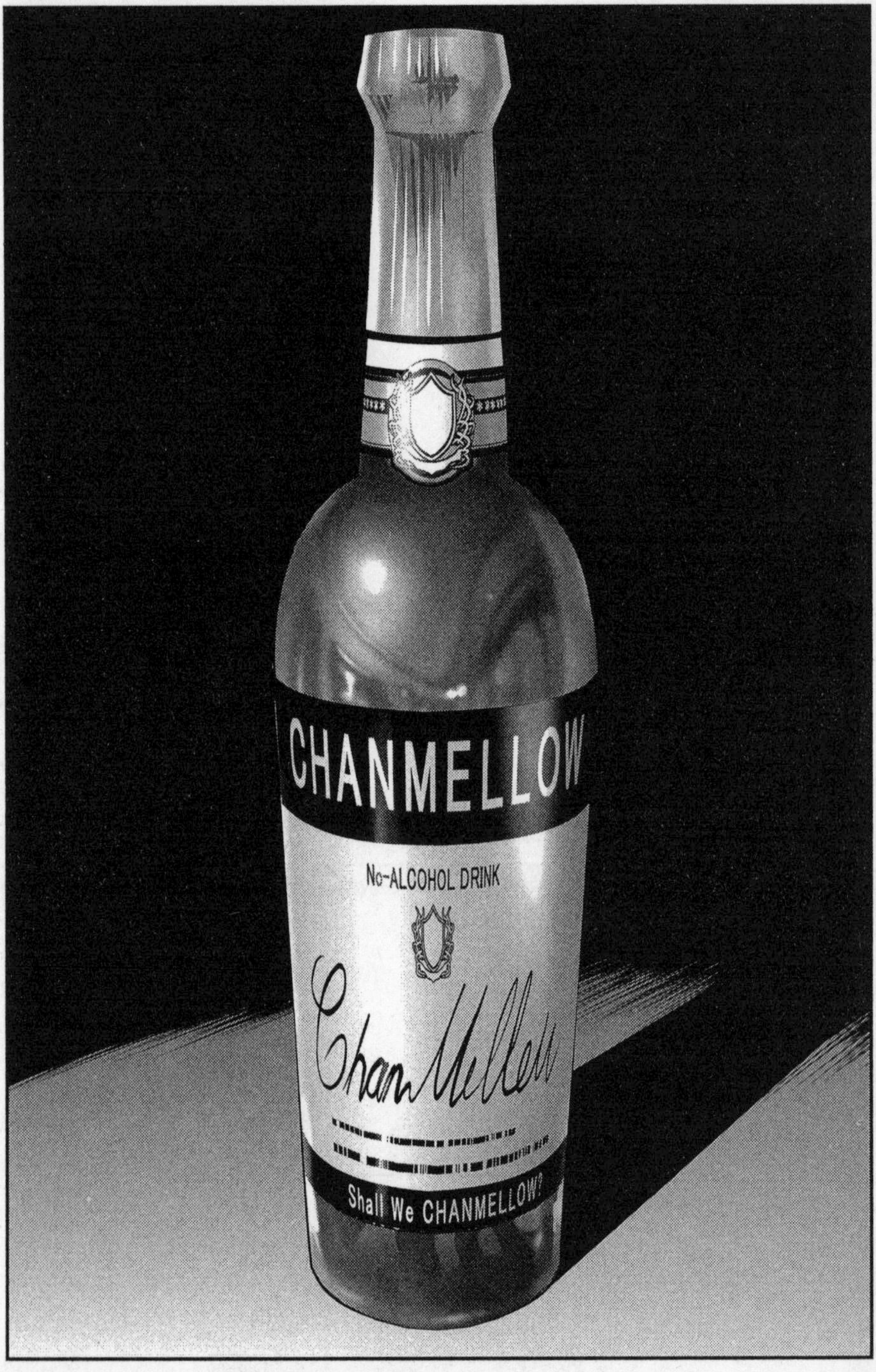
CHANMELLOW
No-ALCOHOL DRINK
ChanMellow
Shall We CHANMELLOW?

CHAPTER 55: THE FALL

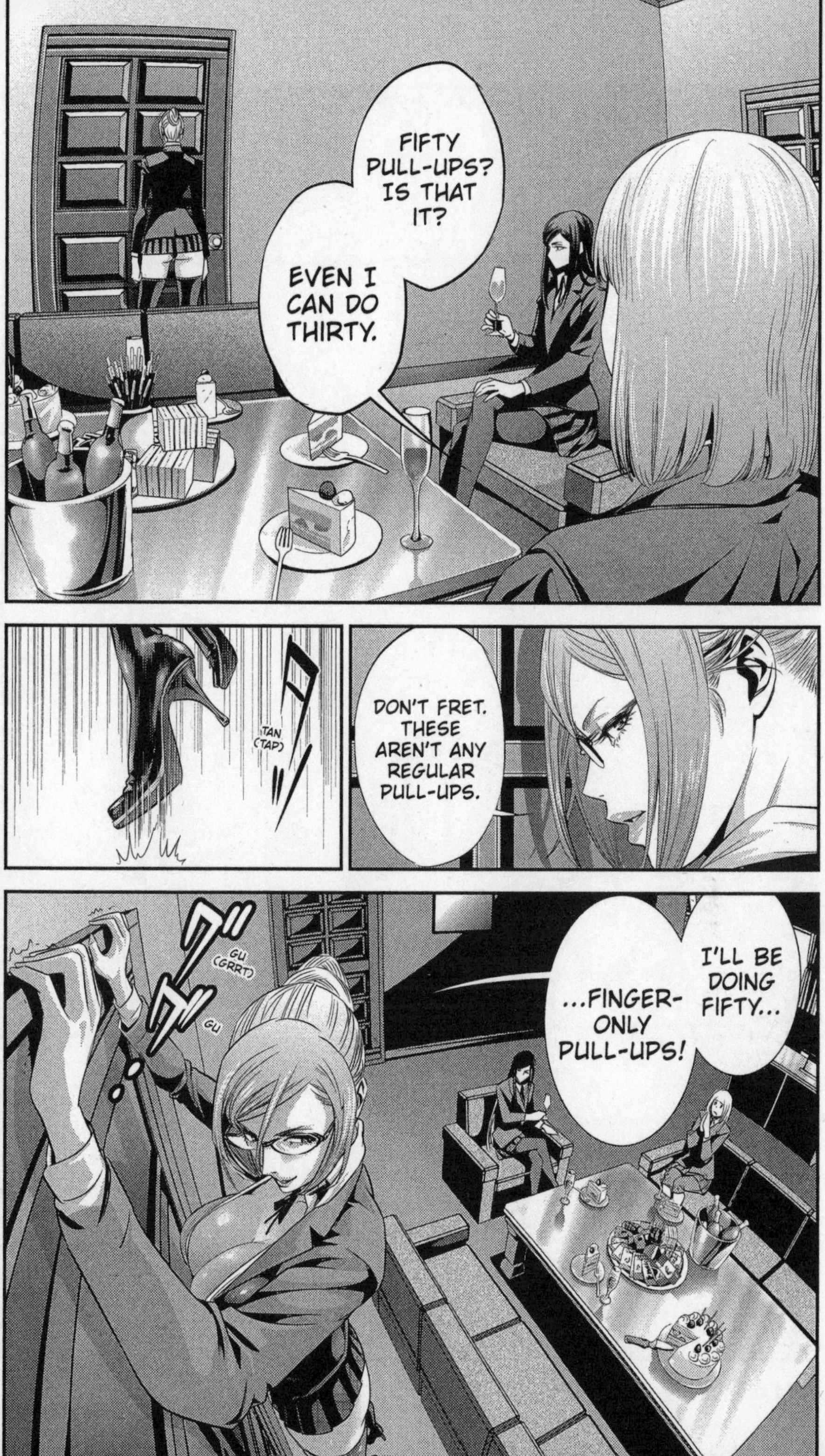
FIFTY PULL-UPS? IS THAT IT?
EVEN I CAN DO THIRTY.
DON'T FRET. THESE AREN'T ANY REGULAR PULL-UPS.
TAN (TAP)
I'LL BE DOING FIFTY...
...FINGER-ONLY PULL-UPS!
GU (GRRT)
GU

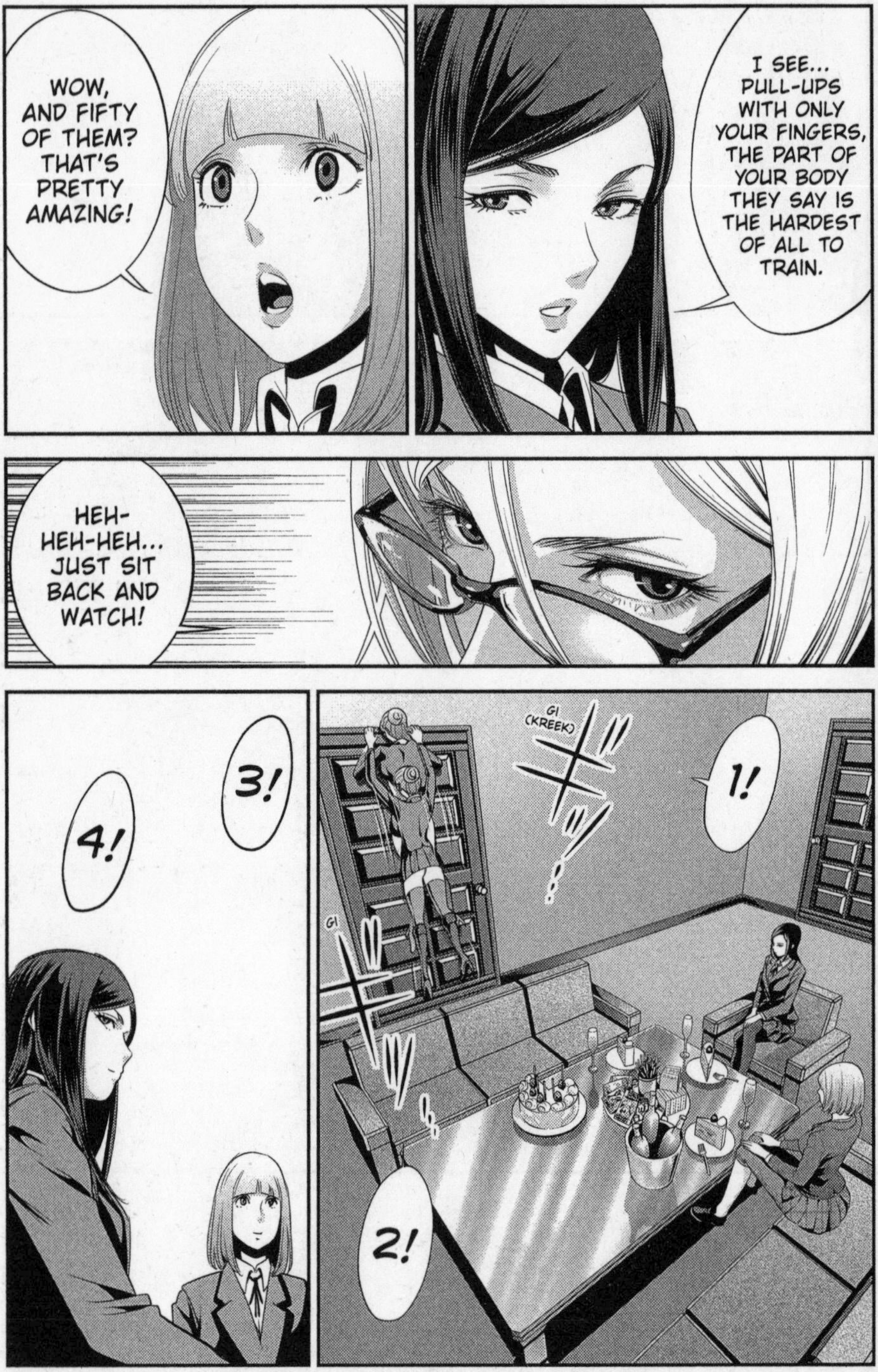
I SEE... PULL-UPS WITH ONLY YOUR FINGERS, THE PART OF YOUR BODY THEY SAY IS THE HARDEST OF ALL TO TRAIN.
WOW, AND FIFTY OF THEM? THAT'S PRETTY AMAZING!
HEH-HEH-HEH... JUST SIT BACK AND WATCH!
GI (KREEK)
1!
GI
2!
3!
4!

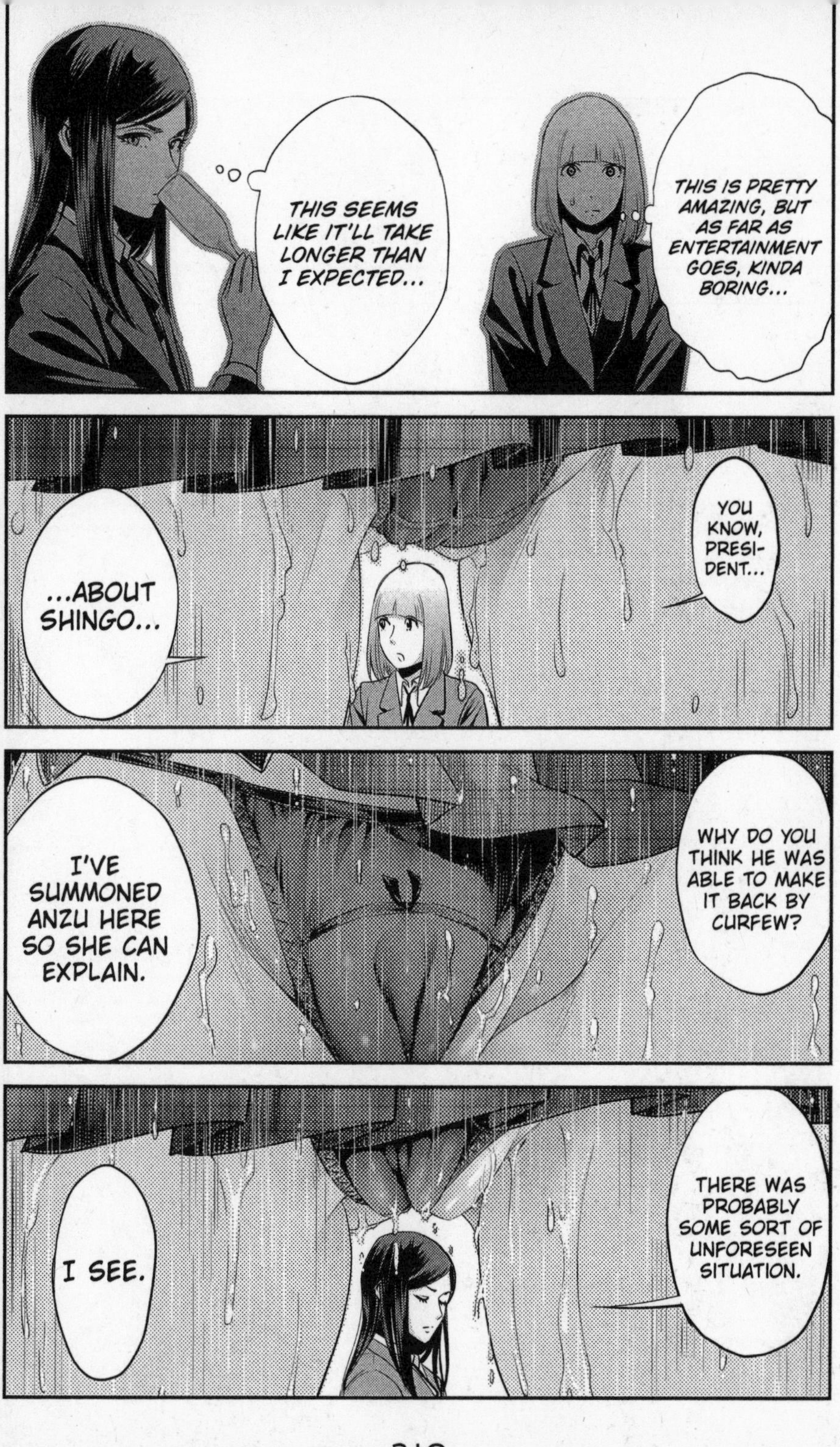
THIS IS PRETTY AMAZING, BUT AS FAR AS ENTERTAINMENT GOES, KINDA BORING...
THIS SEEMS LIKE IT'LL TAKE LONGER THAN I EXPECTED...
YOU KNOW, PRESI-DENT...
...ABOUT SHINGO...
WHY DO YOU THINK HE WAS ABLE TO MAKE IT BACK BY CURFEW?
I'VE SUMMONED ANZU HERE SO SHE CAN EXPLAIN.
THERE WAS PROBABLY SOME SORT OF UNFORESEEN SITUATION.
I SEE.

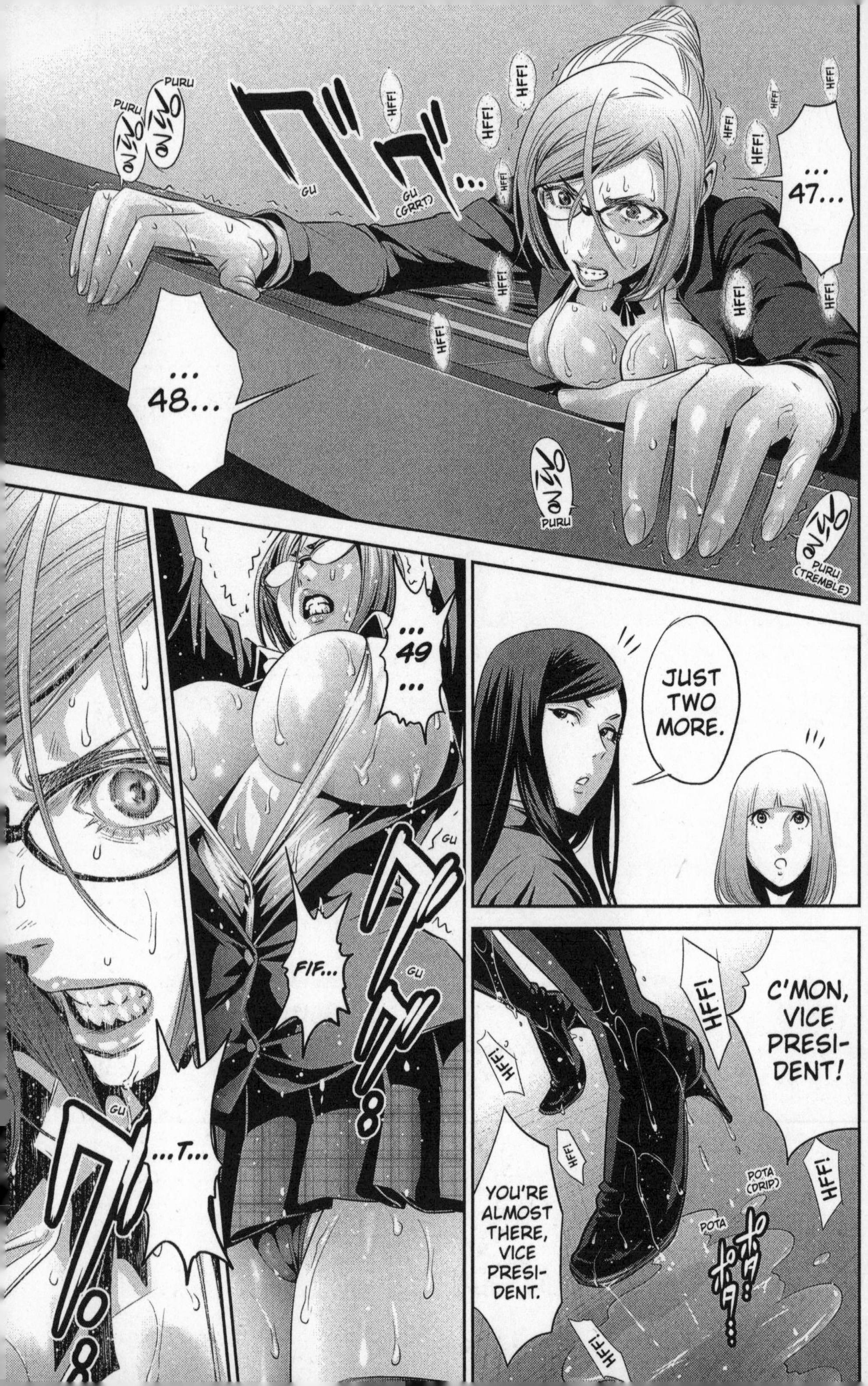
HFF!
HFF!
...
47...
HFF!
HFF!
HFF!
HFF!
GU
GU
(GRRT)
PURU
PURU
HFF!
HFF!
HFF!
...
48...
PURU
PURU
(TREMBLE)
JUST
TWO
MORE.
C'MON,
VICE
PRESI-
DENT!
HFF!
HFF!
HFF!
HFF!
YOU'RE
ALMOST
THERE,
VICE
PRESI-
DENT.
POTA
(DRIP)
POTA
HFF!
...
49
...
GU
FIF...
GU
GU
...T...

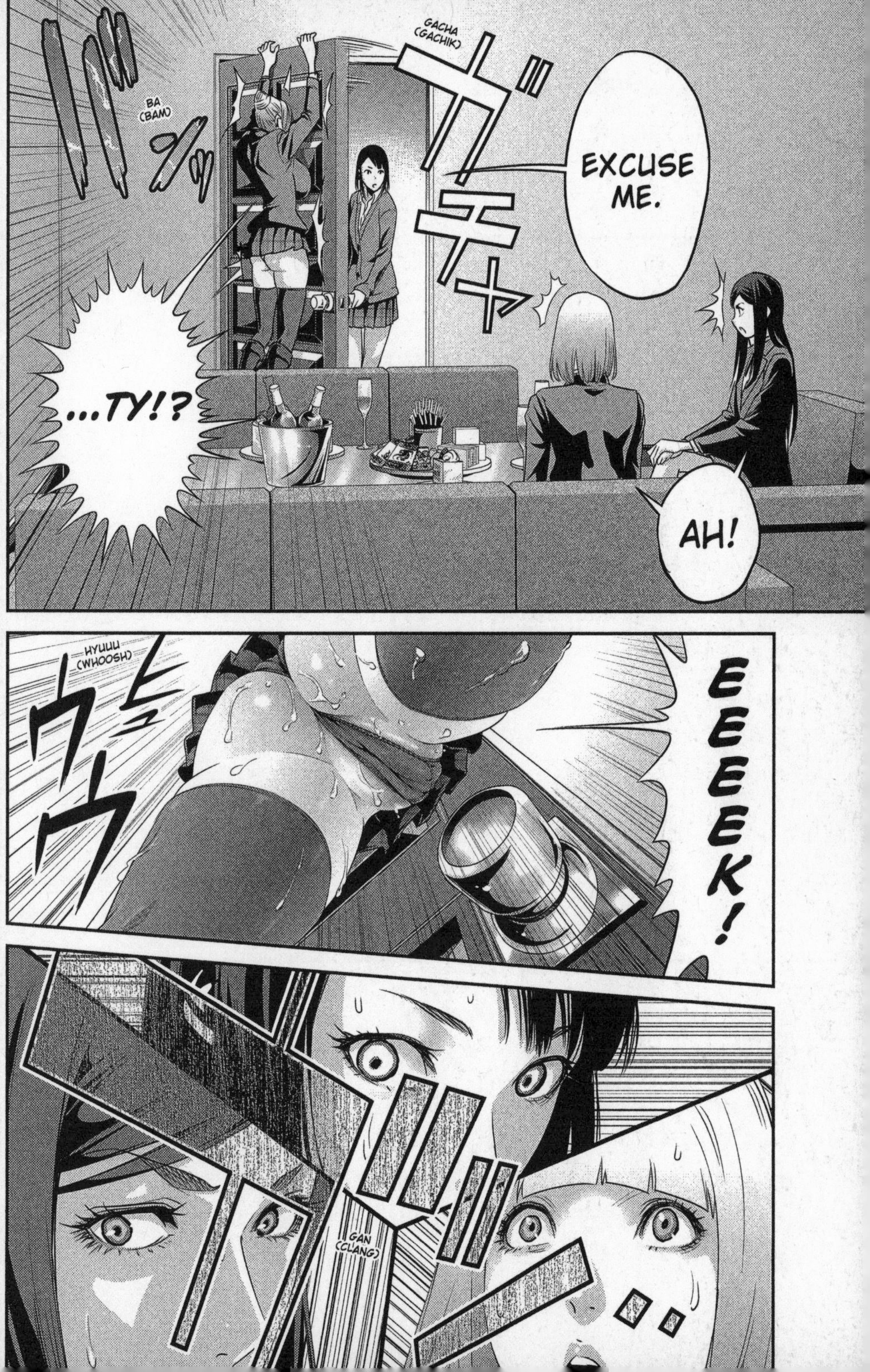
EXCUSE ME.
GACHA (GACHIK)
BA (BAM)
...TY!?
AH!
EEEEK!
HYUUU (WHOOSH)
GAN (CLANG)

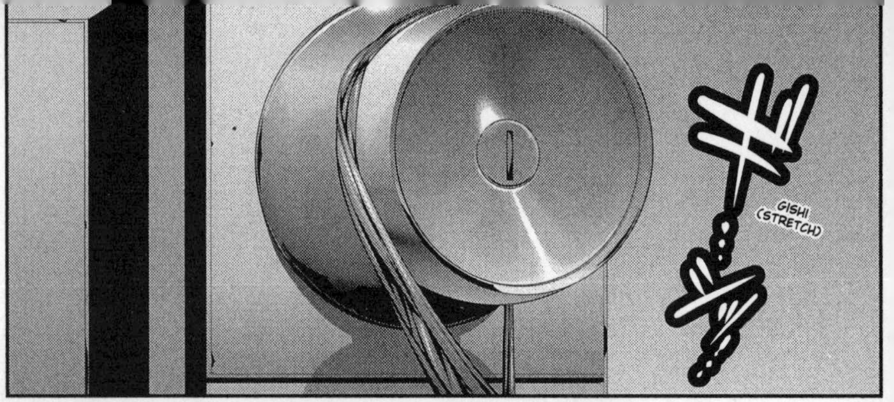
GISHI
(STRETCH)
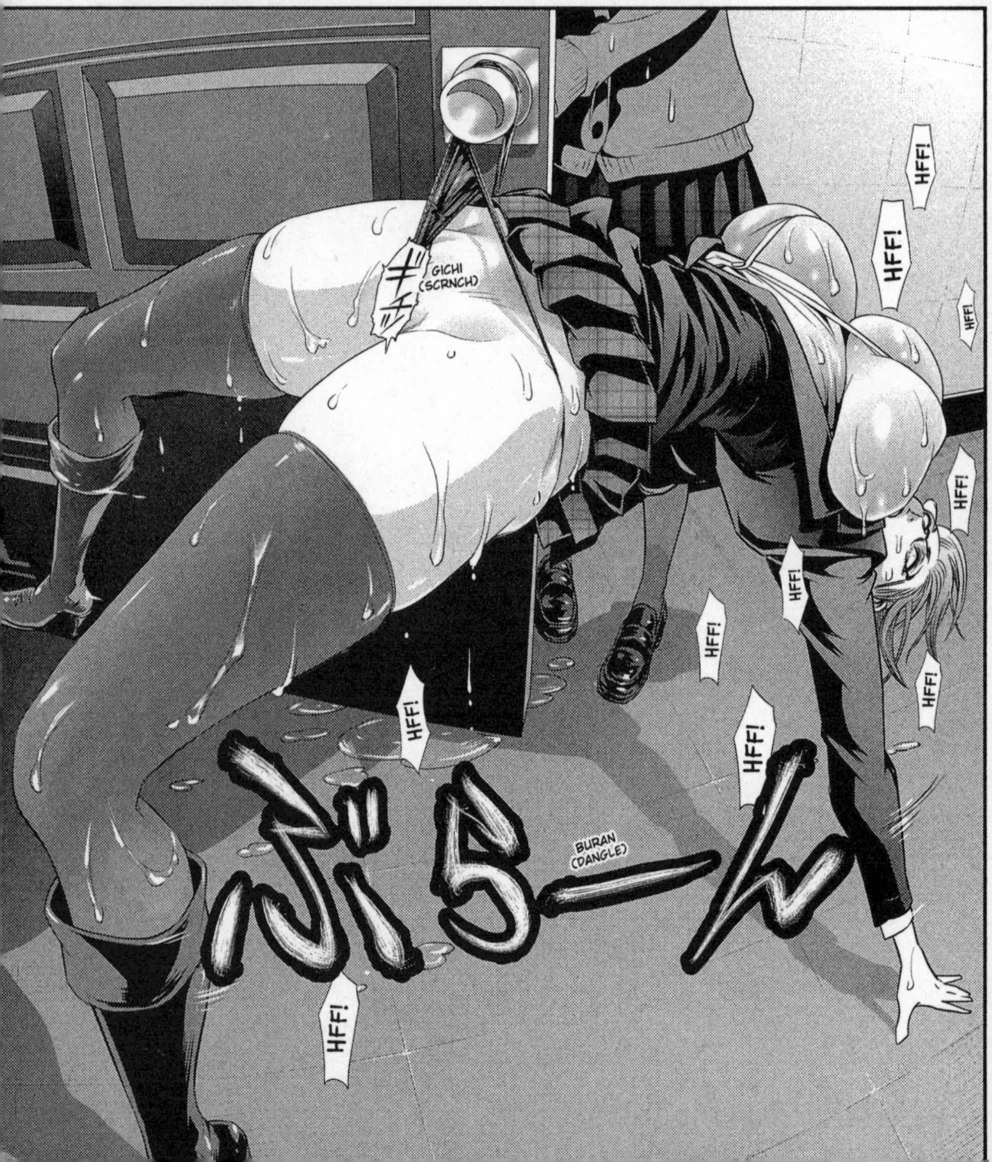
HFF!
HFF!
HFF!
GICHI
(SCRNCH)
HFF!
HFF!
HFF!
HFF!
HFF!
HFF!
BURAN
(DANGLE)
HFF!

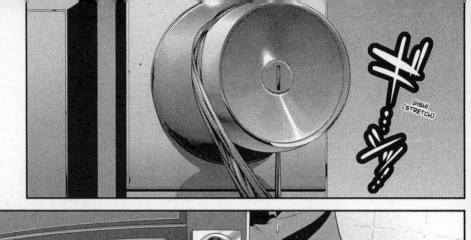

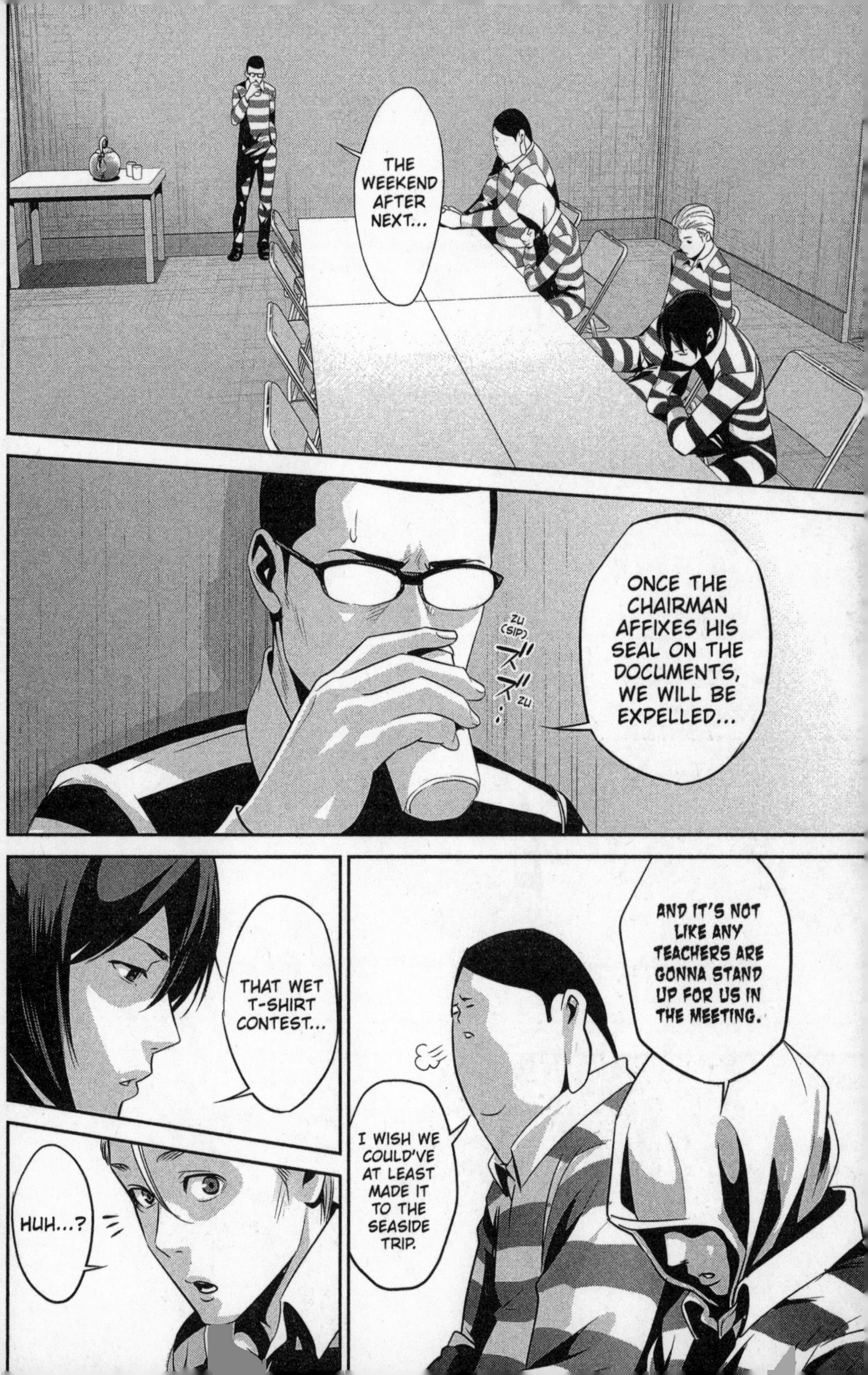
THE WEEKEND AFTER NEXT...
ZU (SIP) ZU
ONCE THE CHAIRMAN AFFIXES HIS SEAL ON THE DOCUMENTS, WE WILL BE EXPELLED...
AND IT'S NOT LIKE ANY TEACHERS ARE GONNA STAND UP FOR US IN THE MEETING.
I WISH WE COULD'VE AT LEAST MADE IT TO THE SEASIDE TRIP.
THAT WET T-SHIRT CONTEST...
HUH...?

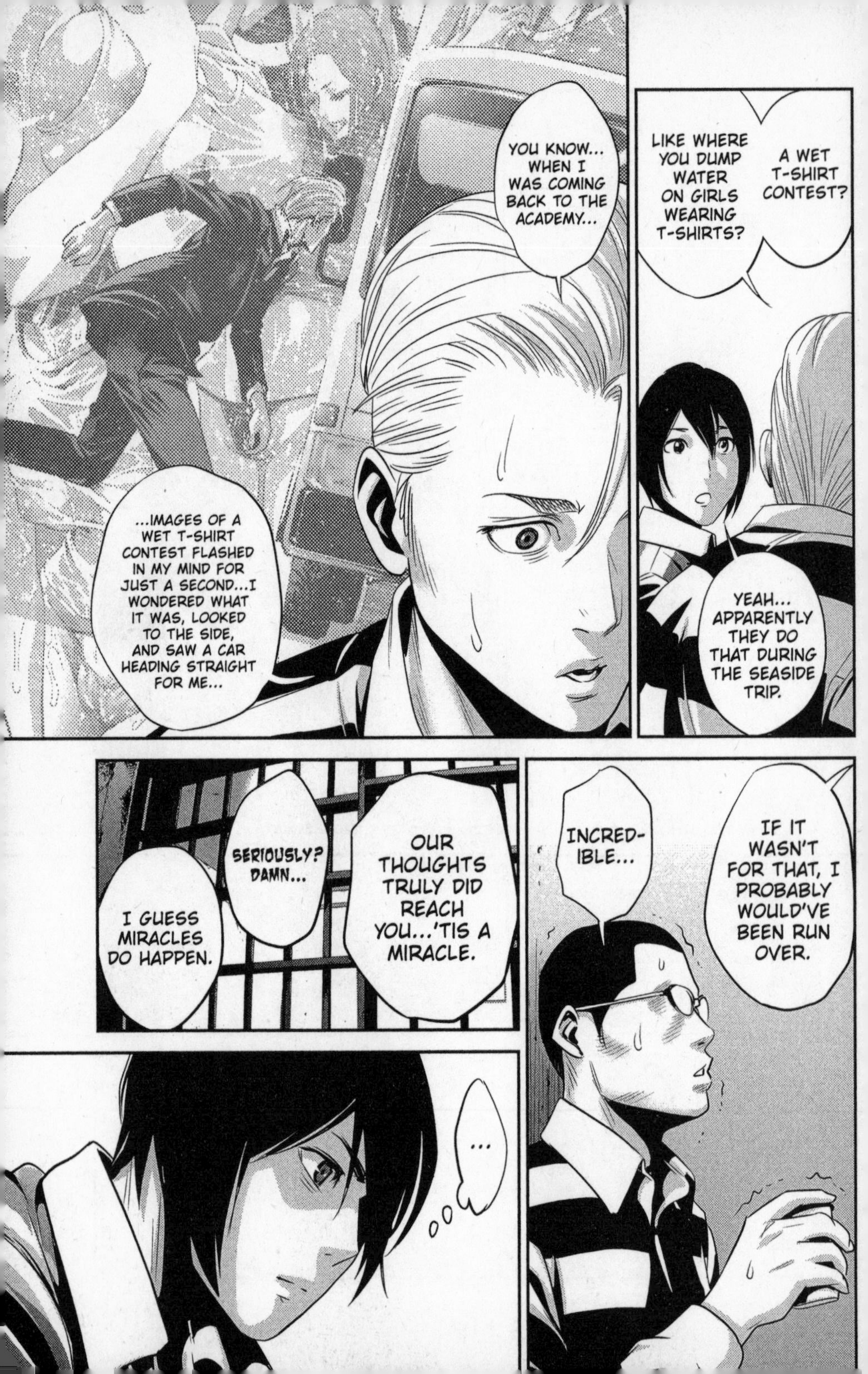
A WET T-SHIRT CONTEST?
LIKE WHERE YOU DUMP WATER ON GIRLS WEARING T-SHIRTS?
YEAH... APPARENTLY THEY DO THAT DURING THE SEASIDE TRIP.
YOU KNOW... WHEN I WAS COMING BACK TO THE ACADEMY...
...IMAGES OF A WET T-SHIRT CONTEST FLASHED IN MY MIND FOR JUST A SECOND...I WONDERED WHAT IT WAS, LOOKED TO THE SIDE, AND SAW A CAR HEADING STRAIGHT FOR ME...
IF IT WASN'T FOR THAT, I PROBABLY WOULD'VE BEEN RUN OVER.
INCRED-IBLE...
OUR THOUGHTS TRULY DID REACH YOU...'TIS A MIRACLE.
SERIOUSLY? DAMN...
I GUESS MIRACLES DO HAPPEN.
...

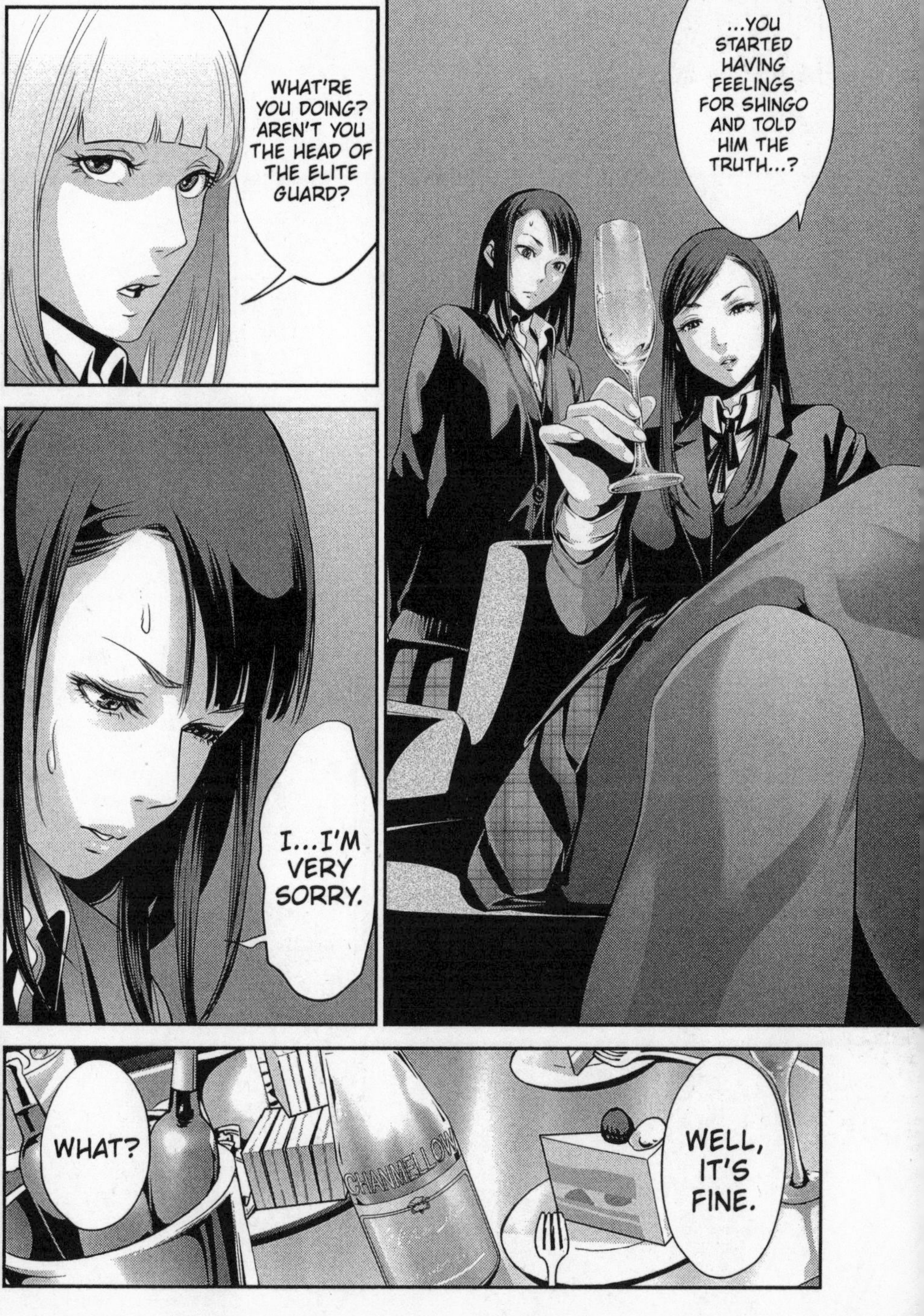
...YOU STARTED HAVING FEELINGS FOR SHINGO AND TOLD HIM THE TRUTH...?
WHAT'RE YOU DOING? AREN'T YOU THE HEAD OF THE ELITE GUARD?
I...I'M VERY SORRY.
WELL, IT'S FINE.
WHAT?
CHANNELLOW

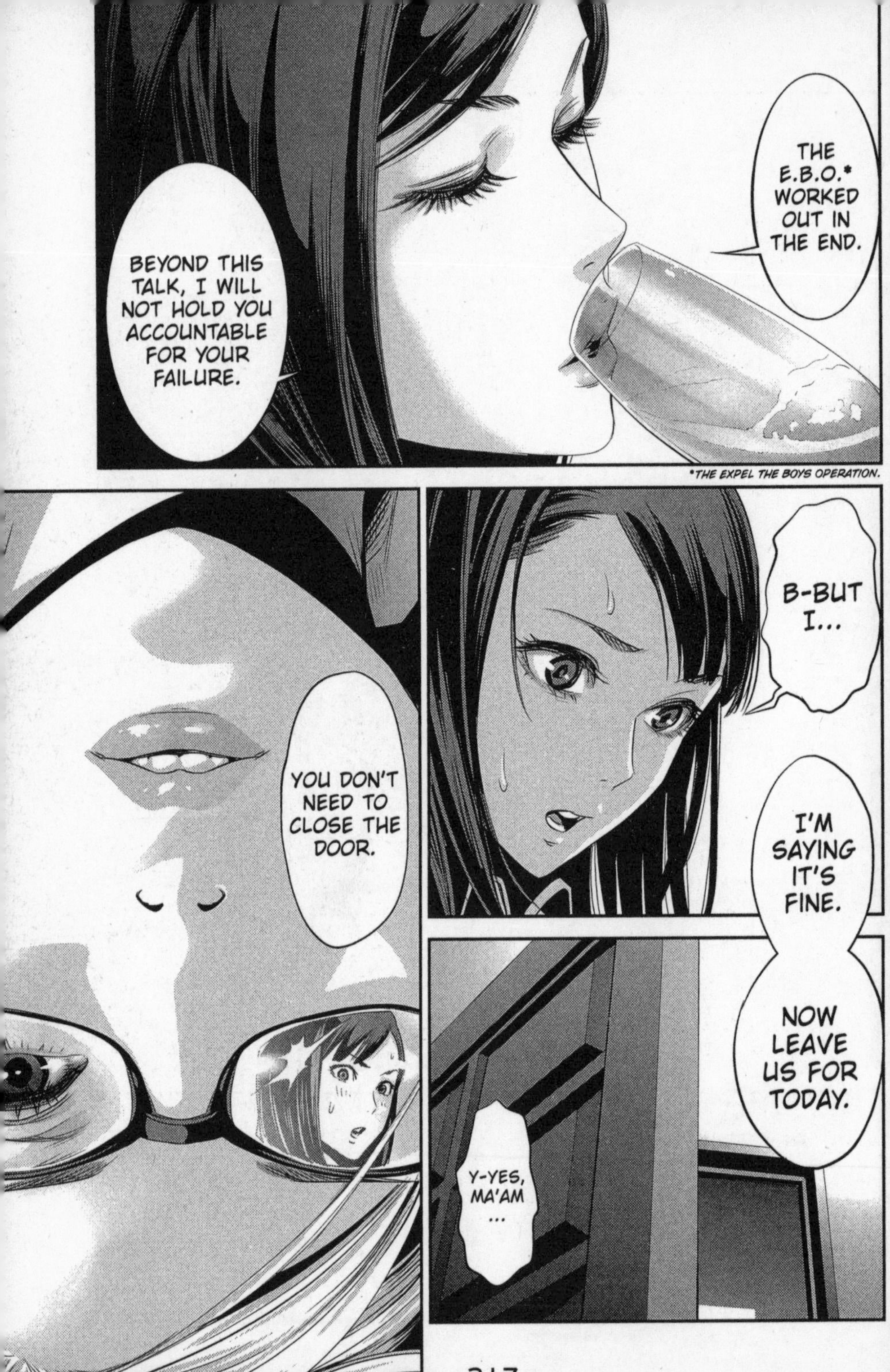
THE E.B.O.* WORKED OUT IN THE END.
BEYOND THIS TALK, I WILL NOT HOLD YOU ACCOUNTABLE FOR YOUR FAILURE.
*THE EXPEL THE BOYS OPERATION.
B-BUT I...
I'M SAYING IT'S FINE.
NOW LEAVE US FOR TODAY.
Y-YES, MA'AM ...
YOU DON'T NEED TO CLOSE THE DOOR.

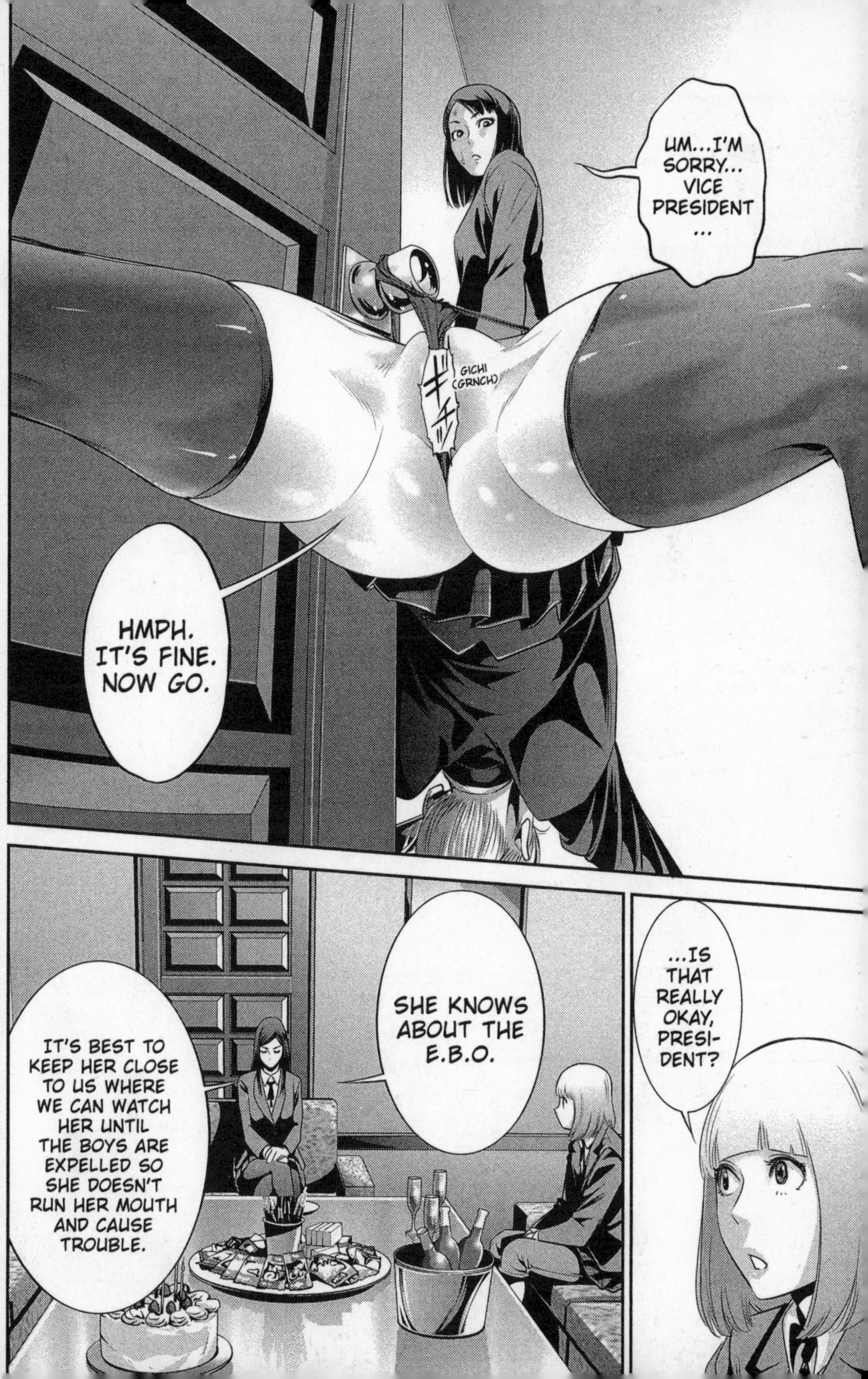
UM...I'M SORRY... VICE PRESIDENT ...
GICHI (GRNCH)
HMPH. IT'S FINE. NOW GO.
...IS THAT REALLY OKAY, PRESI-DENT?
SHE KNOWS ABOUT THE E.B.O.
IT'S BEST TO KEEP HER CLOSE TO US WHERE WE CAN WATCH HER UNTIL THE BOYS ARE EXPELLED SO SHE DOESN'T RUN HER MOUTH AND CAUSE TROUBLE.

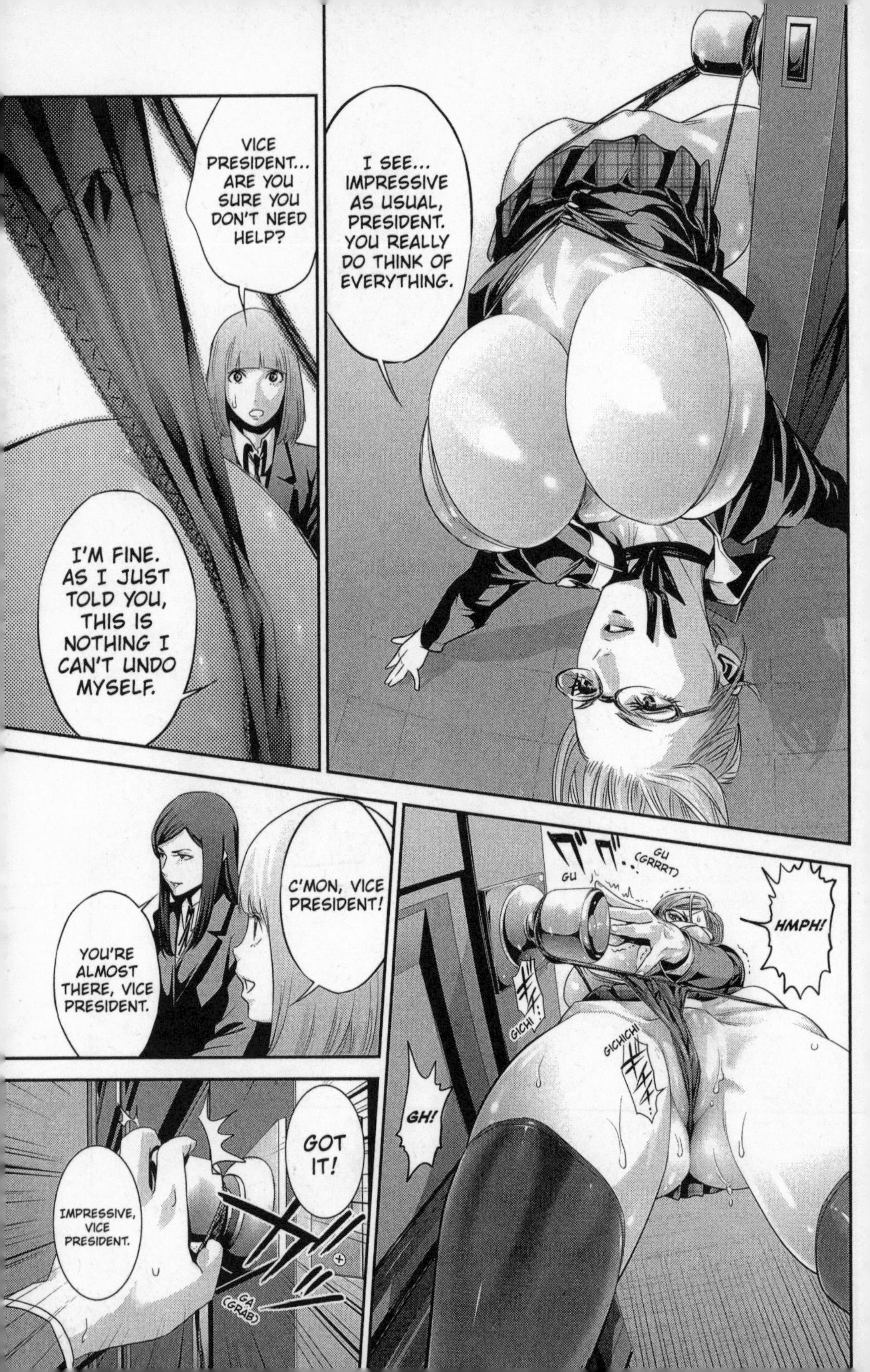
I SEE... IMPRESSIVE AS USUAL, PRESIDENT. YOU REALLY DO THINK OF EVERYTHING.
VICE PRESIDENT... ARE YOU SURE YOU DON'T NEED HELP?
I'M FINE. AS I JUST TOLD YOU, THIS IS NOTHING I CAN'T UNDO MYSELF.
GU GU (GRRRT)
HMPH!
GICHI
GICHICHI
GH!
C'MON, VICE PRESIDENT!
YOU'RE ALMOST THERE, VICE PRESIDENT.
GOT IT!
IMPRESSIVE, VICE PRESIDENT.
GA (GRAB)

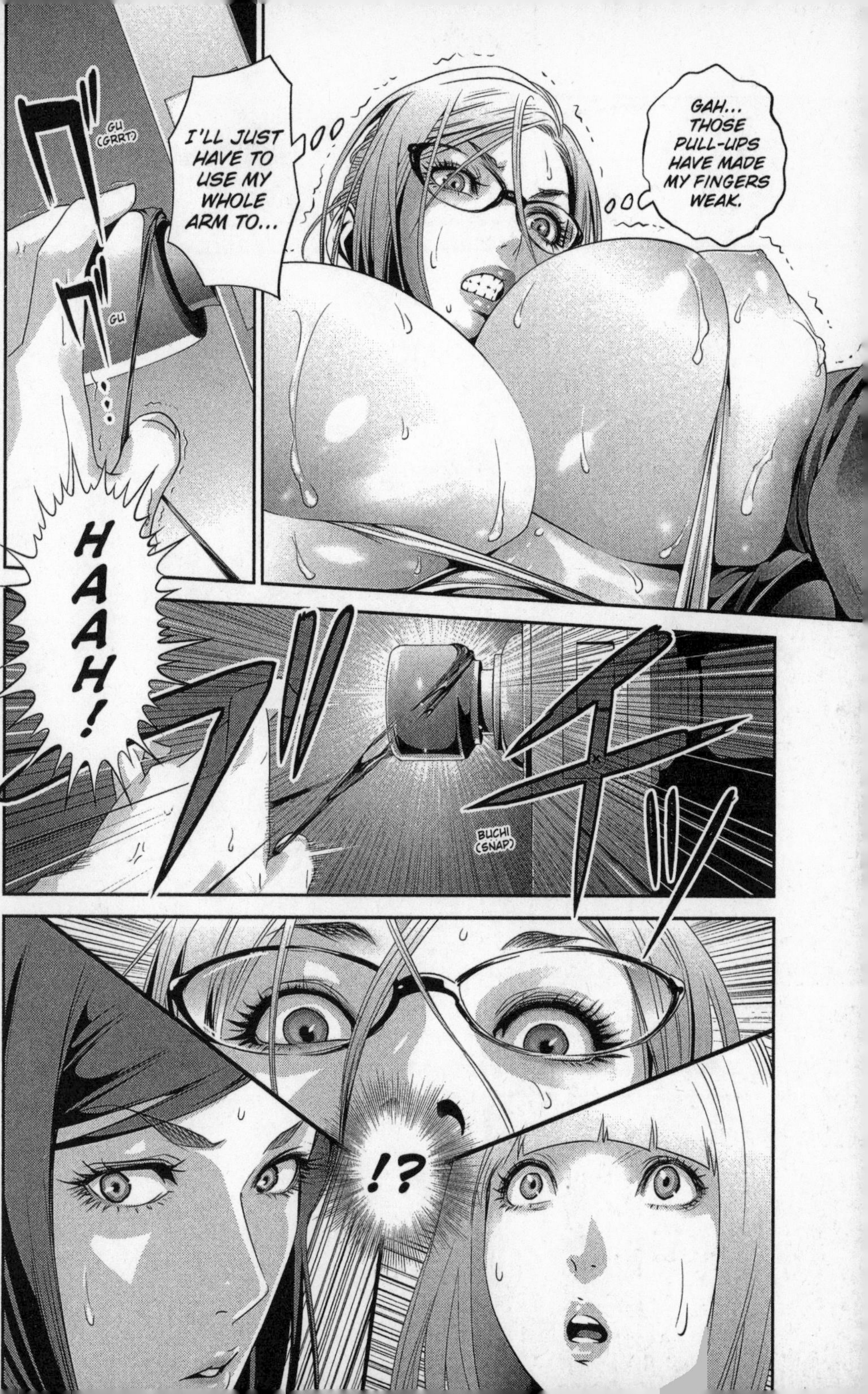
GAH... THOSE PULL-UPS HAVE MADE MY FINGERS WEAK.
I'LL JUST HAVE TO USE MY WHOLE ARM TO...
GU (GRRT)
GU
HAAAH!
BUCHI (SNAP)
!?

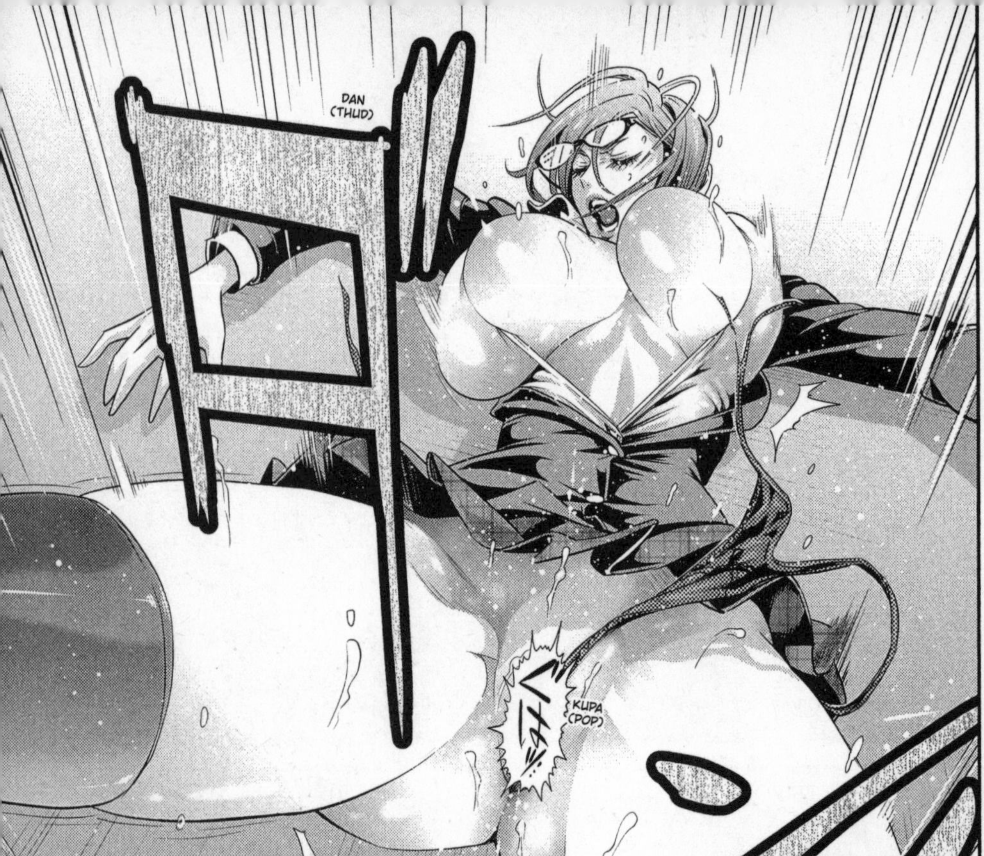
DAN
(THUD)
KUPA
(POP)

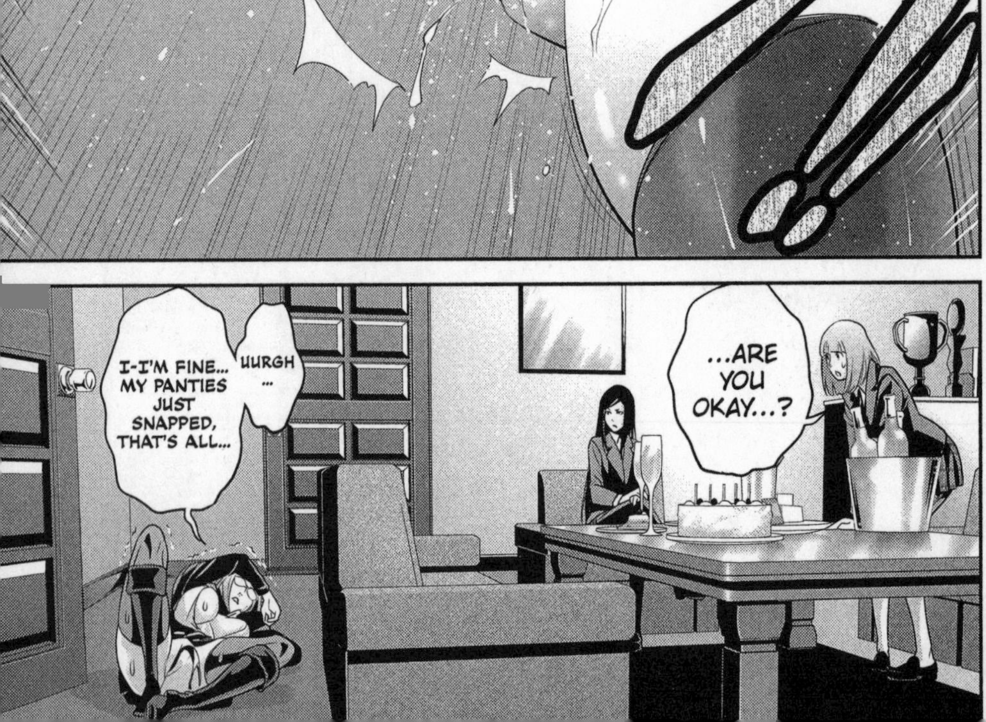
...ARE YOU OKAY...?
UURGH ...
I-I'M FINE... MY PANTIES JUST SNAPPED, THAT'S ALL...

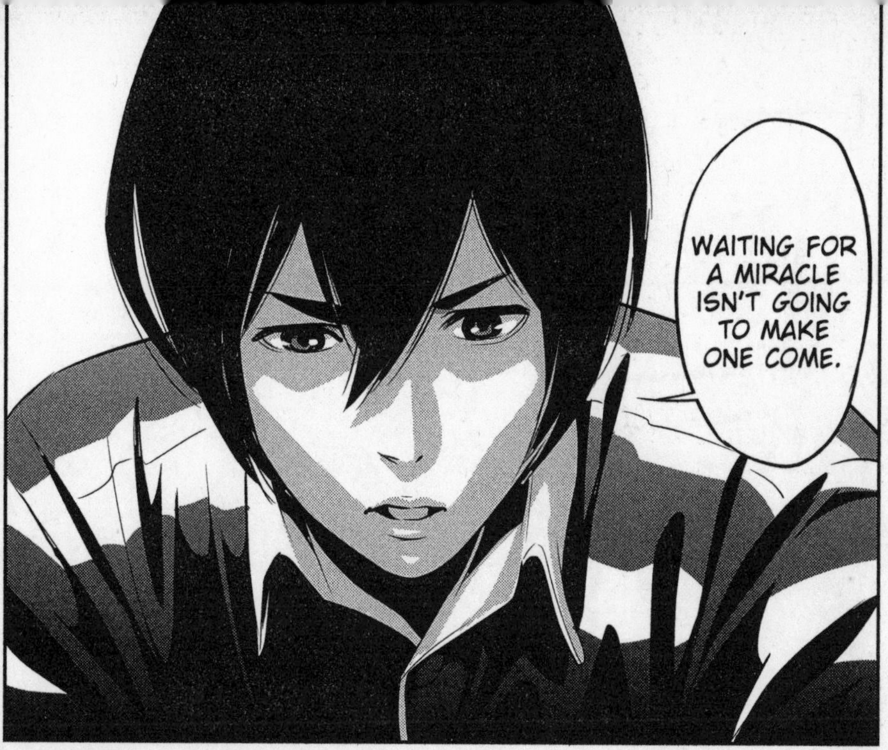
WAITING FOR A MIRACLE ISN'T GOING TO MAKE ONE COME.
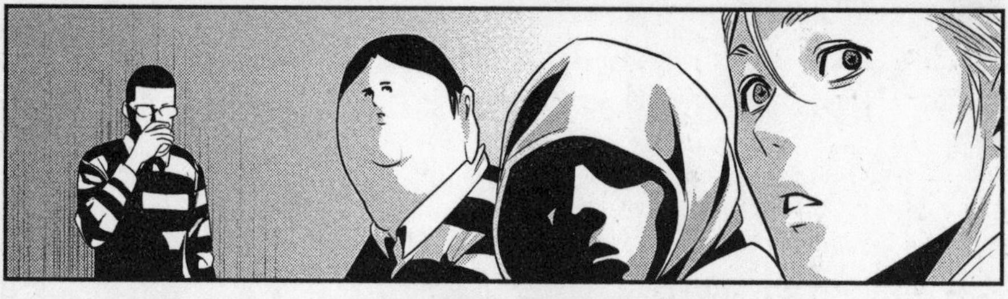
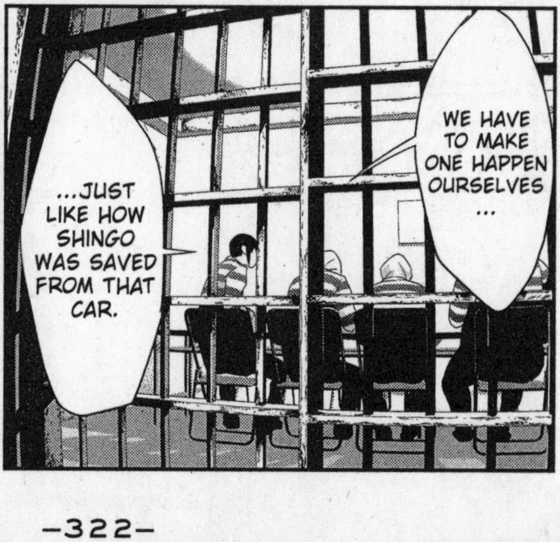
WE HAVE TO MAKE ONE HAPPEN OURSELVES ...
...JUST LIKE HOW SHINGO WAS SAVED FROM THAT CAR.
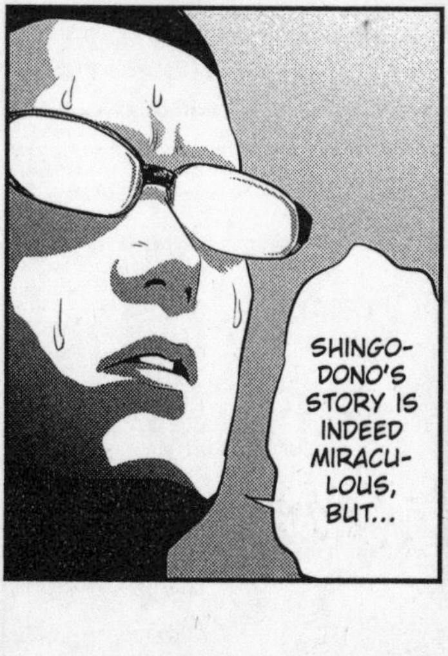
SHINGO-DONO'S STORY IS INDEED MIRACULOUS, BUT...

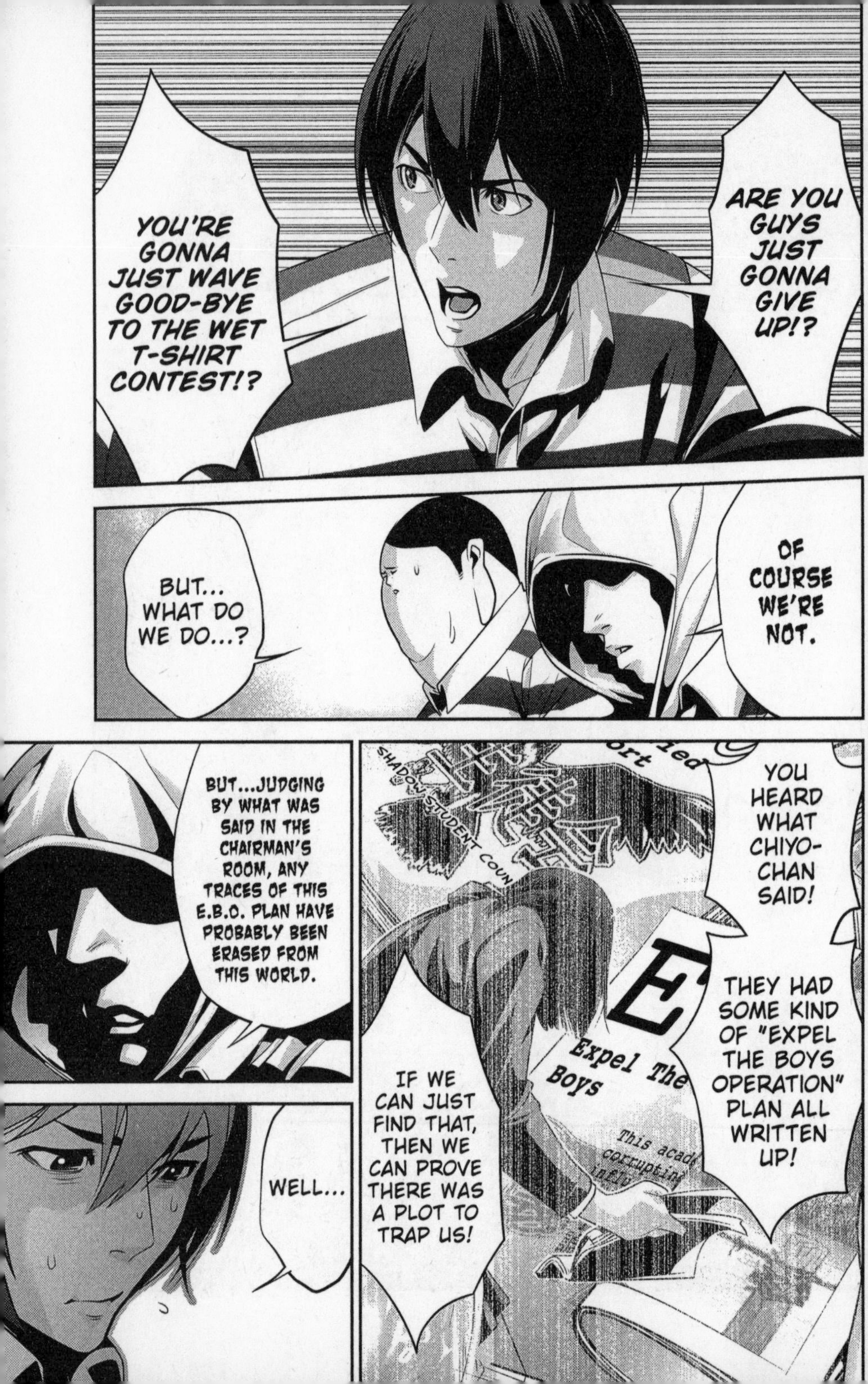
ARE YOU GUYS JUST GONNA GIVE UP!?
YOU'RE GONNA JUST WAVE GOOD-BYE TO THE WET T-SHIRT CONTEST!?
OF COURSE WE'RE NOT.
BUT... WHAT DO WE DO...?
YOU HEARD WHAT CHIYO-CHAN SAID!
SHADOW STUDENT COUN
E
Expel The Boys
THEY HAD SOME KIND OF "EXPEL THE BOYS OPERATION" PLAN ALL WRITTEN UP!
IF WE CAN JUST FIND THAT, THEN WE CAN PROVE THERE WAS A PLOT TO TRAP US!
BUT...JUDGING BY WHAT WAS SAID IN THE CHAIRMAN'S ROOM, ANY TRACES OF THIS E.B.O. PLAN HAVE PROBABLY BEEN ERASED FROM THIS WORLD.
WELL...

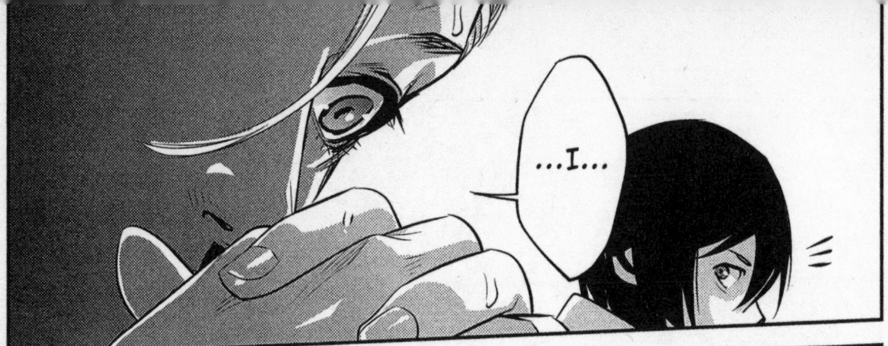
...I...

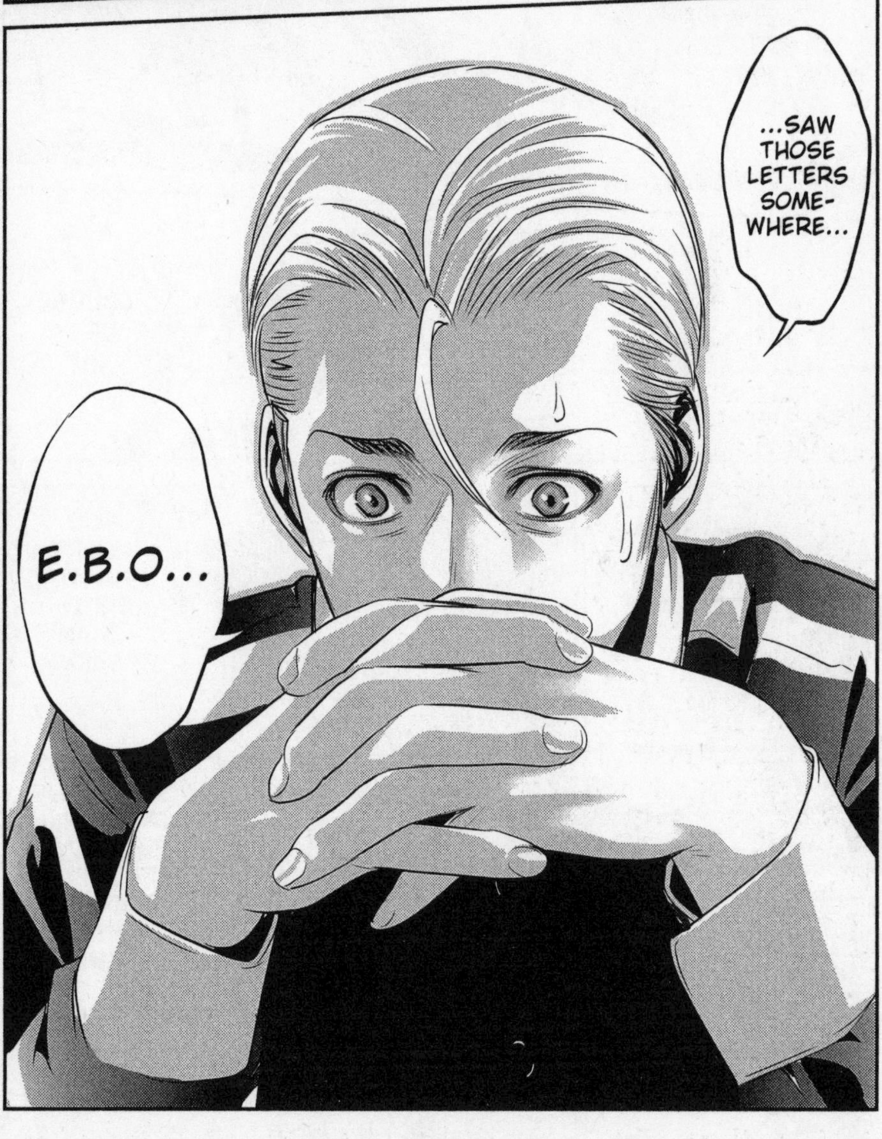
...SAW THOSE LETTERS SOME-WHERE...
E.B.O...

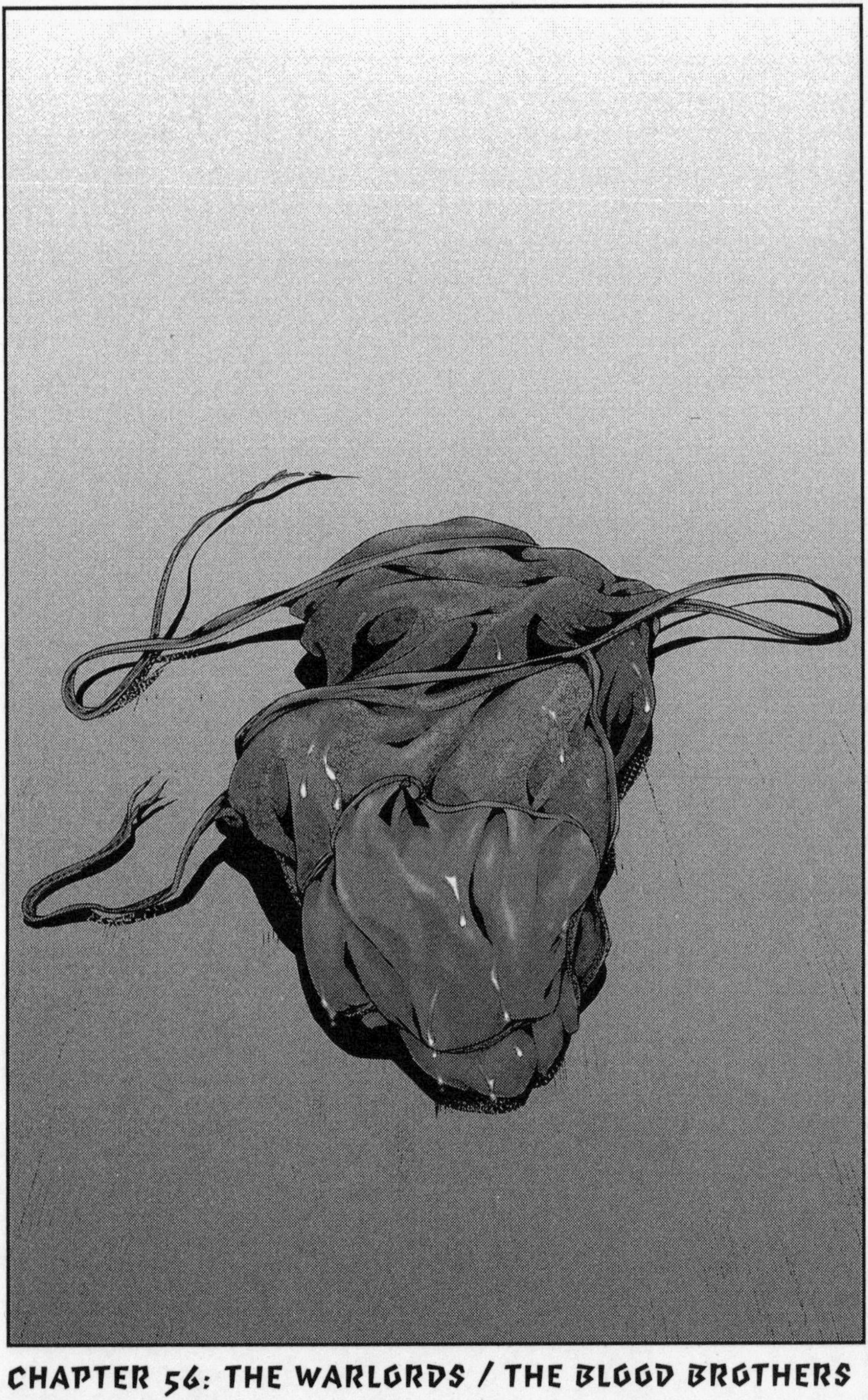

CHAPTER 56: THE WARLORDS / THE BLOOD BROTHERS

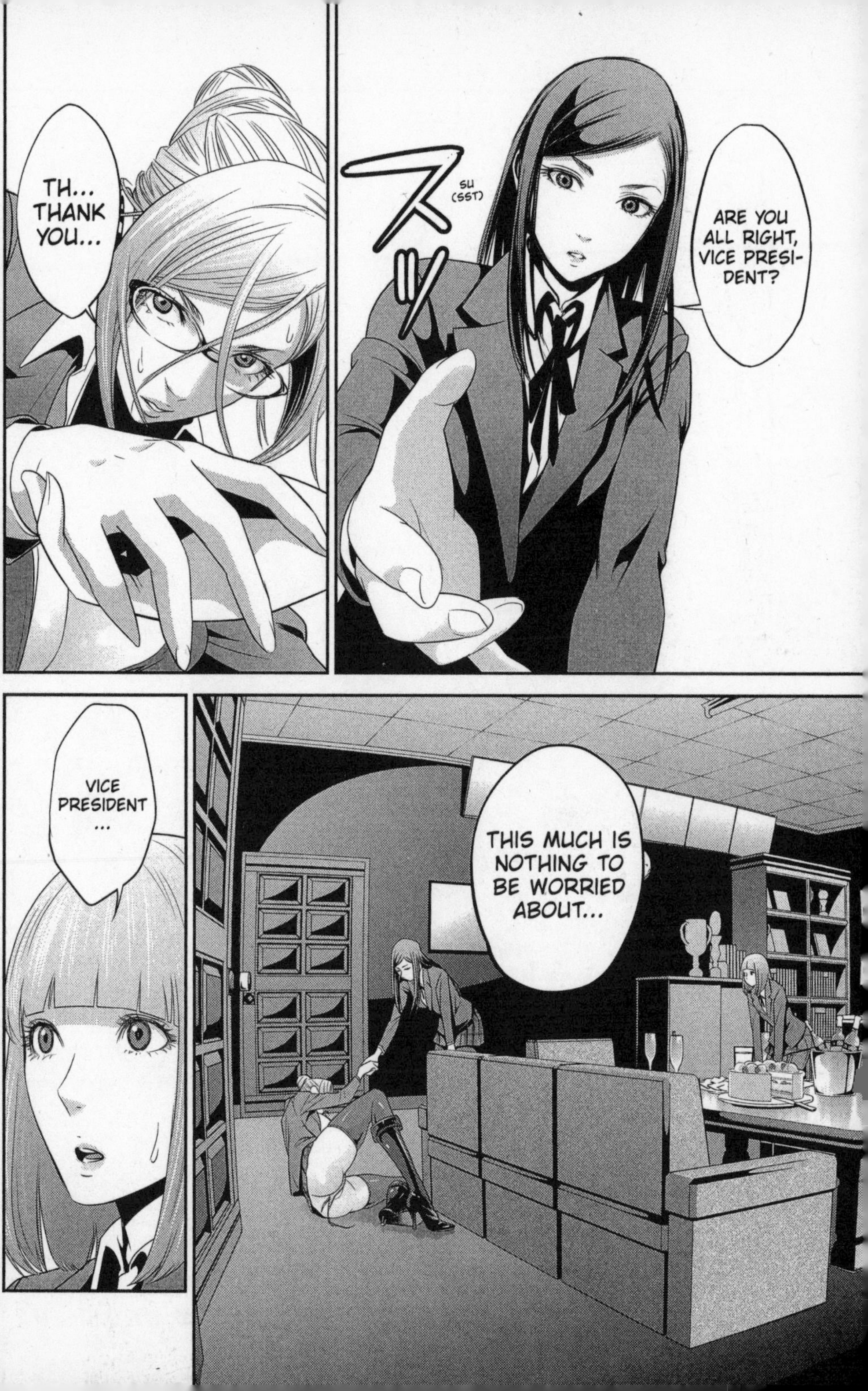
SU (SST)
ARE YOU ALL RIGHT, VICE PRESIDENT?
TH... THANK YOU...
THIS MUCH IS NOTHING TO BE WORRIED ABOUT...
VICE PRESIDENT ...

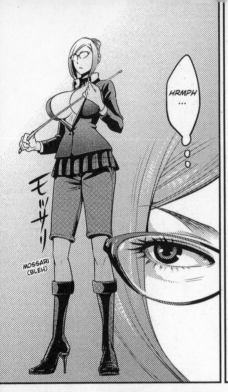

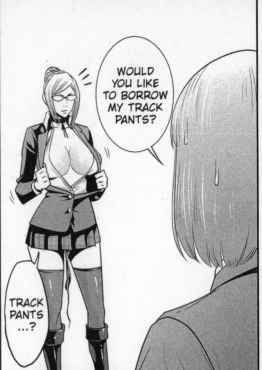

WOULD YOU LIKE TO BORROW MY TRACK PANTS?
TRACK PANTS ...?
HRMPH ...
MOSSARI (BLEH)
NO, BUT THANK YOU FOR THE OFFER.
REALLY ...?
I HAVE MY REGULAR ROUTINE TO GET TO.
GOSO (RUSTLE)
I'LL BE TAKING MY LEAVE HERE.

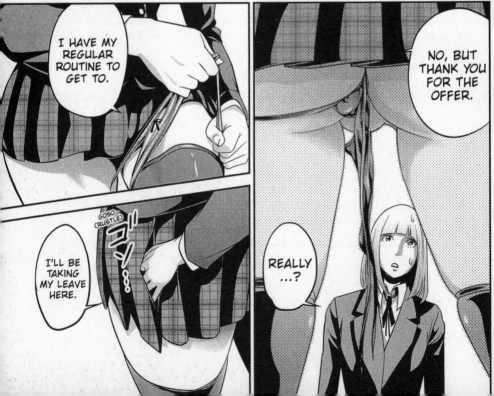

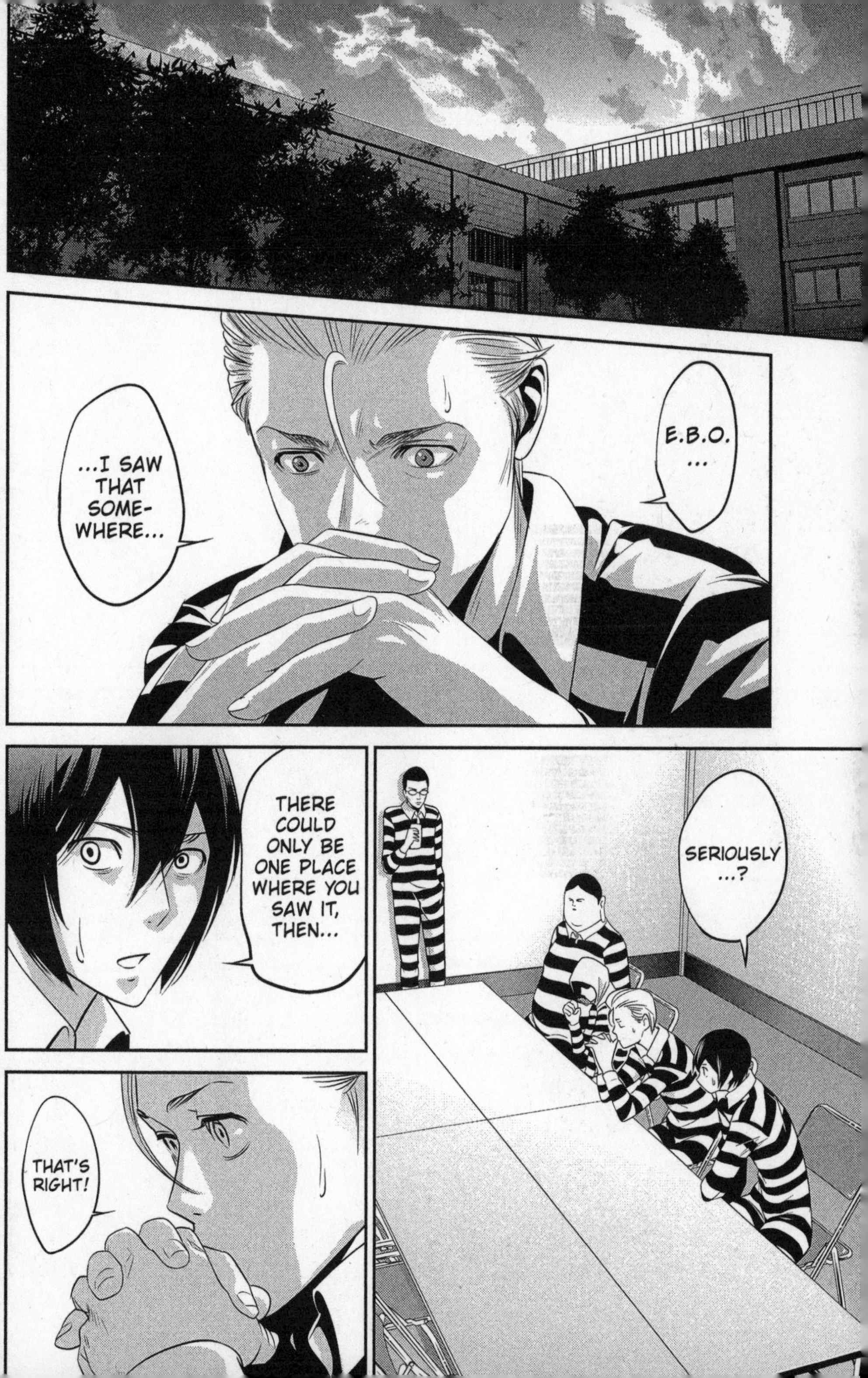
E.B.O. ...
...I SAW THAT SOME-WHERE...
SERIOUSLY ...?
THERE COULD ONLY BE ONE PLACE WHERE YOU SAW IT, THEN...
THAT'S RIGHT!

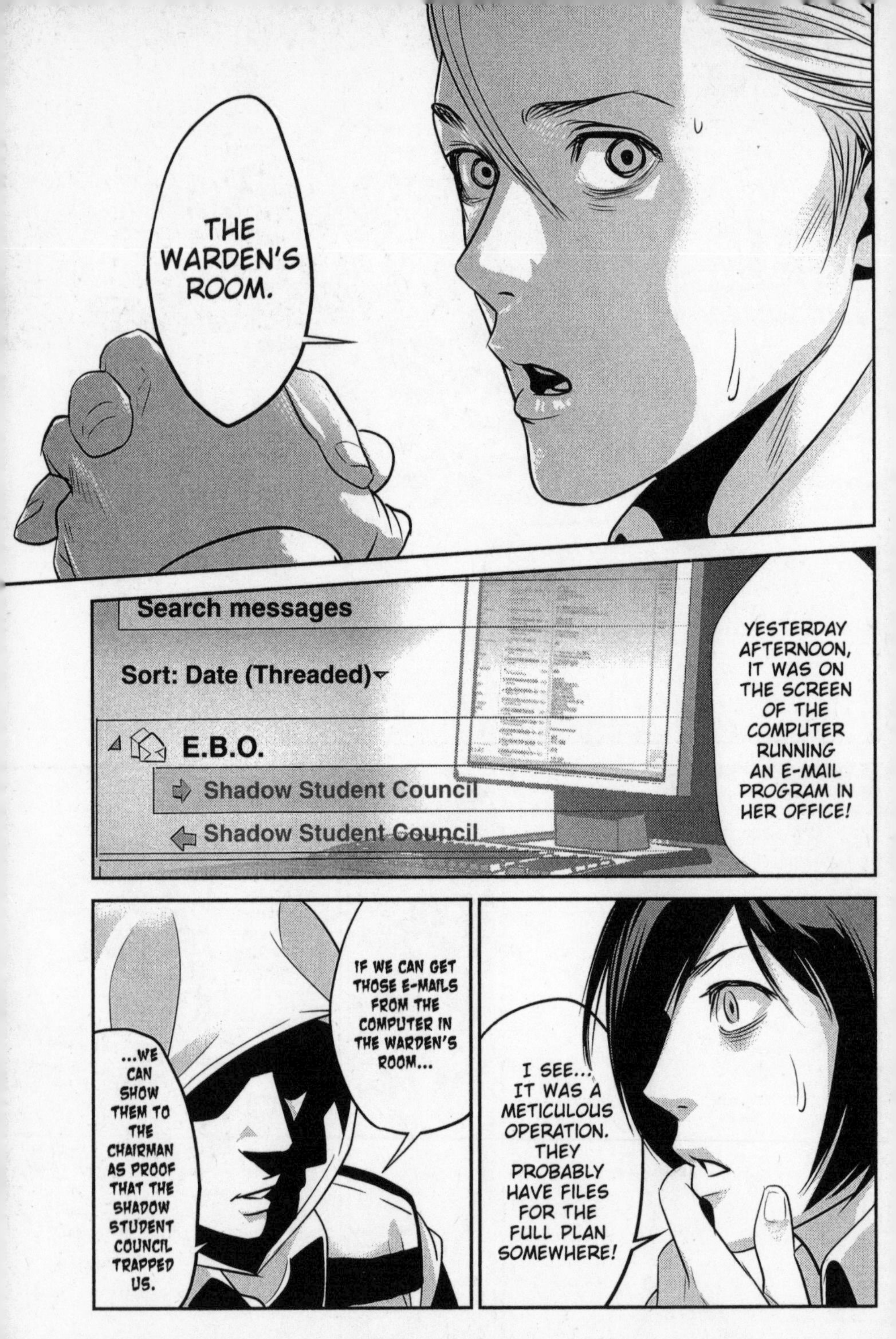
THE WARDEN'S ROOM.
YESTERDAY AFTERNOON, IT WAS ON THE SCREEN OF THE COMPUTER RUNNING AN E-MAIL PROGRAM IN HER OFFICE!
Search messages
Sort: Date (Threaded)
E.B.O.
Shadow Student Council
Shadow Student Council
I SEE... IT WAS A METICULOUS OPERATION. THEY PROBABLY HAVE FILES FOR THE FULL PLAN SOMEWHERE!
IF WE CAN GET THOSE E-MAILS FROM THE COMPUTER IN THE WARDEN'S ROOM...
...WE CAN SHOW THEM TO THE CHAIRMAN AS PROOF THAT THE SHADOW STUDENT COUNCIL TRAPPED US.

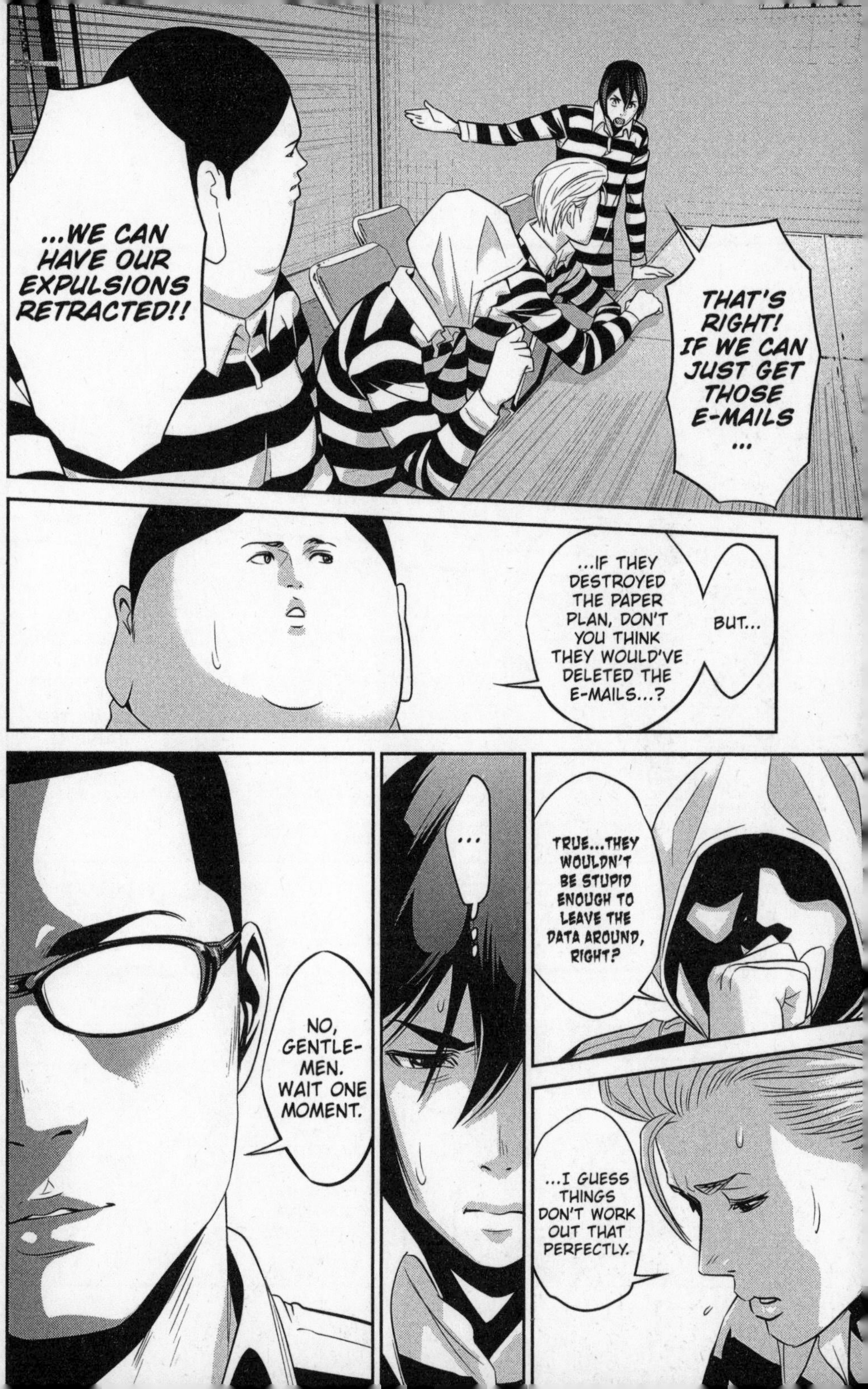
THAT'S RIGHT! IF WE CAN JUST GET THOSE E-MAILS ...
...WE CAN HAVE OUR EXPULSIONS RETRACTED!!
BUT...
...IF THEY DESTROYED THE PAPER PLAN, DON'T YOU THINK THEY WOULD'VE DELETED THE E-MAILS...?
TRUE...THEY WOULDN'T BE STUPID ENOUGH TO LEAVE THE DATA AROUND, RIGHT?
...I GUESS THINGS DON'T WORK OUT THAT PERFECTLY.
...
NO, GENTLE-MEN. WAIT ONE MOMENT.

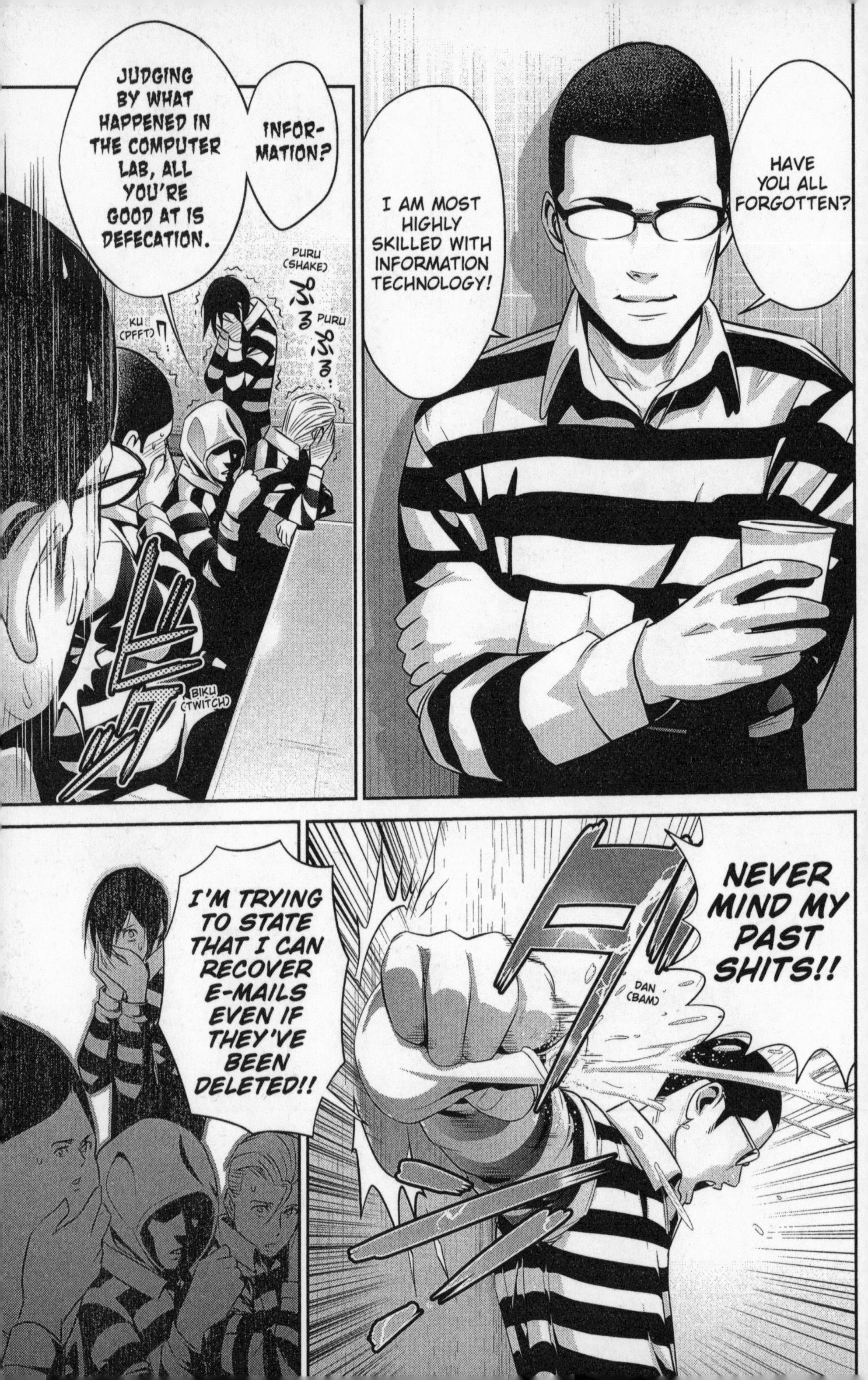
HAVE YOU ALL FORGOTTEN?
I AM MOST HIGHLY SKILLED WITH INFORMATION TECHNOLOGY!
INFOR-MATION?
JUDGING BY WHAT HAPPENED IN THE COMPUTER LAB, ALL YOU'RE GOOD AT IS DEFECATION.
PURU (SHAKE)
ぷる
PURU
ぷる
KU (PFFT)
BIKU (TWITCH)
NEVER MIND MY PAST SHITS!!
DAN (BAM)
I'M TRYING TO STATE THAT I CAN RECOVER E-MAILS EVEN IF THEY'VE BEEN DELETED!!

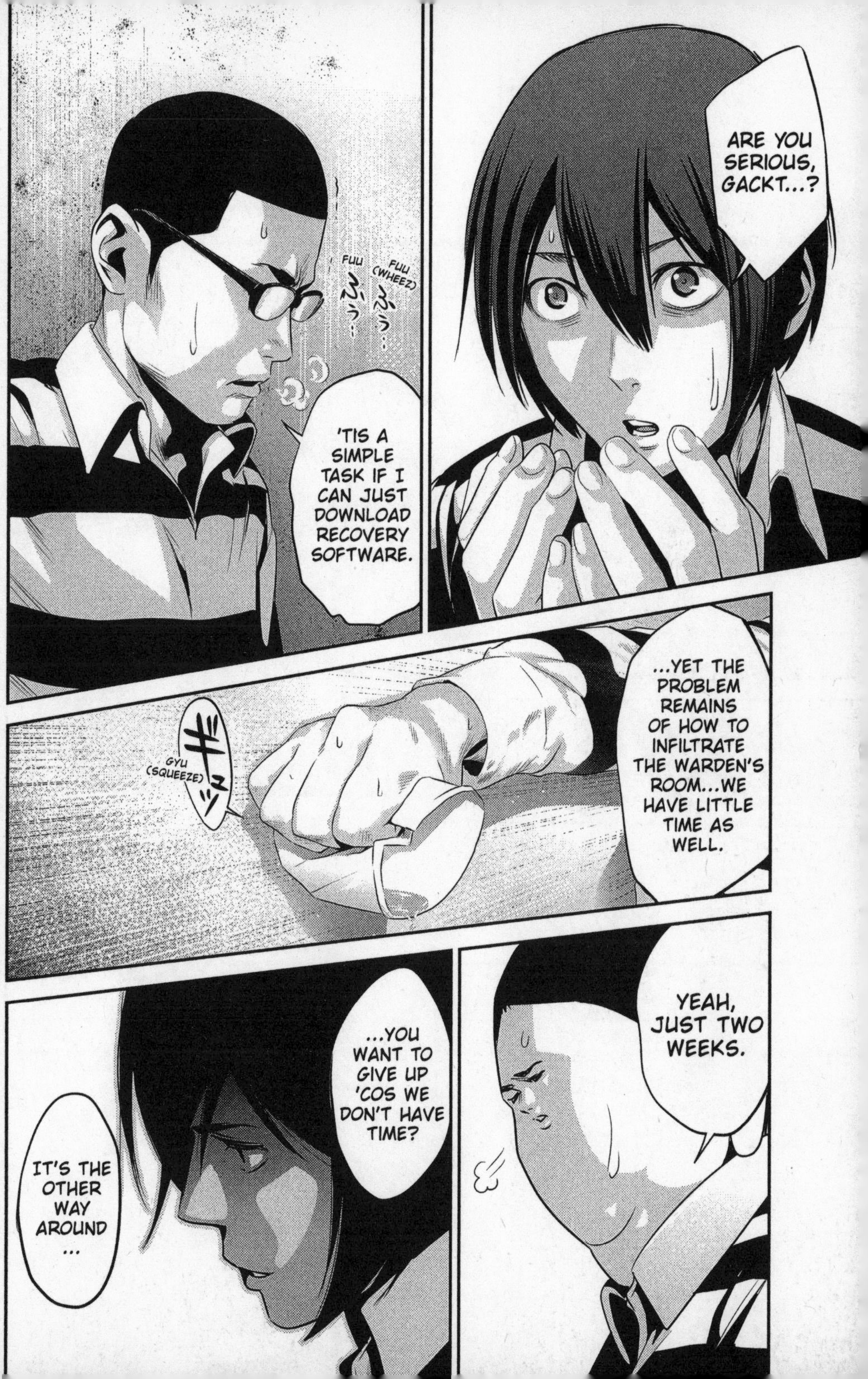
ARE YOU SERIOUS, GACKT...?
FUU FUU (WHEEZ)
'TIS A SIMPLE TASK IF I CAN JUST DOWNLOAD RECOVERY SOFTWARE.
...YET THE PROBLEM REMAINS OF HOW TO INFILTRATE THE WARDEN'S ROOM...WE HAVE LITTLE TIME AS WELL.
GYU (SQUEEZE)
YEAH, JUST TWO WEEKS.
...YOU WANT TO GIVE UP 'COS WE DON'T HAVE TIME?
IT'S THE OTHER WAY AROUND ...

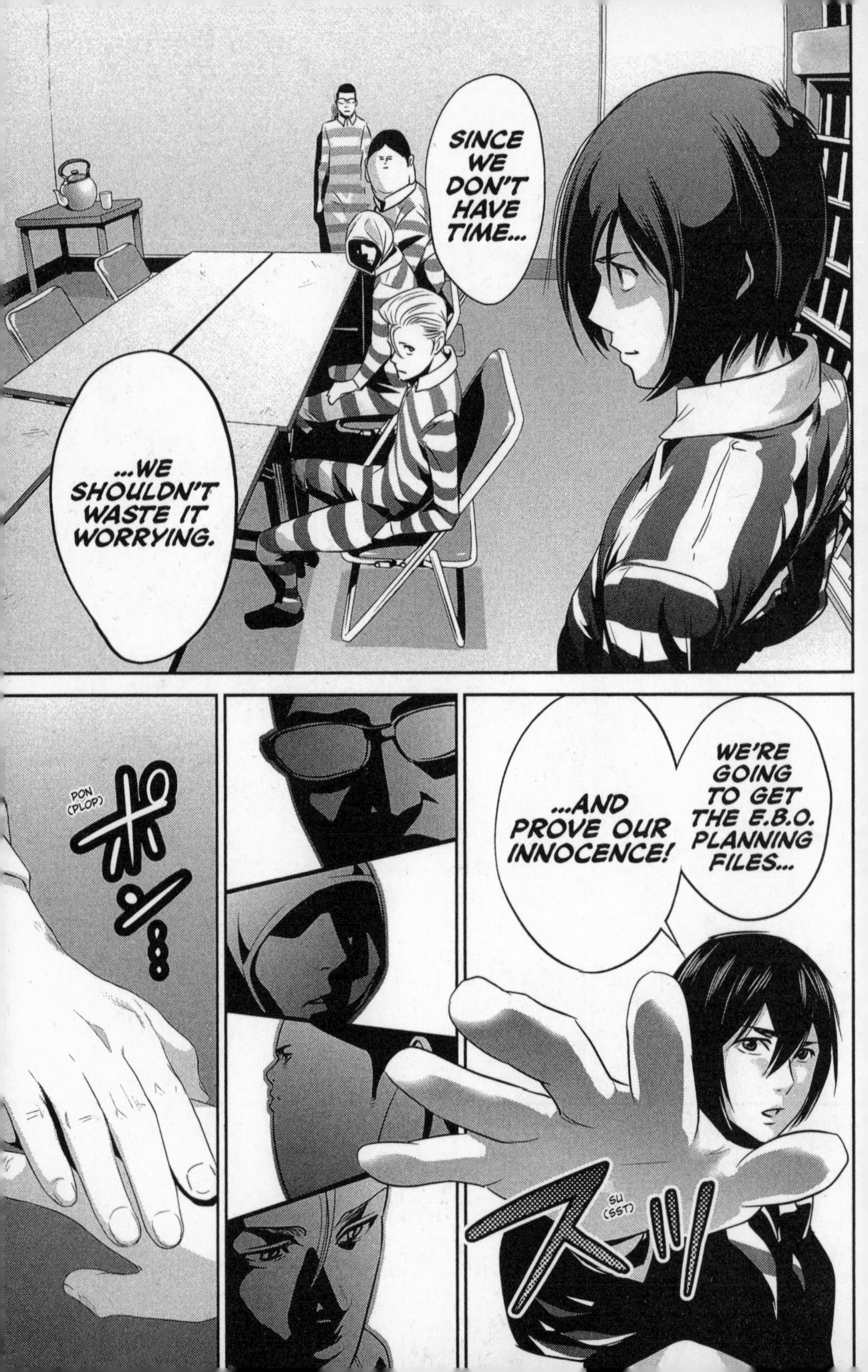
SINCE WE DON'T HAVE TIME...
...WE SHOULDN'T WASTE IT WORRYING.
WE'RE GOING TO GET THE E.B.O. PLANNING FILES...
...AND PROVE OUR INNOCENCE!
SU (SST)
PON (PLOP)

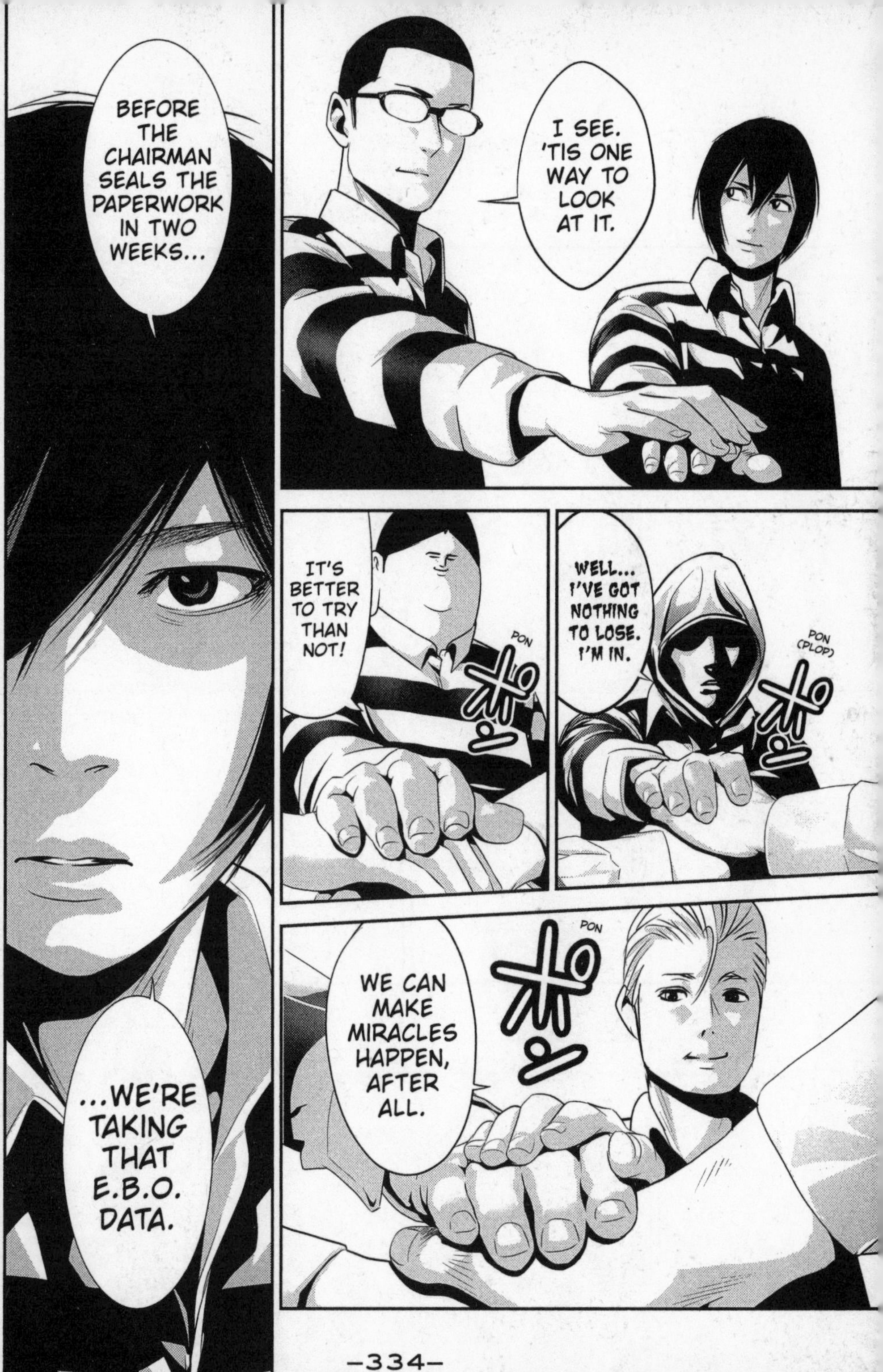
I SEE. 'TIS ONE WAY TO LOOK AT IT.
WELL... I'VE GOT NOTHING TO LOSE. I'M IN.
PON (PLOP)
IT'S BETTER TO TRY THAN NOT!
PON
WE CAN MAKE MIRACLES HAPPEN, AFTER ALL.
PON
BEFORE THE CHAIRMAN SEALS THE PAPERWORK IN TWO WEEKS...
...WE'RE TAKING THAT E.B.O. DATA.

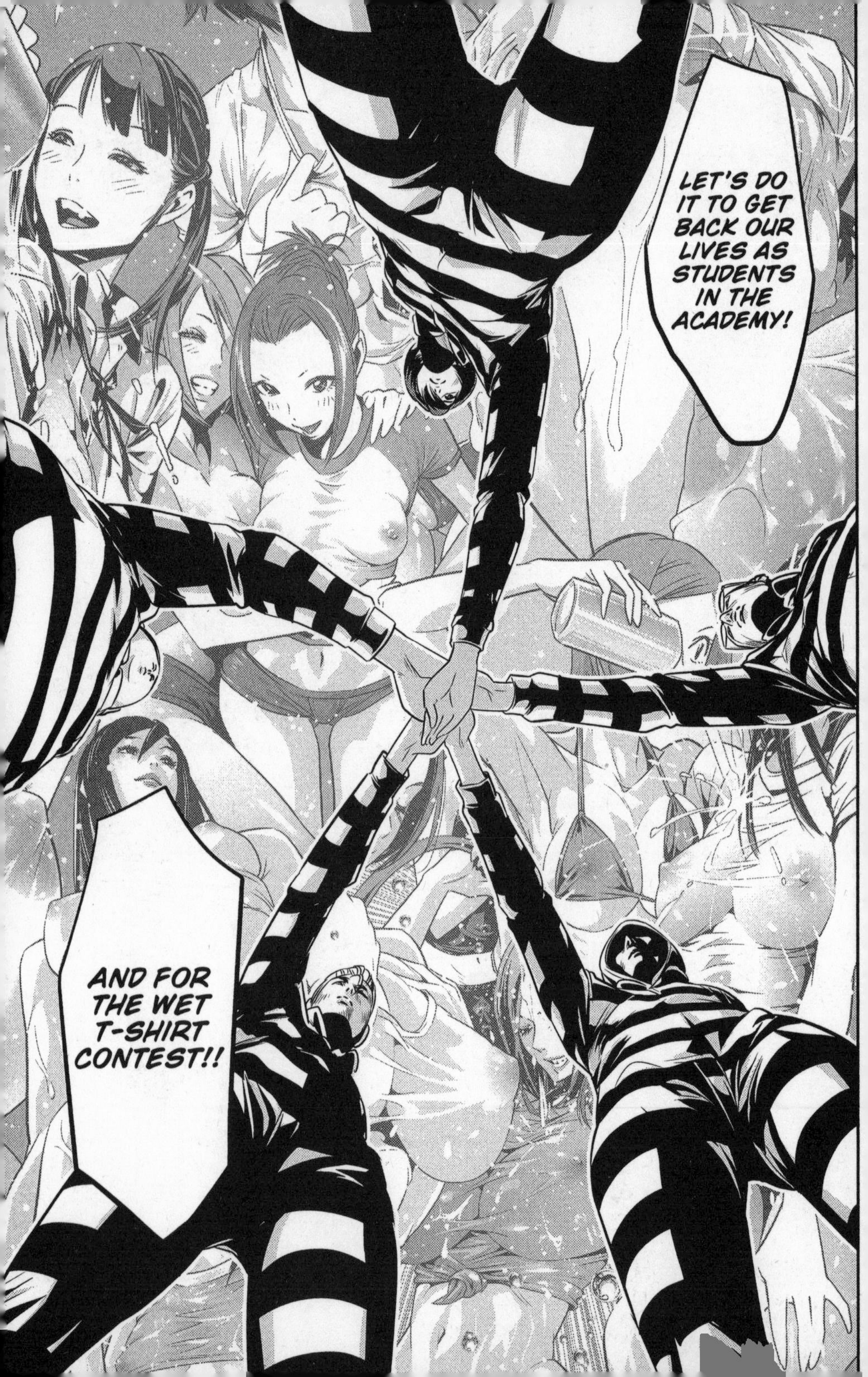
LET'S DO IT TO GET BACK OUR LIVES AS STUDENTS IN THE ACADEMY!
AND FOR THE WET T-SHIRT CONTEST!!

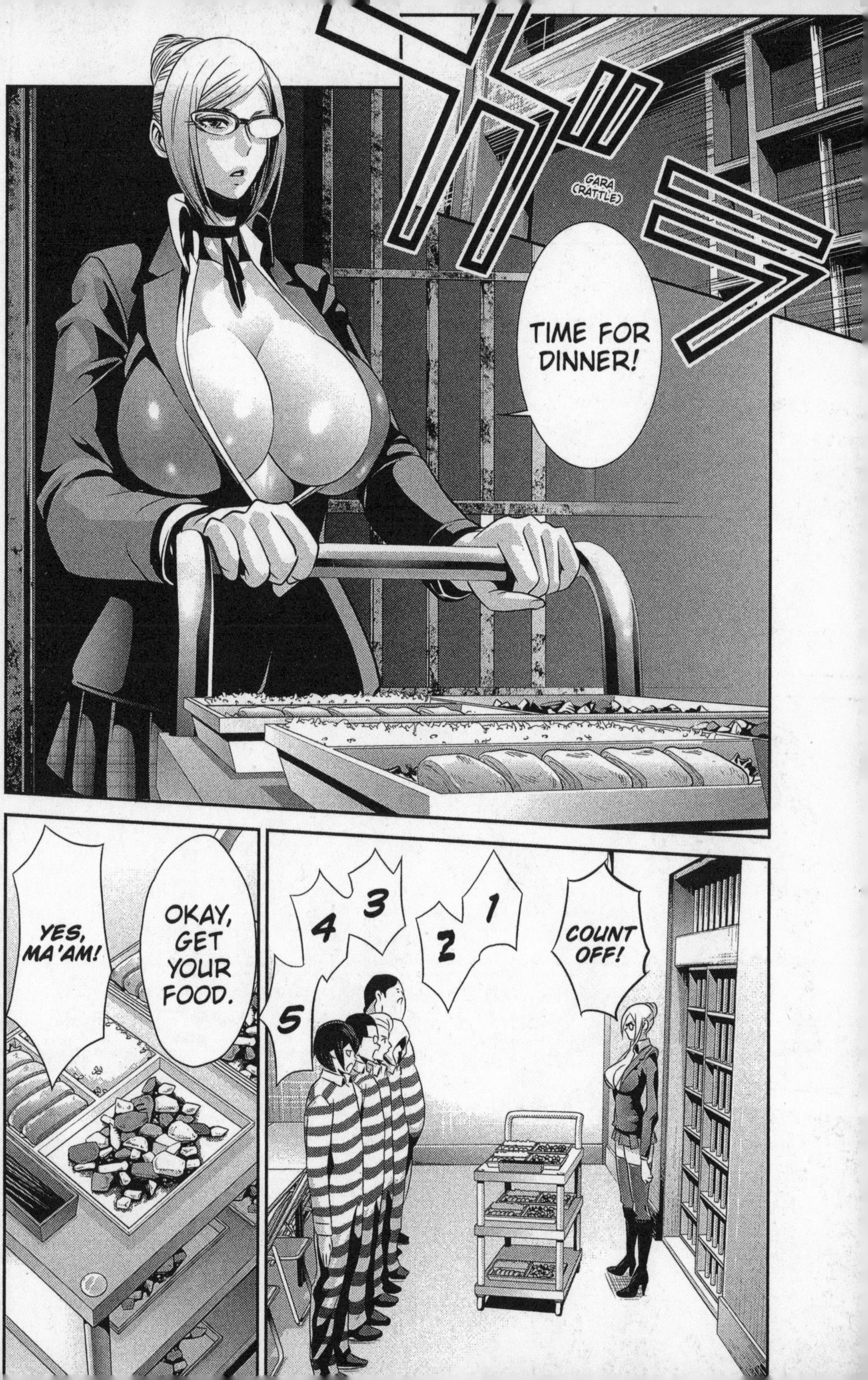
GARA (RATTLE)
TIME FOR DINNER!
COUNT OFF!
1
2
3
4
5
OKAY, GET YOUR FOOD.
YES, MA'AM!

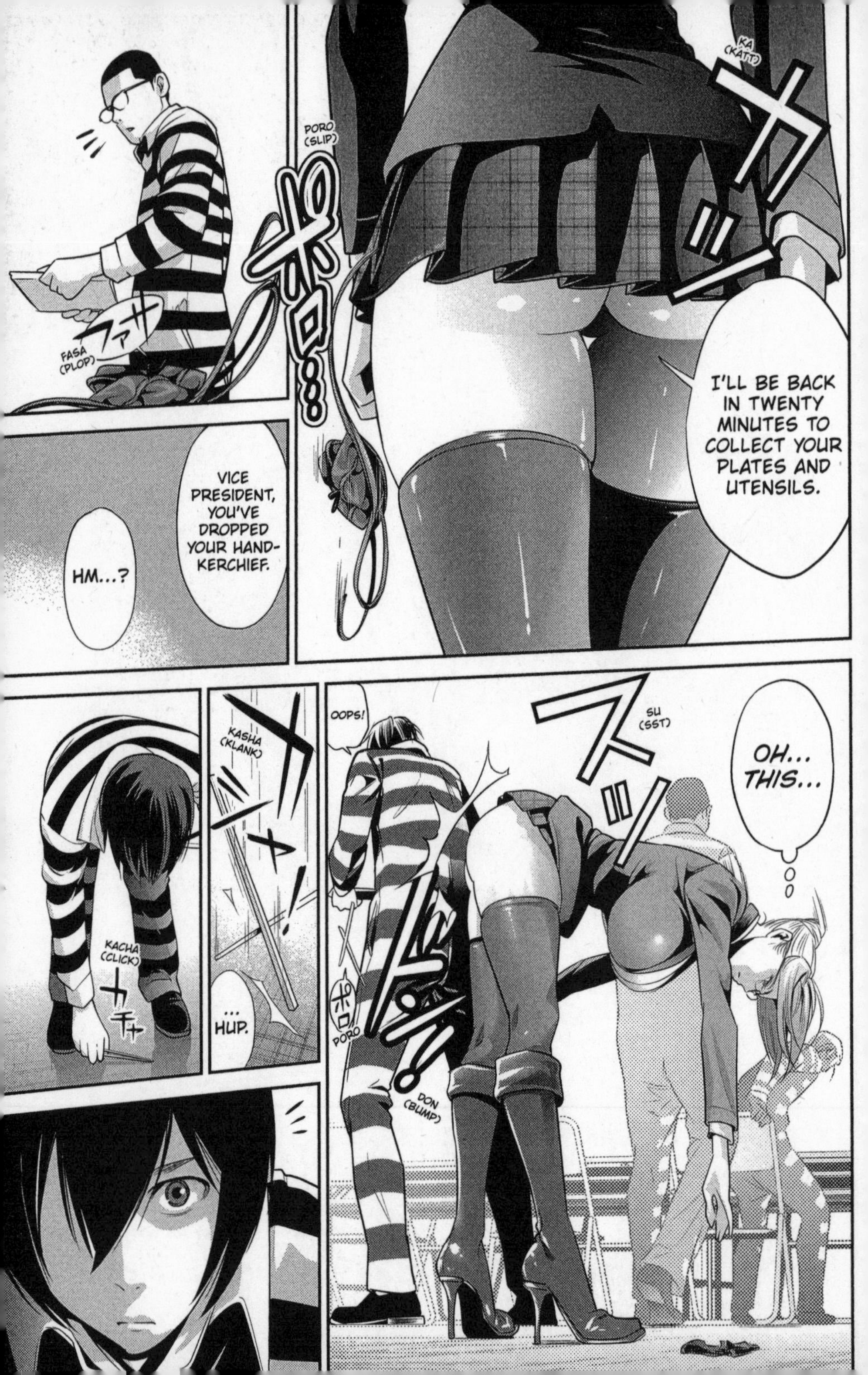
KA (KATT)
I'LL BE BACK IN TWENTY MINUTES TO COLLECT YOUR PLATES AND UTENSILS.
PORO (SLIP)
FASA (PLOP)
VICE PRESIDENT, YOU'VE DROPPED YOUR HAND-KERCHIEF.
HM...?
OH... THIS...
SU (SST)
OOPS!
PORO
DON (BUMP)
KASHA (KLANK)
...HUP.
KACHA (CLICK)

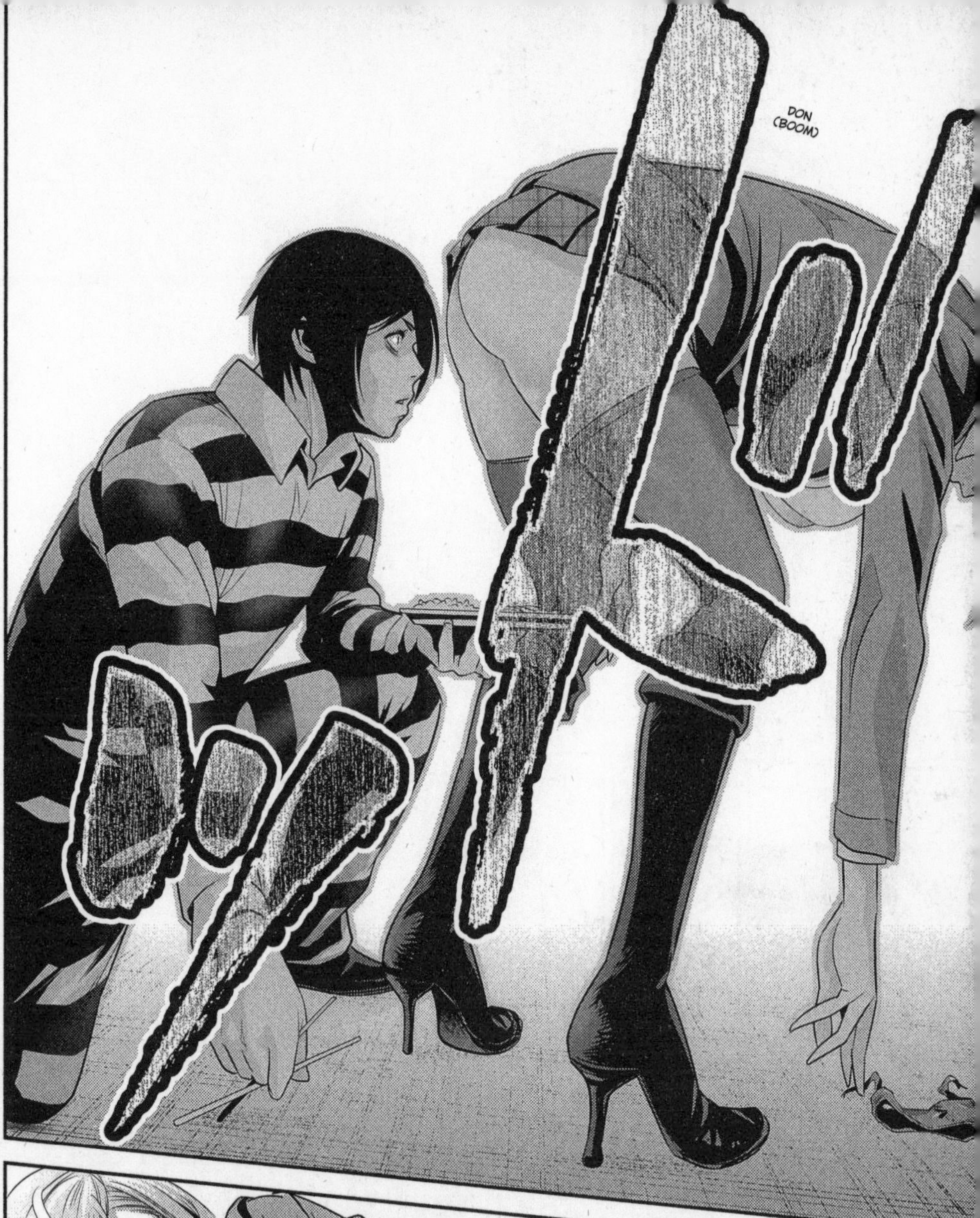
DON
(BOOM)

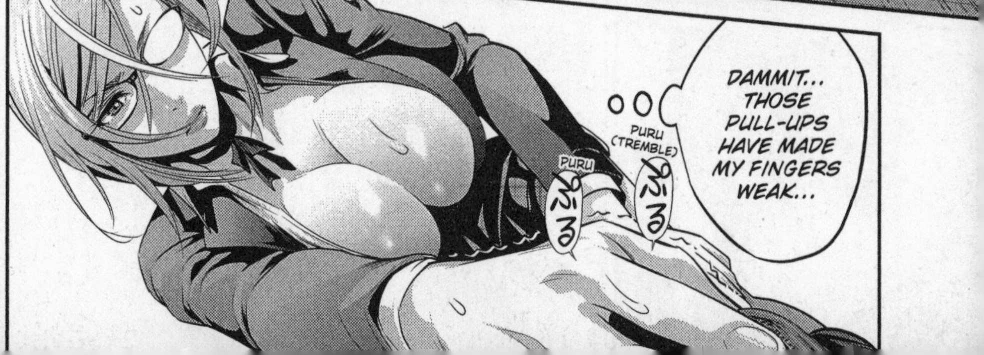
DAMMIT... THOSE PULL-UPS HAVE MADE MY FINGERS WEAK...
PURU
(TREMBLE)
PURU

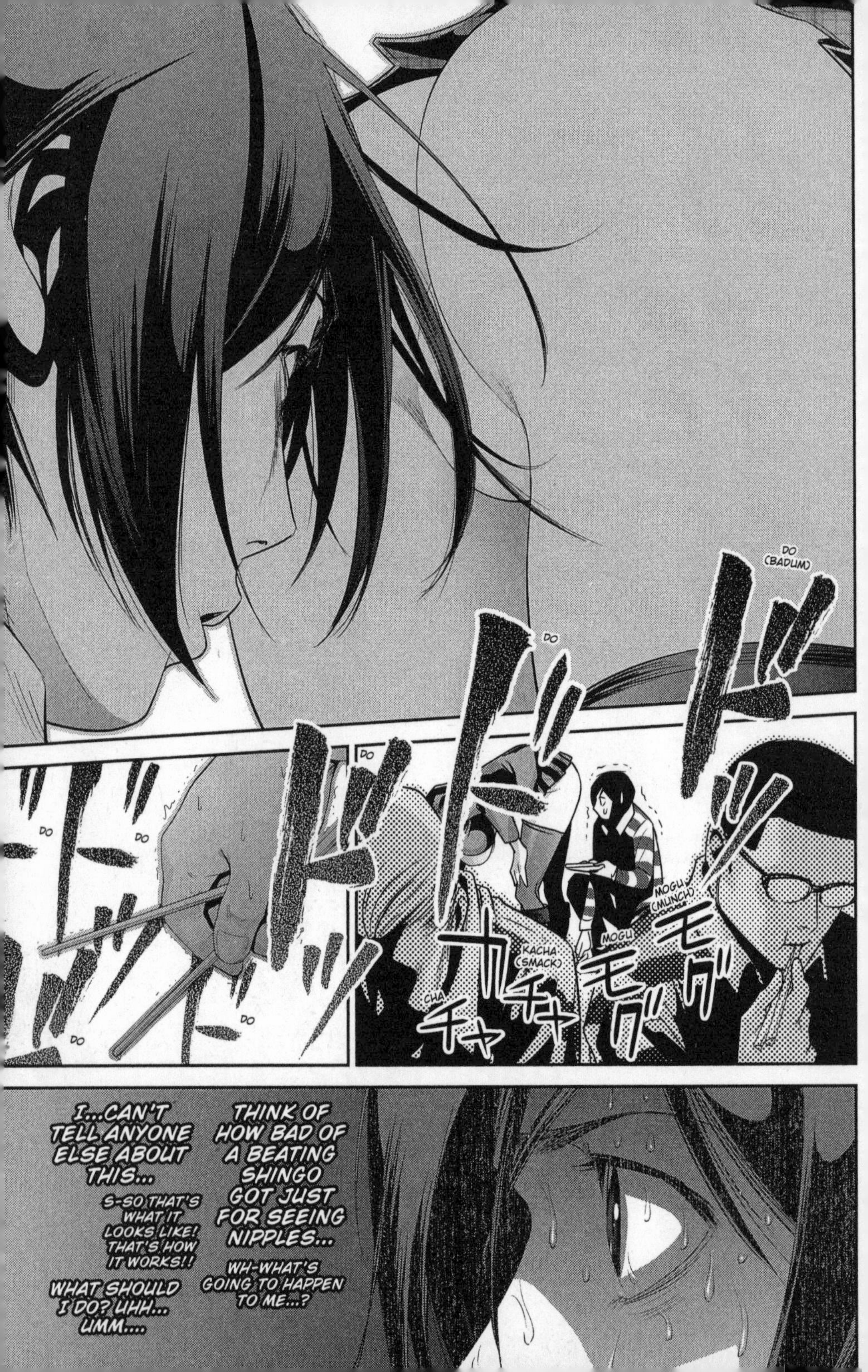
DO (BADUM)
DO
DO
MOGU (MUNCH)
MOGU
KACHA (SMACK)
CHA
DO
DO
DO
DO
I...CAN'T TELL ANYONE ELSE ABOUT THIS...
THINK OF HOW BAD OF A BEATING SHINGO GOT JUST FOR SEEING NIPPLES...
S-SO THAT'S WHAT IT LOOKS LIKE! THAT'S HOW IT WORKS!!
WH-WHAT'S GOING TO HAPPEN TO ME...?
WHAT SHOULD I DO? UHH... UMM....

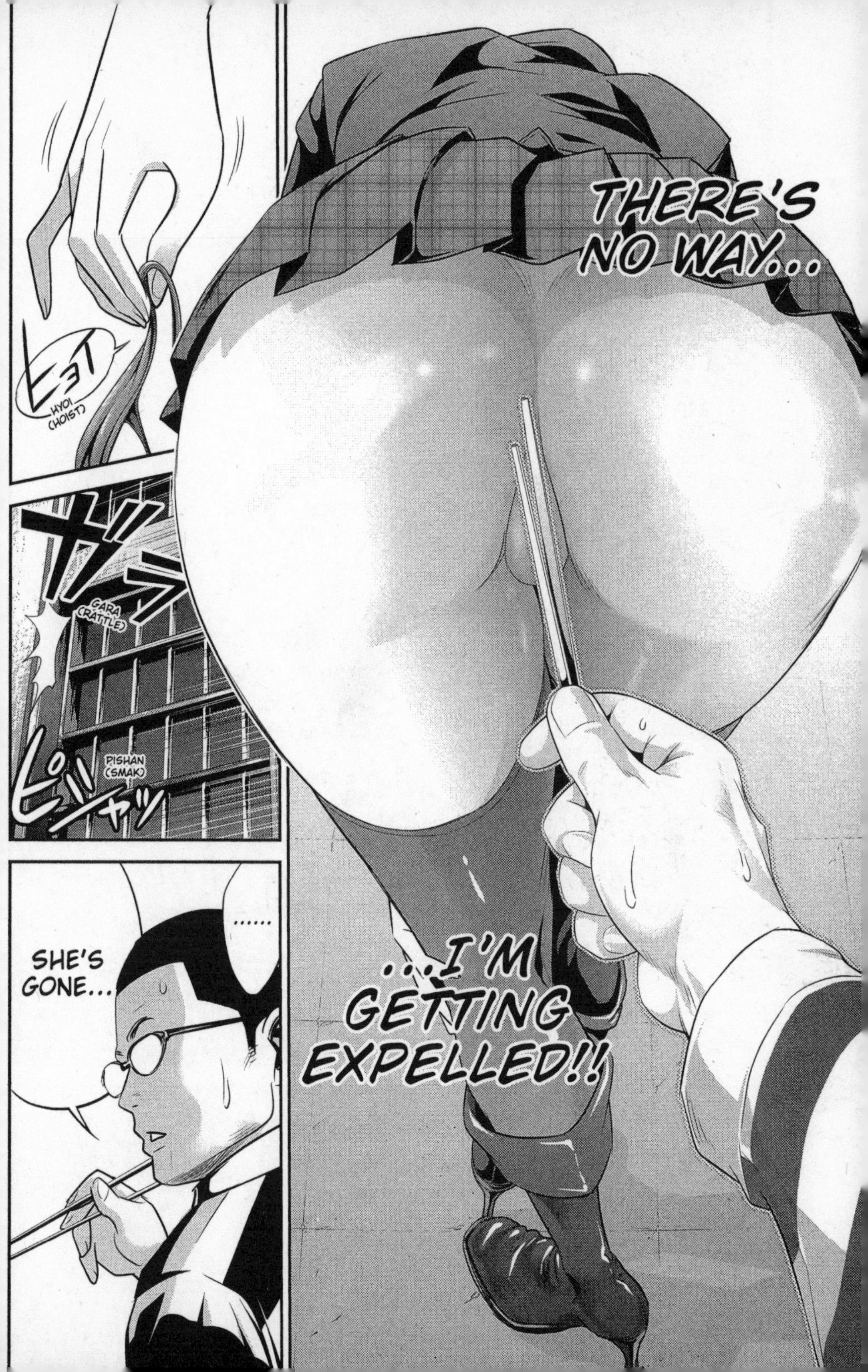

THERE'S NO WAY...
...I'M GETTING EXPELLED!!
ヒョイ
HYOI (HOIST)
ガラ
GARA (RATTLE)
ピシャッ
PISHAN (SMAK)
......
SHE'S GONE...

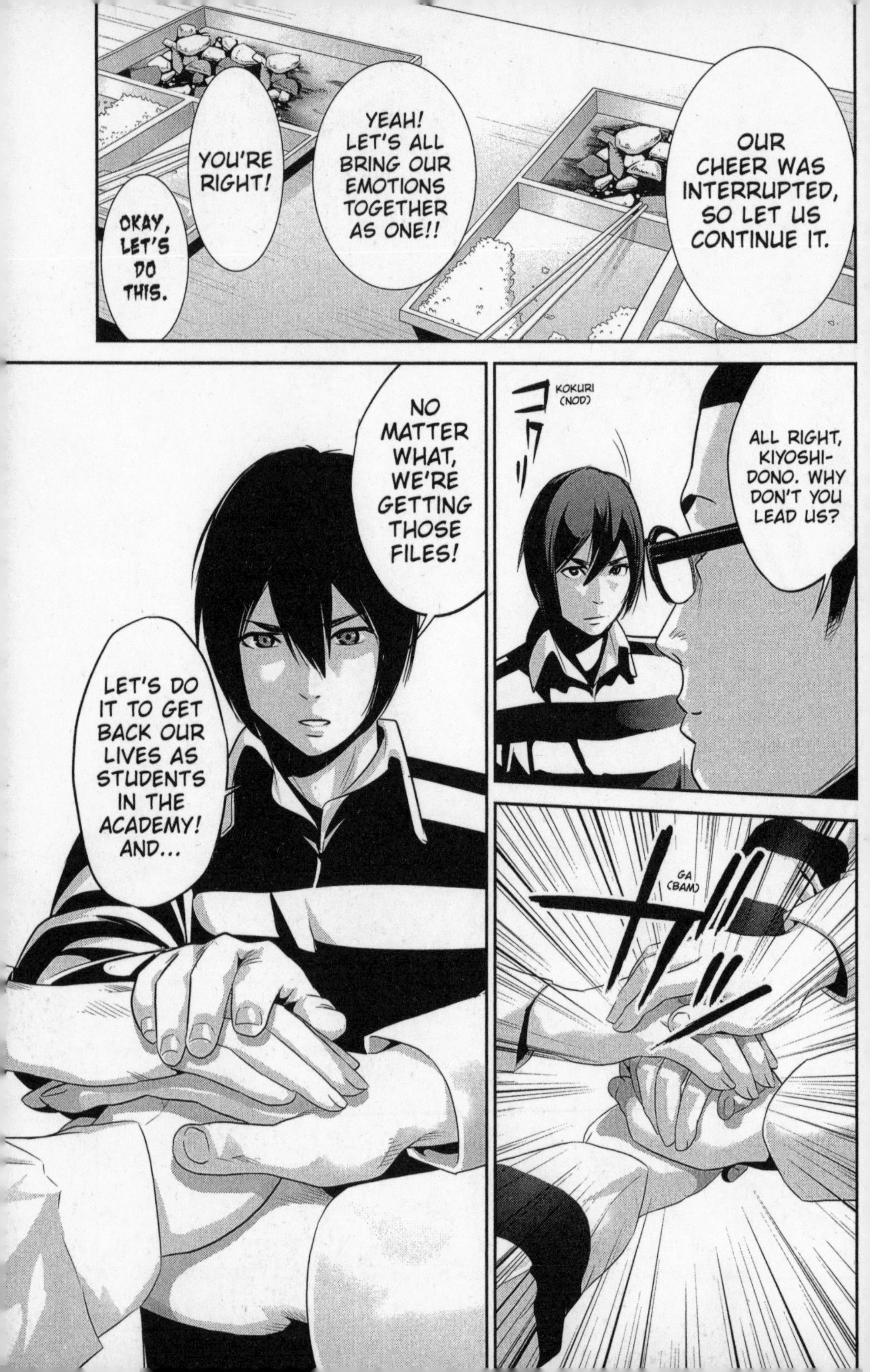
OUR CHEER WAS INTERRUPTED, SO LET US CONTINUE IT.
YEAH! LET'S ALL BRING OUR EMOTIONS TOGETHER AS ONE!!
YOU'RE RIGHT!
OKAY, LET'S DO THIS.
ALL RIGHT, KIYOSHI-DONO. WHY DON'T YOU LEAD US?
KOKURI (NOD)
GA (BAM)
NO MATTER WHAT, WE'RE GETTING THOSE FILES!
LET'S DO IT TO GET BACK OUR LIVES AS STUDENTS IN THE ACADEMY! AND...

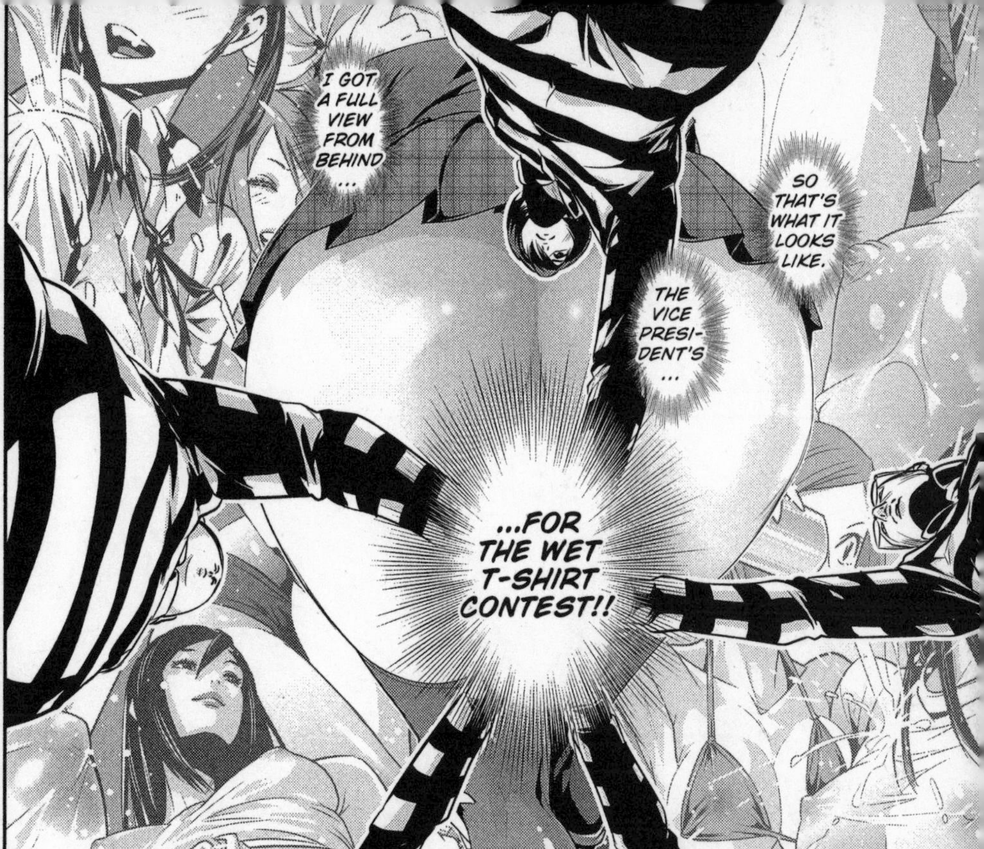
SO THAT'S WHAT IT LOOKS LIKE.
I GOT A FULL VIEW FROM BEHIND...
THE VICE PRESIDENT'S...
...FOR THE WET T-SHIRT CONTEST!!

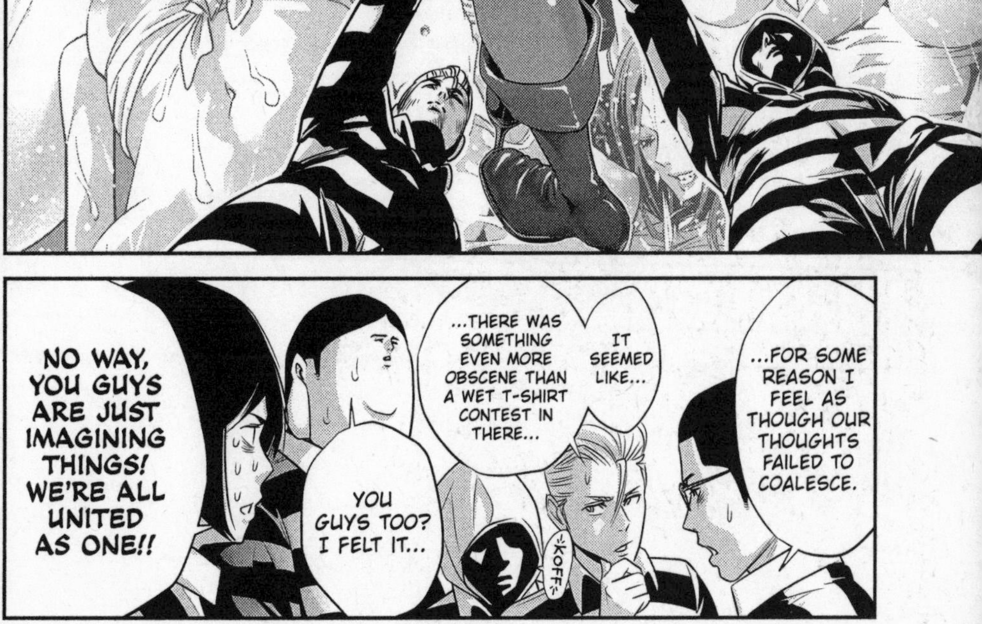
...FOR SOME REASON I FEEL AS THOUGH OUR THOUGHTS FAILED TO COALESCE.
IT SEEMED LIKE...
...THERE WAS SOMETHING EVEN MORE OBSCENE THAN A WET T-SHIRT CONTEST IN THERE...
KOFF
YOU GUYS TOO? I FELT IT...
NO WAY, YOU GUYS ARE JUST IMAGINING THINGS! WE'RE ALL UNITED AS ONE!!

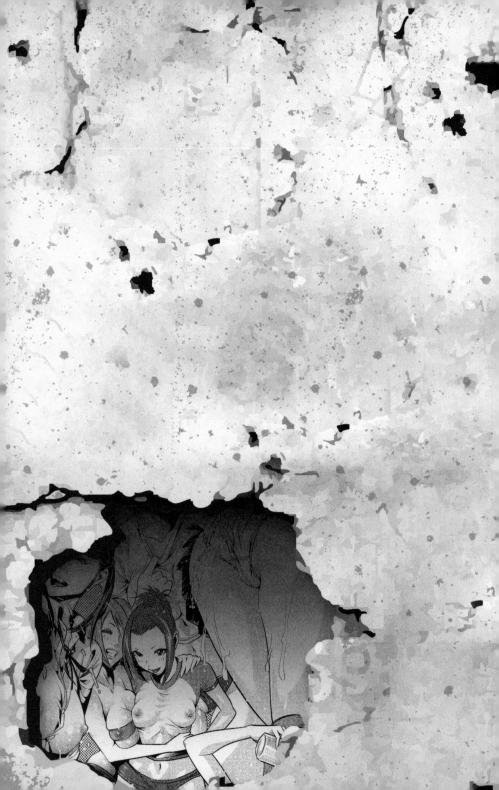

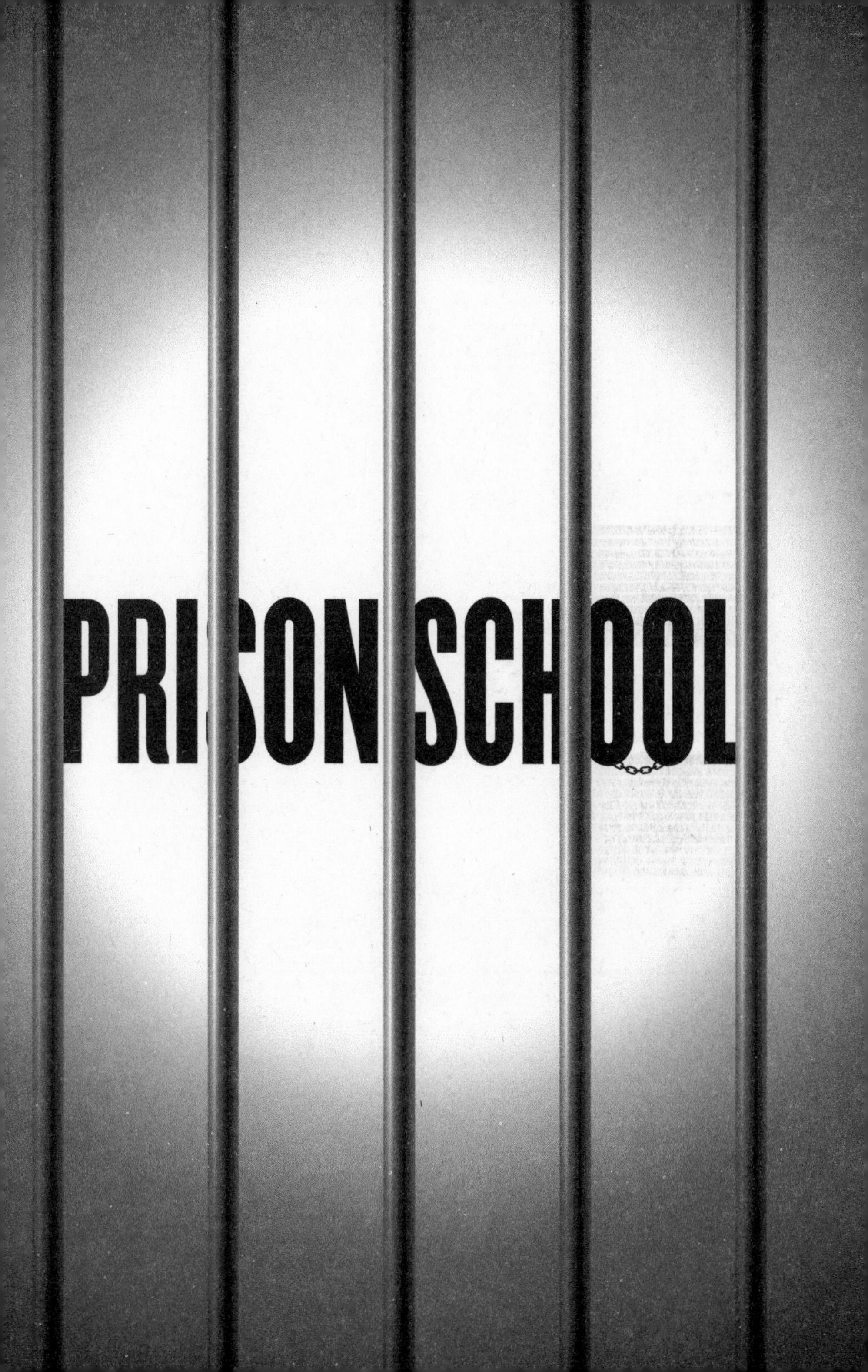
PRISON SCHOOL

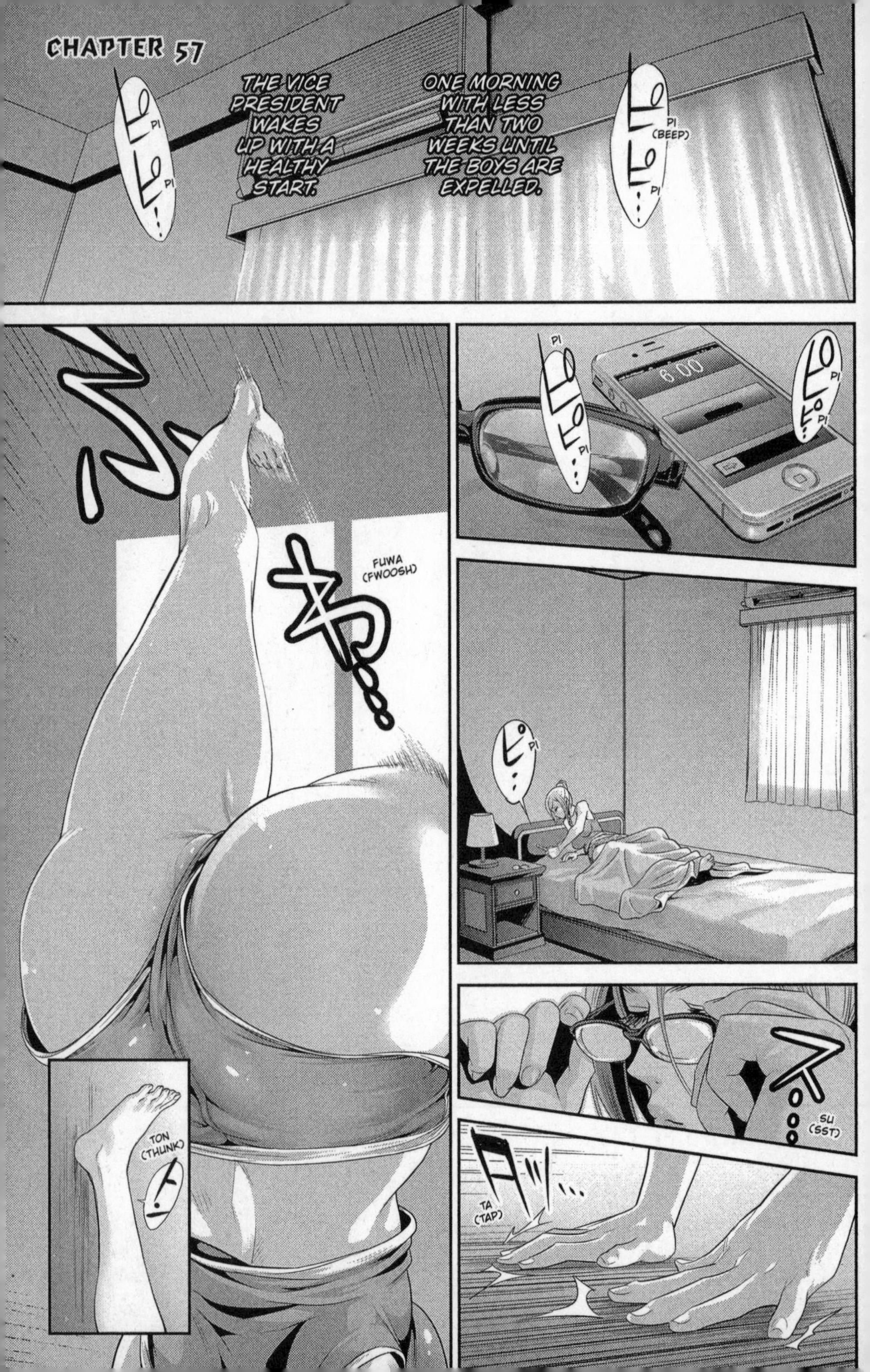
CHAPTER 57
PI (BEEP) PI
ONE MORNING WITH LESS THAN TWO WEEKS UNTIL THE BOYS ARE EXPELLED.
THE VICE PRESIDENT WAKES UP WITH A HEALTHY START.
PI PI
PI PI
PI PI
6:00
PI
SU (SST)
TA (TAP)
FUWA (FWOOSH)
TON (THUNK)

CHAPTER 57: OVER THE TOP

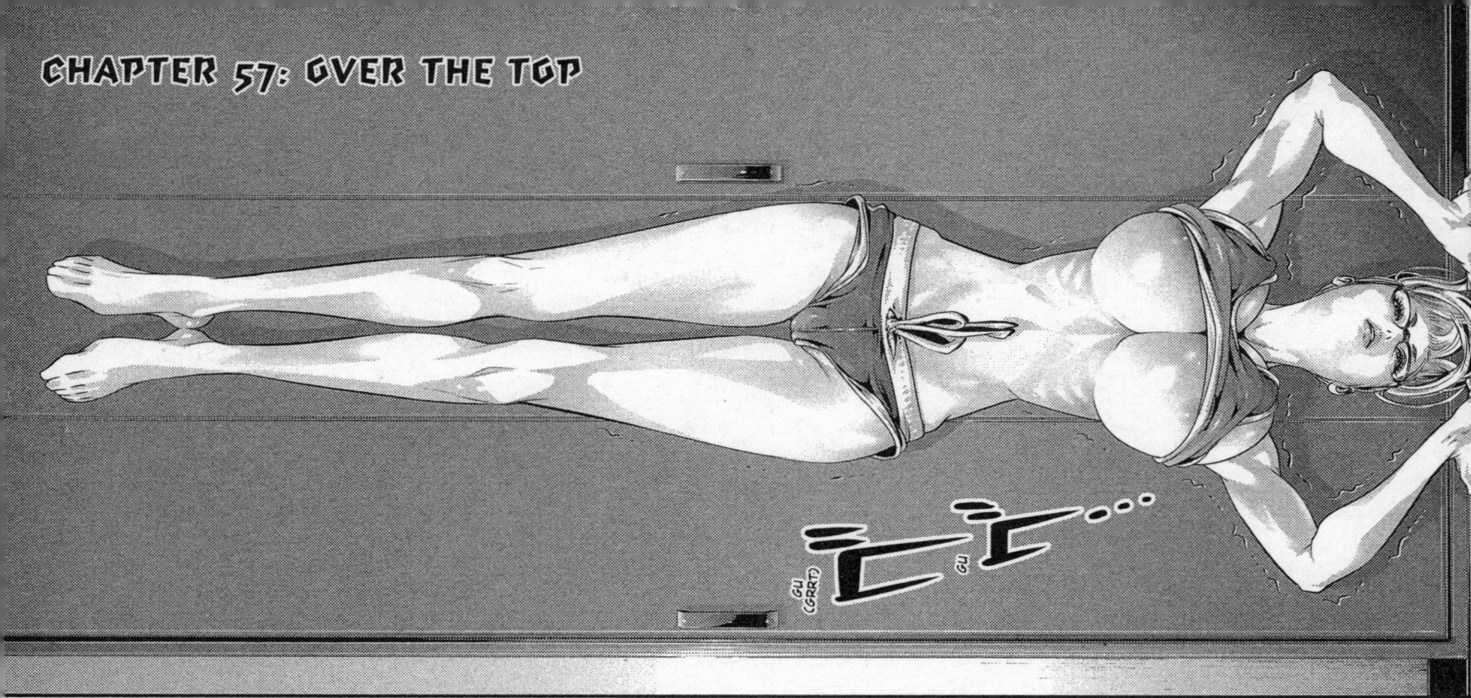

GU (GRRT)
GU

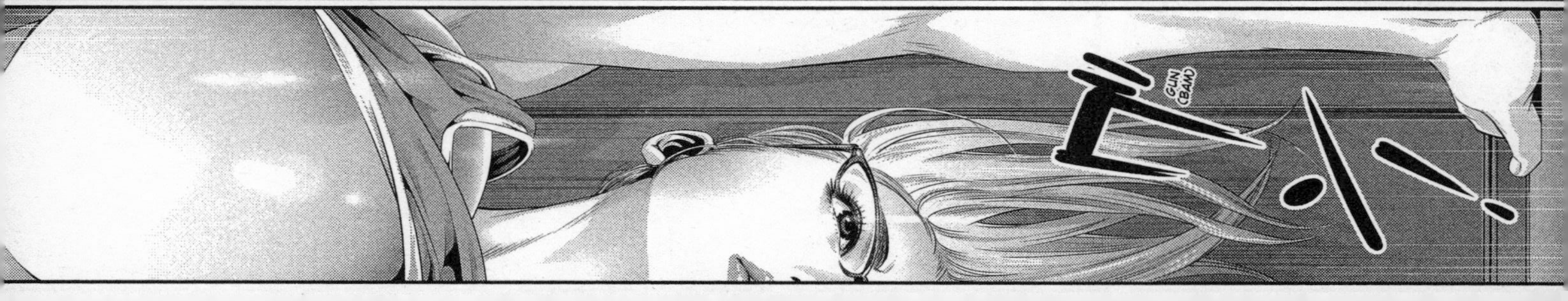

GUN (BAM)

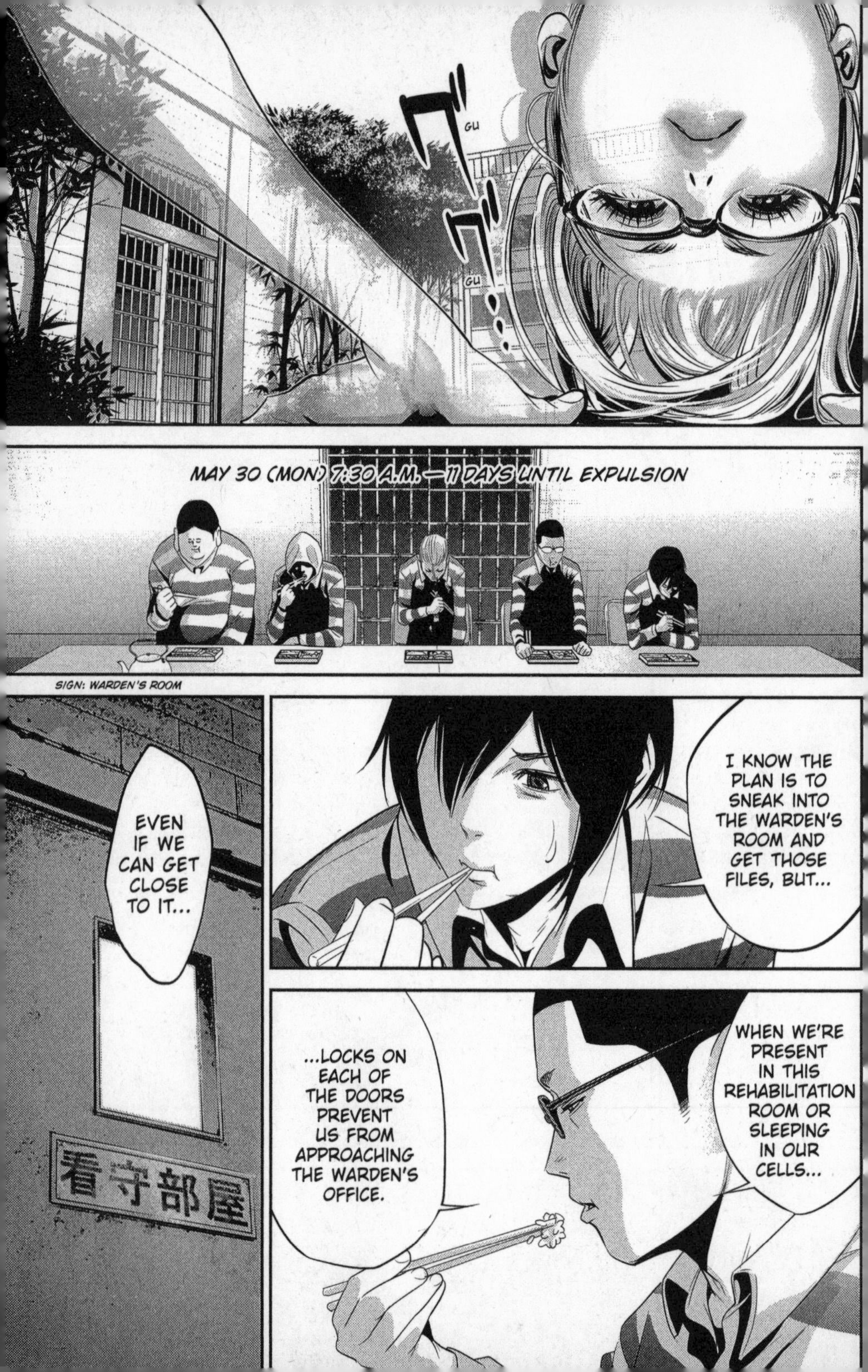
GU
GU
MAY 30 (MON) 7:30 A.M. —11 DAYS UNTIL EXPULSION
SIGN: WARDEN'S ROOM
I KNOW THE PLAN IS TO SNEAK INTO THE WARDEN'S ROOM AND GET THOSE FILES, BUT...
EVEN IF WE CAN GET CLOSE TO IT...
看守部屋
WHEN WE'RE PRESENT IN THIS REHABILITATION ROOM OR SLEEPING IN OUR CELLS...
...LOCKS ON EACH OF THE DOORS PREVENT US FROM APPROACHING THE WARDEN'S OFFICE.

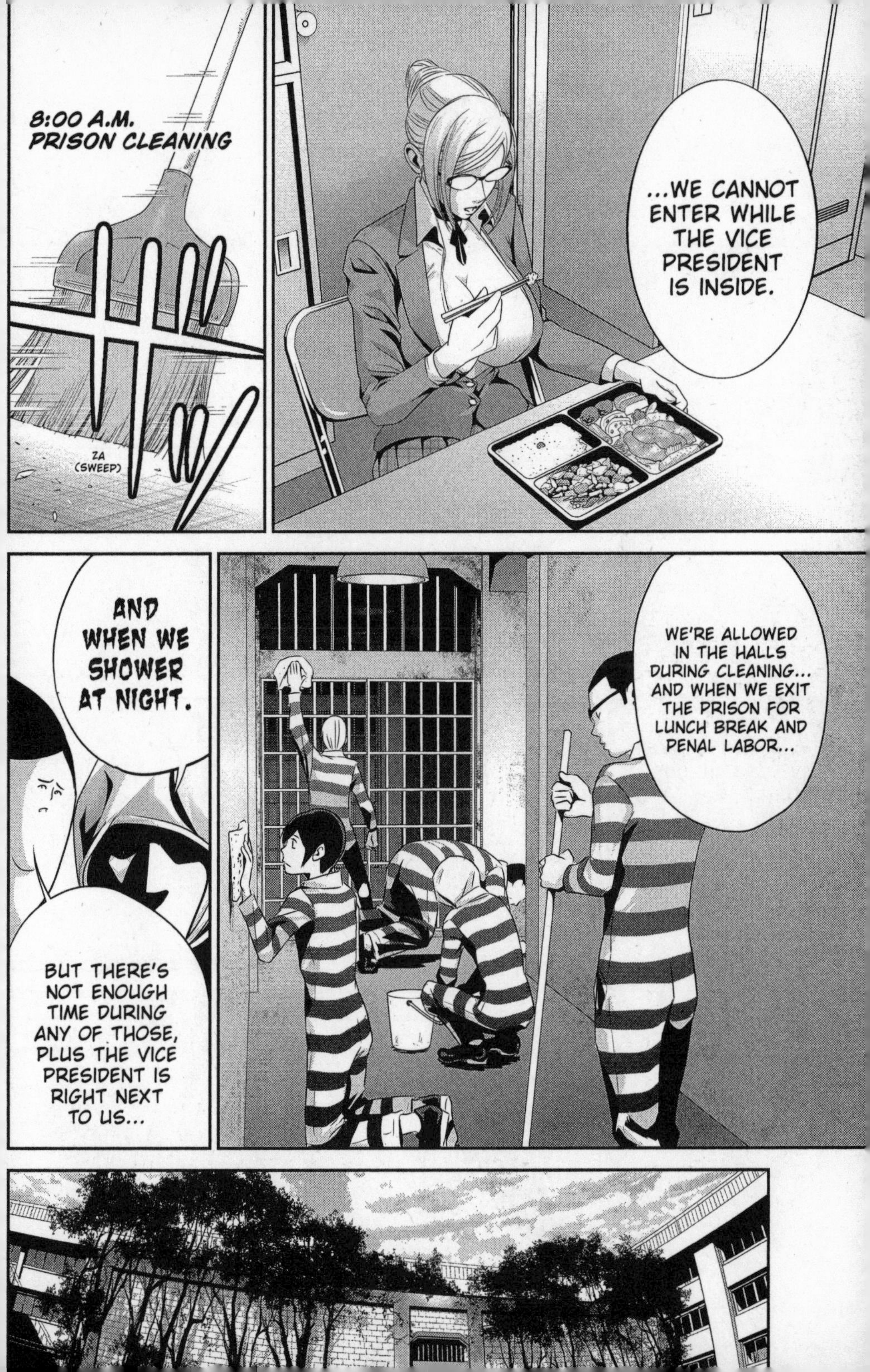
...WE CANNOT ENTER WHILE THE VICE PRESIDENT IS INSIDE.
8:00 A.M. PRISON CLEANING
ZA (SWEEP)
WE'RE ALLOWED IN THE HALLS DURING CLEANING... AND WHEN WE EXIT THE PRISON FOR LUNCH BREAK AND PENAL LABOR...
AND WHEN WE SHOWER AT NIGHT.
BUT THERE'S NOT ENOUGH TIME DURING ANY OF THOSE, PLUS THE VICE PRESIDENT IS RIGHT NEXT TO US...

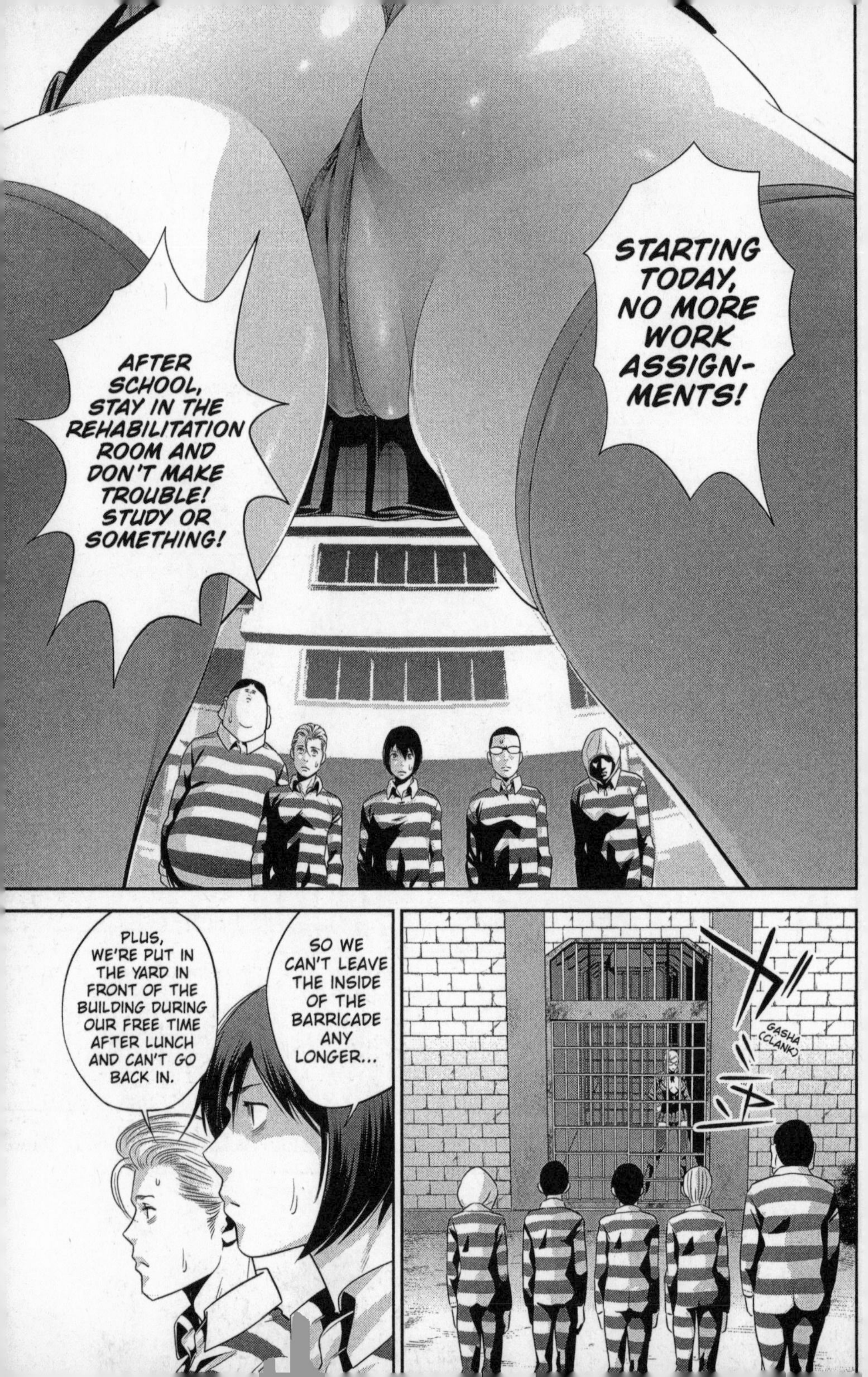
STARTING TODAY, NO MORE WORK ASSIGN-MENTS!
AFTER SCHOOL, STAY IN THE REHABILITATION ROOM AND DON'T MAKE TROUBLE! STUDY OR SOMETHING!
GASHA (CLANK)
SO WE CAN'T LEAVE THE INSIDE OF THE BARRICADE ANY LONGER...
PLUS, WE'RE PUT IN THE YARD IN FRONT OF THE BUILDING DURING OUR FREE TIME AFTER LUNCH AND CAN'T GO BACK IN.

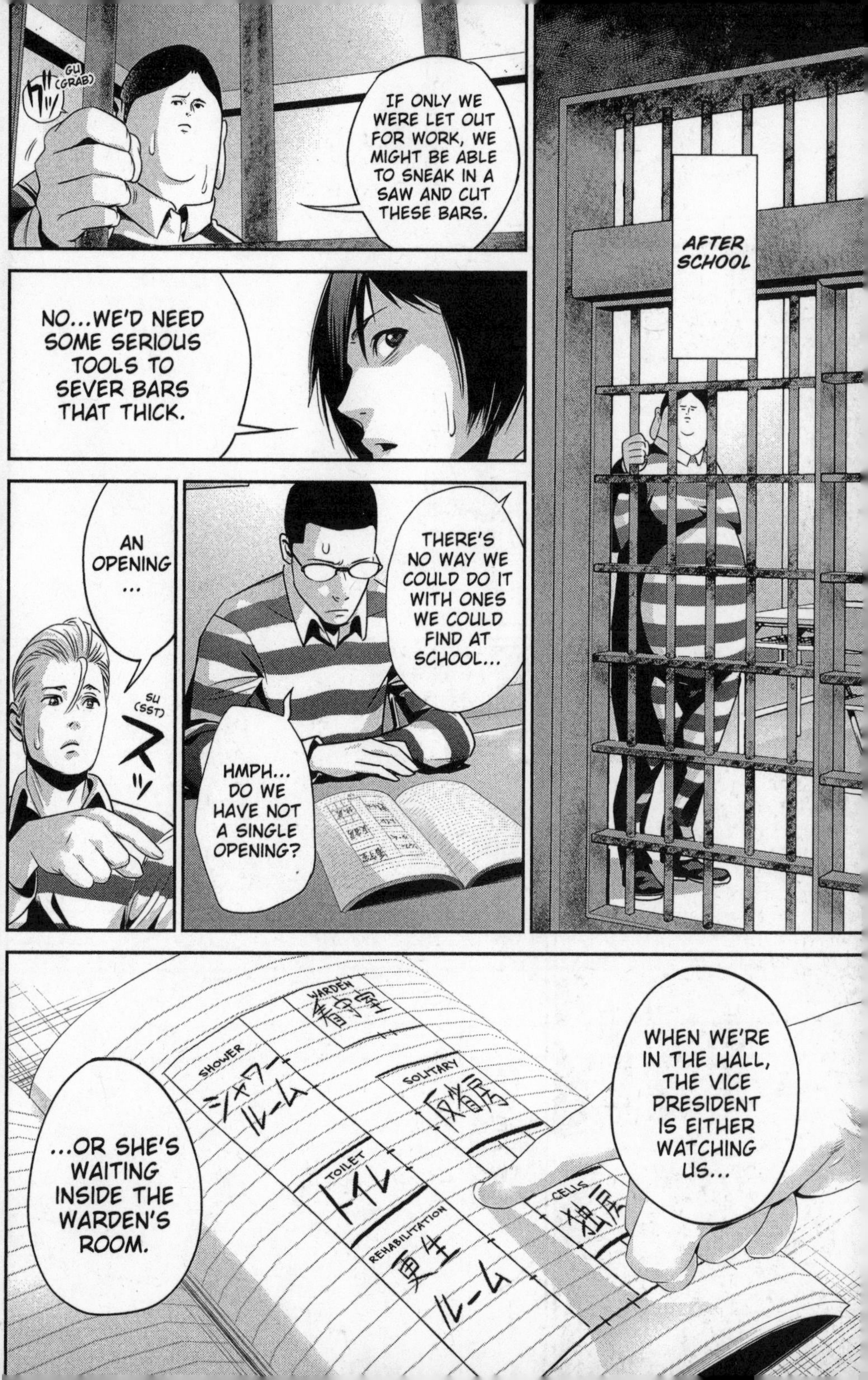
AFTER SCHOOL
GU (GRAB)
IF ONLY WE WERE LET OUT FOR WORK, WE MIGHT BE ABLE TO SNEAK IN A SAW AND CUT THESE BARS.
NO...WE'D NEED SOME SERIOUS TOOLS TO SEVER BARS THAT THICK.
THERE'S NO WAY WE COULD DO IT WITH ONES WE COULD FIND AT SCHOOL...
HMPH... DO WE HAVE NOT A SINGLE OPENING?
AN OPENING ...
SU (SST)
WHEN WE'RE IN THE HALL, THE VICE PRESIDENT IS EITHER WATCHING US...
...OR SHE'S WAITING INSIDE THE WARDEN'S ROOM.
WARDEN
SHOWER
SOLITARY
TOILET
CELLS
REHABILITATION

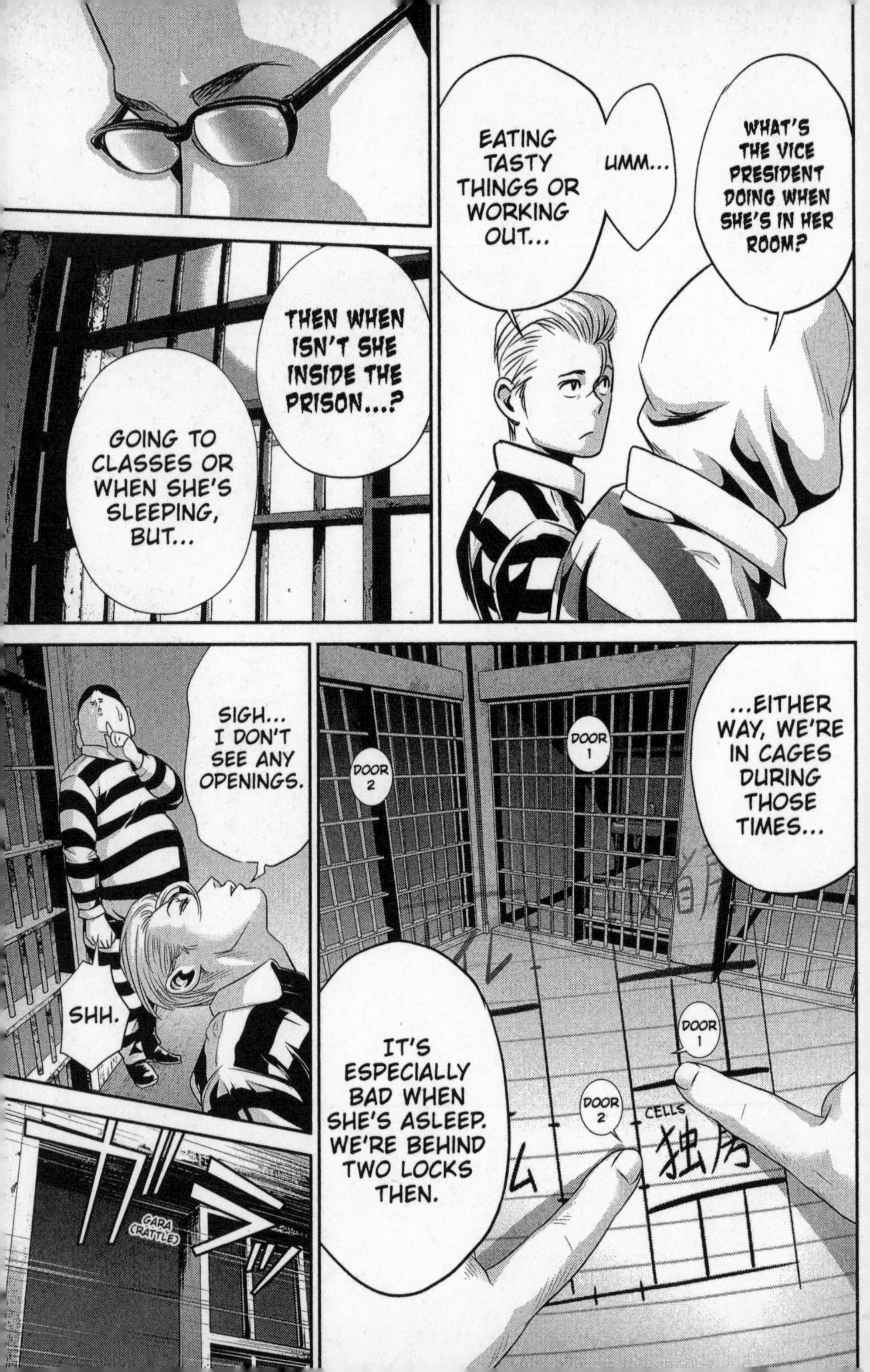
WHAT'S THE VICE PRESIDENT DOING WHEN SHE'S IN HER ROOM?
UMM...
EATING TASTY THINGS OR WORKING OUT...
THEN WHEN ISN'T SHE INSIDE THE PRISON...?
GOING TO CLASSES OR WHEN SHE'S SLEEPING, BUT...
...EITHER WAY, WE'RE IN CAGES DURING THOSE TIMES...
DOOR 1
DOOR 2
IT'S ESPECIALLY BAD WHEN SHE'S ASLEEP. WE'RE BEHIND TWO LOCKS THEN.
DOOR 1
DOOR 2
CELLS
独房
SIGH... I DON'T SEE ANY OPENINGS.
SHH.
GARA (RATTLE)

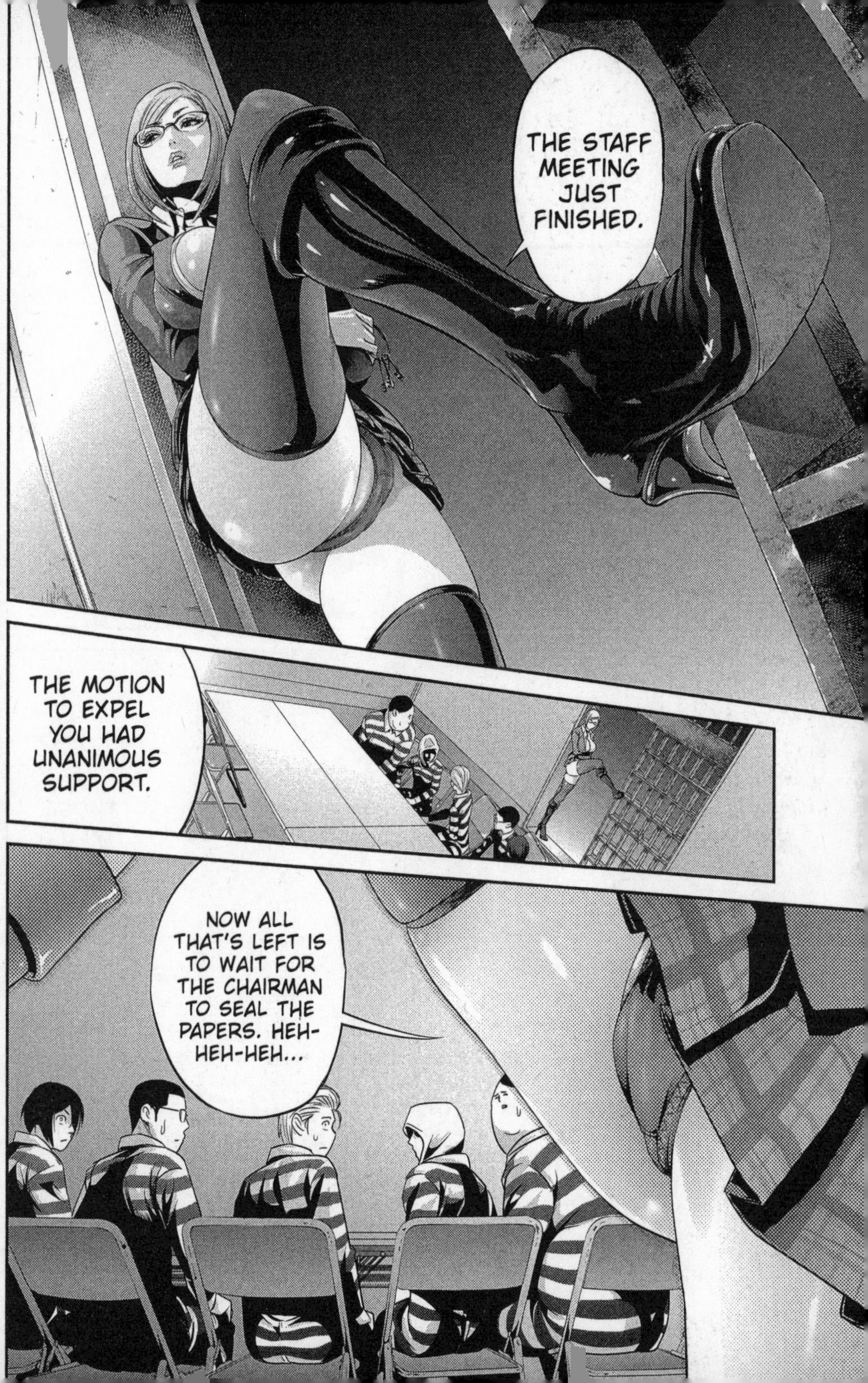
THE STAFF MEETING JUST FINISHED.
THE MOTION TO EXPEL YOU HAD UNANIMOUS SUPPORT.
NOW ALL THAT'S LEFT IS TO WAIT FOR THE CHAIRMAN TO SEAL THE PAPERS. HEH-HEH-HEH...

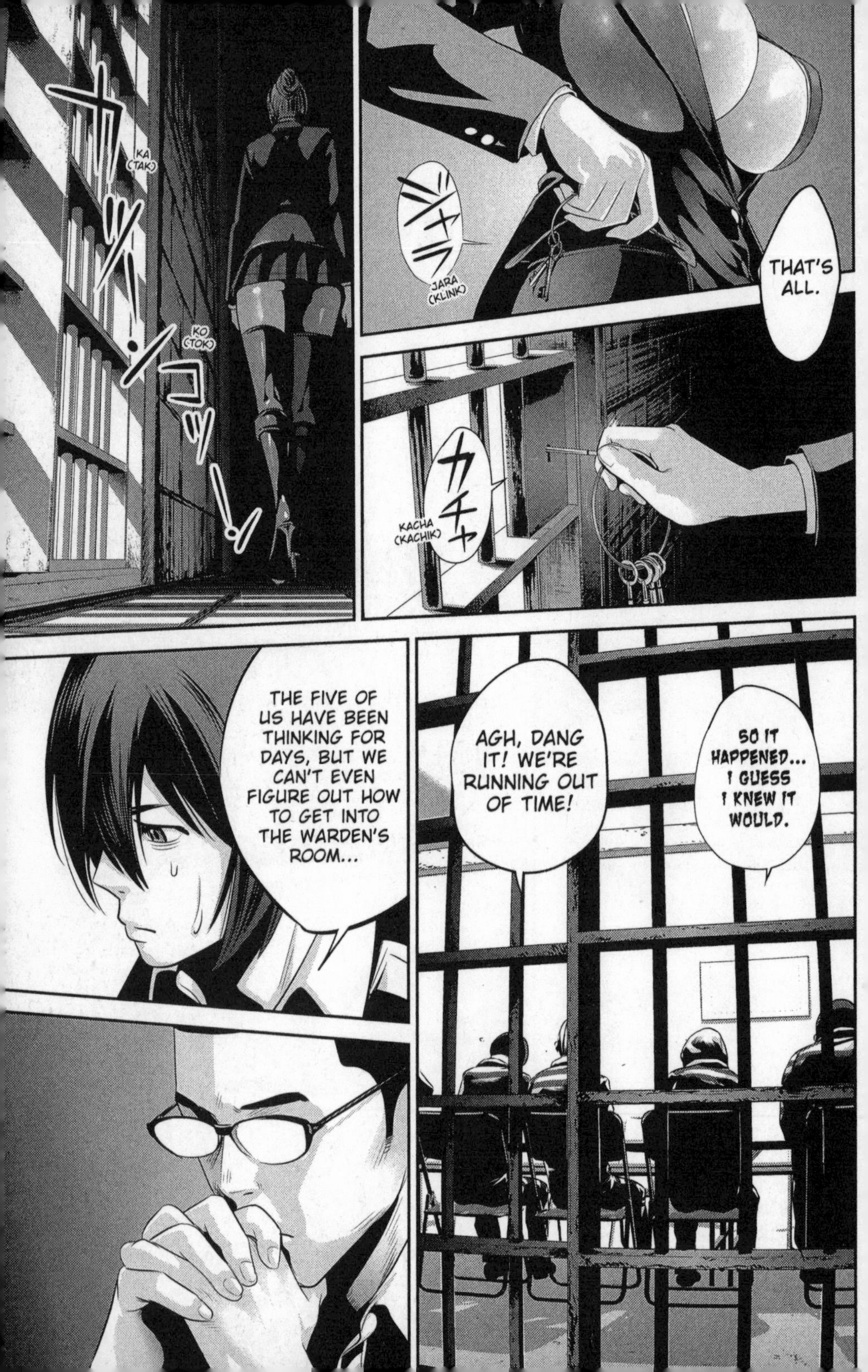

THAT'S ALL.
JARA (KLINK)
KACHA (KACHIK)
KA (TAK)
KO (TOK)
SO IT HAPPENED... I GUESS I KNEW IT WOULD.
AGH, DANG IT! WE'RE RUNNING OUT OF TIME!
THE FIVE OF US HAVE BEEN THINKING FOR DAYS, BUT WE CAN'T EVEN FIGURE OUT HOW TO GET INTO THE WARDEN'S ROOM...

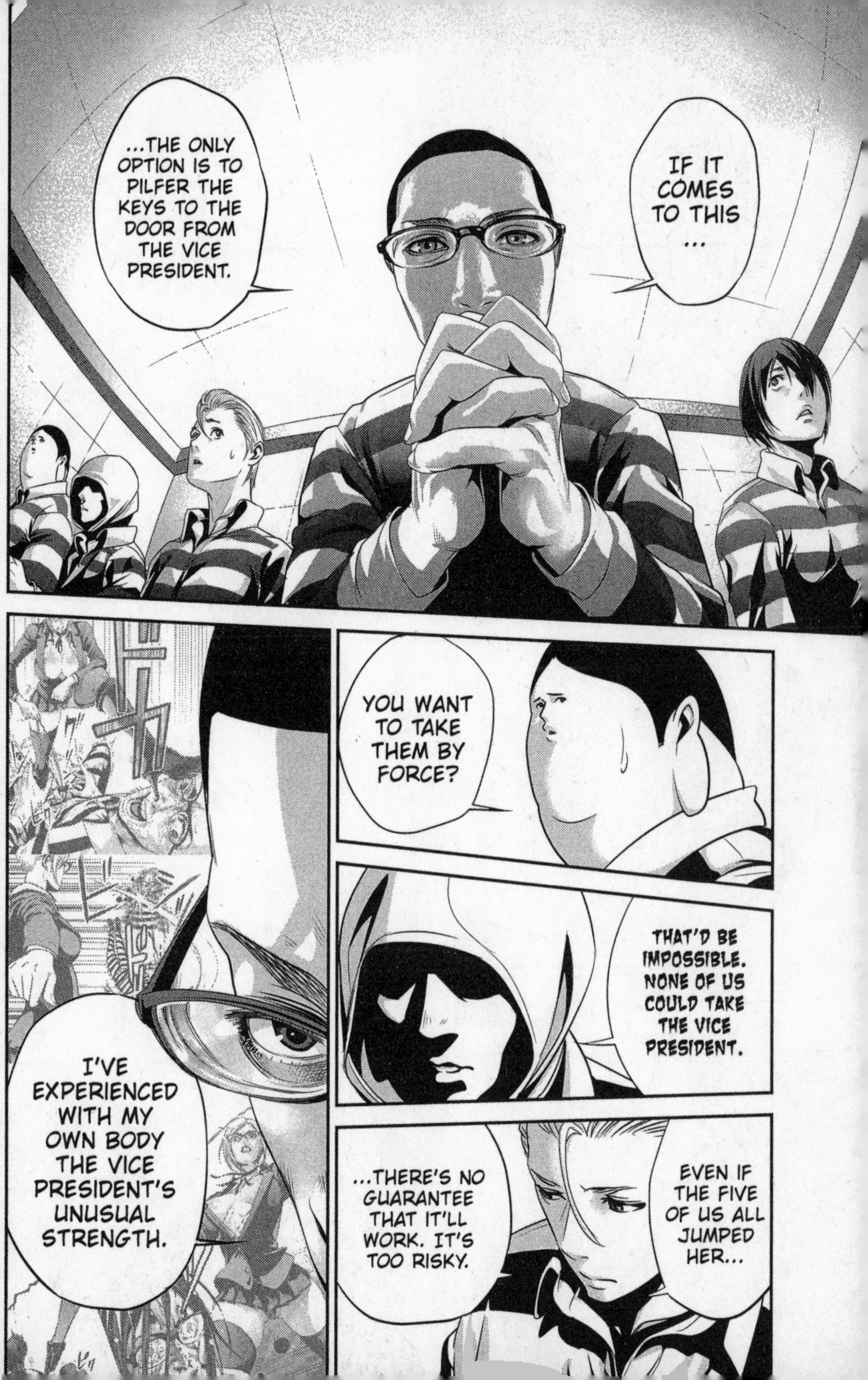
IF IT COMES TO THIS ...
...THE ONLY OPTION IS TO PILFER THE KEYS TO THE DOOR FROM THE VICE PRESIDENT.
YOU WANT TO TAKE THEM BY FORCE?
THAT'D BE IMPOSSIBLE. NONE OF US COULD TAKE THE VICE PRESIDENT.
EVEN IF THE FIVE OF US ALL JUMPED HER...
...THERE'S NO GUARANTEE THAT IT'LL WORK. IT'S TOO RISKY.
I'VE EXPERIENCED WITH MY OWN BODY THE VICE PRESIDENT'S UNUSUAL STRENGTH.

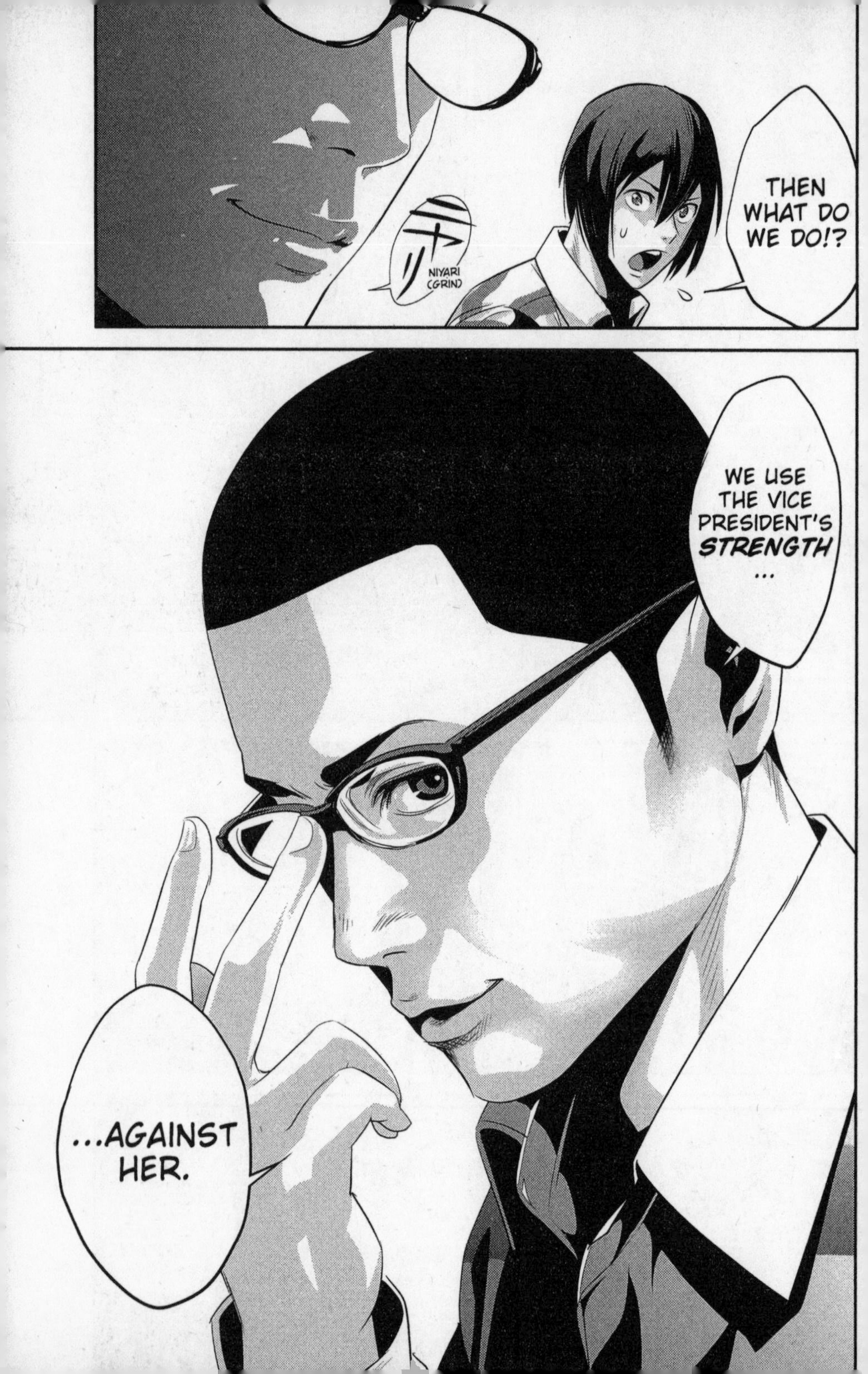
THEN WHAT DO WE DO!?
ニヤリ
NIYARI (GRIN)
WE USE THE VICE PRESIDENT'S STRENGTH ...
...AGAINST HER.

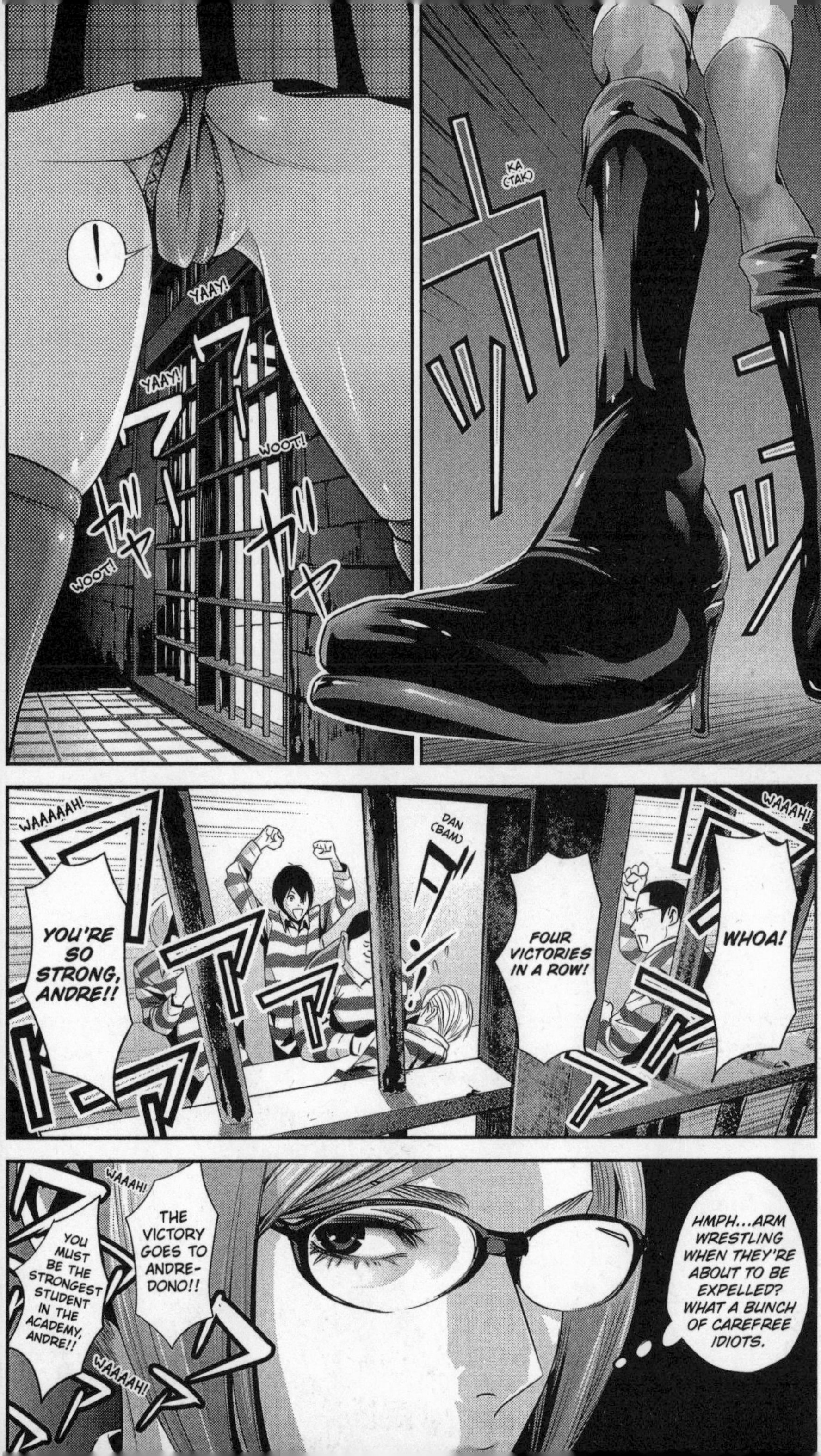
KA (TAK)
KO (TOK)
!
YAAY!
YAAY!
WOOT!
WOOT!
WAAAH!
WHOA!
FOUR VICTORIES IN A ROW!
DAN (BAM)
YOU'RE SO STRONG, ANDRE!!
WAAAAAH!
HMPH...ARM WRESTLING WHEN THEY'RE ABOUT TO BE EXPELLED? WHAT A BUNCH OF CAREFREE IDIOTS.
WAAAH!
THE VICTORY GOES TO ANDRE-DONO!!
YOU MUST BE THE STRONGEST STUDENT IN THE ACADEMY, ANDRE!!
WAAAAH!

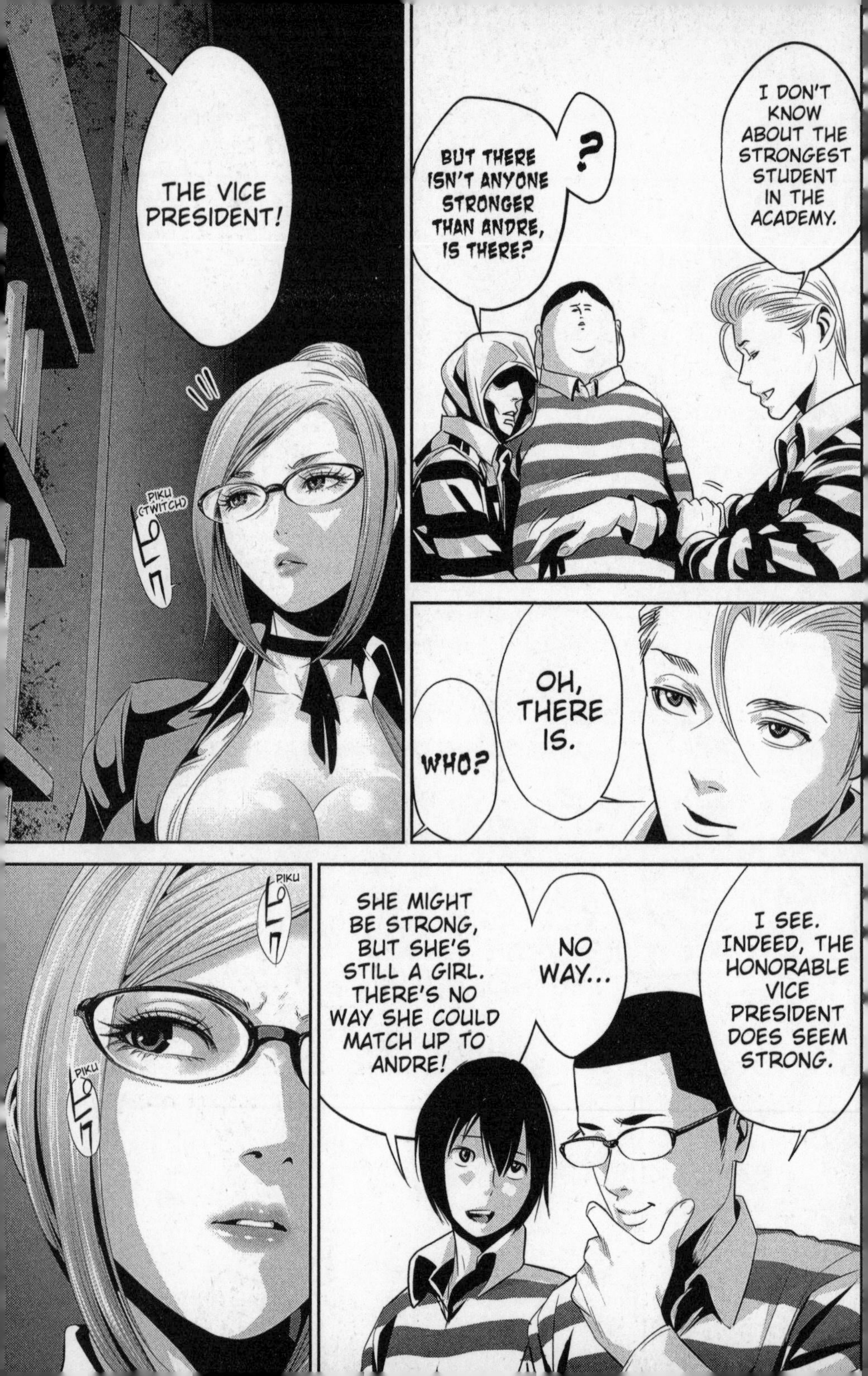
I DON'T KNOW ABOUT THE STRONGEST STUDENT IN THE ACADEMY.
?
BUT THERE ISN'T ANYONE STRONGER THAN ANDRE, IS THERE?
OH, THERE IS.
WHO?
THE VICE PRESIDENT!
PIKU (TWITCH)
I SEE. INDEED, THE HONORABLE VICE PRESIDENT DOES SEEM STRONG.
NO WAY...
SHE MIGHT BE STRONG, BUT SHE'S STILL A GIRL. THERE'S NO WAY SHE COULD MATCH UP TO ANDRE!
PIKU
PIKU

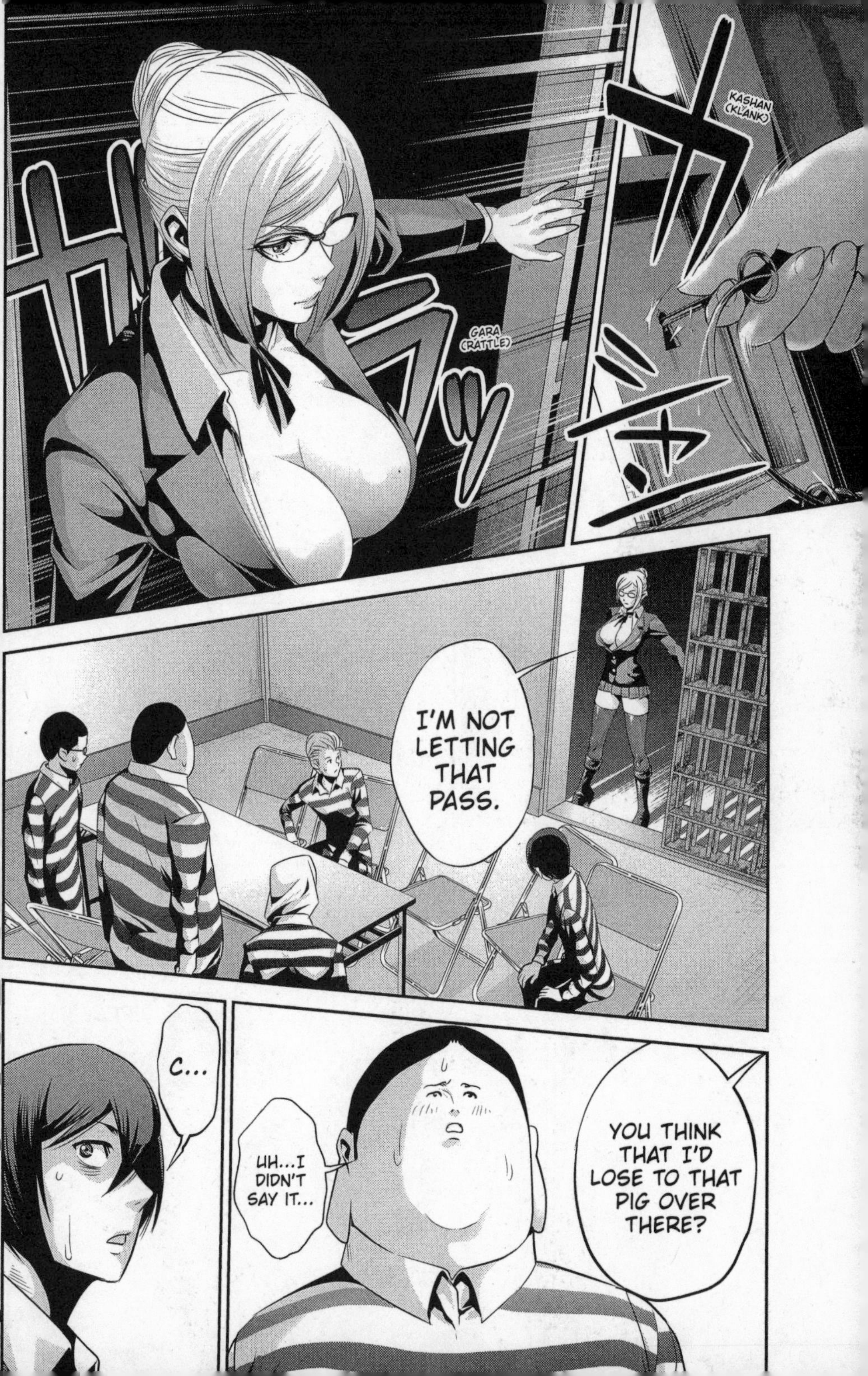
KASHAN (KLANK)
GARA (RATTLE)
I'M NOT LETTING THAT PASS.
YOU THINK THAT I'D LOSE TO THAT PIG OVER THERE?
UH...I DIDN'T SAY IT...
C...

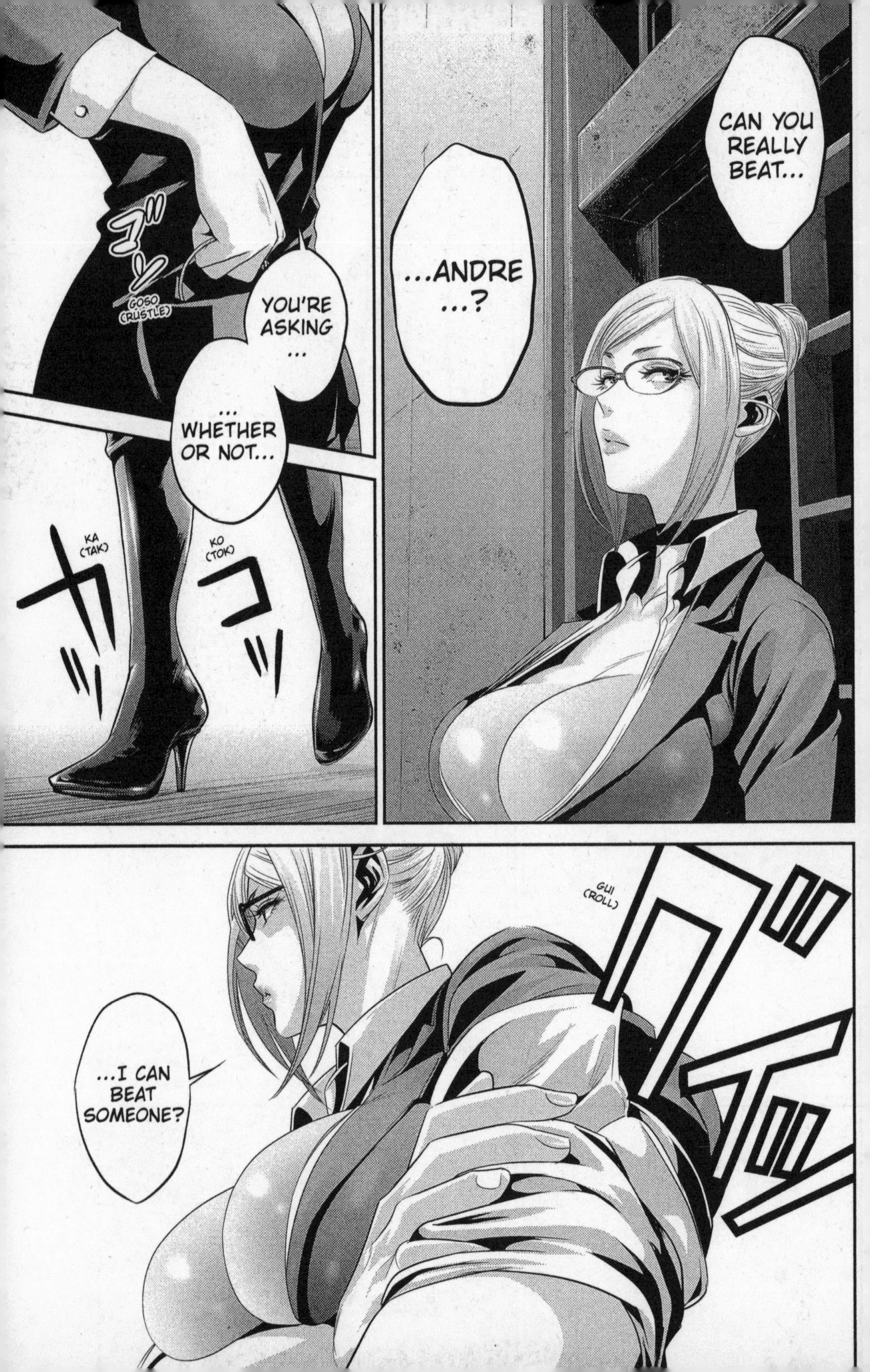
CAN YOU REALLY BEAT...
...ANDRE ...?
GOSO (RUSTLE)
YOU'RE ASKING ...
... WHETHER OR NOT...
KA (TAK)
KO (TOK)
GUI (ROLL)
...I CAN BEAT SOMEONE?

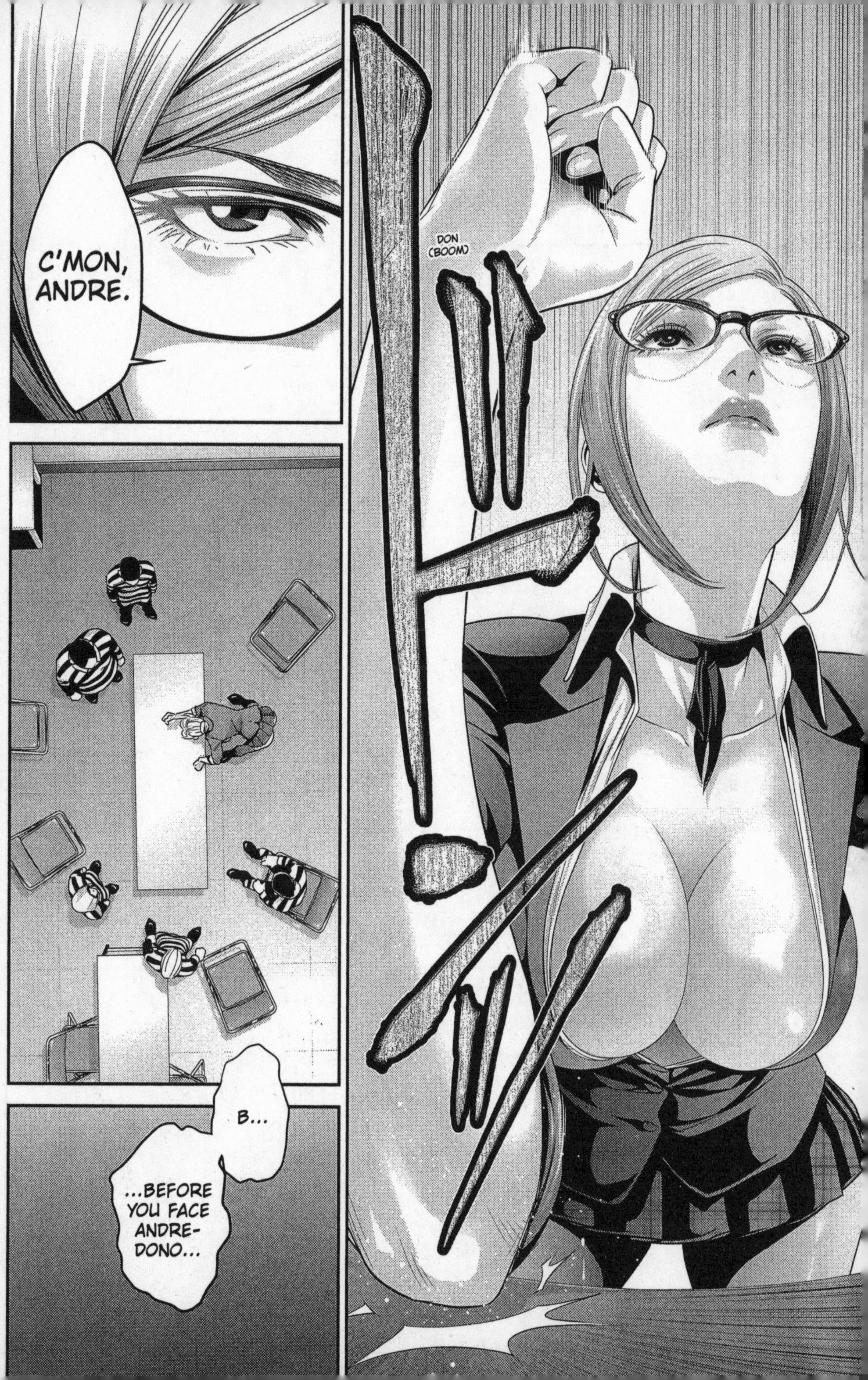
DON (BOOM)
C'MON, ANDRE.
B...
...BEFORE YOU FACE ANDRE-DONO...

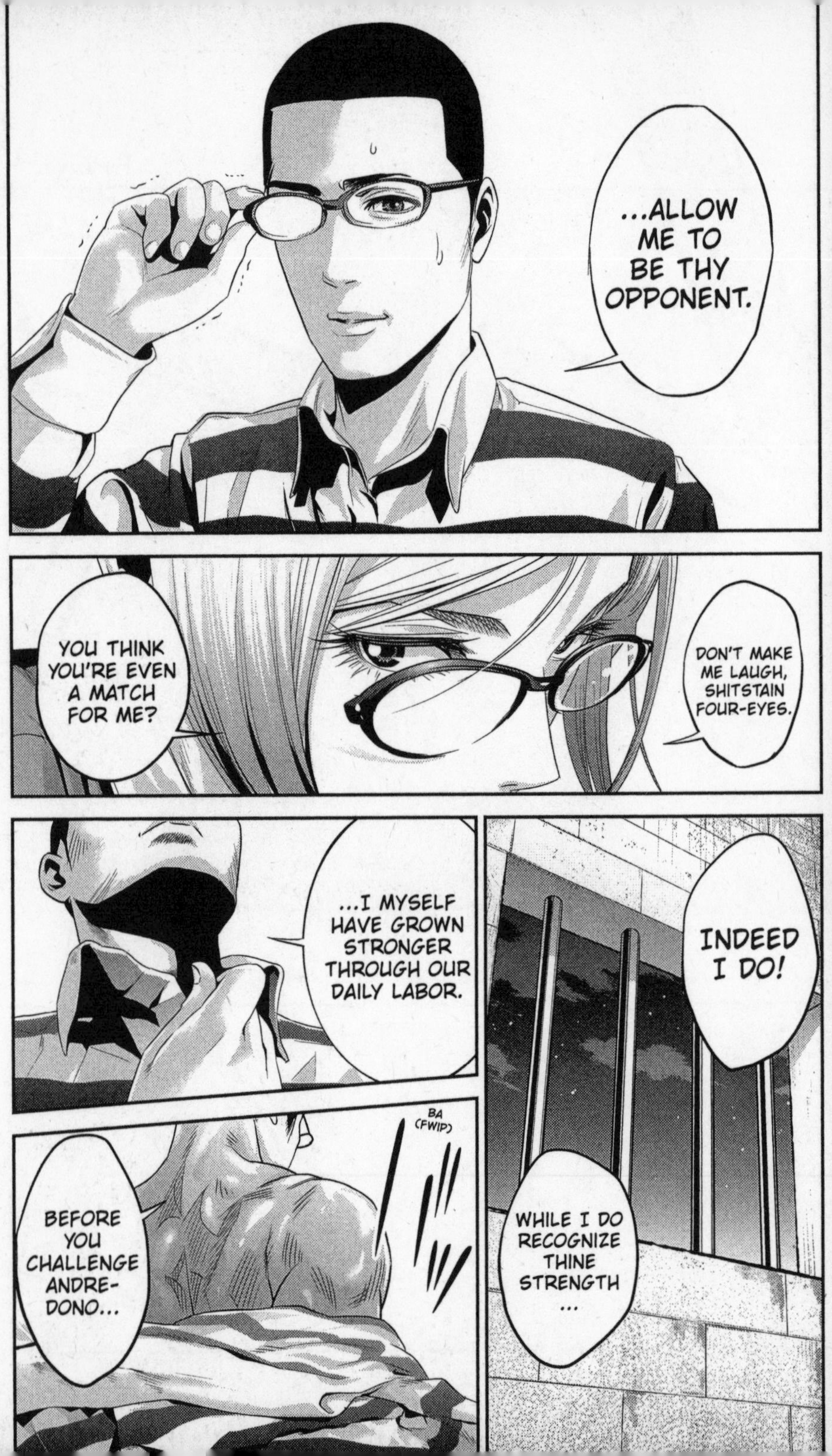
...ALLOW ME TO BE THY OPPONENT.
DON'T MAKE ME LAUGH, SHITSTAIN FOUR-EYES.
YOU THINK YOU'RE EVEN A MATCH FOR ME?
INDEED I DO!
WHILE I DO RECOGNIZE THINE STRENGTH ...
...I MYSELF HAVE GROWN STRONGER THROUGH OUR DAILY LABOR.
BA (FWIP)
BEFORE YOU CHALLENGE ANDRE-DONO...

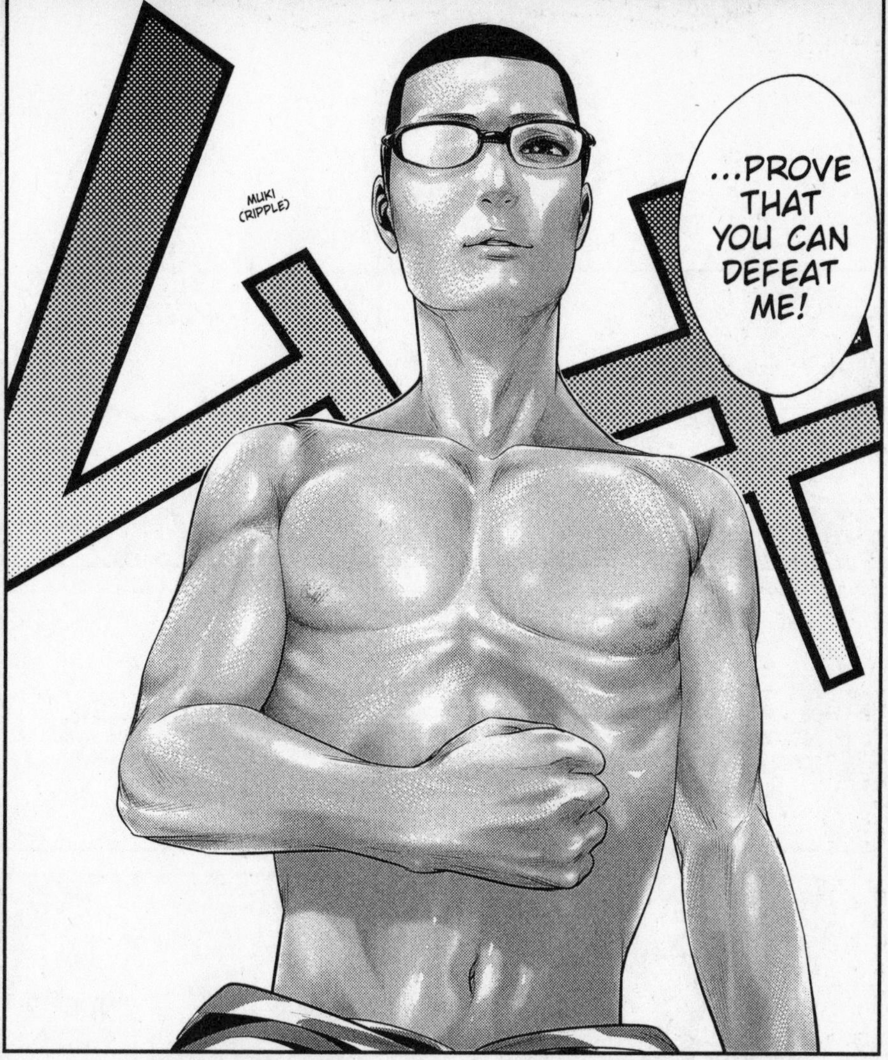
...PROVE THAT YOU CAN DEFEAT ME!
MUKI (RIPPLE)

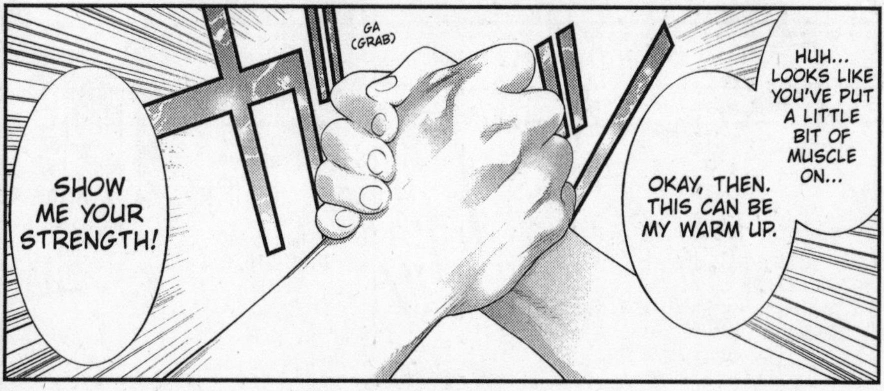
HUH... LOOKS LIKE YOU'VE PUT A LITTLE BIT OF MUSCLE ON...
OKAY, THEN. THIS CAN BE MY WARM UP.
GA (GRAB)
SHOW ME YOUR STRENGTH!

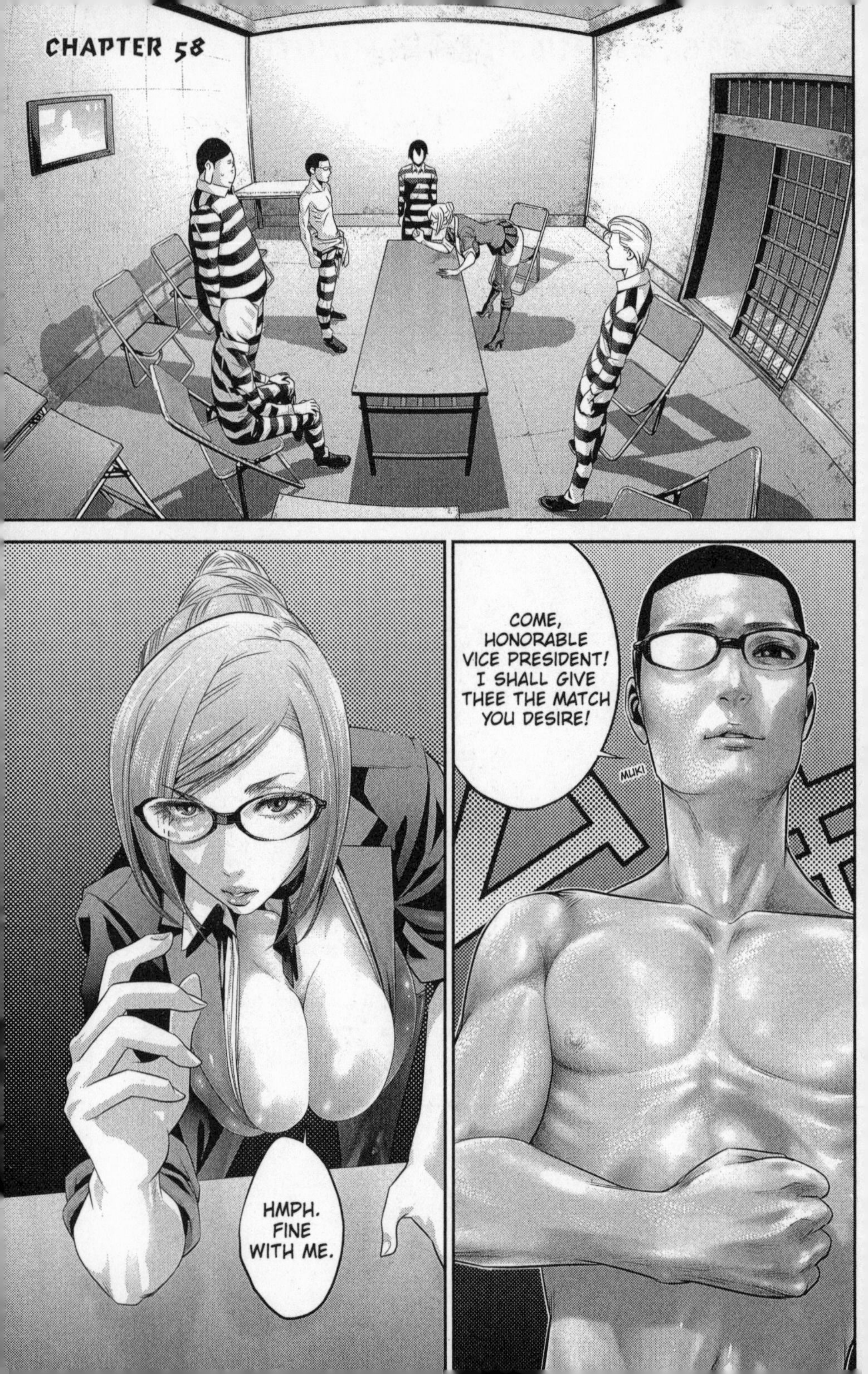
CHAPTER 58
COME, HONORABLE VICE PRESIDENT! I SHALL GIVE THEE THE MATCH YOU DESIRE!
MUKI
HMPH. FINE WITH ME.

CHAPTER 58: MISSION: 10 MINUTES

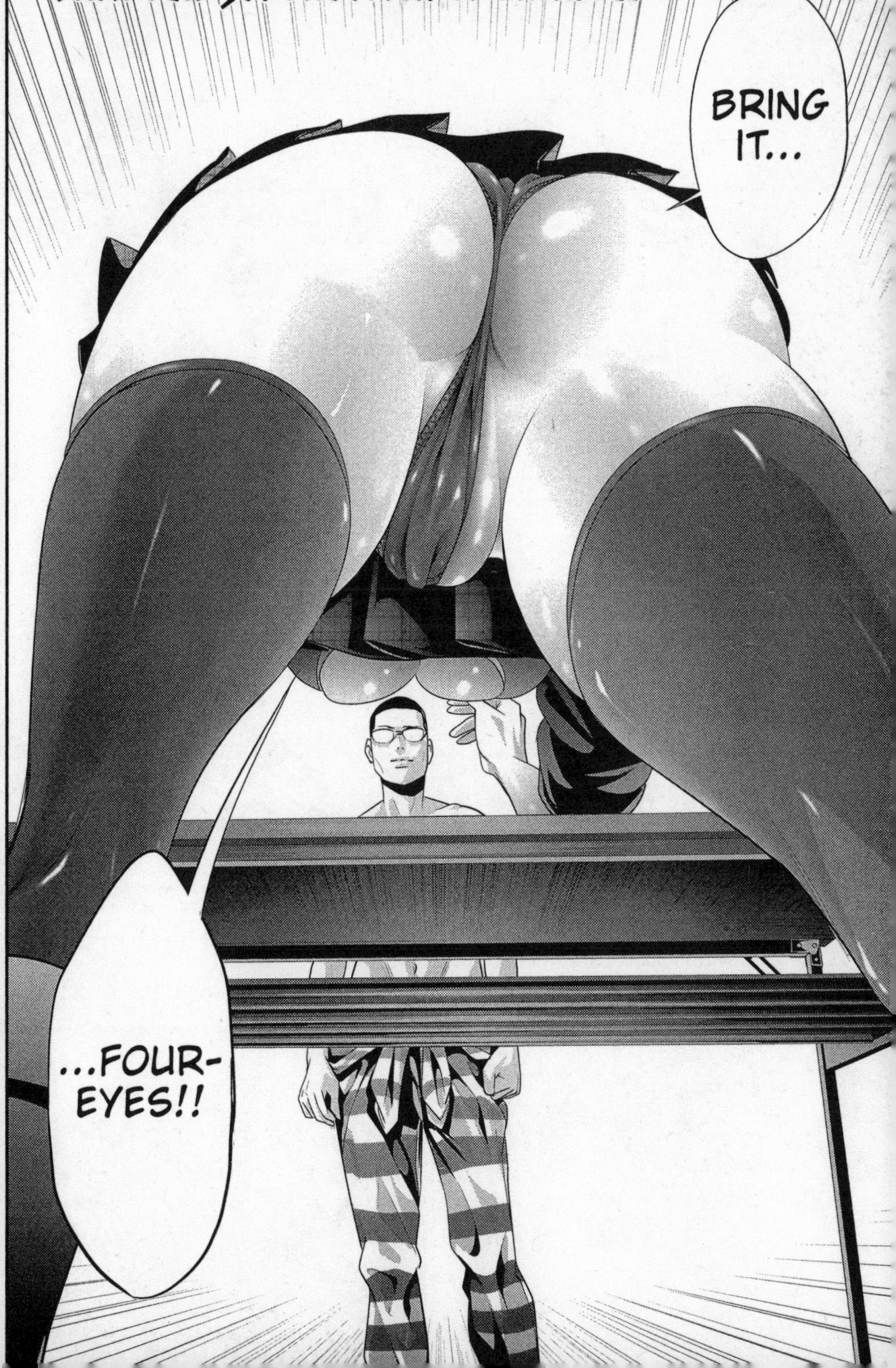
BRING IT...
...FOUR-EYES!!

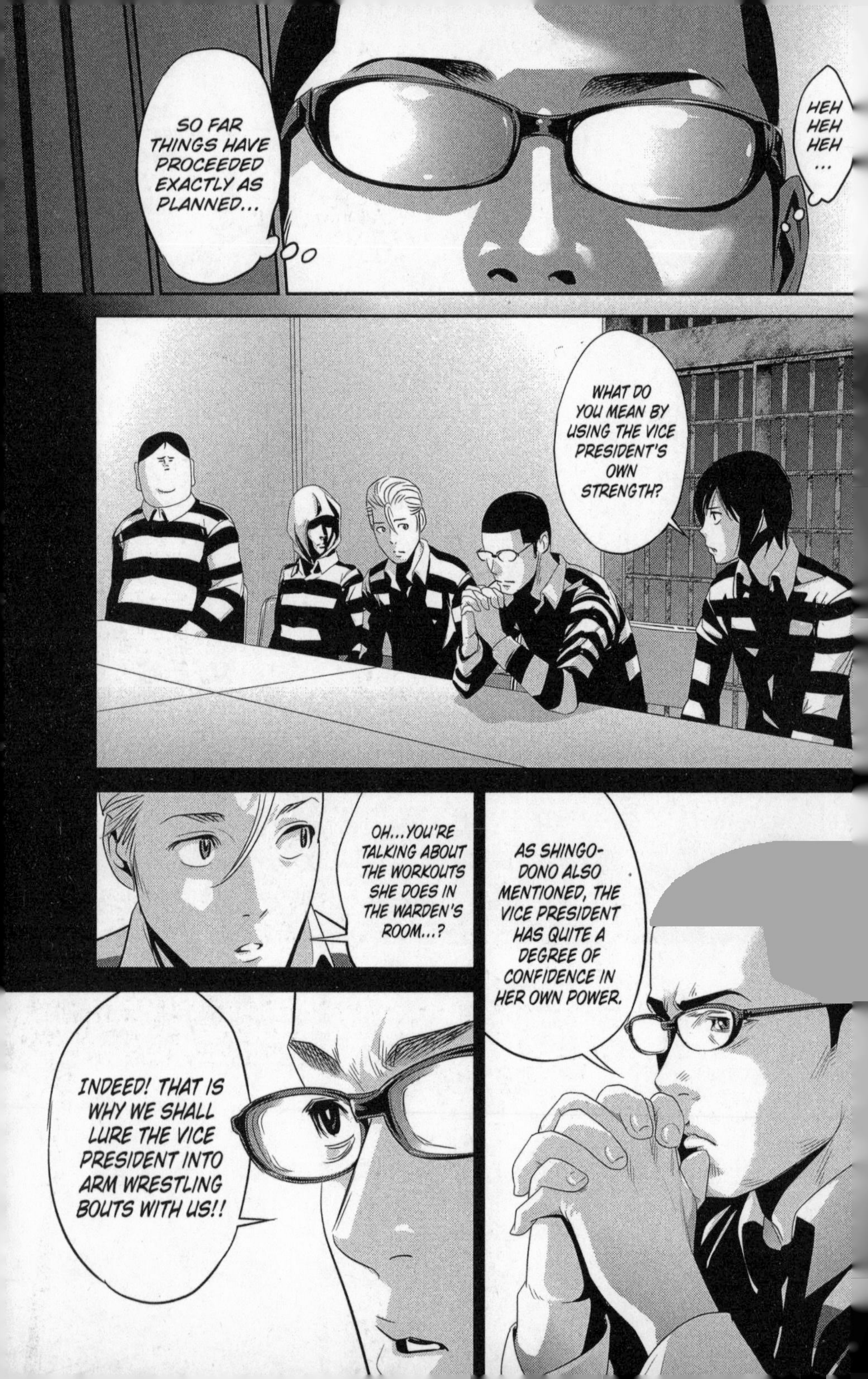
SO FAR THINGS HAVE PROCEEDED EXACTLY AS PLANNED...
HEH HEH HEH ...
WHAT DO YOU MEAN BY USING THE VICE PRESIDENT'S OWN STRENGTH?
AS SHINGO-DONO ALSO MENTIONED, THE VICE PRESIDENT HAS QUITE A DEGREE OF CONFIDENCE IN HER OWN POWER.
OH...YOU'RE TALKING ABOUT THE WORKOUTS SHE DOES IN THE WARDEN'S ROOM...?
INDEED! THAT IS WHY WE SHALL LURE THE VICE PRESIDENT INTO ARM WRESTLING BOUTS WITH US!!

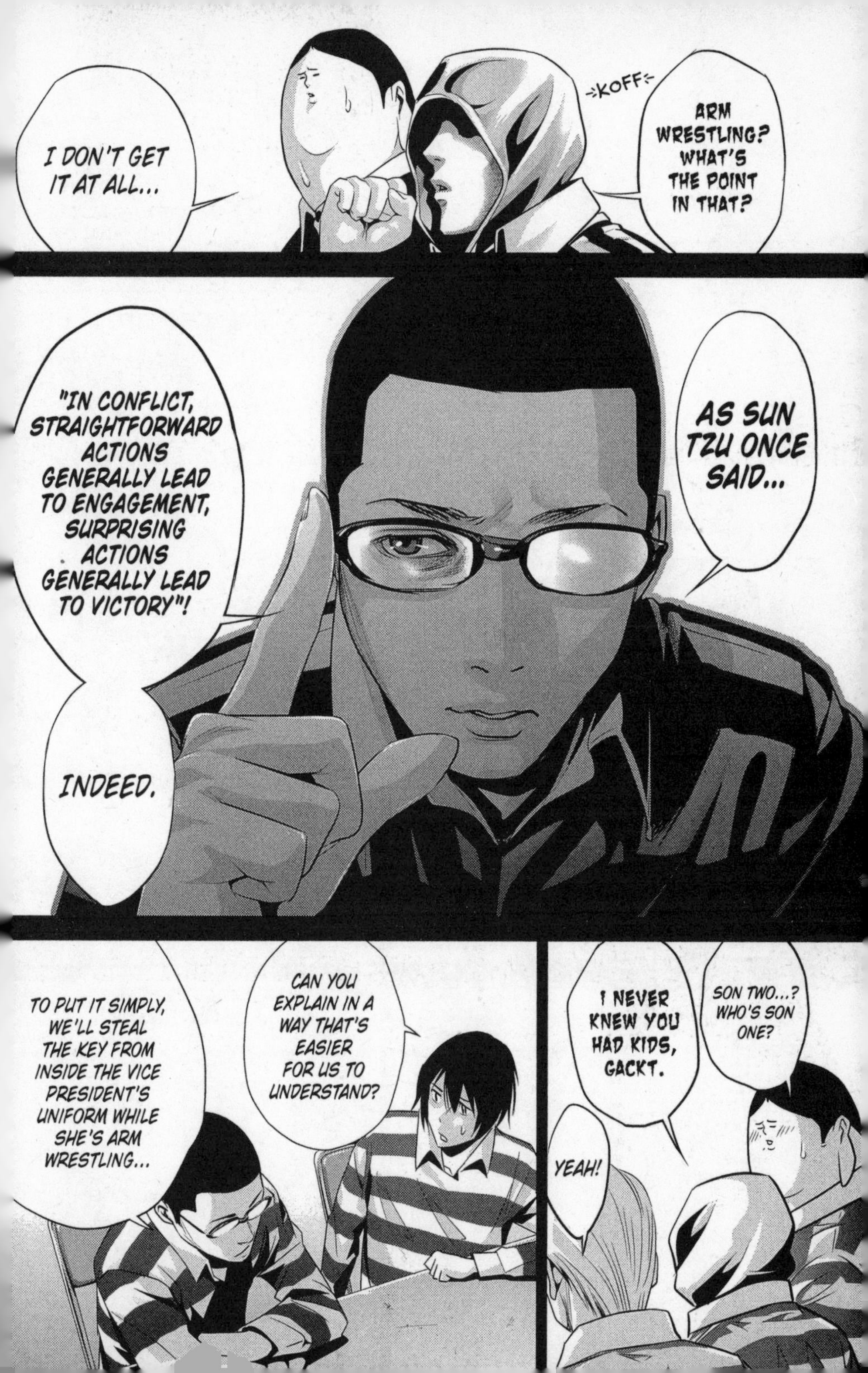
-KOFF-
ARM WRESTLING? WHAT'S THE POINT IN THAT?
I DON'T GET IT AT ALL...
AS SUN TZU ONCE SAID...
"IN CONFLICT, STRAIGHTFORWARD ACTIONS GENERALLY LEAD TO ENGAGEMENT, SURPRISING ACTIONS GENERALLY LEAD TO VICTORY"!
INDEED.
SON TWO...? WHO'S SON ONE?
I NEVER KNEW YOU HAD KIDS, GACKT.
YEAH!
CAN YOU EXPLAIN IN A WAY THAT'S EASIER FOR US TO UNDERSTAND?
TO PUT IT SIMPLY, WE'LL STEAL THE KEY FROM INSIDE THE VICE PRESIDENT'S UNIFORM WHILE SHE'S ARM WRESTLING...

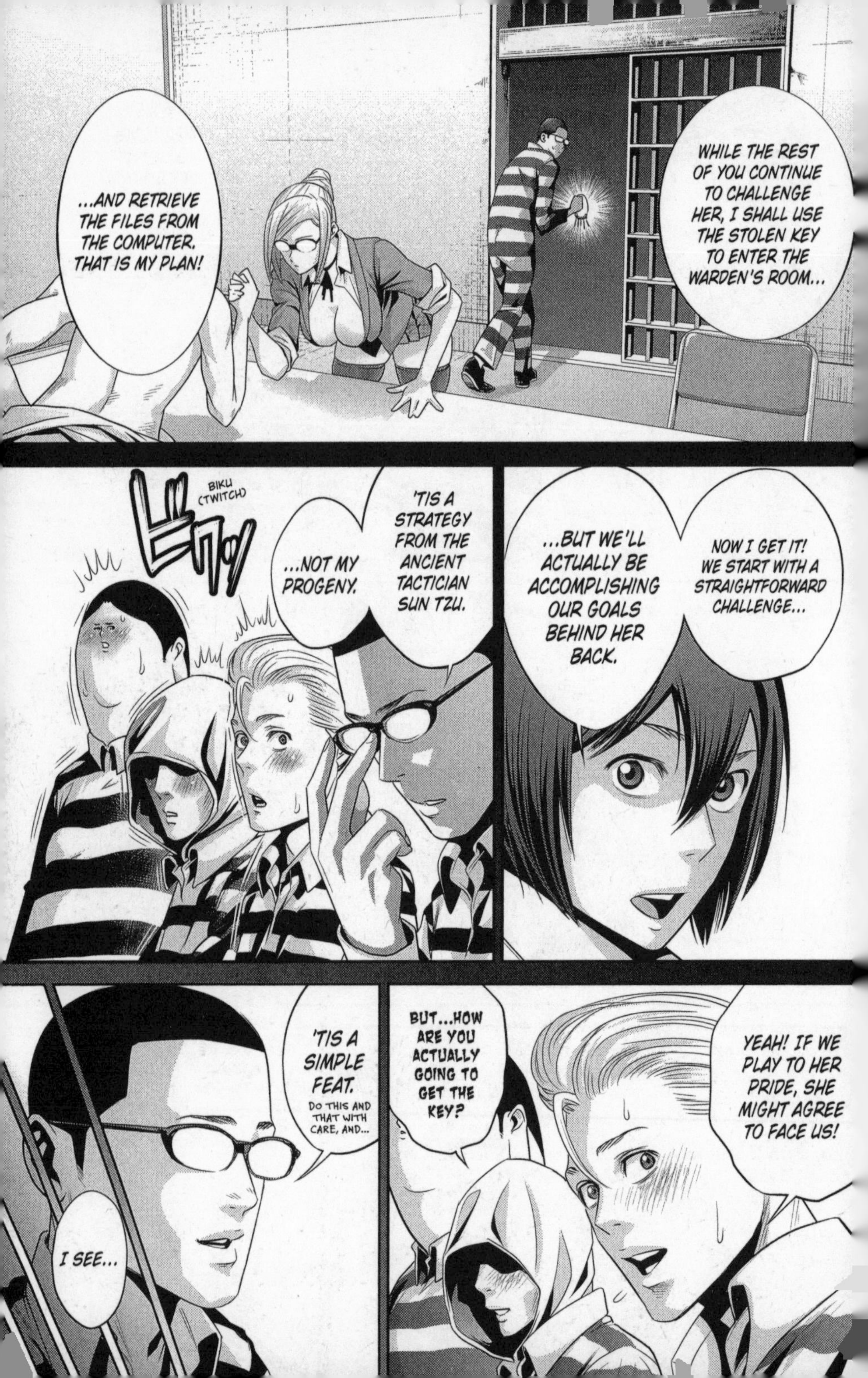
WHILE THE REST OF YOU CONTINUE TO CHALLENGE HER, I SHALL USE THE STOLEN KEY TO ENTER THE WARDEN'S ROOM...
...AND RETRIEVE THE FILES FROM THE COMPUTER. THAT IS MY PLAN!
NOW I GET IT! WE START WITH A STRAIGHTFORWARD CHALLENGE...
...BUT WE'LL ACTUALLY BE ACCOMPLISHING OUR GOALS BEHIND HER BACK.
'TIS A STRATEGY FROM THE ANCIENT TACTICIAN SUN TZU.
...NOT MY PROGENY.
BIKU (TWITCH)
YEAH! IF WE PLAY TO HER PRIDE, SHE MIGHT AGREE TO FACE US!
BUT...HOW ARE YOU ACTUALLY GOING TO GET THE KEY?
'TIS A SIMPLE FEAT.
DO THIS AND THAT WITH CARE, AND...
I SEE...

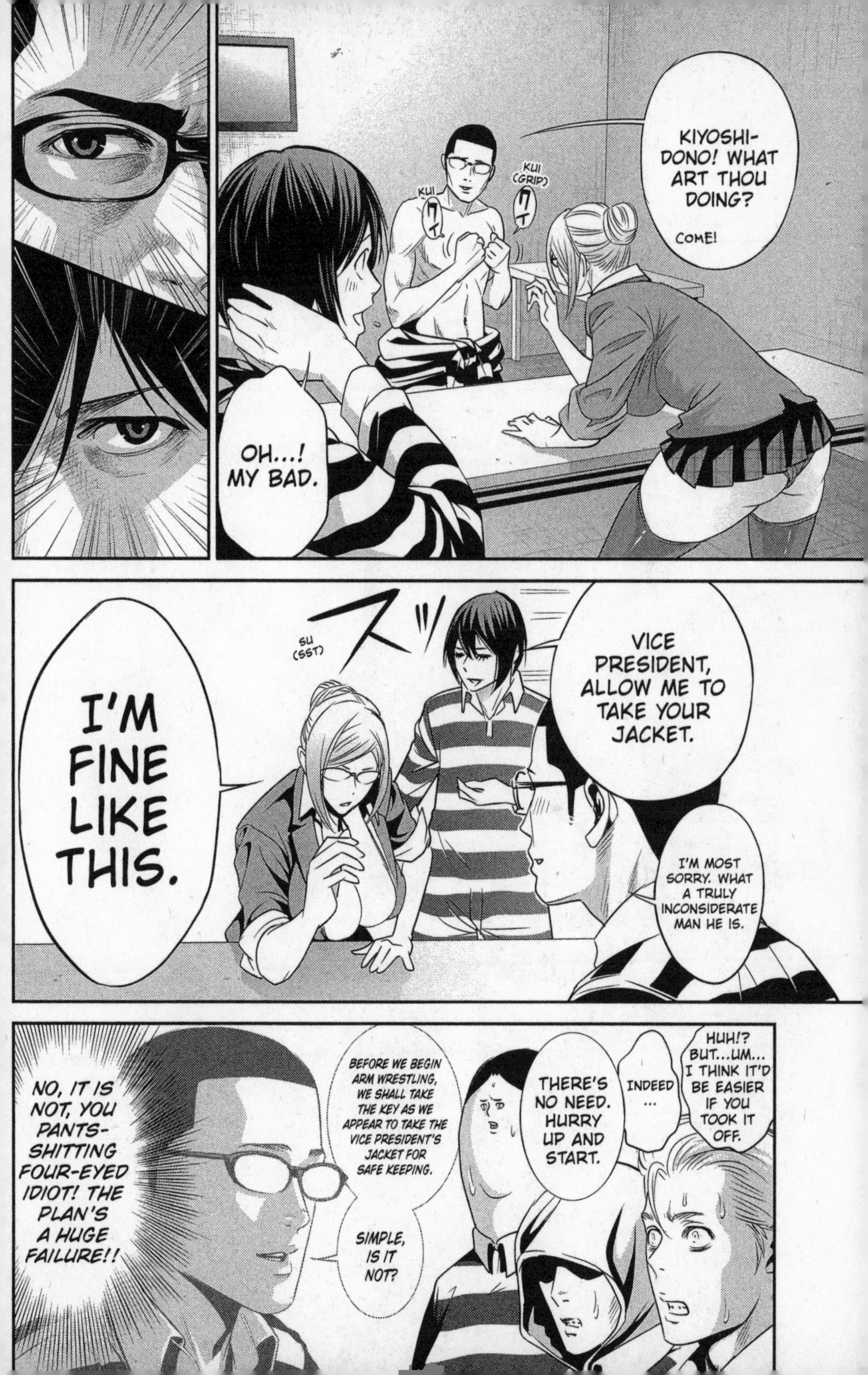
KIYOSHI-DONO! WHAT ART THOU DOING?
COME!
KUI (GRIP)
KUI
OH...! MY BAD.
VICE PRESIDENT, ALLOW ME TO TAKE YOUR JACKET.
SU (SST)
I'M FINE LIKE THIS.
I'M MOST SORRY. WHAT A TRULY INCONSIDERATE MAN HE IS.
HUH!? BUT...UM... I THINK IT'D BE EASIER IF YOU TOOK IT OFF.
INDEED...
THERE'S NO NEED. HURRY UP AND START.
BEFORE WE BEGIN ARM WRESTLING, WE SHALL TAKE THE KEY AS WE APPEAR TO TAKE THE VICE PRESIDENT'S JACKET FOR SAFE KEEPING.
SIMPLE, IS IT NOT?
NO, IT IS NOT, YOU PANTS-SHITTING FOUR-EYED IDIOT! THE PLAN'S A HUGE FAILURE!!

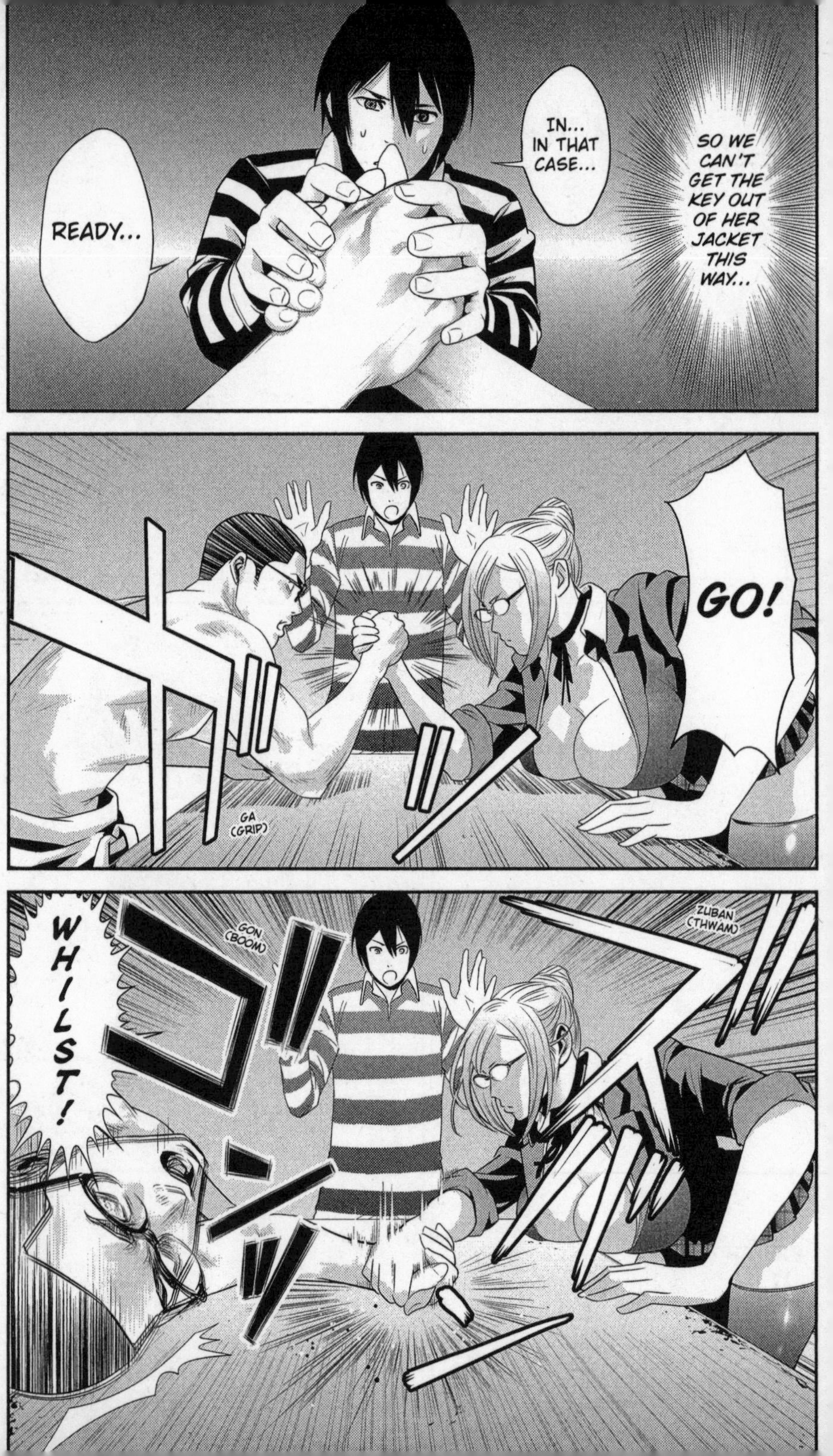
SO WE CAN'T GET THE KEY OUT OF HER JACKET THIS WAY...
IN... IN THAT CASE...
READY...
GO!
GA (GRIP)
ZUBAN (THWAM)
GON (BOOM)
WHILST!

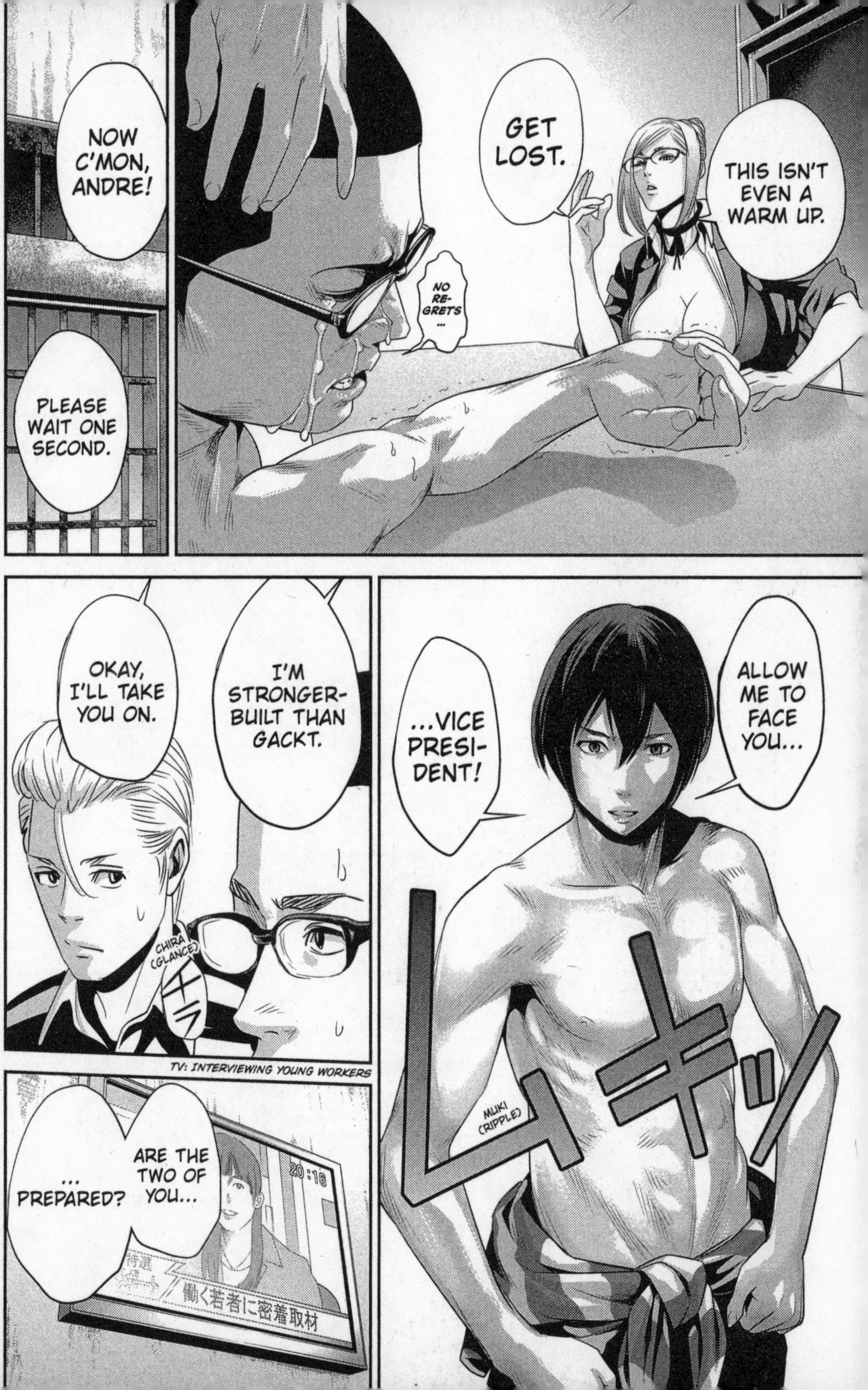
THIS ISN'T EVEN A WARM UP.
GET LOST.
NO REGRETS...
NOW C'MON, ANDRE!
PLEASE WAIT ONE SECOND.
ALLOW ME TO FACE YOU...
...VICE PRESIDENT!
MUKI (RIPPLE)
I'M STRONGER-BUILT THAN GACKT.
OKAY, I'LL TAKE YOU ON.
CHIRA (GLANCE)
TV: INTERVIEWING YOUNG WORKERS
ARE THE TWO OF YOU...
...PREPARED?
20:16
働く若者に密着取材

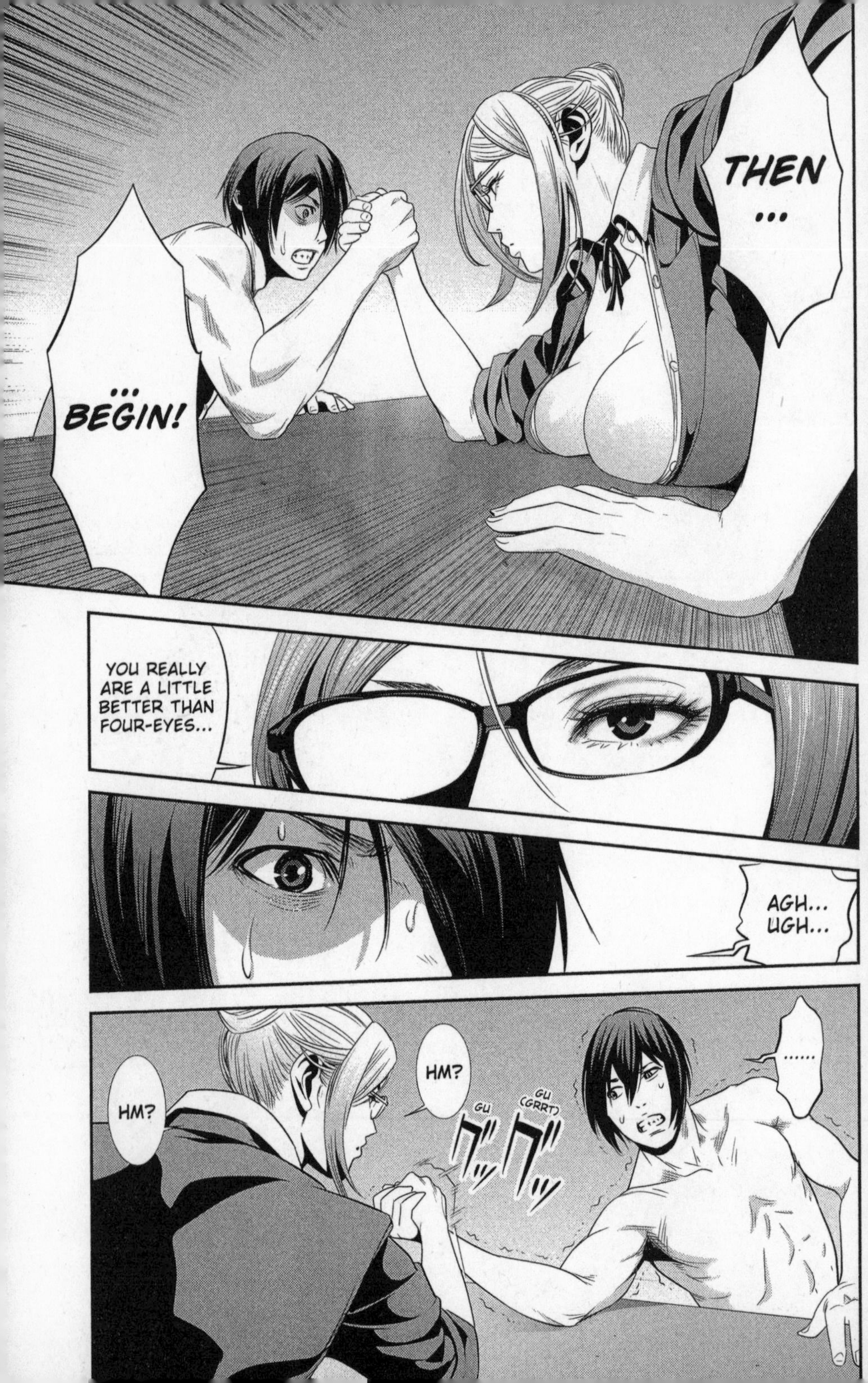
THEN ...
... BEGIN!
YOU REALLY ARE A LITTLE BETTER THAN FOUR-EYES...
AGH... UGH...
......
GU (GRRT)
GU
HM?
HM?

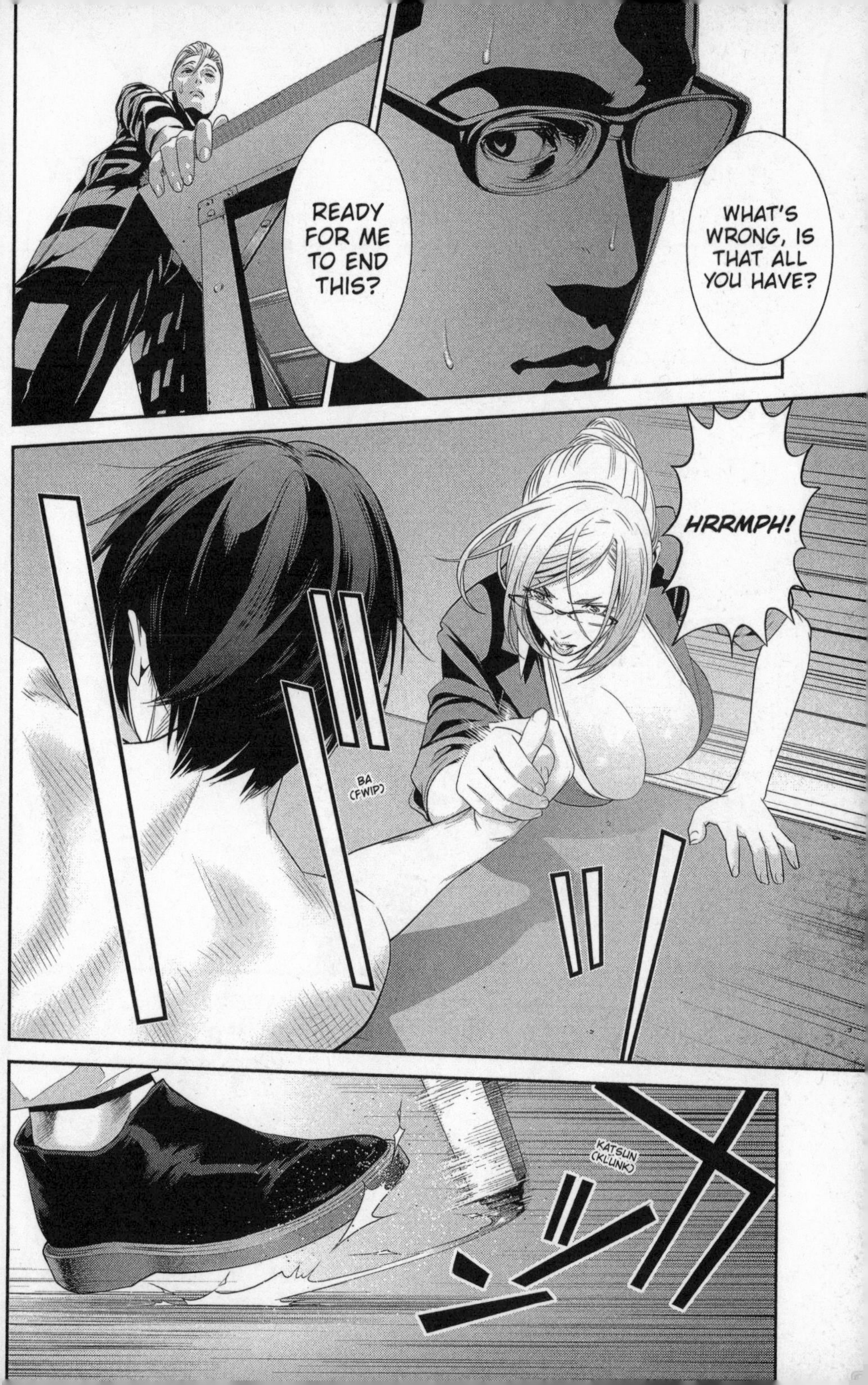
WHAT'S WRONG, IS THAT ALL YOU HAVE?
READY FOR ME TO END THIS?
HRRMPH!
BA (FWIP)
KATSUN (KLÜNK)

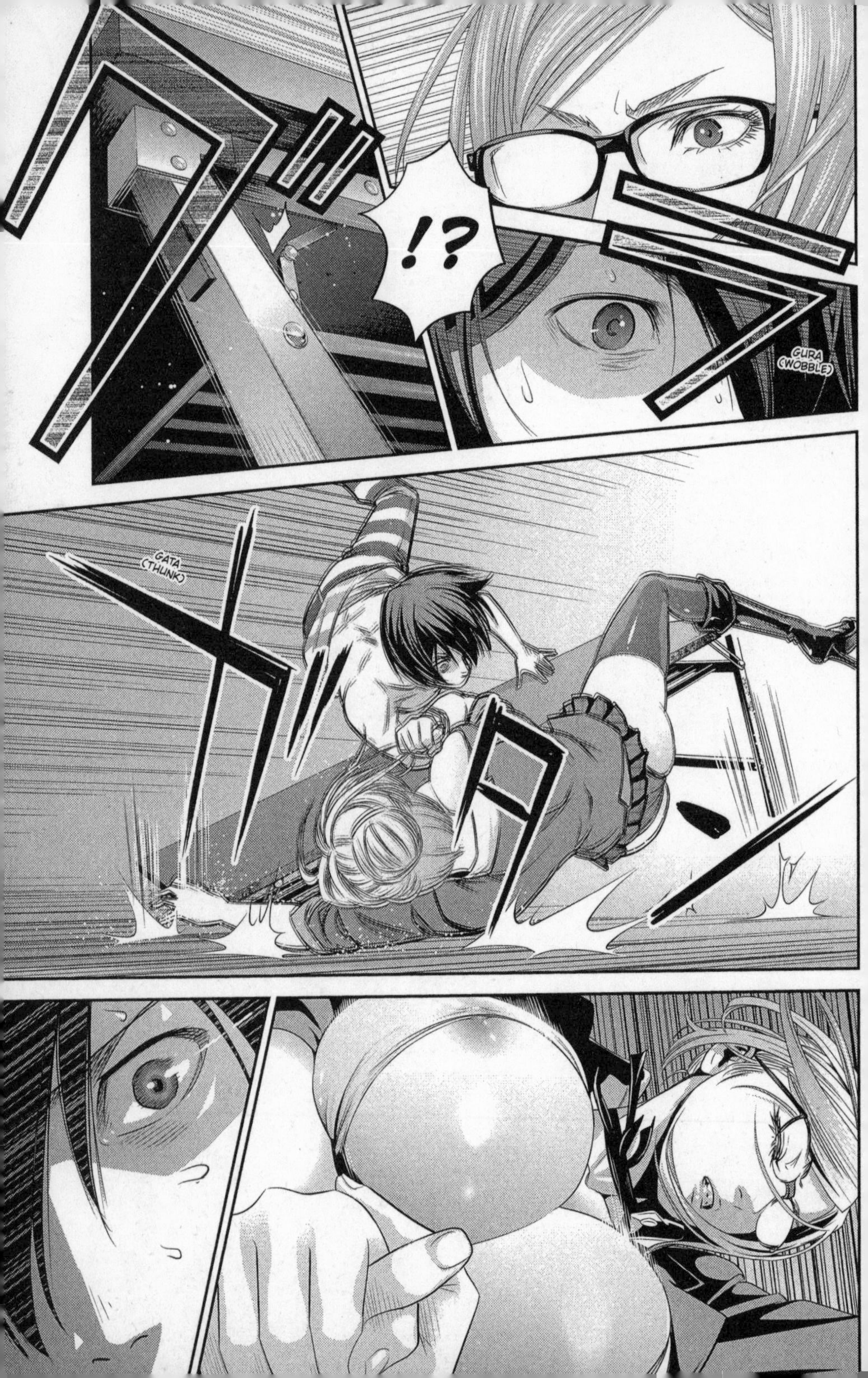
!?
GURA (WOBBLE)
GATA (THUNK)

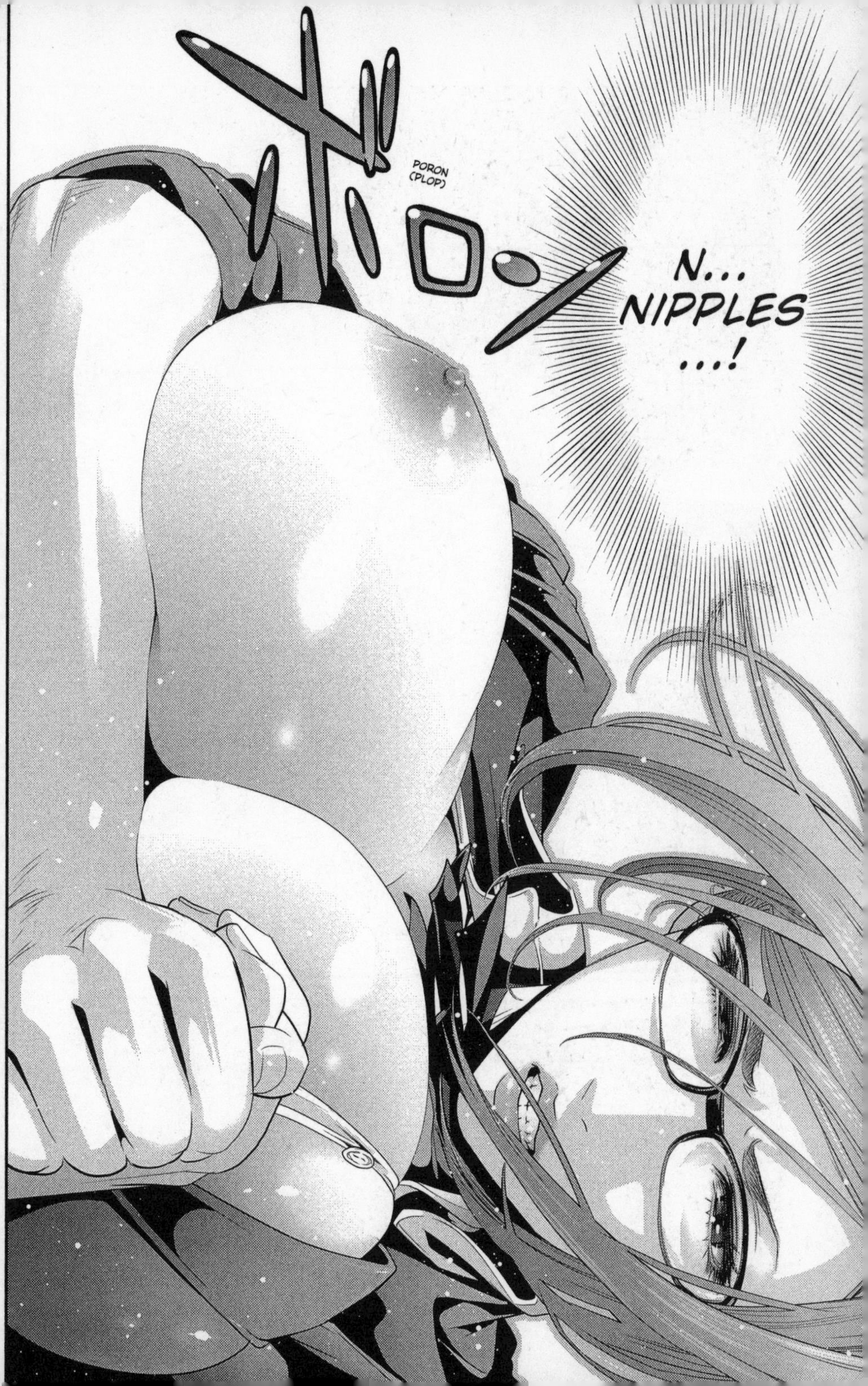
N... NIPPLES ...!
ポローン
PORON (PLOP)

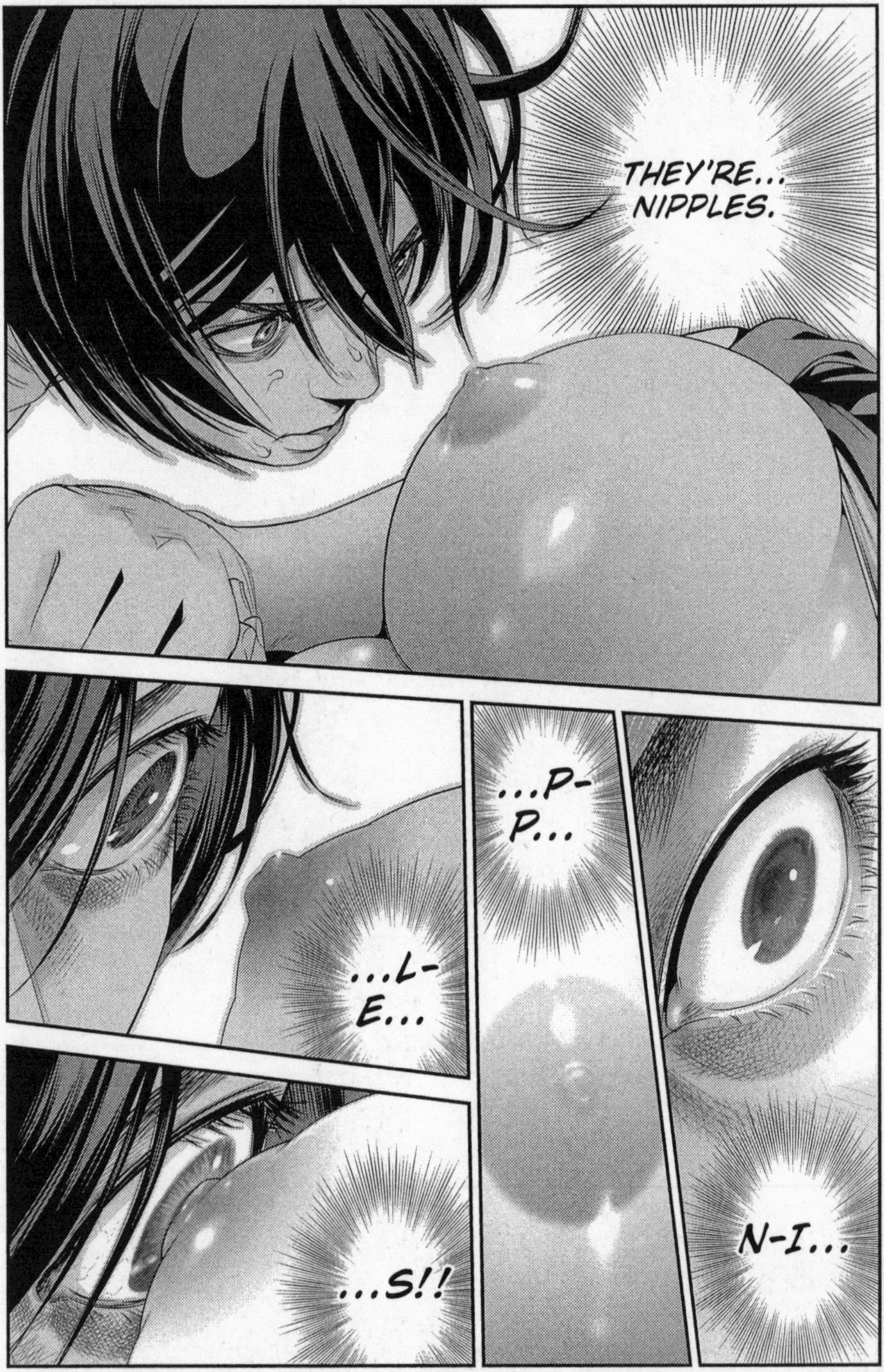
THEY'RE... NIPPLES.
N-I...
...P-
P...
...L-
E...
...S!!

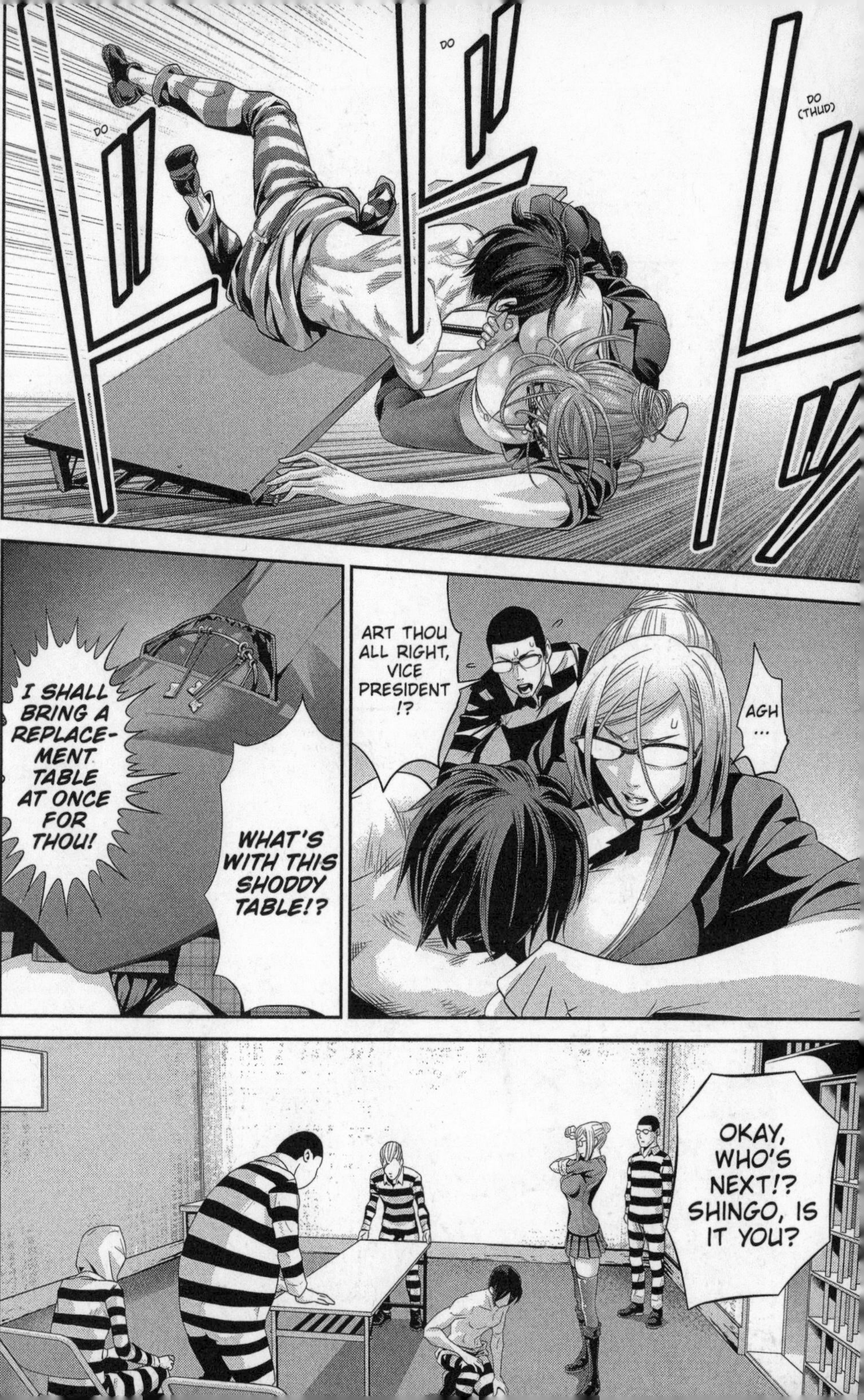
DO (THUD)
DO
DO
AGH ...
ART THOU ALL RIGHT, VICE PRESIDENT!?
WHAT'S WITH THIS SHODDY TABLE!?
I SHALL BRING A REPLACEMENT TABLE AT ONCE FOR THOU!
OKAY, WHO'S NEXT!? SHINGO, IS IT YOU?

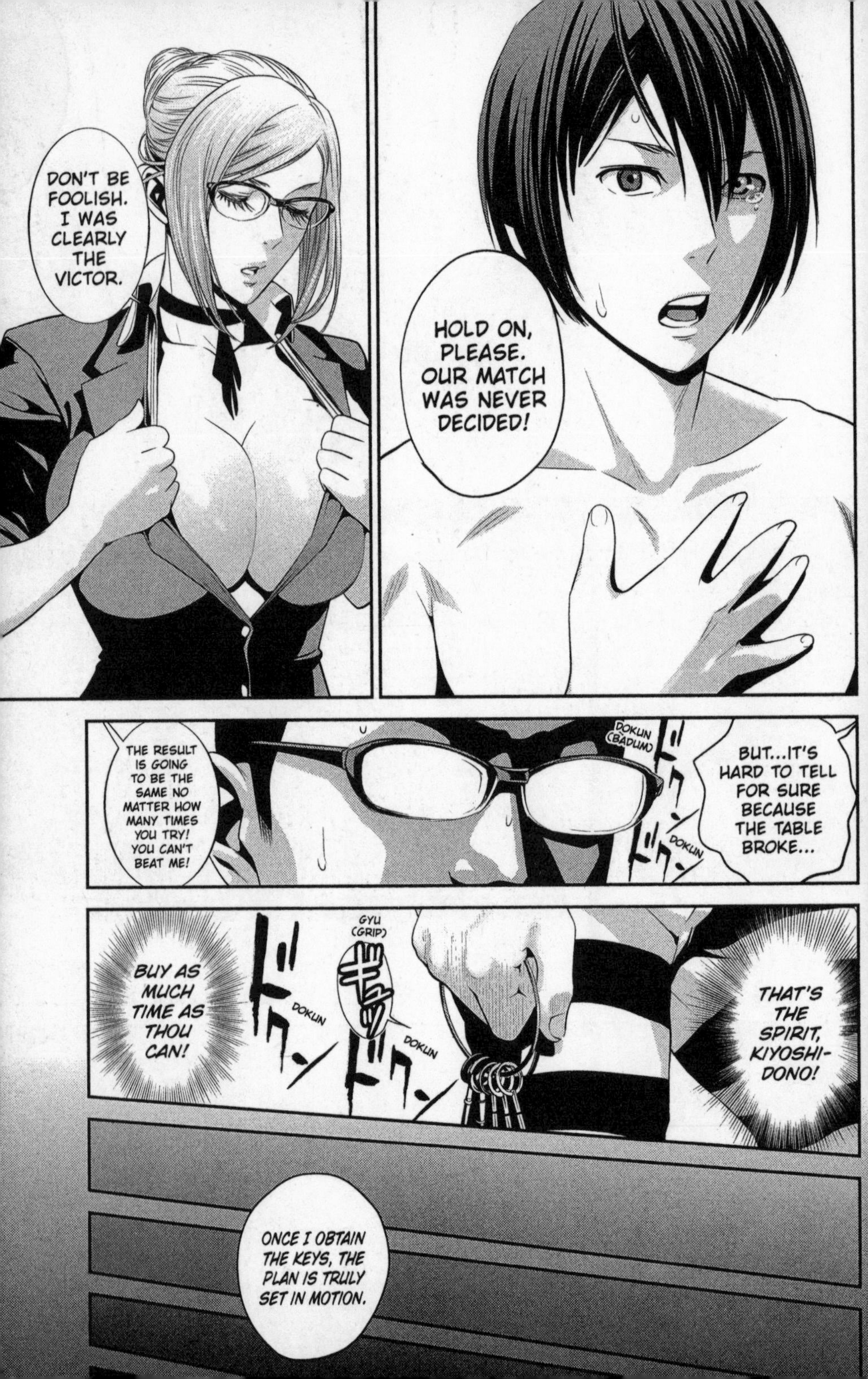
HOLD ON, PLEASE. OUR MATCH WAS NEVER DECIDED!
DON'T BE FOOLISH. I WAS CLEARLY THE VICTOR.
BUT...IT'S HARD TO TELL FOR SURE BECAUSE THE TABLE BROKE...
DOKUN (BADUM)
DOKUN
THE RESULT IS GOING TO BE THE SAME NO MATTER HOW MANY TIMES YOU TRY! YOU CAN'T BEAT ME!
THAT'S THE SPIRIT, KIYOSHI-DONO!
GYU (GRIP)
DOKUN
DOKUN
BUY AS MUCH TIME AS THOU CAN!
ONCE I OBTAIN THE KEYS, THE PLAN IS TRULY SET IN MOTION.

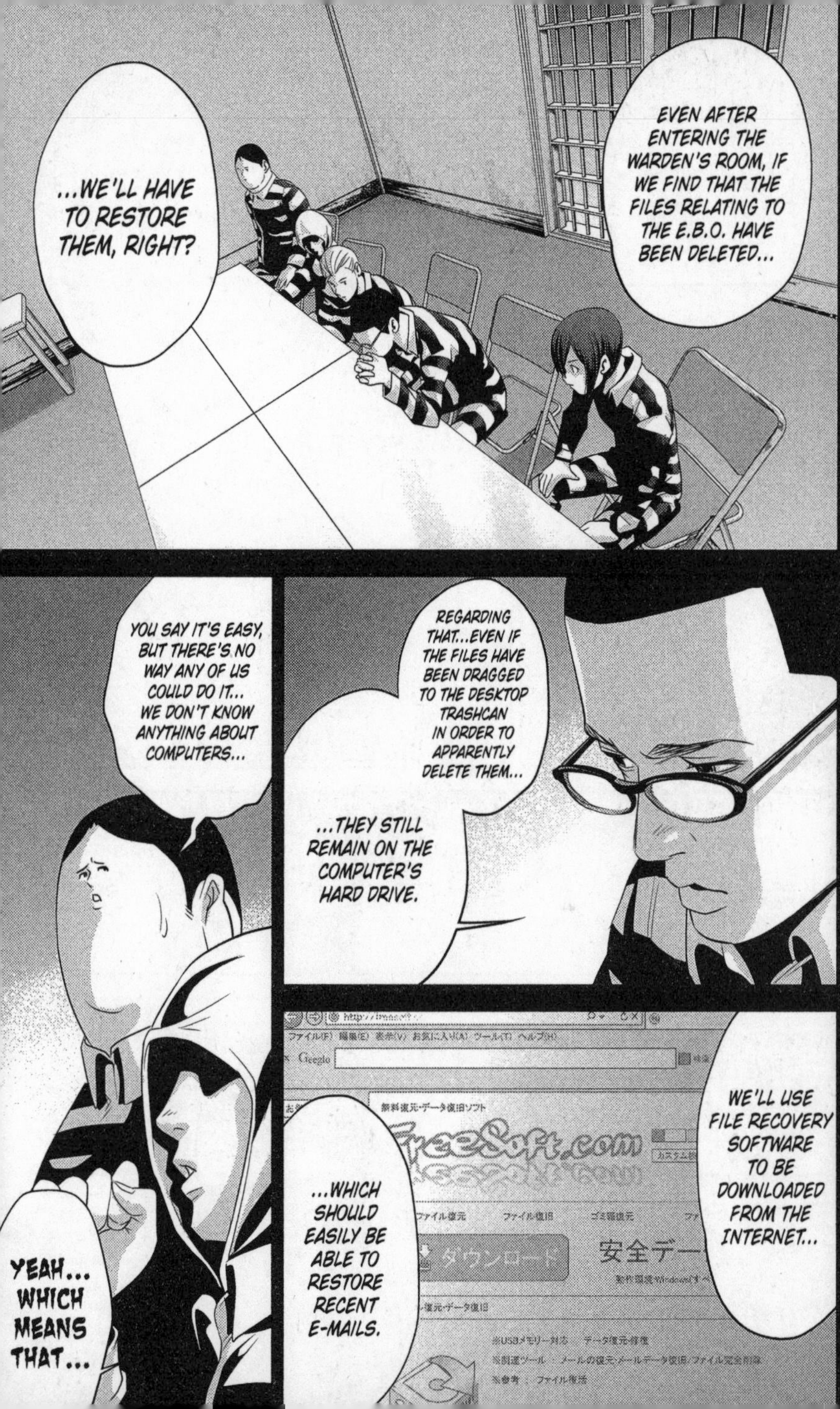
EVEN AFTER ENTERING THE WARDEN'S ROOM, IF WE FIND THAT THE FILES RELATING TO THE E.B.O. HAVE BEEN DELETED...
...WE'LL HAVE TO RESTORE THEM, RIGHT?
REGARDING THAT...EVEN IF THE FILES HAVE BEEN DRAGGED TO THE DESKTOP TRASHCAN IN ORDER TO APPARENTLY DELETE THEM...
...THEY STILL REMAIN ON THE COMPUTER'S HARD DRIVE.
WE'LL USE FILE RECOVERY SOFTWARE TO BE DOWNLOADED FROM THE INTERNET...
...WHICH SHOULD EASILY BE ABLE TO RESTORE RECENT E-MAILS.
FreeSoft.com
ダウンロード
YOU SAY IT'S EASY, BUT THERE'S NO WAY ANY OF US COULD DO IT... WE DON'T KNOW ANYTHING ABOUT COMPUTERS...
YEAH... WHICH MEANS THAT...

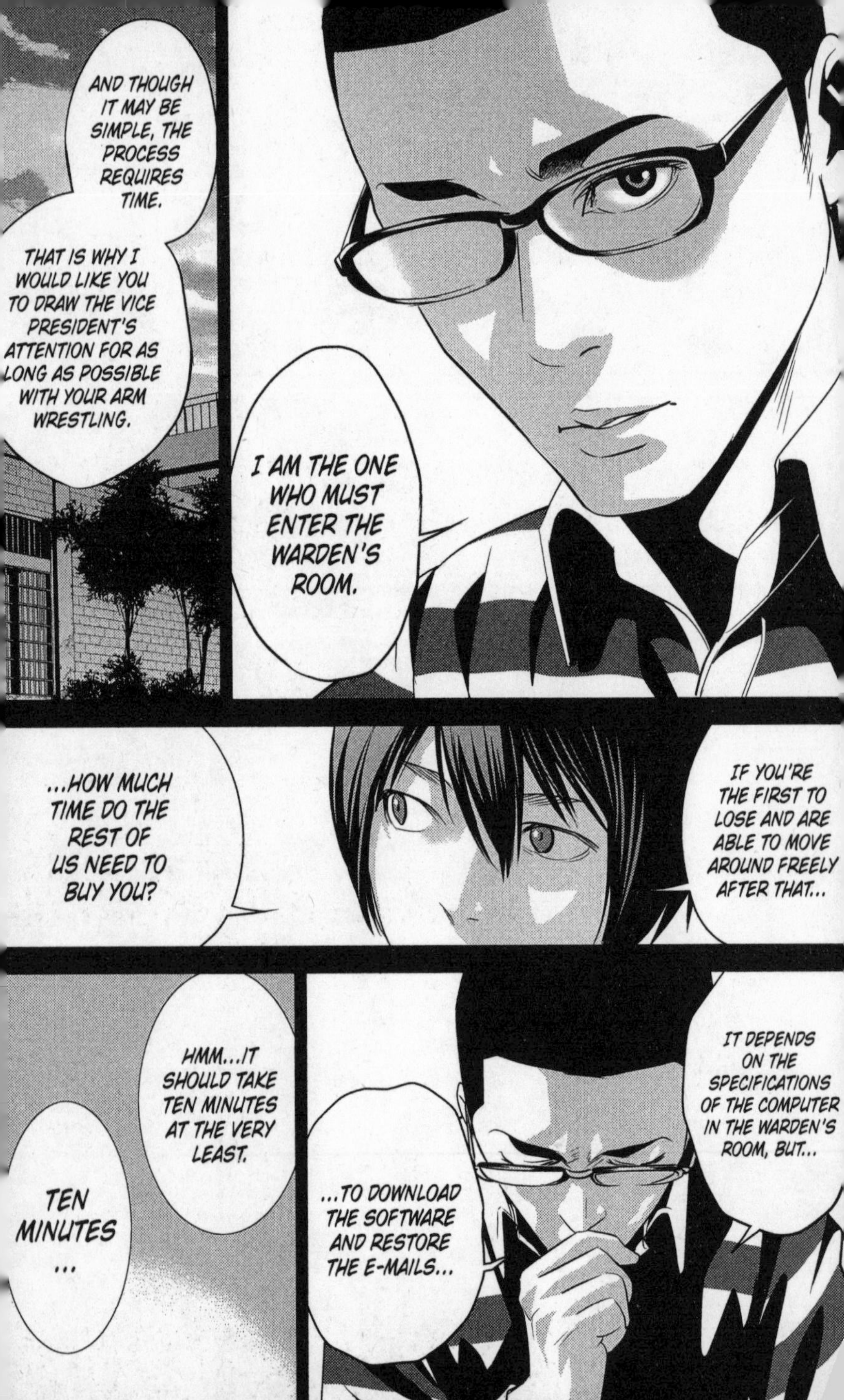
I AM THE ONE WHO MUST ENTER THE WARDEN'S ROOM.
AND THOUGH IT MAY BE SIMPLE, THE PROCESS REQUIRES TIME.
THAT IS WHY I WOULD LIKE YOU TO DRAW THE VICE PRESIDENT'S ATTENTION FOR AS LONG AS POSSIBLE WITH YOUR ARM WRESTLING.
IF YOU'RE THE FIRST TO LOSE AND ARE ABLE TO MOVE AROUND FREELY AFTER THAT...
...HOW MUCH TIME DO THE REST OF US NEED TO BUY YOU?
IT DEPENDS ON THE SPECIFICATIONS OF THE COMPUTER IN THE WARDEN'S ROOM, BUT...
...TO DOWNLOAD THE SOFTWARE AND RESTORE THE E-MAILS...
HMM...IT SHOULD TAKE TEN MINUTES AT THE VERY LEAST.
TEN MINUTES...

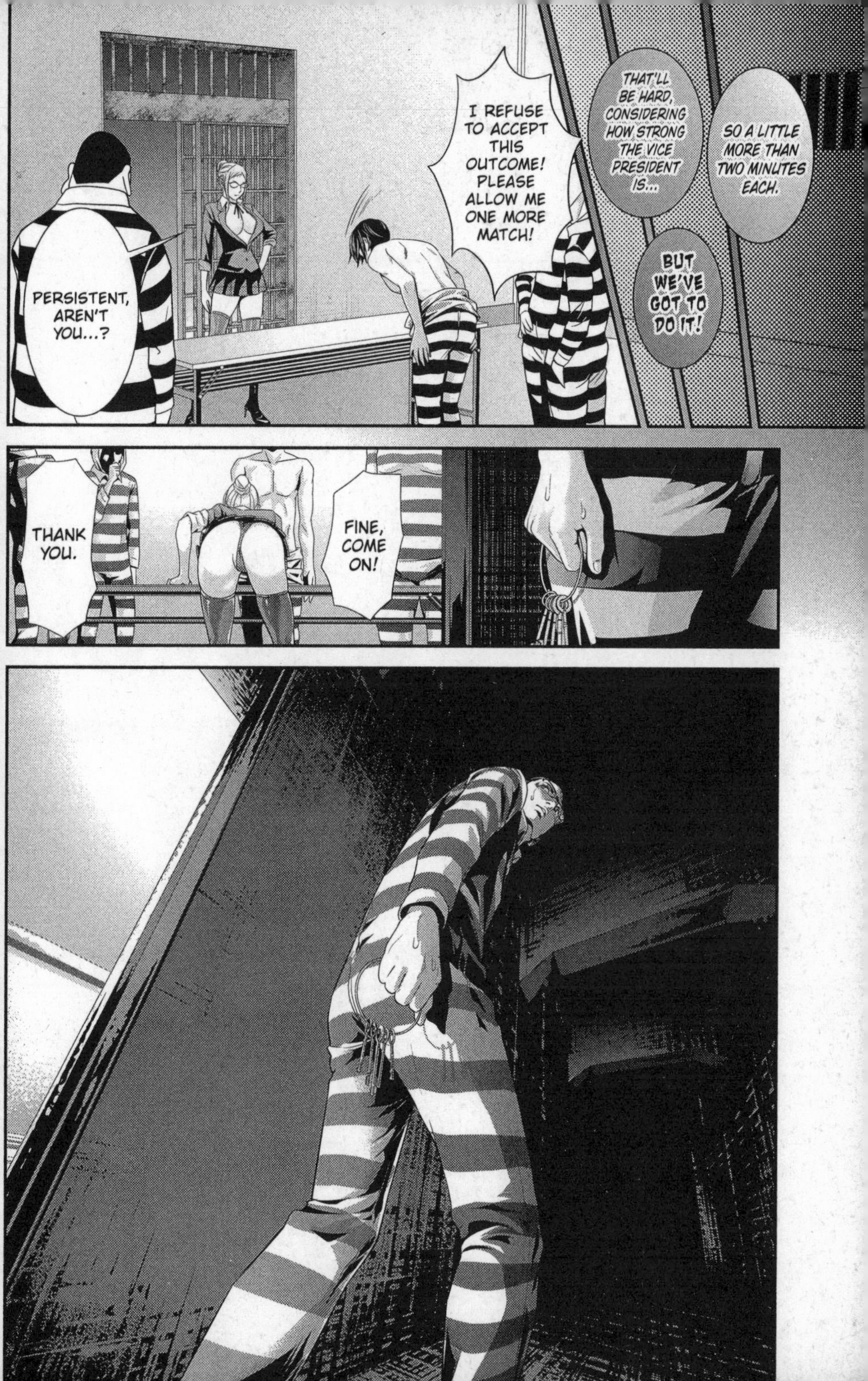
SO A LITTLE MORE THAN TWO MINUTES EACH.
THAT'LL BE HARD, CONSIDERING HOW STRONG THE VICE PRESIDENT IS...
BUT WE'VE GOT TO DO IT!
I REFUSE TO ACCEPT THIS OUTCOME! PLEASE ALLOW ME ONE MORE MATCH!
PERSISTENT, AREN'T YOU...?
FINE, COME ON!
THANK YOU.

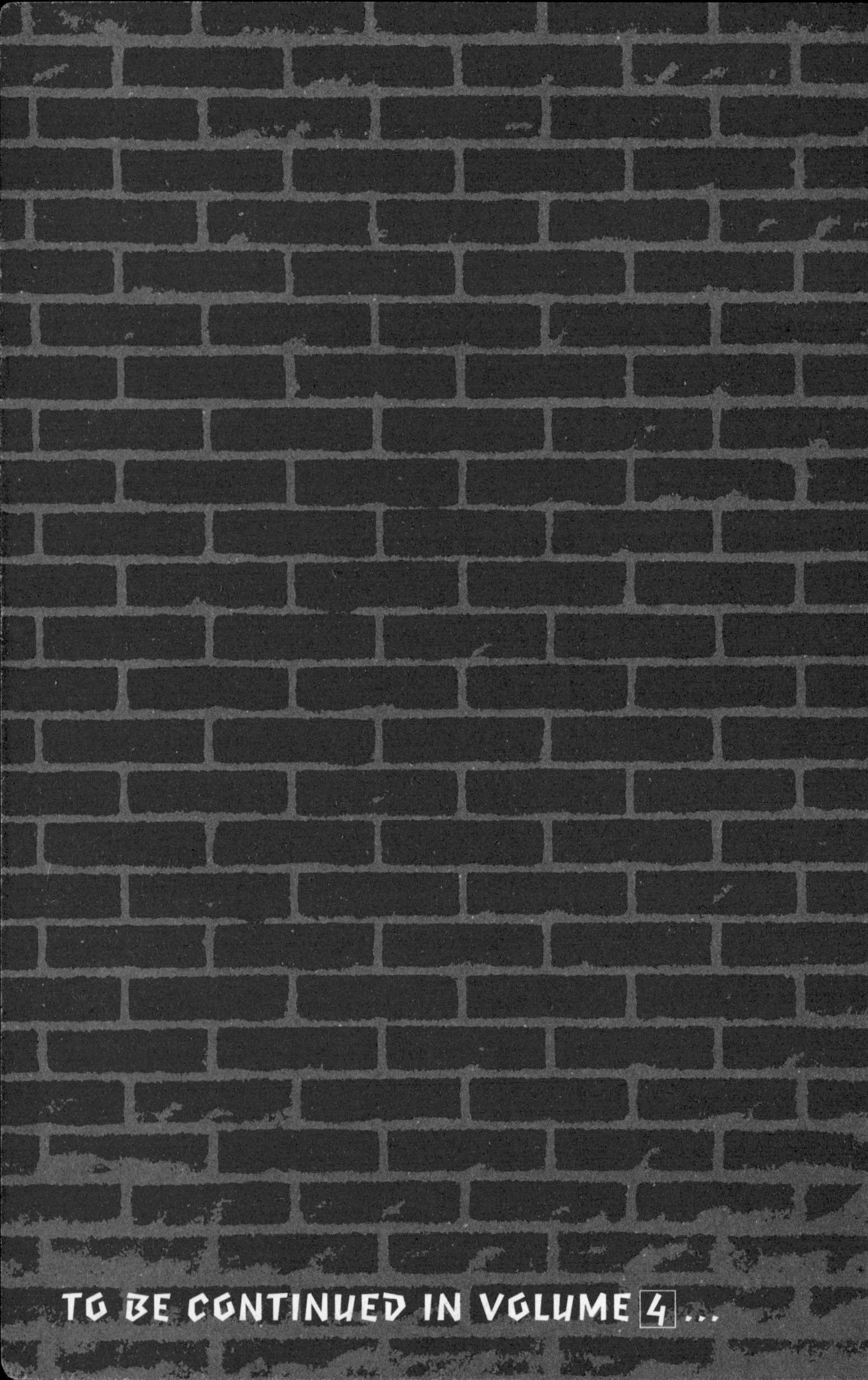
TO BE CONTINUED IN VOLUME 4...

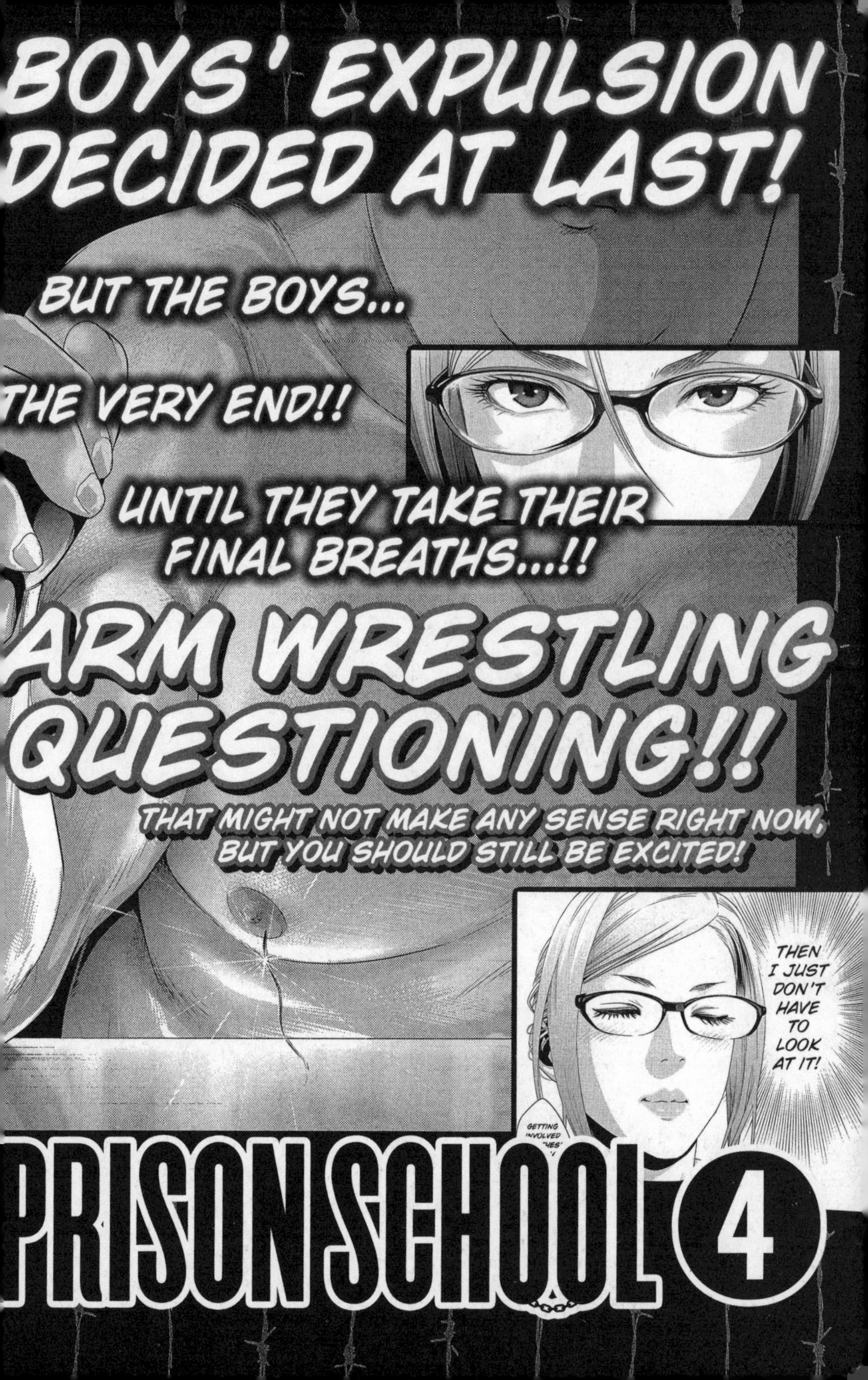
BOYS' EXPULSION DECIDED AT LAST!
BUT THE BOYS...
THE VERY END!!
UNTIL THEY TAKE THEIR FINAL BREATHS...!!
ARM WRESTLING QUESTIONING!!
THAT MIGHT NOT MAKE ANY SENSE RIGHT NOW, BUT YOU SHOULD STILL BE EXCITED!
THEN I JUST DON'T HAVE TO LOOK AT IT!
PRISON SCHOOL 4

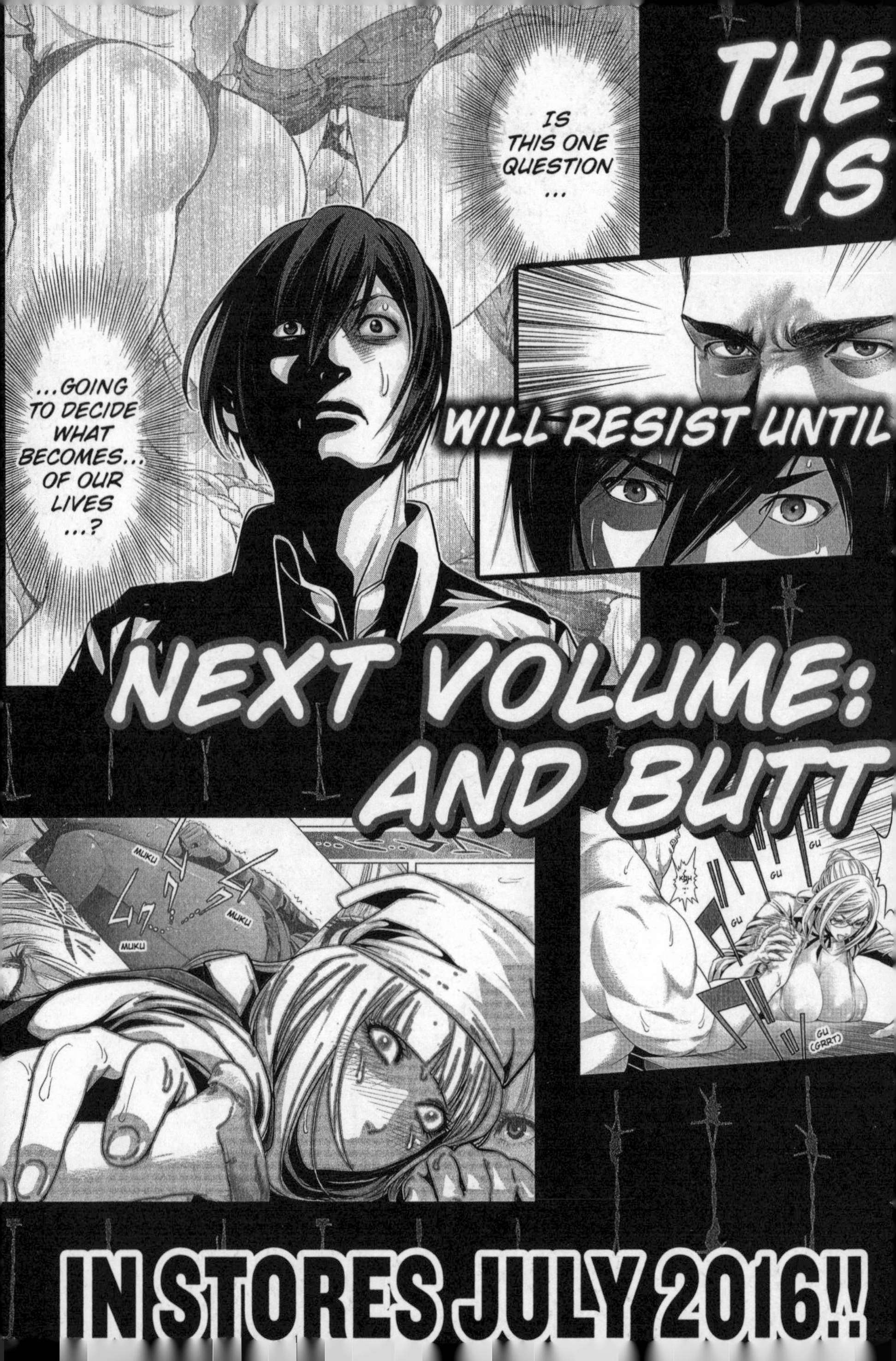
THE
IS
IS THIS ONE QUESTION ...
...GOING TO DECIDE WHAT BECOMES... OF OUR LIVES ...?
WILL RESIST UNTIL
NEXT VOLUME:
AND BUTT
GU
GU
KGH
GU
GU (GRRT)
MUKU
MUKU
MUKU
MUKU
IN STORES JULY 2016!!

TRANSLATION NOTES

Common Honorifics

no honorific: Indicates familiarity or closeness; if used without permission or reason, addressing someone in this manner would constitute an insult.

-san: The Japanese equivalent of Mr./Mrs./Miss. If a situation calls for politeness, this is the fail-safe honorific.

-dono: Conveys an indication of respect for the addressee.

-kun: Used most often when referring to boys, this indicates affection or familiarity. Occasionally used by older men among their peers, but it may also be used by anyone referring to a person of lower standing.

-chan: An affectionate honorific indicating familiarity used mostly in reference to girls; also used in reference to cute persons or animals of either gender.

-senpai: A suffix used to address upperclassmen or more experienced coworkers.

PRISON SCHOOL

PRISON SCHO

AKIRA HIRAMOTO

Translation: Ko Ransom

Lettering: Alexis Eckerman

This book is a work of fiction. Names, characters, places, and incidents are the product of the author's imagination or are used fictitiously. Any resemblance to actual events, locales, or persons, living or dead, is coincidental.

PRISON SCHOOL Vol. 5, 6 © 2012 Akira Hiramoto. All rights reserved.
First published in Japan in 2012 by Kodansha, Ltd. Tokyo.
Publication rights for this English edition arranged through Kodansha, Ltd. Tokyo.

Translation © 2016 by Hachette Book Group, Inc.

Yen Press
Hachette Book Group
1290 Avenue of the Americas
New York, NY 10104

www.hachettebookgroup.com
www.yenpress.com

Yen Press is an imprint of Hachette Book Group, Inc.
The Yen Press name and logo are trademarks of Hachette Book Group, Inc.

The publisher is not responsible for websites (or their content) that are not owned by the publisher.

Library of Congress Control Number: 2015956853

First Yen Press Edition: March 2016

ISBN: 978-0-316-34613-9

10 9 8 7 6 5 4 3 2 1

BVG

Printed in the United States of America